Mrs Oliphant:
'A Fiction to Herself'

Mrs Oliphant:
'A Fiction to Herself'

A LITERARY LIFE

ELISABETH JAY

CLARENDON PRESS · OXFORD

1995

Oxford University Press, Walton Stress, Oxford OX2 6DP

Oxford New York
Athens Auckland Bangkok Bombay
Calcutta Cape Town Dar es Salaam Delhi
Florence Hong Kong Istanbul Karachi
Kuala Lumpur Madras Madrid Melbourne
Mexico City Nairobi Paris Singapore
Taipei Tokyo Toronto
and associated companies in
Berlin Ibadan

Oxford is a trade mark of Oxford University Press

Published in the United States
by Oxford University Press Inc., New York

British Library Cataloguing in Publication Data
Data available

Library of Congress Cataloging in Publication Data
Jay, Elisabeth.
Mrs. Oliphant : a literary life / Elisabeth Jay.
Includes bibliographical references and index.
1. Oliphant, Mrs. (Margaret), 1828–1897.   2. Women and literature—
Scotland—History—19th century.   3. Women novelists,
Scottish—19th century—Biography.   I. Title.
PR5114.J39   1995
823'.8—dc20
[B]   94-3528
ISBN 0-19-812875-4

1 3 5 7 9 10 8 6 4 2

Typeset by Best-set Typesetter Ltd., Hong Kong
Printed in Great Britain
on acid-free paper by
Biddles Ltd., Guildford and King's Lynn

For
Jenny and Bill

Acknowledgements

This book has been written in defiance of Margaret Oliphant's own gloomy verdict upon her life's work: 'An infinitude of pains and labour, and all to disappear like the stubble and the hay'. Nevertheless, her accompanying judgement that her work was worth 'Nothing, and less than nothing' to her when weighed against her children and her friends' has much to commend it as both a salutary and comforting reminder to those preoccupied by lengthy research projects. Few authors, of course, have so much writing to put in the balance as proof of the weight of their affections!

In the course of eight years working on Mrs Oliphant's voluminous output I have had good reason to take her words to heart and recognize the inestimable value of family and friends: they have variously provided antidotes to the 'pains and labour', and much practical help. It is a mark of the interest and encouragement they have offered that in this circle at least Mrs Oliphant's name has become a household word.

For the pleasure I have also derived from the work my first and deepest thanks must go to my editor and friend Kim Scott Walwyn. The confidence she showed in commissioning the work, the breadth of her reading, her unflagging patience, and, above all, her enthusiasm, have all provided a model of author–publisher relations that have helped me to understand the creative flair of that giant among nineteenth-century publishers, John Blackwood.

It has proved impossible to frame a succinct tribute that adequately describes the part played in this book's evolution by its dedicatees, Jenny and Bill Helfrecht, but among the host of other friends who deserve my gratitude the following have provided help that can be more readily specified. Near the beginning a long conversation with Michael Wheeler gave me the encouragement I needed to pursue the experimental structure that I thought might do my subject better service than other tried and tested formulas for considering an author's life and work. As a final draft emerged, Kathleen Davies offered, to my great advantage, to become my first reader. Patrea and Alan More Nisbett offered the kind of hospitality that lent the charm of an exotic holiday to research trips to Edinburgh. Robin Gilbert has been both ingenious and persistent in tracking down the nineteenth-century copies of her works which are so hard to come by. My colleagues Gordon Dennis and Ian Lewis were sufficiently interested in the project to support bids for research time, and Dorothy McCarthy employed her versatile talents to act as a most sympathetic reader and copy-editor.

It is a pleasure to thank the staff of all the libraries who have helped me in the course of my research. Ellen Hall of Westminster College Library good-humouredly explored the resources of the Inter-Library loan scheme for me. David Loach facilitated my progress through various word-processing programs and

Kieran Boyle helped me in the production of the illustrations. Despite the ever-increasing pressures upon them, the English Faculty Library and the Bodleian Library in Oxford have never lost sight of the difference it makes to readers to feel that they are individually made welcome and helped. I should also like to pay tribute to the expertise and friendliness of the staff supervising the Manuscript Room in the National Library of Scotland, who have gone well beyond the call of duty in making sure that no minute of precious research time was wasted.

It is the Trustees of the National Library of Scotland, too, that I must once again acknowledge for permission to quote extensively from the complete manuscript of Mrs Oliphant's autobiography which they allowed me to publish in 1990. I am also grateful for the permission to quote from their extensive collection of Mrs Oliphant's letters. Princeton University Library kindly provided me with micro-film of their archive holdings pertaining to Mrs Oliphant and have granted their permission for quotation from these.

Mr Danvers Valentine has been extraordinarily generous in making available to me his family's collection of beautifully preserved photographs. When I received them, just before the book was due to go to print, it was as if so many of the people I had known only through their letters were given a new lease of life. I am delighted to have been allowed to make them known to a wider public and would also like to thank M. Maurice Lévy for offering his expertise in reproducing them.

Finally, I am fortunate in being able to thank the British Academy for making a research grant, without which it would have been difficult to embark upon a task of this size. I should like to express my gratitude to Westminster College for the research time I have been afforded. Ball State University, Indiana, also deserves mention for the generous conditions of my visiting professorship which allowed for ample research time and the opportunity to make contact with the growing band of Mrs Oliphant's American devotees.

Oxford   ELISABETH JAY
1993

Contents

List of Illustrations

Preface

Mrs Oliphant won a name for herself as an exceptionally prolific and accomplished writer in the highly competitive market of Victorian literature's golden age. Carlyle[1] and Gladstone[2] paid tribute to her non-fiction. Darwin was allegedly an avid reader of her novels,[3] but that, as Mrs Oliphant herself remarked, was a barbed compliment, since he claimed to 'like all if moderately good, and if they do not end unhappily'.[4] Tennyson, whose own writing career outspanned even Mrs Oliphant's, commenting towards the end of his life on her prolific output, told his son that 'she was nearly always worth reading'.[5] Towards the end of her life she attracted a new generation of discriminating readers. Robert Louis Stevenson confessed that he had been moved to tears by *A Beleaguered City*[6] and J. M. Barrie was a prime mover in the effort to secure Mrs Oliphant an adequate memorial.[7] In our own age, however, Q. D. Leavis's informed and impassioned attempt to reinstate her as 'the exemplary woman of letters'[8] has not succeeded, as yet, in restoring her name to the great tradition alongside sister writers such as the Brontës, Elizabeth Barrett Browning, and George Eliot.

Perhaps the name by which Q. D. Leavis and I have both chosen to discuss her seems less inviting than the intimacy promised by talk of Charlotte, Emily, Anne, or Elizabeth. Of recent years it has become even more fashionable to refer, non-divisively, to authors of both sexes by their surnames, but my resolve, in this particular case, to resist the trend, was strengthened by reading Daniel Ferrer's book on Virginia Woolf where I found a similar anxiety of naming disclosed.

I do not feel comfortable with the academic convention of referring to the author of *The Waves* as 'Woolf'. It surprises me that feminist critics should be willing to reduce her to her husband's name in this way . . . Although I feel very close to her after many years of intimacy with her texts, it would seem slightly patronising, or even improper to call her Virginia (after all, I have never been introduced to her, and she was a self-confessed snob). 'Virginia Woolf' is the name she chose as her signature . . . and it shall be repeated here, however cumbersome.[9]

As a later chapter will show, Mrs Oliphant's name was one of her most highly prized possessions; she attached great importance to its correct usage and, furthermore, only permitted its use in circumstances she felt would redound to her credit. Since her first chosen title-page appellation, Margaret Oliphant Wilson Oliphant, proved too cumbersome for regular use, and 'Margaret Oliphant' too frequently risked confusion with her mother, I have chosen, everywhere other than in the account of her childhood, to use the name by which she was professionally known to her contemporaries for the greater part of her career.

Prefatory essays are often used to preview the contents of the ensuing book, but in this case, while the chapter headings might be felt to speak for themselves, it seems important to explain the decisions which lay behind the arrangement of my material.

First, Mrs Oliphant's work raises in particularly acute form the question of the critical relation between the author and the work. It would be foolish to ignore the strong autobiographical impulse in much of her fiction, but to use the fiction mainly as illustrative material for the life becomes little more than a game of literary snap, demeaning the artist by ignoring the creative element involved in the selection and recomposition of these elements derived from 'real life'. She was to describe the process in an early novel, whose heroine is a young novelist.

Agnes's thoughts glided unconsciously into impersonation, and fairy figures gathered around her, and one by one her fables grew, in the midst of the thread of story—in the midst of what people called, to the young author's great amusement, 'an elaborate development of character, the result of great study and observation' . . . Almost unconsciously she had shadowed his circumstances and his story in many a bright imagination of her own; and contrasted with the real ones half-a-dozen imaginary Lionels.[10]

Although we can clearly trace the origins of some of her recurring fictional preoccupations to the concerns of her daily life, it is important to remember that in the earlier part of her life she read her day's writing aloud to her immediate family circle, who encouraged her publishing ambitions. Family copyists do not appear to have recognized themselves in, or at least did not object to, the sons and brothers and dependants whose weakness and lack of backbone caused so much agony to their families in fiction. Mrs Oliphant herself repeatedly decried the public's habit of hunting for the 'originals' behind the fiction of the day. Literary creativity did not lie 'in conscious observation of your neighbour's follies or peculiarities', and she offered tart rebukes to younger novelists who allegedly always had a notebook to hand in which to jot down their observations from daily life.[11] Her objections stemmed partly from her great reserve and dislike of the betrayal of private confidences and in part from her artistic conviction that fiction should stress the universal elements of character rather than transliterate individual foibles. This decision must have represented some sacrifice for her since her private writings reveal her considerable skill as a mimic and satirical anecdotalist, but there were other artistic compensations in the imaginative possibilities thus opened up.

The great 'masters' of the Victorian realist tradition did not hold an unproblematic view of their fiction as simply the powerful expression of personal experience transferred to the canvas of a given imagined social context.[12] In fact what repeatedly struck Mrs Oliphant was the obvious disparity between the life and the work of her fellow novelists. Having read *George Eliot's Life as Recounted in her Letters and Journals*, she could only explain the phenomenon thus to herself: 'I think she must have been a dull woman with a great genius distinct from herself.' By contrast, Trollope's 'talk about the characters in his books' as if they were quasi-real people astonished her 'beyond measure', as something of which she herself would have been incapable.[13]

It would also be simplistic to assume a direct synchronic relation between the life and the art. During the year of most intense grief after the death of her daughter, she was to write two novels, *Agnes* and *A Son of the Soil*, whose subject-matter reflected this, but also her most sustained piece of comic writing, *Miss Marjoribanks*. Moreover, the way in which fictional events and disasters quite frequently seem to prefigure the course that her life was to take can seem weird until we remember the way in which fiction hypothesizes possible resolutions to varied combinations of circumstances. Part of the pleasure Mrs Oliphant derived from her writing was the knowledge that in fiction one could resolve problems which in life itself were chronic, yet much of her strength as a writer came in the resistance she offered to that absolute division between life and the escapist lure of fiction.

In organizing my material I have therefore resisted the temptation to juxtapose chronologically organized chapters upon the life and the writing, partly because the sheer volume of her work makes this cluttered and confusing, and partly because the preoccupations and opinions expressed in her writing do not always fit a neat line of linear development. Furthermore, linearity has a tendency to become conflated with the notion of progress and as such is peculiarly ill-suited to deal with the cyclical rhythm of women's lives. Trying to make a woman's life conform to the implicit lines of increasing self-determination and pyramidal achievement in which a man's life is often conceived does a real disservice to the complexity of the network of sometimes conflicting goals to which a woman's life may tend. For a woman who takes motherhood and work equally seriously, the one may involve her in a process of self-subordination and learning to let go, while the other requires a degree of tenacious self-realization. My resolution to listen to another rhythm drew strength from Mrs Oliphant's own account of her life, which attempted to trace the underlying threads in the fragmentary, non-sequential narrative which she felt best characterized the multi-faceted nature of a working mother's life. If I have not wholly escaped the critical biographer's desire to produce coherence and logical evolution where introspection and observation remind us that each of us daily experiences contradictory desires and emotions, I offer up as a caveat her own picture of an elderly spinster contemplating her life.

She herself was two persons in one, difficult to identify in their separate characters: young Jean Hay-Heriot among the ruins, fresh and sweet as the youngest rose in the garden: old Miss Jean with her shrivelled face surrounded by her 'borders', her wrinkled hand leaning on her cane . . . Which was the real one between these two? which the most true, the past that lives for ever, or the present that is but for a moment?[14]

Her awareness of the slipperiness of such terms as 'the real character', 'the true meaning' or the definitive reading of an event makes her *Autobiography* at times seem like a deconstructionist's paradise. Repeatedly she reminds us that the events of her life, when opened up to subsequent interpretation, seem to offer a multitude of competing meanings, each of which would appear to deny the primacy of the others.

I have therefore adopted a framework for my discussion of Mrs Oliphant's work that allows for the various ways in which her writing mirrored, ironically considered, and sometimes evaded, the concerns of her daily life. I have attempted to show that this most self-aware of women was both creation and creator of the social milieux in which she moved and which she sought to represent. It seemed to me that, despite and because of the energetic debate between essentialism, and the feminine as a social construct, the only firm ground which offered itself was her sense of herself as a woman attempting to evaluate, both in 'real life' and in her fiction, the sometimes conflicting gender roles in which her particular circumstances involved her.

Secondly, I should like to address the two questions I have most frequently been asked during the time I have spent working on this book: 'Is she worth reading?' and 'Where should I start?'. It is all very well quoting to fellow 'Victorianists', happy for any mite which will augment their knowledge of the cultural history of the period, the nineteenth-century praise of her work with which I began this preface, but these same tributes may seem off-putting to many late twentieth-century readers, suggesting either 'earnestness' or the muted tones of a sentimental period piece. Reducing Mrs Oliphant to a phenomenon of cultural history in either of these ways is, in effect, to label her from the outset a minor talent. Mrs Oliphant's case suggests significant variations to the received myth of the Victorian woman writer as anonymous, or, at best, pseudonymous, dependent upon male approval and business skills, and equipped with a temperament, and sometimes a physique, in need of constant nursing. Moreover, the length and variety of Mrs Oliphant's writing career prompts reconsideration of the terms by which we confer minor or major status. George Eliot's career, for instance, has all too often been seen as paradigmatic rather than exceptional; moreover, its shape has been reinterpreted as a myth of progress, so that the activity of literary reviewing thus becomes an apprentice stage for the creative talent and, therefore, regarded as an inferior adjunct to creative talent: money-spinning rather than yarn-spinning. Mrs Oliphant, by contrast, obtained her first commission as a reviewer on the strength of her success as a novelist and short-story writer. She was not merely a product of her culture, but she had a greater hand than almost any other contemporary novelist in forming the standards of that market. If we set Mrs Oliphant's fifty-year stint as a major reviewer for *Blackwood's Edinburgh Magazine* (otherwise known as *Blackwood's Magazine, Blackwood's*, or, by the affectionate diminutive, *Maga*) not against Eliot's monolithic figure but alongside the careers of modern novelists such as Martin Amis, Julian Barnes, Anita Brookner, Penelope Fitzgerald, or Fay Weldon, the practice of combining fiction with reviewing need no longer inevitably be seen as the financial penalty exacted for being a minor artist, but as part of the material that fuels the creative talent. George Eliot's fears of unconscious plagiarism, combined, perhaps, with a desire to have an uncluttered run at her memory's richest vein, virtually precluded her from reading contemporary fiction, excepting that of close friends. Mrs Oliphant, by contrast, claimed, 'I wrote as I read, with much the same sort of feeling. It seems to me that this is rather an original way of putting it (to disclose the privatest thought in my mind), and this gives me an absurd little sense of pleasure.'[15] Her fiction did not change merely according to the dictates of the market, but, fed by her activities as a reviewer, often embodied a response to her voracious reading of other novelists.

Once fired with enthusiasm for Mrs Oliphant's varied *œuvre*, the prospective reader faces the even more difficult question of where to start. Availability is the first hurdle. Despite her prolific output of some ninety-eight novels, fifty or more short stories, twenty-five works of non-fiction, and over three hundred articles published in periodicals, virtually none of this is accessible in its original state outside library collections. Second-hand booksellers have suggested that, like many another author whose star had waned, her fiction was pulped during the Second World War. Within the last decade feminist and other presses have started to republish her fiction, but their selection, understandably, has been based either upon those novels enjoying a high critical repute during her lifetime or upon specialized interests such as the tale of the supernatural. Offering 'tasters' of her work is difficult because of its range and variety, both of genre and tone. Her fiction includes the *roman à thèse* form popular at the outset of her career, historical novels, the regionally based novels of Scotland and Liverpool, a provincial saga, the sensational, tales of the supernatural, and tales of closely observed domestic suffering and joy. Sometimes she would mix these elements within one novel, so that the tone of the novel becomes inconsistent. *Salem Chapel* suffers badly from the sensational plot, which sits ill at ease with the comic realism with which the Dissenting milieu of its setting is depicted. Yet the blending of the various modes at her disposal could elsewhere produce uniquely flavoured creations: *The Wizard's Son* reworks material from her previous work in the supernatural short-story genre, uses both English and Scottish settings, and draws upon her own situation at the time of writing. The transition between *The Wizard's Son* and the pages of the consistently controlled sardonic tone employed by the narrator of the much-acclaimed and often republished *Miss Marjoribanks* suggests the distance to be travelled by the would-be explorer of Mrs Oliphant's fiction.

The opposite side of the coin of this facility for mixing apparently disparate elements was the carelessness which came with profusion. A dominant interest in a character or theme too frequently made her indifferent to the feasibility or mechanics of plot construction. The speed with which she worked, often with as many as three pieces of work on the go simultaneously, did not allow for tightness of structure or the management of overall coherence which might have come with careful revision. Sometimes novels almost burst apart because of the multiplicity of themes, images, and ideas with which they teem.

The Three Brothers provides a fine example of this tendency: it takes as its starting-point a curious will which stipulates a seven-year period during which the three sons of a gentleman's family must make their own way in life before receiving their family inheritance. The ensuing three volumes follow the fortunes of the three brothers, the eldest of whom, disappointed in his love for an adventuress, emigrates to Canada. The second brother's pursuit of his artistic instincts takes us into the most fully realized part of the novel where he falls in love with a widow whose skill as an artist keeps her household afloat. The third brother, a guardsman, negotiates his way between the possibility of a rich marriage to the daughter of a vulgar merchant and the love of the artist widow's daughter. Each of the plots contains an element which raises it above the stereotypical: the adventuress is a 'girl of the period', hard-bitten and determined, but different from her scheming and duplicitous mother. Her reappearance later in the story as the wretched wife of the rich merchant is the crudest plot device, but her portrait contains the germ of subsequent full-length studies by Mrs Oliphant of women who might have been redeemed had love and money been offered together. Her story remains a sketch with unexplored possibilities because Mrs Oliphant's interest switches to the semi-Bohemian world of artistic London, where the second brother finds himself. Drawing upon the spell of married life she had spent in a similar environment, Mrs Oliphant then uses the plight of the widowed artist, Mrs Severn, as a vehicle for an examination of problems central to her own life as a writer. The competing claims upon Mrs Severn made by her art and her financial need, her family and her suitor, are drawn from the inmost concerns of Mrs Oliphant's life and as such grow to dominate the reader's interest in a way that is detrimental to the novel as a whole. This part of the tale, which might well have become a vent for self-pity, gains its cutting edge by allowing us to see the intensity of the widow's dilemma from the point of view of others to whom her self-sacrifice seems akin to passionate egotism. The third, guardsman, brother's situation becomes interesting mainly because the fairy-tale plot allows him to become involved in a tug of love with the widow for her daughter, but even the poor little rich girl whom he abandons is endowed with feelings and thoughts which raise her above the conventional status of passive trophy or 'rich bitch'. The novel has strayed from its titular and narrative origins, but as Mrs Oliphant gathers up the strands she surprises the reader once more by giving a generic twist to the tale: the secret of the will which has ostensibly provided the seven-year period for the proof of manliness and the climactic revelation to which the novel is steered turns out to be a chimera. Land and money have been conventionally distributed, there are to be no fairy-tale rewards. Character, not plot, triumphs: temperament and strength of will, most frequently found in the female characters, are the determining factors. Such an ending draws attention to a further hallmark of Mrs Oliphant's fiction. The deliberate eschewal of conventionally satisfying endings could easily have become an artistic mannerism. Instead, her endings often cast a shadow back over the novel as a whole and raise unsettling questions about the reader's expectations of fiction and of life. By dint of raising conventional endings as a matter for consideration Mrs Oliphant reminds the reader that the narrative strategies and choices of fiction reflect agreed ideologies and acceptable interpretations of experience. It is not in the action of her novels that we find the dissenting voice but in the authorial disposition and interpretation of events.

What emerges increasingly clearly in sustained reading of Mrs Oliphant's correspondence, autobiographical writings, and fiction, is the surprising depth of her self-awareness. Her tongue-tied shyness in social gatherings had allowed her to observe to the full, but reinforced her sense that to others she might well seem stiff, sullen, and self-absorbed.[16] In her letters expressions of justifiable exasperation at the impossible behaviour of relatives are often tempered by a phrase which suddenly disperses the acrimony, admitting that her own behaviour may well seem equally obtuse or high-handed to them. In the fiction this disparity between the subjective and objective view of a character can be used to either tragic or comic effect. Sometimes, she abandons her ironic distance and we are faced with the disruptive effect of what is felt as a more personal intervention. These sudden, disconcerting, relinquishings of the authorial control of unitary tone in her text seem to me characteristic of her writing rather than arbitrary lapses, and for that reason I would hesitate to recommend the carefully controlled *Miss Marjoribanks*, though undeniably a great achievement, as representative of her writing. It is perhaps the apparent 'artlessness' of Mrs Oliphant's flowing prose style, with its conversational cadences and her distrust of the sententious, that has served to conceal this sense of an inner discourse that runs through her work. Yet the complicating sense of irony, so conspicuously lacking in those of her characters who succeed in society's terms, is also fundamental to her work. Absolute self-absorption and an unremitting sense of one's individual value were, she sometimes ruefully reflected, the identifying marks of genius in the case of women such as George Eliot or Charlotte Brontë, or her own creation, Lucilla Marjoribanks. These features, that called forth both pity and envy from her, amounted to an inalienable gender characteristic when they appeared in men. (Ironically enough, this very refusal to project strong female role models, other than in parodic form, may have been responsible for alienating some of her potential feminist readership.)

The sense of men as a race apart suggests one source of the alienation which has so often proved profitable to writers. Consciousness of difference is an impetus to finding a distinctive voice. In Mrs Oliphant's case there were further important factors which helped her to find and maintain a sense of creative unease, so that her point of view never became static or complacent. Two other aspects of her life helped her to resist assimilation into what Matthew Arnold described as the 'tone of the centre'. First, she was born a Scot, but was transplanted at the age of 10 to an expatriate life in the nationally conscious communities of Liverpool. She remained fiercely proud of her Scots ancestry and although she chose to live in England and to give her sons an English gentleman's education at Eton, her attitudes to the English establishment were coloured by her Scottish inheritance. Secondly, her life is proof of the social mobility open to the Victorian middle classes. From her childhood in a humble clerk's home she won for herself a house and position in the heart of Windsor's genteel society where she found herself the recipient of invitations to tea and conversation with her sovereign. Yet the demands upon her purse never allowed her to forget how insecure was her tenure in the realms of upper-middle-class comfort.

Drawing upon this consciousness of difference, I have attempted to write a book which both illuminates the nature of Mrs Oliphant's peculiar achievement and raises wider issues about the most profitable ways of reading women writers.

Part One
Women and Men

1 *Relating the Life*

'It's not the facts, it's the narrative they're arranged to tell', she reminded herself.[1]

Powerful writers lose none of their myth-making capacity when they turn their attention to the art of autobiography. Until very recently John Henry Newman's *Apologia,* or Anthony Trollope's *An Autobiography* provided the framework within which their lives were retold and interpreted by others. In their stories of their own lives they selected, created, and explored the events and emotions that they grew to believe had shaped their subsequent work. The correlation thus provided between the life and the work holds a simple, self-confirming, and therefore compelling, construction for later readers. Mrs Oliphant's *Autobiography* forms no exception to this rule. Therefore, although I have chosen to interweave her life and work throughout this book, it seemed helpful to begin by providing three different ways of looking at her life. The chapter starts by recounting the main events of her life, largely in her own words,[2] while highlighting those aspects that were to prove particularly significant to the nature of her writing. The second section considers her own arrangement of the narrative she wished to present, along with the 'textual harassment' her account suffered at the hands of her first editors. The final section offers some alternative readings of the story of her life.

1. *The Story of her Life*

She was born Margaret Oliphant Wilson in Wallyford, Midlothian on 4 April 1828, the youngest surviving child of Francis Wilson, a clerk. She had two elder brothers, Frank, who was twelve years her senior, and Willie, who was nine years older. In between the two brothers and their little sister there had been a girl and two boys who had died. 'I was born after that period of misery, and brought back life to my mother's heart,' Mrs Oliphant wrote in 1885, and added, 'I know now that I was a kind of idol to her from my birth.' Her parents were almost 40 when Margaret was born and her mother decided to bring up the only daughter she was now likely to have 'with all the delicacies of a woman's ideal child'. With two devoted older brothers and a father who was 'a very dim figure' in her recollection of family life, it is scarcely surprising that Mrs Oliphant was affronted by the prevailing view of a Victorian woman's position that she confronted in her working life. Her mother's devoted attention to her one ewe-lamb was also to provide a model to her daughter when early widowhood made the likelihood of her bearing further children more remote.

During her first ten years she moved twice with her parents, first to Lasswade, near Edinburgh, and then to Glasgow, where her father had obtained a position at the Royal Bank. Around 1838 they moved again when her father obtained a post as a clerk in the Customs House at Liverpool. The seafaring life, witnessed from the comparative safety of the dockside, was to become an important feature in many of her early tales, as was the appalling poverty in such communities caused by fluctuating trade conditions. Her brother Frank soon joined the family in Liverpool, but Willie spent the dangerous and formative two years between the ages of 19 and 21 in Scotland.

It seems probable that Margaret was educated at home by her mother, whose reading habits were eclectic: they ran from the novels to be borrowed at circulating libraries, through the more serious periodicals of the day. The local doctor at Lasswade, David Macbeth Moir, called in to tend the small daughter who had tumbled into the fireplace, was a regular contributor to the Tory *Blackwood's Edinburgh Magazine* and became a firm friend, despite Mrs Wilson's own pronounced Radicalism. Her mother's tales of the former glories of the Oliphant family lent a romantic strain to the daughter's sense of her Scottish maternal inheritance.

Margaret Oliphant's first novel was written, when she was 17, as a solace and pastime while her mother was seriously ill and she herself recovering from a broken engagement. Although she was later to feel that her family had 'lived in the most singularly secluded way', her mother's hospitable tendencies always at war with her father's dislike of 'guests at his table', she nevertheless managed to attract two suitors, a bashful Irish minister from their church, and J.Y., whom she agreed to marry on his return from America in three years time.

He was a good, simple, pious, domestic, kind-hearted fellow, fair-haired, not good-looking, not ideal at all. He cannot have been at all clever, and I was rather. When he went away our correspondence for some time was very full; then I began to find his letters silly, and I suppose said as much. Then there were quarrels, quarrels with the Atlantic between, then explanations, and then dreadful silence. It is amusing to look back upon, but it was not at all amusing to me then.

The episode was to bear fruit both in tales of romantic fidelity, such as *Kirsteen*, and in tales, such as *Old Mr Tredgold*, where the traveller's return serves only to show the gap between tenderly cherished romantic illusion and prosaic reality. Its more immediate effects were also literary: encouraging her to recast her plight in romantic vein in a 'very silly' first novel (later published by her brother as *Christian Melville*), and to develop a certain critical asperity in evaluating her lover's letters.

She was 21 when her first novel, *Passages in the Life of Margaret Maitland*, was published and made a sufficient splash to be mentioned by Charles Dickens and Charlotte Brontë in their letters.[3] Jubilation was tempered by anxiety over her feckless brother Willie, who had embarked upon ministerial training at the English Presbyterian College in London. Precisely why he was sent to London rather than

Scotland for training remains obscure: perhaps he had already disgraced himself in Scotland, or perhaps Mrs Wilson hoped that her nephews, Frank and Tom, with whom he was to share lodgings in St Pancras, would prove a steadying influence. A familiar motif of the fiction in which women have to provide the moral exemplar while realizing their relative powerlessness to transform weak men was preparing itself: Margaret was dispatched to London to see Willie through the last three months of his training and restrain him from his besetting sins of drink and debt. In October 1850 Willie found his first post as minister of Etal in Northumberland, 'a sort of show village with pretty flowery cottages and gardens'. His womenfolk decided, 'with hopes strangely wild', that in such surroundings Willie could not but settle to his 'lowly sacred duties'. The tight-knit family life of the Wilsons, developed in the course of their frequent moves, gave them little insight into the difficulties that Willie would encounter in following a predecessor who had occupied the post for sixty-two years.[4]

Early in 1851 Margaret's cousin Frank, who had squired her around London, came for a visit to the Wilson family, who had recently moved again across the river to more prosperous Birkenhead. When a proposal of marriage came from this cousin, ten years her senior, she was entirely unprepared and refused him. The order of events becomes a trifle confused here. In her *Autobiography* she claimed that Frank's proposal came after Willie's retreat from Etal, but this seems unlikely, both because she makes no mention of her fear of embroiling Frank in these problems as a reason for declining him and because that spring her mother was sufficiently free from anxiety over Willie to plan a literary launch for her daughter. She planned her campaign carefully. Overcoming her general contempt for her husband's side of the family, she took pains to claim acquaintance with some second cousins in Edinburgh. The two older sons, Daniel (1816–92) and George (1818–59), had highly successful academic careers ahead of them. Daniel was to become President of Toronto University and gain a knighthood, while George became Regius Professor of Technology in Edinburgh. At the time of the visit they appeared to their younger cousin to be wholly immersed in literary affairs, writing poetry and, more importantly, involved in an advisory capacity with Nelson's publishing house. Mrs Wilson, however, had set her sights higher than a publishing house known for cheap but improving literature, and so determined to renew her acquaintance with Dr Moir, whose other life as the poet 'Delta' could secure Margaret the coveted introduction to the more prestigious firm of Blackwoods. Mrs Wilson was probably well satisfied with Margaret's entry into Edinburgh literary society, where she had not only made useful commercial connections but acquired a wider circle of friendly but discerning critics. Families such as the Moirs and the Blackwoods were to provide those enduring friends that were to mean so much to a busy woman whose working life often necessitated prolonged visits abroad. The ease with which she knew she could settle back into Edinburgh, and later St Andrews, were to sustain for Mrs Oliphant her sense of herself as a Scottish writer. Furthermore, the recementing of the bonds with their relations in Scotland was to secure a wife for her brother Frank, who married Jeanie Wilson, Daniel and George's youngest sister, who was much of an age with Margaret.

By the autumn Margaret had decided to accept Frank. What brought about her change of heart must remain a mystery. Her tight-lipped comment in the *Autobiography*, 'in six months or so things changed. It is not a matter into which I can enter now', might seem to hint that circumstances rather than romantic inclination dictated the first stages of her reversal. The prospect of acting as housekeeper for the increasingly unstable Willie cannot have made an overwhelmingly attractive alternative. Whatever her initial reasons she was able to write in this vein to Frank the following year: 'I gave you my promise when I was not secure of my heart—I give you my heart now without reserve, with joy and thankfulness, even in this affliction.'[5]

The affliction of which she spoke was Willie's wholesale relapse into alcoholism. 'Without warning, except that his letters had begun to fail, a little, my mother received an anonymous letter about him.' Willie had to be brought home before he could become the subject of church disciplinary procedures. In August he moved with his parents to London, where they had decided to move so that they could spend their retirement near to their beloved daughter, who had married Francis Wilson Oliphant, painter and stained-glass-window artist, on 4 May 1852. For the next two years Willie was encouraged to 'retrieve a sort of fictitious independence' by receiving 10 per cent of his sister's profits for making fair copies of her manuscripts. She lost the opportunity, and, possibly, the habit, of careful revision and gained the first of her dependants. He had in any case already been admitted into a kind of partnership with his sister. It was Willie who had first undertaken negotiations with London publishers on her behalf, and in the process had managed to have four of her novels attributed to his authorship. This involvement did eventually lead him to write a further five novels himself.[6]

The early period of Margaret's seven-year marriage was marred by hostility between her husband and her mother and the stress of dividing her attention between two warring adults and the two baby girls, Maggie and Marjorie, who were born a year apart, on 21 May 1853 and 22 May 1854. Recollecting a period when the jealous rivalry was at such a pitch that she had been forced to keep her daily visits to her mother secret, she wrote, 'I have gone through many sorrows since, but I don't know that any period of my life has ever contained more intolerable moments than those first years that should have been so happy.' With her mother's death in September 1854 the emotional tension lessened, but a residue of guilt remained. In part Margaret, whose life had been wrapped up in her mother's to such an extent that in 1888 she could write, 'I think instinctively still of asking her something, referring to her for information, and I dream constantly of being a girl with her at home', was learning a swift and often painful range of new feelings, not least that motherhood roused her most intense emotions. She seemed genuinely puzzled by the fact that her mother's death was totally eclipsed by the death of her eight-month-old daughter and a day-old son, all three occurring within fourteen months.

People will say it was an animal instinct perhaps. Neither of these little ones could speak to me or exchange an idea or show love, and yet their withdrawal was like the sun going out from the sky—life remained, the daylight continued, but all was different.

Her mother's death also brought about the final break-up of the Wilson family home. Her father seemed, as always, happier in his own company. Frank and Jeanie had remained in Birkenhead, where their four children, Frank, Jeanie, Madge, and Denny were born. Willie took himself off for the time being to write in a clachan on the banks of Loch Lomond.

Throughout these troubled months the writing continued. Although she might claim that her fictions never possessed her, or competed for attention with her family or friends, her writing at the very least provided a rhythm and an imaginative space to counterbalance the successive waves of grief and depression that seemed to characterize her domestic life at this period. Only once, a month after Marjorie's death, did she admit to John Blackwood that she had fallen behind with a proposed article on Dickens.[7] Fortunately, too, she had already stumbled upon a justification for her writing activities that helped her to repudiate the frightening old wives' tales repeated to her by a fellow woman writer, Mary Howitt, the prolific poet, essayist, and translator of Hans Christian Andersen, who told Margaret 'of many babies whom she had lost through some defective valve in the heart, which she said was somehow connected with too much mental work on the part of the mother'. She had already realized that her talent, rather than being seen as a selfish threat to maternity, could be employed as an important contribution to the family budget. In March 1854 she had approached *Blackwood's Edinburgh Magazine* for the chance of the more regular income that would come from reviewing.[8] Professionally speaking this was an important decision, since it was to offer her almost half a century's freelance work and establish her as a powerful critical voice in Victorian literary life. Nevertheless, her habit of referring to herself as Blackwood's 'general utility woman' significantly employed a domestic figure of speech to contain the glories of her achievement within the permissible bounds of lowly female employment.[9]

At this stage in their married life money was needed to support a swiftly growing household. Four children had been born in quick succession: a fourth child, Cyril Francis, always known as Tids or Tiddy, was born on 16 November 1856. Socially too their ideas and needs were expanding: their household at this time supported more than one maid and their professional labours had gained them an entrée into the minor artistic and literary circles of London. These needs were all subsidiary, however, to the larger establishment Frank now envisaged. He set up a workshop near Baker Street, just along the road from their own house, where he could superintend the execution of his own window designs, hoping that this might eventually generate sufficient business to enable him to spend more time as a painter of the large historical and biblical pictures then in vogue. Frank had received his artistic education at the Government Trustees Academy in Edinburgh, under the state interventionist schemes popular in the late 1830s and early 1840s.[10]

However, the growing enthusiasm for church restoration, and his exposure to the ideas of ecclesiastical artists, such as William Dyce and Augustus Welby Pugin, led him to express sympathy with the anti-Erastian views and medieval enthusiasms of a group of artists who had been influenced by the Anglican High Church Movement. Agreeing with William Dyce that 'our glass painters are more money glaziers who dread the introduction of a kind of art which would require better workmen and so diminish the profits',[11] Frank Oliphant, himself a glass-cutter's son, published a pamphlet pleading for the establishment of schools and ateliers where artists and workmen might work side by side.[12] Such work, he remarked, needed to attract patrons, since it could not be expected to be exhibited for sale. His idealism took little account of London art-workmen, who, according to his wife, were 'highly paid, and untrustworthy to the last degree', nor of his lack of business expertise. He had instead concentrated upon artistic research. By 1855, when he published this pamphlet, he had already visited France, Germany, and the Low Countries, examining their traditions of painted glass: only for Italy did he have to rely upon other artists' accounts.

The promise of these years was abruptly shattered in mid-1857 when Frank's tubercular condition first manifested itself. He consulted a Harley Street specialist before they made the decision to disband the business and, supported entirely by Margaret's literary endeavours, to set out for the curative climate of Italy, Frank still pretending that the expense of the trip could be justified by the added artistic expertise it would bring him. Frank's failure to tell her the specialist's grim prognosis left her 'angry and wounded beyond measure' when she finally heard it from a third person. In January 1859 they left for Italy, and Margaret found herself for the first time supervising a travelling group, consisting of an invalid husband, 'ill and worn out, cold and miserable', two small children of 5 and 2, and a maidservant who had never been abroad before. When they reached Italy they were dismayed to find fog and freezing weather, rather than the recuperative sunshine they had longed for. Frank, at times listless, at times restless, and always withdrawn, lingered on, ill, miserable, and self-absorbed. His only worthwhile legacy to Margaret proved to be the friendship of an older painter friend of his, Robert Macpherson and his far younger wife, Geraldine, neé Bate (usually known as 'Geddie'). Robert had initially trained as a surgeon in Edinburgh and it may have been this that prompted Frank to foster the friendship, despite his wife's initial lack of fellow-feeling with this ramshackle family who now ran a photographic business in Rome, further supplemented by Geraldine's activities as engraver and translator. Trust and mutual liking grew as the couple proved themselves 'as good to me as brother and sister', in the days after Frank's death; and it was to this Bohemian partnership that Margaret decided to entrust her brother Willie, who at some point in the early 1860s deteriorated to the point of no longer being able to live independently. In better times he could help run the shop where Robert sold his views of Roman antiquities; during his alcoholic binges the Macphersons could be trusted to keep an eye on him and dole out the allowance that Margaret found herself paying him until his death in 1885. Willie's canny capacity for self-preservation may be gauged by the fact that he survived the death of the Macphersons by a further seven years.

When the good weather came in the summer of 1859 Frank appeared to enjoy periods of remission as they moved from place to place, but when they returned to Rome on 1 October a French doctor told Margaret that the end was in sight. Heavily pregnant, but buoyed up by laudanum, she nevertheless tended Frank night and day until he died, 'quite conscious, kissing me when his lips were already cold, and quite, quite free from anxiety, though he left me with two helpless children and one unborn'.

Margaret had to await the birth of her last child, Cecco (officially named Francis Romano), in Rome on 12 December, before travelling home in February 1860.

When I began the world anew I had for all my fortune about £1000 of debt, a small insurance of, I think, £200 on Frank's life, our furniture laid up in a warehouse, and my own faculties, such as they were, to make our living and pay off our burdens by.

A year of restless movement followed as she took her children around the country, first visiting her married brother Frank in Birkenhead, then taking a house, within reach of friends, on the Fife coast, then moving to Edinburgh for the winter. Here her importunate demands upon her banker-publisher, John Blackwood, were finally refused and, from the depths of her despair, she produced what she ever afterwards regarded as the turning-point of her career, the initial story of the 'Chronicles of Carlingford' series.

Another project at this time, a biography of Edward Irving, a popular Scottish millenarian preacher of the previous generation, commissioned by his relatives, produced new contacts and friendships and launched her into a world where she was regarded as a successful breadwinner, not merely a pathetic relict. It was by way of this project that she became a staunch friend of Thomas Carlyle and his wife, both at one time intimates of Irving. Her work on Irving also effected the introduction to the Story family, who occupied the manse at Rosneath, a lochside parish on the west coast of Scotland, which was to supply her with the setting to several of her Scottish novels, a location for family holidays, and, almost certainly, a suitor. The Reverend Robert Herbert Story, who had recently succeeded his father as minister, was seven years her junior, but they were mutually attracted. She recalled him as a prematurely grey, 'handsome young' man—'a very piquant combination'—whose capacity to spice his conversation with 'witty and profane' allusions to biblical texts taught her to laugh again. She was sufficiently attracted that she remained uncertain for a few months whether her decision to continue 'without any props upon my natural lonely life' had been the right one. Although he was married to someone else within two years, he was one of her last visitors as she lay dying, and remained permanently captivated by her 'lambent eyes' and the attractively low tones of her Scottish accent.[13] Despite the slightly less enthusiastic hospitality of the subsequent Mrs Story, Rosneath clearly retained an especial place in her affections, for it was there that she chose to erect a memorial window to her deeply loved daughter,

Maggie, and to donate a reredos in the form of an illuminated version of the Ten Commandments.[14]

In October 1861, however, perhaps feeling that it would be wise to seal her decision by putting some space between herself and the circle of Scottish friends, such as John Tulloch, Principal of St Andrews, and his wife, 'the Padrona', and the Blackwoods, in whose houses she was likely to encounter Story, Mrs Oliphant moved her family down to London, living near other publisher friends, Henry and Ellen Blackett. Nevertheless, she kept in touch with her Scottish friends and, in November 1863, persuaded by Geddie Macpherson, who had been staying with her, she led a large contingent of mothers and children, including Mrs Tulloch and her two eldest daughters, back to Rome.

Here tragedy struck again. 'It was rotting Rome that did it and I must not think of God as if he were lying in wait for me to take such terrible vengeance on me.' On 27 January 1864, after a four-day bout of gastric flu, her 10-year-old daughter Maggie died. Of all the bereavements that Mrs Oliphant was to suffer this was the hardest. Maggie had been for her, as her name suggested, what she had been for her mother, her one 'ewe-lamb': moreover, Maggie was the only one of her three children whom Mrs Oliphant's mother had known. As she sat, late at night, pouring out her grief into the pages of her journal, she wondered whether when Maggie arrived in heaven, as she surely must have done, 'Was my mother called to receive the child who was her baby as well as mine?' For the next twenty-six years Margaret Oliphant avoided every mention of her daughter's name, calling her instead 'my child, my darling, never that familiar sound'. Nor, after passing through it on 29 May, was Margaret ever to revisit Rome, even to see her brother, although thirty years later, when the death of her sons had distanced the first tragedy, she was briefly tempted, by her work in preparing *The Makers of Modern Rome*, to consider revisiting the city where so much had happened to her.[15]

For the next nineteen months she wandered around Europe, accompanied at first by the Tulloch family, for whose benefit the expedition had partly been organized, and then by her two boys and the two Tulloch girls, Sara and Fanny. They visited Naples and Capri and then returned north, via Switzerland and Paris. Throughout this troubled period abroad the writing continued with barely a pause. Her plans for the future now became wholly wrapped up in providing the best possible opportunities for her two boys. Looking back upon this period, thirty years later, she found herself wondering what would have happened had she done as she 'had half a mind . . . to take an *appartemento*' in the Italian countryside 'and throw myself into the rut of artist life . . . a life not exactly disorderly, but a little wild and wandering and gregarious'. Perhaps the model offered by her 'loving sister, Geddie', whose arrival in Italy, chaperoned by her aunt, Anna Brownell Jameson, a well-known writer on art and literature, had held such promise, but whose life now seemed only to consist of scraping around to find any work that would support the family, played its part in her decision. The prospect of getting sucked into the life of an expatriate colony might also have seemed to have put in jeopardy the chance of being in 'the first rank of novelists', that John Blackwood now assured her was within her grasp. Finally, although she had conscientiously hired tutors and governesses to attend to various subjects, including Cyril and Fanny's Latin, she began to worry that more systematic education was needed: 6-year-old Cecco's English, for example, 'begins now and then to get a little hazy'.[16]

So, in September 1865, she made a decision, which formed a 'turning-point' as dramatic in its way as the one she so often alluded to of 1861 when the Carlingford series had been conceived, and returned to England. There would be no more drifting round Europe, nor would she return to the renting of a series of borrowed houses in the vicinity of friends and relations in England and Scotland. By December she had decided upon an Eton education for the boys. Windsor, within easy travelling distance of her London publishers, was to remain the family base for the next thirty years. The social distance Margaret had travelled in under twenty years by her own literary efforts can be judged by comparing the street in Everton where she and her family had lived in 1849 with the house she now took in the best residential area of the royal borough of Windsor. Success created its own penalties: it created a life-style which not only demanded continuous creativity but assumed a constant or improving market for the product. In her sons' case an aristocratic education, albeit as day-boys, bred aristocratic expectations of life. Relatives and friends alike began to look to this hospitable household for a convenient lodging, or financial help, or literary patronage. Annie Louisa Walker, a distant relative, orphaned and in her mid-twenties, who had hoped to make a living out of literature, was the first permanent addition to the Windsor household. Early in 1868 Margaret's oldest brother Frank's family required urgent assistance. She had seen little of him, his wife, and four children, since an unsuccessful stay with them in early widowhood, but now she was the only relative in a position to help. In poor health, he had mismanaged his financial affairs so badly that he had to leave his job with the Bank of England and slip over the Channel to France. His sister took over his debts, sent his wife and two small daughters to join him, and took the two elder children, Frank and Nelly, back to Windsor. Nelly eventually found a home with a maternal aunt, but Frank received a home and an Eton education from his aunt Margaret. The household had scarcely readjusted before Frank, now widowed and a broken man, crawled back to his sister's house in the summer of 1870 with his two small girls, Madge (7) and Denny (5) to a life of total dependency. A permanent household of eight, and the dogs without which no home seemed complete to her,[17] required either larger accommodation or a reduced standard of living. Feeling herself 'still in the full tide of middle life', Mrs Oliphant opted for the former and resigned herself to doing 'second-class work all my life from lack of time to do myself full justice'.

This ménage continued for five years until the elder boys were ready to leave home, Cyril for Oxford and Frank junior for an engineering career in India. Amidst the atmosphere of farewell festivities her brother Frank died. Margaret continued with her plans to give the three boys a last, joint holiday in Switzerland and dispatched her two nieces, to whom she was still much less close than the three boys, to boarding-school in Germany. Alpine holidays were all the rage with the Victorian middle classes, and on this holiday Margaret made perhaps the last of her really intimate and lasting female friendships when she met Annie Thackeray, with her brother-in-law Leslie Stephen and his family. This holiday was indeed to prove a watershed for her family. For the first time her two small nieces, still aged only 12 and 10, were totally separated from the only home and relations they had known in the last five years. Entering into a house which even their aunt admitted was 'preoccupied by the boys', they had remained 'chilly, scared, distrustful little things'. Now, bereft of their father and brother, and isolated in Germany, they implored their aunt to come and retrieve them. Although she refused to alter the arrangements, her heart was touched and from that moment she adopted them as 'my true children, the unquestioned daughters of the house'.

A period of relative tranquillity and financial security should have ensued. In 1878 she felt justified in buying the house, Nos. 8–9 Clarence Crescent, Windsor, for £1,600, which, she felt, would surely represent a saving against the £105 rent per annum she had been paying.[18] Education, however, still remained an expensive item on the family budget: nor did it look such a good investment as it had during Cyril's brighter days at Eton. He seemed incapable of applying himself to his studies in Oxford and ran up bills at an alarming rate. It was during his time as an undergraduate that Margaret developed the nagging anxiety that his dilatoriness and increasing fondness for drink would leave her with another Willie on her hands. When Cecco's time arrived to go to Balliol she made it an excuse to take a house in Oxford from which she could supervise Cyril's final examination term. 'Notwithstanding all distractions he [Cyril] took a second-class at Oxford,—a great disappointment, yet not disgraceful after all.' While she was endeavouring to find a suitable career for Cyril and plan the future of her nieces, who had just returned to Windsor, news arrived of her nephew Frank's death from typhoid in India at the age of only 25.

Throughout the 1880s family troubles beset her. 'That', she felt in retrospect, 'was the burden and heat of the day: my anxieties were sometimes almost more than I could bear. I had gone through many trials, as I thought, and God knows many of them had been hard enough, but then I knew to the depths of my heart what the yoke was and how heavy.' Cecco showed signs of following his brother's footsteps at Oxford and only managed a fourth-class degree. Efforts to obtain Cyril government patronage failed and Margaret had to support his nominal, but none the less expensive, attempts to live the life of an impecunious barrister. Her own life, Margaret felt, could have been simplified and made more secure by the acquisition of an editorship of the kind of literary journal commensurate with her reputation, but this, she feared, was the kind of prize reserved for men. Instead her busy professional life as journalist, reviewer, novelist, and researcher was further complicated by the problems, both financial and administrative, that sporadic trips abroad for her work or for her sons' health brought with them. Tenants had to be found for the house, paying members of her travelling party had sometimes to be found to finance the travel, and lending libraries and the vagaries of the postal system had to be negotiated in order to ensure the arrival of material and the dispatch of proofs. By the 1880s her expenses always exceeded her income and so she found herself both unable to drive hard bargains with publishers and forced to work without pause.

Cyril's one brief foray into gainful and prestigious employment ended in disaster when his health was pronounced unlikely to survive the climate in Ceylon, where he spent only a matter of weeks as private secretary to the Governor, Sir Arthur Gordon. Cecco was dispatched to Germany to study in the hope that acquiring a thorough knowledge of a further language would improve his job prospects, but worrying bouts of illness, combined with his withdrawn and irascible temperament, cast a gloom over his future. Nor did the girls make the progress their aunt hoped for in the artistic careers on which she launched them: they too resisted her attempts to fire them with the necessary energy to take up independent lives.

During these years she experienced one important source of comfort: the occasional gift of 'a great quiet and calm' in the midst of all her miserable anxieties. The first of these experiences occurred at 'a very black moment' when she had taken Cyril, newly returned from Ceylon, and Cecco with her to St Andrews, and they left her alone every night while they went off to the fashionable Golf Club, seduced by its indolent bachelor charms. Something of her fears and her humiliating, yet compulsive, desire to spy upon her grown sons is caught in this recollection:

I went wandering across the links in the late twilight, almost dark, towards the sea. How clearly I can see the scene now. I went up round the Club to see if I could get a glimpse of them through the lighted windows, but could not, and then I sat down on the seat by the path before you come to the beach . . . I was very miserable, crying to God for them, both, feeling more miserable almost than I had ever done before—when suddenly there came upon me a great quiet and calm, and I seemed stilled and a kind of heavenly peace came over me—I thought after it must have been the peace that passeth all understanding.

The consolation she derived from this sense of the veil between the seen and the unseen being temporarily withdrawn fed itself both into a new departure in her fiction (her tales of the unseen) and into ways of coping with the further tragedies that befell her.

Cyril now seemed perfectly content to idle his days away at home, sponging from his mother for the money necessary to keep up his drinking and socializing. His mother grew to dread the hour before dinner, waiting for Cyril's return, flushed and incoherent, after which 'there would be the usual night of confused guilt and all well next day'. She tried to interest him in work as her amanuensis,[19] entrusted to him a volume on Alfred de Musset, 'of which much was so well done, and yet some so badly done', for the Blackwood's Foreign Classics for English Readers series, of which she was editor. He obtained some employment working for the *Court and Society Review*, but the paper soon folded. Meanwhile Cecco's health caused her constant anxiety; she therefore decided to take him to the Riviera for the worst part of the winter at the beginning of 1889, dropping her niece Denny off in Paris to continue her training as a portrait painter. Cyril was to accompany the party, which also included two paying guests to contribute to the cost. On a railway station in Paris, however, he had some kind of fit and then relapsed into several hours of unconsciousness. His mother and brother stayed behind to nurse him, while the rest of the, now unescorted, party continued. Hotel and medical expenses mounted so swiftly that Mrs Oliphant had to apply to Blackwoods for emergency funds. Cyril eventually made a sufficiently good recovery to continue the journey, but his health, not helped by his drinking habits, was now a continual source of anxiety for his mother.

In July 1889 Cecco was offered intermittent employment as an assistant to the Queen's Librarian at Windsor Castle at the salary of £10 a month. Given his poor degree, his unsociable manner, and his uncertain health, he almost certainly owed this job, involving cataloguing books on genealogy, to his mother's influence. During the following year he was scarcely at home long enough to put in much time at the library: first he accompanied his mother, Cyril, and Madge on Mrs Oliphant's most adventurous journey to date, an expedition to Jerusalem, financed by an advance from Macmillans for another of Mrs Oliphant's popular and evocative accounts of famous historic cities. Typically she managed also to squeeze an article for *Maga*, and some material for her forthcoming biography of Laurence Oliphant, out of the experience.[20] Twice again that year, in May and in November, Cecco was advised to go abroad for his health. On the second occasion, however, his travel plans were interrupted by the sudden and, at least to his mother, unexpected death of his older brother Cyril, after only four days' illness, some time in the night of 8 November. There were no consolations that his mother could take in a life well spent: all with which she could console herself was that 'It will no longer be possible to err', and that in the afterlife God would purify her boy of his foolish weaknesses. Even in her desolation there was a sense of release that she had been relieved of the need 'to take some other steps to save him from himself'. Within a week of the funeral Mrs Oliphant had hustled Cecco abroad to Davos to forestall another death from tuberculosis.

Now in her sixties and with only one of her own children left alive, it is scarcely surprising that Mrs Oliphant lost her appetite for life as the century waned. After Cyril's death she repeatedly wrote that she wished merely to stay alive and fit for work long enough to provide secure futures for Cecco, Madge, and Denny. Madge married William Roderick Harris Valentine, a Dundee jute manufacturer, in July 1893. Although to have one of the children married was an answer to prayer, the bridegroom was not. For a tradesman, as she sardonically commented to Cecco, he had a good turn of phrase and was able to write to his beloved of Dutch art: 'most edifying';[21] he had removed Madge from the cultured environment, to which her aunt had accustomed her, to an atmosphere of vulgar commerce, and he in turn clearly resented his wife's aunt's condescension. Although there were soon Valentine babies, they could never mean as much to Mrs Oliphant as her own children and her adopted children had done, she told Madge.[22]

The valetudinarian Cecco, who 'has known nobody but me, no protector, no provider', was now everything to her: 'the companion, the master, the object of every thought . . . my son—how I have said my son, quoting him for ever—and now', she wrote on 2 October 1894, 'nevermore can I quote him, or tell anybody "Cecco says", words that were always in my mouth'. Returning home in mid-September, from the birth of Madge's first baby, her namesake, Margaret Oliphant Harris Valentine, Mrs Oliphant had found Cecco unwell again, suffering not from his chronic cough but from 'exhaustion after inflammation of the throat and tongue'. For ten days Cecco alternately rallied and relapsed and died near midnight on 1 October, 'his mother holding his cold hands'. As if to convince herself the grand change had not taken place, Mrs Oliphant returned to her desk and her journal within a few hours.

I keep watching and thinking that surely he is coming up the stairs, coming in to stand by me, though it is he who is lying in the next room where he has slept since he was a little boy, always next me with a door between us. He is lying there now on his own bed, looking so calm, so strong, as well as if he had never known what sickness was, his face rounded out, looking as he looked when we went to Pau. God bless him.

After Cecco's death Denny bore the brunt of her aunt's loving affection and rewarded her by changing her name from Wilson to Oliphant by deed poll: Denny indeed thought of her aunt as 'my dear mother'.[23] One by one Mrs Oliphant's responsibilities were falling away from her. She no longer needed the Windsor house, haunted as it was now in every corner by memories of past family life, and in April 1896 she and Denny moved, accompanied by their almost permanent guest, Fanny Tulloch, to The Hermitage, a furnished house on Wimbledon Common. It was clear that Denny would be welcome in the Valentine household, and indeed she was to become their mainstay after her sister and brother-in-law's deaths in 1897 and 1907. Although her aunt claimed to be anxious to secure her last living dependant's future, unremitting work had now become a habit from which she could not break herself. Moreover, as one of the longest-lived of her literary generation she found herself in demand for the retrospective essays and books that publishers felt called for by the coincidence of the Queen's Jubilee occurring in the last decade of the century. In accepting Blackwoods' proposal to write the official *Annals* of the firm she secured a regular £500 per annum while the work was in progress. The last three years did witness one last novel as good as anything she had ever done, *Old Mr Tredgold,* and her valedictory, and finest, tale of the unseen, 'The Library Window',[24] but, despite the laborious research it often entailed, she found non-fiction more agreeable work. By March 1897, however, she told Blackwood, 'I am by no means well and easily worried, which is different from all my habits. And I seem to avoid everything I can possibly leave out in order to be done the sooner'; but then, as if to prove to him how unfounded was his 'apparent alarm lest I should leave you in the lurch', she set off on a fortnight's research trip to Siena on 10 April. Indefatigable though she had always been, she was forced to recognize that the internal pains which intermittently attacked her now could not be attributed to the rheumatism from which she had long suffered. She was suffering from cancer of the colon. On 7 May she wrote to Blackwood, 'I am not any great thing in the way of health and I begin to think will never be any more', yet, she added, this was unsurprising for someone now entering upon her seventieth year and 'though I don't like the pain . . . I feel quite able to work, which is fortunate in a way'.[25]

The end when it came was handled by her with the same composure and efficiency with which she had handled every crisis of her life. She wrote to her various publishers, one by one, asking a last advance from Mr Blackwood to pay for the funeral expenses 'which will either be repaid to you by Denny as soon as my affairs are settled, or else subtracted from the price you may offer to her for these unpublished fragments'.[26] To Mr Craik of Macmillans she suggested that he could possibly get someone to 'write a small preface of my life to enable you to add £100' to the price he might be prepared to pay for the republication of some of her magazine stories. The protracted Jubilee celebrations in London enabled her to make her farewells to Madge and her children, and then to old friends like Robert Story and Lady Ritchie (née Annie Thackeray). And still the writing continued. By the third week in June she was too weak to write for herself but dictated some verses which 'she desired . . . should be sent to Mr Blackwood, thinking they might be printed as a sort of *Envoi* to the Jubilee verses already in his hand'. When she died, a little before midnight on 25 June 1897, 'the names of her boys were on her lips almost at the last, though she had said repeatedly, "I seem to see nothing but God and our Lord" '.[27] After the funeral she was buried alongside her two boys, Cyril and Cecco, in the cemetery at Eton. Despite a flurry of obituaries and a renewal of interest provoked by the posthumous publication of her *Autobiography* in 1899, it was to be another ten years before a public memorial tablet was unveiled to her in St Giles' Cathedral, Edinburgh: a fitting tribute to the Scottish roots by which she had always set such great store.

2. Arranging the Narrative

This simple narrative of the events that befell her does not really explain why an obituarist as fascinated by the special case as Henry James was should remark, 'I know not if some study of her remarkable life, and still more of her remarkable character, be in preparation, but she was a figure that would on many sides still lend itself to vivid portraiture.'[28] In many ways her life was unremarkable. Many Victorian women from the Queen down, as Mrs Oliphant observed,[29] found themselves widowed with a young family to bring up alone; for many widows writing seemed about the only employment compatible with their domestic responsibilities and a notion of gentility. Even the fact that all her children predeceased her was not unprecedented in the days before penicillin, when a man might, without undue morbidity, begin the dedication of his autobiography to his children, seven of whom were to survive him, with the words, 'If any of you should live to manhood'.[30] What was remarkable, as I have indicated in the Preface, was the degree, length, and range of her success as a professional woman writer and the way in which she coped with, evaluated, and viewed her life: in short, 'her character', both as a person and as a writer. Her extraordinariness lay in being able at once to perceive both how the trials that presented themselves were the stuff of ordinary life, requiring mundane fortitude rather than permitting the grandeur of heroic suffering, and how this quality of her life could be exploited to provide exactly the material the nineteenth-century realist novel existed to tell. The author of an apparently patronizingly titled article, 'A Little Chat about Mrs Oliphant', put the matter well when, having praised her photographic realism, he went on to convey his sense that this talent was more than documentary skill. 'And yet there is something more,—there is the imagination which realises the immense pathos of human life,—of life, that is to say, into which no special adventure or misadventure enters, but which simply as *life* is so fundamentally sad, so intrinsically a tragedy.'[31] In a very important sense Mrs Oliphant's life became a fiction to herself. When she came to write the story of her own life she was very well aware that it was a story she was telling and that this required literary decisions and deliberate choices of telling moments and particular emphases.

By 1885, when the notion of something more coherent than journal entries took hold, she had already written two full-length biographies, reviewed numerous biographies and autobiographies, and recently written a series of articles for *Blackwood's* on interesting examples of the autobiographical genre.[32] Instead of beginning with the family genealogy, or plunging straight into her earliest recollections, she mused upon her relationship with the self she found in the earlier pages of her journal.

Twenty-one years have passed since I wrote what is on the opposite page. I have just been reading it all with tears; sorry, very sorry for that poor soul who has lived through so much since. Twenty-one years is a little lifetime. It is curious to think that I was not very young, nearly thirty-six, at that time, and that I am not very old, nearly fifty-seven, now. Life though it is short, is very long, and contains so much. And one does not, to one's consciousness, change as one's outward appearance and capabilities do. Doesn't Mrs Somerville say that, so far from feeling old, she was not always quite certain (up in the seventies) whether she was quite grown up! I entirely understand the feeling, though I have had enough, one would think, to make one feel old.

It is easy to sympathize with the perplexity, verging upon irritation, of her literary executors, Annie Coghill, her erstwhile housekeeper and secretary, and Denny, her niece, as they came to present their relative's account of her life to the public. Impeded on the one hand by their reverence for her own words, and on the other by their desire to reshape the 'autobiographical bits' into the mould of a conventional linear story, they fell between two stools so that their edition begins with a jumble of apologetic footnotes: this has the unfortunate effect of making Mrs Oliphant's reopening of the pages of her life, quoted above, seem like sentimental maundering because the cause of her sorrow has been withheld from the reader. Instead, Maggie's death, which so crucially affected Mrs Oliphant's treatment of her other children, was relegated to a place in the text where her loss is subsumed in the 'major' tragedy of the death of her two adult sons. An instinctive feminist anger at this devaluing of the separate and unique importance of the daughter's death and the intensity of the loss of the mother–daughter bond should perhaps be tempered by remembering that Mrs Oliphant's female editors had only been part of the post-Maggie household and had themselves suffered the trauma of the sons' death. I have written elsewhere and at greater length[33] about the ways in which her first editors misconstrued the nature and form of their relative's autobiographical writings and contrived to present a picture composed to confirm Annie Coghill's epitaph:

Only when the end must be chronicled another hand takes up the pen she has laid down and sorrowfully records the close of a life—not faultless, indeed, but noble, loving, and womanly in the highest sense, and of a literary career full of sound, skilful, and serviceable labours.[34]

Translating this into the terminology of a final school report, the effect is not encouraging: 'Decent and caring character, tries hard, competent worker'. With hindsight one of Mrs Oliphant's greater misfortunes was being forced to leave the narrative of her life to two of the lame ducks who had so consistently flocked to her for care. The letters she penned in the last three or four years of her life show her despair at Denny's apathetic or petulant approach to life, and Annie's constitutional inclination to pessimism had long been a family byword.[35] Their instinctive empathy with the drab and the gloomy found considerable sustenance in Mrs Oliphant's *Autobiography*, though they were also at pains to record their admiration for her 'saving sense of humour' and 'indomitable courage'. They found themselves quite out of their depth, however, when they were confronted with the intensity of her private reflections. The energy and violence of her grief, which led her to berate God and weep alone into the small hours, did not seem compatible with their predilection for drawing-room condolences or their dependence upon the organizational capacity of a woman who even as she lay dying 'spoke to us with all her old brightness, giving such information and directions as she thought might be useful *after*'.[36] So they pared these long outpourings of grief, excruciatingly sharp memories, and theological speculation down to the absolute minimum compatible with her story's intelligibility.

Ironically, it seems to have been the indifference and lack of insight of those about her which stimulated the autobiographical impulse. In 1885, when she wanted to make 'a little try at the autobiography', she sought out the small volume, whose metal clasp and lock are now missing, in which her earliest half-obliterated entries about the burden of her brother Willie's alcoholism had been recorded. The next extant page, written between the death of her husband in 1859 and that of her daughter in 1864, suggests that she had received a proposal of marriage and that after 'some internal struggles' had decided to enter upon a 'natural lonely life'. It was this volume she turned to when Maggie died and letters had 'come to be a pain and trouble to me . . . I have no more heart to write letters—one or two I have written with a kind of vague, foolish hope that some true word of comfort might come to me in reply, but after the pitying, troubled letters I get how can I go on further?' Twenty-one years later, harassed by her sons' indolent, sulky, parasitic life, and further isolated by the death of some of her older friends, she found herself 'having—which, by the way, is a little sad when one comes to think of it—no one to write to of anything that is beneath the surface', and so she turned again to the same volume for recreational pleasure. The desire to fill the void, to remember the damaged, or dismembered, self, to use the magical preservative of the past to ward off the effects of presently experienced, continuous loss are all common impulses to autobiography and would have answered her needs during this period of emotional estrangement from her sons. It is not of course surprising that Annie and Denny deleted her reflection of 1885 that 'No one belonging to me has energy enough to do it, or even to gather the fragments for someone else'. After her sons had both died she sought to persuade herself that she had written the record for them, and in a sense this was so. Like Browning's Andrea del Sarto, a creation with whom Mrs Oliphant repeatedly identified herself, her monologue reflects a desire for self-justification and self-explanation rather than being predicated upon any serious expectation of dialogue. Part of its impulse sprang from the desire to anticipate or blot out the critical voices of friends and relatives, potential biographers one and all, who might have wished to tell the story in a different way. Her wryly self-conscious narrative often makes the apparently naïve disclosure that the persona she has chosen to present is only one amongst many that others might have chosen to construct.

Burying the faults of their lives with them, Mrs Oliphant was able to persuade herself that she had written 'for my boys, for Cecco in particular', but the fact remains that she had shown none of it to them. Her retrospective description of the autobiography as written for her sons may have been a device that helped her to overcome a fear she held in common with many nineteenth-century women, that putting herself forward in this way would seem unnatural and unfeminine. Despite her assertion that she would 'try to change the tone of this record' after her sons died, the transition from intimate reflection to the social and anecdotal was not in fact determined by a sudden consciousness of a changed audience. A letter of 11 March 1890, written while both sons were still alive, already offers 'various fragments of autobiography which may make a publication of a little personal interest' to the publishing firm of Macmillan as one of a number of securities against advances already received.[37] The personae she adopted in several of her later series of articles, writing as from 'The Old Saloon' for *Maga* in 1887, or 'A Commentary from an Easy-Chair' for the *Spectator* in 1888, or 'A Fireside Commentary' from 'A

Dowager' in the *St James's Gazette* (1888), provide further evidence that she did not have to await her sons' death to discover the pleasures and benefits reminiscence could provide. Their deaths, however, may well have removed the unspoken pressure to prove herself as something more than an unheard, disregarded mother, and she now decided 'to try to remember more trivial things, the incidents that sometimes amuse me when I look back upon them'.

The commercial possibilities of exploiting the fact that she had grown old with the century no doubt increased the temptation to accept invitations to undertake literary reminiscence, but the crucial decision to commit herself to autobiography was the one taken in 1885. In her series of reviews of autobiographies for *Blackwood's* she had noted that 'to be an autobiographer at all, a man must possess a certain amount of confidence in himself and in the interest of the world— something of the quality which we call vanity' and that the practice of autobiography helped to 'maintain one's dignity in old age'.[38] Yet this dignity and interest did not, her selection makes clear, reside in worldly greatness. The figures she chose varied from the flamboyant Renaissance artist Benvenuto Cellini to the little-known Alice Thornton, a devout figure of Cavalier times, and in each article she managed to convey the distinctive temperament and mood of the writing by attention to the details of their daily lives the autobiographers themselves saw as important; each in turn 'thrusting their own little tale of events between him and the history of the world, finding their infant or their apple-tree of more importance than the convulsions of nations'.[39] Even in the case of Madame Roland, she concentrated not on the political but on the personal aspects of the life of this famous Girondiste victim of the French Revolution as she reviewed it from the death cell which was to liberate her from the tedium of her bureaucrat husband's company. Unerringly Mrs Oliphant headed for the quality of their domestic relationships and perceptions to give the flavour of these lives, be they male or female, politicians, literary figures, artists, or actors.

So strong was her conviction of the significance of the commonplace detail in conveying the uniqueness of the particular experience that she found herself aghast when she contemplated the written lives of two of her contemporaries who, in their different ways, had been the leaders of the realist school of fiction, George Eliot and Trollope. In George Eliot's case she was able to blame the men in her life for the curious dullness of her *Life as Related in her Letters and Journals*. John Cross, Eliot's husband, was responsible for the hagiographical element, but more interestingly both he, and George Henry Lewes before him, had connived in producing an artificial atmosphere, 'a mental greenhouse', which, in Mrs Oliphant's judgement, had effectively cut Eliot off from the sources of her literary greatness.

The reverential circle that gathered round her in her own house, agape for every precious word that might fall from her mouth: the carefully regulated atmosphere into which nothing from the outer world save the most delicate incense with just the flavour that suited her, was allowed to enter; the ever-watchful guardian who preserved her from any unnecessary contact, are curious accessories little habitual to the possessors of literary genius.[40]

In Trollope's case it was 'his talk about the characters in his books that astonished me beyond measure'. Now, Trollope had undoubtedly attracted a degree of opprobrium for the way in which his posthumously published *Autobiography* talked of novel-writing as a job or a craft much like any other and the businesslike way in which he assessed profits and counselled caution to literary aspirants. Mrs Oliphant had a certain professional sympathy with the desire to fob off aesthetic discussion by reference to the fiction 'trade' but she could not understand the way in which Trollope made his relationship with his characters do duty for his emotional life and veiled his domestic roles as husband and father in almost total secrecy. So when she came to commit the stuff of her own life to paper she had two unsatisfactory models in front of her, that of 'a dull woman with a great genius distinct from herself' where the wonder was the size of the gap between the life and the work, and that of an account entirely directed to the work when, for the public, 'as a matter of fact, it is exactly those family details that are interesting—the human story in all its chapters'. Neither of these made any emotional or literary sense to Mrs Oliphant. It was not merely that her family had been more central to her life but that her work and her domestic concerns had, at every stage, been inseparable. Literally she had always worked in the heart of domestic activity, taking her 'share in the conversation' and never 'shut up in a separate room, or hedged off'; economically her work and the care of her family had been inextricably linked and emotionally she knew both the family and the writing to be necessary to her. 'I have written because it gave me pleasure, because it came natural to me, because it was like talking or breathing, besides the big fact that it was necessary for me to work for my children. That, however, was not the first motive . . .'.

The tension between her life and her work is in fact the underlying theme of Mrs Oliphant's *Autobiography*. She was perhaps one of the very first women writers to explore her own life in terms of the issues feminist criticism has brought to the fore: working conditions, the need for legitimation as a writer, the tendency to compare her work with that of female contemporaries and forebears, the sense of a woman's point of view as necessarily more fragmentary. What obscured her contribution to the construction of a feminist agenda was her unequivocally conservative position in the debate. 'At my most ambitious of times I would rather my children had remembered me as their mother than in any other way, and my friends as their friend.' Nevertheless, she found that when her children were dead and 'friends drop day by day', she could not suddenly separate the spheres in her mind and turn to the writing for consolation, and her autobiography ends with this realization: 'And now here I am all alone. I cannot write any more.'

This carefully chosen ending repays examination. The tone is one of transparent grief, of a woman who has at that very moment laid down her pen, having reached the truly unutterable, unwritable boundary. Autobiography of all genres is the most obdurately resistant to the finality of closure, since the subject's death must always remain outside the text as originally constituted, but this ending is more deliberately premature than most. The reader's attention is focused on the closing image of the bereaved mother/writer, and distracted from too closely enquiring into the nature of the unsayable and unwritable. There is little doubt that this ending was as carefully contrived as any of her deliberately unconventional endings to novels. Half of her *Autobiography* was written after Cecco's death. On Christmas night 1894 she had sat down to take up her life's story in 1860, just after her husband had died. By 30 December she was sufficiently engulfed in the project to begin a second manuscript volume. In the next few months she wrote her way through to 1875, the year when her brother Frank had died, and the children were variously dispatched to India, Germany, and Oxford, leaving only Cecco at home. Several pages before she penned the metrically halting couplet, 'And now here I am all alone. | I cannot write any more', she had written, 'With that year began a new life, one of which I cannot speak much.' It was not her final bereavement that brought her self-inscription to an end, but the growing tension between the fiction and the life. When she looked back from the vantage-point of spring 1894 she recognized the impossibility of telling the truth: 'I do injustice to those whom I love above all things by speaking thus, and yet what can I say?' For which truth was she to tell?

'God alone knows what was the anguish of these years. And yet now I think of *"ces beaux jours quand j'etais si malheureuse"*, the moments of relief were so great and so sweet that they seemed compensation for the pain,—I remembered no more the anguish.' Lately in my many sad musings it has been brought very clearly before my mind how often all the horrible tension, the dread, the anxiety which there are no words strong enough to describe,—which devoured me, but which I had to conceal behind a smiling face,—would yield in a moment, in the twinkling of an eye, at the sound of a voice, at the first look, into an ineffable ease and the overwhelming happiness of relief from pain.

She had found little trouble in relating the main outlines of her life while they could be made to conform to the contours of dutiful daughter, sister, wife, and mother, but, when she reached the stage where the real and the ideal had diverged so irretrievably, she found herself involved in contradictions so profound that she could 'say' only to 'unsay' in the very next sentence: 'a second-class at Oxford,— a great disappointment, yet not disgraceful after all . . . Cecco took the first steps in the same way; but, thanks be to God, righted himself and overcame—not in time enough to save his career at Oxford . . . What a companion he was . . . a most accomplished man, though to me always a boy. He did not make friends easily, and he had few; but those whom he had were very fond of him.' Whilst her sons were still alive her capacity to hypothesize an alternative future, in which they would be neither drunk nor disagreeable, had held her life together, but their death had rendered this an impossible fiction and telling the 'other truth' was both too hard and potentially equally misleading.

By the time that the first major autobiographical urge came upon her in 1885 she had in any case already decided that life was resistant to the formal elegance of art: 'Real life has no ending save in death,—it is a tangle of breakings off and addings on, of new beginnings overlapping the old, of ties arbitrarily cut and arbitrarily pieced together again, and nothing to make the picture, as painters say, "compose".[41] The retrospective mode of autobiography afforded her the opportunity to reflect upon the arbitrary way in which choices, subsequently elevated to the status of decisions, were actually made. Even the chronological breaks in composition were brought into service to demonstrate the intensity of the artist's desire to provide the continuous thread of meaning waging a constant war with life's abrupt discontinuities. To take a very early example, there is as much as a four-year gap between the first and the second continuous entries in her autobiography. The one ends, 'And now perhaps commences a graver era, more guarded and cautious than the past—if experience ever teaches—which, however, I have already concluded it does not.' The opening of the next entry deliberately draws attention to the writerly desire to establish links and trace echoes, but simultaneously underlines the paradox of the resolution to be 'guarded and cautious' when experience cannot teach and there are no premonitory signs to be had.

A graver era, God help me, but I did not know when I wrote the words that I was coming to lay my sweetest hope, my brightest anticipations for the future, with my darling, in her father's grave. Oh, this terrible, fatal, miserable Rome! I came here rich and happy, with my blooming daughter, my dear bright child, whose smiles and brightness everybody noticed, and who was sweet as a little mother to her brothers. There was not an omen of evil in any way.

This fatalism preserves her both from wallowing in egoistical self-recrimination and from being judgemental. When considering other people's criticisms of her as extravagant, or too doting in her children's upbringing, or insufficiently devoted to high art, she concludes with a phrase such as 'It was my way' or 'But so it was' or 'I could have done no other'. Character, she firmly believed, was an unalterable *donnée* and she was exceptionally consistent in her application of this principle. Although brother Willie's life of drink and debt had been a drain upon her purse for over twenty years, when she wrote about him she offered no reproach and he is still 'my poor, good, tender-hearted shipwrecked Willie'. The possession of this strong conviction did not of course prevent her from being irritated by the daily inconvenience caused by the weakness of close relatives, but it is always upon her own unreasonableness in expecting more that she concentrates. Her brother Frank's animal-like dependence upon her in his closing years, or Cyril's feckless improvidence, she admits caused her irritation, but these examples serve also as occasions for remarking the vanity of the human desire to throw off the particular burden fate has assigned. 'What if' fantasies are given particularly short shrift. The capacity for measuring reality against the idealized conventions of human behaviour, so often manifested in her fiction, is frequently to be seen in her reading of her own or others' characters. Brother Frank's recovery from the paralysis of his initial grief at his wife's death provides the opportunity for this reflection.

He was completely shattered, like a man in a palsy, for a time scarcely able to stand or to speak, but not so overwhelmed with grief as I expected. Grief is the strangest thing, or rather it is very wonderful in how many different ways people take those blows, which from outside seem as if they must be final. Especially is it so in the closest of human connections, that between man and wife. People who have seemed to be all the world to each other are parted so, and the survivor, who is for the moment as my poor brother said 'in despair', shows the most robust power of bearing it, and is so soon himself or herself again, that one, confounded and half-ashamed, feels that one is half-ridiculous to have expected anything different.

The changes in pronoun here are indicative both of her surprise at her own almost culpable elasticity of temperament in similar circumstances and of that wider thematic concern of the work to reveal the ways in which life fails to conform to the conventional divisions of tragedy or comedy. This passage also points to a further effect of her retrospective approach. The question of meaning constantly lurks beneath the surface. Which is the truer image, that of the absolute mutual need of a close marriage or that of the robust survivor, and does one necessarily discountenance the other? On the one hand Mrs Oliphant had a compulsive need to believe that her life and her devotion to her children had been worthwhile despite the fact that she had outlived them all, and, on the other hand, the elegiac frame-work in which the story is cast constantly suggests that life is a series of episodes which achieve any significance they may have only in retrospect. The feeling of daily life being made up of trivial moments, only given the sharpness of an etching by a sudden change of mood, is conveyed particularly well in the recollected scene of the arrival of the news of her sister-in-law's death.

We were all assembled, a merry party enough, one summer evening, after an afternoon on the river, at a late meal,—a sort of supper,—when a telegram was put into my hand. I remember the look of the long table and all the bright faces round it, the pretty summer dishes, salad, and pink salmon, and ornamented sweet things, and many flowers, the men and boys in their flannels, the girls in their light summer dresses,—everything light and bright. I have often said that it was the only telegram I ever received without a certain tremor of anxiety. Captain Gun, who was there, had been uncertain of his coming on this particular day, and a good many telegrams on that subject had been passing between us. I held the thing in my hand and looked across at him, and said, 'This time it cannot be from you'. Then I opened it with the laugh in my mouth, and this is what I read: 'Jeanie is dead, and I am in despair'. It was like a scene in a tragedy.

The stark clash of moods and the intersection of past, present, and future in one arbitrary and ill-chosen moment give Mrs Oliphant the feeling of that exceptional clarity of definition only permitted in art. More often it is only the slow unfolding of the years that gives meaning. 'All my little recollections', she wrote as she set to work on her narrative in 1885, 'are like little pictures to which the meaning, naturally, is put long afterwards.' Perhaps the most memorable of these recollected images is one where the absence of subsequent comment suggests the strength of Mrs Oliphant's desire to preserve the memory intact. Characteristically she draws attention to its commonplace and inconsequential elements as being those which endow it with significance.

When I look back on my life, among the happy moments which I can recollect is one which is so curiously common and homely, with nothing in it, that it is strange even to record such a recollection, and yet it embodied more happiness to me than almost any real occasion as might be supposed for happiness. It was the moment after dinner when I used to run up-stairs to see that all was well in the nursery, and then to turn into my room on my way down again to wash my hands, as I had a way of doing before I took up my evening work, which was generally needlework, something to make for the children. My bedroom had three windows in it, one looking out upon the gardens I have mentioned, the other two into the road. It was light enough with the lamplight outside for all I wanted. I can see it now, the glimmer of the outside lights, the room dark, the faint reflection in the glasses, and my heart full of joy and peace—for what?—for nothing—that there was no harm anywhere, the children well above stairs and their father below. I had few of the pleasures of society, no gaiety at all. I was eight-and-twenty, going down-stairs as light as a feather, to the little frock I was making. My husband also gone back for an hour or two after dinner to his work, and well—and the bairns well. I can feel now the sensation of that sweet calm and ease and peace.

It has been interestingly observed that 'a house constitutes a body of images that give mankind proofs or illusions of stability'.[42] Anyone who has ever revisited the derelict site of what was for a time 'home' will swiftly be able to understand how important the physical existence of that space for memories to adhere to is in preserving a sense of continuous identity. On the only occasion Mrs Oliphant made such a visit to the house where she was born she felt no qualms because she had 'no recollection' of this period of her life, and her vague plans as to renting the 'pleasant homely house . . . for the sake of the landscape and the associations' were readily abandoned. Like many middle-class Victorians, the Oliphants rented rather than owned a series of houses and, since such tenancies were the habit of the day, there was less of a tendency to distinguish between the emotional investment in homes that were 'rented' rather than 'owned' than there might be today. The easy tones in which she recounted the casual loss of the house of her birth are in marked contrast to the attitude she displayed to the homes of her memories. Places, houses, and above all her own 'homes', exercised the strongest imaginative pull on Mrs Oliphant. Rome could never be revisited after it had claimed first her husband and then her daughter. After Cyril's death she could not bear to return immediately to the house she now owned in Windsor, 8–9 Clarence Crescent, but rented a smaller house several streets away in Park Street for a couple of months. When Cecco died back in Clarence Crescent in 'the house where almost all the events of my later life have taken place', she found she could no longer bear to live there overlooking the 'Crescent gardens which had been of so much importance in the first chapter of my boy's life'. Just as the past could only achieve its meaning and resonance when it had been unalterably taken away, so it could not be revisited, other than imagin-atively, for fear of destroying it and her sense of self. Repeatedly in the pages of her *Autobiography* she talks of her fantasies of entering the houses of her past life. In 1891 she talks of passing one of her marital homes in Ulster Place in London 'sometimes going to King's Cross, when we have gone to Scotland, and a strange fantastic thought crossed my mind the first time I did so in these latter years, as if I might go up to the door and go in and find the old life going on, and see my husband coming down the road, and my little children returning from their walk'. In 1894 again she remarks, 'I have curious superstitions about localities. I used to have a dizzy feeling sometimes in later years when I passed our old house in Ulster Place that if I had the courage to knock at the door and go in asking no questions I might find, who could tell that all the rest was a dream and that the babies were safe in their nursery and Frank in the studio, wondering what had kept me so long.' Recollecting the house of a neighbour in Clarence Crescent she pictured Cecco aged 'seven or eight years old', going there to make up the numbers at whist, and reflected,

I wonder sometimes if what has been ever dies! Should not I find them all round the old whist-table, and my Cecco, with his bright face and the great blue vein that showed on his temple, proud to be helping to amuse the old people, if I were but bold enough to push into the deserted house and look for them now? I have so often felt, with a bewildered dizziness, as if this might be.

This superstitious feeling about the places which had played host to her past was to feed her tales of the seen and the unseen, where, once the door between the here and now and the hereafter has been pushed open, eternity allows past, present, and future to be experienced simultaneously.

The location of an irrecoverable happiness in a domestic setting is unsurprising, but the quality and 'unconsidered' causes of the peaceful joy repay further examination. Retreating to the middle rooms of the house she is bound about by the comforting, but temporarily undemanding, presence of husband and children. It is a moment in which she consciously luxuriates in her own space and time before returning to the work she had chosen to do, or talking over the day's work with her husband as she did at the end of their day. The knowledge of their assured companionship made her moments of solitude a pleasure, not a burden as they were to become. The gently dispersed light from the street-lamp illuminates the room in such a way as to remind her of the gaiety and allure of 'society' and yet to make her content with the small but safe space of more intimate private life. Work and a motive for work contribute to her felicity, and, if dressmaking suggests to the twentieth-century mind the subservience of literary creativity to domestic bondage, a later chapter will show how sewing came frequently to represent for Mrs Oliphant an alternative to, or a metaphor for, the voice achieved when women resort to penmanship. Her *Autobiography* itself she refers to as attempting to trace the 'thread of my life' which lay below the surface events.

3.   *Alternative Readings*

Mrs Oliphant's own account of her life is insidiously persuasive, partly because of her occasional disarming admissions that hers is a partial view. Her wry self-criticisms and self-deprecations should not, however, blind us to the apologetic functions of autobiography. It is, for instance, observable that although she spoke of herself deprecatingly as a 'fat, little, commonplace woman, rather tongue-tied', she did not take at all kindly to those who accepted this evaluation. One such occasion at the beginning of her literary career in 1853, when an American woman, Sara Jane Lippincott, who wrote under the name of Grace Greenwood, met her at a literary party and 'did what she could in a patronising way to find out who I was', rankled for many years. When Lippincott published *Haps and Mishaps of a Tour in Europe* the following year, she wrote,

Of our party was the authoress of 'Margaret Maitland, of Sunnyside'—a fair Scotchwoman, not over twenty-two, a modest, quiet, lovable person, who seems far from having made up her mind to admit the fact of her own genius. Having wakened one morning to find herself famous, she believes the world to be labouring under some strange delusion, and accounts herself an immensely overrated little woman after all.[43]

This not unfriendly picture aroused Mrs Oliphant's wrath, partly because she resented having first been treated as 'the poor little shy wife of some artist'. She took her revenge three times, first in *The Athelings* (1857), where the poet and journalist Lippincott is turned into a brash, male, sonnet-writing American journalist and lambasted for his vulgarity in repaying private hospitality by using it as the material for his accounts of England for the American press. Her recollection of the episode in her autobiographical writing of 1885 reinflamed her sufficiently to mention the poor woman again in *Effie Ogilvie* (1886), where the daughters of a *nouveau riche* family contemplate putting a small Scottish village on the social map: 'The Americans have not found out Allonby yet,' they said to each other. 'We must ask Miss Greenwood up here.'[44]

Similarly, it was one thing for Mrs Oliphant herself to refer self-mockingly to her own work 'as the boiling of the daily pot', but when 'a bit of a young person' had the temerity to pay a patronizing compliment to her story *A Beleaguered City*, a work which the author herself rated highly, she 'felt inclined to say . . . "indeed, my young woman! I should think something a good deal less than that might be good enough from you"'. 'By which', she added, 'it may perhaps be suspected that I don't always think such small beer of myself as I say.'

As she grew older and her list of achievements longer, she was increasingly resentful of suspected snubs and insults, despite the 'rueful amusement' with which she recounted them. Sir Charles Dilke had the effrontery, on being introduced to her, to begin 'at once to speak of *his* books and his publishers, as if he and not I were the literary person'. When a great Roman Catholic lady took centre stage at a luncheon party by choosing 'as the theme of her conversation her own books, their success or rather their relative successes, the troubles she had with her publishers, and all the rest', Mrs Oliphant complained that she had had her 'little *role* taken from her'. Her mother's insistence that her gift could never justify 'unnatural' behaviour, and her own innate shyness, combined to prevent her from enjoying the larger-than-life role of the literary lion, which she felt that some of her male counterparts embraced all too easily.

I have always thought that Tennyson's appearance was too emphatically that of a poet, especially in his photographs: the fine frenzy, the careless picturesqueness, were almost too much. He looked the part too well; but in reality there was a roughness and acrid gloom about the man which saved him from his over romantic appearance. He paid no attention to me, as was natural.

These reactions were to be mirrored on almost every occasion that she encountered one of her celebrated male contemporaries. She found the male arrogance emanating from Matthew Arnold's prose essays intolerable, but found, when she sat next to him at the Lord Mayor's dinner in 1874, 'that she liked him better in his own person than in his books'.[45] Leslie Stephen's 'great deal of charm' was to overcome her instinctive prejudice against a figure whom she had previously thought of only as the editor of the prosperous *Cornhill*. From all these stories she emerges as a prickly personality whose air of reserve and barely concealed contempt for the social adroitness of which she was deeply suspicious must have made her difficult to deal with.

Male publisher friends like the Macmillans, and more especially the Blackwoods, with whom she frequently stayed, must occasionally have been hurt by the lacerating remarks she could make when she felt she had detected 'an atmosphere of trade' creeping into relations normally conducted under the codes of polite society.[46] Her contemporary novelists, of course, did not all enjoy uninterruptedly harmonious relations with their various publishers, but the boundaries between social intercourse and business were not so marked between men and therefore less easy to transgress. This may well explain why a number of Mrs Oliphant's female contemporaries chose to use male go-betweens in their business negotiations. After the early experiment of using her brother Willie, Mrs Oliphant took financial dealings into her own hands. It seems likely that the fact that her publishers had to deal directly with a woman who could fluctuate so alarmingly between gracious femininity and acerbic business dealings embarrassed them sufficiently frequently for them to feel reluctant to offer her permanent editorial employment.

Her publishers could at least console themselves by reflecting upon her capacity to earn money for them. No such balm was available for the wounded *amour propre* of her male contemporaries whose writings she pronounced upon from the untouchable heights of her anonymous platform in *Maga*. Her position as Blackwood's 'general utility woman' was one of some power, and from time to time male novelists found themselves forced into keeping up civil relations with a woman whom they would dearly have loved to have despised. One of Henry James's notes to her, in which he is clearly replying to her invitation to lend his name to a Scottish friend's new periodical, declares himself 'content to be in any boat to which you bravely—or rashly, or generously, commit yourself',[47] yet the prominence he afforded her reviewing activities in his obituary tribute shows him to have had serious reservations about her powers of discrimination. 'No-one', he claimed, practised criticism 'more in "the hit-or-miss" fashion and on happy-go-lucky lines than Mrs Oliphant'. She had, he asserted, used *Maga* as her own '*porte-voix*'. The way in which the emphases fall in the following sentence reveals that the fact of her gender added insult to the injury sustained from the recklessness with which she exercised the privilege of anonymity. 'I should almost suppose that no woman had ever, for half a century, had her personal "say" so publicly and irresponsibly.'[48] While she was alive Thomas Hardy was careful to welcome 'direct communication with a writer I have known in spirit so long', especially since she seemed in a position to offer him work. He waited till after her death to wreak his revenge for her review of *Jude the Obscure*, caricaturing it as 'the screaming of a poor lady in *Blackwood*'.[49]

Less direct means of revenge were, however, available during her lifetime. Two cruelly acerbic fictional portraits exist, drawn by men who knew her well, of a prolific woman novelist, who justifies her claim to a stall in the literary market-place by presenting herself as a needy widowed mother. It is tempting to interpret them as pictures of Mrs Oliphant, prompted by these men's desire to give fictional vent to the unease and annoyance they felt at a female interloper on their carefully cherished preserve.

When Trollope came to write *The Way We Live Now* in 1873 he had had business dealings with Mrs Oliphant in his capacity as editor of *St Paul's Magazine*, in which he had published her novel *The Three Brothers*. They would also have met at charitable literary dinners, where she was beginning to put her maternal devotion on display by taking her schoolboy son, Tids, as her companion.[50] Lady Carbury, whose spurious literary success is achieved by exercising her feminine wiles upon a series of male editors, publishers, and reviewers, is symptomatic of the fraudulent credit on which the society of this novel operates: she is the literary embodiment of many of Trollope's pet hates and her career bears remarkable resemblances to certain facets of Mrs Oliphant's. Her 'dabbling in literature which had been commenced partly perhaps from a sense of pleasure in the work, partly as a passport into society' had been converted into a money-making venture when 'Tidings had reached her of this and the other man's success, and,—coming near[er] to her still,—of this and that other woman's earnings in literature'. Her ruthlessness is fuelled by a pelican-like willingness to tear out her own breast on behalf of her worthless son, whom she has so indulged 'that even in her own presence he was never shamed of his own selfishness or apparently conscious of the injustice which he did to others'. Carrying her years well at the age of 43, Lady Carbury is a dangerous woman, who declares herself well past the age of romance but uses her good looks, her confidential manner, the intimate tone of her indefatigable letter-writing, and her position as a reviewer, to gain puffs for her latest, slapdash offering, *Criminal Queens*: a work which contained a portrait of Queen Caroline, suspiciously similar to that drawn by Mrs Oliphant in the first essay of her recent series, 'Historical Sketches of the Reign of George II—Queen Caroline'.[51] Lady Carbury takes no pride in the quality of her work, approaching novels, reviews, and even, the narrator suggests, a volume of sermons, had there been money in them, with the same diligence and speed, bent only upon persuading Mudie's lending library and the reading public to give it instant social credibility. A concealed reference to Trollope's own early literary failure with a historical novel, and the pride she manifests in always finishing her work in the time she had allotted herself, show why Trollope felt so vitriolic. Lady Carbury's prolific career is a threat to Trollope because in so many respects it offers a parodic version of his own, and her dishonest achievements threaten to contaminate his by association. By the end of the novel she is shown that a literary woman's proper place is not that of producer, but that of grateful handmaiden, acting as hostess for the literary evenings of her second husband, the editor of an influential daily newspaper. Trollope, who was essentially a kindly man, would have been appalled at the prescience he had shown in his picture of Lady Carbury's worthless son; the venom in which this sketch was dipped seems to have derived from his feeling that his own susceptibility to pretty women made such unscrupulous examples of the species exceptionally dangerous competitors.

At least Lady Carbury is given an interesting and slightly scandalous past that would have enabled all parties to deny that she was based upon Mrs Oliphant, but Henry James's tale 'Greville Fane' has no such saving grace. Part of its impulse may have derived from James's desire to explain his own marginalization as a literary highbrow by vilifying best-selling women novelists as vulgar and talentless,[52] but this neglects the unnecessary humiliations he visits upon Mrs Stormer, his fictional novelist. That the tale has no plot to speak of makes its real-life similarities all the more abundantly apparent. There is no doubt that James knew Mrs Oliphant socially: at least three letters, turning down her invitations with ever more elaborate courtesy, survive and he would also have met her repeatedly at the salon of their mutual friend Mrs Duncan Stewart. Anticipating his later real-life role, James pens the account of his fictional author of some hundred novels from the point of view of a younger male writer who visits her house on the day of her death with the task of composing an obituary notice speaking of 'Greville Fane', as she has been known professionally, 'pointedly but not unkindly'. Yet this tale offers none of the rewards of mystery that characterized such companion pieces as James's study of Browning's two faces, in 'The Private Life'.[53] 'Greville Fane' seems rather to have served as a vehicle for the pitying contempt for Mrs Oliphant's work which he displayed in private conversations with cronies and which he knew he would not be able to offload in his public obituary.[54] For those who wished to read this as a *roman à clef* the clues were made cruelly visible. On the literary side most play is made with Mrs Stormer's enormous contempt for the values of a good prose style or aesthetic form: 'If I hinted that a work of art required a tremendous licking into shape she thought it a pretension and a *pose*.' Mrs Oliphant's admiration for Balzac, another night-worker, is included alongside crueller jibes about the way in which the settings of her tales travelled up the social scale while her personal circumstances grew harder. Her domestic arrangements at Windsor are vividly suggested when the narrator is ushered into 'the small back room' where the novelist worked at a table littered with 'the confusion of scrappy, scrabbled sheets', and he remembers her husband's picture, kept always 'upon an easel in her drawing-room'. The narrator grows more and more reluctant to visit her as she moves through a series of cheaper rooms and houses because he cannot bear to see her sob over the 'extinction of her vogue and the exhaustion of her vein', nor to hear her stories of the harder bargains publishers increasingly drove with her when they realized the extent of her financial desperation. Most obnoxious of all though, the narrator claims, is the spectacle of her son Leolin, educated by tutors and pampered by his mother, contemptuous of his mother's labours and displaying an obvious fondness for drink. The 'knowing' talk about literary life flowing from a young dandy whose mother talks of him as a collaborator while doing all the work herself, makes the hard-working narrator itch to 'kick him downstairs'. Such fisticuffs, even practised at a literary remove, were scarcely Henry James's style and suggest the extent of the frustration he was trying to work off in this ill-tempered piece. There is more than a hint of Madge too in his portrait of Mrs Stormer's daughter, who has been expensively educated into a thoroughgoing snob in Dresden yet is prepared to contemplate marrying for money. In her old age Mrs Stormer persuades herself that Leolin is hampered from producing anything publishable because he has been caught up in the current generation's obsession with 'form'. James at least allows Mrs Stormer to die undeceived as to Leolin's worthlessness, but the son is not let off. His hideous egoism shows itself in not being content to be the one whose selfishness 'had (symbolically) killed her', but determining to profit from her death by rushing to publish every saleable scrap of paper that could be extracted from her table and drawers. It did not perhaps occur to James that this tale effected an equally tasteless plunder without waiting for the subject's death.

In their defence it is also fair to say that all three men, Trollope, James, and Hardy, felt her critical antennae to be more attuned to the desires of the general reader than to the experiments of the conscientious artist and therefore were happy to believe that her success as a novelist must have come about by pandering to the lowest common denominator of public taste. One correspondent to whom Hardy complained replied that Mrs Oliphant was 'a perfect High Priestess indeed—of the Commonplace'.[55] Although the remark was intended as derogatory, Mrs Oliphant herself would probably have found something wryly amusing in this grudging recognition of the critical stance she deliberately occupied.

Many of those who encountered her in later life reported that Mrs Oliphant carried herself with the intimidating dignity of a High Priestess. Even one of her closest friends, Lady Ritchie, née Annie Thackeray, described her as 'a little cold in manner and tart in speech'.[56] J. M. Barrie was never quite so much at ease in Mrs Oliphant's presence as he was in their warm and humorous correspondence: her *grande dame* manner seemed to belong to a former and 'politer age', and 'you never knew it more surely than when she was putting you at your ease with a graciousness that had something of a command in it'.[57] Part of her fascination seems to have lain in her oscillation of mood and demeanour between 'the almost fearsomely correct', the audaciously witty, and the Bohemian. Even those who might have believed themselves intimate with her were sometimes wrong-footed and could not presume upon a cosy familiarity. 'When she pleased she could be very agreeable,' wrote Mrs Story, who was not as enamoured of Mrs Oliphant as her husband had allegedly been, 'but she did not always so please, and when indifferent to her company, she was very silent and took no part in general conversation'.[58] Like many generous and charming hostesses, Mrs Oliphant was at her best when in charge of the arrangements or on home ground. Staying with the Coghills over the New Year period of 1893 she was angered by their apparent neglect of their guests, whose calibre did not in any case please her; she could find no excuse to go away for the weekend, walked gloomily and alone around the lake, and wrote to Cecco, 'I never was good at visiting and naturally this gift does not come with years.'[59] When she did become engaged in conversation her whole manner changed and many of her visitors departed with an impression of eyes that sparkled with fun, scorn, or anger and transferred attention away from her very projecting teeth. Her conversation, however, was not confined to social pleasantries: she was a witty anecdotalist and, if her letters are anything to go by, merciless with pretension wherever she saw it. Even those like Henry James, who were inclined to be dismissive of her literary output, recognized her formidable intelligence. He detected a superior capacity of organization and observation in this woman whose 'sharp and handsome physiognomy' conveyed the impression of 'so much cleverness, courage and humanity'.[60] For all her posing as an anti-intellectual, she was capable of setting in play 'that chord of intelligent antagonism which is so suggestive and makes for such good talk'.

Preoccupied, dogmatic, and hasty-tempered she might have been, but she won herself a series of friends who trusted her completely and were even 'inclined to be somewhat jealous and intolerant of any affections of later date than their own'.[61] Women friends displayed a depth of emotion in writing to her that at first seems odd when her 'coldness of manner' is recalled. Jane Carlyle wrote to her as 'Darling Woman' quite near to the start of their friendship and Geraldine Macpherson always signed herself 'Ever your loving sister Geddie'. Her friendship held two special appeals for women: they knew that she would take an interest in their children and that she would provide a sympathetic and absolutely confidential audience for their tales of marital woe, and this she managed without alienating their husbands or sacrificing her friendships with both halves of a married couple. Her friends' children came for long visits and the relationships often continued into a third generation. One of the Tullochs' many children was to recall, with just a shade of embarrassment at the lavishness of her provision, that 'If you had children she always insisted on your going with her before you left to make a round of the shops, where she would buy expensive toys and books for them'.[62] The memories of her during her own boys' adolescence present her at her most relaxed, a time when 'she seemed to have nothing to do except to manage matters for the young people and to share their delightful and delighted companionship in tea-parties, amateur dramatics and excursions'.[63] As these children grew older she was prepared to use such influence as she possessed on their behalf. [64] Friends, relatives, and aspiring authors could always rely upon her patronage to put them in touch with a publisher, even if she might have private reservations as to their real literary merit. She bound her friends to her with hoops of steel by the inconveniences she would put herself to on behalf of them and theirs. Despite her own hand-to-mouth literary existence she was prepared to finish and see through the press Geddie Macpherson's life of her aunt, Anna Brownell Jameson, in order to eke out the orphaned Macpherson children's income. Her generosity on this occasion humbled Robert Browning into the admission that he might have behaved differently had he taken the trouble to inform himself of Geddie's poverty. Like Mrs Oliphant, he had been alienated by Robert Macpherson's rough ways, 'a butterfly married to a grub', as he put it, but unlike her he had become completely alienated.[65] Mrs Oliphant had managed to discover the trustworthy friend who lay underneath Macpherson's hot-headed, noisy, quarrelsome exterior. Even at her most hard-pressed in the late 1880s Mrs Oliphant made time to devote several months to the 'very troublesome work' of sifting through Tulloch's correspondence in order to write a life, for which she accepted only her expenses, the remainder to go to the widow, for whom the book won a pension from Queen Victoria.[66]

She also seems to have had the loyalty and devotion of her long-staying female servants. She had not come from a family accustomed to keeping servants and the evidence of her novels suggests that she gave considerable thought to the mistress–servant relationship, balancing the need for the servant to feel part of the family network of loyalty and affection against the danger of their coming between parents and children. No good servant, one suspects, could fail to be impressed by Mrs Oliphant's own capacity for work of every sort, and she was prepared to take parental responsibility for them, to the extent of interviewing a French suitor for Esther, a servant of her last years.[67]

Perforce she had taken upon herself the responsibilities of the head of a house-hold, and although she felt that there were a few ritual domestic duties, such as taking the lead at family prayers, that should not be undertaken by a woman, in all the ways that counted hers was the final authority in domestic matters. The role came naturally to her: in her childhood her father had been a mere cipher, while her mother planned, organized, and executed everything from sewing clothes and cooking to extricating Willie from near disgrace at Etal. Her mother had had to recognize one challenge to her supremacy in the form of her son-in-law: after the deaths of her mother and husband Mrs Oliphant became a well-meaning domestic despot. Before her husband's death she had clearly seen herself as an equal in the decision-making process, and the fact that he had failed to tell her the Harley Street doctor's fatal sentence left her 'angry beyond measure' when Robert Macpherson told her, after Frank's death, the true story of the consultation. She attributed the deception to Frank's lack of courage, but it is possible that, being ten years her senior, he had never fully accepted the calm assumption of a woman's right to be consulted in everything that his wife and mother-in-law shared. He was well aware of the substantial nature of their accumulating business debts and it may have seemed sensible to close down the business and pay off the workmen, thus avoiding increasing liabilities, and then take the final gamble that he might recover abroad where life might prove cheaper. Since tuberculosis was characterized by periods of remission, which by Mrs Oliphant's fictional accounts could give both patient and relatives undue bouts of optimism, few sufferers were willing to believe in an absolute verdict. Why burden his wife with a sense of impending doom when all might still be well? His decision undoubtedly affected their relations in his declining months: unable to share his knowledge he seemed to her withdrawn and self-absorbed, and she wrote, years later, of sightseeing expeditions he had 'insisted' on her taking with the children while he stayed indoors, as miserable 'pretences' undertaken 'against my will in obedience to his whim'. Yet watching his wife manage their affairs as they travelled made Frank aware of her organizational skill, and he died 'quite, quite free from anxiety, though he left me with two helpless children and one unborn, and very little money, and no friends but the Macphersons'.

After Frank's death Mrs Oliphant conflated the roles of breadwinner and mother, but working at home meant that she never really distanced herself from the daily implementation of the decisions to which her role as breadwinner entitled her. The adults who joined her household signed up as dependants and were not capable of deflecting the intensity of the emotional energy which was now entirely focused upon her children's welfare. This was to have devastating results.

Out of the five children she raised to maturity (Cyril, Cecco, Frank, Madge, and Denny) only Frank, who must have been about 14 when he came to her, ever achieved an independent existence. After her daughter Maggie's death there was, an onlooker remarked, something 'morbidly passionate' in her love for her boys.[68] Maggie was only 10 when she died, but Mrs Oliphant wrote with a prescient sense of her own possessiveness, 'Had she lived to be married or to sustain any of the great changes of life I must, when the time had come, have stood back and refrained from interfering with her happiness even if to do so had made an end of my own.' When it came to Cyril and Cecco she simply could not let go. Cyril made one bid for freedom in his ill-fated expedition to Ceylon, but after that 'no more melancholy decadence than that of the vivid and sparkling Eton boy into the elderly and deprecating loafer, dawdling about Eton and Windsor, could well be imagined'.[69] Perhaps the saddest record of Cyril's diminished life, capable of asserting himself only by rudeness or indifference to his mother, is to note against his name in the *Eton Lists*, which showed his peer group as barristers, clergy, or landed gentry, the short entry, 'Son of the Authoress: was at Balliol, second in classics 1879. d. at Windsor after a short illness, 1890.' Cecco's behaviour provided a variation on the theme of filial dependence: he became sullen and withdrawn and disliked all interlopers upon his mother's time and affections, including his uncle and cousins. There is a cruel truth to the words Mrs Oliphant wrote the day after he died: 'Cecco, my darling, has been his mother's boy all his dear life. He was born after his father died. He has known nobody but me, no protector, no provider, but his mother.' The imperious behaviour of her 34-year-old son that his mother fondly recalled: 'I wait for his cry of "Mamma"—for he never gave up the childish title—from the other room, a little impatient, knowing full well that everything would be thrown aside to answer it', seems suspiciously like childish attention-seeking to a more detached observer. Mrs Oliphant's 'habit (hardly a wise one) of keeping up baby-names for her sons after they grew into manhood' was picked up by at least one reviewer of her *Autobiography*.[70] Sadly, a note of something like triumph occurs in her valedictory observation of Cecco that 'though he had all a man's experience, save for one boyish inclination towards a pretty girl, he never put any woman near his mother in his heart'. Her disposition to treat romantic attachments with a deflatory cynicism cannot but have sapped his self-confidence: September 1893 found her writing to Denny with grim amusement that she presumed Cecco had a love affair on hand, 'which is ridiculous at his age [33] . . . he sits in the middle of Bexley for hours together saying and doing nothing. The lady must be there I suppose.'[71] She could not be equally certain of Cyril. A week after his death she wrote, 'I never was jealous of his love, never but happy and glad to think he could have friends better and more near to him than I. I am not jealous of the girl who thinks he loved her.—Did he love her: or was no love strong enough to raise the languour of his being?' There is more than a suggestion of a Jocasta-like passion for these sons which could be kept at bay only by keeping them in child-like subservience. When they were apart she would write to 'Cecco mio' daily and complained of her disappointment and misery when the postbag was delivered if he had not responded with similar regularity.[72] In the final year of Cecco's life she had real cause for concern, but it cannot have improved his appetite to have his mother sitting eagle-eyed watching his every mouthful so that she could give a daily report to her nieces in a letter written later in the evening.[73] Something of the tone of her over-anxious maternal supervision can be caught in this excerpt from what she promises will be 'a short letter' written to Cecco, who was wintering abroad.

I am very much afraid that your cough has come back. I hope it may not last. There was an article about colds by a medical man in the *St. James's* the other night in which he recommends (for a simple cold) sitting with your back to the fire so, as to get thoroughly warmed through and keeping your mouth shut when in the open air. I wish you could try to adopt a little at a time, the last of these remedies which would give the best possible protection to your delicate throat. Anyhow eat as much as you can, that is always good. I hope the cuisine is tolerable. Are there not more men in the Costabella than in the Ermitage? I am sorry for you with all those women and children.[74]

Lest there should be a danger of overplaying the latent sexuality in the mother–son relationship, it is only fair to remark that Mrs Oliphant extended the habit of detailed supervision of the minutiae of their lives to her nieces. When Denny was studying art in Paris her aunt's letters questioned every decision she made as to the type of class she attended or the branch of her profession she pursued. When

Denny, back in England, received her first commission she had a letter from her aunt enjoining her to be firm with her patrons, but also giving her detailed instructions as to the size and composition of the picture she was to undertake.[75] Madge's marriage and distant residence in Dundee did not put her beyond the reach of her aunt's advice about how to comport herself in her new social milieu. The nearest comparison Mrs Oliphant could find to the tea-parties to which Madge now found herself invited was the impromptu visits she and Frank had exchanged, at the beginning of their marriage, with the artist Alexander Johnstone and his wife. Denny, who was staying with Madge, was told to tell her sister that the gown Madge had worn to the tea-party the previous day had been inappropriate and that next time she should wear something lighter in weight and colour.[76]

Just as she had misjudged the strength of the little girls' desire for a home when they were small, so their aunt seems not to have appreciated the full nature of their mutual devotion until Madge's marriage effected a definitive separation. Three months later Mrs Oliphant declared herself pleased that Denny should find a welcome in the Valentine household: by the time another six months had passed she was worrying lest 'her little Den' should leave her to live permanently with Madge, the only person Denny really loved.[77] Denny changed her surname to Oliphant to give her aunt some visible proof of her devotion but jealousies still abounded. According to Mrs Oliphant, Denny became jealous if she or Fanny Tulloch presumed to write to Madge without consulting her.[78] Yet, despite the tensions and rivalries, Mrs Oliphant remained the head of their depleted family and the one to whom they turned for help. William Valentine may have resented his aunt by marriage, but he and Madge nevertheless left their seven-months-old baby at Windsor in her care when they wanted to go abroad.[79]

Before proceeding to convict Mrs Oliphant of a rapaciously possessive and domineering love which stunted any young growth with which it came into contact, it is important to remember two mitigating circumstances, one personal, the other cultural. Her over-protective fussiness where her adult sons' health was concerned was, in the event justified, if not successful. She had seen her husband die of tuberculosis and now recognized and dreaded the symptoms. Moreover, the endless reproaches and the constant monitoring of Cyril's drinking sprang also from a dread of history repeating itself. The image of brother Willie's helpless alcoholism haunted her, and modern medical research suggests that she was right to suspect a genetic predisposition to this particular weakness. Her parents had sanctioned her sisterly monitoring of Willie's every move during the final months of his training in London, but her fiction suggests that she found it hard to forgive herself for her lack of trust and the occasional 'spying' to which Cyril's more defiant outbursts reduced her.[80]

Secondly, in a society where gender roles were firmly entrenched, the emergence of a woman as the chief breadwinner in a household had a tendency to leave the men of the family all at sea as to their place in the world, especially if no close role models were readily available. William Gaskell and George Henry Lewes were already well established in their careers before their partners achieved fame and fortune, but Mrs Fanny Trollope swiftly eclipsed her morosely eccentric barrister husband and, by taking a managing interest in the work of her eldest son, Thomas Adolphus, reduced him to the position of her literary satellite. Anthony Trollope may well have had what he perceived as his mother's rejection of him to thank for his independent career as a prolific and successful novelist. Mrs Humphry Ward's husband seems to have accustomed himself to the higher standard of living his wife's exceptional earning powers commanded, and declined from *Times* political leader writer to the post of art critic, which required less stamina. Meanwhile, he squandered his wife's earnings in speculative art purchases. Her son, Arnold, was an even less attractive proposition than Cyril Oliphant. Also the apple of his mother's eye, academically talented and endowed with a vulnerable constitution that permitted too much maternal fussing, he too used the emancipation of under-graduate life at Balliol to embark upon a career of drunkenness and debt. Tied for too long to his mother's apron-strings, he became incapable of managing his own life and, after a brief spell as a Member of Parliament, from which his gambling debts forced his resignation, he declined into a drag on the family fortunes.

The case of the Ward family provides many instructive parallels.[81] The insecurities of Mary Augusta's childhood, brought about by her father, who placed his ideals above the welfare of wife and children, made her determined to keep her own children by her. It is fairly clear that Mrs Oliphant's family dated 'poor Willie's' initial downfall to the period when the family moved to Liverpool and he was left, aged 19, to fend for himself in Glasgow: her own sons were therefore under constant supervision, as day-boys at Eton, and, by way of their mother's occasional bouts of residence, in Oxford. By comparison with Mrs Ward's intentions for her daughters, Mrs Oliphant's insistence that her nieces receive training to fit themselves for independent lives seems strikingly unselfish, even if her increasing need for Denny eventually undermined her niece's desire and capacity for independence. The most remarkable similarity, however, is still to be found in the parasitic lives of the two sons, Cyril Oliphant and Arnold Ward. Bred to expect success, the comfortable life with which their mothers could provide them did not make the struggle for independent achievement sufficiently enticing. It was easier to remain slightly contemptuous of the maternal pot-boiling if they refrained from too committed an attempt to rival the parental literary output. Their descent into an idle male-clubland atmosphere of drink and debt carries with it the suggestion that their instinct for self-destruction was at least matched by their desire to wound their mothers by showing how quickly they could waste the substance it had taken so much effort to create.

By such behaviour, moreover, Cyril was able to demonstrate how Mrs Oliphant's proud boast that 'At my most ambitious of times I would rather my children had remembered me as their mother than in any other way and my friends as their friend' was only one version among the multiple fictions or experimental egos with which her own relating of her life so artfully played. Had motherhood and friendship been the roles to which she had confined herself, neither the *Autobiography* nor the vast collected *œuvre*, in which we catch glimpses of her complicated jugglings of her notion of a woman's sphere and duties with those of the wider world of her work, would have existed.

2 Women's Sphere

Perhaps the household drudge is the natural attendant or double of the goddess.[1]

In 1859 Florence Nightingale had privately printed her passionate outburst, *Cassandra*, on the lot of women of the mid-nineteenth-century leisured classes.[2] Silent suffering, she claimed, had been enshrined by a patriarchal society, as the highest way in which women could emulate the life of Christ. Presenting women with this passive or negative ideal encouraged guilt and self-doubt inasmuch as it refined the moral instincts without providing a sphere in which to exercise them. Women who had been taught to repress and deny their passions wasted their undervalued time in guilty dreams of an Ideal all too often located in a male saviour figure. Marriage did not liberate; it merely completed the systematic robbery and enslavement of women who had been brought up to believe that there was no time they could call their own, without fear of offending or hurting someone. Ironically, Nightingale suffered this bitter denunciation of the psychological deprivations of women, which she had originally assembled as early as 1852, to be silenced by the advice of two male counsellors: J. S. Mill and Benjamin Jowett.

The same decade saw Mrs Oliphant achieve professional status with her novels in print and a platform for her views in *Blackwood's Magazine*. Yet the apparent liberation of a female talent and voice, that had so forcibly impressed Henry James,[3] turns out to be so hedged about with qualifications that Florence Nightingale's case might seem to be validated. That Mrs Oliphant was allowed space as early in her Blackwood's career as 1856 to comment upon 'The Laws Concerning Women' confirms her feeling, expressed in the letter proposing her article, that her views would prove acceptable to John Blackwood, editor and proprietor of *Maga*, and noted for his conservative views on feminist issues.[4] Not only did her 'say' have to receive male endorsement but sought authority by disguising itself as a male voice.

Florence Nightingale had also noted that 'widowhood, ill-health, or want of bread, these three explanations or excuses are supposed to justify a woman taking up an occupation'. The full account of Mrs Oliphant's self-legitimation as a writer belongs to another chapter; suffice it here to note that she had at every stage been freed by necessity from the luxury of guilt or false modesty to see her occupation as a way, albeit pleasurable, of fulfilling a female duty to her family. Circumstances, she contended, had conspired to place 'a commonplace little woman' in an extraordinary position, so giving her the unique opportunity to write on behalf of and for the average middle-class reader. Just as reformers and legislators should be discouraged from making exceptional cases such as George Eliot or Charlotte Brontë into normative examples, so novelists should refrain from using fiction to encourage young girls to dream of the self-aggrandizing heroism their mundane lives would deny them.[5]

In many respects Mrs Oliphant's analysis of woman's position concurred with Florence Nightingale's, but their attitude to this state of affairs was radically different. Where Florence Nightingale's bitter resentment fired a reforming zeal, Mrs Oliphant's approach might at first sight seem to enlist her as a collaborator in female oppression. It is one of the greatest paradoxes of Mrs Oliphant's life and work that, despite her much-bruited 'half-contemptuous attitude' to men, her opinion on the rights of women question seems to place her in what would now be labelled the anti-feminist camp. Before arraigning her as an ultra-conservative whose widely disseminated views served as a drag on the wheels of feminist history, it is worth recalling what distinguished company she kept. George Eliot too found favour with John Blackwood, and the recalcitrance of her novels to feminist annexation has given rise to such twentieth-century articles as 'Why the feminists are angry with George Eliot'.[6] Both George Eliot and Mrs Oliphant were painfully aware of the limitations imposed upon women's lives by the unthinking tyranny of cultural tradition, but wanted to distinguish these from the sacrifices which, consciously embraced, might bear fruit in the refinement of the moral spirit. Despite their divergent credal positions, both authors saw the prevailing metaphoric understanding of Christianity as a religion of suffering and self-sacrificial love as intimately related to man's highest moral and spiritual aspirations.

Naturally, during the course of a half-century's writing, cultural constraints changed, and Mrs Oliphant's sensitivity to variations in the climate of opinion ensured that the lines demarcating unreasonable restrictions from morally profitable opportunities for self-sacrifice fell differently as the years went by. Like Trollope, Mrs Oliphant was inclined to believe that Parliamentary legislation often offered little more than a belated rubber-stamp to opinions that had gradually come to reflect the will of the country at large. This scepticism as to the real significance of legal change played an important part in her slowly changing approach to the question of female suffrage. As a girl she had discovered that it was perfectly possible for a woman to play an active role in politics when she had helped to collect signatures for the women's petition to Parliament at the time of the Anti-Corn Law agitation. Moreover, being brought up in a family which had been 'tremendously political and Radical, my mother especially and Frank',[7] convinced her that married women did not need the vote to make their views tell. For the rest of her life she clung tenaciously to the view that, in marrying, men and women became 'one flesh' and entitled therefore to only one vote, but, as her earliest article on the subject was at pains to point out, women enjoyed absolute authority where it really counted, on the domestic front.[8]

As England entered the 'age of equipoise' and left behind it the last wave of Chartist fervour and memories of European revolutions, Mrs Oliphant's sense of the illusory nature of the power to be gained through suffrage increased. In her essay upon John Stuart Mill and his 'mad notion of the franchise for women', as she light-heartedly abbreviated the contents of her article 'The Great Unrepresented' to John Blackwood,[9] she suggested that two classes of society were already alienated from the voting process: the working classes failed to exercise the privilege for which they had fought, and the upper classes believed their vote worthless in the face of the publican and shopkeeper classes who seemed to carry elections. Furthermore, Mill's campaign for single women to receive the vote was based upon a false premiss in suggesting that women would feel their lot improved by the insulting inference that they had been yearning for 'equality' with men from whom they knew themselves to be different and to whom they in any case often felt superior.

By 1869 she still felt that Mill's arguments were wrongly grounded, but was prepared to support the vote for single women, though she wryly noted that widows, who might be supposed to feel deprived of their previous share of the married vote, could not be seen clamouring for this way of expressing their sense of life's most serious matters.[10] In 1880, when Principal Tulloch offered her the chance to air 'the Grievances of Women' in the pages of *Fraser's Magazine*, of which he was editor, she declared the current legal position with regards to single women to be indefensible. 'I think it highly absurd that I should not have a vote, if I want one—a point upon which I am much more uncertain.' She also paid grudging tribute to those women who had 'dared ridicule' so that those, like her, who disliked public meetings and platforms might benefit from the treatment these activists had received, thus 'bringing into the open the superior patronizing way in which some men regard women'.[11] Behind this thanks, nevertheless, lies the implicit criticism, often made explicit in the earlier articles, that women who were prepared to indulge in the discussion of marital and sexual politics such campaigning involved had come close to endangering feminine modesty and dignity.

Her consistent preaching of these now unfashionable womanly qualities is inclined to make modern readers squirm, especially when it leads to explaining why married women are of course excluded from the professions because of their need for periodic retreats from society to bear 'the proud shame of childbirth and pregnancy'.[12] Yet an insistence upon this model of womanhood carried a hidden advantage. In acknowledging this as an ideal, rather than claiming it as the norm, Mrs Oliphant was able to escape the bonds of essentialism, and this in turn liberated her to see that changing mores implied the possibility of an interpretative change in the understanding of what constitutes feminine 'modesty' or 'dignity'. Although she herself remained of the opinion that women were most fulfilled in marriage, family responsibilities, or, when needs must, in the types of employment which most nearly replicated these conditions, by 1889 she was driven to admit that the belief in woman's right to an independent career was no longer embodied 'in a sect, or a party, but an atmosphere, and it breathes through almost every educated household in the land'.[13]

Since, in view of the much-publicized surplus of women, one could not know if a daughter would marry, prudence had long dictated female education and training.

Mrs Oliphant in practice had always favoured women's education. Under her auspices Fanny Tulloch had shared a Latin tutor with Cyril back in 1865, but her scepticism as to the value of a classically based English education,[14] which she overcame in the case of her boys, was absolute in the case of her nieces: Madge and Denny were sent to Germany on the grounds that English boarding-schools did not provide a comparably useful education. Their subsequent artistic training reflected Mrs Oliphant's belief that art could be justified as a feminine profession by its kinship, on the one hand, with ladylike accomplishments and, on the other, with the demands of genius; training, moreover, provided the technical substructure for an artist to fall back upon when inspiration failed.[15] Better still, 'the highest work', she wrote to Madge, 'you can have at home and do at leisure with credit and profit'.[16] Marriage to Frank had shown her that art provided a passport to a world beyond the confines of the social milieu in which one was born. As Rose Lake, the mistress of Carlingford's School of Design, repeatedly reminds her innately less genteel elder sister, 'the true strength of our position is that we are a family of artists. We are everybody's equal and we are nobody's equal. We have a rank of our own.'[17] In the course of *Miss Marjoribanks* (1866) 'poor Rose' has to sacrifice the career, of which she has dreamed, to her family's need for a housekeeper. 'Little Rose', 'Poor Rose': these diminutives are employed to remind us of a stature at odds with the girl's sense of her own dignity; she is gently laughed at by her creator, though her diminished prospects are none the less sympathetically presented. As so often when Mrs Oliphant portrayed artists, art serves as a metaphor for her own writing career, and the treatment of the sacrifice Rose felt compelled to make echoes Mrs Oliphant's own half-derisive reporting of several crises in her own life when she found herself 'making a kind of pretence to myself that I had to . . . make a great decision, to give up what hope I might have had of doing now my very best'.[18] In a later novel, *The Curate in Charge* (1876), written just after her brother Frank added his family to her other responsibilities, art is once again presented as a suitable career for a girl, but the necessary professional training can only be achieved at the expense of a sister who stays at home to tend to her young half-brothers and sisters. Such were the kinds of sacrifice and choice 'which almost any artist is compelled to make', Mrs Oliphant reminded her niece, Madge. Yet the same letter also removes the choices, which might have given the girls independent careers, from them. 'If I were dead', the letter continues, 'it would be a choice you would be obliged to make . . . But as long as I am here at your back I grudge it for you.'[19]

Mrs Oliphant seems to have had difficulty in conceiving of any profession other than literature, and possibly art, which was compatible with the status and nature of middle-class womanhood. Music, for instance, was a more ambiguous vocation. When its aim of breadwinning was uncomplicated by any selfish consideration, music teaching, like any other form of governessing, was compatible with the instincts of a lady, as the short story 'My Faithful Johnny'[20] shows. To be a performing artist, however, exposed women to public attention in an undesirable manner which almost put them on a par with actresses. Among the great professional actresses Fanny Kemble was to win absolution from Mrs Oliphant because she had allegedly always disliked acting and had only taken to the boards as an act of self-sacrifice on behalf of her family.[21] An early novel, *The Athelings* (1857), indulges in gentle mockery of suburban preoccupation with gentility, but the plot of the novel as a whole endorses and rewards the careful nurturing of middle-class values and Mrs Oliphant concurs with a middle-class mother who claims that before allowing any daughter of hers to make a living by singing in public, 'I should rather a hundred times take in work myself, or do anything with my own hands, than let my girls do this. It is not respectable for a young girl. A public appearance! I should be grieved and ashamed beyond anything.'[22] Those who actively seek and enjoy such self-display automatically remove themselves from the ranks of gentle-women. Barbara Lake's use of her voluptuous contralto as a method of gaining access to a higher social circle in *Miss Marjoribanks* serves to distinguish her from her respectable sister Rose, whose artistic integrity remains unimpaired by the necessity to gain a living. In an otherwise uninteresting novel, *Within the Precincts* (1879), the topic is given a further airing. Lottie Despard is brought up to believe herself a gentlewoman, but, on her dissolute father's remarriage to a vulgar seam-stress, she finds herself in need of a means of gaining her own livelihood. Her beautiful voice, which has been for her, as for Barbara Lake, a passport to coveted social progress, is also almost the means of her undoing in attracting the attentions of Rollo Ridsdale, a cad of aristocratic lineage, who plans to gain a living by exploiting her talents. The fact that he inadvertently falls in love with her makes no essential difference to his plans as an impresario, though he is prepared, while his fortunes appear uncertain, to contemplate a secret marriage to her.

In former times, perhaps, a man would have thought it necessary to pretend at least a desire to snatch his bride from the exposure of publicity, from the stage, or even from the concert-room—a determination to work for her rather than to let her work for him; but along with circumstances sentiments change, and the desire of women for work is apt to be supported from an undesirable side by those who once would have thought their honour concerned in making women's work unnecessary.[23]

The unlooked-for death of his elder brother and his succession to the family title lead Rollo to abandon Lottie in compromising circumstances. The stale re-working of the classic Victorian discussion of what constitutes gentility (birth, breeding, or an innate sense of moral values) is given a further dimension by allowing music and the status of musicians to complicate an already fine-drawn set of distinctions. There is a choice open to Lottie which would allow her to practise her gift and retain the reader's respect, although it conflicts with Lottie's own prejudice that a gentlewoman never works for her living. The organist at the abbey whose precincts give the novel its title has fired her artistic ambition by his inspired playing of sacred music, but the fact that he is both a confirmed bachelor and a foreigner (he is of Anglo-Italian extraction) suggests that if she accepts his offer of a musical training she will also have to forfeit social acceptance and marriage.

'Happiness dies,' the organist tells her, 'love fails, but art is for ever.'[24] It seems probable that the imminent return of Madge and Denny from their German boarding-school prompted Mrs Oliphant to consider the niceties involved in balancing artistic flair, financial need, and social considerations 'within the precincts' of the Royal Chapel at Windsor. Her failure, in real life, to cast her lot unequivocally on the side of a woman's duty to her art is reflected in the cop-out ending to the novel, where Lottie's reputation is saved by marriage to a devoted minor canon. Lottie's voice, endangered by the illness contracted after waiting in the open all night for Rollo, recovers sufficiently to allow her private satisfaction but has been too enfeebled for her ever again to contemplate public performances of secular operatic music.

Before dismissing Mrs Oliphant's intricate sense of gradation in the acceptable combination of vocation and profession as mere Victorian snobbery, it is worth remembering the careful contrasts and parallels George Eliot erected in *Daniel Deronda*. For the Princess Halm-Eberstein the satisfaction of her dramatic and operatic talent proved incompatible with either the filial or maternal feelings that 'most other women feel—or say they feel'.[25] Mirah is justified in using her vocal talent in private drawing-rooms to earn a living but runs away from her father's exploitation of her voice for financial and social aggrandizement. Gwendolen's presence at Mirah's London début underlines the boundary between them. Mirah's genius, need, and personal modesty justify her professional career, whereas Gwendolen's theatrical aspirations have been exposed by Klesmer as a desire to trade on a meagre talent in a manner more self-gratifying than governessing would have been. As so often happened in Mrs Oliphant's case, it was her plotting that let her down. Where George Eliot effected a plot which, despite considerable use of melodramatic device, provided a framework for the careful measurement of genius against selfish motivation and financial need, Mrs Oliphant's plot has insufficient substance to bear the weight of a serious discussion or resolution of the issues. Pitiable though Lottie's plight is, she never attains the tragic forlornness and absolute need of Mirah, and Rollo's disreputable intentions establish her womanly purity as a gentlewoman in a way that obscures the more interesting issue of whether she was right to feel that accepting work would inevitably endanger her frail grasp upon the claim of gentility. George Eliot maintains her moral clarity by relying upon extreme cases to make her point: Mrs Oliphant, as usual, saw things in more muted tones, and the evasiveness of this novel may well reflect her suspicion that social prejudice rather than morality dictated the answers to Lottie's dilemma.

When Mrs Oliphant read the life of her American contemporary, Louisa May Alcott, which told how this daughter of an intellectual, but improvident, household resorted to plain sewing and even to domestic service as an honourable means of earning a living, she reacted with 'a certain abashed admiration'. In England, she commented, social embarrassment would have prevented former friends taking Alcott into domestic service. 'If, however, this story is true, and a good and brave girl can go to service in America without ceasing to form part of the best society, it is so much the better for America.'[26] Her reviews of this late period reflected the social trend towards the acceptance of women's rights to a career which would give them purpose, dignity and independence,[27] but in her fiction such desires remained little more than protests symptomatic of some other social malaise.

Only once did Mrs Oliphant mention in her novels the possibility, to which her articles gave cautious approval,[28] of women becoming doctors. In *Sir Tom* (1883) Lucy, formerly the heroine of *The Greatest Heiress in England*, finds herself embroiled with her older husband's set of worldly friends. Anxious to free a young girl, Beatrice, or Bice, from a life that promises only pleasure-seeking and fortune-hunting, Lucy tells her:

There are so many things that girls can do, there are things open to them that never used to be—they can even be doctors when they are clever. There are many ways in which they can maintain themselves.

'By trades?' cried Bice, 'by work? . . . We hear of that sometimes: and the doctors—everybody laughs; the men make jokes, and say they will have one when they are ill' . . . 'There is no question of working', said Bice with decision, 'neither for women, neither for men. That is not in our world.'[29]

Lucy's suggestion and her offer of financial backing to save Bice from the prospect of marriage to a rich dullard are greeted as merely naïve. Lucy's notions, derived from a puritan middle-class upbringing, make no inroads on this world-weary upper-class society, but this is partly because Mrs Oliphant never allows any vocational glamour to attach to woman's work. Doctoring is seen merely as a way in which clever women 'can maintain themselves'. Like other forms of female employment of which she approved, doctoring was allowable because it seemed merely the professional extension of a skill which good women naturally had occasion to practise: nursing. When Lucy's child falls ill a woman doctor is not summoned. Instead it is Lucy, with a mother's instinct, who recognizes the turning-point in the child's fever, and Bice's world of social frivolity is briefly dented by a desire to dance helpless, admiring attendance upon this madonna and child.

Two late novels, *The Railwayman and His Children* (1891), and *The Marriage of Elinor* (1891), use minor characters to allude to the phenomenon of 'the girl of the period' and her assumption of a right to an independent career. In *The Railwayman and His Children*, a novel which again explores the clash of class expectations, 'the girl of the period' is a serious-minded, pragmatic young woman whose interest in a career is little more than a studied rejection of the opportunist, scheming life of her cynical and debauched father. Resenting raffish males of her own class and the oafish assumption of the newly rich that to be idle is a proof of gentility, she is convinced that 'Honest work is the only salvation' and 'to be of use' the only purpose in life.[30] One might have expected Mrs Oliphant thoroughly to endorse these propositions, but the girl lacks charm: she is cold-blooded, humourless, and, it is suggested, asexual. Her enthusiasm for a profession rather than a particular vocation seems to stem from a deep-seated disgust with the idle men she encounters. Her half-masculine dress as she stalks the streets of London, accompanied only by a mastiff, is indicative of a desire to take over the world from inefficient and effete males rather than to show what a woman's contribution might be. Mrs Oliphant's interest remains at the level of social psychology and we never find out what employment exactly the girl attains in the closing chapter. *The Marriage of Elinor*, which alludes in passing to a modern world where girls go to Girton and then waste their expensive education by marrying poor curates,[31] is principally concerned with an old-fashioned girl who is ill-yoked to a member of the minor aristocratic 'fast set'. The dissolute husband is virtually written out of the plot, but his sister, Lady Mariamne, forcibly reminds the reader what happens to those who have gone 'too fast' and for whom 'the pace' had been too much. Her desperate attempts to retain her one property, her beauty, are repellent enough, but more important is the rebellion waged by her daughter, the inappropriately named 'Doll'. She has rejected the flirtatiously effusive image of womanhood in favour of a cold and strident invasion of male preserves. At social gatherings she heads straight for male groups where her voice can be heard raucously 'laying down the law' in legal and medical discussion.[32] A short story of the same era, 'A Girl of the Period' (1891), completes the picture of Mrs Oliphant's hostility to female ambitions which seemed to her to threaten her ideals of womanhood. The story is a thinly disguised sermonette on the culpable ignorance, conceit, and utter self-centredness of young girls who presume to reject the wisdom and experience of their parents. By the end of the tale it is conceded that a girl might reasonably prefer to study art in Paris to 'doing the season', but this is carefully segregated from more fanciful notions such as complete equality between the sexes or between the social classes. Her mistaken and aggressive championing of these causes has led her to become ridiculous even in her own eyes and nearly caused real harm to those less well off than herself.

Retrograde as Mrs Oliphant's attitudes of the 1890s now seem, they do in fact represent some progress from the views given currency in her earliest fiction. *Merkland* (1850) introduced Miss Marjory Falconer, a militant champion of the rights of women. Her attire is masculine and she resorts to the horsewhip, or cameraderie with the local lads, to achieve her ends, thus drawing down a lecture upon herself from the heroine, who claims that, by attracting gossip, Marjory has demeaned the name of woman. The heroine offers instead a vision of woman's fulfilment in 'Household strength and loftiness, and purity', and adds for good measure, 'I do utterly contemn and abominate all that rubbish of rights of women, and woman's mission, and woman's influence, and all the rest of it: I never hear these cant words, but I blush for them.'[33] True to this teaching, Mrs Oliphant proceeds to demonstrate that Marjory's views were a temporary affectation and by the end of the novel the girl of this period has been squeezed back into an acceptable mould by marriage and motherhood. The late tales, disapproving as they may be, at least acknowledge that the social conditions which have given rise to such desires have wrought a change too radical for mere suppression or reversal to be effected. There were, Mrs Oliphant conceded, in an article for the *St James's Gazette*, no longer any easy conventions to draw upon in establishing whether it was appropriate for a middle-class girl to work. The possibility of earning an independent income was of course more satisfying to a girl than being dependent upon a miserly pension eked out to her by a brother merely bent upon preserving the family name from disgrace, yet all too often woman's 'progress' had become a further kind of enslavement, as brothers, husbands, and sons grew idle and content to live upon their female relative's earnings: an *ad feminam* argument which seems unlikely to have applied among the schoolteaching classes of which this article purportedly spoke.[34]

As she grew older so her scepticism increased: the school of life taught as its second rule, she claimed, 'Never be too sure of the badness or wretchedness of other classes and systems.'[35] Perhaps temperament and circumstance were the only sure guidelines: in an amusing letter to Madge of 2 December 1896, Mrs Oliphant drew a picture of a certain Madame Blanc, a head of department for the French paper, *Revue des deux Mondes*, who had against all her feelings and habits been forced for the first time in twenty years to play the roles of wife, mother, and grandmother. 'I suppose the ideas of the time do get into one's head however much one may disapprove of them,' she wrote, 'and therefore I am not inclined to object so much to this woman who declines to take the cow's part as I used to be. I always would have been a cow-woman myself you know.'[36]

Back in 1858 the didactic heroine of *Orphans* had refused so much as to believe in the very existence 'of that hypothetical woman which has no genius for children'. This novel had explicitly tackled the question of what a rich single woman of 28 should do with her life in an era when 'there were no Miss Nightingales' to raise nursing abroad as an exciting proposition. This girl's disposition, like her author's, made her shrink from believing that 'maiden ladies might be improved in mind and circumstances by being permitted to attempt surgery, to make watches, or to keep books'. Instead she decides to collect around her an assembly of poor relations whose 'far-off bonds of relationship . . . were just sufficient to add piquancy to dislike, and vehemence to emulation';[37] a recipe for female heroism that Mrs Oliphant clung to unwaveringly both in her own life and in her fiction. This prescriptive novel is predicated upon Mrs Oliphant's belief that many girls derived their expectations of life and their role models from fiction. Working on this assumption Mrs Oliphant decided that it would be the business of her fiction to provide role models that did not glamorize a woman's lot. During her career her novels moved slowly away from the prescriptive to the descriptive, but the mission to deprive the image of womanly self-sacrifice of any hint of heroic allure if anything intensified.

For this view of the function and dangers of fiction Mrs Oliphant looked to the authority of her own experience. Her own novel-writing had begun as the day-dreaming of a teenager attempting to console herself for a broken engagement and the enforced passivity of tending her mother's sick-bed. 'I wrote a little book in which the chief character was an angelic elder sister, unmarried, who had the charge of a family of motherless brothers and sisters, and who had a shrine of sorrow in her life in the shape of the portrait and memory of her lover who had died young.' Years later, Mrs Oliphant related in her *Autobiography*, brother Willie published the novel *Christian Melville* 'on his own account, and very silly I think it is, poor little thing'.[38] The phrase 'poor little thing' applies as much to the writer as to the novel itself, which bears the clear marks of the young author's wish-fulfilment. Mrs Oliphant, whose chance of freedom and importance had been snatched from her by the broken engagement, fantasizes a narrative in which her fictional counterpart is transposed from disregarded youngest child to the eldest daughter, whom the mother's swift demise liberates so that she may gain tragic stature by practising a form of domestic sainthood which gains the admiring love of an extended family. The heroine's shrine to her departed lover keeps her ever conscious of her sorrow, and as the novel charts the passage of years her brave smile becomes 'more sad than other people's tears'.[39] By the time Mrs Oliphant came to write the series of novels featuring Clara Crofton (*Orphans*, *Lucy Crofton*, and *Heart and Cross*) married life had taught her that a woman's daily lot was not conducive to such angelic evenness of temper nor did it permit the self-pitying egoism of constantly revisiting the wounds the past had inflicted. In the second novel of the series the rich benefactress has married, but lost her only baby. She has to learn that the self-indulgence of prolonged private grief is potentially damaging to her role as wife. The second baby, promised by the end of the novel, is perhaps too patly provided as a reward for facing the full desolation of loss for the readers to grasp the real bleakness of Mrs Oliphant's code of self-sacrificing love which exacts a full look at the worst and a total acceptance of it. Perhaps she herself scarcely realized the full stoic implications of her creed before the loss of her husband deprived her of further babies and Maggie's death revealed the hard furrow she would have to plough.

I cannot stop and go no further. I must go on to places, among people who know not of her, the awful routine of life has commenced again. I have no longer any power of revival, any new hope to rise in my heart. That does not matter. I must go on. I must endure. It is the lot God has appointed to me.[40]

Mrs Oliphant was well aware that publishers preferred happy endings and so she occasionally used a comic or parodic form to encode her message. From her earliest reviews she had represented Charlotte Brontë's *Jane Eyre* as the revolutionary initiator of novels pleading the rights of women,[41] and it was to this book she turned, towards the end of the century, for a clearly discernible and well-known narrative structure, ripe for conversion to bear her own very different construction of a woman's place in the world. The novel which resulted, *Janet* (1891), is one of Mrs Oliphant's most literarily allusive works, which, while employing a plot derived from the Gothic tradition, also makes teasing reference to the anti-Gothic novels of Jane Austen. When Mrs Oliphant's governess heroine hears a demonic outcry late at night which she cannot reconcile with the staid manservant who comes and goes between the servants' quarters and the locked wing of the house in which she is employed, the text directs us to *Northanger Abbey* rather than Grace Poole and Bertha Mason.

Needless to say that Janet had read 'Northanger Abbey', and had been taught to smile at the investigations of our dear little Catherine, and their amusing issue: though, to tell the truth, her sympathy with Catherine Morland's thirst for adventure had been more strong than her amusement in the result, which disappointed her a little too.[42]

Like Janet, the reader is encouraged, in the course of this narrative, to recognize the 'disappointment' of the desire to identify with Gothic-loving heroines as her passport into a mature perception of life. From the opening of the novel all that makes Jane Eyre's predicament exceptional and therefore instantly pitiable is deliberately undermined. Janet has been well treated by the aunt who raised her and failed only to make provision for her ward in her will. She then spurns the generous, albeit unexciting, proposal of a middle-aged country doctor who 'wanted to save her from the life of a governess'. She prefers to embrace the novelistic allure of the 'heroine as victim' role of governess. Earlier novels had shown Mrs Oliphant's very qualified endorsement of governessing as suitable female employment: its virtue was that it offered women who had no choice but to work, employment in domestic circumstances, but its disadvantage was that, while overtly signalling a life of sacrifice, it could covertly excite a spirit of independence in young women who had real domestic ties closer to hand.[43] Having derived her picture of the governess's lot from the pages of *Jane Eyre*, the *Family Herald*, and *Martin Chuzzlewit*, Janet is much disappointed by the friendly welcome that awaits her in the cosy domesticity of the Harwoods' house in St John's Wood. The trials she faces, such as they are, are the rudeness and belligerence of her spoilt 14-year-old charge (no Adèle she) and irksome minor reminders of her servile status, such as not being invited to dine with the family when guests are expected. Janet's faulty readings persist: she fails to see that the placid, determinedly cheerful, invalid Mrs Harwood, her employer, offers a woman's reinterpretation of Rochester's role. Mrs Harwood has not banished her discarded spouse to the servants' quarters, but has protected and suffered vicariously for a husband whose bankruptcy and ensuing insanity would otherwise make him prey to creditors and the lunatic asylum. The entrance to the sealed wing leads directly off the hall: it is always in sight. Skeletons in closets, Mrs Oliphant reminds us, are not, as novelists like Thackeray suggest, confined to the recesses of personal memory.

The real skeleton is very different: it haunts the house in the form perhaps of a ruined son, a debased and degraded brother. . . . It is always in the minds of those to whom it belongs. In the midst of laughter, in the happiest moment, it gives a tug at their hearts, as if it held them in a chain, and the smile fades, and the sweetest tints grow grey.[44]

Like her author, Mrs Harwood lives not only with ever-present fears of disgrace but with the nagging fear that this weakness might prove hereditary. Her suffering is exacerbated by her need to preserve the smiling exterior, to guard the social niceties. It would be little exaggeration to suggest that in almost every novel by Mrs

Oliphant an occasion arises where at some point in a domestic crisis it is the woman's part to preserve an appearance of normality for the sake of the servants, guests, or neighbours. Men can ride or walk off their emotions or retreat to the library: women's lives simply permit no time or space to indulge their private grief. Unlike Rochester who can travel abroad to dim the memory of his fatal marriage and whose conscience apparently convinces him that his marriage is invalidated by his wife's lunacy, Mrs Harwood lives a life of self-incarceration, bound by her enduring devotion to husband and children. The enforced passivity of female heroism is given symbolic force by her confinement to a wheelchair. Again this encourages Janet and the reader to mistake her for one of the self-indulgent women, so frequent in Victorian fiction, whose hypochondriacal invalidism is an expression both of their real impotence and their desire for sympathetic attention. Mrs Harwood's paralysis, in the event, seems to be a form of psychological identification with her husband's sufferings, for at the moment of his greatest danger she makes a supreme effort to overcome even this handicap and rises from her wheelchair to defend him.

Janet may well have been prompted by Mrs Oliphant's involvement in writing *The Victorian Age of English Literature*, in which she had identified Charlotte Brontë's creation, Rochester, as a new type of hero who had had the unfortunate effect of calling forth a new kind of heroine: 'the maiden on the tip-toe of expectation, no longer modestly awaiting the coming of Prince Charming, but craning her neck out of every window in almost fierce anticipation, and upbraiding heaven and earth which kept her buried in those solitudes out of his way'.[45] Rochester's other role, as Jane's lover, is entrusted to a specious young barrister, Charles Meredith, who, like his literary progenitor, tries to prove his eligibility by provoking female rivalry. His easy patronage of women, 'like a man in an old novel who kisses the maid and gives her half-a-crown, and is what he calls civil to every girl', merely serves to fuel another female fantasy that to whatever depth she has to sink to win him, once won she will be able to save him from himself.[46]

The impact of the Gothic climax of this novel, which discloses the mad husband and father to the appalled eyes of his ignorant children, is deliberately dissipated by its failure to bring a satisfactorily tragic resolution. Janet, who expects to be reviled for her part in betraying the family's secret to strangers, is humiliated by the discovery that she does not count sufficiently to inspire such reactions. Even her final acceptance of the country doctor's second proposal is a muted affair: she comes to him chastened by her failure to attain heroic stature and he has suffered no transformation. Meredith's interest in denouncing the bankrupt is bought off by an engagement to the daughter, whose fortune he will enjoy if he colludes in perpetuating the fraud upon the creditors. Meredith himself compares the plot of the novel in which he finds himself with Maupassant's *Pierre et Jean*, which Mrs Oliphant had recently reviewed for *Blackwood's Magazine*.[47] Such a commendation is, as one might expect, double-edged. Mrs Oliphant had found the subject-matter of a mother's adulterous liaison with a family friend and her eldest son's discovery that his younger brother is the product of this liaison, revolting, and it is a mark of Meredith's degeneracy that he finds this suitable to discuss with single women (it is also, of course, a more plausible equivalent of Rochester's penchant for telling 'stories of his opera-mistresses to a quaint, inexperienced girl' like Jane Eyre).[48] Mrs Oliphant did not consider Maupassant suitable reading for her married niece Madge.[49] Nevertheless, her review did pay tribute to the artistry and fine sense of domestic tragedy of Maupassant's tale: it contained no cathartic outbursts and afforded no scope for displays of self-sacrifice. 'Great scandals are not in the way of the ordinary and commonplace people among whom, all the same, the greatest tragedies may be enacted.' Ordinary people are concerned 'only how to go on, and spread a decent veil over the tragedy and continue to live'.[50] Meredith's greatest sin is his cynical exploitation of the mother and daughter's willingness to suffer in silence.

Mrs Oliphant makes no attempt to hide her conviction that men are complicit in, exact, or take advantage of, women's renunciations and hidden suffering. In her earliest fiction, especially in those novels set on the edges of Edinburgh and Liverpool lower-middle-class life, subsequently published in Willie's name,[51] many a young man unwittingly relies financially on the sewing or washing his womenfolk take in. They steel themselves to make this sacrifice of their precarious social dignity, but, for fear of compromising his, are always anxious to hide their labours. In this early fiction the women perform these feats with a saintly demeanour for the sake of men of earnest good-will, but once freed from sensitivities about Willie's *amour propre*, Mrs Oliphant soon progressed to drawing pictures such as that in *Harry Muir: A Story of Scottish Life* (1853) where womenfolk pinch and scrape and sew in Glasgow tenements to support the indolent, the ungracious, and the wastrel. The ridiculous contortions to which women silently submit to satisfy peremptory male desires are nicely illustrated in a passage from *The Last of the Mortimers* (1862) where a low-ranking army officer's wife finds herself stealthily taking in the land-lady's laundry in order to pay for a maid to care for their baby of whom the self-centred young husband is becoming jealous.[52]

Such silent sacrifices on account of men who merited so little on their own account took place at every level of society, but the female suffering that occurred in wealthier families tended to be psychological. It was difficult, Mrs Oliphant felt, to take wholly seriously the material sacrifices of the comfortably off. The first chapter of *Innocent* (1873) makes gentle mockery of the widowed Mrs Eastwood who had '*put down her carriage*, I dare not print such words in ordinary type', to pay off the debts her son has contracted at Oxford.

She said very little about the reasons for this very serious proceeding, but it cannot be denied that there was a grandeur and pathos in the incident, which gave it a place in what might be called the mythology of the family . . . She would not receive any condolences, and yet even she got a certain subtle pleasure, without knowing it, out of the renunciation. It was the hardest thing she had ever been called upon to do in her life, and how could she help being a little, a very little proud of it?

There is, in this humorous deflation of any attempt to upgrade mundane economizing into a grander sense of sacrifice, something very reminiscent of Mrs
Oliphant's amusement at her own momentary 'half-sincere attempt at a heroical
attitude' when her brother Frank threw himself on her sisterly devotion in 1870 and
she had felt it difficult to maintain the pose of 'nobility' in the face of clear duty and
of her own aversion to all trivial economies.[53] Yet Frank's untroubled assumption of
his sister's provision did grate, and Mrs Eastwood finds that this is merely the first
of many sacrifices her son demands and that her daughter angrily points out would
not have been asked 'if papa had been alive . . . but because mamma is a woman,
Frederick and everybody think she should give in continually'.[54]

In the later novels the capacity of weak men to exploit women's quiet sacrifices
is perceived by the author, and some of her female characters, with a cool-headed
sense of derision which can make discomfortingly bitter reading. Mrs Oliphant was
not unaware of how such an attitude must affect her popularity. In 1870 she had
accounted for Jane Austen's fall from favour with the Victorian public by referring
to her 'fine vein of feminine cynicism':

It is the soft and silent disbelief of a spectator who has to look at a great many things without
showing any outward discomposure, and who has learned to give up any moral classification
of social sins, and to place them instead on the level of absurdities. She is not surprised
or offended, much less horror-stricken or indignant, when her people show vulgar or
mean traits of character, when they make it evident how selfish and self-absorbed they
are, or even when they fall into those social cruelties which selfish and stupid people are so
often guilty of, not without intention, but yet without the power of realising half the pain
they inflict.[55]

Catherine Vernon, the despotic benefactress of the Vernon family in *Hester* (1883),
finally arrives at the bitter knowledge that it is her very capacity and power to help,
born of long years of self-sacrificing work for the family bank, that has turned the
heir, for whom she would have done anything, against her. By 1883 Mrs Oliphant's
own son, Cyril, was well set upon a career of resentful and self-destructive spending of the resources which represented a lifetime of his mother's sacrifices for him.
Yet *Hester* deliberately repudiates any possibility of a new mould for womankind
being developed to counter the cruelty, betrayal, and exploitation that had so easily
adhered to the old ideal. When Catherine's niece, Hester, abandoned, as her aunt
had been at the tale's inception, by the man she loved, wishes to emulate her aunt's
career in banking, Catherine rejects this, despite her feeling that Hester has the
makings of 'an excellent man of business . . . it can't be'.[56] When pressed for a
reason all she will give is that by the time she herself 'saved the bank' she was
already an old maid and the only way she could fulfil her womanly duties was to
repeat the decision of the Crofton heiress to gather relatives around her whose 'far-
off bonds of relationship . . . were just sufficient to add piquancy to dislike, and
vehemence to emulation'.[57] For all the irony of the paragraph that concludes this
novel, leaving Hester between two devoted suitors, neither of whom 'wrung her
heart . . . What can a young woman desire more than to have such a possibility of

choice?', the dilemma is the author's as much as Hester's. While Hester has a home with her mother and is young enough still to marry and take up a woman's domestic cross of suffering, no other honourable course is open to her. Male abuse of women's capacity to suffer did not, in Mrs Oliphant's eyes, justify women in abandoning the old ideals. The suffering and waste that occur in the pages of *Hester* remain a woman's tragedy rather than a man's fault.

The late novels constantly revert to the question of whether there is a female code that exists independently of male understanding, appreciation, or abuse of it. In *Joyce* (1888), a novel largely ruined by the improbable behaviour the plot demands of the characters, the heroine is raised by foster-parents, a ploughman and his wife, in Lowland Scotland. In this context her career as a schoolteacher is seen as perfectly proper, though her schoolmaster fiancé, who holds Ruskinian views on women, feeling 'profoundly that to be able to keep his wife at home, and retain her altogether like a garden enclosed for his private enjoyment, was a supreme luxury', holds that her desire to continue working after marriage showed 'a great deal of that ambition which is more appropriate to a man than a woman'.[58] Since it was Ruskin's motives and manner Mrs Oliphant disliked rather than his conclusions, this element of the plot is quickly dropped when Joyce's true father is discovered and carries her off to a Thames-side haunt of the English middle classes. Joyce is ill at ease with her newly acquired family, but her innate gentility has always been a stumbling-block to her happiness with her humble Lowland schoolteacher fiancé. She falls in love with Norman Bellendean, a scion of a well-born Scottish family, who had first met her when she was a protégée of the big house in her Scottish parish, but he is slow to overcome his sense of the social degradation involved in such a marriage and his aunt, Joyce's former Scottish benefactress, has other plans for him. Appealing to Joyce's sense of gratitude to the Bellendean family, she asks Joyce to step aside so that Norman may marry her daughter. Racked by guilt over her betrothal to the increasingly obnoxious schoolmaster, and haunted by the accusation of ingratitude, Joyce seeks advice from a variety of disparate sources as to whether it is a woman's highest duty to sacrifice herself. The voice of male religious authority, the canon of the Thames-side parish, firmly rebuts this female understanding of Christian duty, though he is driven to admit that 'on this point good women are all fools, and the better they are the greater fools they are'.[59] Everyone is entitled to happiness and no one, he says, must feel it incumbent upon him to sacrifice himself for another, especially if such an act might humiliate the recipient. Joyce, however, feels that the views of a disregarded spinster schoolmistress ring truest when she claims that sacrifice is a woman's lot. Her dilemma leaves her no space in which to turn.[60] The life of a spinster schoolmistress is incompatible with the pride of her newly acquired middle-class family: and so Joyce quite simply disappears beyond the margins of the realist text and is last heard of as a legendary cultivating force, living with her two foster-parents, on a remote island off the north coast of Scotland. The ending concedes that it may no longer be possible for the young to practise the old female code in late nineteenth-century society. Moreover, though Joyce has kept faith with the old ideal, her sacrifice is not understood, nor does it benefit anyone with whom the story has led us to sympathize. Norman leaves for India and turns into a misanthropist, and the schoolteacher and Norman's cousin make other successful marriages.

The sense that this ideal of female self-sacrifice, upon which she had been raised, might have become unintelligible to the English middle classes at the close of the century may have led Mrs Oliphant to seize upon her friend Christina Rogerson's story from her Scottish family's history[61] to explore the question in a more remote setting in *Kirsteen: The Story of a Scotch Family Seventy Years Ago* (1890). Certainly the pilgrimages south, undertaken by both Kirsteen and Joyce, consciously echo Jeanie Deans's famous journey in Sir Walter Scott's *Heart of Midlothian*, and the sense that Kirsteen shares Jeanie's indomitable energy, while Joyce's initial spirit is cowed and can only flourish on the fringes of civilization, has more to do with the deadening historical march of English middle-class morality than with inherent differences in character between these girls. Ostensibly Kirsteen's plight is harder than Joyce's in that she faces the boorish violence of a tyrannical father whose brutality had been nourished by a period of service running a slave plantation. Like so many of Mrs Oliphant's despotic fathers, Kirsteen's father inflicts his worst blows at the psychological rather than the physical level, 'not without intention, but yet without the power of realising half the pain'. This story measures with especial subtlety the pain women experience when they realize that their standards of loving self-sacrifice are not even comprehensible to those for whom they make these sacrifices but are merely perceived as a weakness to be exploited. Kirsteen's father, the poor and brutal Laird of Drumcarro, is prepared to spend what money he has on launching the sons who will bear the family name of Douglas, but his daughters are totally neglected 'as unlucky accidents, tares among the wheat, handmaids who might be useful about the house, but who had no future, no capabilities of advancing the family, creatures altogether of no account'. The women in his family react to this in different ways: the mother 'sank only into invalidism—into a timid complaining, a good deal of real suffering, and a conviction that she was the most sorely tried of women'.[62] The eldest daughter, Anne, has had her name and image wholly effaced from the family records for defying her father and linking the Douglas name with that of a lowly doctor. Kirsteen, who runs away from home to avoid marrying her father's choice, nevertheless disapproves of Anne's course of action: 'It was shameful to her family. It was forgetting all that was most cherished. I may be sorry for her . . . but I cannot approve her.'[63] The third daughter disguises complete self-interest under the mask of subservience to men, and the youngest girl is almost seduced because she cannot accept that it is a woman's lot to 'be patient and bide at home'[64] waiting for the man who truly loves her to play the active role of gaining fame and fortune.

Kirsteen has a finely developed sense of morality enabling her to respect her father's code of conduct where this does not absolutely challenge her own integrity. In novel after novel Mrs Oliphant makes it clear that it is not a woman's duty merely to yield unquestioning obedience to any man, since this would effectively be abnegating a woman's most treasured possession, her moral sense. Kirsteen cannot marry her father's choice of suitor, kindly though he is, because she has already given her heart elsewhere to a lad who is, as yet, in no position to marry her. Her decision to leave home and find work is supported by the author because it is Kirsteen's only self-respecting option: she has been 'forced into independence'. Whether Kirsteen's successful career in London as a mantua-maker to the aristocracy was part of Christina Rogerson's original tale is unclear, but Mrs Oliphant perceived the choice of the humble trade of dressmaking as integral to the moral development of her tale. 'I think no shame of my work,' asserted Kirsteen, 'but I will not put my father's name in it, for he is old-fashioned and he would think shame.'[65] Being forced into independence is never confused by Kirsteen with an opportunity for self-assertion. The end of the novel puts this to the test. On his deathbed her father unbends sufficiently towards her to take up her offer, of money she has made in her trade, to purchase one of the old family properties. The sum needed is greater than her resources and will condemn her to even harder work at the trade that her father despises and yet is prepared to exploit. For him it is merely a matter of filial obedience, for her it is the moment that transforms independence into an act of silent submission. ' "Ye speak justly", she said, with a little heaving of her breast. "For them to whom it's natural a little may suffice. But I that do it against nature am bound to a different end." '[66] His one stipulation in accepting the money is that she shall not have used the Douglas name in connection with her 'dirty trade'. The voluntary abnegation of the family name she made many years before is ignored and treated as a final piece of enforced submission. Her family's subsequent attempt to distance themselves from her society gives an ironic twist to the way in which a woman is forced to interpret 'That best portion of a good man's life, | His little, nameless, unremembered acts | Of kindness and of love'.[67]

Kirsteen's lover dies a hero's death abroad, but his memory is untarnished and undimmed and when we last hear of Kirsteen she is a sprightly and hospitable old lady living in Edinburgh in the 1850s 'in one of the most imposing houses, in one of the princeliest squares' of the city.[68] By implication, therefore, we can assume that in Mrs Oliphant's formative years those who had kept faith with the old ideal of womanly self-sacrifice could still gain an honoured position in middle-class Scottish society.

One of the last novels Mrs Oliphant ever wrote tolled the death-knell of her ideals. *Old Mr Tredgold* (1895) is a novel which suggests that her dispirited sense of being 'on the ebb tide' of her popularity had less to do with her continuing ability to respond to changing literary fashions than with her awareness that the entire moral framework upon which she had based both her life and her work was now regarded as outmoded. The sadness behind this novel derives from its appreciation of the bleak isolation which will be the reward of any woman attempting to practise the old ideal of absolute purity and integrity among the denizens of late nineteenth-century England. Katherine Tredgold, the standard-bearer of Mrs Oliphant's ideals, is the older and disregarded daughter of a rich and cynical, self-made old man who has retired from the City to the Isle of Wight. The island setting is important first in suggesting the vulgar luxury of southern retirement homes and then, as carefully placed references to *Othello* indicate, in conveying the claustro-phobic frustrations of the life lived in these small village communities. The younger, spoilt daughter, Stella Tredgold, strains to escape the island's ambience from the opening pages of the novel. She is irresistibly drawn to yachting adven-tures, even if they threaten to compromise her reputation, and eventually elopes with a husband who can offer her the excitement of travel to India. Mrs Oliphant, however, in an unwontedly self-disciplined plot, confines us to the slow pace of island life and to sedentary drawing-room scenes in the house where Katherine spends seven years growing old caring for her irascible and spiteful father. Faithful to a childhood memory of romance, she turns down two proposals from the rector and the doctor, but the rejection of two suitors who are so central to village life makes her less welcome in the community. Her allowance is sent secretly to support the extravagant life-style of her monstrously egotistical sister, and she devotes herself to trying to restore Stella, whom she believes the old man has disinherited, to her father's favour. It is in any case Katherine's intention to divide the inherit-ance she anticipates equally with her sister. When old Mr Tredgold dies it is found that he has left almost his entire fortune to Stella, who has no intention of sharing her inheritance with Katherine, whose dowdy life of self-sacrifice, Stella argues, is sufficient proof that she does not need a larger share. Even the consolation of the return of Katherine's youthful lover turns into a further disappointment, for, though free to marry her, he has accepted second-best, married for companionship, and is now a widower with a child. By the conclusion of the novel we have learnt with Katherine that energy, unprincipled egotism, and financial power have the uppermost hand in this world, but we have also been invited to see Katherine as unreasonably inflexible in the integrity of her private ideals. We are tempted to feel with Lady Jane, the doyenne of local society, both 'an awed sense that here was a creature who was outside of her common rules'[69] and to wonder what right an ageing, poor, single woman has to take herself so seriously and cling so tenaciously to her outmoded idealism.

The novels written after 1880, as her life entered that phase of Promethean torture 'of which I cannot speak much',[70] are particularly cogent in depicting the real powerlessness of women to affect the lives of those they love and their own consequent frustration. In the early novels, depicting women in the harsher eco-nomic circumstances of lower-middle-class life, there was a consolation to be found and an outlet for energy in the hardness of the physical toil a woman could take upon herself. In *The Melvilles* (1852), another of those novels set in the Liverpool environment of her adolescence and published by her brother on his own account, the father's untimely death leaves a widow and her son and daughter in much reduced circumstances. The daughter's education at home has not prepared her adequately to pursue a career such as teaching, and Mrs Oliphant reminds her

comfortably-off novel-buying public to 'remember those of you who have independent ambition those who have not: To endure hardship and labour demands a
kind of heroism—to endure to be useless is the hardest fate of woman.'[71] In fact the
daughter is kept fully employed taking in plain sewing and performing the menial
domestic services for which the family had previously kept a maid, but she still
envies her brother's freedom to leave the confines of the house and make the
dispiriting rounds of local firms seeking a humble clerkship.

The wealthier middle-class heroines of the later novels cannot exhaust themselves in physical labour; they can only wait. In the psychological strains of enforced passivity Mrs Oliphant detected the nineteenth-century version of the
Gothic tales of terror and suspense. In *Sir Robert's Fortune* (1894) the heroine is
banished to a secluded country mansion unless she will fall in with her rich uncle's
plans. The rich uncle acts in his niece's material interest by endeavouring to
dissuade her from thinking of an avaricious and penniless young advocate as husband, and his only, though sufficient, cruelty is a total disregard for her personality
and wishes. With the stakes of Sir Robert's fortune before him her lover engages in
a long-drawn combat with her guardian in which Lily becomes the powerless
victim. Motherless and superficially educated 'in the way that English boarding
schools managed so well', Lily embarks upon the 'waiting' which she optimistically
assumes will break her uncle's will if cheerfully undertaken.

Her present circumstances were quite usual features in the novels before the age of Sir
Walter: a residence in an old castle or other lonely house, where a persecuted heroine had the
best of reading, and emerged quite an accomplished woman, was the commonest situation.
She said to herself that there would be plenty to do: that she would not leave a moment
without employment: that her life would be too busy and too full to leave any time for gazing
out at that window, watching the little bit of road, and looking, looking for someone who
never came. Having drawn up this useful programme, and decided how she was to spend
every day, Lily, poor Lily, all alone—even Beenie (her maid) having gone downstairs for a
long talk with Katrin—seated herself, quite unconsciously, at the window, and gazed, and
gazed without intermission, at the little corner of the road that climbed the brae, and across
the long level of the unbroken moor.[72]

Lily has now become a mere spectator. To measure the degree of Lily's final
disillusionment the novel provides us with a comparison in the shape of the local
minister's daughter, Helen Blythe. Helen's worldly disadvantages are outweighed
by her father's real need of her and her conviction in a woman's redemptive powers:
she chooses to sacrifice herself to filial duty and to impose a penitential exile upon
her scapegrace lover. Lily's secret marriage and childbearing tie her to a husband
who finds no great hardship in the 'waiting game' he has chosen to play and who
has few qualms in abducting their child to ensure the deception continues. Furthermore, the knowledge of her own duplicity sours Lily's life because she feels she can
only offer a parody of female devotion when her uncle arrives at a real need of her.
The end of the novel would appear to mirror rather than offer comment upon
Gothic strategies: the child is returned, and Lily's husband reigns in her uncle's

stead, only to be deposed by a melodramatically untimely death. Yet the novel does not end with Lily's 'deliverance from difficulties beyond her power to solve'. Instead it ends some years later when she and her child have settled near Helen and her 'partially reformed' husband and children.

She was now a great deal better off, her life a great deal brighter, with all manner of good things within her reach, than Helen, on her little bit of land, pushing her rough husband, with as few detours as possible, along the path of life, and smiling over her hard task. Lily was a wealthy woman, with a delightful boy, and all those openings of new hope and interest before her in him which give a woman perhaps a more vivid happiness than anything strictly her own. But the one mother trembled a little, while the other looked forward serenely to an unbroken tranquil course of college prizes and bursaries, and at the end a good Manse, and perhaps a popular position for her son. What should Lily have for hers? She had much greater things to hope for. Would it be hers to stand vaguely in the way of Fate, to put out ineffectual hands, to feel the other currents of life as before sweep her away? Or should she ever stand smiling, like simple Helen, holding the helm, directing the course, conscious of power to defeat all harm and guide towards all good? But that only the course of the years could show.

That Lily's position bodies forth Mrs Oliphant's image of herself as widowed mother is immediately apparent: what makes the ending more remarkable is the comparison it offers to a novel of the previous year, *A House in Bloomsbury* (1894), which contained within it a replica of Lily's story without the apparently happy ending of the restoration of the child. Miss Bethune, who has resumed her maiden name, has chosen a lonely life in Bloomsbury in preference to returning to her Scottish properties which only serve to remind her of the misery of her past loss. Yet Miss Bethune is in a sense happier than Lily in that she has no further hostages to offer to fortune: in the face of ambiguous evidence she chooses to treat a nameless young Scot as her long-lost son and she is free to deploy her wealth in private acts of patronage despite her suspicion that the recipients will turn out to be unworthy. Her 'feminine cynicism' and her hard-won independence protect her from further hurt.

Women can only achieve indifference to the blows of fate at a great cost. One of the many ironies of the novel *Hester* is embedded in its title, which would appear to offer the *Bildungsroman* expectations of a novel such as Jane Austen's *Emma*. Mrs Oliphant's novel does indeed depict the process of a girl's education, but the plot and the times conspire to deprive Hester of any but a passive role. Since in Mrs Oliphant's world women are the repositories of the highest moral truths, rewards for moral progress cannot be incarnated in Knightleyesque form. Experience in this novel has to prove its own reward, and experience serves only to teach the limited utility of middle-class girls. Hester's anxiety to offer understanding to the man she loves and his desire that she shall be nothing more than an unthinking emotional prop is neatly captured in the following exchange.

'But tell me, only tell me a little more.'
He shook his head.

'Hester', he said, 'that is not what a man wants in a woman; not to go and explain it all to her with pen and ink, tables and figures, to make her understand as he would have to do with a man. What he wants, dear, is very different—just to lean upon you—to know that you sympathise, and think of me, and feel for me, and believe in me, and that you will share whatever comes.'

Hester said nothing, but her countenance grew very grave.[73]

The promised exchange does not take place: her treacherous lover is offering false currency, but, more importantly, in his eyes she has no positive contribution to make, nothing of value to offer, and she knows that she cannot supply the credit of unquestioning belief that he requires.

The Prodigals and their Inheritance (1885) again makes use of a financial metaphor to demonstrate a woman's powerlessness at the centre of competing male strategies. Squire Chester has disinherited his two worthless sons and made his daughter Winifred the heiress on the condition that she makes no attempt to share the inheritance with her brothers. Winifred is merely a pawn in her father's unforgiving war with his sons and the pathos of her position arises from her 'inability to soften judgement on one hand, or to reduce rebellion on the other'. She can only await her father's death and trust herself to another male, a crafty lawyer, to outwit the Squire at his own game. In this novel the males conspire to deprive the heroine even of the supposed consolations of the womanly virtues of 'sympathy' and 'belief'. The characters of her father and brothers create 'the most horrible of all the tortures that women have to bear, to see the men belonging to them, whom they would so fain look up to, breaking down into ruinous failure'. Her doctor-suitor and her father alike mock her desire to nurse her dying father 'as very fine in a woman's novel. Taking care of her old father, the sweet girl! a ministering angel, and so forth.' This womanly function has now been usurped by professionals. Her brothers unthinkingly collude with the father in seeing her merely as an obstacle in the path of their desires, but the worst blow is the incapacity of her suitor to recognize that she does not wish him to interpose between her and her brothers. 'A woman has often many pangs to bear between her husband and her family. She has to endure and maintain often the authority which she does not acknowledge, which in her right he assumes over them, which is a still greater offence to her than to them.' His belief that 'A woman should put everything into her husband's hands' once again denies this woman any independent existence, and the very act of divesting herself of the property, an act in accordance with womanly ideals, deprives her, in male eyes, of independent value and reduces her to an object whose worth is determined by her new proprietor's labour to protect her.[74]

Florence Nightingale had complained that middle-class women's occupations were deliberately trivialized so that they were prevented from developing an inherent value.[75] Mrs Oliphant's view was that women's household labours, which enabled the work of the breadwinner, had a value which men refused to admit lest it diminish their self-estimation. In 'The Grievances of Women' (1880), having called attention to the way in which working-class women's labour retained greater visibility, she went on to relate an anecdote about a happily married couple of her acquaintance. The husband, it seemed to her, supported the myth of his pre-eminence by denying credit to his wife's work and treating her as an object whose value directly reflected his earning capacities. He declared himself 'shamed' by her 'shabby gloves'. 'One would think', he said, 'that I could not afford to buy you gloves.' Adopting the feminist strategy of substituting a female for a male voice here, Mrs Oliphant suggested, revealed the vulgar ingratitude underlying the words. In campaigning for professions for women, too many women, she felt, had failed to recognize that this was implicitly endorsing the view that a middle-class woman's work in the home was worthless.[76]

In noting that society at large would accuse a woman who drew attention to her capacity to support a man, of tasteless vulgarity, Mrs Oliphant is suggesting that codes of conduct are rooted in those ideologies which are acceptable to the prevailing orthodoxy and not in a timeless and innate appropriateness. Marthas, as she frequently reflected, were 'made' and not born, and for every Martha in her tales there is a Mary whose temperament has allowed her to interpret 'a woman's lot' after another fashion.[77] It is usually men, often after their first disappointment in love, who use the word 'women' as a collective pejorative, and that, as one of her fictional mothers reflects, is 'curious when you come to think of it' since these same young men have often been nurtured by a mother and sisters whose different personalities should have impinged upon them.[78] Whereas Mrs Oliphant's ideal woman sees men, in their very helplessness, as appropriate objects upon which the virtue of loving self-abnegation can best be practised, her fictional sisters some-times employ the prevailing standards for female behaviour in a wholly different spirit. There are, of course, the sirens who haunt the pages of *Sir Tom* or *The Sorceress* who devote their energy to pleasuring men. Since Mrs Oliphant did not believe in absolutely evil human beings, such women interested her only in so far as their position reflected an interesting combination of character and circumstance. In a society which elevated marriage as the highest prize for a woman, those whose ambitions made them unwilling to accept poverty and the single state as God-given might well learn to see men as their prey rather than as offering a sphere for their protective instincts. The prize once achieved, such women, she observed, often made excellent wives and mothers because they identified the welfare of their husband and children with their own welfare and ambition.

Mrs Oliphant derived great entertainment from describing a subtler form of the misappropriation of the womanly ideal to foster the ambitions of girls whose temperament did not lead them to embrace the ideal of self-abnegation. Such girls as Lucilla Marjoribanks and Phoebe Tozer are endowed with too great a sense of selfhood to derive pleasure from the secret practice of self-sacrifice and yet their absolute acceptance of their middle-class milieu and its aspirations is expressed in that tag which Oliphant had defined since her earliest writing as the hallmark of the middle classes: 'I cannot beg and to work I am ashamed.'[79] Lucilla and Phoebe are recognizably fictional cousins, yet, as so often when Mrs Oliphant's plots or characters echo one another or consciously recall the work of other writers, it is worth paying attention to the variations she works upon her theme.[80]

As has frequently been remarked, the plot and circumstances of *Miss Marjoribanks* (1866) owe something to Jane Austen's *Emma* (1816). Lucilla, like Emma, is well aware of the advantages accruing to a girl who finds herself at the head of a widowed father's comfortable establishment and who can therefore enjoy the pleasure of household management without the immediate need to hunt out a husband. Lucilla consciously embraces the ideal of womanhood and determines to embody that 'picture of angelic sweetness and goodness . . . Woman the Reconciler, by the side of those other characters of Inspirer and Consoler of which the world has heard'. The first difficulty she encounters is that of her father, the doctor, who, as his profession suggests, is wholly unlike the valetudinarian Mr Woodhouse, and rides roughshod over her girlish attempts to fulfil the heroic 'duty of an only child to devote herself to her father's comfort, and become the sunshine of his life, as so many young persons of her age, have been known to become in literature'.[81]

The real egoism of Lucilla's ambitions for her life is highlighted first by the covert war she has to wage with her father in order to get the servants and the local community to acknowledge that a middle-class woman's work in the home can be seen as a serious career, and secondly by the contrast with another prematurely motherless household, where poverty ensures that the female sacrifice demanded is real and disagreeable. Lucilla, in the dominant metaphorical mode of the novel, can operate as 'an adventurous general' whereas the children of the parallel family are seen as mere 'soldiers of fortune'. The mock-heroic metaphor is important in this novel for a variety of reasons. It signals the way in which Lucilla plans the campaign of her life, applying those practical calculations so often assumed to be distinctively male to the deployment of her resources, and regarding the obstacles she encounters, usually male, as so many challenges that, once defeated, can be displayed as trophies. As in Pope's *Rape of the Lock*, however, the implications of the mock-heroic genre are complex: there is an obvious comedy in the disparity between the trivial domestic events and the importance they assume in the mind of the major protagonist. Yet Pope's use of the device also contrived to suggest a deeper irony in the unthinking adoption by a so-called Christian society of the mores advocated in pagan literature. The level-headed pragmatism and messianic egoism with which Lucilla decides to convert a woman's constricted sphere into a field for heroic conquest suggest that Lucilla can only succeed because of her limited vision and sensibilities. Although overtly practising womanly virtues, she comes near to sacrificing a feminine appreciation of life. The terms of the approval her unsentimental father accords her on the day before he dies suggest that she has succeeded on male terms. If only she had been physically male she would, in his opinion, have made a far better heir than her sentimentally disposed, impractical cousin Tom. Indeed, her retention of her maiden name, even in marriage, underlines this ambiguity in gender characteristics. Yet along with his grudging admiration for achievements which would have been better rewarded in the male sphere goes the doctor's slight contempt for Lucilla's 'prudence' in arranging her prospects.

When examined closely, the 'principles' by which Lucilla guides her life are in fact pragmatic strategies rather than ethical convictions, so that she sees no shocking disparity between these two statements: 'It is one of my principles never to laugh about anything that has to do with religion', and 'It is one of my principles always to flirt in the middle of company'. Nor does she see any point in parliamentary candidates confusing the electorate with detailed 'confessions of faith'. ' "After all", said Lucilla, with fine satire, of which she was unconscious, "what does it matter what people think? I suppose when it comes to doing anything, the Whigs and the Tories are just the same." '[82] This fine disregard for sentiment and moral vision in favour of the pleasure of management has several limiting consequences: Lucilla neglects the ends in favour of the means and is in danger of being disheartened when, having become 'a Power in Carlingford', she is unsure where to channel her energies.[83] Moreover, her absorption in the day-to-day acquisition and maintenance of Power blinds her to the extent to which she is still circumscribed by male actions and decisions. Finally, readers may be inclined to sympathize with the publisher's regret as to the novel's 'hardness of tone', for Lucilla's prosaic nature denies us any outlet for emotion. Mrs Oliphant defended herself thus:

to bring a sudden change upon her character and break her down into tenderness would be like one of Dickens's maudlin repentances, when he makes Mr Dombey trinquer with Captain Cuttle. Miss M. must be one and indivisible, and I feel pretty sure that my plan is right. It is the middle of the story that is always the trying bit—the two ends can generally take care of themselves.[84]

The ending did, however, cause Mrs Oliphant more of a problem than she admitted here. Even she was not prepared to have Lucilla calculate wholly cold-bloodedly the respective merits of her cousin and his rival suitor, and so Lucilla is permitted the momentary respite of genuine tears, uncharacteristic though this is. This is not the only admission that Lucilla's attempt to treat 'a woman's lot' as a male career has come dangerously near defeminizing her. Cousin, now husband, Tom has to have a career as a county Member of Parliament mapped out for him as a way of getting him out of the way of Lucilla's 'proper sphere of influence'.

In *Phoebe Junior* Mrs Oliphant overcame the problem by creating a character at once highly feminine and able to manipulate the womanly ideal in such a way as both to derive self-satisfaction and refrain from openly assuming a male mode of operation threatening to potential husbands. From the first Phoebe is more constrained than Lucilla. Mrs Oliphant may have deplored the arrogant and self-centred tone of Matthew Arnold's criticism and found fault with some of his prejudices, but she had thoroughly digested the cultural implications of his social analysis.[85] Not only is the heroine, a metropolitan Dissenting minister's daughter, liable to be made to recognize her social inferiority by the wealthier elements in her father's congregation, but she is then transplanted to Carlingford, 'a little Tory borough, still holding for Church and Queen', where she is reminded of her social marginality by being brought into contact with the Anglican rector's family. It is not society alone, however, that constrains Phoebe to adopt the womanly ideal of duty and self-sacrifice: she is temperamentally suited. The tone of the novel is less ironic than *Miss Marjoribanks* because Phoebe does not have to spend the time Lucilla does rationalizing her desires into accordance with her duty: she is a good-hearted girl who willingly undertakes a 'domestic mission', which she does not abandon, even when it becomes unpleasant, for fear of hurting her grandparents, vexing her parents, imperilling her brother's interests, or 'her own, which, to do her justice, was the last thing she thought of, and yet was not undeserving of notice in its way'.[86] Phoebe is even physically better adapted to the role she chooses than Lucilla; Lucilla is always in danger of outgrowing or exploding the role she has chosen: when still at school 'she had made the painful discovery that her gloves were half a number larger, and her shoes a hairbreadth broader than those of any of her companions'. Phoebe, however, 'possessed in perfection the hair of the period' and 'a warm pink and white complexion', which had 'the boundaries between the pink and the white been a little more distinct, would have approached perfection too'.[87]

The picture given so far may prompt the question as to how Phoebe actually diverges from a true incarnation of Mrs Oliphant's womanly ideal. The answer is in part provided by the ambiguous chapter-heading, 'Self-Devotion', which de-scribes Phoebe's behaviour in putting her family first when deciding where her duty lies, and yet calculating perfectly on her own ability to 'show to the admiring world what a Dissenter's daughter could be, and what a dutiful daughter was'.[88] The novel also avoids the monotony of tone towards which *Miss Marjoribanks* veers, by multiplying the number of women's parts in such a way as to define Phoebe's attitudes more precisely. She is contrasted with two women who in their different ways display the true womanly ideal of self-sacrifice: Ursula May, the eldest daughter of and housekeeper to a poverty-stricken and irascible rector, and Anne Dorsett, a baronet's daughter who, in taking on her young niece and nephew, becomes 'the maiden-mother, who is a clearly-defined type of humanity, though rare perhaps, like all the finer sorts'.[89] Any tendency we may have to suspect Phoebe's careful calculation of absolute cynicism is offset by the provision of the baronet's second daughter, Sophy, who 'laughs at love and all that nonsense', resents the practice of 'training up girls to unnatural high-mindedness', and feels it would be better to teach them 'to play their cards properly' in the marriage stakes.[90]

This novel overcomes the problem of allowing a girl to make a middle-class woman's domestic mission into a career without calling her femininity into ques-tion by resolving Tom Marjoribanks' role into two separate characters, one of whom, Reginald May, plays the romantic hero, evoking in Phoebe the knowledge that 'the feeling he might inspire would be a warmer and more delightful one than that which would fall to Clarence Copperhead', her final choice. Yet Reginald's very masculine perfection is against him: 'He was very tender in his reverential homage, very romantic, a true lover, not the kind of man who wants a wife or wants a clever companion to amuse him, and save him the expense of a coach, and be his to refer to in everything.' For Clarence, however, she felt 'a kind of habitual affection, as for the "poor thing, but mine own, sir" of the jester'.[91] Tom Marjoribanks had to combine the function of the idle and inept cousin, whom Lucilla can easily dismiss or manipulate, with the charm and forcefulness of the hero who has suffered a sea-change in his years of exile. Phoebe's, and her creator's, real cleverness resides in divining that she can only continue to make a career out of womanly self-sacrifice if she chooses the candidate who needs her 'to undertake the charge of him, to manage, and guide, and make a man of him'. The final proof of Phoebe's success, misread by many as a disappointing marginalization of the heroine, is the almost perfect mimicry she achieves of true womanly self-sacrifice.

And Clarence got into Parliament, and the reader, perhaps (if Parliament is sitting), may have had the luck to read a speech in the morning paper of Phoebe's composition, and if he ever got the secret of her style would know it again, and might trace the course of a public character for years to come by that means. But this secret is one which no bribe nor worldly inducement will ever tempt our lips to betray.[92]

Phoebe gives her talent and voice to her husband just as readily as Mrs Oliphant made over those early novels to brother Willie, yet, like her creator, she finds that by sacrificing her right to open acknowledgement as an author she manages to reach a wider audience. Clarence's personality, such as it was, quickly becomes effaced by an anonymous 'public character' with a distinctive style. Phoebe has, in effect, discovered her author's secret and found a way in which a woman might have 'her personal "say" publicly' in a man's world.

3 A Woman in a Man's World

> It did not indeed enter into Jack's mind to realise what he should do were he
> Elly; for that is one inalienable peculiarity of the human constitution that no
> male creature can put himself in the place of a woman, as almost all female
> creatures imaginatively place themselves in that of some man. It is the one
> intimate mark of constitutional superiority which makes the meanest man
> more self-important than the noblest woman.[1]

Mrs Oliphant was justly renowned in her fiction and her private life for the 'half
contemptuous' view she took of men. Her readiness to publicize her view of men as
a separate and inferior race was remarkable in an age when two of the most notable
fictional exponents of the injustices suffered by women, George Eliot and Charlotte
Brontë, often used male mentor or saviour figures to monitor or reward a woman's
moral progress. If Mrs Oliphant's tales do not represent marriage as the reward for
woman's moral progress neither do they repudiate marriage and motherhood as
desirable goals, for in these relationships women find their best hope of attaining
moral excellence. Her contempt for men is tempered always by her sense of them
as the necessary raw material upon which women practise the daily self-denial
which will sharpen their moral faculties.

She was willing to admit that character and circumstance could yield as great a
variety in the moral composition of her male as of her female characters. It was just
that, even at their best, men rarely showed the sensitivity or altruism of which her
female characters were capable. It is easy to point to the inadequacies of the men in
her immediate family as an explanation of her attitude to men in general. It is also
worth noting that, unlike Elizabeth Gaskell, Charlotte Brontë, and George Eliot,
Mrs Oliphant had a close relationship with her mother that persisted into adult life
and never sought validation from the men in her family for her writing. Nevertheless, such was her maternal partiality that she believed her sons could be raised to
be different: when she talked to mothers with grown-up sons she 'sat and listened
and laughed within myself at the thought that my beautiful little boys could ever
grow into men like them'.[2]

Moreover, her well-known view of men as a race apart did not preclude close
friendships with individual men: it may even have contributed a certain piquancy
to these relationships. Robert Macpherson was able to begin a letter asking a favour,
'Dear Maggie, I know I am very selfish! "but then, men are all more or less so" as
you might say.'[3]

Nor did it deter male readers: her obituary in *The Daily Chronicle* observed that
'Men read and enjoy her books: she is perhaps as much a men's as a women's
novelist'.[4] George Eliot, whose liaison with Lewes hampered the freedom of her

social intercourse with women, is often thought of as the Victorian female novelist who was most at her ease in depicting male characters. Though it is a crude gauge, it is worth observing that Mrs Oliphant's novels and short stories divide about equally in offering a man or a woman as the main character. The arrival of brother Frank and his son, and the numbers of young men whom her sons introduced into the Windsor house, meant that Mrs Oliphant was always in a position to observe male habits of thought and patterns of behaviour at close quarters. In her earliest novel criticism she had found fault with Thackeray's penchant for incorporating slang in the dialogues of his male characters,[5] but, in the novels written after her sons' adolescence, she grew very adept at catching the tone affected by idle young men of their class and justified her breaches of decorum on the grounds that reproducing the 'force' of the language they employed 'in private moments' was a tool of which the realist novel should avail itself.[6]

Family circumstances may well have attuned her ear to the distinctive inflexions of male speech, but she also had almost half a century's experience, in her capacity as a reviewer for *Blackwood's Edinburgh Magazine*, of assuming a male persona and imagining herself into a male perspective. It has been suggested that George Eliot's adoption of a male pseudonym indicated her 'ambiguous view of the woman writer' and her consequent desire to distance herself from identification with such writers as she had stigmatized in 'Silly Novels by Lady Novelists' or in the opening paragraph of 'Woman in France: Madame de Sablé':[7] 'Eliot knew what the legacy of Wollstonecraft and Fuller meant for her, but she had forgotten the legacy of female self-hatred and masculine misogyny which every "cultured" woman writer internalizes.'[8] In her anxiety to avoid the failings she diagnosed in so many women's writings, which, 'when not a feeble imitation . . . are usually an absurd exaggeration of the masculine style, like the swaggering gait of a bad actress in male attire',[9] she sought what, by her own definition, must have seemed the middle course, 'a critical cross-dressing' which attempted a fit so perfect that its disguise should prove impenetrable. So, with Lewes's help, she assumed the doubly authoritative voice of a man and a clergyman in the negotiation with John Blackwood over *Scenes of Clerical Life*. Mrs Oliphant's response to these tales provides an interesting comment upon the nature and extent of Eliot's identification with her chosen role, for, after several years of personal experience in the use of a male voice, she professed herself unable 'to believe that the author of the "The Scenes of Clerical Life" is a woman'.[10]

For Mrs Oliphant the act of male impersonation had been a professional decision, dictated by her view of *Blackwood's Magazine* as the 'most manly and masculine of magazines'.[11] Discounting those novels handed over to brother Willie, it never seemed to have occurred to Mrs Oliphant to wish to adopt a male pseudonym for her fiction. Nor had there been any attempt to delude her publishers. Indeed, in 1896, while working her way through the Blackwoods' papers for her history of the firm, she discovered that her 'very girlish simplicity' had so appealed to the Blackwoods that they had nicknamed her 'Katie' after the title of the first fictional manuscript she had sent them.[12] According to John Blackwood's daughter, he continued patronizingly to refer to her as 'a wonderfully clever (little) woman'.[13] Moreover, Mrs Oliphant never lost sight of her own identity in this game of critical cross-dressing. The danger of such confusion occurring was what struck her when in 1853 she met Rosa Bonheur, the French artist, who in 1857 was to gain authorization from the French police to wear male clothing. 'With her hair cut short and divided at one side like a man's,' wrote Mrs Oliphant, 'she was, indeed not very distinct in the matter of sex so far as dress and appearance went.'[14] Regardless of the gender she was currently supposed to be inhabiting, Mrs Oliphant's awareness of the prejudices operating against women coloured everything she wrote. For instance, when she wrote an article entitled 'Silly Women' she followed it up three days later with one on 'Silly Men': the subject of both was ostensibly British attitudes to Irish politics, but the first article starts with an attack upon St Paul's contemptuous attitude to women, and the second with her observation that 'silly men' are always thought of as individuals while the phrase 'silly women' has too frequently been used as a generic grouping.[15]

Adopting the stance of a male reviewer for *Blackwood's* was an acknowledgement that she had decided to place her talent in direct competition with men. At the start of her *Blackwood's* career she was well aware that she was in danger of exciting the ire or professional contempt of such long-established *Maga* hands as Professor Aytoun.[16] Mrs Oliphant's mother may have been a 'fervent Liberal . . . and therefore completely opposed to *Blackwood's Magazine*', nevertheless she had not allowed political prejudice to interfere with her keen enjoyment of its literary contributions.[17] Neither Mrs Oliphant nor her mother ever seemed to have considered it appropriate to apply for reviewing work in the pages of periodicals specifically intended for the women's market. Mrs Oliphant's reaction to Blackwood's publication of a volume of ninety stories for women in 1876 showed her to be suspicious of the patronizing attitude implicit in such a policy of literary apartheid. Remarking that not all women shared the taste of girls in their twenties, she continued, 'I am almost sorry to say I don't feel myself much sillier than the majority of men I meet, though perhaps that may be because the men in Windsor are not lofty specimens.'[18] When it came to selling fiction she was well aware of the different areas of the market catered to by various publishers. She decided not to offer *Maga*, *The Days of My Life* (1857), a story told in the first person by a woman character, since the tones of 'a womanish story-teller like myself' might prove 'wearisome' in the magazine's 'manly' pages.[19] Indeed, as she candidly admitted in 1861, when Blackwood rejected two of her articles, 'I should be glad to console my *amour propre* by thinking that the stronger fare to which you are accustomed has given you a distaste for my womanish style. One finds it always odd somehow to account for being stupid in one's own person.'[20]

The refusal to take refuge in the consoling thoughts of misogynistic dismissals of 'womanish' writing is indicative of Mrs Oliphant's rejection of stereotypical judgements and her endeavour to arrive at a careful discrimination of good and bad writing by women. She could be harsh, on occasion, to women she believed were in danger of trivializing the art of novel-writing. In May 1875 she found herself confronted with a pile of worthless fiction and wrote, 'We are disposed to be a little lenient to those which have feminine names on the title pages, for there can be no doubt that quantities of women able to read and write have very little to do, and no way to earn a little pocket-money; so that their attempts in this line may be excused at least.'[21] She might choose to use the chivalry associated with her male garb to avoid particularizing the individual failures of these dabblers in literature, but she was not normally led to apply very different standards in her aesthetic judgement of male and female novelists. Poetry was a different matter, and Elizabeth Barrett Browning was labelled 'as the greatest Woman-poet whom England has known. No woman,' she added, 'so far as we know, has ever been a great poet, or attained the level of the highest.'[22] The two volumes of *The Victorian Age of English Literature* made no attempt to segregate male and female authors, but considered them together under the different generic headings. Sisterly solidarity did not, in Mrs Oliphant's mind, necessitate a policy of positive discrimination, nor did it prevent her rebuking any female novelist who departed from her own 'womanly ideal' in the presentation of her subject-matter: thus the conversation between Rochester and Jane Eyre was both 'womanish' in its false perception of male character and 'unwomanly' in displaying 'a degree of refined indelicacy possible to a woman which no man can reach'.[23]

Yet, far from Mrs Oliphant being endowed with 'a bitter competitiveness', or being 'a woman not given to feelings of *esprit de corps* as her writings on her sister authors indicated',[24] she frequently sought to give reviewing space to 'that half of the world' who had hitherto been 'for the most part voiceless and always swordless'.[25] In her earliest series of articles on contemporary fiction she began her article on 'Modern Novelists Great and Small' by reminding her readership that this was 'the age of female novelists'.[26] By the midpoint of her career, and freshly elevated to the editorship of Blackwood's Foreign Classics series, she might speak self-mockingly of a Miss MacDonald's manuscript on Heine as 'much too woman-ish for a calm and experienced professional like myself', but this did not deter her from accepting the work, for 'gush is not a bad thing in a new writer and there is appearance of stuff enough to cut down'.[27] Or again in 1886 in the December number of *Maga*, whilst apparently colluding with the magazine's manly tone by selecting novels by three men, she contrived to end her review with this obser-vation: 'The novels we have selected for this brief survey are all written by men. It would be unjust to the other half of the creation to say that we could not find others equally worthy of consideration from feminine pens: but space at present forbids the addition.'[28]

Occasionally she found the demands forced upon her by her male persona at odds with her literary taste. She confessed to Blackwood that she preferred Richardson to Fielding. 'I suppose that is one of the differences between men and women which even Ladies' Colleges will not set to rights. Pray don't tell of me; if

I betray my sentiments in public they shall be laid upon the heavily burdened shoulders of what Clarissa would call "my sex", and your contributor shall sneer at them as in duty bound.'[29] This letter might be presumed to prepare us for an article in which Mrs Oliphant embarks upon an act of double betrayal in denying her own tastes and sneering at them as 'womanly'. In fact the article does no such thing.[30] Instead she uses her disguise for an act of sabotage. Initially she appears to collude with·'the present fashion' and 'to sneer at Richardson' for his fondness for women's company and gossip, adopting the dismissive tones of a man of the world: 'And then his knowledge of the world! Richardson's knowledge was only of a good sort of people, and secondary litterateurs, and—women, who are not the world, as everybody knows. This curious distinction of what is life and what is not, which has prevailed so widely since then, probably originated in the eighteenth century.' At every point in the article she presses the feminine nature of Richardson's experience, his commonplace life, his ordinary duties, his role as midwife to others' inferior literary productions, as a means of asking her readers to reconsider the critical prejudices of the time. Riding on the back of Richardson's ability to reproduce the delights of female conversation, she manages a diversion in which she sets out to defend women against the universal claim of their educational inferiority. Encoded in this overtly male essay are the highest terms of praise her critical vocabulary knows: the words that are on the face of it terms of abuse, such as 'ordinary', or 'commonplace', are, as her autobiography makes clear, the precise source of interest to the discerning novel reader. By the time she reaches a discussion of the individual novels she has contrived to shake the conventional critical vocabulary so free of its normal pejorative associations that she can afford to claim that the greatness of *Clarissa* resides partly in Richardson's creation of Lovelace as 'a feminine ideal'. This act of genius stemmed from Richardson's habit of 'contemplating the world from a woman's point of view', so that he understood that women are not attracted by milksops or by 'the frank animalism of Tom Jones', but by their tendency to identify with a man who enjoys intrigue, sentiment, and emotion and who desires universal conquest whilst at the same time almost despising those whom he hopes to 'dazzle and beguile'. In this article Mrs Oliphant appropriated the male voice to educate male readers into an understanding of the woman's point of view. Occasionally a 'male' point of view happened to coincide with her own, and then she would adopt the habit she described in *Whiteladies* (1875), speaking of an elderly spinster who exhibited 'one very common weakness to which independent women are especially liable'.

She had the old-fashioned prejudice that it was a good thing to 'consult a man' upon points of difficulty which occurred in her life. The process of consulting, indeed, was apt to be a peculiar one. If he distinctly disagreed with herself, Miss Susan set the man whom she consulted down as a fool, or next to a fool, and took her own way, and said nothing about the consultation. But when by chance he happened to agree with her, then she made great capital of his opinion, and announced it everywhere as the cause of her own action, whatever that might be.[31]

Such an occasion presented itself in her first article on women's rights when she was offered the lead article in *Maga*.[32] Yet even here, though apparently adopting 'the husband's point of view', her arguments often proceed from a position of ambivalence rather than from a straightforwardly anti-feminist platform: 'justice' is not likely to be achieved by reversing present inequities; laws are ineffectual instruments for interfering in a domestic relationship.

Thirty-three years after her first attempts at assuming a male voice, Mrs Oliphant decided that her persona in *Maga* needed a hormonal boost and she negotiated a new monthly review of books under the general title 'The Old Saloon' which was to run from January 1887 to December 1892. The choice of title was indicative of her intentions. These views were to emanate from a male enclave, the saloon, not from the salon of a literary lady. The first article of the series placed the writer in the imagined library which had seen *Maga*'s heyday in 1845: 'Here we sit . . . here in the winter nights, with laughter as of the demigods, Homeric, inexhaustible.' The setting, in fact, conjures up the library at Strathtyrum, John Blackwood's country house at St Andrew's, which his daughter described as lined with books and old engravings, the floor littered with corrected proofs, the air smelling pleasantly of cigar smoke.[33] John Blackwood had been known as a clubbable man, and the atmosphere of this *Maga* sanctum, the library, so often identified in Mrs Oliphant's novels as a distinctively male space, is less welcoming to women. *Maga*, as the article parenthetically observed, 'has her ladies too, but shall we own it, loves them less'. There was doubtless some personal animus in this remark, but it also contributes to the general strategy of the article, which was designed to demonstrate how the old spirit of *Maga* found no difficulty in harmonizing with the male-dominated literary world of the late 1880s. Freed from the towering pre-eminence of George Eliot's presence, the world of higher literary culture was increasingly 'edging women out'. This was in part a matter of male domination of the means and network involved in literary production. Mrs Oliphant was all too aware of these processes at work and deliberately used her access to literary periodicals to counter the influence of the male literary mafia. Writing to John Blackwood to defend herself against a reader's attack on her critical reception of Augustus Hare's *Memorials of a Quiet Life*, she wrote, 'The tremendous applause which has greeted this performance is a good specimen of the sort of thing which I am anxious to struggle against—the fictitious reputation got up by men who happen to be "remembered at the Universities", and who have many connections among literary men.'[34] In 1888 hers was a dissentient voice raised among the general eulogies consequent upon Matthew Arnold's death. Why, she asked, should Arnold merit commemoration in Westminster Abbey? In her opinion it was 'that Matthew Arnold's reputation is very greatly that of a man borne upward on the shoulders of his friends'.[35] Male clubland's increased purchase upon 'the world of culture and influence' seemed to go hand-in-hand with a market interested in subjects which, by their very nature, allowed women only a very minor place. Rudyard Kipling, whom Mrs Oliphant saw as 'the most powerful of our young writers', had, in her opinion, won popularity by his 'manful perception of life as something more than love-making'.[36] Mrs Oliphant's first 'Old Saloon' article paid due tribute to tales of empire and boys' adventure stories by a lively appreciation of Admiral Hobart Pacha's *Sketches from My Life*, which, 'were we a boy again, such as once we might have been', would have made a welcome Christmas gift. However, even in this article, which was ostensibly devoted to male authors and male subjects, she managed to introduce the suffering and marginalization of talented women by lingering on the domestic tragedy and wastage of Harriet and Mary Shelley in her review of Dowden's life of the poet.[37]

Mrs Oliphant's own increasing sense of being 'on the ebb-tide', as a producer of fiction which still attended mainly to domestic life, may have led to her choice of name for her last male persona in the final series of articles she contributed to *Maga*, 'The Looker-On', but it did not prevent her from appreciating the real success of this new wave of male-oriented fiction. Heralding Robert Louis Stephenson's *The Master of Ballantrae*, which had appeared in serial form, as a new departure in publishing, she wrote, 'the writer of fiction, if he be but strong enough, need think of none of the conventional requirements with which smaller hands are compelled to recommend their art, and that neither a love story, nor a heroine, nor a cheerful picture of human life, nor indeed anything that can be called a picture of human life at all, is necessary to him who has the power.'[38] Condensed in that choice of 'smaller' rather than 'less skilful' hands is one of Mrs Oliphant's most strongly felt perceptions of the irony of her life. A quarter of a century before she had been reading of Charlotte Brontë in Elizabeth Gaskell's *Life* and confided to her private journal:

I don't suppose my powers are equal to hers—my work to myself looks perfectly pale and colourless beside hers—but yet I have had far more experience and, I think, a fuller conception of life. I have learned to take perhaps more a man's view of mortal affairs,—to feel that the love between men and women, the marrying and giving in marriage, occupy in fact so small a portion of either existence or thought.[39]

As a widowed mother she had been forced to accept full responsibility as family provider, and as a writer she had had no husband to manage her financial affairs and negotiations, yet she was doubly hampered by being a woman. For one thing, she had no wife 'to stay at home and take care of things, and hear all I had to tell her when I came back'.[40] 'Perhaps no popular authoress lived so completely out of the world', said one of her obituaries,[41] alluding to her decision to base herself in Windsor. Moreover, she felt that, despite the chance of literary transvestism that *Maga* had afforded her, she had been constrained, by the expectations of publishers and the reading public, to concentrate her fictional output upon precisely those areas of heroines, love, and marriage that her wider experience had taught her to regard as trivial.

It may have been that the opportunity, given her by *Maga*, to adopt the male voice, to speak, as it were, from the centre rather than the margins of the culture, exacerbated her sense of grievance. While editors could impose censorship more or less subtle upon the matters a woman could discuss, and publishers might presume to intrude their notions of best-selling formulas upon novelists, this served as a creative irritant to an artist as practised as Mrs Oliphant at subverting the stereotype, whether by appropriating the male voice to discuss female concerns or by using clichéd subjects and plots to present a wholly distinctive view of life. It was perhaps while she was working on the *Annals* of the Blackwoods Publishing House that Mrs Oliphant noted with admiration a letter from George Eliot refusing to give John Blackwood a detailed synopsis of the plot of *Adam Bede* and giving as her reasons, 'the soul of art lies in its treatment and not in its subject'.[42]

Just as Mrs Oliphant very frequently used her opportunities as a reviewer to rebuke the false impressions that novels of the day gave of women, so she used her novels to redress the impression so frequently given of men in women's fiction. She diagnosed the rise of the Rochester school of hero as allied, on the one hand to the Rights of Women movement, and on the other to Carlyle's elevation of the strong heroic mould. Detecting implicit patronage in old-fashioned chivalrous love-making, women now preferred to imagine a sustained warfare in which the woman gained recognition of equal status from the sheer volume of the armoury the hero needed to achieve his conquest. That these heroes spoke to an emotional need in women rather than corresponding with the alliances contracted in real life could be gauged, Mrs Oliphant felt, by considering the sheer unlikeliness of such unions as 'the stately Margaret Hale' with the 'churlish and ill-natured Thornton' in Elizabeth Gaskell's *North and South*. The fictional conventions that often seemed to deprive heroines of mothers also seemed to leave them without 'the good gift of an irate brother, to exchange civilities with the love-making monster'.[43] Male freedom from domestic ties or supports was something that Mrs Oliphant's fiction was to redress: her heroes do not emerge as knights clad in strong armour but come with a full accoutrement of womenfolk anxious to protect their lad, but also well able to demonstrate his deficiencies as a son or brother. Her own practice of inviting long-term female guests seems to have been part of a deliberate coeducational policy, fighting against that tendency for men and women 'to look upon each other as hero and heroine in the brief drama whose stilted rules are supposed to affect the life of one of them from beginning to end'.[44]

Just as the Carlylean search for authority located in a strong leader could so easily become debased into the worship of force so, she claimed, the Rochester/Thornton hero deteriorated, in the hands of the sensational novelists, into a mere animal. She laid the fault unequivocally at the door of women novelists whose maidens of romance 'wait now for flesh and muscle, for strong arms that seize her'. Not only did the girls of her acquaintance, and she presumed of her readership's, 'not pant for indiscriminate kisses' but had these male characters been drawn 'from the man's point of view' the frankness of their animality 'would at least be repulsive'.[45]

The reasons for men being used, in women's novels, as an objective correlative for unfulfilled female desires were, as Mrs Oliphant tried to explain in this letter to Isabella Blackwood, interestingly complex.

the reason why, as you say, I give softness to men rather than to women, is simply because the men of a woman's writing are always shadowy individuals, and it is only members of our own sex that we can fully bring out, bad and good. Even George Eliot is feeble in her men, and I recognise the disadvantage under which we all work in this respect. Sometimes we don't know sufficiently to make the outline sharp and clear; sometimes we know well enough, but dare not betray our knowledge one way or other: the result is that the men in a woman's book are always washed in, in secondary colours. The same want of anatomical knowledge and precision must, I imagine, preclude a woman from ever being a great painter; and if one does make the necessary study, one loses more than one gains.[46]

As Mrs Oliphant was to discover, a Victorian woman who dared to express her honest assessment of men was swiftly labelled a misandrist. Some women, who had cause like her to find the men of their family unsatisfactory, allowed, instead, an element of redressive fantasy to creep into their picturing. Girls with appalling fathers, she observed, had a tendency either to be disgusted by the male sex as a whole or to devote longing worship to the search for a true man.[47] Herself agonizingly familiar with the half-contemptuous sympathy drunken, self-pitying men evoked in their relations, Mrs Oliphant was particularly astute in judging the process by which the Brontë legend, nurtured by Elizabeth Gaskell, had exaggerated the tyranny of Patrick and the tragic-victim status of Branwell to accord with the male monsters of the sisters' fiction, rather than recognizing that the girls found 'the high-spirit and peculiar temper' of the one and the ordinary 'ne'er-do-well' character of the other insupportable, and rewrote their relatives' parts so as to give them a dignity and power worthy of a gifted woman's opposition and eventual capitulation.[48]

Mrs Oliphant's own portrayal of men was in keeping with the scepticism she expressed to Isabella Blackwood about the profit to be had from a scientifically precise study of them. The strength and the characteristic bias of her pictures of men derive not from attempting to fathom gender difference from a male or 'neutral' perspective, but from capitalizing upon the limitation of knowing them only from a woman's point of view. Though she had welcomed the advent of male story-tellers who could tell exclusively masculine tales of companionship and adventure, she deplored the effect that the growth of gender separation in late nineteenth-century society was having upon fiction which presumed to describe the interaction of the sexes. The 1890s, with their division between male clubland and the 'female family stranded in the drawing-room', had brought forth the 'New Woman' novel, or 'the Girl of the Period' under a new name. These women differed from their sisters of the *Jane Eyre* school in dismissing and belittling men rather than moulding them into worthwhile opponents. It had always, she observed, been a problem for a novelist who wished to present a strong woman to refrain from the simple device of surrounding her by male ciphers.[49] In her now infamous critique of Hardy's *Jude the Obscure*, Mrs Oliphant paused to indict women novelists as largely responsible for the tradition which had culminated in Jude as the passive victim of Sue's 'fantastic' behaviour. George Eliot and Mrs Humphry Ward were named as the chief offenders in creating the tradition of women's mysterious moral influence. Romola, Dorothea, and Marcella were sisters to 'the sublimated school-girl of the romance, capable of subduing men by the sheer force of their high-minded convictions.[50] Even Christian moralists had succumbed to this myth. Mrs Oliphant was ruefully amused by the way in which men like Dean Stanley and Jowett spoke so glibly of the importance of the female influence in a man's life when women were all too aware 'how the youngest about us maintain its little individuality, and how easily our counsels are ignored'.[51]

Only in a very early novel does a woman effect her husband's salvation and then only at great cost. *Lilliesleaf: Being a Concluding Series of Passages in the Life of Margaret Maitland* (1855), is particularly interesting in its development of this thesis. Mary, the married heroine of this tale, had refused, in the preceding novel, to marry the charming but self-indulgent young Scots laird, Allan Elphinstone, in the hope of reforming him. Only God, she claimed, could claim that privilege. The sequel investigates the state of their marriage after the birth of their four living children. Mary's involvement in domestic affairs has left her husband free to indulge his spendthrift ways and to create a scandal by dallying after a local aristocrat's French maid. Mary's spinster aunt, Margaret Maitland, reminds Mary of her duty to enter fully into her husband's life and inclinations. So Mary, to her husband's surprise and embarrassment, decides that she will leave her children behind in Scotland and accompany her husband to the fleshpots of London society. Her decision discomforts Allan because he has grown to justify his increasingly separate existence by recourse to the myth of the angel in the house, referring to Mary as the 'pure flower at home' to whom he can retreat when jaded by his worldly excesses. Mary's private agenda for her life in London is to be able to open Allan's eyes to his need for a job which will provide a focus and sense of responsibility commensurate with his wealth and abilities. Like many of Mrs Oliphant's heroines she alights upon her husband's election to Parliament as the suitable goal and remedy. Marital experience, however, has convinced her that open upbraiding of his thoughtless self-indulgence will only widen the gap between them and so, odious though it is to her, she throws herself into the shallow round of his social circle. So convincing is her performance that her friends are temporarily deceived into seeing her as heartless and pleasure-loving and her husband is appalled by the reflection she offers him of his own inclinations and habits. Mary's course of action, which necessitates separation from her children, exacts a terrible toll and the awakening she has effected in her husband is paid for by her own collapse. The price Mary pays for exerting a woman's influence comes close to endangering her very personality because she has had to sacrifice both her natural inclinations and the respect of others for her moral superiority.

Lilliesleaf can also be read as offering an assessment of standard Victorian thinking upon the relative moral responsibility enjoyed by men and women. While Mary may enjoy a better-developed moral sense by virtue of her sex, temperament, and manse upbringing, Allan is not exculpated on any of these counts. Mary's determination to share every portion of his life presents a direct challenge to the male habit of mind which, by locating morality in the home and in the domestic angel, liberated the outside world for the man to enjoy free from moral consideration.

Of course Mary's ability to challenge stereotypical thinking is dependent upon choosing a setting where women can accompany men in most aspects of their lives. When Dickens or Conrad makes the same point about the separation men make between their domestic and public lives in their pictures of Wemmick in *Great Expectations* or Charles Gould in *Nostromo*, it is difficult for us to imagine Miss Skiffins or Emilia Gould transforming their loved ones' thinking by pursuing them into the law-courts or the silver-mine. It might seem easy to criticize Mrs Oliphant's novels for their failure to enter imaginatively into the male world of work, but, apart from the brief glimpses of factory life and political meetings in her early novels, we mainly see her subsequent lawyers, doctors, clerics, and squires exercising their professions in a more domestic environment. Though women may envy their menfolk their apparent freedom, all too often these lives are in fact circumscribed and her world allows them almost as little chance as their sisters for the display of glamorous heroics. Her novels and articles repeatedly deplored the dearth of opportunity which confronted middle-class youths. Since a sense of vocation, rather than inheritance, was increasingly regarded as a prerequisite for the ministry, fewer opportunities presented themselves to wealthy young men when they came down from university and the choice seemed to be whittled down to India or the bar. For poorer gentlemen the choice was even grimmer: Branwell Brontë's plight seemed to Mrs Oliphant no less harsh than his sisters:[52] a man in his position could contemplate only the servitude of tutoring, a bitter pill which tutors in both *Margaret Maitland* and *Lilliesleaf* find hard to swallow, or exile in the colonies. As is the case with their fictional sisters, such men must learn to bow to the dispositions of Providence: even those men who are allowed the ostensibly heroic activities of surviving the hazards and rigours of a sailor's life, or enlisting for active service in India or the Crimea, are allowed a degree of adulation only in so far as their choices have involved the enforced sacrifice of the marital bliss which they would have preferred.

Male characters who seek out a life of heroic adventure are invariably depicted as riding roughshod over more immediate domestic needs and emotional sensitivities. As readers we are shown the years of silent suffering endured by mothers, sisters, and sweethearts rather than the achievements of the absent hero. All too often heroic renunciations turn out to be little more than a way of a young man justifying to himself the more common procedure of kicking over the traces and asserting himself only by rejecting his family's standards. Mrs Oliphant drew several full-length fictional portraits of the opportunities for false heroics provided by the fields of nineteenth-century politics and religion. *He That Will Not When He May* (1880) tells the story of a misguided young Oxford undergraduate who renounces his patrimony to show solidarity with radical working men. On his first day of work at a picture-framer's shop,

Somehow, Paul could not have told how, he felt himself a sort of sacrificial offering to justice and nature, making the most eloquent of protests against wrong, tyranny, injustice, and everything that was evil in society. With the dignity of a noble victim, and with a conscious-ness of innate, inborn, but most illogical superiority to fate, he drew the glue-pot and the tools towards him, and began to do the workman's work. Nothing could have been more illogical . . . Yet it was with a smile of unspeakable superiority that he began his first day's real work, enjoying the sensation of voluntary humility, of doing what it was beneath him to do.[53]

An implausible plot subsequently deprives him of his patrimony, but still Paul Markham has not learnt the lesson of doing his best within the sphere in which God has placed him. He angrily rejects his local rector's offer to make over the family living to him. 'Paul might have been a missionary after the apostolic model,' comments the narrator, 'but a clergyman with very little to do and a wife to do the great part of that little for him—no, he said to himself, no!'[54] The rector's *laissez-faire* mode of conducting his pastoral duties is partly responsible for Paul's need to invent for himself a mould into which he can pour his youthful radical ideals.

A variety of factors seems to have contributed to Mrs Oliphant becoming par-ticularly adept, in the 1860s, at putting her finger on the pulse of contemporary metaphysical dilemmas. Doubtless her encounters with Robert Story and John Tulloch, Scotland's new generation of religious leaders, helped, as did the breadth of her reading as a reviewer. Her work on the life of that searcher after apostolic purity, Edward Irving, had heightened her sense of the way in which the prevailing materialism of the nineteenth century could easily lead the youthful reformers to confuse the voluntary self-martyrdom of worldly renunciation with the quieter, less dramatic practice of spiritual values she herself favoured. *The Perpetual Curate* (1864) offers two variant readings, within the Anglican context, of such a mis-taken conception of Christian heroism. Both characters seem animated by that widespread Victorian male nostalgia for an illusory heroic past when warriors could sing,

> the joyful Paean clear,
> And, sitting, burnished without fear
> The brand, the buckler and the spear—
>
> Waiting to strive a happy strife
> To war with falsehood to the knife,
> And not to lose the good of life . . .
>
> To pass, when Life her light withdraws,
> Not void of righteous self-applause,
> Nor in a merely selfish cause—
>
> In some good cause, not in mine own,
> To perish, wept for, honoured, known,
> And like a warrior overthrown.[55]

The eponymous hero is one of Mrs Oliphant's most attractive, not least because, unusually for her male characters, he occasionally displays that capacity for con-

sidering the alternative view of one's own conduct which is so often the basis of the
moral humility lauded in her fiction. At the outset of the novel he is a poorly paid
'perpetual curate', much in need of a permanent living if he is to be able to propose
to the girl he loves. His Evangelical aunts come on a tour of inspection to discover
whether his reputed Ritualist views should be considered as disqualifying him from
the living for which they have always intended him. The embattled rigidity of their
Evangelicalism is no less a stumbling-block to an idealistic young man than was the
Laodicean apathy of the rector in *He That Will Not When He May*.

On Easter Day, Frank Wentworth went to church with a half-conscious, youthful sense of
martyrdom, of which he was half-ashamed. St Roque's was very fair to see that Easter
morning. Above the communion-table, with all its sacred vessels, the carved oaken cross of
the reredos was wreathed tenderly with white fragrant festoons of spring lilies, sweet
Narcissus of the poets; and Mr Wentworth's choristers made another white line, two deep,
down each side of the chancel. The young Anglican took in all the details of the scene on his
way to the reading desk as the white procession ranged itself in the oaken stalls. At that
moment—the worst moment for such a thought—it suddenly flashed over him that, after all,
a wreath of spring flowers or a chorister's surplice was scarcely worth suffering martyrdom
for. This horrible suggestion, true essence of an unheroic age, which will not suffer a man to
be absolutely sure of anything, disturbed his prayer as he knelt down in silence to ask God's
blessing. Easter, to be sure, was lovely enough of itself without the garland, and Mr
Wentworth knew well enough that his white-robed singers were no immaculate angel-band.
It was Satan himself, surely, and no inferior imp, who shot that sudden arrow into the young
man's heart as he tried to say his private prayer; for the Curate of St Roque's was not only
a fervent Anglican, but also a young Englishman, sans reproche, with all the sensitive, almost
fantastic delicacy of honour that belongs to that development of humanity; and not for a
dozen worlds would he have sacrificed a lily or a surplice on this particular Easter, when all
his worldly hopes hung in the balance.[56]

This passage neatly captures the mixed motives that inspire Frank's Ritualist
practices. The sensuous over-abundance of 'fragrant festoons' is curiously at odds
with the austerity of Wentworth's intentions and the rhythm of the sentence throws
the emphasis on to aesthetic narcissism rather than the sacred vessels or simple
wooden cross. Frank's desire to see his disagreement with his aunts in the light of
a holy war persuades him, rather than the narrator, to identify the 'horrible suggestion' as a Satanic shaft. His decision to abide by his principles, even though they
have been foolishly invested in non-essential symbols, has little to do with spirituality and everything to do with that dangerously nebulous, characteristically nineteenth-century concept: conduct becoming in a gentleman.

Gerald Wentworth, Frank's oldest brother and holder of the Wentworth family
living, embodies the second way of misconceiving Christian heroism. Gerald has
decided to secede from the Anglican Church to embrace the authority which
Roman Catholicism seems to him to offer. In the mistaken belief that he can become
a Catholic priest by the simple expedient of discarding his wife and family, he has
mentally divested himself of these responsibilities and, at the end of the novel,
shorn of his profession, he stands idle, 'a man whose career was over'. The deliberate self-martyrdom involved in renouncing his living has also involved him in

repudiating two of the fundamental keystones of Mrs Oliphant's moral system: his family and his work.

Her daughter Maggie's sudden death in the course of this novel's composition seems to have given even sharper focus to Mrs Oliphant's pondering of man's desire for certainties and ideals and their inevitable disappointment in 'a world in which every event is an enigma, where nothing that comes offers any explanation of itself'.[57] The contemporary popularity of novels with a 'religious' setting allowed her the perfect vehicle in which to discuss this negotiation between the ideal and the real. *A Son of the Soil* (1865) changed the ecclesiastical backdrop, but once again the debate overspills the confines of the narrowly doctrinal and broadens into a consideration of what remains possible or can be explored to provide an honourable course for the nineteenth-century male of heroic temperament. The title is indicative both of the way in which the hero, Colin Campbell's, essential nobility and unworldliness are rooted in the moral integrity of the Scottish farm at Ramore on the Holy Loch, and of the apparent wealth of opportunity opened to a lad from humble origins by way of education. Refusing the repeated offers of patronage extended to him by an English aristocrat, whose son he twice saves from drowning, Colin doggedly pursues his way through a Scottish university education and eventually wins himself both a scholarship to and a double first at Balliol. The two averted drownings signify the way in which the novel deliberately discountenances the possibility of a nineteenth-century hero enjoying the simple muscular satisfaction of perishing 'in some good cause, not in mine own | . . . wept for, honoured, known | And like a warrior overthrown'. On the second occasion, when Colin, by now a humble tutor in the baronet's household, saves the heir, he nearly dies, and his and his mother's reflections are undoubtedly fuelled by Mrs Oliphant's own bitter sense of injustice when her own much-valued daughter had died and she looked at the way God 'had sowed children broadcast about this world, how they swarm untaught, uncared for by the score in these Italian villages, living in beggary and wretchedness'.[58] Though the episode offers a channel for these personal emotions, the novelist's transforming art retains the upper hand and none of those affected by the incident are allowed the reactions conventionally associated with heroic exploits. The hero himself experiences no warm spiritual afterglow but, confined to his bed, speculates endlessly on 'the mysterious inequalities and injustices of life'. Attempts to see himself as part of an epic of biblical dimensions fail him.

It spoke of the wicked great in power, flourishing like the green bay-tree, and of the righteous oppressed and suffering for righteousness' sake; which was in its way a comprehensible statement of the matter. But the facts did not agree in Colin's case. Harry Frankland could not, by any exertion of dislike, be made to represent the wicked, nor was Colin, in his own thinking, better than his neighbour.

Nor is the flirtatious niece of the house suddenly converted by his bravery into a true and repentant lover. Harry Frankland's mother makes repeated sallies to the sick-room, brimming over with gratitude to her son's deliverer, but underlying her sympathy is her view that 'it was rather natural than otherwise that the tutor should suffer and that her own son should be saved' and she is offended by Colin's blunt rejection of the role convention has assigned to her.

'I have no right to your gratitude. Your son and I have no love for each other, Lady Frankland. I picked him out of the canal, not because I thought of the importance of his life, but because I had seen him go down, and should have felt myself a kind of murderer had I not tried to save him. That is the whole. Why should I be supposed to have any special regard for him? Perhaps . . . I would have given my life with more comfort for any other man.'[59]

Having put paid to muscular Christianity, the novel allows Colin to explore the alternative routes to the Christian heroic ideal, encoded in Roman Catholicism, Tractarianism, and Evangelicalism, but he finally returns to Scottish Presbyterianism rather in the spirit of the protagonist of Browning's *Christmas Eve*, critical of its shortcomings but feeling that it provides the best available expression of his own religious yearning. Just as Colin has to discover that no one religious institution embodies the ideal, so he is forced to recognize that he will never find the ideal creature of his dreams, 'she who could have divined the thoughts in his mind and the movements in his heart before they came into being'.[60] By the end of the novel he has instead offered the chivalrous protection of marriage to a girl who is his undoubted intellectual inferior and can never enter 'the innermost chamber, the watch-tower and citadel of his heart'. Yet even this 'sacrifice' provides no absolute heroic satisfaction: for Colin, 'not withstanding that he had many gleams of insight, did not always know what he would be at, or what it was precisely that he wanted', and so we cannot feel that a marriage that holds him back from becoming his Church's leading reformer is entirely disastrous. Was he right to marry a girl who fell so short of his ideal companion? Again the answer is ambivalent: he can offer Alice 'affection, tenderness, protection', all of which she will reciprocate, yet he is conscious of the effort he has to make in reconciling himself to the reduced expectations of such a marriage while she regards their union as Providential. Finally the novel confronts the question of whether this can be considered a happy ending and judges that Colin 'was as happy as most people are', since although his sights have been lowered from the vision of heavenly perfection he still has youth, health, and genius on his side. The final paragraph suggests the third sense in which the title is to be understood: Colin has had to come to terms with the limitations of the human condition. The relentless pursuit of either his ecclesiastical or female ideals would have led him into inhumane cruelty to a girl who, whatever her limitations, is devoted to him. This novel may address Mrs Oliphant's understanding of the human condition, but it does not lose sight of the variations dictated by gender. Arbitrary circumstances interpreted by the orthodox as the ways of Providence may seem to have forced a choice upon Colin that he would prefer to have avoided, nevertheless the novel reminds us that Colin always had the option of running away, of not proposing to Alice. Moreover, Colin 'has his work to do in the world' as a minister and this can help him to triumph over the limitations of his marriage, for, as the last sentence of the book puts it, 'a man can live without that last climax of existence when everything else is going on so well in his life'.

The conditions attaching to proposals of marriage, Mrs Oliphant believed, provided clear demonstration of sexual inequality. Moreover, this was an area where the greatest discrepancy between the conventions of contemporary fiction and social reality could be seen. While many of her heroines are forced to lie in a state of eager but suspended anticipation of the moment when a lover can be brought to declare himself, the noblest and least worldly of her male characters are one with their more cynical brethren in indulging in a period of decidedly unromantic calculation before offering themselves. The Reverend Morley Proctor, fellow of All Souls, whose unworldliness has rendered him inadequate to fill the position of rector of Carlingford, is determined in his 'intentions' toward the middle-aged spinster, Miss Wodehouse; nevertheless he is greatly perturbed by the thought that he will be taking on a penniless woman together with her younger sister and linking his name with that of their vagabond brother. Mr Proctor is probably the humblest man ever to have entered the purlieus of Carlingford, 'But, to tell the truth, Mr Proctor was not in a state of very deep anxiety about his fate. The idea of being refused was too unreasonable an idea to gain much ground in his mind.'[61] From the days of her first published novel Mrs Oliphant had registered a protest against the universal male assumption that ' "a" womenfolk want to be marriet'.[62] Male writers, she claimed, were responsible for the persistence of this myth. Reviewing Trollope's *The Claverings*, she complained that its hero was obviously the creation of a male author who seemed to believe that no stupidity or infidelity was too great to make a man unacceptable. 'Women', she observed, 'are neither so passive nor so grateful as they are made out to be.'[63] Passivity or gratitude were expected by men because, in the first case, pride would not allow them to conceive that their proposals had been in any way elicited from them and, in the second, their sense of the freedom they had sacrificed demanded a woman's unstinting admiration. Yet the most romantically inclined of her heroes rarely makes the uncompromising self-sacrifices of which women are capable. Her short story, 'The Lily and the Thorn',[64] and the related novel *Young Musgrave* (1877), both feature young men who apparently sacrifice their good names for the girls they love. In both cases these reckless lovers endure exile and the name of murderer to save the neck of their loved one's demented brother. In the novel the implausibility of the Gothic short story is embedded within the larger framework of the realist novel, and the events of the short story are related as having occurred many years before the main action, which is designed to address the question raised in the epigraph, 'Touching Sacrifice'. The sacrifices of these wildly impetuous lovers emerge paradoxically as both less considered than the daily rituals of submission women silently undergo and more calculated, and therefore less selfless, than the subsequent hero-worship they receive would suggest. If a man is to gain the chief object of his desire that must, Mrs Oliphant argues, at least blur the concept and clarity of his much-vaunted sacrifice.

The novel *John* (1870) demonstrates Mrs Oliphant's view that even honourable men seem utterly incapable of appreciating a woman's understanding of sacrifice as the central tenet of Christianity. John is destined to follow his father into the priesthood when he encounters Kate Crediton, the flirtatious daughter of a banker. Although John appears in heroic guise, saving her from the consequence of a riding accident, and her father's bank from a fire, she does not throw herself at his feet but demands that he sacrifices his uncertain but genuine sense of vocation, for a job in her father's bank. Having succumbed to the goddess of materialism, John finds life sterile and futile. Discussing this with his mother he asks her what has been the point of her twenty years of parish work since the visible results are negligible. She responds by asking him whether the world was worth Christ's sacrifice. John dimly recognizes that his sacrifices for Kate have been illusory in so far as he has expected her to provide ample recompense for his losses. Perhaps, he surmises, 'Life means a great deal, after all—more than just what you call happiness'; nevertheless he is shocked when his mother endorses this view, which for him has represented a glimpse into the abyss of depression, and says, 'Believe me, my own boy, the only comfort is doing God's work.'[65] Mrs Oliphant appears unable to envisage a resolution in which a man could embrace total self-surrender, and the novel closes feebly with a sudden change of heart on Kate's part so that she is now willing to become a clergyman's wife. The contrast established between John's selfless mother and his dilettante father, the rector, shows the gender difference at its most extreme: a point the author humorously underlines when the rector, upset by the son's sudden interest in his mother's self-sacrificing way of life, starts to worry whether John has been infected with Comtism, a creed renowned for its high estimate of women.

Few men, Mrs Oliphant thought, would believe a woman worth the suspension of their powers of choice implied by Mr Ruskin's view 'that a good girl should have seven suitors at least, all ready to do impossibilities in her service, among whom she should choose, but not too soon, letting each have a chance'.[66] Indeed, to submit to a woman's whim in this fashion would be seen in Victorian society, she claimed, as a sign of adolescent infatuation or effeminate weakness. The numerical disproportion that had left half a million single women as a surplus on the marriage market bolstered a man's sense of his strength as a purchaser at the same time as it rendered a woman most sensitive to the 'immoral randomness' of the process which could so transform her life. The inflated sense of self-worth such statistics produced inclined men increasingly to dislike women who presumed to affect a degree of independence, to overrate their own powers of discrimination, and to resent any suggestion that a particular choice had been arrived at by the manipulation or seductive wiles of women. Their economic and social power had contributed to their emotionally limited natures since they had never been required to study others with the self-protective fear that developed the powers of observation and imaginative skills of a subject people.

Even the best-natured of men in Mrs Oliphant's fictional world can display an insensitivity tantamount to emotional cruelty when seen from the perspective of the women whom it affects. The plot of *Joyce* (1887), which focuses on whether women should still see self-sacrifice as the ultimate feminine ideal, is nourished by the well-meaning stupidity of Colonel Hayward, one of a series of male characters whose success in the male world of Indian commerce and military service has been achieved at the expense of feeling the softening influences of a continuous female presence.[67] His first wife, after a hasty marriage in India, ran back to England when she grew to believe their marriage to be irregular. Tied to his post the Colonel makes such limited efforts as are possible to trace his pregnant wife, but, as time elapses, presumes her dead and remarries. By now retired, he is thrilled to discover his lost daughter, who has been raised by a Scottish ploughman and his wife. The pleasures afforded by the reunion of long-lost relations, so beloved of the Gothic tale, are held up for closer inspection by contrasting the Colonel's delighted recognition with the more complex and sombre reactions of his second wife and adult daughter. Secure in his sense of his own integrity, it never occurs to him that the discovery will exacerbate all the anxieties from which his second wife has always suffered as to the validity of her marriage. Nor can he make any sense of the difficulties experienced by a girl brought up as a Scottish peasant being suddenly translated to a genteel Southern life and finding, moreover, that her stepmother is anxious to conceal her origins. The subtext of this tale underlines the absolute and peremptory power of a man to change women's lives: a power before which women can only acquiesce, as the stepmother does, or retreat. The first wife retreats from life itself, runs away from her marriage, goes insane, and dies; the daughter too can only resist her father's wishes by retreating wholly from the world of English middle-class society and effectively writing herself out of the story. Middle-class Victorian family life affords no space to women who wish to question male decisions. An alternative version of this tale in which the Colonel becomes quiveringly sensitive to the feelings of the women whom he has unwittingly injured would invalidate his position as a leader of men. An affable man, he is simply unequipped even to perceive, let alone sympathize with, the wretchedness of his wives or daughter.

Once or twice in her domestic fiction Mrs Oliphant did draw pictures of men who respond sensitively to the emotional needs of those around them, but these men, by her definition, behave like women and meet a woman's fate. *Ailieford, a Family History* (1853), a long rambling tale made over to her brother Willie, pursues the story of another Willie, also the middle brother of a Scottish family. The hero and narrator is a dreamy lad with an especial capacity to attract women's confidences and unable to commit himself fully to fulfilling his own career with either the hard-headed practicality of his elder brother or the impulsive adventurousness of his younger brother, Jamie. Soon after the tale opens Willie becomes engaged to Mary, a girl of great common sense, who is uncomplainingly tending her alcoholic father. When brother Jamie starts to go astray in Edinburgh, Willie's mother instantly enlists Willie to keep him on course and Willie finds himself increasingly slipping into a maternal role. Jamie's impulsive marriage leaves Willie financially committed to the support of this new household and forced into the role of confidant to his sister-in-law. His fatal incapacity to adopt a male stance and assert the primacy of his own concerns loses him his own fiancée. The extent to which he has adopted a woman's view of affairs is indicated when he renounces his male desire to impose 'a strong restrictive system' upon the wayward Jamie, and learns instead to recognize Christ as the sacrificial victim who 'only laid the silken ties and distinctions of individual love'.[68] Despite Willie's precautions his brother's escapades result in the couple being forced to flee the country and the hero suddenly finds himself unencumbered and purposeless. The third volume sees the hero as voluntary exile and language tutor in Germany. Here he falls in love with a girl to whom he has never spoken but whose entire life he creates in his own imagination. This unmasculine activity receives its punishment when the girl receives him as her friend and confidant but marries a more robust English gentle-man. During the eight years he wanders Europe his guilt about his ingratitude to his mother gathers force and finally he returns only to find her on her deathbed. The rest of his life is spent providing support in turn for his father, with whom he cannot attain any meaningful relationship, and then for the orphaned children of his emigrant brother. Like a woman, all he has to look forward to is seeing his loved ones depart. The responsibilities Willie undertakes and the guilt he feels mirror key incidents in the author's own life, yet ultimately the novel casts Willie as a failure, a mere spectator figure. Had she been a man, Mrs Oliphant implies, none of these sacrifices would have been asked of her: indeed, a man is encouraged to prove his manliness by obdurately resisting appeals to self-sacrifice.

A much later novel, *The Second Son* (1888), again casts the middle son in the role of the passively reflective spectator figure who acts out of love rather than a due regard for his worldly prospects. Edmund Mitford is contrasted with his brutally acerbic and quarrelsome father and with his two brothers, the one an unthinkingly obstinate replica of his father, and the other a caddish guardsman. After all the will-shaking, in which the plot abounds, is over, Edmund, by the rule of primogeniture now the rightful heir, is in fact left, symbolically, with only his mother's portion. Moreover, the county neighbours quickly accept the guardsman as Squire despite his transgressions, which include manslaughter and attempted seduction, because he displays a manly ability to surmount inconvenient obstacles like guilt.

To the world at large, moral and emotional sensitivity on a man's part were too apt to look like feeble indecisiveness. Women in particular are unimpressed by male passivity and stoicism. As one of her heroines, Nettie Underwood, finds, 'She half despised her lover, as woman will, for obeying her—almost scorned him, as woman will, for the mere constancy which took no violent measures, but only suffered and accepted the inevitable. To submit to what cannot be helped is a woman's part.'[69] If a man took 'violent measures' his female admirers could persuade themselves that these were evidence of a passion strong enough to move him out of his characteristic self-absorption.

Given Mrs Oliphant's need for her sons to supply her with the love and affection of which she felt her daughter's untimely death had deprived her, and her view that successful English gentlemen, which she wished them to be, could not be required to possess much in the way of self-abnegating sensitivity, it is perhaps scarcely surprising that her sons received a mixed message and turned out both passively dependent and selfishly resistant to her emotional requirements.

In 1875, when her boys were still on the point of achieving great things, Mrs Oliphant wrote, in her role as narrator of *Whiteladies*, 'Men and women, I fear, will never be equal in this world, were all conventional and outside bonds removed tomorrow', and adds that 'it will be a strange world, when, if ever, we come to expect no more from women than we do from men; it being granted, sure enough, that in other ways more is to be expected from men than from women'.[70] Yet it has to be said that Mrs Oliphant's fiction is no more specific than her sons' lives were to be in offering precise illustration of 'other ways' in which more might be expected from men.

If women were expected to make the home their major sphere of influence, it might seem reasonable that men should be encouraged to pursue an active career in the outside world. Even here, however, men were scarcely to be trusted with their independence: 'It is indeed one of the marks of "female tribulation", to be shut up apart, and leave the great events outside to be transacted by those incautious masculine hands, in which, at the bottom of her heart, a woman seldom has perfect confidence where her own supervising influence is withdrawn.'[71] Her novels recommend a career for men as the least dangerous channel for their energies or the most suitable corrective for their natural failings. Moreover, careers open to country gentlemen offer the advantage that they can be overseen by their wives. When Lucilla Marjoribanks decides to marry her cousin Tom she swiftly alights upon the notion of his running an estate to counter his desire to provide her with a life with nothing to do 'but enjoy yourself and take care of yourself'. 'The thing that we both want', she contends, 'is something to do.' Within a chapter the necessary diversion for her husband has been reshaped into a vision of her husband standing as the county Member for Parliament, for this was 'but the natural culmination of her career that . . . held out to her the glorious task of serving her generation'.[72] In Mrs Oliphant's novels Parliamentarians gain none of that respect for selfless service to their country that they are sometimes accorded by Trollope or George Eliot: being a Member of Parliament is merely the most suitable activity for a country gentleman.

Mrs Oliphant's commitment to the Victorian work ethic was absolute. Her heaven, like Robert Browning's, is a city still under construction, where the inhabitants delight wholeheartedly in their various crafts because competition no longer exists and the certainty that God will perfect the work removes all fear of failure.[73]

From her first published novel she raised her voice against every manifestation of 'idle set' (a Scotticism for idleness), whether the offender was a young girl without a piece of sewing to occupy her listless hands, or an aimless young man. Throughout her fiction she deplored the dangerous condition of all these upper-middle-class young men with sufficient income to support themselves without the need to work. By the time Cyril reached 21 she had begun to realize the ironies of her position as mother to a son protected from this fate only by lack of income. As she wrote to John Blackwood, 'If all these boys of ours had but two thousand a year what delightful fellows they would be! I fear that is what our modern education trains them for, more than anything else.'[74] Her devotion to the work principle was so great that it even mitigated her moral disapproval of 'men of the period'. Such men as the barristers Cosmo Douglas of *In Trust* (1881) or Dewsbury of 'A Girl of the Period' (1891),[75] who hang back in their wooing because of worldly calculations, may offend against codes of the heart, but they are not to be regarded as wicked: their commitment to raising themselves from humble origins by dint of their own hard work is commended up to the point when it involves using others. It may even be that it is their ruthless self-control which provides their initial attraction for girls more accustomed to society idlers.

Mrs Oliphant reserved her deepest scorn for 'the rigorous route of pleasure-seeking' indulged in by men who love 'those fictitious bonds of engagements, appointments, and all the pretences at an occupied life'.[76] Her idle young men are not as they are sometimes in Trollope's fiction, partially redeemed by their prowess on the hunting field or at the weekend shooting party. (Privately Mrs Oliphant disliked such activities so much that she felt one might 'rather be a butcher at once which is an honest trade'.[77]) The fashion for educating boys in the style of muscular Christianity had gone so far, she was inclined to feel by the 1870s, that young men found great trouble in adjusting to the desk-work necessary for success at university or in bar examinations.[78] The purpose of education, in her view, was that of preparing a man for life. In part this view stemmed from her early acquaintance with the Scottish educational system, which favoured a wider, more vocationally oriented training than that offered by the English public school and university system. Matching the education to likely future prospects therefore played a part in the choice of school and university. There was little point in subjecting a boy to a classical education if he was destined to a clerk's desk.[79] Eton for her represented the English system at its best. It was distinct from its Scottish counterpart in that it eschewed professional training and engaged instead to teach its pupils 'the art of mastering yourself'.[80] The preparation she believed Eton gave for adult life also allowed her to be caustic at the expense of Rugby's regime, which, according to *Tom Brown's Schooldays*, addressed itself in morbidly earnest fashion to 'the moral depravities and low vices caused by the boys breakfasting alone, and cooking sausages themselves'.[81] Two of her novels, *The Story of Valentine and His Brother* (1875), dedicated 'To my Eton boys: C.F.O., F.R.O. and F.W.', and *Sir Tom* (1883), pay fulsome tribute to the school and its educational system and she was happy to seize the chance to devote articles in *Maga* to singing its praises.[82] Eton had been chosen for her sons partly because 'mere intellectual gifts without some weight of character fail generally to make much impression on the school'.[83] Yet as she looked back on Cyril's unprofitable life she recognized that easy success at Eton had done little to prepare him for the sustained self-discipline required to gain distinction at Oxford.[84] Swift as always to seize the moral responsibility, she blamed her own attitudes—her 'foolish way of laughing at the superior people, the people who took themselves too seriously,—the boys of pretension, and all the strong intellectualisms'—for his failure: 'this gave him, perhaps, or helped him to form a prejudice against the good and reading men, who have so many affectations, poor boys, and led him towards those so often inferior, all inferior to himself, who had the naturalness along with the folly of youth.'[85]

When her sons chose Benjamin Jowett's Balliol as their college they came under the aegis of a man whose penchant for cultivating those destined to form the ruling classes of the Empire attracted charges of snobbery, but Mrs Oliphant saw nothing amiss in this policy. In a late story, 'The Whirl of Youth' (1893), she carefully distinguishes between 'tuft-hunting' and the avowed principles of a Warden of an Oxford college who believes 'it is a finer thing to exert influence over those who will have a great deal of power in their hands, than over those who will have none'.[86] This Jowett-like figure is shown defending the university experience to a disenchanted wealthy young undergraduate. His artistic proclivities may mean that the scholarly life is not ultimately for him, the Warden argues, but it is important to recognize the university as a testing-ground for developing the moral power to resist the sin of idleness.

At worst the Oxford system seemed to her to offer a breeding-ground for the selfishly dilettante life of the idle bachelor. From the first her novels had deplored the self-cocooning habits and smugness of confirmed bachelors, but from the point at which Cyril went up to Oxford in October 1875 she found a new form in which to incarnate male selfishness. Inclined always to seek excuses for Cyril's poor performance, she laid the blame at the door of college tutors who were so caught up in ivory tower living and fostering similar minds that they neglected those undergraduates who required to be kept up to the mark.[87] Although it seems likely that Cyril's favourite vices would have excluded him from the Pater circle, nevertheless Walter Pater became for Mrs Oliphant the archetype of contemporary male vice. Her fictional world may have been emptied of heroes and villains and her theological world devoid of absolute sin, but Pater's cultivated aestheticism was capable of raising her religious hackles. In his *Studies of the History of the Renaissance* she detected 'an elegant materialism' and absolute egocentricity which manifested itself 'amid all the collected prettiness of modern-antique decoration, putting up their delicate atheisms, like their old china, on velvet shelves and conspicuous brackets'.[88] The visionary idealism divorced from assent to Christian dogma proffered by *Marius the Epicurean* must have struck the last nail in Pater's coffin. Pater's neo-classical interests are devalued as mere 'bric-a-brac collecting' in Mrs

Oliphant's writing.[89] Her bachelor collectors of fine china are representative of an enervated age where artistic creativity has degenerated into decking 'dim altars with ephemeral wreaths of evanescent flowers'.[90]

The Curate in Charge (1876) provides the most fully developed portrait of the cultivated dilettante bachelor don. Chapter 8 gives us a minutely detailed account of the artistic taste on display in his rooms as a check-list for recognizing the species. Only the saving fact that this young ordinand has never felt himself to have 'outgrown Christianity' separates Reginald Mildmay from the full flowering of a spirit that was shortly to reach its literary apogee in Henry James's portrait of Gilbert Osmond.[91] Slowly Mildmay begins to tire of the melancholy perfection of his surroundings. 'After all, a man cannot live for china; for aesthetic arrangement, for furniture, however exquisite; or even for art, when he is merely a critic, a commentator, and amateur—not a worker in the same.' In his deliberations as to how to achieve a sense of life beyond his scholarly commitments Mildmay begins to articulate the kind of limited but measurable moral growth available to one of Mrs Oliphant's heroes. He contemplates a life of philanthropic endeavour, but finds himself 'in such a self-discussion as many women are. If he works, what is the good of it? It is to occupy, to please himself, not because the work is necessary to others.' Finally, he resolves to put his ordination vows to the trial and accept a college living. Noble though his newly awakened impulses may seem, he finds that the real challenge to his cloistered self-indulgence lies not in the exigencies of parochial duty, where he finds himself shamed and inadequate in the face of poverty and illness, or irritated by the trivia of parish business, but in his first encounter with the elderly curate's curiously assorted family.

Mildmay felt a thrilling sensation of newness as he sat down at the tea-table, and looked on, an interested spectator, at all that was proceeeding under his eyes. This in its way was evidently life . . . It was life, not the quiet of books, and learned talk, and superficial discussion, but a quiet full of possibilities, full of hidden struggle and feeling. Mildmay felt as if he had come out of his den in the dark like an owl, and half blinking in the unusual light, was placed as spectator of some strange drama, some episode full of interest, to the character of which he had as yet no clue.[92]

The concluding scene, in which he proposes to the curate's daughter in the full acceptance of the family responsibilities she brings with her, sets the seal upon his moral evolution. Yet that very proposal scene is also used by Mrs Oliphant to underline the distance to be travelled between a man who has achieved heroic status by the nobility of his choices and a woman whose nature and circumstances have conspired to present her with a path of silent self-sacrifice since adolescence.

But Mr Mildmay had first a great deal to say. He gave her the history of his life since August, and the share she had in it. . . . He had so much to say, that . . . he scarcely remarked the little response she made. But when it came to her turn to reply, Cicely found herself no less impassioned, though in a different way.

'Mr Mildmay,' she said, 'there is no equality between us. How can you, such a man as you, speak like this to a girl such as I am? Don't you see what you are doing—holding open to me the gates of Paradise; offering me back all I have lost; inviting me to peace out of trouble, to rest out of toil, to ease and comfort, and the respect of the world.'[93]

Women will always be unequal, in Mrs Oliphant's opinion, as long as they have nothing but unquantifiable goods such as love and care to offer. Cicely does in fact have a small salary and a post as parish schoolmistress to prove her 'material' worth, but the job is socially demeaning and its true value can only be measured by the family relationships and responsibilities it underwrites. By and large the men of Mrs Oliphant's fiction reach their moral apogee at the point when they are prepared to take on or acknowledge familial responsibilities, yet once marriage has been embarked upon, or a reconciliation with alienated wives or parents is effected, little beyond cordiality and financial provision is expected of them. Even her finest masculine characters tend towards solipsism, and, unchecked, this tendency develops into full-blown autocracy of the type voiced by the humble peasant farmer, father of Isabell Carr: 'I'm in my ain house, where I've aye been king and priest. Providence gi'ed me the charge ower you, and it's your business to obey. . . . ye're mine to dispose of baith by God's law and man's.'[94] Her women, by contrast, are defined by their relationships, as friends, sisters, lovers, maiden aunts, daughters, wives, or mothers.

4 Women in Relationship

> Nothing could be more characteristic than the stories she used to tell, such as women tell among themselves, half in anger, half with a sense of injury, half (a woman's mood may have many halves) in amusement, especially when the trouble is past, of those deprivations women have to bear, and which no suffrages nor freedoms, political or otherwise, can help them out of . . . These stories would make a little collection, best appreciated, perhaps by women— stories of men thoughtless and indifferent, of careless husbands, and unthought of sacrifices.[1]

This vision of a feminist press, expounded only a year before Mrs Oliphant's own death, was inspired by the death of her old friend Lady Cloncurry, a former society beauty, and noted for her anti-suffragist views. The paradox is informative: on the one hand one could reasonably argue that 'thoughtless and indifferent men' had littered the pages of Mrs Oliphant's fiction from the beginning, but she conceives of 'these stories' as a new departure because they would be written for women. She knew that success as a writer had depended upon her capacity to appeal to male as well as female readers, and this had involved muting part of her personal convictions.

Twentieth-century feminist criticism of novels by Victorian women has frequently pointed to the divergence between the radical message overtly preached in the novels and the traditional 'male' plots to which even the most rebellious of their female characters eventually conform. Mrs Oliphant deserves recognition as a precursor of this critical tradition. In a late essay she identified one of the factors that had always dissatisfied her in that apparently revolutionary novel, *Jane Eyre*. Despite its campaigning fervour for a new perception of women's rights, the novel had succumbed to at least one facet of the stereotypical misogynistic representation of women. In total disregard of the evidence of mutual trust and support experienced between women, supplied by Charlotte Brontë's letters, Brontë as novelist had followed 'the thirty-ninth article of fiction' by depicting female characters as naturally jealous of other women who appear more attractive to men.[2] Mrs Oliphant's diatribe of the 1860s against novels of sensation had focused upon the detrimental effects of such a fictional creed. She observed that the physical magnetism of the heroes lauded by the Braddon school of women novelists (stigmatized by the name of their most successful representative, Mary Elizabeth Braddon) too often had to be given substance by a plot which represented these heroes as both object and cause of bitter female rivalry. 'The fact is', wrote Mrs Oliphant, 'that a great many of the women who write live very contentedly in the society of other women, see little else, find their audience and highest appreciation among them, and are surrounded, backed up and applauded, by their own sex in a way which men would be very slow to emulate.'[3] The extent to which such pictures distorted actuality mattered to an author so supremely conscious of the complex relation between fictional codes and the stuff of everyday life, but it mattered even more because the ideology implicit in the picture was being transmitted to the next generation by way of those family readings of which the English were so fond.

Strikingly female rivalry rarely forms the central strand of her plots. Once in *Ombra* (1872) she seems to have contemplated it, but at the end of the second volume the titular heroine's character suddenly changes when security in love not only removes the proximate cause of her jealousy but also rids her of a naturally jealous temperament. In the context of a novel which continues to make play with allusions to Coleridge's Geraldine and Christabel[4] the volte-face is ridiculous, but the apparent failure of nerve in depicting a woman driven by jealousy actually serves to underline Mrs Oliphant's belief that among women jealousy is circumstantial rather than intrinsic. The women who flirt and scheme on plot fringes to secure the undivided attention of yet undecided men are represented as to be pitied for the 'unfeminine' behaviour to which their desperate need for marriage has driven them. In part, these women exist as antitypes to the code of behaviour Mrs Oliphant's novels preach as the feminine ideal. Ombra's early behaviour is stigmatized thus: 'She thought, with some recent writers, that the doctrine of self-sacrifice, as taught especially to women, was altogether false, vain and miserable.'[5]

In the few cases where female jealousy receives serious treatment the enmity is not motivated by rivalry in the marriage stakes but derives from far deeper emotional well-springs. In *The Heir Presumptive and the Heir Apparent* (1891) it is a woman's passionate instinct to protect her children that leads her to drive her rival insane and contemplate the murder of her rival's son. In *The Two Marys* (written in 1872) it is shown as easier for a stepdaughter to surmount the ill-will engendered by her suitor's apparent attachment to her widowed stepmother than to overcome the coldness and distrust implanted years before when her close relationship with her father was disturbed by his remarriage. Sisterly jealousy on behalf of a brother's reputation is also sympathetically treated, even if it involves transgressing the law, in as far as it can be accounted an altruistic expression of female passion.[6] Indeed, the men that such devoted sisters subsequently marry are inclined to interpret this passionate behaviour as an unlimited fidelity to the male that augurs well for their treatment as husbands. These men occupy the position of poor readers. Blood-begotten loyalty is perhaps the only force to triumph over the natural solidarity of the oppressed that otherwise exists between women. In *The Wizard's Son* (1884) pragmatic Katie articulates the position to her rival.

'If he has good taste, of course I know whom he will choose.'
'Katie!' cried Oona, with a violent blush, 'if you think that I would submit to be a candidate—a competitor—for any man to choose——'
'How can you help it?' said Katie, calmly. 'It appears it's nature. We have a great deal to put up with, being women, but we can't help ourselves. Of course the process will go on in

his own mind. He will not be so brutal as to let us see that he is weighing and considering. And we can have our revenge after, if we like: we can always refuse: Come, Oona, I am quite satisfied. You and me, that are very fond of each other, we are rivals. We will not say a word about it, but we'll just go on and see what will happen. And I promise you I shall be as fond of you as ever, whatever happens. Men would say that was impossible—just as they say, the idiots, that women are never true friends. That is mere folly; but this is a problem and it will be very interesting to work it out.[7]

As Katie is at pains to point out, the hero's decision defines him, not them. There is no attempt to suggest, as so often in Victorian women's novels, that either girl can or needs to accommodate her behaviour to present him with an all-encompassing model of femininity: their differences are temperamental rather than moral.

Female friendship without the presence of the 'interesting problem' presented by the intrusion of a male suitor is a subject that Mrs Oliphant rarely gives any degree of prominence in her fiction. Personally she disliked the times when her family became 'just a household of women',[8] for women living alone were deprived of that daily budget of news of the outside world to which even the idlest of men had access.[9] Many of her close female friendships were founded upon the small change of shared intimacies as to the exigencies and follies of her friends' husbands. In later life she was to recall the brief but intense friendship of this nature she had enjoyed with Jane Carlyle in terms of 'that fine scrutiny, *malin* but tender', which saw 'through and through' her husband, Thomas Carlyle, and provided Mrs Oliphant with a 'constant suppressed interest which gives piquancy to life'. The flavour of such a relationship is captured in Mrs Oliphant's recollection of a conversation they had one day when out driving together. Mrs Oliphant had 'foolishly' remarked upon 'the way in which Mr Carlyle alone, of all his peers, seemed to have trodden the straight way'. 'My dear,' was Mrs Carlyle's barbed reply, 'If Mr Carlyle's digestion had been better there is no telling what he might have done.'[10] Women like Jane Carlyle, Geddie Macpherson, or Mrs Tulloch felt free to unburden their minds to her knowing that she would respond sympathetically but incline them to see their particular grievances as symptomatic of 'woman's lot' rather than inciting rebellion. The searing experience of the tension between her mother and husband taught her to distrust women like Mrs Bate who 'constantly encouraged Geddie in her little rebellions against her husband'.[11]

Since the married state represented the natural order, female friendship held most allure for Mrs Oliphant when it could be seen as offering relaxation from the rigours of heterosexual relations. Contrary to popular opinion, she claimed, women actually enjoyed that period after dinner they had together while the men lingered over their port.[12] The pleasure derived from male absence is important enough to deserve validation in heaven: in one of her tales of the afterlife Mrs Oliphant's Little Pilgrim listens at length to male historians and poets at work in the heavenly city and then finds herself 'glad to be by the side of a woman after talking with so many men'.[13] Yet, although the spinster pilgrim is allowed the 'feminine' reward of deriving pleasure from the texture of her female companion's cloak, such a potentially exclusive relationship cannot go unchecked, and her new-found friend uses their time together to lecture to her on the fact that married love retains its special status in heaven.

One of those 'unconsidered moments' of happiness whose significance only became clear in retrospect was an all-female expedition to the Continent under-taken in 1863 before Maggie's death: 'the little party of women, all of us about the same age, all with the sense of holiday, a little outburst of freedom, no man interfering, keeping us to rule or formality'.[14] She could see the value of religious sisterhoods in as far as they provided restorative companionship to which the wounded could make temporary retreat,[15] for in times of grief women were instinc-tively better than men at offering comfort to other women, even those they scarcely knew.[16] During her pregnancy in Italy, when Frank was slowly dying, because she had no woman to go to for comfort Mrs Oliphant took to straying into a room in the Pitti where 'the great picture of the Visitation—Albertinelli's—hung alone . . . it seemed to do me good to go and look at these two women'.[17] It was the mother–daughter relationship, in which female wisdom was handed down, that Mrs Oliphant missed. Although she frequently invited her friends' daughters to stay, they remained proxy daughters and were not encouraged to become reverential acolytes of the variety she so scornfully observed congregated around Mrs Duncan Stewart or George Eliot.[18] Onlookers might claim that Mrs Oliphant too attracted admirers who were unworthy of her, but her close female friends, like Mrs Tulloch or Geddie, or Mrs Ritchmond Ritchie, were usually women of considerable strength of character and often of some literary attainment. Others, like little Nelly Clifford, she valued for the selfless quality of their lives, or, as in the case of Christina Rogerson, who had been embroiled in the Dilke scandal, for a certain pertinacity in the face of adversity. Her frank estimate of her own limitations combined with an independent spirit to disincline her to unequal friendships. In 1861 she wrote as follows to Isabella Blackwood:

As for your question about whether I think a woman sure to dislike one of her own sex who comes out when she cannot, I answer most decidedly no. There are many women who, obliged to be inactive themselves, follow the labours of other women with such generous sympathy and admiration as makes me feel very small when I think of it. To be perfectly candid, I don't think I could do it, otherwise than very imperfectly myself. I imagine I should find it very hard to play second for any length of time, or in the estimation of anybody I much cared for; but I do believe there are women who can do that most magnanimous of acts, and I honour them accordingly.[19]

Yet they remained for the most part unhonoured in her fiction. One such made a brief appearance in *The Three Brothers* (1870). Mrs Severn, the widowed artist of the tale, employs a governess who, 'though she was sometimes troublesome, and almost intrusive in her vigilance . . . loved her friend with the intense affection of one woman to another—generally of a lonely woman to one more fortunate than herself—which is so seldom appreciated and so little understood, but which some-times rises to the height of a passion'.[20] The relationship probably remained undeveloped, in this already loosely structured novel, because it had already provided Mrs Oliphant with the germ of a short story for her series of tales, *Neighbours on the Green*. In 1871 she published 'Lady Isabella' as part of this series in the *Cornhill Magazine*. It deals with the passive 35-year-old Lady Isabella of the title, who lives with an energetic widow in a relationship which she openly characterizes as that of 'wife' to Mrs Spencer's husband. Mrs Spencer tries to disguise her joy at the return of a former suitor but is helpless in the face of the bitterness of Lady Isabella's perception of what their marriage will mean to her: 'Then I am nothing to her, nothing to her.' The narrator then offers a comment which illuminates Mrs Oliphant's own sense that in a society where marriage is upheld as the ultimate prize alternative narratives command little respect.

We are all in the habit of laughing at the idea of friendships so close and exacting, especially when they exist between women. Next to a man's wife deserting him, or a woman's husband, I know nothing more hard. . . . I suppose to be married is the happiest; but still I was very, very sorry, grieved more than I can say, for the woman who was forsaken; though she was only forsaken by another woman and not by a man. However that, I fear is a sentiment in which I should find few sympathizers.[21]

Elsewhere in her fiction female community is seen as the consolation conferred upon those who by reason of age, or disappointment in love, are excluded from the race for the greatest prize. On the only occasion, in *Whiteladies*, when a still marriageable woman voluntarily opts for life with two elderly spinsters it is implied that she does so because, lacking in the higher sensibilities, she chooses, like an animal, to live with those who have always treated her kindly.

The ideal adult relationship, Mrs Oliphant felt, would be that enjoyed between a man and a woman without hint of sexual involvement, or the embarrassment of unfounded but lubricious gossip circulating: 'that companionship of man and woman which, after all, is the greatest and most lasting happiness of marriage— better, more delicate, complete and sufficing, than any tie between man and man or woman and woman'.[22] She was fulsome in her praises whenever she thought she had found evidence of such a relationship. She left her *Maga* essay on William Cowper unamended to demonstrate to her readers her intense sense of shock and disappointment when, half-way through writing about the beautiful friendship achieved between the poet and Mrs Unwin, she stumbled across evidence, in another biography she was consulting, which suggested that the friendship had indeed been marred by unfulfilled promises of marriage.[23] Yet she had to admit that part of the pleasure she herself derived from reading about such relationships was the enjoyable suspense as to whether the friendship would wither away or slip beyond the permissible boundaries.[24] Only once in her fiction did she pursue the topic. In *Carità* (1877) a middle-aged widow and widower find themselves drawn close by their need to discuss their respective children, but Mrs Oliphant's instincts prompted her to bring the man to the point of a declaration, however pragmatically conceived, and, after marriage has been dismissed, the friendship inevitably suffers.

Along with that other relationship she herself would dearly have loved to have enjoyed, the close adult companionship of brother and sister, the topic, lacking sustained romantic interest, was inimical to sustained development in a three-decker novel.

Once single women had safely passed the age where they could be seen as irresponsible or predatory in their attitude to eligible males they were accorded remarkable respect in the world of Mrs Oliphant's fiction. Notably their fondness of good-natured gossip, their supposed lack of vested interests, and their constant availability to receive confidences or perform menial tasks made them ideal narrator figures. Although local opinion may occasionally stigmatize pairs of spinsters as 'old cats'[25] such characters rarely do more than indulge in gossip or a little well-intentioned interference. Spinsters in her novels are far less likely to be presented as selfish than their bachelor counterparts because their plight more often derives from lack of opportunity than deliberate choice.[26] They merit respect rather than pity, however, because they are in a position most nearly to approximate to Mrs Oliphant's womanly ideal: a life of altruistic self-sacrifice. From her earliest novels she stresses that spinsters need not automatically assume that they will be deprived of all the benefits accompanying marriage, for the frequency of death in childbirth left many children motherless. Mrs Oliphant would surely have been comforted if she could have foreseen that her spinster niece, Denny, whose future she had agonized over, was so soon to be called into active service as a proxy mother when her aunt and sister died within weeks of one another. Her own experience, as a single parent to brother Frank's motherless children, was to confirm her also in the belief that it was impossible to become an adoptive parent without also feeling the pangs incumbent in such a relationship.[27] One of her saddest portraits is that of the last days of Catherine Vernon in *Hester* (1883), a woman who, like Mrs Oliphant, had made herself responsible for a large extended family, but had taken one young relative, Edward Vernon, and admitted him to a son's place in her heart, only to be betrayed by him.

Yet it is this Achilles heel in her otherwise 'masculine' demeanour that guarantees her the dignity of a tragic death in which 'her heart fails her'. At the end of the novel she refuses to endorse her young relative, Hester's, desire to tread the same path by becoming 'a man of business' and so to transcend the miseries into which affairs of the heart must lead. Women like Catherine Vernon, it is implied, present dangerous role models. 'I think you are like me, Hester. We were kept apart by circumstances; perhaps it is possible we might have been kept apart on purpose.'[28] This 'purpose', interestingly, remains undefined in terms of character or plot motivation and seems more akin to the combination of natural and social forces represented as working together at the end of E. M. Forster's *Passage to India* to prevent the interracial friendship proposed by two of the less conventional characters. The ending does, however, pay full tribute to the paradox of a woman's position. If Catherine has been 'saved' from her masculine trait of using her intellect to distance herself from her emotions, by capitulating to a woman's distinctive organ, 'the heart', where does this leave Hester? The novel's ironic closure calls attention to this by leaving Hester to be wooed by two men, 'good men both, who will never wring her heart . . . What can a woman desire more than to have such a possibility of choice?'

Although her novels often present the single woman's lot as contented and useful and certainly no unhappier than some marriages, equal understanding is given to single women beyond the prime of life who make unromantic marriages. Perhaps prompted by contemplating the position of her niece Madge, who, in her late twenties, was soon to have to choose between spinsterhood and the attentions of a jute manufacturer with whom she was not in love, Mrs Oliphant explored the matter in the opening chapter of *The Railwayman and His Children* (1891). Here a 40-year-old spinster is brought to consider a proposal from an honest and success-ful 'railwayman' of lower social origins than her own. Her own immediate family being dead she has no other prospects than acting the role of unpaid companion or governess in friends' houses where she will always feel herself *de trop*. She accepts his proposal because it will provide her with duties, a home, and the promise of friendship; nevertheless she shrinks from the physical intimacy marriage will entail and is 'startled' when her suitor approaches her and offers 'for the first time, to touch her forehead with his lips'.[29] The pragmatic basis of her decision is counter-balanced or morally validated by the integrity of her subsequent conduct as wife and stepmother.

The life of even a poor spinster could be perfectly acceptable, as Mrs Oliphant had opportunity to observe in the case of her cousin, Annie Walker. In *The Wizard's Son* she drew a picture of just such a 'sensible woman with much kind feeling' toward her provider and son 'though she was not perhaps the kind of person from whom any high degree of unselfish devotion was to be looked for', yet even she was surprised by the degree of insensitivity and the nature of the calculations involved in Annie's sudden decision to marry an elderly rich widower after eighteen years of living in the bosom of the Oliphant family. 'Well!', she wrote, 'let us console ourselves that the price of all that is not a pleasant one to pay.'[30]

Mrs Oliphant rarely missed a chance to comment upon the astonishing fact that women's morals had not been thoroughly corrupted by the knowledge that 'It is always possible, not only for a girl, but even for a woman who has reached the middle of life, to have her position and prospects changed in a moment as by the waving of a magician's wand—and that probably not by any virtue or any exertion of her own, fortuitously, accidentally, by what seems more chance and good for-tune'. In *The Heir Presumptive and the Heir Apparent* this thought fuels the entire plot: a wife whose marriage has been the result of carefully calculating the odds between the life of an impoverished, uncultivated Northern squire's daughter and the probable acquisition of wealth and title through marriage to a younger son, is indeed 'demoralized' by having her prospects dashed when her husband's 60-year-old brother, Lord Frogmore, marries the much-put-upon spinster companion, Mary, whom she has been exploiting. Mrs Oliphant attempts to secure our understanding of the woman's subsequent murderous impulses by producing a further 'control' figure, Agnes, Mary's sister, who in turn cares for her parents, her sister, and her nephew and whose life of largely unacknowledged service wins for her only the reputation of 'a grim spinster'.[31]

Mrs Oliphant's fiction leaves us in no doubt that it is an independent income that secures the power base from which an elderly single woman can raise her voice even against the brutal tyranny of men who hold their wives and daughters in terrorized subjugation. Elderly female servants often retain independent judgement, but money is necessary to command a hearing. It is the same social law that underlies the tragic events of *Kirsteen* and the comedy of *Miss Marjoribanks*. Lucilla Marjoribanks' strength derives from an awareness of the rules commanding social intercourse that is in inverse relation to her self-awareness. For the greater part of the novel Lucilla, like her literary predecessor, Jane Austen's Emma Woodhouse, is enabled to play personally and vicariously with the pleasant frisson of matchmaking without fear of being burnt, because her father's income underwrites her freedom to pick and choose. Marriage can be deferred until it promises to fulfil a perceived need. In Emma's case she is brought to marry by the prospect of losing Mr Knightley, but in Lucilla's case Mrs Oliphant has to remove her income in order to reduce the virgin queen to the status of a mortal woman considering spinsterhood in straitened circumstances as an inducement to marriage. Emma is never forced to recognize in Miss Bates a picture of her own future, merely to understand that her own queenly eminence brings with it certain responsibilities to the least of her subjects. In all respects save one Lucilla is more conscious than Emma of the social responsibilities incumbent upon her, but Victorian ideology demanded that she be made to realize the antisocial nature of her aspiration to solitary rule. Victorian novels do not easily provide space for heroines who deliberately embrace spinster-hood. Personality changes are foreign to Mrs Oliphant's authorial creed and so Lucilla is brought to heel by the sudden loss of her father and her income. She is then forced to contemplate a vision of the future embodied in the two Miss Ravenswoods who have thus far provided Carlingford's model for a life of 'genteel economy'.[32] To a woman of Lucilla's spirit, who finds that she has no vocation for the totally selfless life of the foundress of a charitable institution, marriage to a reasonably malleable husband is an exercise in damage limitation, and, had her cousin Tom, for whom she had always felt a vague preference, not turned up in the nick of time, she would have accepted with equanimity 'the possibility afforded to her' by the local Member of Parliament's proposal.[33] The ending of the novel reminds us that Lucilla's heroic trajectory 'when she rose like the sun upon the chaos of society' has descended into a marriage to her cousin with which a 'few remaining malcontents' among the readers will be dissatisfied. In this narrative acknowledgement of an alternative perspective Mrs Oliphant reminds us of her kinship with George Eliot, who returns Dorothea to the realms of the possible in marrying her to Will rather than envisioning a feminist Utopia. Lucilla too might have been seen as an exceptional woman who demonstrated 'a certain (spiritual) grandeur ill-matched with the meanness of opportunity'.[34] Lucilla's optimistic assessment of her life remains intact because she entertains none of the disturbing questions as to social values that the authorial irony implicitly raises for less sanguine readers. Such 'malcontents' are inclined to conclude that, like Dorothea, Lucilla found for herself 'no epic life wherein there was a constant unfolding of far-resonant action'. Instead she colluded with society's restricted view of a single woman's appropriate sphere and made herself a figure of fun by blindly determining to treat this trivial arena as a field suitable for heroic enterprise.

Of all her former glories as virgin queen of Carlingford, Lucilla finally retains only the name, Lucilla Marjoribanks. Lucilla was the creation of a woman who had also, after circumstances had changed, married a cousin but determinedly proclaimed her double right to the title of Oliphant. Indeed, this novel alone out of all Mrs Oliphant's titles proudly proclaims the heroine a spinster. It may have been Mrs Oliphant's private conviction 'that the love between men and women, the marrying and giving in marriage, occupy in fact so small a portion of either existence or thought',[35] but as a professional novelist she recognized the market value of titles featuring female Christian names that offered promise of romantic addition in the course of the novel. Once again a comparison of *Miss Marjoribanks* with *Phoebe Junior* proves instructive: where the former title suggests the history of a mature single woman, the latter promises a process of maturing into seniority which, in a girl's case, will almost certainly be marked by the acquisition of a new identity given by a marital surname. The title *Phoebe Junior* offers a further signal: it is fathers and sons who are usually distinguished in this way, not mothers and daughters, in whose case it is generally assumed the daughter will distinguish herself from the mother by acquiring a husband, and it is upon this assumption that the novel concentrates. Phoebe is endowed with the epithet and mental characteristics that Victorian society would happily have accorded her elder brother, had she had one, but she is placed in the heroine's role. In this way Mrs Oliphant offers her most pungently concentrated commentary upon the inequities of men and women as they contemplate marriage. For marriage, as Phoebe is aware, is the chief Career (and it is in capital letters she always thinks of it) held open by Victorian society to a woman.

The point of the story is not to suggest that Phoebe would have been happier as a man—indeed, the young men of the tale, for all their braggadocio, are often reduced to the position normally occupied in romantic tales by their romantic 'sisters'. A careful account of her education reveals that, far from being an eccentric misfit, Phoebe is very much the product of the muddled thinking of a generation who encouraged their daughters to pursue every educational opportunity without considering the wider ambitions this would nourish, but then thought to check undesirable vocational enthusiasm by simultaneously patronizing 'Mr Ruskin's theory that dancing, drawing and cooking were three of the higher arts which ought to be studied by girls'.[36] Phoebe is therefore mentally conditioned to devote her energies to a Career, but socially conditioned to locate this Career in marriage. Any father would have been proud of the sacrifices she is prepared to make for success in the family business. There is indeed a poetic justice in this auburn-haired beauty becoming the working heir to the self-made Copperhead fortunes that her husband, 'a perfectly useless piece of humanity', is so woefully unequal to. At every stage of her progress, from the moment when she leaves home to attend to a threatened family inheritance, to the interview she carries out on her suitor's behalf with a reluctant father-in-law, Phoebe is given the role normally entrusted to her heroic counterpart. Mindful that success, and not happiness, is the name of the male career game, she reluctantly relinquishes a suitor who touches her heart in favour of 'the object' who will best suit her uses. Despite the fact that her story is contrasted with a more insipid and conventional figure of romantic fiction, Phoebe is not a Becky Sharp. She is not an adventuress, for there is integrity in her decision to renounce the chance of sexual gratification and the vision of a higher kind of existence in the dedicated pursuit of her Career. Only once does Phoebe lose conviction in the worth of her enterprise: significantly it is at the moment she has secured her prize, Clarence. Her tradesman grandfather is overcome by Phoebe's good fortune and proceeds to do homage to her indolent, loutish intended.

The girl sat by them languidly, though with a beating heart, wondering, as girls will wonder sometimes, if all men were like these, braggards and believers in brag, worshippers of money and price. No doubt, young men too marvel when they hear the women about them talking across them of *chiffons*, or of little quarrels and little vanities. Phoebe had more brains than both of her interlocutors put together, and half-a-dozen more added on; but she was put down and silenced by their talk.[37]

To the undiscerning male world the success she has so diligently laboured for appears no different from the 'demoralising' chance of meeting with male approbation for which conventional girls hope. Phoebe is right to be dismayed for a number of reasons. All her carefully calculated stratagems have attained nothing more in the eyes of society than her conventional female friends might have aspired to, and were she to declare her stratagems she would be denounced rather than admired. Her triumph perhaps resides in abstaining from cynicism by managing, in her own eyes at least, to reinfuse a woman's restricted prospects and silent achievements with a certain glamour by relabelling them.

Phoebe is fortunate to come from the classes where she can persuade herself that a Career is a reasonable ambition. Rich girls have an even harder time in Mrs Oliphant's novels than poor ones because, although they are so constantly warned of the danger of being a prey to fortune-hunters, they more often find themselves having to propose to a poorer suitor and thus displeasing him by affronting his masculinity and depriving themselves of their romantic dreams.[38]

Rich girls seem to offer particularly convincing proof of the thesis that a woman's only power is 'the power of refusal'.[39] The heroine of *The Greatest Heiress in England* (1879) reluctantly accepts the proposal of a man who is far from perfect (a man who finds he cannot declare his love because 'it was a word he had already soiled by ignoble use') on the grounds that he represents an escape from 'running the gauntlet through a string of suitors'. In the sequel, *Sir Tom* (1883), she finds that her 'greatness' is much reduced by marriage. Her middle-aged husband dismisses as bizarre nonsense the conditions of her father's will that have secured her wealth and attempted to provide a suitable education in worldly wisdom. The father had stipulated that she was to dispose of half of her fortune by finding individuals to whose lives a bequest could make an appreciable difference. In effect Sir Tom wishes to truncate this education. For him the matter is simple: he has rescued her from the merely avaricious and he has a husband's right to overturn the foolish innocence of her schoolmaster father's provisions. Neither Lucy nor Sir Tom has intended to deceive the other; they have merely harboured different assumptions as to the change marriage should effect. Sir Tom sees no need to temper his opinions or change his social circle but expects that his wife will accommodate herself entirely to his needs and requirements. The irony of his position lies in his failure to realize that the innocence he valued in his betrothed had its roots in the moral integrity of her upbringing and cannot be smothered or disguised to suit his convenience.

As her sobriquet, 'the greatest heiress in England', announced, Lucy at least enjoyed the dubious distinction of being a much-valued prize in the marriage stakes. Less wealthy girls, Mrs Oliphant thought, often suffered earlier disillusion from the gap between their dreams of an ardent lover desperate to achieve married bliss and the harsh reality that decreed that, once having gained a girl's emotional support, many young men were unanxious to proceed too rapidly to the married state with the expenditure and responsibilities that would entail. Indeed, such caution, though disappointing to the girl concerned, was often deemed praiseworthy in a society where men were judged by their capacity as breadwinners and women for their spiritual qualities of patient devotion. The matter is treated with comic compassion in *The Perpetual Curate* (1864) where Mrs Morgan, the rector's wife, is often to be found, in moments of tension, tending her maidenhair fern as if recollecting the ten years during which her husband had forced her into prudently waiting for the diminished pleasures of a financially secure middle-aged existence together. Her longing for the lost life they might have had together is 'as Sanscrit' to a husband who can only see in those years a schooling in patience particularly appropriate for a parson's wife.[40]

With the prospect of a career before them, young men rarely find themselves reduced to marrying for money alone, although even this motive was generally deemed acceptable by society, if regrettable in a close relative such as a brother or cousin.[41] By contrast, girls, who often held no other hope of improving their lot, were regarded with social opprobrium if they actively sought the security of marriage. The inequity of this state of affairs was repeatedly underlined by Mrs Oliphant in pictures of flirtatious, marriage-hunting girls, cordially despised by their female peers and exploited by the young men whose vanity they flattered, who yet turn into good and caring wives. As one such girl expresses it, she can afford fine feelings 'now I have got one who is going to stand by me, who knows what I mean, and will put no bad motive . . .'.[42] Such girls are not held up to the reader's admiration, but we are reminded that the likely success of their marriages is based upon the knowledge of men they have acquired in the course of their successive disappointments. Given the power men have at their disposal, women, and especially the impressionable adolescent readers of novels, have a duty to themselves to develop a certain scepticism about their 'rescuers'. 'Nothing vexed her more', wrote Mrs Oliphant's obituarist in the *Daily News*, 'than to see a woman worshipping a man.'[43] Trollope came in for particular and repeated criticism on account of his pictures of women 'who look upon their future husbands as demi-gods'.[44] It was not merely that she found the wooing rituals practised in Trollope's novels out of kilter with her own experience: she found the idealized expectations they aroused positively harmful. She particularly disapproved of the convention that, until the moment of the proposal, a girl should remain unawakened, never admitting to herself, and much less to any female confidante, her growing fondness, not yet identified as love, for her husband to be. Like Prince Charming's kiss, his proposal was to awaken her virgin and as yet dormant affections. In Mrs Oliphant's novels, however elderly or humble she may be, the bride to be is rarely unaware of the impending proposal and is therefore usually in better command of the interview than the luckless male. Even nervous, spinsterly little Miss Wodehouse, in *The Perpetual Curate*, is primed by 'a certain feminine instinct' as to the probable purpose of her hesitant and fumbling suitor's visit to her the day after her father's death. It is even hinted that 'in her youth Miss Wodehouse might have come to such a feminine crisis before'.[45] This suggestion is important. In Mrs Oliphant's view the Prince Charming pattern of courtship was just as likely to frighten an unprepared girl into an immediate refusal, subsequently regretted.[46] Moreover, the theory that the ideal romantic heroine remained unconscious of her budding love until liberated by a proposal could only make women unreasonably ashamed of emotional prescience or unreciprocated affection. 'A man feels no such shame to have given his love to a woman who loves him not . . . it is a disgrace to her and to all womankind—or at least so the girl feels in the first agony of discovery.'[47] The plot of the short story in which this questioning of the convention occurs, contrives to suggest that the false shame so induced can effectively kill a girl's chance of happiness by suggesting to her that she has somehow misused and exhausted her store of emotions so that any subsequent relationship can only be a tepid affair compared with the first.

Alternatively, fidelity to a romantic code that binds a girl to her first untutored choice can leave a sensitive and honourable girl beleaguered in unconfessed misery when she finds the man unworthy of her love. Mrs Oliphant's own early betrothal at 17 and her subsequent heartbreak when things went wrong led her to moving depictions of the trapped desperation experienced in this situation.[48] An emphasis upon the absolute nature of first love left a girl no room for the infatuations and innocent mistakes of real life. Sensible mothers, in her fiction, are undismayed when their daughters are driven to reveal their love for men who can for one reason or another 'be nothing to them' now, but seek to prevent any damaging displays of such emotion.[49] True to this philosophy, Mrs Oliphant wrote sympathetically but firmly to her 19-year-old niece, Denny, after 'a disappointment': 'I wish it to be simply said that you found you had no such feeling as you supposed for the young man and had written to him to say so.'[50] Though the young man had undoubtedly behaved badly, it was imperative that the true version was not allowed to become current in Windsor, where it would have the effect of damaging Denny's reputation. Denny should have known from her aunt's novels that a poor girl's reputation was her most valuable attribute since she had nothing more material to offer. Denny, however, proved resistant to this view of life. Three years later her aunt had cause to remonstrate with her for embarking upon a series of art lessons in Paris where she and another girl were left unchaperoned with a male model. When Denny stood on her dignity and accused her aunt of impugning her character she was told not to be so silly: the propriety of Denny's behaviour was not in question but her reputation was.[51]

As this response indicates, Mrs Oliphant was neither a hypocrite nor a prude: her attitude to the sexual mores of her society was pragmatic rather than fuelled by reforming ardour. In her tales girls can even recover from the scandal of an unconsummated elopement, but only if gossip chooses to recognize the irreparable blackguardism of the would-be seducer.[52] In these circumstances his loss of reputation is treated by relatives as a question of social esteem, not as a sin. His punishment is equivalent to that meted out to unwise but unfallen women: to be talked of as '*planté-là*'. To trifle with the reputation of a girl of your own class was not the act of a gentleman. The point is well made in 'A Widow's Tale' (1893) where Mr Fitzroy, a ne'er-do-well bachelor, counts, in his low-minded way, upon a certain licence in sexual matters as more likely in a widow and embarks upon a shameless flirtation with her. Astonished by her maidenly outrage when he attempts to compromise her, he reluctantly proposes marriage only when he realizes that if he is publicly spoken of as 'an infernal cad' he will lose his precarious standing as a man of honour with his many creditors. His gallant proposal takes the form of reminding the widow that if she is 'not a fool' she will deliver herself into his hands rather than face social ostracism. From her point of view the matter is complicated by the fact that, although she recognizes him to be unprincipled and brutally insensitive, she is sufficiently physically attracted to him not only to accept his proposal but to abandon the young children of her first marriage to her sister's care. Two years later she returns from the Continent alone, a sadder and a wiser woman.

Sexual attraction, in Mrs Oliphant's view, was an inadequate recipe for a happy marriage. For one thing it too often took no account of social class: therefore, once sexual gratification had been obtained, there were no shared cultural assumptions upon which to build marital companionship. Once the *égoïsme à deux* of the lovers is dispelled and they attempt to establish their own social circle, embarrassment and alienation follow. One of Mrs Oliphant's least attractive novels, *Mrs Arthur* (1877), concentrates exclusively upon the impossibility of a truly happy relationship between a man of upper-class origins and a worthy girl of lower-class suburban stock. Although we are asked to admire the proud integrity of the Bates family, 'a happy ending' is only achieved by separating the husband and wife for long enough for the wife to realize that the marriage can only be resumed when she has changed her identity by taking a crash course in upper-class attitudes and values. Neither she nor her family could be accused of having 'led on' their paying guest, but the gratification of his desires has to be paid for by her total submission. The same point is being made more subtly and more palatably when Phoebe Junior sets aside the warm pleasures offered by thoughts of the young Anglican curate, Reginald May, because she can foresee, from his and his father's behaviour to his sisters, that he would not prove malleable in marriage and she would be expected to submerge her Dissenting background in his cultural identity.

In one short story Oliphant does imagine the case of a woman for whom sexuality and sexual desire form the basis of her decisions. In the conventional sense of a mystery tale *The Mystery of Mrs Blencarrow* (1890) is a failure since the plot-line becomes obvious too rapidly, but the tale becomes more interesting when, as the title suggests, we attend to the central character, a widow of some five years' standing who has been left a country estate 'in trust' for her five children. It is hinted that her former husband was so doting that he made unusual arrangements, virtually excluding his own family and leaving everything at his wife's immediate disposal. Yet, despite her husband's family's unhappiness, no one could accuse her of being a selfish or scheming woman. On the contrary, she seems devoted to the children who are destined to inherit. Her undue influence over her doting husband, we must therefore conclude, was not intellectually manipulative. Her behaviour gives no cause for scandal, but local gossip is fed the interesting rumour that she has made a second, secret marriage. Mrs Blencarrow is finally driven to confess to the rector that she has indeed married her steward, Brown, whom we discover to be the figure making clandestine visits to her late at night. The marriage has not made either of them happy and its disclosure will damage her children. The rector is nonplussed since the dilemma with which he is confronted is not within the moral boundaries of his normal remit. Neither the rector nor the reader can understand what prompted this marriage to a man whom we have only seen as a faintly menacing, boorish figure who seems out of place in her rooms. Only at this late point in the story are we suddenly allowed to see him in his natural habitat, outside, skating, describing 'sweeping and wonderful circles about the pond, admired by everybody. He was heavy in repose, but he was a picture of agile strength and knowledge there.' The mysterious aspect of this upper-class widow's personality that has led one husband to slavish devotion and has in turn prompted her to an act wholly out of keeping with her otherwise conventional behaviour, is instantly illuminated. In the event Brown is happy to be bought off and make his departure for Australia. What brought them together, he reflects, was also the undoing of their relationship, for, once married, Mrs Blencarrow had been disgusted by 'all my natural ways'.[53]

These two stories of widows who succumbed so disastrously to their physical natures lend a further dimension to the portrait J. M. Barrie tried to draw of Mrs Oliphant. Throughout his description he concentrates upon the glimpses of a discrepant personality lurking just under the surface of the imposing *grande dame*, Windsor's Other Widow. 'She could be almost fearsomely correct, and in the middle of it become audacious (for there was a dash of the Bohemian about her).' Rather than concentrating, as her women friends did, upon the industry with which she kept her 'lovely hands' busy with 'dainty sewing or knitting',[54] he drew attention to a certain sensuality: 'she gave you the impression of one who loved to finger beautiful things'. His pen-portrait served as the Introductory Note to the posthumous collection *A Widow's Tale and Other Stories*, and he used the opportunity to indicate what he perceived as the closeness of authorial identification with these women 'no longer in the first flush of their youth, of whom Mrs Oliphant wrote always with abundant sympathy, and latterly as if she loved them the best'.

Yet these women had made their mistakes within marriage. Throughout the vast corpus of her fiction Mrs Oliphant never placed the 'fallen woman' topic at the centre of her story. There are, it is true, stories where gullible girls agree to plans which leave them alone with their would-be seducers, and yet the outraged victim always escapes physically unscathed to leave the villain gnashing his teeth in impotent fury at the uncomprehending innocence of the girl.[55]

Her reluctance to give attention to this topic seems to have stemmed not so much from prudery as from a sense that it would prove difficult to handle with the moral realism she esteemed.[56] It is true that in 1855 she denounced the subject of Mrs Gaskell's *Ruth* as too distressing for fiction likely to be read by pure young women, but by 1892 she readily admitted that this novel would no longer shock anyone.[57] Her own move into literary Bohemia had inevitably led to encounters with couples whose liaisons had not been sanctioned by marriage: in the mid-1860s in Paris she had, for instance, met 'old Father Prout', a former Jesuit priest 'and the old lady about whom he circled'.

I don't know if there had been anything wrong in their connection. It was certainly patriarchal then, they were so old and such born commanders and so entirely at ease with each other. It was wicked of me I fear, but it amused me to think that these old people had perhaps indulged in a grande passion and defied the world for each other. I thought no worse of them somehow! which I am aware is a most immoral sentiment.[58]

She admired the uncensorious spirit of a woman like Jane Carlyle who lived cheek by jowl in Cheyne Walk with openly acknowledged mistresses and displayed a robust common sense in dealing with an incident of attempted sexual harassment in the street: looking at the man with 'one can well imagine what immeasurable scorn', she 'uttered the one word "Idiot!" and went upon her way'.[59] Nevertheless,

Mrs Oliphant maintained, whatever the accommodations of private life, moral discrimination was important.

As a reviewer she was speedily forced to recognize that her own cautiously discriminating attitude in the matter of fiction likely to be seen by adolescent girls did not seem to be shared by the novel-buying public at large. The melodramatic fiction of the 1860s she diagnosed as a disagreeable facet of the age of equipoise in that it offered excitement to a public palate in search of new sensations. She described Mrs Henry Wood's *East Lynne* as a clever but immoral novel in which the heroine was made interesting only as a consequence of her fall and 'nothing can be more wrong and fatal than to represent the flames of vice as a purifying fiery ordeal, through which the penitent is to come elevated and sublimed'.[60]

The women of easy virtue who have walk-on parts in Mrs Oliphant's novels are drawn in deliberate defiance of a tradition which justified playing with sin by effecting touching redemptions. To effect these redemptions usually required that the sinner should be made exceptionally young, innocent, and morally sensitive, so that her capacity for redemption might be left in no doubt. Having achieved moral salvation, the heroine then achieved sainthood and avoided problems of social ostracism, by dying early. Such girls, in Mrs Oliphant's view, were figments of the middle-class imagination.[61] As a servant tells her young mistress, who is planning to sublimate her sorrows by becoming a missionary to fallen, and therefore presumably miserable, women, her work will be in vain: many of them have heard the message of redemption—'they know it all, every word'—but their easygoing natures militate against their forming any desire to exchange their pampered, happy lives of freedom for the rigour of a penitentiary.[62] The good-hearted whore who appears in this tale, *A Country Gentleman and His Family* (1886), illustrates Mrs Oliphant's thesis. In order to gratify the honourable intentions of a young Englishman in California she agreed to marry him, but left him when the restraints of married life became irksome. Her good nature extended to attempting to free her husband by faking her own death. In order to prolong a melodramatic plot she reappears at the church where her husband has just wed the country gentleman's sister. Although the plot is unconvincing, it is entirely consistent with the girl's character that the impediment she represents should be removed by disclosing that the Californian marriage was invalid because she had previously been through a similar ceremony with a lover in her yet more remote past. The main plot of the same novel is also concerned with the bearing of past relationships upon the present: the country gentleman of the title is an Oxford undergraduate who falls in love with an older woman, the widowed Lady Markland. There is ample evidence to suggest that her early and brief former marriage was less than perfect, nevertheless her spoilt young idealist of a second husband cannot bring himself to accept her history or the evidence, in the shape of a young son, of a past life that did not include him. His morbid jealousy forces the breakdown of this marriage, whereas his sister learns to live with the knowledge of her husband's chequered past.

Like women, the men in her novels enter into mistaken relationships and marriages, but for them the long-term effects seem less catastrophic. 'A man is none the worse for things that would ruin a girl for ever.'[63] When early marriages to lower-class girls are revealed at some later date, the middle-class women of Mrs Oliphant's fiction at least take comfort from the fact that their sons and brothers were not dead to all sense of honour.[64] The most extreme example of this attitude can be found in *Oliver's Bride* (1885), allegedly based upon 'a true story', in which Oliver, who is all set to marry the significantly named Grace Goodheart, is summoned to the deathbed of a prostitute whom he had initially seduced. Although he knows that other men have subsequently treated her worse than he did, he feels honour-bound to go through the wedding ceremony which is her deathbed request. Grace, who knew in general terms that Oliver 'had a past', not only forgives and marries him after the prostitute's death, but admires him for his act of atonement and self-martyrdom.

It is a commonplace of Victorian novel criticism to comment upon the double standards operating in Dickens's private life and his fictional portraits of fallen women. A facile reading of Mrs Oliphant's fiction might suggest that she too colluded with a system that condoned male sexual escapades outside marriage, while condemning women who took the same liberties to banishment from good society. What distinguished her treatment from Dickens's is the explicitness with which she raises the conventions operating in middle-class society. As a reviewer she was outspoken on the issue. Amidst the awed public adulation that characterized the general response to George Eliot's demise, Mrs Oliphant raised a dissenting voice: she attacked the double standards that had allowed her fellow-novelist to be received at her own evaluation as a 'great moral teacher' while enjoying a relationship that was 'morally wrong (without doubt!)' and would not have been tolerated by the public 'in a duchess or a dressmaker'.[65] There is a similar deliberation in the way that her fiction of this period draws attention to the inequities implicit in the rules governing polite society. *The Wizard's Son* (1884) contrasts the lot of the eligible but impecunious spinster and bachelor.

Perhaps she likes too, poor creature, the little excitement of flirtation, the only thing which replaces to her the manifold excitement which men of her kind indulge in—the tumultuous joys of the turf, the charms of play, the delights of the club, the moors, and sport in general, not to speak of all those developments of pleasure, so-called, which are impossible to a woman. She cannot dabble a little in vice as a man can do, and yet return again, and be no worse thought of than before.[66]

'Those developments of pleasure' available to the middle-class man, but not to his sister or prospective bride, are addressed even more bluntly two chapters later in the course of an abortive proposal scene. The girl puts the worst case that gossip has to offer against the man and, in passing, rejects the notion of a woman having a duty to make a morally redemptive self-sacrifice.

'Why should I be asked to step in and save you, from—bitter folly or anything else? And this life that you offer me, are you sure it is fit for an honest girl to take? The old idea that a woman should be sacrificed to reform a man has gone out of fashion. Is that the role you want me to take up?' Katie cried, rising to her feet in her excitement. 'Captain Underwood (whose word I would never take) said you were bad, unworthy a good woman. Is that true?' 'Yes', he said in a low tone, 'it is true.'

When the crestfallen hero finally finds a good woman to accept him he is still looking for a Christlike figure able to absolve him and offer him 'a new life' as though he were 'born again'. The quasi-allegorical nature of this scene might be thought to remove the reader from the uncomfortable reality of human trans-actions, but at the critical moment Mrs Oliphant deliberately reminds us that Oona is but a woman: 'What woman can bear to hear out such a confession, not to interrupt it with pardon, with absolution, with cries to bring out the fairest robe.'[67] The allusion to the parable of the Prodigal Son not only reminds us of Mrs Oliphant's habitually feminine perception of the sacrificial aspect of the Godhead, but aligns this sheltered young girl with the parental role of forgiveness based upon love and knowledge of former wrongdoing. Oona is forced to recognize, before marriage, that her lover is 'no hero', a discovery, the narrator remarks, 'which is often made in after life, but by degrees, and so gently, so imperceptibly, that love suffers but little shock'.[68] Psychologically it seems implausible that Oona's carefully nurtured innocence could survive such a blow, and Mrs Oliphant's comments seem here more appropriate to the slow discoveries that she was making as a mother of two sons. The remark made in her *Autobiography*, after the death of her bachelor son Cecco: 'I think, though he had all a man's experience, that save for one boyish inclination towards a pretty girl, he never put any woman near his mother in his heart', perhaps suggests how few illusions she retained in this area.[69]

In a novel written only two or three years before Cecco's death, she portrayed an aristocratic mother, determined to protect the family inheritance from the marital scheming of a lower-class girl, as relieved to allow her simpleton son the licence of an unaccompanied visit to London. She 'thought cynically, with a woman's half-knowledge, half-suspicion of what that meant—that life as seen in London would cure him entirely of Patty and of the dangers that were concentrated in her . . . Whatever he might do in London, she, at least, could not see it.'[70]

Mrs Oliphant's practice as reviewer and novelist provides interesting comment upon the Podsnappery of her society. She frequently repeats her belief that many girls received their knowledge of human behaviour from fiction and this lays a certain educational responsibility upon novelists. Although she consistently de-nounced works of fiction that seemed deliberately to exploit sordid subject-matter, evasive silences were seen by her as reneging on the artist's responsibility. One of her short stories, 'Norah: The Story of a Wild Irish Girl' (1871),[71] provides an interesting exploration of the artist's dilemma. The story was clearly intended to belong to the loosely linked series *Neighbours on the Green*, which examines the mores of a closely knit and rather old-fashioned provincial community from the viewpoint of a good-hearted, middle-aged woman. The plot of this particular tale involves the maliciously attempted seduction of a newcomer by one of the community's ne'er-do-well sons, Everard Stokes. The narrator feels herself trapped between a desire to say nothing of Everard's reputation, out of friendship for his widowed mother, whose survival has depended upon her ability to blind herself to his wrongdoing, and a desire to speak out for the sake of his intended victim, the young Irish girl. The narrator's perplexities are worsened by the fact that the 'audience' for her warning tale is to some extent an unknown quantity. The feckless, nomadic life led by these impoverished members of the minor Irish aristocracy makes their forthright manners and easy sociability attractive to the reserved occupants of the Green, but the narrator finds it hard to fathom the degree of experience or naïvety that lies beneath their outspokenness. When she and Everard's sister give socially coded warnings as to Everard's reputation these are brushed aside by the assurance that Lady Louisa and her daughter Norah expect young men to 'have a past' in which some girl has been involved. Both the tactful warnings of the narrator and the more explicit but generalized cautions about male behaviour given by the Irish mother prove insufficient to prevent a headstrong girl making her own almost disastrous mistake. The educative activities of both the narrator and the mother have been dangerously hampered by different kinds of deeply embedded taboos. The weight of things unsaid comes to the surface at the end of the tale. The Irish mother's 'foreignness' allows her to voice the unspeakable truth.

'. . . men are but men,' said Lady Louisa . . . We don't talk of such things before the girls, but ye can't mend the creatures, and ye must just swallow them as they are. Sure, when I can't answer for me own boys, I've nothing to do with casting stones at Everard Stoke.'

The life stories of the inhabitants of the Green pay silent tribute to the truth of this statement, but, judged by their social decorum, Lady Louisa's admission has a certain shameless garrulity about it. Meanwhile, Mrs Oliphant, as their creator, has been enabled to air such matters 'before the girls', while also voicing her scepticism as to whether any educative fiction can be effective before experience has schooled her readers' understanding.

Since it must be impossible to predict a tale's moral effect without a precise knowledge of audience, the artist's only safeguard is to tread the mean line, between hypocrisy and a culpably naïve idealism, by clinging to social realism. At the heart of her literary reservations about George Eliot's novels was her judgement that her later heroines, such as Romola and Dorothea, were over-idealized until they became 'the sublimated school-girls of the romance', and that the sinners like Tito were pursued by their author with 'a vindictive and terrible' vengeance.[72] A young female reader of *Middlemarch* in one of Mrs Oliphant's novels confesses that, although her heart is wrung by the picture of Rosamond 'getting worse and worse' and she 'supposes it is true to nature', such pictures seem to conflict with the evidence of her own eyes.

'People are not bad like that in life', said Nora, 'they have such small sins,—they tell fibs—not big lies that mean anything, but small miserable little fibs; and they are ill-tempered, and sometimes cheat a little. That is all. Nothing that is terrible or tragical.'[73]

The point was more succinctly and acerbically made in a letter Mrs Oliphant wrote to John Blackwood:

Many thanks for Middlemarch which I have read with great interest—but not, may I say? with the delight I expected—these superior heroines are very awful people, and of course poor Miss Brooke has got to have her heart broken—I wish George Eliot would not be so harsh upon all mediocrities—for after all mediocrity is the rule and only a very few of the human race can be superior.[74]

Paradoxically it was the distortions of the idealists such as George Eliot or Mrs Humphry Ward that had led ineluctably to the novels of the 'anti-marriage league'. By overestimating the reforming powers of 'women's mysterious influence' these novelists had opened the doors to fiction which exaggerated women's power in the opposite direction. Sue Bridehead, in Hardy's *Jude the Obscure*, incurred Mrs Oliphant's disgust for managing to combine the doubly implausible roles of seductress and Jude's moral mentor, 'holding him on the tiptoe of expectation, with a pretended reserve which is almost more indecent still'.[75]

Hardy's famous posthumous attack upon Mrs Oliphant's article 'The Anti-Marriage League' (as 'the screaming of a poor lady in *Blackwood*') appeared in a decade which established debunking Victorian figures as a fashionable literary pastime.[76] In one swipe Hardy effectively consigned her to the sidelines of literary history and gave undue prominence to an article whose 'headline of horror' has caused it to be more frequently alluded to than read. By caricaturing her as a shrill female prude, Hardy brutally misrepresents the stance of the article, which took advantage of the assumption that anonymity was at least as likely to conceal a male as a female voice, to raise the ways in which novels like Hardy's *Jude*, and the works of the popular novelist Grant Allen, dangerously distorted society's notions of both male and female roles. The specific novels mentioned are used as exemplars of a tendency she detects by which the educative and representative functions of fictions are being eroded, in novels that purport to discuss serious issues, but in fact treat them irresponsibly. The emotional hysteria of which Hardy accuses her is his attempt to dismiss the ironic logic with which she argues her case for the moral necessity of realism. In these novels, she claims, emphasis is repeatedly given to motherhood as 'a development necessary to a woman's full perfection', yet the concept of the indissoluble bond of marriage is simultaneously under attack. Her article concentrates upon the social consequences of this realignment of social mores. The fictional arrangement by which Jude's eldest son simply murders his illegitimate siblings can scarcely be accounted an adequate solution to the problem. Nor did it seem any more reasonable to her that a mother driven by adulterous inclination should expect to deprive the legitimate father of his children.

The plight of the children involved in marital breakdown was not merely a useful weapon to be deployed in her attack upon the novelists of the anti-marriage league: in each case where she herself wrote of a marriage ending in separation there were children to be taken into account. It is instructive to compare Mrs Oliphant's treatment of this subject with George Eliot's. When Janet returns to the dying lawyer Dempster, or Lydgate 'takes up his burden' for life,[77] their thoughts and emotions are untroubled by the complicating factor of considering their spouse's suitability as a father or mother. They make their decisions in an adult environment where marriage can be seen as the most testing human relationship in which to express the Feuerbachian notion that 'God is Love Himself'. By contrast, Mrs Oliphant's definition of the ideal state of marriage emphasizes its contribution to society and its mutuality:

that faithful union of two upon which pure and progressive society is built, which is expressed not in one action but in a hundred, which means the perfect fellowship of joy and sorrow, of interests and of hopes, of mutual help, support, and consolation, which is more certainly to be obtained in marriage than in any other connection or companionship on earth.[78]

It was not until late in her career that Mrs Oliphant brought the problem of marital breakdown to centre-stage in her novels. Where earlier novels had raised the issue it usually remained peripheral to the main narrative considerations. In *The Minister's Wife* (1869) Isabel does have to choose between the child of her first marriage and the peremptory desires of her murderously despotic second husband, but the decision fails to carry moral resonance because the reasons for his enforced exile are sufficient to ensure that readers never consider the alternative of her accompanying him into exile. In *Carità* (1877) the selfish behaviour of grown sons is partly attributed to the mother's self-centred decision many years before to leave her husband to pursue his career in India alone. *Madam* (1884) proved unsuccessful as a forum for examining a failed marriage because the central character's experiences are never sufficiently established as the focus of interest: a failure of nerve on the author's part resulted in the wife's plight deteriorating into melodrama and the plot being handed over to the romantic complications of an insipid stepdaughter. This novel did, however, establish the dilemma that would be developed in later tales: a mother is forced to choose between her children and the demands of an insatiably jealous and increasingly tyrannical husband, but the psychological traits that lead a woman to this impasse are never explored and her children are too easily exploited by the novelist as ciphers through which to punish her betrayal of the duties of motherhood.

In *A Country Gentleman and His Family* (1886) marriage and its breakdown are eventually given pride of place. A young man, who has been accustomed to rule the roost over his widowed mother and sisters, becomes besotted with a young widow who already has a young son by her former marriage. Mrs Oliphant's personal objection to widows remarrying serves as the only flaw in the woman's position, making her feel like 'a Magdalen, ah, worse than Magdalen, though she was doing nothing'. The slow process of disenchantment is well handled as we see the wife's attempts to humour her sulky boy of a husband, her anxious forethought to prevent occasions for displeasure, and her oppressed sense of being punished for unde-clared 'sins'.[79] Matters are brought to a head when her husband focuses his un-reasonable, and therefore unassuageable, jealousy upon her son and forces her to choose between them. Reflecting that a woman can have other husbands while children represent unique God-given chances, the wife is certain that her loyalties must lie with her son and the twin baby daughters of the second marriage.[80] As the novel ends the father exiles himself abroad.

It has been assumed that *A House Divided Against Itself*, which appeared in the same year, was a sequel to *A Country Gentleman*, but it would be more appropriate to describe it as an alternative version of events and Mrs Oliphant seems to have made no demur against the novels' simultaneous publication in serial form either side of the Atlantic. It is as if the self-questioning that was so inclined to overtake her in her autobiographical writings, just as she had adopted a definitive stance, overcame her as she came to the end of a novel in which the narrator's sympathies had been unequivocally and unilaterally given.

The second account complicates the moral clarity with which blame and sym-pathy are apportioned in the first, partly by exposing us to other participants' views, and partly by treating the matter retrospectively when the children of the marriage have themselves attained marriageable age. Mrs Oliphant uses one other obvious ploy to discourage us from reading *A House Divided Against Itself* merely in order to see what happened to the protagonists of *A Country Gentleman*: though the names and arrangements bear a very close resemblance they are sufficiently distinct to suggest a relationship of close analogy rather than direct descent. Markland becomes Markham, Warrender: Waring; and one of the twin daughters has been carried off to Italy to be brought up by her father. As the story unfolds we find the 'innocent' stepson disclosing how his manipulative behaviour had driven a wedge between husband and wife when she found herself unable to control her son and yet was unwilling to allow her new husband to attempt to do so. To the fresh eye of the unsophisticated Italian twin, Lady Markham's renowned 'sweet malleability' seems as much a matter of calculation as do her matchmaking plans for her children. The husband has remained 'what is called sensitive—that is, impatient, self-willed, and unenduring'.[81] His 'gentlemanly' behaviour has consisted of allowing his wife to keep one of the twins, although legally he could have laid claim to both, but this has not extended to informing the daughter living with him of her mother's existence. In the upbringing of the children both parents have been unduly influenced by the attempt to redress the wrongs they imagine themselves to have sustained. Lady Markham's daughter has been allowed an unprecedented degree of freedom of self-determination, until the moment when this brings her into conflict with her mother's will. Her Italian sister, however, has been brought up, like Henry James's

Pansy Osmond, to accept that it is a woman's duty to yield unquestioning obedience to her father.

Recognizing that the code of female self-sacrifice she had so long preached simply did not speak to a younger generation, Mrs Oliphant's tales of the 1890s explore what might be considered sufficient cause to justify female rebellion. Her remaining tales of innocent wives deserted and betrayed by cruel and manipulative husbands, such as *A House in Bloomsbury* (1894), or *Sir Robert's Fortune* (1894), place the crucial events in a bygone world of rural Scotland. The new generation of heroines resent what they see as the moral accommodations practised by their mothers in their attempts to respond to the competing interests of husbands and children. The narrative thrust of *The Duke's Daughter* (1890) largely supports a daughter's bitter impatience with her mother's fence-sitting: 'I sometimes feel that you think nothing is wrong—altogether.'[82] The *Marriage of Elinor* (1891) proceeds from a similar premiss. Elinor's condemnation of her mother, 'You put up with things. You think perhaps they might have been worse. In every way that's your philosophy. And it's killing, killing to all life',[83] forms the well-spring from which she draws the rules with which she conducts her own marriage. When her louche and fraudulent husband refuses to drop his gambling or abandon his flirtations, Elinor deserts him, retreating, with her mother, to the Lake District, where, for the next eighteen years, she devotes herself to the upbringing of the baby whose appearance triggered her decision. Her maternal devotion is unquestioned, but Elinor's actions do not receive the author's unqualified endorsement. Throughout the years of hiding, her mother and her lawyer cousin, both of whom loved her and disliked her husband, repeatedly remind her of the cost of her headstrong pursuit of a personal morality at odds with society's conventions. Their major disapproval is reserved for her refusal to divulge his parentage and expectations to her son. Although she may represent her decision to arrogate complete parental powers for herself as taken in her son's interest, she comes dangerously close to losing his love when she absolutely refuses to enter into explanations with him on the verge of maturity. Moreover, the ending of the novel provides an ambiguous commentary upon the central plank of her self-defence. She has claimed to fear the father's corrupting influence upon the son, but when contact is eventually re-established, the father, much weakened by the ravages of a profligate life, is converted to a premature old age of harmless indolence through his very fear of corrupting his son's wholesome integrity. Whether this represents a triumph for the mother's educational policy or an indictment of a self-righteous woman whose wrongs led her to confuse her husband's moral weakness with real viciousness and caused her to ignore his 'decency' in leaving her unmolested to raise their son, is left a moot point. As in *A House Divided Against Itself* the marital saga ends in the promise of a reconciliation that satisfies social proprieties, though offering little prospect of positive happiness. 'The Story of a Wedding Tour' (1893) finally dispenses with this nod to social convention: it is the story of an orphan girl acquired by a wealthy vulgarian as wife, servant, and object of beauty. A week into their wedding tour fortune suddenly presents her with some money, a room of her own, and the chance to escape.

A sudden energy of resolution seized her. She put on her hat again, and as she looked at herself in the glass encountered the vision of a little face which was new to her. It was not that of Janey, the little governess-pupil; it was not young Mrs Rosendale. It was full of life, and meaning, and energy, and strength. Who was it? Janey? Janey herself, the real woman, whom nobody had ever seen before.[84]

The exhilaration is unmistakable and reminiscent of 'the climbing joy' experienced by Lady Car upon the sudden death of her brutish husband.[85] Such moments evoke a warm response of imaginative sympathy on Mrs Oliphant's part, even if approval is tempered by the penalty subsequent events exact. Given the direct challenge they offer to the dominant code of patient self-sacrifice enacted in her novels, the energy generated by these liberating moments of self-realization is significant. Mrs Oliphant's own life had been marked by accidents of fate that could conventionally only be viewed as tragic losses, but retrospectively assessed might be interpreted as milestones in her own development. When her mother's feuding with her husband was brought to an end by her mother's painful death, she was conscious of 'something like a dreadful relief'. When she looked back upon Frank's own death the image of re-creation is stronger than that of desolation: 'When I thus began the world anew . . .'.[86] It would not be surprising if, looking back upon all she had achieved since Frank's death in 1859, she could see that she had been freed by the necessities of widowhood into a life of continuous creativity.

Another aspect of her personal life in the early 1890s may have prompted this re-evaluation of the limits of a woman's justifiable subordination in marriage. The subject crops up in the most unexpected places: in the opening pages of *The Annals of a Publishing House* she refers to the way in which England has swallowed up a Scottish name and enterprise 'like a husband with his wife, an equally dignified and considerable if not so wealthy name'.[87] In July 1893 Madge had married William Valentine and by October her aunt was writing of her to her sister Denny, 'I think I understand all her moods of mind—and that breaking against the bars of the cage which is most hurtful to one's self, and does no good anyway.'[88] Only a week before she had congratulated herself that, though not to her taste as a person, William Valentine was the answer to her prayers in terms of the material provision he offered her nieces.[89] Like the heroine of 'The Story of a Wedding Tour', Madge found herself pregnant soon after her marriage, and this, if it did not reconcile her to Dundee, at least provided a reason for commitment to the marriage. In 'The Story of a Wedding Tour' the heroine manages to hide herself and her son from her husband in a remote village in France for some ten years, until the emotional impact of a chance encounter on a railway station results in her husband's death from a fatal stroke. But death, as Mrs Oliphant was so aware, is no guarantee of resolution, and the story continued to gnaw at her imagination to produce three loosely related sequels, 'John' (March 1894), 'The Whirl of Youth' (October 1893), and 'A Mysterious Bridegroom' (March 1895).[90] John is the child of the brief marriage and eventually hears, by way of local gossip, that his mother has lied in allowing him to believe her a widow. He finds himself heir to substantial wealth, but having 'lost what I believed in'. The mother now disappears from view: the cost for her has been high, but her decisions have eventually ensured John's opportunity to thrive as a talented painter. The final story, in late-Shakespearian romance fashion, employs the younger generation to right the wrongs wrought and endured by their elders. John falls in love with a girl from the heartlands of bourgeois respectability, an Anglican rectory. Like Madge she has been trained to support herself as an artist, but this marriage is set fair to extend her artistic horizons rather than cancel them. The rector and his wife undergo an educational process, in the course of which they learn to distinguish between 'the essence of the artistic temperament' and mere 'noisy bohemianism'. The acceptance of John, the artist, in the household of an Anglican rectory might be taken as the final justification of his mother's desperate flight from the stultifying vulgarity of mere financial security.

Failed or failing marriages notoriously provide finer grist for the mill of the realist novelist than successful ones. No reader of *Middlemarch*, one supposes, ever wished to spend longer in the company of the Garths at the expense of time spent with the Casaubons or Lydgates. Mrs Oliphant's view of the marital relationship, however, enabled her to find crevices and nooks within which to lodge the hints of irrefragable individuality upon which the novelist's art of characterization must depend. D. H. Lawrence's theory of resistance to the fusion or 'oneness' of individuals in marriage was to serve him well in drawing an absorbing picture of the successful marriage of Tom and Lydia Brangwen in *The Rainbow*. Mrs Oliphant does not, like Lawrence, celebrate the notion of difference, but she does acknowledge it. We have no way of gauging the quality of her own marriage to Frank in the five years left to them after the death of her mother had removed the chief source of friction. The few glimpses yielded by the *Autobiography* suggest a man who wished to mould his wife to the life he had mapped out for his family, whether this involved trying 'in vain (as I can now see) to form me and make me attend to my social duties',[91] or eating up her earnings in the business venture he was temperamentally unsuited to run. Their final months together were coloured by his, to her inexplicable, caprices and self-absorption and retrospectively soured by her discovery that he had known himself to be dying from the outset of their journey to Italy.

The memory of the unequal yoke of her parents' marriage would, if anything, have confirmed the view that she held by 1864 when she wrote of 'this innermost chamber of the heart which no man except a husband can enter and he but a little'.[92] The following picture from an otherwise unnoteworthy novel, *In Trust* (1881), is a measure of the distance that can separate the thoughts of a couple who have survived the longest and most harmonious of marriages. Here we have the hearthside scene after the husband has threatened to change his will in favour of his stepdaughter, merely as a means of coercing his elder daughter into compliance with his wishes.

Thus the two sat within a few feet of each other, life-long companions, knowing still so little of each other—the man playing with the hopes and fears of his dependants, while smiling in his sleeve at the notion of any real occasion for those hopes and fears; the woman much more intent upon the problematical good fortune of her child than the existence of her own other half, her closest and nearest connection, with whom her life had been so long identified. Perhaps the revelation of this feeling in her would have been the most cruel disclosure had both states of mind been made apparent to the eye of day. . . . to know that his wife could look his death in the face without flinching, and think more of his will than of the event, which must precede any effect it could have, would have penetrated through all his armour and opened his eyes in the most dolorous way. But he never suspected this.[93]

The contrived nature of the incident lying behind this exploration of disparity and its narrative function in preparing for the husband's sudden death might be thought to deprive this particular observation of typicality. However, Mrs Oliphant is often at her best in providing just those mundane details that give substance to fictional relationships. In *A Poor Gentleman* (1886) Edward Penton, the discontented and impoverished gentleman of the title, returns home, disgruntled by his discovery that he is heir to the estate he has always coveted but lacks the funds to live up to his inheritance: this is expressed in another hearth-side scene where he pokes and rakes the fire violently, rails at his wife for its poor state, and then rejects her offer to get it made up. Yet, in the midst of his petty grievances, he searches for a way of expressing his sense of his own new-found dignity and marks it by an uncharacteristic gesture of physical affection; laying his hands on his wife's shoulder, 'My dear', he says, 'do you know you're Lady Penton now?' Towards the end of the novel, although the family fortunes have improved, marriage retains its familiar contours. The new Lady Penton contemplates the 'chiffonier with plate-glass back and brass ormolu' from her old home which has so long 'formed her highest idea of grandeur' and reluctantly confesses that it will not do for the great house to which they are moving, only to discover that her husband 'has never much liked the thing'.[94]

A certain irritability combined with a degree of oversolicitousness in guarding one another from their secret anxieties characterizes the relations of the happily married elderly couples who are a recurrent feature of her fiction. These couples, such as Colonel and Mrs Chiley in *Miss Marjoribanks*, Captain and Mrs Temple in *Within the Precincts*, or Captain and Mrs Morgan in *Hester*, are either childless or estranged from their children and grandchildren by a daughter's unfortunate marriage. These couples' withdrawal into a life much occupied with valetudinarian concerns, though it may initially seem to offer a warm nest of emotional comfort, comes in the course of the novel to have something of a pathetic consolation in its nature. In these marriages there is an element of role reversal: the husband fusses over the wife, reducing her to an object to be cosseted, and so she loses both the *raisons d'être* of a woman's married life: children and household duties. The position of these wives, psychologically speaking, is little better than those wives and mothers whose husband's refusal to acknowledge their 'careers' drives them to seek compensatory attention in feigned ill-health. Lucilla's mother, Mrs Marjoribanks, had been one such 'who had devoted all her powers, during the last ten years of her life, to the solacement and care of that poor self which other people neglected. The consequence was, that when she disappeared from her sofa—except for the mere physical fact that she was no longer there,—no-one, except her maid, whose occupation was gone, could have found out much difference'.[95] When, in Mrs Oliphant's novels, these Victorian anorexics have the good fortune to outlive their spouses and find themselves with a reduced income and children to feed, they make a speedy recovery to blooming good health.

Romantic love, or *égoïsme à deux*, as Mrs Oliphant more normally labels it, has little to do with a woman's married life. 'The beautiful new world of love and goodness into which the happy bride supposes herself to be entering comes to bear after a while so extraordinary a resemblance to the ordinary mediocre world which she has quitted that the young woman stands aghast and bewildered.'[96] The sense that for most women the real centre of their lives is quickly transferred from a suitor to home and children helps to explain why so many of Mrs Oliphant's suddenly bereaved wives make so swift a recovery. For some, of course, widowhood provides a fresh taste of freedom. Even relegation to the Dower House could provide unexpected pleasures.

Mrs Mountford had never known the satisfaction, almost greater than that of dressing one's self—the delight and amusement of dressing one's house and making it beautiful. She had been taken as a bride to the same furniture which had answered for her predecessor; and though in the course of the last twenty years something had no doubt been renewed, there is no such gratification in a new carpet or curtains, which must be chosen either to suit the previous furniture, or of those homely tints which, according to the usual formula of the shops, 'would look well with anything', as in the blessed task of renovating a whole room at once.[97]

This picture was penned after Mrs Oliphant herself had had twenty years' experience of widowhood. Unsurprisingly, her view of the perplexities of widowhood had been less sanguine immediately after Frank's death. With a touch of Swiftian satire she had used a *Blackwood's* review to advocate the introduction of suttee into Britain as a form of public entertainment which could not be considered cruel if compared with the 'tedious fate nature ordains for those whom society has done with'.[98] The recurrent concerns in her fiction of this period seem to offer corroboration to the hints in her journal that she considered remarrying within a couple of years of Frank's death. A higher adult mortality rate combined with the frequency of large families combined to encourage remarriage. Its conveniences for single-parent families were obvious enough. Some authors contrived to extract romance from the delicate process of weaning widows from their grief and loyalty to the dead and offering them a second chance of happiness, yet this was perhaps more easily achieved in a comic setting where the painful transference could be facilitated by using or exploding stereotypes, as Thackeray does for Amelia Sedley in *Vanity Fair*. Alternatively the widow could be wholly detached from her former married life and reconsigned to the care of her paternal family, as in the case of Trollope's Widow Bold in *Barchester Towers*. Bold may be a name acquired through marriage, nevertheless its resonance attaches to Eleanor as she re-enters the marriage market after a pause whose brevity is measured by the tender age of her baby. Widows gained their comic reputation for predatoriness as much from the unspoken fears aroused by their sexual experience as from the other financial and romantic needs they shared with other 'single women of a certain age'. The uncertainty as to how to classify them socially is seen in the tendency to categorize widows in fiction either as scheming women bent upon securing the advantages of a second marriage or as saintly sufferers dedicated to a life of semi-conventual seclusion.

Being widowed prematurely gave Mrs Oliphant cause to consider these stereotypes carefully. When married she had herself been guilty of drawing stereotypical predators such as the 'nice' Mrs Herbert of *Orphans* (1858) who unsuitably presents herself for the second time at the altar, sporting the orange blossoms associated with virginity.[99] At about the time she must have been considering the Reverend Robert Story's proposal she aired the popular prejudice on this matter in a two-part story for *Blackwood's*, 'Mrs Clifford's Marriage':[100] the chapter headings for the first part tell their own story: 'The Ladies' Opinion', 'What the Gentlemen Said', 'What the Children had to Say', 'Her Own Thoughts', and 'The Marriage'. Mrs Clifford, mother of five young children, is permitted to remarry, but not before her creator has put her through the mill of malicious gossip and well-intentioned advice. Moreover, we are treated to the full embarrassment of the couple's nuptials surrounded by a congregation whose opinions they know all too well. At the 'terrible' moment when Mrs Clifford is forced to repeat the words of the marriage vow she breaks down, and the episode does not end until we are firmly reinstalled in the world of gossip and speculation rife at the wedding breakfast after the couple have left. The second part is an anticlimax: despite the new husband's high-handed and illegal attempts to deprive his eldest stepson of the estate, the couple eventually settle down to a life 'no unhappier than that of most married folk'. The problem Mrs Oliphant experienced with the second part of the tale was that she could not imagine a mother irresponsible enough to remarry without having secured the best arrangements for her children, nor a man sufficiently two-faced to marry a mother of five solely for her wealth.

According to her journal, Mrs Oliphant had made the decision against remarriage fairly easily, experiencing 'some hours very fanciful and some internal struggles which there is no comfort in recalling, but no harm to speak of'.[101] In her fiction of this period she was at least content to allow for the chances of success and happiness outweighing the misgivings that had influenced her. It was her daughter Maggie's death, rather than Frank's, that seemed to have given definitive shape to her views on widowhood and remarriage. From 1864 onwards it is difficult to think of a widowed mother in her fiction who remarries without either suffering herself or being forced to see her loyalties split between her new husband and her children by the previous marriage. The simple explanation would be that Mrs Oliphant was forced to comfort herself for a pointless self-sacrifice on behalf of a child old enough to remember Frank by reassuring herself that 'It is not, nor it cannot come to good'. The relationship between Maggie's death and her elevation of widowhood to a semi-religious status, to default from which could only be accounted 'a sort of atheism, a giving up of the religion of the immortal',[102] seems more complex. The shock of the abrupt termination of her relationship with Maggie, 'who would have been at least for all the set years of her youth my constant companion by night or day', prompted Mrs Oliphant to intense speculation about relationships beyond the grave.

Do they sleep until the great day? Or does time so cease for them that it seems but a matter of hours and minutes till we meet again? God who is Love cannot give immortality and annihilate affection; that surely, at least, we must take for granted—as sure as they live to love us. . . . They neither marry nor give in marriage our Lord said, but if heaven was ignorant of the bonds of nature it surely would be no heaven for the spirits of men. Do they dwell in families, in long succession of kindred and race? Was my mother called to receive the child who was her baby as well as mine?[103]

In this light, keeping faith with a dead husband can be seen as a witness to and guarantee of a personal immortality which will permit even more strongly desired reunions to take place.

After Maggie's death even the widowers who make second marriages, often to provide homes for the devoted governesses who have brought up their children, become anxious as they approach death. The elderly schoolmaster, father of 'the greatest heiress in England', explains his dilemma thus to his daughter:

People say that you show how happy you've been with the first when you get a second, but I don't go in with that. When I think of facing these two women and not knowing which I belong to, I—I don't like it, Lucy. Lucilla was always very considerate, and made great allowances, but there are things a woman can't be expected to put up with, and I don't like the thought.[104]

Since Mrs Oliphant believed men to be by nature less morally and spiritually sensitive, she could afford to treat their anxieties on this head with 'humour and half-ludicrous pathos'.[105] The cluster of portraits of widowers considering remarriage drawn in the period 1877–8[106] may have been sparked off by discussing Leslie Stephen's behaviour with Annie Thackeray, her great friend and his sister-in-law. In a gossipy letter she wrote of him, to John Blackwood, 'He appeared the most heartbroken of bereaved husbands two years ago, as well as the most melancholy of men—he is now just on the eve of a second marriage.'[107] Stephen could perhaps be forgiven on account of his children and his disbelief in immortality, but when a man like Laurence Oliphant, who had aspired to higher things, succumbed and married his assistant, claiming her to be a medium who brought him into close contact with the spirit of his first wife, Mrs Oliphant's scorn was sufficient to prevent her visiting him as he lay dying.[108]

There was nothing light-hearted in her almost obsessive treatment of the subject of widowed mothers in the years immediately following Maggie's death. The morbid novel *Agnes* (1865) has a consolatory would-be suitor hovering in the background by the end of the novel, but Agnes is understandably too bowed down with grief over the appalling accidental death of her son to show any interest in him. He exists partly to attest to the continuing eligibility of a girl whose simple dignity has raised her from blacksmith's daughter to a baronet's family, and partly as an excuse for Mrs Oliphant to give vent to her own frustrations: 'To live that vicarious life which is called living in one's children, it is necessary to avoid all personal crises, and those moments of individual existence which will arise by times, even in the mind of a woman, before age has calmed everything down.'[109] In *Madonna Mary* (1866), which appeared the following year, the widowed mother of three infant sons actually acquires her creator's sobriquet, 'Madonna', and is left, uncourted, 'To judge for herself, and do the best that in her lay, and take all the responsibilities upon her own head, whatever might follow; to know that nobody now in all the world was for her, or stood by her, except in a very secondary way'.[110] Three years later things had changed and the widowed heroine of *The Three Brothers* (1870) is no longer a *madonna pietà* grieving for her children, but has been transformed to an artist breadwinner and has acquired the honorary title of Padrona. When a younger suitor appears for her hand, she finds that her children have filled a husband's place, and when, worse still, her much-cherished daughter receives a proposal, she finds she is 'content, more than content to work late and early, to spare herself in nothing, to labour with both hands, as it were, never grudging. Only her children, that was all she asked to have!'[111] Moreover, her very renunciation of the personal consolation of marriage gives her a saintly elevation that she would lose, even in her lover's eyes, were she to descend to accept mortal consolation. Yet even this widow remains vulnerable at one point, and for the first time Mrs Oliphant allows herself the fictional exploration of a wound her imagination had opened up for her at Maggie's death: 'Had she lived to be married or to sustain any of the great changes of life I must, when the time had come, have stood back and refrained from interfering with her happiness even if to do so had made an end of my own.'[112]

Widowed mothers merely exemplify more purely, because their love is uncontaminated by the consolation sometimes proffered by a husband, the self-sacrificial heroic ideal of womanhood incarnated in motherhood.

Recently, Mrs Oliphant's presentation of motherhood has been attacked as on the one hand a 'resort to popular sentiments about mothers and religion',[113] or an over-personal identification, resulting in demands for pity that the reader does not wish to give.[114] The first criticism is astute in diagnosing the link between motherhood and religion in her writing but less so in attributing this to popular Victorian mythology. In the light of her reviewing experience of early Victorian novelists Mrs Oliphant clearly believed that she was fighting against the popular trend in her portraits of mothers. From her earliest days as a critic she had condemned

Dickens's portraits of motherhood for succumbing either to sentimental stereo-typing or producing degrading caricatures. 'Mrs Nickleby', she wrote to John Blackwood, 'is a picture which I always regard with both disgust and resentment, as every one must I think who has honoured a mother, as a mother should be honoured.'[115] Given this outburst against Dickens's portrayal of the weak-minded, self-pitying Mrs Nickleby, it may seem surprising that in 1861 Mrs Oliphant could write to Isabella Blackwood of her plans for the development of Mrs Fred Rider, a mother who was to be widowed and then remarry in *The Doctor's Family*: 'Now that you have read a little more of it, you will see that I want to represent one of my women as a *fool*, which character, I think, wants elucidating, and has not received its due weight in the world of fiction.'[116] Susan Rider, in addition to being languid and unreasoning in Nickleby fashion, is also capable of being 'insolent' and 'spite-ful' when crossed, or of exerting her feminine charms sufficiently to attract a rugged Australian Bushman as a second husband. The ease with which she finally abandons one of her own children should surely have provoked 'disgust and resent-ment' in those who 'honour a mother', but Mrs Oliphant is careful to emphasize to Isabella Blackwood that Susan Rider is a 'secondary character' in the story. She is contrasted with her single sister, Nettie, whose selfless efforts on behalf of her 'family' embody Mrs Oliphant's ideal of 'motherhood', which she never confined to biological parentage. Having vested respect for motherhood in Nettie, Mrs Oliphant can then afford to treat Susan with greater realism than Dickens can Mrs Nickleby: as evidence of Mrs Nickleby's children's noble-minded integrity they continue to treat her with filial devotion and respect despite her obvious folly and selfishness. Not only does one of Susan's young children prefer to stay with his aunt rather than return to Australia with his feckless mother, but Nettie, in the midst of her selfless slavery, retains an acerbically realistic sense of her sister's egotism and her own exploitation.

Feeble and foolish mothers abound in her fiction, although very few are without some plaintive attachment to their offspring. For the majority of her female charac-ters the maternal instinct is innate, but, inasmuch as it is an instinct requiring careful moral discipline, it could also be held responsible for some of the less attractive ways in which human love appeared to operate. In *The Heir Presumptive and the Heir Apparent* (1891) a mother's outrage at a threat to her children's inheritance prompts her to contemplate the murder of the cuckoo in the nest. Although in this case Mrs Oliphant's view served as the basis for high melodrama, more often it enabled her to avoid the temptations of the stereotypical. Few authors are better at both acknowledging the repetitive patterns of human behaviour that lie behind such stock figures as the wicked stepmother or the interfering mother-in-law and allowing us to see why the particularities of their circumstances drive them to repeat the mistakes of generations. Stepmothers in her tales are in general terms far better disposed than stepfathers to the children their marriage brings as an inheritance: this makes good sense since the proposal they have received is usually predicated upon their ability or willingness to fill the vacant post of 'mother'.

However, when, subsequently, the interests of the children they have themselves conceived conflicts with that of their stepchildren, it can scarcely be considered surprising that they harbour a certain partiality for their own. Although the plot of *In Trust* (1881) depends upon just such an opportunity presenting itself for a mother to further her daughter at the expense of her stepdaughter, all three women accept this as 'natural' if not commendable and they continue to live together in relative amity. Mrs Oliphant's own experience as substitute mother to her nephew and nieces, whose presence was sometimes sharply resented by her own sons, could not but have given her an insight into the prejudices to which maternal love inclined.

Similarly, her own history had revealed to her something of the rivalry and jealousies to which the maternal heart might succumb in contemplating an off-spring's marriage. No evidence survives of her relation with Frank's mother, but her own parents' decision, so soon after her marriage, to move from Birkenhead to London to be near her mother's best-loved child cost Margaret the most 'intoler-able moments' of her life as 'the silent (not always silent) conflict' over her mounted to such a pitch that she was forced by her husband's 'foolish ideas about a mother-in-law' to steal 'to her daily though she never crossed my doors'.[117] In *Lilliesleaf* (1855) she draws her only portrait of this period of 'a fretting, carping, restless old woman, neither lovely to see nor to hear', causing trouble by her endless criticisms of her daughter-in-law's handling of her son's misbehaviour, but her peripheral presence in the novel seems designed merely to add one more element to the wife's suffering rather than to encourage understanding of the position of mothers-in-law. Two other novels of this period contain the narrator's endorsement of the trouble in store for those who plan on housing a mother-in-law and her child under the same roof.[118] It is possible that her mother's death made the 'in-law' relationship too painful to revisit immediately: it was not until *A Beleaguered City* (1879) that the topic received a fresh airing. Even here the contrast between mother-in-law and daughter-in-law is developed only to the point of proving that women's tempera-ments are more varied than the complacent, generalizing Mayor believes. Whatever the reason, in later fiction we are treated only to mothers admitting to themselves their fears of exclusion and loss as they see a son or a daughter heading happily toward marriage.[119] As she grew older and her sons reached marriageable age, her fictional mothers occasionally look back ruefully upon the jealousy they felt as young wives of the affection expressed by a husband for his mother, and pray against hope that history will not repeat itself.[120] Even fictional probing of the scar tissue did not lessen the pain when it came. In one of those apparently freakishly prescient scenes her psychologically exploratory form of fiction sometimes gave rise to, *Kirsteen*, written the year before Tiddy's death, presents us with a bereaved mother who cannot admit that a mere lover could have shared a mother's place in her son's affections: 'Calamity had made her severe and terrible, she who had once been kind . . . "Lassie", said Mrs Drummond, "What are you, a young thing, that will love again and mairry another man, and have bairns at your breast that are not his?" '[121] Kirsteen's fidelity 'even unto death' puts the mother to shame, but when, some four months after this episode had been published, Mrs Oliphant found herself in the same position as Mrs Drummond she was inclined to be no more generous in yielding place to a lover.[122]

In her later novels she was inclined to represent the bond between widowed mothers and their sons as closer than and therefore more vulnerable to disappointment than any other. When reading the opening chapters of *The Wizard's Son* one has cause to be grateful that nightly family readings of the work in progress had fallen into desuetude. With unsparing hand Mrs Oliphant transferred on to the novel's canvas the unbearable mundane reality of the embattled relations to which a widowed mother and her son have been brought.

Home! This is what it had come to be; and nothing could mend it so far as either mother or son could see. Oh terrible incompatibility, unapproachableness of one soul to another! To think that they should be so near, yet so far away. Even in the case of husband and wife the severance is scarcely so terrible; for they have come towards each other out of different spheres, and if they do not amalgamate there are many secondary causes that may be blamed, differences of nature and training and thought. But a mother with her child, whom she has brought up, whose first opinion she has implanted, who ought naturally to be influenced by her ways of thinking, and even by prejudices and superstitions in favour of her way![123]

At first sight this rhetorical apostrophizing of home and motherhood may seem set fair for a celebration of just the kind of vaguely religious maternal piety for which she has been criticized. But though Walter Methven, the son, may be a Prodigal, his mother's capacity to produce an atmosphere heavy with unspoken reproach constantly mars her capacity for the saintly self-sacrifice to which she aspires in her best moments.

The plot of this novel gives frank recognition to the fact that Walter Methven's salvation depends upon finding an independent path in life: the drama of his life lies elsewhere, and it is not under his mother's tutelage but through his long-forgotten father's patrimony that he finds himself. Attempted *rapprochements* with his mother bring her as much pain as balm, since both of them are aware that he can only revert to a childhood habit of casting his burdens upon her, and she is trapped, even in her most strenuous efforts of selflessness, by her consciousness of previous rebuffs. Mrs Methven's habitual self-control, the product of the years in which she has sought not to drive her son from her, turns into a scourge when she witnesses the consolation offered to an apparently bereaved mother who has never had cause for self-restraint in her relation with her daughter. At the end of the novel she learns more readily than some to welcome a daughter-in-law because she recognizes that she had not really 'possessed' her son for many years. The sombre power of this tale of the supernatural in part depends upon its refusal to allow fairy-tale reversals of fortune to interfere with the relentless evolution of familial relationship. The characterization of Mrs Methven, who is conscious of the partial truths implicit in others' criticism of her single-minded devotion to her son and only too aware of the part that her thwarted ambition plays in souring their relationship, perhaps pro-

vides the best qualification to the criticism that Mrs Oliphant's vision of motherhood as a woman's mode of fulfilment seeks a pity for disappointed mothers that as
readers we are unwilling to give and, in real life, placed impossible demands upon
her sons.[124] The poignant assessment of the ravages wrought by the sensation of
powerlessness, contained in *The Wizard's Son*, was penned at a time when Mrs
Oliphant's own anxiety over Tiddy's indifference and seemingly calculated disregard of her wishes was best represented for her by the 'image of Shelley's
"Prometheus"'.[125]

There can be little doubt that her anxious fussing over her constitutionally weak
sons did produce a sullen resentment in them that lodged itself as a poisoned dart
in the maternal heart, but it is a tribute to her integrity as an artist, rather than a
proof of her evasive sentimentality, that she was prepared to place these matters at
the centre of her fictional agenda. Knowledge of her personal sufferings at this time
may, of course, tempt us to lend a greater degree of sympathy to Mrs Methven than
the narrative actually warrants, but Mrs Oliphant's own resistance to over-identi-
fication with the particular case was aided by her capacity to identify the dilemma
she represented here and elsewhere as endemic to the Victorian ideal of womanhood rather than a purely personal cause of suffering.

The novel *Harry Joscelyn* (1881) is a particularly compelling example of her
ability to draw upon personal anxieties but to reallocate temperamental tendencies
and conflicting desires and emotions amongst a variety of characters from whom
total authorial approval or identification is always withheld. When the novel appeared, she could reasonably have expected that her days as maternal provider were
numbered: Tids and Cecco were adults and her youngest niece was 16. The novel
depicts a family similarly poised upon the brink of change: the elder children have
already flown the nest, and, within chapters, two of the remaining three have left,
the daughter to make a pragmatic marriage while the son, maddened by his father's
brutal tyranny, flees to start a new life under an assumed name. After thirty-five
years of marital tyranny the mother has been reduced to a nervous, ineffectually
fretting cipher. What makes the first volume interesting is the way in which Mrs
Oliphant encourages us to divide our sympathies equally between the feeble mother
and her stolidly unemotional daughter. We share Joan's affectionate contempt for
her mother's 'half-fictitious' fussing: 'What good could it do? Why couldn't she sit
down and get her work, and occupy herself?', and yet the amusement that Joan
displays at her worthy suitor when he appears as 'a man in love', though we know
Mrs Oliphant herself to have experienced this reaction, is presented as evidence of
an altogether too phlegmatic nature. Furthermore, Joan's unflinchingly hard-
headed approach to life, it is suggested, may result in another kind of deprivation
and misery.

'It's hard to say what's the good of us women', she said, 'to rear children and never have them
but when they're babies, and think all the world of them, and watch them go away. Phil and
me, we are best without any, though that's a hard trial too. But, mother, don't you make a
fuss, poor dear. It's the way of the world, and it's the course of nature, and there isn't a word
to say.'

The mother's wretchedness is compounded when she looks at her married sons, with 'the slow coming down of heart and hope by which a woman arrives at the fact that her child is not ideal, nor even excellent, nor superior in any way to the coarsest common pâte of man'. Nevertheless, in the course of the years that pass while we follow the career of the exiled son, Harry Joscelyn, life changes too in the parental home. Although there has been no visible act of contrition, the father has mellowed and drawn closer to his wife in their shared solitude. The various children's determination to make peace with their parents speaks for the devotion which their mother had inspired in them, and, as the last page approaches, the reader confidently predicts a happy ending for all. Typically the twist comes in the final sentence of the novel, which, in the very act of celebrating the mother's transformation from disregarded victim into a successful wife and mother, returns us as readers to contemplate not just the message of this particular fiction but motherhood and our evaluation of it. 'She saw her children now and then, and they were all happy and in no need of her. What could any woman desire more?'[126]

The ironies implicit in that final question are multiple. Mrs Oliphant's own dearest wish in 1881 was to launch her indolent children upon independent careers, but she was also profoundly aware that what society at large would see as the proof of her success as a mother would for her be the recipe for personal loneliness and loss. With one open-ended question she had raised the ghost of many Victorian women's fears (fears that have been complicated rather than allayed by late twentieth-century patterns of working motherhood); if the greatest part of women's efforts, love, and imagination are poured into fulfilling their children's needs, what is left for them when those needs have been fulfilled?

Although her *Autobiography* does labour her consciousness of her special plight as a widowed mother, it is noteworthy that the question as it is raised in this novel is deliberately applied to all mothers. From the days of her own cosseted childhood Mrs Oliphant had recognized women's tendency to wish to fulfil themselves and make up for their own disappointments or frustrated ambition through the lives of their children. When her own children were still quite young she had written of a mother who suddenly found her plans frustrated by her son whom she had been preparing to stay in his own home, working as his father's curate, to improve upon his father's life, and to carry out and develop her own. The educational development of mother and child are paralleled in this story, *John* (1870). Just as the son has to learn not to expect the girl he loves to recompense him for everything he feels he has lost in life, so his mother has to learn that she cannot depend upon her son to undertake the role her husband has so lamentably failed to fill. Her son is shocked by the heartfelt and painful conviction shown by his mother when she assures him that she has discovered that outside 'the comfort of doing God's work' there are no certain rewards to be depended upon. The final proof of this mother's altruism are the preparations she undertakes to help him live an independent life away from home.[127]

Many of her fictional mothers find it well nigh impossible to believe that their sons are not, as Mrs Methven implied, 'possessions' to be cherished, protected, and appropriated as the mother's property. Such an assumption is dangerous for a variety of reasons. For one thing the children may show an unfortunate genetic disposition to resemble their disappointing father. Alternatively, it could be the similarity between mother and son that eventually brings the mother's wishes to nought. A late story, 'The Member's Wife' (1893), rests upon this thesis. When Mr Vickers, an ailing parliamentarian, wishes to give up his seat over Gladstone's Home Rule policy, his wife is mortified by the social come-down this will involve for her. From the moment when her husband abandons his seat she transfers all her energies to preparing her schoolboy son to retrieve the seat and her social position. Her machinations ensure that five years later her son secures the seat, but it is already becoming clear to the mother that the calculating, ambitious spirit she has passed on to and encouraged in her son will prove her own downfall since he will not brook any further exercise of her power.[128]

The contribution made by heredity to a child's disposition was a subject that came to obsess Mrs Oliphant and was most often represented through experiments to efface the paternal inheritance. This tendency was probably partly shaped by her inability to imagine maternal love that could manifest itself in total self-effacement. Only one early story, Orphans (1858), written when her own family circumstances seemed stable, even fleetingly attempts to imagine the circumstances that might lead an impoverished widow to 'give up' her children to a rich benefactress. Once Mrs Oliphant had taken the decision to keep her own children by her at all costs, even if this should involve moving to Harrow or Windsor to secure them an education as day-boys, she was simply incapable of imagining any but the most melodramatic of plots that might effect a separation between mother and children. Secondly, it must have seemed to her that such hereditary defects as she could identify and guard against in her own family had all been transmitted through the male side. Her husband's death from tuberculosis made her always nervous for the state of her sons' chests. More importantly, however, she feared a hereditary element in the chronic alcoholism and accompanying indolence that afflicted her brother Willie. The memory of her father's phlegmatic indifference to everything in his declining years, revived by the all-too-present picture of her brother Frank's repetition of this pattern, must have provided an unflattering contrast with the seemingly boundless energy and resolve of Mrs Oliphant and her mother. Modern science provides some support for heredity as a factor in the predisposition to alcoholism, but since Mrs Oliphant's conviction pre-dated these findings the reasons that led her to espouse it are more interesting than their coincidental rightness.

Her novel, The Son of His Father (1886), written during that dreadful period when she had reason to believe that Cecco was following the same path of drunken dissoluteness already taken by Tids, once again serves both as an illuminating representation and, in part, a self-critique of her beliefs about the hereditary transmission of the disease. The story tells of a tight-lipped, self-controlled mother who ensures that her son is brought up unaware of the scandal his father's drinking, debts, and fraud have brought upon the family. Even though there is no chance of her son being contaminated by the example of a father he believes to be dead, the mother watches him anxiously at every turn for any evidence of a weakness she fears may be hereditary. Here, as in other tales where mothers spy on their grown sons,[129] the mother's distrustful behaviour is sympathetically explored and yet also deplored as resulting in behaviour no more morally admirable than that which it is seeking to combat. Mrs Oliphant's unexplored assumption that the predisposition to alcoholism was a hereditary problem in the male line also emerges very clearly in this tale where the mother makes no comparable effort to hide the evidence of the father's history from her young daughter.

The relative contributions made by parents of either gender was clearly much on her mind at this period when she was driven by Tids's excuse that his life might have been very different had he had a father's example to follow.[130] She had long felt that a son's maternal inheritance was to be judged in moral terms. Lady Byron, for instance, had received some of the blame for her son's subsequent life because she had failed to inspire him with noble ambitions 'at her knee'.[131] Mrs Oliphant's tales of the supernatural, that burgeoned at this period, repeatedly reverted to an exploration of how far moral, spiritual, and emotional characteristics might be said to be gender-determined and whether there might not be a case for radical reconsideration of traditionally assumed distinctions in order to reap the benefits of cross-fertilization. Two stories of this period, the one a supernatural tale, 'The Portrait',[132] and the other a three-volume novel, *The Second Son*, both provide pictures of male adult households from which the mother's presence is absent. The civilizing influence of the drawing-room gives way to the business-dominated life of 'the library', mealtimes are silent or rancorous affairs, and first the ability and finally the desire to express love disappear.

For all her obsessive interest in the mother–child relationship, children themselves play surprisingly little part in her fiction. Her memories of her own childhood, apart from her intense relationship with her mother, were confined, she found in 1885, to a little collection of pictures 'against a vague background'.[133] Early in her career she had tried her hand at writing improving books for children,[134] and was prepared in later life to write for more secular publications like the American magazine *St Nicholas*. She was, nevertheless, keenly aware of 'the limitations that are required for youth. All the complications of love-making are to be left out, I suppose?—which is hard upon a novelist.'[135] One of her early domestic sagas, *Lilliesleaf* (1855), written when her own children were young, did depict a family of four children, sketching in their different personalities with remarkable economy, but usually young people only entered the world of her novels when they were on the verge of joining drawing-room society. By her last decade she openly admitted that she shrank from the task of portraying large fictional families: 'Only Miss Yonge can keep so many threads in her hand and make the reader to see the individuality of each.'[136] In fact this had been true for the majority of her career. Children still in the nursery served, in her work, as constituting the moral task for responsible orphaned heroines. Their illnesses and their easily diverted affections came in useful when Mrs Oliphant wished to evoke sympathy for distraught or estranged mothers. Nevertheless, for most of her career when her eye rested, however briefly, upon fictional children in a normal state of health, she was able to view them with humorous detachment. Only in the very last years was she tempted to draw sentimentalized pictures of lisping tots.[137] In one of her earliest reviews she had criticized Dickens's pictures of childhood suffering as overdone on the grounds that children lived 'in the present moment' alone.[138] It seems possible that she actually underrated her own children's capacity and need to grieve. She encouraged the notion of children's innocent, thoughtless good humour in the midst of adult desolation, partly because it increased the pathos of the adult suffering as seen in the mother who bears all for her children, and partly because it helped her to achieve the public control of her own grief, necessary for a widow to make her way in the world. In the *Autobiography* she makes no mention of how her 6-year-old daughter reacted to her father's death: we are merely left with the touching cameo of the toddler, Cyril, with his beaming little face, comforting his mother unconsciously and singing children's hymns. Until Cecco's outburst a week after his brother's funeral, when he insisted that Cyril was not to be buried under a veil of silence, the strain she had imposed upon her own children by never allowing Maggie's name to be mentioned seems never to have occurred to her.[139] It is possible to catch a glimpse of an emotionally suffocating regime, with the accompanying guilt and resentment that the boys must have felt for their 'bravely' widowed mother, from a remark in the narrative of *The Story of Valentine and His Brother*:

Strangely enough, children show little curiosity in most cases about the parents they have lost. It seems so natural to them, to accept what is, as absolutely unchangeable, the only state of affairs they have ever known, as the state which must be and to which there is no alternative. The very idea of an alternative disturbs the young mind and wounds it.[140]

And yet the tone of these remarks is so robustly commonsensical that it may seem wilfully unjust to raise the spectre of psychological damage done to children by a monster of maternal egotism. The truth, as so often, probably lay somewhere in between; or rather she was both by turn, the responsible mother protecting her children from unnecessary suffering, and the *madonna pietà* figure, heavy with the unspoken grief she insisted it was her right to bear alone.

The complex interweaving of cherished ideologies, honest intentions, and self-deception, tested against a web of particular circumstances and temperaments, that makes up familial relationship is difficult enough for the immediate participants to apprehend, let alone later biographers. The problem is compounded when the main witness is so expert at chameleon-like changes between a variety of artfully constructed experimental egos.

Something of this interpretative challenge can be seen by looking at the figure of Lady Car, who appears in two novels during the course of which she enacts most of the women's relationships to which this chapter has been devoted. In *The Ladies Lindores* (1883) and *Lady Car* (1889) she is by turn depicted as daughter, sister, wife, mother, widow, and remarried. Like Chaucer's 'patient Griselde' her role as the absolute incarnation of the ideal of the self-sacrificing female is easy to identify: it is far harder in both cases to decide how the narratives as a whole evaluate the attempt to live by that ideal. Lady Car has been cited as an example of the way in which Mrs Oliphant used female characters, who cling to the concepts of duty and fulfilment through motherhood, as vehicles for a self-pity which readers are reluctant to endorse.[141] Instead they feel manipulated into offering a compassion that is unjustified because the author has never confronted the root of her character's, and, by implication, her own troubles, which stemmed from making parasitic and impossible demands upon others for her own fulfilment. Yet the passivity with which Lady Car embraces the notions of filial obedience, wifely subservience, and maternal sacrifice, despite the repugnant circumstances in which she is forced to practise them, is the subject for animated debate among other less malleable, but by no means immoral, girls of her own age within the novel. Lady Car's younger sister, Edith, resolutely refuses to marry the very agreeable heir to a dukedom to gratify her father's ambitions. She also criticizes her mother's habit of 'trying to find reasons for what my father wishes, whether it is right or wrong' in defiance of her own conscience. Edith and her friend, Nora, agree that the Bible commands conjugal obedience, but feel that 'there must be distinctions'. Examining the matter impartially Nora even opines that the fault lay with Lady Car. Lord Lindores had not imprisoned or starved his daughter into compliance: 'He had insisted, and she had not been strong enough to stand out. Was it not her fault rather than his?'—a point that the majority of Mrs Oliphant's tales of parents attempting to thwart the course of true love would wholly endorse. Nora even finds herself defending Lady Car's undeniably boorish, tyrannical husband: 'Perhaps she aggravates him a little', she remarks, 'by the absolute submission with which she receives every jibe he throws at her.'[142] When this husband dies suddenly, Mrs Oliphant provides us with a measure of the self-repression that even Lady Car's passive nature has had to apply to conform to the expectations of the dutiful wife. She retires to her room and refuses to see anybody. Her servants interpret this as her consummate act of devotion, going through all the rituals of mourning even for a husband who has bullied her shamefully. The scene the reader is then shown was, as a contemporary reviewer observed, one of the most shocking in Victorian literature. In the privacy of her own room Lady Car gives utterance to her otherwise unspeakable and uncontrollable joy:

Oh, shut out—shut out the light, that nobody might see! close the doors and the shutters in the house of death, and every cranny, that no human eye might descry it! . . . was he dead?— was he dead? struck down in the middle of his days, that man of iron? Oh, the pity of it!— oh, the horror of it! She tried to force herself to feel this—to keep it down, down, that climbing joy in her.[143]

Buoyed up by her sudden sense of release she finds the courage to defy her father and marry a former suitor whom he had dismissed. Yet so ingrained is her practice of self-subordination that her only way of manifesting her love is to prepare a temple for this man, a library in which he can achieve the great works to which she will be the willing handmaiden. Her second husband reveals himself as unworthy of her worship because he is quite content to live the life of a dilettante gentleman on the fruits of her first husband's fortune. Furthermore, he begins to perceive that her desire for him to achieve something worthy of her adulation has turned her into a harsh judge by whose standards he will always fail. Her son is discovered as a lout and a cheat and she does not have that recourse of unhappily married women, 'children in whom to live a new life'. When the men, whom she has used for her self-fulfilment and self-definition, fail her, her self-abnegation is revealed as lack of identity and she falls 'into a sort of petite santé' and slowly fades away in early middle age. It is, of course, possible to read all this as a thinly veiled attack upon Cyril for failing to live up to his mother's ambitions and behaving with scarcely concealed contempt for her values, and the tale betrays a certain envy for a woman whose financial security allows her the luxury of escaping her disappointment in an early death, but the narrative would also suggest that Lady Car's sacrifices have arisen from a combination of passivity and sentimental self-indulgence. She has neither the energy nor the need to find a means of survival that might lead her to oppose others or create a role for herself. The poem she starts to write about 'the dawning of a genius' comes to a halt when she is forced to realize that her son, who was to provide its subject, has been so obdurately resistant to the image in which she has hoped to mould him. Lady Car emerges as, at best, a pathetic woman whose romantic sensitivities are doomed to disappointment, and, at worst, as a woman who embraces the role of victim so readily that she has an uncanny knack for forcing her menfolk into the position of bullies, tyrants, and sullen resentment. Mrs Oliphant, by contrast, had the good sense to turn her disillusion into the hard-paying stuff of anti-idealist fiction. Although Lady Car's misfortunes are not entirely brought upon herself and the strength and power of patriarchal assumptions in these novels is felt to be unjust, it is difficult to see her as either a role model or an unconsciously employed vehicle for eliciting sympathy. Against Lady Car it is worth remembering the praise Mrs Oliphant lavished upon England's Queen Caroline for practising the kinds of accommodation 'that we see continually employed in private life when a clever and sensible woman is linked (unfortunately not a very uncommon circumstance) to an ill-tempered, headstrong and shallow man'.[144]

Part Two
A Woman of Ideas

5 A Scottish Widow's Religious Speculations

1. 'The Fancies of a Believer'

> Of course it could hardly be expected that she should treat ecclesiastical
> questions either with knowledge or with fairness; and she did not.

Such was the obituarist's verdict in *The British Weekly: A Journal of Social and
Christian Progress*.[1] More than a suggestion of a desire to pay off old scores against
a woman who could 'say more easily than most people the things that sting and
blister' pervades this article, and nowhere more clearly than in this imputation of
ignorant prejudice to a woman who had five religious biographies to her credit,
numerous fictional evocations of ecclesiastical dramas, and substantial experience
as a reviewer of religious writings.

As early as 1855 *Blackwood's* had entrusted its new recruit with an essay on
contemporary theology under the remit of her series on Modern Light Literature.
With the Broad Church as her subject, she devoted her attention to F. D. Maurice
as its most contentious figure. Adopting the ground of the average churchgoer, the
review questions whether sceptically inclined theological debate addresses the
needs of the ordinary worshipper who seeks consolation from religious beliefs and
the voice of humane authority from its clergy. Proceeding according to 'the logic of
feeling about what it is appropriate to believe', she expressed her reservations about
Maurice's teaching. Her criticism hinged upon his progressive 'patronage' of the
teaching of the Patriarchs and upon his interpretation of Atonement, which, in
reading Christ's death as a proof of God's love for man, belittled the Crucifixion as
divine overkill—'the only instance on record of waste of means and unnecessary
expenditure on the part of God'.[2]

Her repeated denunciations of the Doubt infesting Victorian religious debate
might lead one to identify her as a fundamentalist, but her eclectic reading and
interest in eccentric religious positions give the lie to this. In as far as she disapproved of the Broad Church position it was because it seemed to purvey equivo-
cation and uncertainty: nevertheless, when her daughter died, she did not hesitate
to write to Maurice to see if his theology had any consolation to offer.[3] The bedrock
security, as she saw it, of her own faith in God's existence allowed her outbursts
against God's unfathomable ways that outdo Job's and caused offence to some
readers.[4] The heavenly guide who conducted her Little Pilgrim back to earth to
witness the lamentations of bereaved parents tells his pupil that although they are
undoubtedly 'to blame' for their excessive grief, none can be found, even in heaven,
to do so because throughout they 'clung to Him still'.[5] She wholly refused to

recognize any kinship between inadequacy in meeting the tests of faith and actual disbelief.

Disbelief is not granted a voice in her fiction. The one apparent exception to this rule is Halbert Melville, who falls prey to a diabolic seducer peddling 'the captious search for seeing flaws and incongruities' under the name of 'truth-seeking'. Halbert's mental and spiritual disintegration is taken seriously enough, but since the specific nature of his doubt is never revealed, a 'sea-change' is easily effected during a period of self-exile in America. Welcomed once more by family and friends he is enabled, as a minister, to redeem his erstwhile spiritual seducer. Halbert's ominously veiled references to 'the profligate company into which he had fallen during his period of unbelief aligns *Christian Melville* (1856) with the prevailing orthodoxy at the time of its composition (1845): that morality was inextricably bound up with Christian belief.[6] Like many another Victorian, Mrs Oliphant's reading of Tennyson's *In Memoriam* was to be highly selective and largely ignored his bold defence of the moral integrity compatible with 'honest Doubt'.

The young men luxuriating in doubts which incapacitate them for the ministry, who occasionally make an appearance in her fiction, are invariably dismissed as immature, indolent, and self-opinionated.[7] It is possible that her early diatribes against 'the schoolboy vanity of modern criticism and the solemn coxcombry of intellectual unbelief' were fomented by daily exposure to Sebastian Evans, her husband's young and well-to-do collaborator, who took up the stained-glass-window business while 'drifting' because his doubts 'would not let him go into the Church'.[8]

Even in the heart of orthodox Anglicanism Mrs Oliphant diagnosed an increasing inability to speak to the extremities of the average worshipper's need. The rationalizing clerical liberalizers of her middle period give way in the later fiction[9] to men who are socially and spiritually inadequate to deal with the challenges with which they are faced and leave the moral tide of life to be carried by their womenfolk. Apparent exceptions only prove the rule. In 'The Golden Rule' (1891),[10] a country vicar goes to London in a conscientious attempt to enlighten his black sheep son's prospective bride and wealthy father-in-law as to his son's dismal record. The self-imposed agony of his position, however, is interpreted by the girl and her father as a piece of wholly anachronistic chivalry in an age when an American girl frankly welcomes a weak young man whom she can mould to her own design. A tale which ostensibly prizes honesty as the best policy actually reveals its central character, the vicar, as a failed father and priest in a world where the promise of material reward is more likely to effect moral reformation than is well-meaning sermonizing. A couple of years later 'A Mysterious Bridegroom', one of a loosely linked series of short stories, openly founded its comic success on the woeful combination of worldly naïvety and entrenched bourgeois morality of a vicar whose daughter's happiness is to be entrusted to an artist of unknown background. [11] The *Pall Mall*'s illustrator served Mrs Oliphant well in recognizing the significance of the scene in which the vicar's wife pursues him to his den and carries on her argument by remorselessly tidying away his books, thus removing his last fortification against the concerns of daily life. The Established Church, Mrs Oliphant believed, had long ago bankrupted itself spiritually by elevating scholarship over pastoral concerns or by dissipating its energy in inept social work. *The Rector* (1862) embodies the former criticism with all the clarity available to an author brought up in the Scots tradition, which offered a non-élitist education and system of preferment to lay student and ordinand alike. Mr Proctor, 'cloistered in All Souls for fifteen years of his life', embarks upon the parochial ministry without preparation, so that he may give his elderly mother a home. Yet the genteel comedy the tale seems to promise soon finds itself encompassing more serious issues. Faced with a distraught soul seeking the Church's consolation on her deathbed, the Reverend Morley Proctor has neither the habit of spirituality nor the experience of practical ministry to draw upon.

> For the first time in his life he set himself to inquire what was his supposed business in this world. His treatise on the Greek verb, and his new edition of Sophocles, were highly creditable to the Fellow of All Souls; but how about the Rector of Carlingford? What was he doing here, among that little world of human creatures who were dying, being born, perishing, suffering, falling into misfortune and anguish, and all manner of human vicissitudes, every day? . . . Was he a Christian priest, or what was he?[12]

This comparatively early tale allows Proctor, and Anglicanism, a second chance; it concludes with an epic allusion, reduced, as was Mrs Oliphant's way, to the diminished possibilities of nineteenth-century life, when we see Proctor, self-expelled, for the second time, from his now 'uneasy paradise' of All Souls, 'setting forth untimely, but not too late, into this laborious world'; a vision which is given some substance when he makes a brief reappearance in *The Perpetual Curate* (1864).

After she had taken up residence in the ecclesiastical purlieus of Windsor Mrs Oliphant became less inclined to take so rosy a view of the Church's capacity to reform itself. In 1871 she produced a blistering response to the view that the Anglican Church provided a trained body of men strategically sited throughout the kingdom to remedy the nation's ills. She painted instead the bitter and ineffectual sacrifice made by urban priests and the society-oriented lives enjoyed by the croquet-playing curates of 'gay Rectors', the triviality of whose pastimes was an admission of the hopelessness of their task.[13] In *The Curate in Charge* (1876) the Anglican system of patronage is blamed for this malaise—a cause probably suggested to her by her friend John Tulloch's success in reforming the rules of Scottish patronage in 1874. Yet, however low her incumbents sink into egoism, listlessness, indolence, disillusion, debt, or fraud, her fiction reveals none of the thoroughgoing clerical hypocrites who skulk through the pages of so many contemporary novelists. This was not a matter of chance. 'That there are bad men and vulgar men, I do not doubt, among the servants of the churches,' she told John Blackwood, 'but I cannot help resenting the perpetual reproduction of such a filthy reptile as [Dickens's] Chadband as a type of the class and I condemn it quite as much on behalf of *art* as of truth.'[14] Poor, hopeless brother Willie's ministerial failure had shown her that the ordained 'were but men as other men', reacting as their temperaments disposed them to the trials of daily life.[15] Moments of honest self-analysis, and a vague, if ineffectual, desire to help others are perhaps the highest to which even her finest fictional clerics aspire, and they are not vouchsafed the transcendent or visionary experiences occasionally granted to the laity in her works.

The clergy whom she valued as personal friends, Robert Herbert Story and Principal John Tulloch, were active men, ecclesiastical leaders, university administrators, both, in their time, moderators of the general assembly of the Church of Scotland, not theologians, philanthropists, or saints. Yet the very talents which attracted her to these men epitomized the predicament of the nineteenth-century world as she saw it. They were good men in their way, conscientious administrators, caring fathers and husbands, and yet unable at the times that counted most, of bereavement and grief, to penetrate further into the mystery of things than Mrs Oliphant herself. [16] The genial liberalizing spirit with which Tulloch, in particular, wished to reinterpret the Church of Scotland to itself, simply failed to address 'the terrible enigma God had given' her to read in the death of her daughter. The best he could do was to recommend Tennyson's *In Memoriam* as 'an embodiment of the spirit of this age, which he says does not know what to think, yet thinks and wonders and stops itself, and thinks again; which believes and does not believe, and perhaps, I think, carries the human yearning and longing further than it was ever carried before'. This did not take her any further than her 'own thoughts', which were 'much of the same kind', and certainly offered none of the authority for which she, like so many contemporaries, occasionally yearned.[17] To Mrs Oliphant, who believed in calling a theological spade a spade,[18] Tulloch appeared 'naturally tolerant almost to excess of every independent belief or disbelief'.[19]

Tulloch's son was outspoken on the matter of Mrs Oliphant's own dogmatic streak.

In fact it was difficult to discuss any such matters [of belief] with her so impatient was she of argument on the subject. Somehow it seemed to me she could never understand or sympathise with those who took views differing from her own, and she was not slow to pour ridicule on you or your favourites if they were not hers.[20]

It was perhaps this trait in her personality that had excited her interest in three of the five men whose religious biographies she was to write. Passionately held convictions had led Irving, Montalembert, and Laurence Oliphant to occupy sometimes beleaguered positions on the nineteenth-century religious landscape. Although these biographies were commissioned work, these three men seem to have appealed to her creative sympathy in a way in which Thomas Chalmers and John Tulloch, her other subjects, did not. The biography of Chalmers (1780–1847), the Evangelical churchman and professor, who had emerged as the first moderator of the free Church of Scotland after the disruption of 1843, is frankly dull stuff. Despite her reputed admiration for this man whose thinking on Erastianism and social matters seems to have left its mark upon the practices of the Wilson and Oliphant families, the biography is little more than a competently executed précis of the standard four-volume work by Chalmers's son-in-law, Hanna. It was written to order for Methuen's English Leaders of Religion series—a series which was to include other 'brief lives' such as Handley Moule's *Simeon* and R. H. Hutton's *Cardinal Newman*. The years that had elapsed between Mrs Oliphant's youthful espousal of Chalmers's teaching and her biography (1893) had revealed that the figures to whom she subsequently warmed, such as Erskine of Linlathen and Campbell of Row, had been progressives, whereas Chalmers's role during the time of their ecclesiastical prosecutions could at best be interpreted as cautious reticence and at worst as cowardly silence. Tulloch's biography, undertaken at the family's request, proved 'very troublesome work: a world of letters to read':[21] it brought her neither financial profit nor the gratitude of the Tulloch family, who, it was claimed, 'passionately disliked and disavowed it'.[22]

It was not only the strength of their convictions that attracted Mrs Oliphant to Irving, Montalembert, and Laurence Oliphant. They shared two further character-istics: first, they were, in their various ways, 'outsiders'; secondly, they each exhibited an extraordinary combination of worldliness and a naïve enthusiasm for the supernatural. These two factors, linking men of otherwise disparate beliefs and circumstances, provide a key to Mrs Oliphant's own religious position and writings.

To start with the notion of 'outsider' status. These men may seem unlikely cases for invoking mirror recognition in a female biographer, but she had begun work upon the first two in early widowhood at a time when she felt herself very much a solitary figure bravely fighting the establishment (in this case the world of male publishers) for recognition. Moreover, by the time of her first article upon Irving she had, like him, experienced Scottish religious life, both in Scotland and in its exiled version, and had come into contact with the more eclectic experiences London had to offer. She had glimpsed something of the excitement and ensuing bitterness that accompanied breakaway movements in her childhood experience of the 1843 disruption in the Church of Scotland, and her family's 'warm' advocacy of the Free Church predisposed her to sympathize with seceders rather than with a conservative remnant. Out of the vagaries of Irving's spiritual pilgrimage she was able to sculpt the life of one of the last romantics, who died 'isolated, deluded but unstained'.[23] In later life she openly admitted the partisan attitude she had adopted in her research procedures. The Catholic Apostolic Church had been impressed by the tenor of her 'trailer' article in *Blackwood's* and Henry Drummond, one of its leaders, had invited her to visit them because 'he had a notion, which my Roman Catholic friends always share, that since I went so far with them I must go the whole way'.

These good people thought, partly because of their deep sense of their own importance, and partly by a trick of sympathy which I had, and most genuine it was, that I was interested beyond measure in them and their ways, whereas it was in Irving I was interested . . . They were disappointed accordingly, and not pleased with the book.[24]

Faced with the social rank, wealth, and apparent complacency of this sect, it is not surprising that her sympathy grew for the man she perceived to have been hounded to his solitary grave by his followers. Her subject's desolate plight became further entwined with the pattern of her own life when she returned alone to pursue her research in Scotland after Frank's death. Carlyle's verdict upon her biography suggests the extent to which she had succumbed to the biographer's besetting temptation of refracted autobiography.

All Mrs Oliphant's delineation shows excellent diligence, loyalty, desire to be faithful, and indeed is full of beautiful sympathy and ingenuity; but nowhere . . . are the features of Irving or of his Environment and Life recognisably hit, and the pretty Picture, to one who knows, looks throughout more or less romantic, *pictorial*, and *not* like.[25]

Montalembert too was always associated in her mind with the same traumatic period when she 'began the world anew'. Taking pity upon her, John Blackwood had given her Montalembert's *Monks of the West* to translate and she had been particularly grateful for the author's praise of her laborious efforts. Her first meeting with him took place during the emotionally susceptible time of 'the first anniversary of my Maggie's death' when 'the tears . . . were never far from my eyes'. A second encouragement for identification with this one-time leader of French Catholic opinion, whose campaigns for religious liberty were successively outflanked by Papal authority and Catholic bigotry, was the sense that both she and Montalembert spoke English as a 'second' mother tongue; she was fascinated by the very Frenchness of his thought and behaviour, expressed as it was in faultless English.[26]

Laurence Oliphant, to whom she discovered herself distantly related, was another exile, whose travels embraced three continents. His restless craving for excitement and his impatience with society's imperfections led him to throw up his career as a Member of Parliament and join an autocratically run religious community in America. If she could not sympathize with this or any of his subsequent enthusiasms, she did recognize the edge that a life lived mainly outside England gave to his perceptions of the vicissitudes afflicting the English governing classes.

It was Laurence Oliphant too who most flamboyantly embodied the paradoxical combination of cynical philosopher and visionary idealist. On the one hand his sardonic manner and odd comings and goings led to the suspicion that he was a spy, and on the other hand he was credulous, illogical, and prepared to suffer any humiliation for ideas he believed in. According to one close friend, Mrs Oliphant's biography was a triumph of tact in 'telling the whole truth without showing how his "divagations" made him absurd'.[27] As she thought back over the years Mrs Oliphant realized that it was the same mixture that had fascinated her in Henry Drummond, that 'caustic wit and man of the world' explaining to her his sect's esoteric ecclesiology, and Montalembert, 'keen and sharp as a sword, and yet open to every belief and to every superstition, far more than I ever could have been who looked at him and up at him with a sort of admiring wonder and yet sympathy, not without a smile in it'.[28]

The attraction she instinctively felt to these men's heroic follies, tempered always by her more reserved character, provides a way of understanding Mrs Oliphant's own religious voyage from Scottish Free Churchism to a loose inclusion within the world of Anglicanism—a progress which seemed singularly hard for her obituarists in the English religious press to understand. Her position as reviewer for *Blackwood's*, a magazine with feet in both camps, Edinburgh and London, no doubt helped her to retain a creative marginality. An aside in her early review of F. D. Maurice, describing Calvinism as 'that bête noir of the popular English understanding', certainly suggests that she was already conscious of the widely differing traditions she would have to negotiate.[29]

She had been brought up in the Evangelical Calvinist wing of the Scottish Church. It is not clear at exactly what date she transferred her allegiance to the Church of England, but Chalmers's typically Evangelical lack of interest in a particular Visible Church would have made this decision easier. It would be all too easy to stigmatize her for engaging in the usual shift from what would in England have been branded as Dissent to the Establishment as she moved up the social ladder, but her reasons for effecting this transition were more complex and personal than this. Nor was she ashamed of her religious upbringing. In 1859 she sent a paper on Chalmers to John Blackwood, saying that she had confined herself to 'historical' views of the Disruption, knowing how strongly he and she disagreed on this issue.[30] Her partisanship must have leaked into the article sufficiently to prevent Blackwood publishing it.

Moreover, the Wilson family did not equate Free Churchism with English Dissent. It remains a mystery as to why Willie was sent to the English Presbyterian College in London for his ministerial training rather than its Scottish equivalent; one can only surmise that he had already discovered ways of indulging his weaknesses in Glasgow and that the Wilsons felt, mistakenly, that sharing a house with his Oliphant cousins in London would provide a guarantee of good conduct. When he embarked upon his Presbyterian ministry in Northumberland his family argued that its spiritual parent was the Free Church of Scotland, which they, in turn, persuaded themselves 'was the direct successor of the 2,000 seceders of 1661'— those Anglican clergy forced to take issue with the State and leave their livings. His mother and sister had made a deliberate effort to reinterpret Willie's situation as Dissenting minister of Etal and see him as the natural incumbent of this small Puritanical backwater so 'like a Scottish parish' and to ignore the prior claims of the Established Church by defining it and the parsonage as 'quite exotic' or foreign to the temperament of the place.[31] These accommodations, subsequently characterized as half-conscious by Mrs Oliphant, underline the way in which a natural pride in the religion of their upbringing was threatened first by the question of their Church's 'legitimacy', that Chalmers's defection had raised, and then by their sense of themselves as 'Dissenters' in an alien country.

Her earliest novels, written while she was still living amidst the expatriate Scottish community of Liverpool, repeatedly displayed a concern to explain and defend the Free Church tradition to the English audience her London-based publishers would attract. In *Margaret Maitland* (1849) the narrator's brother and nephew join the Free Church exodus and are thus involved in what Mrs Oliphant was to describe in Chalmers's biography as 'the real dramas enacted in country manses when ordinary parish priests and their families, careful of principles, but also mindful of all the details of renunciation, were forced to forfeit their manses and kirks'.[32] Her next novel, *Caleb Field: A Tale of the Puritans* (1851), a historical romance set in plague-ridden seventeenth-century England, is at pains to present the variety to be found within the Presbyterian ministry: the scholar, the flamboyant preacher, and men of practical goodness. The tale's dedication to Robert Barbour 'of that church in England which claims to represent the brave gentle presbyterians of 1665' signals her intention to give fictional substance to her identification of her brother's ministry with the Non-Juring tradition of the seventeenth century. Her final chapter makes explicit the novel's challenge to the Dissenting stereotype, 'half fool, half fanatic whom men of these latter days have foisted into the ancient Presbyterian Church of England'. The two ensuing Scots novels, *Merkland* (1850) and *Adam Graeme of Mossgray* (1852), respectively defend the congenial traditions of manse life and attempt to blacken the survivors of the Disruption, who, it is alleged, have had to fill their vacant posts with less educated men, whose consciousness of newly acquired status makes them a prey to vulgar ostentation and pomposity. By contrast, *The Melvilles* (1852) claims that the ministers recruited by the Free Church in Liverpool were nature's gentlemen. During the earlier years of their sojourn in Liverpool the Wilson family were noted for their 'warm Free Churchism': brothers Frank and Willie 'filled my mother's cup of happiness' by their involvement.[33] According to a visitor to Liverpool in 1845, Willie's determination to learn sufficient Latin and Greek to qualify for ministerial training dated from this period when he had first exerted himself 'to uphold the cause of Presbyterianism in that city, after the crisis caused by the Disruption'.[34] Their sister's social life seems also to have been conducted in this milieu: she found herself wooed by a young Irish minister and completed a three-volume novel, which she subsequently burnt, 'very much concerned with the Church business'.[35] Yet the degree of cultural shock sustained by this Scots-born family as they came to perceive the discrepancy in position enjoyed by Dissenters and Anglicans in England emerges in the fiction. To the Wilsons the division which had opened up in the Scots Church was a matter of recent and therefore potentially reversible historical accident rather than of deeply entrenched religious or political prejudice.

What form her worship took in the years immediately after she left Liverpool is unclear: we know only that, however critical she was becoming of a tradition which, by placing preaching at the centre of its worship, encouraged self-importance in the preacher and boredom in the congregation, she still regarded attending between one and three sermons a week as normal.[36] A letter of 1856 to John Blackwood gives the clearest statement of the alternatives under consideration.

About 'the shepherds'—a few years ago it was my fortune to see a great many specimens of the class. I don't like English dissent though I am a Free Church woman and a most prejudiced and partial lover of presbytery and of all the forms and modes of my own church. I like the English Establishment a great deal better than the English sectarians with whom perhaps I might differ less in doctrine—but (I suppose I ought to be ashamed to say) I have fully more sympathy for the fervid poor preacher though he be ungrammatical, than for the chilly intellectualists, who, so often, hold the higher places in dissenting churches. I think Dickens is one of those men to whom religion is but a system of mild and sentimental prettiness—I think in his heart he would prefer Charles Honeyman and I think every man who associates systematically, as he does, religion with vulgarity and meanness, deserves a heavier whip than any small switch of mine.[37]

The prejudice she had conceived against English Dissent was clearly one reason for changing her affiliation. 'It is said', wrote the Dissenting historian of the priests of Etal, 'that Mrs Oliphant was favourably disposed to dissent at one period of her life, but that what she considered the unbrotherly treatment of her brother by the Berwick presbytery aroused in her breast contempt for dissent in every form.' The manner of Willie's enforced defection from his Presbyterian ministry, which had involved anonymous letters from the congregation and fast footwork by the Wilson family to prevent public notoriety, aroused bitterness because the minister who had preached the sermon at his ordination gave it as his opinion that Willie could and should have been reclaimed for the Church's service rather than summarily condemned.[38] As the plot of *Salem Chapel* makes clear, the experience also brought home to Margaret Oliphant the absolute dependence upon his local flock's good opinion of the isolated Dissenting minister in England, in contrast with the support available to the occupant of the manse or rectory.

The Northumberland experience showed how beleaguered 'a literary priest' (such was Willie's sobriquet) could be in a small Puritanically disposed Dissenting community. Their Scottish background had accustomed the Wilsons to the more democratic assumptions of a community where the candidate for the manse had probably been educated alongside the laird's son and the dominie. George Eliot was not alone in criticizing the implied egalitarianism of Dissent and the Establishment in *Salem Chapel*: 'And certainly no dissenting life I ever came in contact with in the provinces, could furnish an example of a dissenting minister being invited to visit by a lady of title on a first interview in a shop.'[39]

As a picture of English provincial society such familiarity may have lacked verisimilitude, but the point of the episode for Mrs Oliphant was that the meeting took place in the bookshop. She is at pains to explain how Vincent's education has led him to frequent Masters', a London-based booksellers, not the tract-laden bookshop normally favoured by Evangelicals and Dissenters. It is Vincent's humili-ation and sense of pique when he discovers that shared literary interests cannot be converted into social coinage that fuels his series of lectures on Church and State.

It was the cultural isolation of English Dissent that Mrs Oliphant focused upon when she came to characterize its contribution to *The Literary History of England in the End of the Eighteenth and beginning of the Nineteenth Century.* The writings of John Foster, the Baptist minister and essayist, she thought, conjured up 'a gloomy Dissenter, shut up by circumstances in a small circle, sitting among his little group of intellectual persons with a heartfelt sense of aggrieved superiority (and contemplating most things in heaven and earth as subjects to be discussed by letter or by word of mouth)'.[40] The hypothetical world of fiction, however, allowed her to formulate protests against social arrangements that diminished or ignored shared cultural concerns. The unlikely friendships and alliances formed in *Salem Chapel* stem not so much from the failure to observe Dissenting life as it was lived at the tea-party and chapel meeting, but from a desire to underline the waste such a system invited. Arthur Vincent and Reginald Northcote are not, as the *Nonconformist* pointed out, typical products of Homerton College's training for the Congregational ministry; they are liberally educated gentlemen who are confused when their pride in their ideological position is confronted with the real touchiness and pettiness of an underprivileged community and when the status of Christian gentleman, upon which they presume, is repudiated by the Establishment.

Mrs Oliphant has been attacked for 'the ludicrous inadequacy' of her 'solution to the differences between Church and Dissent . . . based on ignorance of the problem and the issues',[41] and it is true that the amity achieved in *Phoebe Junior*, where urbane Dissenters enjoy the democratic world of love and music with their Anglican peers in a rectory drawing-room, presents an unlikely idyll. Yet, in the case of both *Salem Chapel* and *Phoebe Junior* the novel's resolution makes clear that these scenes of social intimacy have indeed been idyllic interludes. Northcote 'mistakenly' renounces both political commitment and the Dissenting ministry for the sake of an Anglican bride. Vincent's pride ensures that he retains the name of Independent even though he rejects the realities of the Dissenting ministry and opts instead for earning a livelihood as editor of a philosophical journal. The freemasonry of literature alone provides a niche for these dispossessed souls, and it was in the mildly Bohemian circles of literary London that Mrs Oliphant attempted to gain the only foothold now conceivable for her displaced brother. The extent to which she blamed the world of English Dissent for an exclusivity, which they had turned from a sign of oppression into a badge of virtue, surfaces at its most bitter in *At His Gates* (1872), which contains a vignette of a Dissenting minister who, despite his evident intelligence and probity, proves acceptable to artists but is marginalized by the class-conscious. When a severe stroke prevents him from continuing an active ministry he earns a living by editing a Dissenting journal, but when his handicap becomes more serious, he is relieved of this post. By the end of the novel his total paralysis embodies the abject powerlessness of a Dissenting minister deprived of both the need and support of a flock.

It was not Willie's shipwreck alone that had affected his sister's slow estrangement from Free Church Presbyterianism. The minor literary and artistic circles of

1a. Mrs Oliphant in her early thirties.

b. George Wilson (1818–59); Janet Aitken Wilson (1786– 1864).

2a. Principal Tulloch.
2b. John Blackwood.

2c. Robert Herbert Story in
1860.

3a. Cecco and Cyril Oliphant.

3b. Cyril.
3c. Cecco.

4a. Denny as aunt and 'mother'.

4b. Madge and Denny.
4c. Madge and Denny at school in Germany.

5a. Windsor 1874, Cecco, Mrs
Oliphant, Cyril, and nephew
Frank.
5b. Cyril. Frank Wilson.
Cecco.

c. Frank and Nelly Wilson.

6a. Lady Ritchie (Annie Thackeray).

6b. 1881 Portrait of Mrs Margaret Oliphant.

7a. Great-aunt Margaret with
the Valentines, 1896.
7b. Madge, Margaret and
William Valentine.

7c. Cecco in Nice.

8 Mrs. Oliphant's drawing-room and study

London, to which Frank and Margaret's talents gained them access, offered a wider array of religious allegiance. There were kindly Anglican clergy like Mr Laing, the perpetual curate of St Pancras.[42] It also seemed possible to combine Christianity with less orthodox practices. Many of their friends and acquaintances from the 1850s were involved in the wave of spiritualist interest currently sweeping America and England. Samuel Hall, a periodical editor, and his novelist wife, Anna, and William and Mary Howitt, both prolific essayists, were promoters of the notorious American spiritualist Daniel D. Home (whose antics were to be immortalized in Robert Browning's poem 'Mr Sludge the Medium'). The Howitts' eldest daughter discovered herself to be 'an art medium producing wonderful scribble-scrabbles which it was the wonder of wonders to find her mother, so full of sense and truth, so genuine herself, full of enthusiasm about'.[43] Her publishing friends the Blacketts, and Dinah Mulock, to whom she had introduced them, held evening parties where spiritualism was practised 'half as entertainment and half as consolation'.[44] Mrs Oliphant's awareness of the psychological appeal of spiritualism prevented her from either censorious disapproval or taking it too seriously. As her own need for consolation grew greater she became ever more conscious of the emotional continuum that led other, seemingly sophisticated, friends to confuse the levities of table-rapping, occasionally practised in her own drawing-room,[45] with naïve belief in direct communications from the spirit world. In Laurence Oliphant's case she was particularly acute about the psychosexual problems that inspired some of the communications he allegedly received and about the way in which a desire to provide legitimation for physical intimacy led his two successive wives to discover hitherto unsuspected talents as types of medium.[46] Her level-headed assessment of the bodily and mental fatigue that often lay behind the desire for reassurance provided by physical manifestations did not desert her when, shortly afterwards, she began to experience 'momentary contact' with her dead son, Tids. In logging these occurrences she is careful to acknowledge that they may have been 'only some trick of the mind' or nothing more than a dream, but this freed her to admit that, whatever their origin, they offer 'great comfort'.[47]

Trips abroad, at first with Frank and then with the children, had continued the process of her religious odyssey. She endeavoured to do her Sunday duty wherever she found herself, and this led her into the expatriate communities cared for by Anglican clergy abroad. The sudden appearance, after Frank's death in Rome, of a series of gossipy and interfering Evangelical clergy in the pages of her fiction suggests that she had experienced similar intrusions in her grief. It was at that point that she discovered the devout unintrusive atmosphere, conducive to solitary prayer, afforded by Roman Catholic churches abroad.[48]

The close friendships she made in the course of early widowhood also led her to review her attachment to the Free Church wing of Presbyterianism. Within a year or so of her 'faithful cavalier',[49] Robert Story, allegedly proposing to her, and after holidaying with the Storys, Tullochs, and Cairds, the new leaders of moderate opinion within the Church of Scotland, her writing showed a notable shift of bias.

The heroic mantle was transferred from the Evangelically disposed seceders of 1843, who had gone out 'arrayed in those robes of sacrifice which can be and often are made the most offensive livery of arrogance and self-regard', to those who had stayed behind, enduring contumely for their attachment to the loaves and fishes of preferment and experiencing the loss of so many of the flock they had previously nurtured.[50] From 1862 she badgered John Blackwood to allow her to write articles on the last half-century of Scottish Church history, 'no fear of too much free Church sympathy now—I have seen that blunder by dint of living in Scotland'.[51] A further plea, the following year, for an opportunity in *Blackwood's* to expand upon the subject-matter she had worked up for a review of Story's life of his father as 'Clerical Life in Scotland' indicated how far her flirtation with the Establishment had now taken her: 'I think if I were living in Edinburgh I should give a series of ecclesiological teas and try to organise a female movement for the general seduction of the young clergy into Ritualism.'[52] By the end of the decade she was expressing herself disappointed with the headway made by the Story party within the Scottish Church, and sought Blackwood's permission to use the pages of *Maga* for polemical purposes.[53] Failing in this, she instead contributed an introductory chapter to Story's *Life and Remains of Robert Lee* (1870), where she made public her severance from the Free Church movement, which was now retreating 'back to the ancient intolerances, the old bigotries, the stern bondage of tradition' all too often associated with Presbyterianism. Lee's efforts to stem the drift of cultivated Scots to Anglicanism by securing the use of the Book of Common Prayer in Scottish Churches met with her full approval.

The extent to which she had imbibed the small change of clerical discussion emerges in *A Son of the Soil*, planned during the summer of 1863 at Rosneath and written in the company of the Tullochs, with whom she was travelling when Maggie died one-third of her way into the novel. The immediate concerns of the Established Church found a place in the novel's texture when the hero, 'a young Scotchman and Presbyterian, strongly anchored to his hereditary creed, and yet feeling all its practical deficiencies',[54] adumbrates his desire to infuse the Presbyterian Church with the glories of a Catholic tradition which could offer a liturgy adequate to the celebration of Christian festivals and a form of prayers for public worship. The hero's dilemma also incorporated Mrs Oliphant's own internal debate as she contemplated the religious implications of establishing a permanent home in Scotland or England. The hero, as the title implies, eventually decides to work within the kirk, although he is aware that preferment lies by way of the English chapel attended by wealthy Scots landowners. Yet his ecclesiastical odyssey enables him to distinguish between the anti-Dissenting interest of a Scottish kirk, whose Presbyterian faith nevertheless also predisposes it to anti-episcopalianism, and the 'foreign concerns' of the Anglican High Church movement, obsessed with such matters as priestly authority, church restoration, and the formal observance of saints' days.

Mrs Oliphant's final position, as 'a churchwoman who found early communion a help,[55] and preferred the prayers of the Anglican liturgy to the uninspired repetitions of Scots ministers' individual composition, yet 'in one of her many sorrows . . . wished the presence of one who would pray with her "not out of a book"', was notably 'impatient of ritual',[56] and was incensed by her niece's Scots husband requiring thrice-daily church attendance in the 1890s,[57] suggests that for her the virtue of Anglicanism was its eclecticism. Just as the theology and politics of English Dissent had held little interest for her, so she concerned herself only with the broad outlines of the Anglican compromise. She was quick to defend herself against Blackwood's complaint that she had misunderstood the nature of a perpetual curacy,[58] but far more damning than the terminological inaccuracies in *The Perpetual Curate*, which was to deal with 'all three parties in the Church', is the lack of doctrinal interest displayed by Frank Wentworth, the High Church perpetual curate, who is only interested in the domestic turmoil his brother's impending secession to Rome will create, since 'between Rome and the highest level of Anglicanism there was no such difference as to frighten the accustomed mind of the Curate of St. Roque's'.[59] Mrs Oliphant embraced Anglicanism, in the Arnoldian spirit, as the inclusive national Church of her adopted home,[60] and drew the line only at such flagrant transgressions of its elastic boundaries as were implied by Dean Stanley's invitations to non-Anglicans to preach in Westminster Abbey.[61] The wide umbrella of England's established Church guaranteed a haven for her idiosyncratic mixture of lay dogmatism and unorthodoxy.

The shifts in her affiliation, and her scepticism as to the absolute authority of the Church leaders she knew, combined with her instinctive sense of privacy to develop a highly personal sense of inner religious life. Commenting upon Mary Howitt's conversion to Roman Catholicism, she found it difficult to understand how an intelligent woman could submit to an authoritarian Church but surmised 'that there are many, especially among what is called the cultured classes, to whom sermons are a heavy burden, and who are apt to fall into a neglect which is scarcely intentional'.[62] She may have found church attendance a means 'to get through Sunday' in the years after both sons were dead, but in the years between the deaths of her two sons she attended church only once a month, preferring to remain at home paying bills, or reading, but chiefly thinking of her boys, 'one of whom is— we know not where he is or how employed in the great and terrible Unseen, and the other whose change of countenance I watch so anxiously'.[63] Although her unspoken prayers were so often to do with her immediate family, she shrank from open or shared displays of piety. As she read Archbishop Tait's memoirs she commented,

We are none of us pious like him and his wife, not praying together or talking as they do— too little, I know, too little. Sometimes Cecco has written to me, and I to him out of the depths of our hearts but we have scarcely prayed together except that one night, before Tiddy was carried away to his grave. I think he would not have liked it from me, the two boys had that impression, got I don't know how, that a woman should not lead in that way—at least I think so.[64]

There are two points to be made about this reflection. First, prayer had always seemed to her a solitary practice. In her *Autobiography* she recalled an occasion when she was 'in great straits' and asked a friend to pray with her; the ensuing paragraph mulls over the experiences that might possibly have led to this and concludes, 'I have never asked any one else to do that for me.'[65] Certain portions of her *Autobiography* are almost a continuous prayer, thinking through events in the presence of a God whom she implores, berates, but always acknowledges. Even when she declared to Annie Coghill, 'I have lost confidence in any prayer of mine', she immediately continued the sentence with the phrase 'but as one must pray whether one will or not'.[66] In times of severe distress she would carry around her prayers, in written form, in her purse.[67] For her prayer was the voicing of concern and, as a writer, this 'voicing' was necessarily a solitary act, even if carried out against the backdrop of family life. Indeed, she ruefully admitted that she had perhaps neglected her sons' formal religious education in the conviction that they, like her, conducted this inner debate: she and Cecco, for example, had only managed to share their innermost concerns on paper.

Secondly, she attributed the absence of a sense of familial religious community to the problem of gender-defined roles: it was a general nineteenth-century assumption that although the moral and religious upbringing was the mother's special responsibility, the priestly function of leading formal worship, even at family prayers, fell to the male. Yet, even as she acknowledged her collusion with this prejudice, she was clearly puzzled as to how her boys could have imbibed it, given their reliance upon her guiding hand in every other aspect of their lives. Since her autobiographical musings over the perplexities of life often took the form of informal communing with God, it was in this quasi-religious context that her puzzling over gender-related considerations emerged particularly clearly. If popular mythology portrayed woman as both chaste and maternal, to be reverenced and protected, yet silenced and helpless in the presence of males, where was she to take her place? Chaste and maternal she had elected to be, and her friends, in particular the rejected suitor Robert Story, reinforced her appropriation of this part of female spirituality by nicknaming her Madonna Mia (it was for her married friend, Mrs Tulloch, that the name 'the Padrona' was reserved). It is hard to divine in what spirit the sobriquet was originally bequeathed, since her independence and her acquisition of a voice so markedly departed from the popular iconography associated with it. When she recalled asking Nelly Clifford to pray with her, the singularity of the occasion lay for her in the way it challenged her image of herself as someone who 'asked help' from no one but God.

Nowhere does Mrs Oliphant's sharp awareness of the ways in which the parabola of her life so spectacularly converged with and diverged from the 'womanly ideal' of continuous self-sacrifice emerge more clearly than in her 'Stories of the Seen and the Unseen'. As the earlier chapter on the womanly ideal illustrated, throughout her life she displayed unswerving allegiance to silent self-sacrifice as the mode by which a woman might most closely attempt the imitation of Christ. As the years passed, however, her fiction displayed an increasing sense of the bleakness of adherence to this ideal in a world which no longer reverenced it and only recognized its practice in order to exploit it. More disquieting still was the dawning revelation that the conflict between the ideal and the forces of cynicism could no longer be so readily externalized into a battle between the female victim/hero and an uncaring or exploitative world but might be located deep within. At the simplest level this can be illustrated by the paradox of a woman, whose tales advocate and extol silent self-sacrifice, voicing on almost every page of her *Autobiography* the sacrifices that have been required of her. At a more complex level the ambiguities of her own position opened up what at times threatened to be a theological abyss.

The nineteenth-century notion that transformed the image of maternity from an inherited curse to a domestic icon of love fulfilled through sacrifice[68] was one that had initially appealed to Mrs Oliphant. This is how she imaged her mother: 'poor mother, poor bright, thwarted, wasted Love incarnate as she was, lived between her daughter who was taken from her, and her son, who was an anguish to her'. The mother–daughter relationship had been encouraged to grow into a reciprocity of suffering until the final days when neither mother nor daughter ever voiced their knowledge of the mother's approaching death, but endured 'a struggle of a month or two, much suffering on her part, and a long troubled watch and nursing on mine'.[69] In Mrs Oliphant's own recollection of the mutuality of love and suffering enshrined in this relationship we might be tempted to see a precise illustration of F. D. Maurice's preaching of the 'fellowship of mutual love' effected by Christ's redemptive sacrifice.[70] It is interesting therefore to recollect how her early review of Maurice had rebuked him precisely for finding the Crucifixion an embarrassment and for undervaluing the extent of God's sacrifice upon the Cross by speaking of it as a proof of His love rather than as a uniquely terrible test of His love.

Whatever her misconception of Maurice, the entire thrust of her article was designed to reinstate sacrifice at the centre of Christianity and to repudiate any interpretation which seemed to undervalue the extent of the suffering implicit in absolute love. For Maurice's reading of the Atonement had consequences for the appreciation of earthly sacrifices: in interpreting Abraham's offering up of his only son Isaac he saw a proof of man's love for God, a human impulse to thanks-offering. To Mrs Oliphant such a reading implied that all the pain and carnage involved in Old Testament sacrifices could only be seen as insane cruelty and waste: the suffering involved in human self-sacrifices was only bearable, to her mind, in as far as they could be interpreted as 'shadows of one Infinite Sacrifice'.[71] Understanding the Christian life chiefly in terms of sacrifice raised further problems. If Maurice's theology seemed to make sacrifice one of the ends of creation rather than the only means to salvation, her understanding seemed to link motivation and the perceived success of the sacrifice too closely. At times, as we shall see, even Christ's sacrifice seemed to her unavailing in achieving resurrection of the only kind that humans could readily understand,[72] and her own sufferings increasingly seemed out of proportion if judged by visible results. For experience had already taught her that the suffering involved in sacrifice might outweigh the desiderated bond of love between the victim and the beneficiary of that sacrifice. The crucifixion, 'an act of saving love', might be imaged as a sacrifice which cemented indissolubly the bond of love between the victim and those beneficiaries who recognized the greatness of his sacrifice and the love that produced it.[73] Yet Mrs Oliphant's own wish to enter into this absolute bond of reciprocal love and suffering with her mother had, she felt, been tarnished. The suffering engendered by the emotional tug-of-war between her husband and his mother-in-law etched the reality of her own suffering in her mind far more deeply than the reward of love; yet this does not suffice to explain the bitter conviction, manifested in her late fiction, that the virtue implicit in sacrifice must be its own reward and bears no necessary fruit in those for whom it is undertaken. In her mother's death the concept of maternal love as a reflection of Christ's redemptive love had suffered no diminution. Indeed, her mother's death at this point had perhaps helped to freeze the image of selfless love as incarnated in the maternal role in a way that might not have survived had her mother's isolation and growing debility begun to make more pronounced demands upon her. The fiction contrives to suggest that her husband's death, and her subsequent refusal to contemplate the remarriage which would have involved renewing competing claims upon her affections, allowed her more fully to invest sacrificial love in the figure of the sorrowing mother. Her easy acceptance of the title 'Madonna Mia', apparently unmarred by any consciousness of blasphemous identification, suggests her Protestant upbringing had not encouraged her to submerge her own sufferings in those of the Virgin Mary. Rather Mary's sufferings, and even God's sufferings as Father, were intelligible to her only in as far as they replicated the desolation of bereaved human mothers. Despite her criticism of F. D. Maurice for allegedly undervaluing Christ's sufferings on the Cross, her own picturing of God's sacrifice has little to do with Christ on the Cross and far more to do with a desire to identify with God the parent who permitted His son to be sacrificed; but this same image in turn begets its own troubles for an author brought up to worship a male-gendered God while always aware of male inadequacy.

When Maggie had died, aged 10, her mother had spoken of God almost as a divorced mother might do of a former spouse to whom she had had to entrust a child.

She is with God, she is in his hands. I know nothing, cannot even imagine anything. Can I trust her with Him? Can I trust Him that He had done what was best for her, that He has her safe, that there has been no mistake, no error, but only his purpose in all, and that he is keeping her now in the position most happy for her, that even my own human judgement, when enlightened, will approve as best?[74]

Agnes (1865) was Mrs Oliphant's first full-blown fictional response to the theological perplexities into which her daughter Maggie's sudden death had thrown her. In the last chapter of this dreadful tale of repeated loss, bereavement, and death, where Mrs Oliphant's separation from her own parents, her husband's death, and finally her child's death are revisited, we are reminded that this mother's story is in no way an exceptional case. The free-thinking parson, unable to comfort her amid his own 'bewilderments and perplexities', allows her to pour forth her own speculations.

'I think sometimes that there is a kind of mass being always said in the world', said Agnes— 'a kind of repetition every day of His sacrifice; not because of any priest's saying, but because of God's appointing. Perhaps it is only fancy; and some of us are always being chosen to carry it on. We ought to be glad; but at the end even He was not willing, except because it was God's will—any more than we are willing. It is hard to be put up on the cross to show other people how blessed they are; but that is not what I wanted to say. Sometimes I think it is to keep up and carry on the spectacle of loss, and pain, and anguish; and I have my mass to say, though I am not willing. Sometimes it comforts me a little; I think He would have raised them all like Lazarus, if it had been possible; and it was not possible; and now we have all to put on our priest's garments, and hold up the host, that all the world may see. We were a long time in Italy!' she said, with a faint smile, breaking off.[75]

Agnes's final remark reveals Mrs Oliphant's fear that this doctrine of repeated sacrifice comes dangerously near an understanding of the sacrament at odds with Protestant teaching. The authorial narrative, therefore, proceeds to demonstrate a suitably low estimate of the elements in the Eucharist whilst also underwriting Agnes's general proposition that God's sacrifice is not unique.

Agnes's view of the inefficacy of Christ's sacrifice to achieve the only kind of resurrection in which she is interested receives authorial collusion when Agnes stands by her dying son's bedside. The syntax fails to reveal whether it is character or narrator who exclaims, 'Ah, my God, was it as hard to be crucified?' This understanding of the Atonement has already led Agnes into jealous rivalry with God—'He who had taken to Himself the supreme luxury of dying for the world He loved; and yet He would not let her die for the son of her heart'.[76] The plot of this novel as a whole shows Mrs Oliphant's desperate search to create analogues by which she can interpret God's role in the matter of her daughter's death. After the death of Agnes's husband his estranged relatives approach her for the custody of the child whom they wish to bring up as befits the heir to the baronetcy, but even the Lord Chancellor is convinced that, despite her humble origins, a mother's care is best and finally the relatives resort to kidnapping Walter, who dies in his bid to escape and rejoin his mother. When the lawsuit for custody is first initiated, Agnes's father reminds her that 'there are women who have to consent to give up their children altogether', but Agnes responds that God is more merciful than men and she feels that 'None of them would take my child quite away from me, not even Sir Roger'.[77] In the event, God is shown as harsher than even the relatives, who act out of selfishness not from any desire to harm the child. By concentrating upon God as an alternative, but far more powerful, guardian or parent, Mrs Oliphant has effec- tively separated the sufferings and power of the Father from the enforced and, to an extent, unavailing sacrifice of the Son. Conceptualizing God as an omniscient parent had the advantage for her of creating a divinity who, though he might on occasion be inscrutable, was also prepared to behave indulgently to his children.[78] Such a figuration in turn legitimated His earthly disciples' attempts to adopt a

Providential role in the lives of those for whom they were responsible. In an interesting passage in the *Autobiography*, where Mrs Oliphant discusses a period in 1872 when her attempts to support two households seemed to be foundering, she described herself as 'miserably anxious, not knowing where to turn or what to do ... waiting upon God' to reveal to her some new outlet for her talent. When the man from the *Graphic* turned up with an offer, his visitation was seen as prompted by God ('Our Father in heaven had settled it all the time for the children'). Nevertheless, in the next paragraph she is swift to take charge of life again and to organize this Providential gift to the best possible advantage.

It was not, however, the story which I had finished at the time which I gave them ... It was always a struggle to get safely through every year and make my ends meet ... Good day and ill day, they balanced each other, and I got on through year after year ... I might say now that another woman doing the same thing was tempting Providence. To tempt Providence or to trust God, which was it?[79]

The final question indicates Mrs Oliphant's own perception of the extent to which she had relied upon a highly individual interpretation of God to allow her to do so much. If God's ways are mysterious, and from an earthly point of view arbitrary, this frees His creatures from petty calculation, or meticulous plotting, but, since God's interventions cannot be counted upon to occur in accordance with a human programme of perceived need, His creatures would be wise to bestir themselves in every way available and deploy every resource to hand.

This combination of trusting in God and keeping one's powder dry has, of course, had notable precedents in Protestant history, yet in Mrs Oliphant's case the recognition of that precise blend of faith and works allowed her to pay tribute to Catholics like Montalembert or Catherine of Siena,[80] and helps to explain the total repudiation of the self-imposed sufferings of the hypochondriacal middle-class female who so frequently appears in her novels. These women who have embraced physical debility as a way of avoiding confrontation with authoritative males and used their only weapon, their body, to gain attention, often regain their capacity to become effective parents if their husbands predecease them.

Effective parenting, however, as interpreted to mean enacting the role of Providence on earth, brings us back to the heart of Mrs Oliphant's theological problems. When Cyril died, she prayed to God the Father that 'Thou wilt cradle him in Thy arms. Thou wilt comfort him as one whom his mother comforteth.'[81] It comes as something of a surprise to remember that this was not an infant death, but the death of an adult aged 33, who had been inclined, even on his deathbed, to resent her maternal solicitations. 'I'll tell you what you are afraid of,' he had told her. 'You are afraid of the time when the doctors will say I may go out again.'[82] The inability of mothers to exercise a Providential role over their adult sons was the nub of her theological perplexity. Having concentrated upon an understanding of God the all-powerful and all-caring parent to validate her exceptional career as a working mother she had had comparatively to neglect an identification with God as victim.

After the death of her last son, Cecco, she wrote a signed article entitled 'The Fancies of a Believer' in which she wrestled with the problem of suffering. Although her discussion claims to be predicated upon an assertion of moral freedom as God's gift to humanity, the article mainly focuses upon the place of natural evil in the shape of untimely death rather than upon the implications of human sin. The article accentuates the division, already detected in her writing, between God the Father and God the Son. All of us, she remarked, are moved alike by two things:

they are the impossibility of securing that those whom we love should choose, as we hope we have done, the worthier way; and the other, and to some the more terrible, as more evidently beyond their power to effect one way or the other—the impossibility of securing the lives of those we love, or of saving them from being suddenly seized and hurried away from us by irrevocable and incurable separation of death.

At the centre of human perplexity then, Mrs Oliphant suggests, is the desire to invoke God as a superior parent who will intervene to secure our loved ones, fighting against our recognition that the exercise of this power must negate the gift of free will. Such consolation as is offered is dependent upon a supernatural economy in which God has planned the sacrifice of His son before the world was created, to save us all from ultimate damnation, though not from the earthly consequences of our wrong choices. Her religious speculations effect no union between God the creator-parent and God the victim, whose suffering was disproportionate to its achievements. Either God is all-powerful, in which case why do we suffer? Or He is helpless (rather than showing His power by voluntarily divesting Himself of it), and, as she flatly concludes, all of this, of course, limits the power of prayer.[83]

That title, 'The Fancies of a Believer', adopted, one suspects, to ward off charges of unorthodoxy by pleading guilty to the lesser crime of whimsicality, suggests where and how she had attempted to explore and then negotiate between these two positions.

2. Tales of the Supernatural

It was in the world of fancy, or fantasy, in her *Stories of the Seen and the Unseen*, in the liminal spaces between the here and the hereafter, in the uncharted regions of the hereafter itself, that Mrs Oliphant discovered a place to ponder further upon irresolvable paradoxes and gender-related confusions. These uncolonized spaces permitted an indirectness of approach that itself proves disruptive of reader expectation. Within a particular tale two stories often compete for our attention: a male protagonist and narrator, for instance, may stake a claim while a female ghost's silent presence intrigues in direct correlation to the suppression of her narrative.

The first problem that arises in trying to discuss Mrs Oliphant's 'Stories of the Seen and the Unseen', perhaps the least contentious title in that it sidesteps matters of genre, is the difficulty of agreeing what is covered by this collective name: the American (1889) and British (1892) versions of this anthology included different tales and the earlier publication conflated the kinds of narration that twentieth-century critical procedures would encourage us to distinguish. While it is clearly the case that all the stories from *A Beleaguered City* (1879) onwards fulfil the basic requirement of fantasy in expressing or telling of a dimension of experience not available within the prevailing realist tradition, not all of them attain that further resistance to meaning and closure that keeps the reader in a creative sense of dissatisfaction and avails the writer of a chance to express or rid himself of intransigent problems and subversive concepts.[84] Those that do make out a space, hovering between the limitations of the terrestrial and the freedom of the supernatural, enable the exploration of problems that might be self-destructive or blasphemous in real life. A mechanical division could easily be made between those tales that chart the landscape and activities of the afterlife and those where the story makes sorties into an alternative world from an earthbound base. Such a division, however, neither accounts for the difference in the power to disturb, exerted by different stories in the first class, nor, when we come to the second class, does it distinguish sufficiently between largely allegorical tales, such as 'A Visitor and His Opinions',[85] and a tale like 'Old Lady Mary',[86] which includes a dimension more akin to the tales of the afterlife. Since their very variety (surprising in so small a corpus) resists theoretical categorization, it is more rewarding to consider the impulse that generated these ventures into an alternative mode from the general tenor of her realistic fiction, and the nature and chronology of the problems and anxieties explored in these tales. The enterprise seems to receive further justification from her own sense of these stories as different in kind and origin from her usual fiction. 'Stories of this description', she wrote to William Blackwood, 'are not like any others. I can produce them only when they come to me. I should be glad to do one for the New Year number, but nothing suggests itself.' A month later she referred to 'Old Lady Mary' as a tale that had 'presented itself' unexpectedly.[87]

It has been traditional to ascribe Mrs Oliphant's turning to the supernatural as a source of inspiration to commercial perspicacity. The 'Little Pilgrim' tales were certainly a financial success, and her very first venture into the genre followed a vogue for comic responses to the 'Christmas fantasy' originated by Dickens's *Christmas Carol* (1843). In some ways her 'Christmas Tale' was too carefully contrived a piece of literary parody, one suspects, to be readily enjoyed by the average periodical reader, and so when Blackwoods came to republish it the tale was retitled 'Witcherley Ways: A Christmas Tale' to alert the reader to its deliberately playful use of the supernatural.[88] The game that the narrator has played with us only becomes clear in retrospect when he wakes from a dream that we have been led to conceive of as taking place in his waking life: the tale explodes, or rather fizzles out, at the point of crisis just as the narrator is to meet a parricide, and we realize that the extravagances of the Gothic setting have been employed to lead us away from an allegory demonstrating that the New Year can only come of age at the expense of the death of the Old Year. Mocking allusion is made to *Wuthering Heights* in the name and character of the old servant, Joseph, and in the tale's dream and nightmare sequences, which are fed by the narrator's reading habits, but the essentially parodic nature of the whole is given away by the mingling of devices from different genres: the tale starts at the fairy-tale time of *undermeles*, alludes to desolate wasteland landscapes opening up at street corners, involves family curses, and makes passing reference to Rosicrucian ancestors.

It was another twenty years before Mrs Oliphant appeared to realize the non-parodic potential of these devices, and market forces may again have played their part. Ghost stories were in vogue in the second half of the nineteenth century. Their appeal may have lain in the disruptions they offered to a mechanistic explanation of a world increasingly dominated by sceptical materialism. A spate of non-fictional books appeared, attempting to bridge the gap between science and spiritualism: R. D. Owen, *The Debatable Land between this World and the Next* (1872), A. R. Wallace, *Modern Spiritualism* (1874), Balfour Steward and P. G. Tait (anon.), *The Unseen Universe* (1875), and this area of investigation was given respectability when men like Leslie Stephen, Ruskin, and Symonds founded the Society for Psychical Research. Gladstone, an honorary member, made the astonishing observation that psychical research was 'the most important work, which is being done in the world'.[89] As a reviewer Mrs Oliphant noted the warm reception given to two recent American books: E. S. Phelps's whimsical exploration of the afterlife, *Gates Ajar* (1868), and Mrs Whitney's, *Hitherto: A Story of Yesterday*, which she put down to 'the extraordinary pressure of the unseen everywhere, without, however, any relapse into the vulgar supernatural'.[90] In the following month's number of *Blackwood's* she embarked upon a reappraisal of Coleridge and singled out *The Ancient Mariner* for its 'crossing the borders of the unseen' and 'Christabel' for its investigation of 'the mystery of evil, an unseen harm and bane'.[91]

The title of her second tale of the supernatural, 'The Secret Chamber', is itself an indication that she had begun to see how she might use the genre as a literary equivalent to those Sunday evenings she had long set aside as a time to 'fantasticate' about the perplexities of her private life.[92] The concept of 'the secret chamber' as a receptacle for a woman's inmost concerns and anxieties probably stemmed from the biblical account of Mary, of whom we are told that, unlike the shepherds, who blazoned abroad the tale of angelic appearances and Christ's nativity in a stable, 'Mary kept all these things, and pondered them in her heart.'[93] Mrs Oliphant literalized this image in *Lucy Crofton* (1859), where the heroine, unbeknown to her husband, regularly retreats to a secret room which she has turned into a shrine for her dead baby. The allegorical application of 'The Innermost Room' in a house to represent that portion of a woman's life accessible only to the beloved dead or Christ Himself occurred in her poem of this title, published in *Blackwood's* in March 1867.[94]

The cumulative resonance of these usages is present in a later tale of the supernatural where we are told of Old Lady Mary,

She did not forget the dark day when her first-born was laid in the grave, nor that triumphant and brilliant climax of her life when every one pointed to her as the mother of a hero. All these things were like pictures hung in the secret chambers of her mind, to which she could go back in silent moments, in the twilight seated by the fire, or in the balmy afternoon, when languor and sweet thoughts are over the world.[95]

Like its predecessor, 'The Secret Chamber' was also a Christmas tale for *Blackwood's*.[96] Ostensibly it is concerned with a turning-point or rite of passage: the coming of age of young John Randolph, Lord Lindores, who is to be initiated by his father into a family secret. In the middle of the night Lindores is taken by his father to an old lumber-room in the heart of the family portion of the castle through which he enters 'a little intermediate place—this debatable land between the seen and the unseen' *en route* to the innermost chamber where he encounters the ancestral head of the family, Earl Robert. Lindores is offered power in return for his unquestioning allegiance to Earl Robert in all matters of family business, which will always be directed 'for the furtherance of the race'. Young Lindores is enabled to overcome this vampiric wizard, but there can be no final exorcism, partly because Lindores' father, who had succumbed to Earl Robert, still lives, and partly because the secret chamber has no identifiable material location.

As Mrs Oliphant was writing this tale she was experiencing her first real problems with her eldest son, who was, like Lindores, on the brink of his majority and an undergraduate at Oxford. Cyril was exhibiting those tendencies described in the Randolph race as making 'quite a wonderful start' and then 'falling back into mediocrity'. In November 1876 Cyril told his mother that he was 'gradually giving up all hopes of my first'.[97] Had he, his mother must have wondered, fallen prey to the losing streak that bedevilled her brothers? It is at the moment when Lindores looks into the mirror and sees not himself, but an innumerable company of his ancestors looking back at him, 'some mournfully, some with a menace in their terrible eyes', that he comes closest to paralysis of the will. But the story is also one about a boy achieving freedom from a possessive power, and Lindores' response to Earl Robert, 'Is it for this that you oppress a race, and make a house unhappy', for all its Gothic overtones carries within it the nub of the struggle that was to smoulder for the rest of Cyril's life between the son and his mother. There is a lingering sadness to this tale, whose plot does not end with Lindores' victory over Earl Robert but with his father's denial of what has taken place. His attempt to hide the truth of the family secret from the castle guests and ultimately from himself must deprive him forever of the solace of sharing his burden.

Such anxieties lie hidden deep within a tale whose ghost-story features are crafted with a sure hand. The narrator adopts the stance of an educated man of the world, well aware that secret chambers and family ghosts are a commonplace of the folklore surrounding Scottish castles. Lindores arrives by courtesy of the Great Northern Railway to encounter an ordeal in which even at the heart of his adventure 'a gleam even of self-ridicule took possession of him, to be standing there like an absurd hero of antiquated romance' with a 'rusty, dusty sword' in his hand.

When he first sees Earl Robert he reviews the logical explanations for the phenom-enon: 'what could it be but optical delusions, unconscious cerebration, occult seizure?' Cheek by jowl with the world of nineteenth-century sceptical materialism exists the castle whose architecture displays the remnants of Celtic art and Runic cords. The entrance to the secret chamber is effected via the lumber-room contain-ing the rubbish jettisoned as outmoded by successive generations: it is from this supply of relics that Lindores' father takes 'an old sword with a cross handle' and gives it to his son, 'whether as a weapon, whether as a religious symbol, Lindores could not guess'. The narrative never discloses whether the old symbol really has potency or whether it merely serves as a visual encouragement to Lindores to pray to God .

Little over a year later Mrs Oliphant began work on *A Beleaguered City*, envis-aged again as a Christmas story.[98] It was a tale over which she took unusual pains, revising it carefully, and consequently she was fiercely proud of it.[99] Formally the piece is experimental: a succession of narrators recount this tale of a French city, possessed by the spirit of materialism, which is then briefly taken over by the 'unseen forces of those who knew the meaning of life being dead'.

It has been customary to point to Mrs Oliphant's own knowledge of the French religious scene, gleaned whilst working on Montalembert during the 1860s and 1870s, supplemented by her acquaintance with the work of the French biblical critic Renan, to account for the setting and format of this book, whose narrative deliber-ately raises questions as to the status and reliability of eyewitness accounts akin to those posed by the Gospels. Actually, Mrs Oliphant knew little of Renan, other than mediated through the work of her friend Tulloch,[100] and is as likely to have grasped the complicating possibilities of the split narrative from Wilkie Collins's *The Moon-stone* or Browning's *The Ring and the Book*. The literary nature of her inspiration in this piece is beyond question. She herself cited De Quincey as her source, claiming to have found a passage in his work 'about the possibility of the dead coming back, besieging the living and turning them out of their places', and her recent efforts at popularizing Dante had exposed her to a method of embodying spiritual truth in contemporary clothing.[101] Ostensibly the story is concerned with the inadequacy of the polite bourgeois morality, in the ascendant in France, to cope with the sudden irruption of spiritual concerns that have hitherto been dealt with by institutional-izing them. The tale's French setting allowed the Victorian reader the instant pleasure of xenophobic outrage at a country where enlightened scepticism and bourgeois respectability are openly privileged; the disconcerting parallels with British middle-class attitudes are slower to emerge. At the allegorical level the tale's disclosures are unspectacular: unthinking idolaters easily change their god when circumstances prove him inefficacious, and the humble and naturally devout, rather than those honoured by the human community, are the only ones to whom the unseen visitation comes as a delight. The tale derives its impact from the specificity with which the various narrators endeavour to communicate the inarticulable experience at its centre, from the fussy pomposities in the self-congratulatory account of M. le Maire, to the visionary narrative of Paul Lecamus, who despite his unique responsiveness 'to those mysteries which have been my life-long study' can find no metaphor or literary analogue adequate to conveying his experience. Time and again his narrative stumbles against the barriers of articulation: 'It was beyond knowledge or speech.' Moreover, the intensely personal nature of his encounter with these unseen forces, amongst whom he feels his dead wife's presence, leaves him hesitant as to the 'public signification' of the account that M. le Maire has requested of him. His use of the word 'signification' is intended to take us back to that phrase, 'la vraie signification de la vie', which, emblazoned on the doors of the cathedral, has been the notice served by the dead upon the uncomprehending inhabitants of Semur. Lecamus's reputation for 'impracticable and foolish opinions' has led to his status as a good citizen being brought into question: this distancing from the camaraderie of male citizenry, combined with his desolate yearning for his wife and the subsequent events of the story which bring him close to M. le Maire's wife, all serve to associate him with the female portion of Semur's population who, like him, are 'slow to understand a system that compartmentalizes private and public signification'. For the reader the fascination of this tale partly consists in the way it raises questions about an element of its signification apparently inaccessible to the narrators: the nature of the women's role.

M. le Maire's narrative repeatedly manages to associate women and religion as two aspects of life that can be accommodated within a sceptical male-dominated world by according 'respect to their prejudices'. This process is designed to neutralize their disruptive potential and to provide an agnostic with a spiritual insurance policy. He is struck by 'the extreme justice (not to speak of the beauty of the sentiment)' with which he explains to his wife, 'Take courage . . . this world will never come to anything much different from what it is. So long as there are *des anges* like thee to pray for us, the scale will not go far down on the wrong side.' His materialist understanding conceptualizes these matters as an affair of weights and balances.

The *bon Dieu*—if, indeed, that great Being is as represented to us by the Church—must naturally care as much for one-half of His creatures as for the other, though they have not the same weight in the world; and consequently the faith of the women must hold the balance straight, especially if, as is said, they exceed us in point of numbers. This leaves a little margin for those of them who profess the same freedom of thought as is generally accorded to men—a class, I must add, which I abominate from the bottom of my heart.

Women have been given their compensatory affinity with heavenly concerns precisely because this is territory outside the pale of the known and the valued. When M. le Maire searches for explanations for the inexplicable events that ensue he automatically turns first to the women's part in their causation. Yet his sceptical rationalism prevents him from giving serious weight to their imprecations. He sees their instinctive revulsion at impiety, repeatedly expressed in the words 'It is enough to make the dead rise out of their graves', as a merely coincidentally apt use of cliché rather than as a formula encoding deeper truths. The trickery that he initially assumes must account for the supernatural inscription on the cathedral doors is attributed, by M. le Curé, to the nuns who are attempting to 'move heaven and earth' to prevent the secularization of their hospital. The official representative of the Church makes even M. le Maire uncomfortable when he appears to be 'abandoning his own side' by speaking of the nuns as if, like witches, they cannot be trusted to use their spiritual powers responsibly: 'It is never well to offend women . . . Women do not discriminate the lawful from the unlawful: so long as they produce an effect it does not matter to them.' The agnostic had been happy to accord them (meaningless) angelic status, but the world of official religion is driven to finding a more remote diabolic territory for them to inhabit.

At every point of the tale the women are marginalized. Structurally their narratives are left to the end, but not allowed a conclusive voice since the final chapter is given back to M. le Maire. Moreover, the two female voices, empowered only by virtue of their relation to M. le Maire, declare themselves hesitant witnesses. Madame Dupin, his wife, whose maiden name, Champfleurie, suggests the pastoral complement she was to provide to her husband's urban status, would have liked to be the representative chosen to re-enter the occupied city but she accepts that 'perhaps it was better that the messenger should not be a woman; they might have said it was an attack of the nerves. We are not trusted in these respects, though I find it hard to tell why.' His widowed mother acknowledges her triple inadequacy as a female narrator 'because in the first place I have not the aptitude for expressing myself in writing, and it may well be that the phrases I employ may fail in the correctness which good French requires; and again, because it is my misfortune not to agree in all points with my Martin'. As the plot unfolds the women are evacuated to the surrounding countryside where they care for the young, the old, and the infirm with a growing disregard for the insistence upon social hierarchy that underpinned all male planning. Here they are condemned to await the outcome of an affair negotiated by a man whom even his own mother acknowledges as an unlikely intermediary given that he is 'a person of the world and secular in all his thoughts'.

Readmitted to the now totally deserted city, M. le Maire goes to the male enclave, the library, 'where my father and grandfather conducted their affairs', in search of a message from the unseen visitors. He finds an implicit message to heed the past, conveyed in the restoration of his grandfather's desk to its central position, but looks in vain for 'any writing, any message to me'. Instead he finds the sign of the angelic visitation in his wife's rooms where the embroidered veil she has wrought for their dead child's shrine has been folded away and an olive branch laid in its place. That a non-verbal communication should have been employed by angelic forces, using a woman's handiwork and a woman's space, sets the seal upon the association patronizingly alluded to by M. le Maire's compliment to women as 'des anges'. In a moment of illumination, when the cathedral towers first pierce the sepulchral gloom surrounding the beleaguered city, the Mayor suddenly experiences a moment of conversion: 'I have loved, I have won honours, I have conquered difficulty; but never had I felt as now. It was as if one had been born again.' As an agnostic he associates his rebirth with the re-emergence of a patriarchal landmark 'which we had been born to love like our father's name', but for the reader the significance of his conversion lies in the following paragraph:

When we had gazed upon them, blessing them and thanking God, I gave orders that all our company should be called to the tent, that we might consider whether any new step could now be taken: Agnes with the other women sitting apart at one side and waiting. I recognised even in the excitement of such a time that theirs was no easy part. To sit there silent, to wait till we had spoken, to be bound by what we decided, and to have no voice—yes, that was hard. They thought they knew better than we did; but they were silent, devouring us with their eager eyes. I love one woman more than all the world; I count her the best thing that God has made; yet I would not be Agnes for all that life could give me. It was her part to be silent, and she was so, like the angel she is. . . . *Mon Dieu!* but it is hard I allow it; they have need to be angels.

As M. le Maire himself points out, the conversions effected by this abrupt collision with another world are short-lived and his is shorter than most. His brief moment of enlightenment is quenched when, as the populace re-enter the city, he remembers that he is still wearing 'my scarf of office, which had been, I say it without vanity, the standard of authority and protection during all our trouble: and thus marked out as representative of all, I uncovered myself after the ladies of my family had passed, and without joining them, silently followed with a slow and solemn step'. Vesting himself in officialdom once again, he resumes his patronizing 'respect' for the ladies. At the celebratory service he and his brother citizens displace the female worshippers and make the walls ring to a sound 'Mâle and deep, as no song has ever risen from Semur in the memory of man'. He is oblivious to possible ironies in the women's remarks: 'The *bon Dieu* is not used to such singing . . . It must have surprised the saints up in heaven . . . It is not like our little voices, that perhaps only reach half-way.' On this occasion their words coincide with his prejudices and so they are allowed 'signification'.

This was figurative language, yet it was impossible to doubt that there was much truth in it. Such a submission of our intellects, as I felt in determining to make it, must have been pleasing to heaven. The women, they are always praying; but when we thus present ourselves to give thanks, it meant something, a real homage.

The occupation of the city soon becomes entwined in myth, superstition, and self-interested deceit and this in turn returns M. le Maire to the fold of bigoted agnosticism: 'though gentle as a lamb and open to all reasonable arguments, I am capable of making the most obstinate stand for principle'. Now that he takes the religious threat seriously, women find themselves placed beyond the bounds of his tolerance: he is outraged that the male-led cathedral celebration is not perceived as sufficient, and when some of the citizens suggest that the chapel should be restored to the convent hospital this is his reaction: 'And now they would insult the Great

God Himself by believing that all He cared for was a little mass in a convent chapel. What desecration! What debasement!' Ironically he now finds himself isolated from the majority and patronized in the very terminology he had formerly applied to women: 'The best men have their prejudices. M. le Maire is an excellent man; but what will you?' He finds himself condemned to bear the women's lot and suffer from knowing that his perceptions will go unheard and disregarded. Almost despite himself he ends his account with a tribute to the disregarded: Lecamus the visionary, and Agnes his wife. In her silent ministrations and his tombstone lie the only meaningful record of these experiences.

This tale of reversals, of the dead displacing the living, of the unseen dictating terms to a secular community, had afforded Mrs Oliphant the opportunity to explore the fears and prejudices which lurk beneath and support any dominant ideology. The exceptional nature of the events that take place provides its own commentary upon the seismic proportions of the revolution in contemporary thought that would need to occur before male complacency is shaken into taking account of the forces it has tamed by institutionalization. *A Beleaguered City* had not attempted a vision of an alternative society; rather, the incursion of these mysterious discomforting powers that the community is afraid to face had laid bare the assumptions upon which a supposedly rational, materialist society based itself. Contemporary women readers, though they might not agree with her analysis, were not slow to perceive the point of her tale. One of her correspondents, a Blanche Airlee, who disapproved of the notion that souls remained gendered in the after-life, chose the xenophobic option the tale offered in an attempt to deflect its implications: 'I do not quite like the divisions you have made between men and women. I daresay it is true in France.'[102] The story was written at a point in Mrs Oliphant's career when private concerns forced her to take stock of the position in which women found themselves: her nieces returned from their German boarding-school in the spring of 1879 and a future needed to be planned for them. In the couple of years that this tale took to come to fruition she published two novels that reflected many aspects of its feminist concern: *Within the Precincts* and *The Greatest Heiress*, and in the year after the tale's publication she first offered a cautious tribute, on behalf of 'voiceless women', to those feminist campaigners who had brought 'into the open the superior patronizing way in which some men regard women'.[103]

The next tale of the unseen, 'Earthbound',[104] further explores issues raised in *A Beleaguered City*, such as maternal anxiety and the need for men to be educated or jolted into seeing women as being as various in temperament and role as men. M. le Maire's two female relatives had both been mothers, but whereas his wife saw only the goodness of God in the visit of the Unseen, the mother feared a God who might require 'us to give up all if we would be perfected'. The death abroad, in October 1879, of Mrs Oliphant's nephew, Frank, had reopened the wounds of bereavement and confronted her with a picture of herself as a woman who cared too passionately about her loved ones to entrust them willingly to God's care. The

Gospel tale of Mary and Martha lurked behind the contrasting pair of women, united only in their love of Martin Dupin, and was to surface openly in novels and tales from this point.[105] 'Earthbound' voices Martha's anxieties in a variety of ways: in the image of the bereaved mother with whom the tale opens, forced to reserve her grief for her locked room while organizing a Christmas house-party that will include a suitor for her younger daughter. Her family preoccupations link her to their eighteenth-century ancestress who haunts the grounds, condemned to the vicinity because she had been overfond 'of the house and the trees, and everything that was our own. I thought there was nothing better, nothing so good.'

The quest of Edmund Coventry, the male protagonist in this tale, has also to do with discrimination. M. le Maire has been briefly jolted into a glimpse of women as other rather than necessarily inferior, but there is no evidence that he perceives the distinctions the reader is led to make between, say, the nature of his mother and his wife. Edmund Coventry has to learn to discriminate between the unavailable spirit bound forever to her obsession with the place and the younger daughter of the family with whom he is staying and, like her ancestress, also called Maud. His meetings with the apparition, visible only to him, have aroused him from the easy indolence of bachelor life to a state where he sees 'that one ought to select one's path, to settle, to take up the more serious part of life', and like some knight of medieval romance he wanders the neighbourhood trying to find a mortal woman who incarnates the girl of his dreams. The living Maud is understandably dis-pleased by the sense that Edmund has been aroused by the notion 'of a different kind from any he had met before: a new woman, a creature born to influence him', and proceeds to lecture him upon a young man's commonest error, that of judging women by their dress alone. From his description of the visionary girl's attire she hypothesizes that he has encountered the keeper's niece, a London dressmaker. 'A girl like that may walk like a lady and dress like a lady. She has got to be among ladies most of her time . . . Indeed, sometimes they talk even, just as nicely as we do.' Armed with this advice Edmund goes to see the young dressmaker and emerges 'pleased with his own discrimination'. At the crisis of the tale Mrs Oliphant invokes Dante to signal the story's meaning. Alluding to an embrace refused in purgatory because such a thing between shades is impossible, though the desire is itself a measure of love, the apparition tells Edward, 'You will do what is appointed; but do not be sorry, you will like to do it.' It still remains for him to learn to discriminate between fraternal and conjugal love, as is emphasized by her farewell, 'Goodbye, brother—goodbye!' When Edmund recovers from his traumatic encounter he is ready to recognize in the living Maud not the 'sister' with whom he has grown up as her father's ward, but a potential wife. The apparition's deliberate retreat from Edmund is immediately succeeded by 'a roaring of echoes, a clanging of noises, a blast of great trumpets and music' in Edmund's head: a mental echo of the shout of triumph that marked the liberation of earthbound souls at this point of Dante's *Purgatorio*.[106] The story does not reveal whether the ghostly visitant has been liberated from her earthly sojourn by her educative role, but Edmund learns to distinguish between the comfort and pleasure provided by the women of his guardian's demesne and the possibility of married happiness offered by a particular girl whom he must love for herself. So great has been his previous confusion that after his marriage to Maud he never revisits Daintrey.

'The Open Door', of January 1882,[107] again used the challenge to conventional assumptions afforded by the supernatural, to investigate Victorian middle-class constructions of gender. By now Cyril was 25 and well embarked upon a career of idle dissipation much resembling brother Willie's, and Cecco had begun to show signs of following suit. The story's narrator, a brusque military man, is frankly puzzled by young fellows of 25 'with no notion of what they are going to do with their lives'. His unconscious answer is to oversee the upbringing of his delicate surviving son with a great emphasis upon 'manly' behaviour. Mrs Oliphant was well aware that even her friends had begun to attribute her sons' indolence to the pampering lavished upon them by their widowed mother. The comments so frequently proffered to single mothers about the need boys have for a strong male presence, even if galling to a woman of her particular experience, must have given her pause for thought. The fictional parents decide, like Mrs Oliphant, upon a day-boy's career for their delicate son; nevertheless the child falls ill from concern at hearing a ghostly voice in the ruined part of their rented Edinburgh estate. The voice, finally audible even to his father and the sceptical local doctor, can be heard by the sill of an open door in the ruins of the former house crying, 'Oh, mother, let me in.' The child recovers when the elderly local minister exorcizes the spirit of a former parishioner, 'Willie', by telling him to 'Go home to the Father'—a feat only accomplished when he prays to God to let the dead mother 'draw him inower'. The prodigal son, suggestively named after Mrs Oliphant's brother, is saved through the mother. Yet, as so often in her tales of the supernatural, the enigma is provided, not so much by the surface plot of ghostly visitation, but by the reader's disconcerting suspicion that the real centre of interest lies elsewhere. Thirty years' experience in learning to subvert her male persona in *Blackwood's* reaps its reward in tales like *A Beleaguered City* and 'The Open Door'. It is the Colonel, rather than his son, who is most enduringly affected by this encounter with the unseen. To preserve his position as the decisive and effective parent the Colonel is forced to confront those very irrational forces he most distrusts and dismisses as feminine. His narrative has already dismissed 'that fool of a woman at the gate' and proclaimed that the most effective way of allaying his wife's anxieties is to refuse to take any notice of them. Events force him both to recognize the inadequacy of 'manly' fortitude as a code to life and to accommodate previously denied or suppressed facets of life within his definition of 'manliness'. Physical courage, embodied in his soldier–butler, gives way before the unseen. The local doctor's scientific materialism makes no headway with his son's health and moreover begins to irritate the Colonel by its obstinate reductionism. Only his son and the elderly minister, unembarrassed by his tearful tussle with the wandering spirit, seem free from terror and able to concentrate upon 'succouring' a poor fellow creature in misery. If by the end of the tale the Colonel's fear of 'the hysterical' is no less, at least he has been convinced that his former 'male' template does not meet all cases and his narrative ends with the sentence, 'Things have effects so different on the minds of different men.' (A far less subtle tale, 'The Portrait' of 1885, was to investigate the spiritual sterility of the male ethos by alternately removing and replacing feminine influence in a young man's life.[108])

'The Lady's Walk',[109] a short story of the same year as 'The Open Door', repeated these concerns and introduced a new theme that was also to haunt the next tale of the supernatural, 'Old Lady Mary': the power to provide for the next generation. As in 'Earthbound' and 'The Portrait', we have a tale of female doubling. The spirit of an ancestress walks the grounds of the Ellermore estate anxious to alert the family to impending threats. There is a strong physical resemblance between her and the current mistress of Ellermore, Charlotte, the eldest daughter, who vowed to her dying mother to devote herself to the care of her siblings. Eventually the ancestress and her descendant have to accept that they cannot avert the series of disasters that occur, but Charlotte exorcizes or liberates the ghost by distinguishing between legitimate self-sacrifice for those entrusted to one's care and attempting to usurp God's position by playing Providence. The departing ghost's rueful reflection, 'I have never done any good—just frightened them, or pleased them', is an uncomfortable echo of Mrs Oliphant's private lamentations over her inability to influence her obstinately indifferent sons. The tale is told, however, by a bachelor barrister intent on marrying Charlotte. His wishes lead him to interpret Charlotte's role as virgin-mother as enslavement, 'a poor sort of reward for a good woman. There is such a thing as being too devoted to a family. Are they ever grateful? They go away and marry and leave you in the lurch.' In the course of the tale the narrator learns 'to bear the woman's part': although he is allowed to provide sympathy from the sidelines he begins to feel 'rage at his impotence to help'. Finally, he finds himself in a position to provide the money to save the family estate but can only do so as an altruistic sacrifice since he is not to be rewarded by marriage to Charlotte, whose undivided attention seems so important to her immediate family.

Mrs Oliphant attempted only one full-length novel of the supernatural, *The Wizard's Son* (1884). It is not wholly successful because the expanse of the three-volume novel encourages the realist traits of her fiction, sometimes to the detriment of the carefully controlled ambiguity between natural and supernatural explanations that can be maintained within the sparer confines of the short story. To give a brief example: Walter Methven's experiences as hero are clearly based upon those of the protagonist in 'The Secret Chamber', young Lindores; but whereas Lindores is crisply presented as a type of young aristocrat enduring an archetypal rite of passage, Methven's story is complicated by a series of closely explored relationships and the temporal demands of the novel that necessitate annually repeated confrontations with his 'wierd'. Mrs Oliphant encounters similar problems to those faced by other Victorians who sought to incarnate spiritual conflicts, previously expressed through allegory, in narrative form, though her heroine, Oona, a Scottish version of Spenser's embodiment of true religion, has a mother and lover whose failings allow her slightly better anchorage in the mundane world than Tennyson's Arthur was ever to achieve in the world of the *Idylls of the King*.

Yet these weaknesses are not a simple matter of artistic mismatch: they are endemic to the nature of the enterprise in a novel that sets out to discuss what kind of heroic absolutes are available to upper-middle-class Victorian gentlemen. Walter Methven, brought up by a widowed mother in the aptly named southern town of Sloebury, is suddenly catapulted, by unforeseen inheritance, to the position of Lord Erradean and a Scottish lochside landscape, which manages to accommodate the Gothic attributes of Walter Scott's Ravenswood estate,[110] a high place where the devil takes those whom he wishes to tempt, and an enchanted isle, together with the substantial holiday home of a rich and vulgar Glaswegian magnate.

The wizard, an Erradean ancestor, whose Darwinian challenge to Walter to submit personal ideals and goals to the 'furtherance of the race' so clearly echoes that of Earl Robert in 'The Secret Chamber', has a curious role in the novel. Like Hogg's satanic double in *The Private Memoirs and Confessions of a Justified Sinner* (1824) this satanic warlord is sometimes felt to be an aspect of Methven himself; more than this, it slowly becomes apparent that the wizard's kingdom is not limited either to this one family or to the ancestral estate, and Walter's own world-weary talk begins to carry overtones of Job's tempter as he proclaims that he has been 'wandering up and down the earth, seeking I don't know what'. Sometimes, however, the tempter is perceived as an external presence: a group of well-to-do sightseers see him only as a distinguished statesmanlike figure and this, Mrs Oliphant argues, is what the devil amounts to in the nineteenth century—the spirit of compromise. Although absolute goodness and love exist as heavenly ideals in her work, the fight they engage in is not with absolute evil, which she can conceive of no one desiring, but with the devils of indifference, fatalism, and the acceptance of the second best. The wizard serves to give an allegorical reading to Walter's encounters with five women, the chief of whom are his mother, defeated and embittered by her failure to influence her beloved son; the magnate's daughter, an embodiment of sceptical common sense who would save him from his vagaries, but in so doing deaden him to his spiritual yearning; and Oona, whose love finally enables him to rout the wizard. The scene where Walter is eventually driven to make his 'confession of love' to Oona is one of the most extraordinary that Mrs Oliphant ever wrote. Oona becomes the Christ figure from Holman Hunt's *Light of the World* as she tells him that the 'Lord stands at the door and knocks, till you are ready to let him in', and he responds, 'the house is yours, and all in it. Open the door to your Lord, whom I am not worthy to come near and to everything that is good. It is yours to do it. Open the door!' The scene is immediately reintegrated within the parameters of the realist novel when they realize that 'they had forgotten Hamish', who is rowing their boat and worrying over the reputation of his young mistress, who seems to be succumbing to the romantic overtures of a none too savoury local landowner. The attempt to pull the moment back into 'the common life which was so near' is no mere bathos, for Oona, despite her Christlike capacity to grant absolution and give love 'unmerited, unextorted, unalterable', can only do this by virtue of being a woman.

her hands fluttered with longing to clasp him and console him. What woman can bear to hear out such a confession, not to interrupt it with pardon, with absolution, with cries to bring forth the fairest robe? She touched his head with her hands for a moment, a trembling touch upon his hair, and said, 'God forgive you. God will forgive you,' with a voice almost choked with tears.[111]

In the moments of her transcendence it is clear that it is as a woman that she mediates Christ. 'She looked at him with the pity of an angel, with something of the tenderness of a mother, with an identification and willingness to submit which was pure woman.' Moreover, in these moments it is repeatedly stressed that it is 'like a mother' that she interprets God's role of welcoming the prodigal son. Oona is the transfigured version of Walter's mother ('like his mother' only 'brilliant with celestial certainty'), whose life is embittered by her thwarted desire to redeem him. The poignant and penetratingly self-critical analysis, offered by Mrs Oliphant earlier in the novel, of an embattled home where moral disapproval and obstinate resistance wage silent warfare under the sardonically amused gaze of a distant cousin 'who was not of the class of peacemakers to whom Scripture allots a special blessing',[112] makes one grateful that the practice of reading the day's writing to her sons and cousin Annie had fallen into desuetude.

3.   Tales of the Afterlife

Mrs Oliphant's stories of the afterlife itself do not , for the most part, hold much to attract a twentieth-century reader. Their combined aim of consoling the bereaved and justifying the ways of God to men by adopting a heavenly perspective results in episodic narratives where each event offers a message, free from the troubling dualities and lack of closure observable in her finest tales of the unseen. The desire to console, by offering as real these imagined heavenly places, destroys the tension implicit in the earthbound stories, where the appeal of the unseen, the other life, derives precisely from a final uncertainty as to whether it can or will ever be attained. In her *Autobiography* she repeatedly reverts to the mingled pain, pleasure, and 'bewildering dizziness' of allowing herself to play with the notion of entering the doors of her past homes in the unrealizable hope of finding her previous life going on there unaltered. In almost all of her successful tales of the supernatural we find a door, which both is and is not there, either because it is intermittently accessible, or because, although it exists, it is apparently devoid of meaning, made obsolete by later architectural modifications. Allowing the imagination to create a liminal world, where past, present, and future can coexist, permits the unseen to find a point of entry. As Mrs Oliphant lay dying she dictated a last poem whose first lines express her sense of death itself as such an opening.

On the edge of the world I lie, I lie,
Happy and dying, and dazed and poor,
Looking up from the vast great floor
Of the infinite world that rises above
To God, and to Faith and to Love, Love, Love![113]

It was her sense of the here-and-now and the hereafter as a continuum that allowed her to depart so very strikingly from the conventional deathbed scene whose staginess arose from a need to forestall the uncertainty of eternal justice and realize the dramatic finality of the Last Judgement in mortal surroundings. For the same reason her stories of the afterlife are more interesting for the commentary they offer on her earthly concerns than for any compelling visionary revelations or innovativeness in speculative theology.

When God appears in these stories it is usually in the person of the Son and He is felt more as a presence confirming 'the peace of God that passeth all understanding' than as a personal Saviour. The work of God the caring father is left almost entirely to the agency of the spirits of ex-mortals and to female spirits at that. Among the most interesting aspects of Mrs Oliphant's Utopia are the roles played by women which both mirror and offer models for their earthly roles. Women find work in heaven because the holistic tendencies of their earthly concerns with caring, nurturing, and healing are in high demand in an afterlife which accepts such a diversity of life's outcasts. Inasmuch as they have always done this work on earth, yet been largely invisible in the public authority structure of the Church Visible, they are peculiarly suitable in a role which leads sinners to God rather than usurping His role. The 'Little Pilgrim' series was in fact inspired by the sudden death at 58 of Nelly Clifford, a Windsor neighbour and 'a woman of the angel kind' who despite being 'generally reputed rather a silly little woman' had devoted herself successively to a senile mother and a debilitated brother.[114] When her fictional prototype, 'the Little Pilgrim', reaches heaven she discovers that the history recorded there is of a very different kind from that on earth: it concerns itself with the good works performed by those whom earthly history has ignored.[115] The heavenly Book of Life begins to look suspiciously like twentieth-century feminist history. Mrs Oliphant's often perfunctory attitude to the Victorian novelistic conventions of romantic themes and intricate plotting had long been founded upon a belief that there were other tales scarcely permitted by the limits of the genre. *The Minister's Wife* (1869) had ended with this characteristic comparison of the melodramatic tale of a short marriage, recorded within the novel, with the subsequent unrecorded narrative of a widowed mother's life: 'the other, long, tranquil, with no facts at all to speak of, marking the passage of the years—nothing to tell; but yet, perhaps the life that bulks most largely in the records in the skies'.

Mrs Oliphant's heaven allows full recognition to female modes of spirituality while freeing them from the earthly disadvantages of gender. In heaven earthly marriages are perpetuated but, since spiritual equality has now been gained, 'it is no longer needful that one should sit at home while the other goes forth'. The family unit, which in some earthly homes shows forth God's grace, is reconstituted in heaven so that the bereft and lonely on earth have a heavenly 'home' where they may return to their parents in the interstices of their work for God. The vital nature of their healing mission removes any sense of a mere return to dependence upon paternal structures. Moreover, the 'liberation' of married women from domestic servitude enables due value to be given to a sense of female community.[116] Most women find themselves particularly at home in heaven because their experience has already taught them something of divine altruism. In 'Old Lady Mary' (1884) Mrs Oliphant used the exception to prove the rule. A rich old woman, Lady Mary, whose 'whole life went on velvet, rolling smoothly along without jar or interruption', dislikes the troubling thought of contemplating her own death and therefore neglects to secure adequate provision for a young relative, little Mary. On her arrival in purgatory she was 'somewhat astonished . . . being used, wherever she went, to a great many observances and much respect' to find herself surrounded by people 'so busy with their own occupations that they took very little notice'; she also finds herself unable to intervene on others' behalf with the easy patronage to which she was accustomed. Worse still, her purgatorial desire to remedy the wrong she has done her young relative brings her back to earth, where she learns what it is to be wholly disregarded, except by children. In effect her purgation is accomplished when she arrives at an understanding of the altruistic sufferings of less privileged women. By the end of the tale the significance of the shared name is discovered when Lady Mary learns what it is to be a dependent woman and benefits from her relative's unsought forgiveness while aware that she herself has not had the power to right wrongs.

In the 'Little Pilgrim' series of tales some departed spirits learn for the first time the female capacity for secret suffering: they come to understand what it is to shed tears for those they have left behind, knowing all the while that their earthly mourners cannot be troubled by the capacity of the departed to feel sorrow. In heaven the silent ministrations and unregarded sacrifice of women's earthly sojourn help them to participate in the paradox of the Godhead. Now that they share the Father's will there is no tension between earthly and divine parentage, although, interestingly, Mrs Oliphant still finds it hard to accept a divine Father whose commitment to free will allows wrongdoing and alienation: prolonged discussion or lament upon such matters is a distinctive feature of her afterlife. Mrs Oliphant's heaven is in fact used to validate the absolute primacy of the mother–child bond. In the first tale the divine education of a fallen woman is entrusted to her dead child.[117] In the second tale, where 'The Little Pilgrim Goes Up Higher', the climax of her joy in the Heavenly City is reserved for the concluding episode where she is reunited with her mother, now restored to full health and mental competence. Her father too is in heaven, but his role is peripheral: he merely serves to make up the numbers of the average family structure and the Little Pilgrim shows no interest in asking him questions. In the last of these tales, 'The Land of Suspense', a tale so 'personal' it hurt to publish it,[118] a young man, clearly modelled on Cyril, finds himself a dispossessed person in a corner of God's kingdom, where, in accordance with his self-centred, aimless earthly life, he has neither work, responsibilities, nor affection to define him. Slowly he loses the resentment he felt on arrival that his reception did not measure up to his earthly home, which was 'never closed to me before; never have I failed of entrance there and welcome, and my mother's light always burning to guide me'. The young man whose excuse on earth has been 'If my father had been here' finds the Prodigal Son's reception in heaven less fulsome than the one his earthly mother had accorded him. In heaven such a welcome can only come when his will is in tune with the Father's. Seeing a younger brother's immediate access to heaven his anger and despair is transformed, not by divine intervention, but by the agency of his mother. His egoistic misery is interrupted by his sudden awareness of his mother, still on earth and now doubly bereft. He visits the temple in the woods to pray for her and leaves it 'with the gift of a blessing he has not sought'. Healed by his altruistic prayers he is now ready to be welcomed into the heavenly city.[119] This image of salvation, effected through the mediation of Christ by the oppressed and dispossessed, interestingly anticipates the mode of liberation theology; yet such images of mediation can be misleading in failing to distinguish between the idea of Christ identifying with the suffering of the poor and oppressed and any romanticized notion that the poor and oppressed are necessarily spiritually superior or nearer to God.[120] Christ identifies with them, they are not identical with Christ. Mrs Oliphant, I think, often failed to make this distinction. It is true that when forced to articulate her position in non-fictional form she reminded her readers that Christ differed from humans in that he had a life he could choose to take up and lay down freely,[121] but in her fiction she had long ago ceased to use the images of mothering as a way of making God intelligible and gradually reduced the Trinity to a deeply caring single parent wounded by her children's rejection.

As Mrs Oliphant lay on her deathbed she dwelt on two things: the death of St Catherine of Siena and the words from Corinthians 3: 15.[122] The two images are telling. St Catherine was an appropriate patron for Mrs Oliphant: the Sienese saint's sense of mission had been honed and disciplined and, to an extent, moulded by her family's decision to remind her of her womanly duty by setting her domestic chores and denying her the privacy to devote to her inner life. Her best known works were done from home; she became the recipient of mystical experiences and her caring, nurturing role earned her the title of 'Mamma' from her followers. The words from Corinthians may seem a more curious epitaph: 'If any man's work shall be burned, he shall suffer loss: but he himself shall be saved, yet so as by fire.' It is perhaps not surprising that such a text should have caught the imagination of so prolific an author: it was not by her works, as she had always known, that she would be saved.[123] But the penitential fires of suffering 'that shall try every man's work of what sort it is' she must have hoped would reveal and justify the ways in which the passive agony of a woman's life established an identity with the sacrificial suffering of God.

'Blessings not sought' are part of Mrs Oliphant's understanding of the role of prayer. It was thus she explained to herself the moment of mystic visitation she had received on the golf-links at St Andrew's in 1884 as she wandered desperately miserable 'crying to God' for the reformation of her sons who were at that moment carousing in the Golf Club. 'A great quiet and calm' descended upon her precisely at 'that blessed moment when I was not asking for it, not thinking of any consolation for myself, only help and deliverance for them'. She was to revisit the experience many times in her writing and always with the same sense of wonder that 'This is what is meant by the answer of prayer'.[124] In this way too she was able to accept a doctrine of purgatory without embracing the efficacy of prayers for the dead: these could only be understood as an expression of human concern or forgiveness, which may be a balm to the departed but cannot influence God, whose careful provision for each soul is 'as if there were not another in the world'.[125]

It is customary to refer to the vague popularism implicit in Mrs Oliphant's attempts 'to give topography to the world beyond the grave',[126] and it is true that her landscape of the afterlife offers a curious mixture of Dantean allusion, travel brochure writing, and illustrations in primary colours occasionally obscured by the filmy mists of angelic presences. Of far greater interest are the theological implications behind the imprecise lineaments of her post-terrestrial world.[127] Any suggestion of a static heaven or hell, characterized by atrophy, indolence, and hopelessness implicit in 'fixed states', was anathema to someone as imbued with the Victorian work ethic as Mrs Oliphant. Her tale 'The Land of Suspense' embodies in acute form the move away from a predominantly Calvinistic eschatology so characteristic of the nineteenth century. The notion of 'a land of suspense' presumably derives from Calvin's attempt to distinguish his teaching from various Anabaptists who believed that the soul slept between death and the Last Judgement: 'The souls of the faithful, after completing their term of combat and travail, are gathered into rest, where they await with joy the fruition of their promised glory; and thus all things remain in suspense until Jesus Christ appears as the Redeemer.'[128] The horror of the young man who finds himself wandering in a place outside the city derives from his growing awareness that this is a place which perpetuates the style of his life on earth, devoid of responsibility, of thoughts of past or future. Yet Mrs Oliphant cannot envisage a state of perpetual suspended animation: even here some souls slowly disintegrate without work or feelings to cement their sense of identity. The oscillation between hope and dejection which was characteristic of her own earthly life finds its way into the eschatological narrative so that the spirit finds himself alternatively depressed, by the energy and purpose of the souls of the saved passing through on the Lord's work, and possessed by the hope that intermittently God Himself will pass by. The final chapter effects the transposition of the wandering soul to the city of the saved.

The interrelation between the various stopping-off places on Mrs Oliphant's eschatological map is hard to conceptualize. Where the Land of Suspense exists in relation to the place where newcomers await their first meeting with God in the first tale of the 'Little Pilgrim' series would be difficult to say. The transition from earth to the hereafter is in every case so gentle that most newcomers are slow to recognize the changeover other than by external signs such as 'unfamiliar clothes', or 'perpetual daylight'. Since Mrs Oliphant's afterlife is physically, morally, and emotionally a continuum of earthly life, its existence comes as a shock, not to the sinner, but only to the agnostic and the sceptical materialist. To William Blackwood, attending George Eliot's funeral in 1880, she wrote, 'There is something very solemn in the thought of a great spirit like hers entering the spiritual world which she did not believe in. If we are right in our faith, what a blessed surprise to her!'[129] For high-minded agnostics like Eliot or Leslie Stephen Mrs Oliphant was sure that immortality would provide 'surprise and relief', but for the 'earthbound' spirits, 'to whom it seems to be easy enough to be without hope and without God—either by reason of an easy temper which takes anything lightly and does not trouble to think, or for other reasons', the notion of resurrection would surely be a change too traumatic for a loving God to wish to impose. Therefore she was tempted to espouse the conditional immortality theory that was gaining ground in Britain by the 1870s: 'Is it perhaps', she asked herself in her autobiographical musings, 'a theory to take into consideration that we are not all intended to be immortal, that some may always stop and cease when this world is over, thinking no more and wishing no more, and being taken by God, as it were, at their word?'[130]

Her combined emphasis upon a God understood as love, and upon the coherence of the earthly and the afterlife, inclined her to accept the temporally and spatially intermediate state. The possibility of believing in an intermediate state of consciousness, without subscribing to the doctrine of purgatory, seems to have been suggested to her when reading Gladstone's *Studies Subsidiary to the Works of Bishop Butler* (1896). In her review she wrote approvingly of Gladstone's notion, derived from Butler, which provided for the development of latent seeds of good 'in persons who had not during this life in any manner perceptible to us actually crossed the line which divides righteousness from its opposite, but might make such further advances as would effect that transition'. This intermediate state, as she developed it, was 'the halting place in which those who were too ill for blessing and too good for banning might be stricken violently out of their half-virtues' and seemed to allow for more active intervention than Butler's seed-bed.[131]

Her conception of a 'halting place' was also much influenced by the Dantean model that stressed the possibilities of purification afforded by an all-pervasive Divine Love. As a reader of Dante she had always preferred 'the sunny hillsides of Purgatory' to the tedious theological arguments that go on in heaven.[132] Moreover, her conviction of personal immortality took a stronger form than it did for many Victorians in that it did not merely presume the survival of an individual soul but interpreted personal salvation as an individually designed package. When Old Lady Mary, from the tale of the same name, finds herself dead she makes haste to enquire her precise location from the spirit who has been earmarked to greet her.

'I suppose,' she said rather timidly, 'that we are not in—what we have been accustomed to call heaven?'

'That is a word', he said, 'which expresses rather a condition than a place.'

'But there must be a place—in which that condition can exist.'

She had always been fond of discussions of this kind, and felt encouraged to find that they were still practicable. 'It cannot be—the Inferno, that is clear at least,' she added with the sprightliness which was one of her characteristics; 'perhaps—Purgatory? since you infer that I have something to endure.'

'Words are interchangeable,' he said; 'that means one thing to one of us which to another has a totally different signification.'[133]

Each soul would appear to experience a species of immediate personal 'judgement' or allocation of a particular door by which they arrive in the afterlife, whether in the land of darkness, the land of suspense, or the hinterland of the heavenly city. The concept of definitive 'judgement' was abhorrent to her. When a busy man rushes into the afterlife asking for immediate directions to the 'Judgement-Seat' he is told that his sense of urgency and need for conventional assurances is misplaced because 'it does not feel like that when you are there'.[134] So attached was Mrs Oliphant to the conception of the continuous personal process of self-judgement that she used the phrase 'Dies Irae', traditionally reserved for the Last Judgement, as a title for a late story that deals with the spiritual awakening of a girl hovering between life and death. The sightseeing tour of heaven and hell that her soul is given by the Blessed Damozel turns out to comprise scenes from her home town.[135] Even her last story, 'The Land of Suspense' (1897), written under the influence of Gladstone's 'unfashionable outspokenness' on the grimmer aspects of eternity, concludes with a reference to the last day but is immediately qualified by 'But of that day knoweth no man, not even the Son, but the Father—as was told us by our Lord'.[136] The strength of Mrs Oliphant's resistance to the idea of closure in her realist fiction seems to translate, in the further dimension to earthly life provided by the hereafter, into a sceptical attitude to the concept of Last Judgement. Theologically she found that the concept limited the notion of a God for whom 'we have never found the boundary of His mercy'. 'Nor has it ever been fathomed among us', the Little Pilgrim is told by a heavenly sage, 'how long He will wait, or if there is any end.' The blinding finality of the resolutions such a catastrophist ending supposed was wholly at odds with the notion of free will which was so implicit a plank to her understanding of a God who permitted wrongdoing and suffering. Instead, the drama of a judgement which presumes a separation between God and the spirit on trial is replaced by the internalized 'trial of conscience' which is replayed endlessly throughout a man's earthly life as he stands as both criminal and judge arraigning himself for sins committed and opportunities neglected. The time spent in the various areas of the afterlife merely prolongs and accentuates the intensity of the experience of self-conviction that should have taken place on earth.[137]

For some, such as the fallen woman who has been subject to the Sisters' threats of damnation in her reformatory, this initial meeting with God is sufficient to reconcile them to all further suffering, even that of hell, as part of God's plan and therefore not to be feared but embraced as an aspect of His love.[138]

It seems likely that Mrs Oliphant's theology demonstrates in accentuated form the ramshackle process of accretion and deletion according to personal preference practised in an age which Principal Tulloch had justly characterized as one which 'does not know what to think, yet thinks and wonders and stops itself, and thinks again; which believes and does not believe, and perhaps I think, carries the human yearning and longing farther than it was ever carried before'.[139] A theology which looks forward to 'the time that our Lord might come', but seems to make Christ's harrowing of hell and passage through purgatory an intermittently repeated affair, and then separates this absolutely from any belief in final judgement, raises further problems.[140] Endlessly to defer or even to deny closure is to destroy anticipation and to ensure the collapse of narrative tension, as is evident in the first three of the 'Little Pilgrim' stories. The success of her endings in her realistic fiction derived more from the deliberate tampering with the absoluteness of conventional 'happy endings' than from an abdication of the authorial capacity to imagine a closure however provisional. In the later tales of the afterlife, however, Mrs Oliphant began to develop a paradox, derived from Dante, in which tension was again implicit: in 'On the Dark Mountains' the Little Pilgrim learns 'that there is that which is beyond hope yet not beyond love. And that hope may fail and be no longer possible, but love cannot fail. For hope is of men, but love is the Lord.'[141]

It may seem surprising that an author who had 'always veered away from' talk of eternal punishment should have turned her attention in the late 1880s to hell and its approaches. Possibly Cyril's behaviour had by now begun to temper her earlier optimistic attachment to the virtues of the universalist teaching of Campbell of Row or Erskine of Linlathlen. In the first 'Little Pilgrim' tale, after all, it had even been suggested that Satan himself might not be beyond redemption.[142] She had first become acquainted with the teaching of these Scottish divines back in the 1860s when researching for her *Life of Irving*: they preached that 'unless Christ had died for all, and unless the Gospel announced him as the gift of God to every human being' then Christ's atoning sacrifice was belittled into 'so much suffering reduced to paying for only a few'.[143] After his expulsion from the Church of Scotland, Campbell of Row had continued to worship in the church at Rosneath where her friend Robert Story's father had been the minister, and when the son, encouraged by Mrs Oliphant, wrote his father's *Memoir*, she found herself frankly puzzled by the prominence he gave to the bitter controversy that had surrounded Campbell's teaching. Campbell's creed, she claimed, had been largely absorbed by the Church of the 1860s and exactly expressed what she herself now believed.[144] What she of course meant was that these beliefs were largely shared by the liberal members of the Scottish Church whom she counted among her closest friends: Story and

Tulloch. She herself certainly shared with such men as Campbell and Erskine a strong sense of heaven and earth as a continuum, a belief in the importance of sanctification rather than a total reliance upon appropriating the merits of Christ, and her writing on religious matters could with even greater reason than theirs be criticized for centring the Christian faith in human experience rather than in the events of the Gospel.[145] Nevertheless, in later life she began to feel that the pendulum had swung too far towards consolatory preaching and that there was a strong case for preaching hell to 'those who grind the faces of the poor, and oppress the weak and cheat, and betray, and hurt'.[146] The heroine of 'Dies Irae' (1895), for example, trusting exclusively to the merits of Christ, has seen no need for the exercise of personal charity. Morever, 'being deeply imbued with the latest sentiments', she did not believe in hell.[147] Since the redemption, we are told, the roads between heaven and hell are always open, but the will to embark upon the arduous journey may well have become atrophied. For Mrs Oliphant hell carried no implication of divine vengeance. 'Is there condemnation?' asks the Little Pilgrim. 'It is no condemnation,' answers her heavenly instructor. 'It is what they have chosen— it is to follow their own way.'[148]

Her pictures of hell are incomparably superior to her pictures of heaven. This is not merely a question of the absence of sentimentality—the use of the diminutive 'little' in the titles of the early tales of the afterlife is indicative of this flaw. It is rather the case that her visions of hell employed her strengths as a writer of realist fiction. Satan and his devilish minions do not occupy centre-stage, if indeed they exist at all, for, as was hypothesized in heaven, life in hell is like life on earth and pain is felt only when one wishes for something different. 'Dies Irae' images the terrors of hell as like being forced into realizing for oneself the living anguish and cruelty concealed in the statistics of the Society for the Prevention of Cruelty to Children without being able either to avoid or remedy them. Yet her pictures of hell are fuelled by more than a sense of social injustice.

'The Land of Darkness' dispenses with the pious instructors who accompanied the Little Pilgrim and relies instead upon the self-important voice of a first-person narrator who embodies the traits of the self-centred, bibelot-collecting idlers Mrs Oliphant so despised. Throughout his journey through hell we are shown the interplay between his language and assumptions, derived from the gentlemanly code of England's learned classes, and the modus vivendi in a country that has done away with civilized self-restraint. Law, order, social hypocrisy, or a sense of fellow-feeling have all been discarded in favour of the unbridled pursuit of self-advancement. 'The Land of Darkness' is a fable demonstrating how 'the survival of the fittest' (whether of the individual or the race) would work not in the context of the long-term evolutionary process, but in an ostensibly cultivated industrial and urban society. An extra dimension of horror is lent by the fact that in hell society's failed experiments cannot be killed off, but survive as objects of contempt whose suffering serves as the index of others' comfort. The anxieties manifested in this tale are in one sense typical of many another Victorian dystopia: the fear of machines that replace and tyrannize over the human labour force; the distrust of scientific materialism. Undoubtedly some of the physical tortures, including crucifixion in the interest of moral science, are horrific, but the truly disturbing quality of the tale lies elsewhere. Dante is once again Mrs Oliphant's openly acknowleged source, but the use of colloquial dialogue and the taut dramatic narrative sometimes carries more obvious echoes of Bunyan. Like *Pilgrim's Progress* too, the tale derives some of its nervous energy from its ability to disconcert the reader: the interest stimulated by the convention of realist fictions is held in creative tension with our sense of allegorical intent. Take the following passage:

'You mean you have got no rooms to put them in', said the master of the shop. 'You must get a house directly, that's all. If you're only up to it, it is easy enough. Look about until you find something you like, and then—take possession.'

'Take possession'—I was so much surprised that I stared at him with mingled indignation and surprise—'of what belongs to another man?' I said.

I was not conscious of anything ridiculous in my look. I was indignant, which is not a state of mind in which there is any absurdity, but the shopkeeper suddenly burst into a storm of laughter, he laughed till he seemed almost to fall into convulsions, with a harsh mirth which reminded me of the old image of the crackling of thorns, and had neither amusement nor warmth in it; and presently this was echoed all around, and looking up, I saw grinning faces full of derision, bent upon me from every side, from the stairs which led to the upper part of the house and from the depths of the shop behind—faces with pens behind their ears, faces in workmen's caps, all distended from ear to ear, with a sneer and a mock and a rage of laughter which nearly sent me mad.[149]

As readers we start to enjoy a comedy of manners, observing the priggish hauteur of the narrator played off against the colloquial chumminess of the shop-keeper. If anything, our sympathies incline to the frank pragmatism of the shop-keeper. Very abruptly, however, the mood changes to one of grotesque distortion and demonic possession. The biblical reference to the thorns begins to suggest that we should search for a parabolic interpretation, but suddenly the diabolic grinning faces start to resume the form of workmen enjoying a joke at the gentry's expense. Has the slipping of the mask to reveal demonic derision had any objective reality or is the workmen's involvement in the scene a hallucination prompted by the narrator's inner insecurities? Imprisoned within the narrator's discourse we have no evidence by which to judge the people we encounter, yet the irrational violence of his reactions makes us suspect that some at least of his sufferings are self-induced, the product of a disturbed state of mind. The dynamics of reading reinforce the tale's perception of hell as located in the paranoia of an alienated mind. The frenetic aimlessness of the narrator's pursuit of anything which will distract him from his knowledge of absence and meaninglessness finds its perfect resolution in a dramatic ending that paradoxically resists closure. Towards the end of the tale the narrator is ineluctably drawn to feelings of identity with two men who, having experienced all hell has to offer, determine to start upon the terrible journey to God. He repudiates the first companion with the assertion 'There is no love'. By the time that the second offer is made by a man whose power and self-control in hell have won his admiration, everything inclines us to feel that he will repent at the last, but the tale closes with the narrator flinging aside his companion and turning back to the maddening pursuit of the imperfect. 'On, on across the waste! On to the cities of the night. On, far away from the maddening thought, from hope that is torment, and from the awful Name!' The strength that the rejection has taken is the measure of the desire that tortures him.

4.   Death and Closure

Pre Jubilee Sunday, 1897: They sent to bring Alfred Tennyson's poems last night. There was one that she [Mrs Oliphant] wanted. In it he says Death should have another name and that is 'Onward'.[150]

. . . there nearly always comes a point in Mrs Oliphant's novels where almost any writer of the younger school, without a sixth part of her capacity could have stepped in with advantage. Often it is at the end of a fine scene, and what he would have had to tell her was that it was the end, for she seldom seemed to know.[151]

The figure of a narrator 'hell-bent' on resisting a satisfying end to his tale provides a telling image of Mrs Oliphant's fictional strategies in the matter of death and closure. The deathbed never forms the final climax of her stories, and endings invariably reach out beyond the chronological limits of the novel, prompting the reader to contemplate either the unpredictable dilemmas with which the future may confront them, or the diminished life now available to those already restricted or maimed by their past experiences.

Practical observation conspired with religious belief to encourage Mrs Oliphant to use her novels to mount a consistent and absolute repudiation of the cloying sentimentalities of conventionally pious deathbed scenes. As early as 1858 she laid out the grounds of her campaign in an article on 'Religious Memoirs' largely devoted to the prodigiously successful *Memorials of Captain Hedley Vicars*. Noticing that death held 'something like a professional place in the agencies of modern piety', Mrs Oliphant produced a double-pronged attack upon 'the cold undertaker touch of those biographising fingers'. Aesthetically speaking, she deplored the 'unrounded hieroglyphs of piety' created by writers anxious to stick close to commercially profitable formulas.[152] 'People are as different in their dying as in their living', remarks an experienced hospital matron in one of her later novels.[153] It is the theological dimension of her argument, however, that forms the most striking aspect of her critique. Deathbeds, she roundly asserted, were not a Scriptural method of teaching, and the contemporary habit of identifying 'the manner of death' as the real test of Christianity flew in the face of experience: 'Death is not a religious act, nor a meritorious sacrifice', nor was she inclined to feel that the contemplation of death was a spiritually profitable act.[154] In a scene that directly challenges Evangelical teaching of the kind popularized by Mrs Sherwood's *Fairchild Family* (1818), Edgar Arden is invited to view the corpse of one of the family's eldest retainers. Where his pious counterpart would have seen evidence of the corruption of the flesh and the hope of the life to come, Edgar, in the disillusionment wrought by his private circumstances, sees merely that you 'Do your best for a hundred years, suffer your worst, take God's will patiently, go on working and working: and at the end this—this and no more'.[155]

Mrs Oliphant's own religious biographies bear witness to her integrity in the matter of presenting death. Irving is shown to be delirious as death approaches. Lest there should be any temptation for the sentimental to mistake his murmurings for a miraculous last-minute endowment with the gift of tongues that Irving's preaching had fomented, Mrs Oliphant prosaically asserts that the 'unknown tongue' was subsequently identified as a recitation in Hebrew of Psalm 23.[156] Tulloch's deathbed, which she had doubtless been made to relive many times by his family, contains an element of pathos in the dying man's repeated but, she insists, 'unconscious' cry of 'Jeanie, Jeanie' for his wife, but the narrative coda is uncompromisingly deflationary: 'Human nature always longs to know something of the steps by which the traveller reaches the goal; but in his case, as in so many others, that consolation was not given.'[157] By the time that she came to write Laurence Oliphant's biography in 1891 Mrs Oliphant seemed positively to welcome opportunities for exploding the language of conventional piety. One paragraph ends, 'Murmuring something about the angels all around and about, Lady Oliphant died', and the next begins, 'She had been greatly deceived in her life and suffered much.' The scepticism becomes still more overt as the account continues: 'at all events it was with her son's hand in hers, and her Lowry's beloved face bending over her, nearer than any angel, that this good woman . . . passed into the eternal home'. When she came to record the son's death Mrs Oliphant mentioned that 'he was heard to hum and sing in snatches the hymn, "Safe in the arms of Jesus"', a 'homely strain' that, she speculated, would have caused him a wry smile at his own expense when he first picked it up at an American 'revival'. A bystander at his deathbed had told her that Laurence's last words were for 'more light', and she is driven to ponder whether this was 'because the darkness was really gaining on him', or whether it was an example of the way in which death itself had become a second-hand experience: was it merely 'some wandering recollection in the confused musings of a mind shut up from all immediate influences' which led him to use the dying words attributed to Goethe?[158]

Tempted to produce consolation for her close friends, Mrs Oliphant made one foray into the world of the child's deathbed vision. *Little Pilgrim in the Seen and the Unseen* was inspired by the death in 1883 of 10-year-old Wladimir Tarver, at whose birth 'Mrs Gamp-like'[159] she had presided. The liberty afforded by the 'Little Pilgrim' format allowed her to indulge in a flight of fancy where the dying child sees his, and her, old friend, Nelly Clifford, alias the Little Pilgrim, coming for him, but honesty compelled her also to emphasize that such terrestrial proofs of eternal bliss did not exist: 'his eyes opened wide and he saw her where she stood. He cried out "Look! mother, mother! . . . Look! she has come for me!" he said; but his voice was so weak they could not hear him nor take any comfort.'

In her treatment of death, as in so many other areas of her writing, Mrs Oliphant's reconsideration of the traditional modes of presentation was based upon her desire to be true to 'the human story in all its chapters'.[160] In almost every tale, including her comic novels, a character whom we have known dies. When members of her own family died she did not resort to a separate 'mausoleum' book but turned instinctively to the volumes of autobiographical jottings as the appropriate place to record their deaths. Honesty compelled her to admit that her mother's and her eldest brother's deaths were accompanied by a certain sense of relief in the emotional tensions of family life, but the vigil she kept at the premature deathbeds of her husband and three children required more detailed analysis. The fidelity with which she logged her own changing emotions of disbelief, agonizing attentiveness, and occasional moments of nervous levity, makes these deathbeds seem individual, nevertheless certain similarities emerge which provide clues for identifying the distinguishing features of her fictional handling of death. In each case death is remarkable not for its definitive finality but for the confusion and uncertainty with which it is surrounded: only in the last three weeks did she recognize that the tubercular symptoms her husband had been displaying for two years were to be terminal, and from that point the laudanum she was prescribed to check her pregnancy pains confused and numbed her reactions. When Cyril fell ill she had great difficulty in distinguishing between a possible recurrence of the symptoms which had preceded a violent fit some two years before and the 'nights of confused guilt' associated with his drinking. His own 'confused and cloudy condition' produced a mirror response in his watchers over the ensuing five days, so much so that the moment of death itself became obscure. In the days after his death Mrs Oliphant became uncertain as to whether he had died on Saturday night or Sunday morning.[161] In Cecco's case there were ten days of alternating improvement and relapse, and then, 'he was very ill all Monday; it is only yesterday, but it seems to me so far away—only at the very last he made a rally, that the doctor and even I were deceived, but then [he] suddenly fell back and in a few minutes breathed as peacefully away as ever an infant did. . . . He knew nothing about it . . .'.[162]

Death as a spiritual and physical event is so unremarkable for those who die that in her tales of the afterlife they initially find it hard to believe that they have made any transition. The significance of the event can only be registered by the bereaved. It is in this contrast between the gradual journey of death and the catastrophist aftermath for the living that the shocking absoluteness of death is felt:

instead of my sweet, living, loving child I have but a curl of the dear hair and another name upon the marble out at Testaccio [Rome's Protestant cemetery]. Those curls I was so proud at were never more beautiful than when they were all rippling back with gold string through them from her dear head as she lay ill.

God knows I would give all the noble thoughts in the world for that one impatient quick cry of 'Mamma' from the next room, the empty room, whence he has been taken away for ever . . .[163]

There is, of course, a certain contrivance about these deliberately selected contrasts between continuing motion and absolute cessation, but this sense of artifice is designed to contribute to a further and more subtle effect. Inasmuch as these stark juxtapositions satisfy an emotional desire to sum up the experience in a neat oxymoron, the aftermath deliberately undermines the definitive moment. Writing appreciatively of Henry James's fiction, Mrs Oliphant noted the way in which he contrived to suggest that, 'Life is no definite thing with a beginning and an end, a growth and a climax; but a basket of fragments, passages that lead to nothing, curious incidents which look of importance at first, but which crumble and break in pieces, dropping into ruins.'[164] Each of her images of intense grief is submerged and then dissipated in the subsequent paragraphs detailing the peremptory demands made by 'the awful routine of life.' The repeated occurrence of this narrative strategy within the *Autobiography* serves both to reveal any representation of finality as illusory and to throw the emphasis upon the daily and the commonplace as most likely to yield such meaning as life or death have to offer.

The eschatological framework of Mrs Oliphant's view of life prevented her from a total denial of meaning. The closing paragraphs of *Madonna Mary* (1866) are interesting in this respect. The sufferings of the eponymous heroine, a recently widowed mother, bear clear traces of Mrs Oliphant's own recent history. Though she never wavers in her faith, Madonna Mary's selfless piety is outraged by the simplistic Providential explanations of her miseries that she receives from a doctrinaire Evangelical, Mrs Kirkman. The story's repeated use of coincidences, all of which contrive to work against the widow's interests, encourages the reader to form a more cynical view of life than the widow herself does, and the novel's concluding pages allow for this response. The widow's self-centred and embittered sister writes to her, 'I wonder often, for my part, if there is any meaning at all in it. I am not sure that I think there is. And you may tell Mrs Kirkman so if you like.' Although the sister's position in the novel's moral hierarchy invites us to be critical of her interpretation, the fact that she is allowed the last voice gives a certain weight to this alternative reading of events. Even more disquieting is the possibility, raised in later novels, that a capacity to assume purpose and meaning in life may be entirely dependent upon one's temperament and disposition.

The Ladies Lindores (1883) perhaps came as close as Mrs Oliphant was ever to get to expressing the two warring sides of her own personality, tempted at times to see herself as 'stranded upon this desolate shore', and at other times to recognize a culpable elasticity of temperament that allowed her to 'keep on with a flowing sail' and to pilot herself and others through the worst of adversities.[165] As is so often the case in Mrs Oliphant's fiction this novel ends with a battery of rhetorical questions as to the new possibilities raised by its apparent closure. Lady Lindores has come to perform her maternal duties at her daughter, Lady Car's second marriage. Lady

Car's emotionally sensitive, but essentially passive, character led her to accept her father's dictate in her first marriage, despite her own dreams of marriage to a less socially acceptable suitor. The sudden death of her tyrannical husband has left Lady Car free to marry her first suitor, but her growing awareness of the enervated dilettante manner the intervening years have developed in him altogether distinguishes the long-desired outcome from any sense of 'a happy ending'. The novel ends, however, by depicting her equally put-upon mother's psychological voyage into the unknown.

She went home that night, travelling far in the dark through the unseen country, feeling the unknown all about her. Life had not been perfect to her any more than to others. She had known many disappointments, and seen through many illusions: but she had preserved through all the sweetness of a heart that can be deceived, that can forget to-day's griefs and hope again in tomorrow as if to-day had never been. As she drew near her home, her heart lightened without any reason at all. Her husband was not a perfect mate for her—her son had failed to her hopes. But she did not dwell on these disenchantments. After all, how dear they were! after all, there was tomorrow to come, which perhaps, most likely, would yet be the perfect day.

Within this passage the narrative voice moves from a condescending view of the gullibility associated with such optimism into a state approximating collusion with Lady Lindores: such phrases as 'after all', and 'most likely' are those a woman uses to persuade others to her optimistic view of life. Narrative empathy in this case was prompted not merely by a shared capacity for optimism but by authorial identification with 'the trembling interest of observation with which a mother watches her child on the brink of new possibilities.' The maternal anxiety that characterized Mrs Oliphant's refusal to allow her own children to effect the break necessary to begin an independent adult life was complemented by an authorial disinclination to effect the clean break for her characters which might have been achieved by definitive endings to her novels. The authorial version of this trait turned out more happily to have a commercial advantage in that it allowed her to resurrect characters whose fate had been left in the fictional limbo of a non-conclusive ending.

At the conclusion of *Sir Robert's Fortune* (1895) the latent comparison between author and mother offered in the final picture of Lady Lindores is more self-conscious. After the death of her selfishly scheming husband the heroine of this tale is left to the full enjoyment of her child and a financially secure future. Throughout the novel her lot in life has been contrasted with that of the suggestively named Helen Blythe, the daughter of an impoverished manse.

They were different in every possible respect, but above all in their view of existence. Helen had her serene faith in her own influence and power to shape the other lives which she felt to be in her charge, to support her always. But to Lily there seemed no power in herself to affect others at all . . . the one mother trembled a little, while the other looked forward serenely to an unbroken tranquil course of college prizes and bursaries and at the end a good Manse, and perhaps a popular position for her son. What should Lily have for hers? She had much greater things to hope for. Would it be hers to stand vaguely in the way of Fate, to put out ineffectual hands, to feel the other currents of life as before, sweep her away? Or should she stand ever smiling, like simple Helen, holding the helm, directing the course, conscious of power to defeat all harm and guide towards all good?

Since Helen's capacity to steer the bark of life seems predicated upon a naïve assumption as to her powers, the prose rhythms seem to be directing us to give a negative answer to the novel's final question.

Lest it should be thought that Mrs Oliphant's habitual resistance to absolute closure was little more than a habitual tic, amounting to an artistic failure of nerve, she reported that it was 'the middle, that fatal period, which is always my most dangerous moment' in a novel.[166] Her last three-decker novel, *Old Mr Tredgold* (1895), offered readers her considered view on the artistry of endings. The age of the aesthete, she noted, had declared happy endings to be vulgar and less true to life than tragic endings. This reversal of fashion, in her opinion, merely mirrored the mistake of preceding generations. The only 'end' that life had to offer, she re-affirmed, was that 'which we hope is exactly the reverse of an ending'. The novel closes by offering the reader alternative futures for the spinster daughter left alone with a maid and the modest sum of five hundred pounds per annum. Mrs Oliphant's apparently old-fashioned disinclination for new literary fashions in fact disguises a shrewd deployment of modernist techniques: the full weight of a decisive reading is transferred from the vagaries of the individual character's temperament to the discernment of the reader. 'A vulgar happy ending' is on hand for the reader prepared to privilege escapist inclination over fidelity to the charac-ter's temperament. With a positively Jamesian relish for using slang to place readers who choose this option, the disillusioned Katherine Tredgold is described as being in a good position to marry, having as they say, 'two strings to her bow'. Those who prefer unhappy endings are offered the picture of Katherine brooding in rural seclusion over life's inequities, and finally those who share the author's preference for endings which contain their own denials are catered for: 'She would have liked to have gone abroad, to have done many things; but what can be done, after all, by a lady and her maid, even upon five hundred pounds a year?'

Mrs Oliphant's conviction that endings, either tragic or happy, were untrue to her sense of life as 'a mystery without close' did not blind her to the novel reader's desire for resolution as a pleasure often thwarted by life itself.[167] Women, her novels observe, are rarely permitted the enjoyable act of closure, however temporary, afforded by slamming a door and walking out after a domestic quarrel. In an article of 1889 pondering 'Success in Fiction' she attributed the current popularity of Rider Haggard or Stevenson's tales of adventure to a public emerging 'fascinated yet unsatisfied' from the 'purposively inconclusive endings of Henry James's art'.[168] One of her own last tales, 'Queen Eleanor and Fair Rosamond', made conscious play with the gap she had identified between popular convention and 'truth to life'. The tale's structure enacts its message. When a middle-class wife and mother discovers that her husband has established a bigamous marriage elsewhere, the position of her children and the undoubted innocence of the second wife do not allow her the moral outrage and decisive action that convention, embodied here in a male friend's advice, dictates. Rather she suffers her husband's sporadic and uninformative visits, never able to learn where he comes from, what prompted his bigamy, or whether 'it had all been worth it'. The title's allusion to the legend of Henry II's queen, who had allegedly resolved a similar situation by poisoning her supplanter, is foiled by the way in which the tragic potential of Mrs Oliphant's tale is drained away into 'tragi-farce at the end, that is the most terrible of all'.[169]

The originality of Mrs Oliphant's treatment of deathbeds sprang from her perception that they epitomized this dynamic tension between a desire for definitive closure and a sense of the irresoluble: bystanders inevitably looked for indisputable signs of recovery or cessation, and were shortly to have to cope with the finality of loss, while the dying themselves were more inclined to look at death as transitional. Indeed, the moment of release experienced by the most heartbroken of relatives when death breaks the tension is something her novels frequently register. As she perceptively diagnosed, this tension needed to be re-created for those not actually present at the deathbed. Relatives welcomed a letter recounting the final moments of those who had died abroad, especially if these included some sense that the dying person had made some acknowledgement of being aware of an imminent meeting with God. *Carità* (1877) includes the portrait of a family for whom the memory of the father they have abandoned in India is remote and misty. One morning, just as the wife is thinking of making some token of *rapprochement*, they receive a letter communicating his death and are thrown into a state of almost comic uncertainty as to how to behave: 'In such a case as this "the bereaved family" did not know what to do. How were they to gain that momentary respite from the common round? If the blinds were drawn down, and the home shut up, according to the usual formula, that would be purely fictitious; for of course he had been buried long ago.' In the same novel a woman, dying of a lingering illness, meets her end abruptly when an overdose of medicine is innocently administered and her husband, deprived of the final moments, remains emotionally numbed for much of the novel, despite the fact that such an unlooked-for end forestalled suffering which would have been particularly hard for his pleasure-loving wife to bear.[170]

Once convinced that death is more likely than recovery, relatives display a desire for death to take place in a seemly manner compatible with the semi-fictional conventions of pious deathbed literature. The first volume of *The Sorceress* (1893) contains one of Mrs Oliphant's longest-drawn-out deathbeds, lasting four chapters. Mrs Kingsward, a good wife and mother, has finally succumbed to her weak heart and is slipping away from her family, comforted by gazing at a picture of St Catherine of Siena floating into heaven supported by angels. The doctor has already declared that there is nothing he can do, but her husband, Colonel Kingsward, is dissatisfied by 'such infidels' who 'would let a soul rush unprepared' into the presence of the Supreme Judge. Anxious to get her into 'the state of mind becoming a dying person', he summons the rector and assembles the children, but his rigorous military code is offended by the way his wife, knowing that it would be better for the younger children to 'go and finish their game', evades formal farewells, and

even more disturbed by the smile with which she greets the rector: 'the same smile
of welcome with which she would have greeted her kind neighbours had she been
in her usual place in the drawing-room'. In the midst of his carefully assembled
scene the narrative conflates Mrs Kingsward and the picture of St Catherine
'floating away' so that, cheated of any final moment, the Colonel is forced to accuse
his children of being 'lost to all feeling' rather than admit that death itself has
disappointed his own emotional needs.[171]

Sometimes Mrs Oliphant produces tragicomedy out of the desperate efforts
made by distraught relatives to get the dying to approach death with due solemnity.
May (1873) starts with the episode of a debauched young man sustaining a fatal
injury. Unaware that he is dying, the severity of his plight nevertheless persuades
him to consider turning over a new leaf, but, despite his devoted sister's prayers and
entreaties, he dies without ever confessing himself of the major stain on his conscience. While his sister is busy, in vain trying to mould him into 'an evangelical
conqueror, a saint-like personage in robes of white and crown of glory', the total
unsuitability of the material she has to work upon is further revealed by the wildly
inappropriate snatches of conversation between her uncle and a comic ostler that
keep floating up from the inn-yard below.[172] Such was Mrs Oliphant's scepticism
about deathbed repentances that although she would have liked to have believed
that her son Cyril had finally made his peace with God she nevertheless honestly
records that it was only at the very last with 'the phlegm rattling in his throat' that
'he spoke, muttering and low, of seeing God' and that those outside the room
claimed to have heard him mention Jesus, though she herself had not.[173] In one
early novel, *The Laird of Norlaw* (1858), written contemporaneously with her piece
on 'Religious Memoirs', she took particular pleasure in illustrating that 'God does
not always make the Christian death-bed sublime'. Three lingering deaths go
spectacularly wrong: the Laird himself calls out the name of his first love, not that
of his devoted wife, in his death throes; an emotionally debilitated young woman is
being preached into a deathbed conversion when the sudden reappearance of her
wicked husband distracts her attention from other-worldly concerns; and, in the
final volume, a good-hearted elderly minister dies striving to make a last witness,
but a stroke has made him unintelligible and his niece merely pretends to understand him in an effort to soothe his parting moments.[174]

Only the death of children escapes Mrs Oliphant's wry humour, though here too
she was determined to challenge sentimental prejudice. The only thoroughgoing
piously sentimental deathbed she composed occurs in *The Melvilles* (1852) where,
in a scene that owes much to Jo's death in Dickens's *Bleak House*, a little boy dies
with the words of the Lord's Prayer on his lips; but even here the scene is prefaced
by a furious repudiation of the callous notion that children's deaths can be accepted
more easily in the persuasion that this will enable them to reach God faster.[175] Mrs
Oliphant grew deeply to dislike the pathos with which Dickens surrounded the
death of young children, claiming that his deathbed scenes derived their power not
from artistry but from unfairly tapping 'the personal recollections which any
allusion to a feeble or dying child inevitably recalls'.[176] In the other two children's

deaths drawn at any length in her work she is careful to focus attention upon the parents' emotions rather than upon the child's innocent piety. In *Agnes*, a novel written in the immediate aftermath of Maggie's death, a child of comparable age lies dying and 'it did not occur' to his mother to disturb him with 'conversations about death and heaven'. Instead she tells him stories that seem to entertain him. *Agnes* becomes the receptacle for the full weight of Mrs Oliphant's own anger against a God who deprived her of her only daughter, and so deep is her resentment at this sudden interruption of a child's life ('Thus it all ended, God knows why') that the narrator refuses to offer any consolatory vision of the child's transition to heaven, choosing to distance herself from the language of pious consolation by quotation marks: 'And then it was all over in two days, and the little life became perfect, "rounded with a sleep".' Mother, narrator, and reader alike in this book are left with the finality of loss: 'That was how it ended abruptly, like a thread suddenly snapped upon the wheel, when nobody was thinking; and no one yet could understand the dread certainty, the blank and final repose, which had succeeded to so much anxiety and suspense. He was dead, and hope was dead, and with hope fear; and yet, at the same time, the eager throbs of the old anguish had not learned to cease contending with the awful stillness of the new.'[177]

To underline the contrast between the sudden and irrevocable loss sustained in death and the unsatisfyingly indistinct contours of life, Mrs Oliphant deployed her chapter headings. The child's death, recorded in chapter 60, 'How it ended', is succeeded by two further chapters entitled, respectively, 'After the end' and 'Conclusion'. Faced with the intransigence of life itself, the artist can only 'wind matters up' in provisional fashion, reminding us that for the living even the most tragic incidents are only phases. Tales of disappointed love are characteristically signed off with phrases such as 'However, he is young, and things may mend', or 'But it may be that Effie's wounds are not mortal after all'.[178] These remarks do not diminish the particular suffering depicted within the tale, but serve to remind us of the 'condition of mortality' where only death itself appears to be capable of effecting absolute rupture. Yet this rupture too can be seen as a matter of 'illusion' or perspective. For Mrs Oliphant the act of narration provided an analogy through which she could image her religious faith to herself. 'And the story ends, being like all stories, no story of life, but only a bit out of life', she wrote as she decided to 'break off' her tale of *The Three Brothers*. In her role as artist she was forced to determine a point at which to effect a rupture, though knowing that, by an equally arbitrary act of the imagination, her characters' lives could be almost infinitely extended. The characters within her tale, however, can no more know what their future lives might have held than mortals can conceive of the continuity which the afterlife offers. In her tales of the afterlife characters are enabled to see their deaths as merely transitional, but in her novels characters seem obdurately trapped by their concept of death as a boundary.

Her conviction of continuity combined with her belief that death is the point at which God reveals most clearly that 'each is to Him as if there were not another in the world'[179] to preserve her fictional deathbeds from the conventional piety that overcame most other Victorian novelists. The two concepts worked hand in hand to guarantee a sense of the individual character's singularity at the very moment when an appeal is made by many novelists to the stereotypical and the sentimental in an effort to cover over the abyss of the unknown into which their tale threatens to disappear. By contrast Mrs Oliphant's characters are never more fully themselves than when death approaches: 'A man may "lose his head" as we say at the time of his marriage, or of any other great crisis in his life, but he rarely loses his head at the moment of his death.'[180] Death comes most easily in her novels to those who have had the insubstantiality of earthly life impressed upon them by the death of those they have cared for: they are also disposed to accept death more readily because of the prospect of reunion it affords. The most interesting of her deathbeds in her novels depict those characters, most frequently male, whose lives have been dedicated to comparatively harmless self-gratification. These portraits often re-explore the shock with which Mrs Oliphant had registered her husband's lassitude and growing self-absorption that was to culminate in a death 'quite, quite free from anxiety, though he left me with two helpless children, one unborn, and very little money, and no friends'.[181] If we are to judge by *Agnes*, Maggie's death prompted her also to re-examine the feelings associated with Frank's death. Agnes's husband, Roger Trevelyan, dies slowly, 'without very much more suffering, but also without any special intensification of feeling, or sense of awakening to the solemn things that lay before him. He made all the responses quite faithfully and humbly, and received all the consolations of the Church, without ever getting beyond the idea that he supposed he should be happy and not mind, and yet that, on the whole, it was strange and a little hard.' In a telling parallel to the later scene of her son's death, Agnes finds Roger incapable of deriving much spiritual consolation from the Bible: instead she is condemned to amusing him by reading an interminable novel. Roger is, in death as in life, a mildy petulant child.[182]

The Primrose Path (1878), an over-lengthy novel of trivial concerns, contains one fine cameo of old Sir Ludovic, thrice a widower, approaching his death. He finds that 'what he believed had not much to do with what he felt'; he hopes, by visiting his local church, containing the family burial place, to be able to raise his mind to the contemplation of 'the last things', but a lifetime of antiquarianism as a mode of shielding himself from anxiety or responsibility has atrophied his spiritual responses. Possible reunion with all three wives troubles more than it consoles, and he has only a dull sense of the 'wide, vague, confusing desert of the unknown' to which he is bound. On his deathbed he relapses into trust in the only thing on which he has ever relied—a conviction of his aristocratic lineage: 'Sir Ludovic was never a more high-bred gentleman than in this last chapter of his life. He was bored beyond measure, but he never showed it.'[183]

Since Mrs Oliphant conceived of judgement as a continuous process, death served her well as a summatory point without becoming the earthly enactment of Final Judgement that it did in the work of novelists who were too uncertain about the hereafter to miss this chance of doling out rewards and punishments. In keeping with her growing attachment to the notion of conditional immortality, the relatives of very worldly characters are allowed to express themselves incapable of imagining a 'spiritual non-bodily existence' for the departed. When, in *Innocent* (1873), the suddenly bereaved husband of a vulgar termagant realizes that he has been set at liberty, he nevertheless feels pity for his wife.

How could any imagination follow Amanda into the realms of spiritual existence? Her life had been all physical—of the flesh, not of the spirit; there had been nothing about her which could lead even her lover to think of her as otherwise than as a beautiful development of physical life . . . Her soul—what was it? Frederick had never cared to know. He had never perceived its presence in any secret moment. But he was not impious, nor a speculatist of any kind; he indulged in no questions which the most orthodox theologian could have thought dangerous.[184]

Scepticism of this nature was useful to a novelist. Even in a very early work such as *Harry Muir* (1853), written before she became much acquainted with death, she was able, on the one hand, to deliver a dramatic deathbed in which the fate of the ne'er-do-well's family depends upon his ability to repent his fecklessness and survive long enough to summon his lawyer, and, on the other, to make the drama credible by admitting how much of a mystery death remains, eluding the understanding or control of doctors, lawyers, pious relatives, and the author. Harry Muir's grieving sister exhorts him to cast his eyes heavenward.

And the dim eyes turned upward to the roof—to the human mortal screen built between him and the sky; and saw, not the heavens opened, and Jesus standing at the right hand of God, but only a household of weeping women, half frantic with love and eagerness, crying aloud for him before the everlasting throne, where mercy sits and judgement; and a blank numbness was on Harry's soul.

The scene is emblematic in showing how Harry has always thrown all moral and spiritual responsibility upon his womenfolk. The lawyer arrives only in time to hear Harry deliriously muttering 'the texts and the psalms which he had learned as a child'. The incipient sentimentality accompanying reversion to childlike innocence is arrested by the uncertainty we share with the bystanders as to whether such unconscious recall is sufficient to 'cancel out' a lifetime's careless wrongdoing. In earthly terms his reflex response to spiritual concerns comes too late for him to attend to his neglected duties: there can be no deathbed reversal of a lifetime's processes, but despite the fact that 'No human speech could move him now, or reach his veiled and hidden soul . . . the way was all open to God'.[185] Although such a scene has its roots in tract literature it also shows how early Mrs Oliphant recognized that faith, and, for that matter, realism, had little to do with clear-cut doctrinal assertions. Her novels may repeatedly criticize ministers whose latitudinarian tendencies render them incapable of proffering effective consolation to the bereaved, but she never confused orthodoxy with faith. Death in her novels often reveals to a clergyman how he has unwittingly confused a profession with a spiritual vocation.

Perhaps the most daring use she made of these convictions was in *A Rose in June* (1874) where a whole chapter is devoted to the death of a country clergyman, Mr Damerel, whose life had been one of cultivated aestheticism nurtured at the expense of his ever-anxious wife.[186] In cruder hands this could well have degenerated into a tract illustrating the circle in hell reserved for false shepherds, but instead we are encouraged to feel a muted version of the 'grief and pity' his wife feels as she watches the inability of the intellectual and aesthete to respond adequately to the unique mystery of death. Damerel, 'who was no sceptic' and 'believed what he had been taught and what he had taught in turn to others', reviews the literature of death, both liturgical and poetic, and finds nothing that quite corresponds to his own predicament. 'He was not thinking of his sins, nor of reward, nor of punishment, nor of rest from his labours (which had not been many).' He is troubled only by philosophical uncertainty: 'He was departing alone, the first of his generation; curious and solitary, not knowing where he was going. To God's presence; ah, yes! but what did that mean?' Just at the point when the chapter is in danger of settling into easy moral condemnation of a theology totally divorced from experiential faith, Mrs Oliphant jolts the reader's complacency. Mr Nolan, the hard-working Irish curate, who exemplifies all the Christian virtues his rector does not, leaves the deathbed disgusted by the rector's mental levity and self-centredness, only to find himself 'shivering with something like cold, as he looked up at the stars. "I wonder, after all, where he is going?" he said to himself with a sympathetic ache of human curiosity in his heart.'

That capacity for pitting the certainties of orthodoxy against the unfathomable mysteries of man's spiritual condition is one of the greatest strengths of Mrs Oliphant's fiction. It is also typical of her fictional studies of the clergy that neither of these clerics, despite their early promise of simple stereotypical contrast, is confined to a one-dimensional landscape. The breadth of her own experience was capable of translating itself into a 'sympathetic ache of curiosity' on behalf of even the least admirable and least spiritually aware of her male characters.

6   A Woman and the Wider World

I was reading of Charlotte Brontë the other day, and could not help comparing myself with the picture more or less as I read. I don't suppose my powers are equal to hers—my work to myself looks perfectly pale and colourless besides hers—but yet I have had far more experience and, I think, a fuller conception of life. I have learned to take perhaps more a man's view of mortal affairs,—to feel that the love between men and women, the marrying and giving in marriage, occupy in fact so small a portion of either existence or thought.[1]

1.   'Far More Experience'

(a)   The length and the breadth of it

Mrs Oliphant was only 35 and had half of her life still to come when she made this comparison of herself with Charlotte Brontë, who had died at the age of 39. Although she was nine years younger than her sovereign and was to predecease her by four years, her memories and her exceptionally long writing career effectively spanned the period normally characterized as 'Victorian'. She shared to the full her age's self-consciousness about the speed with which change was being effected and its passion for constant reassessment to determine whether change could be equated with progress.

Her role as occasional essayist offered a further inducement to comment upon the nation's penchant for erecting benchmarks of change. Such events as the New Exhibition of 1862 prompted comparisons with the political climate in which its illustrious predecessor of 1851 had taken place. Peace had given way to war and the royal instigator of the nation's euphoric self-congratulation, the Prince Consort, was dead. The architectural fantasies of Paxton and Sir Gilbert Scott had given way to 'the school of accidental architecture', but encouragement could be derived from the international friendship symbolized by the picture collection which, for her, formed the crown of the new exhibits.[2] Her penultimate essay in *Blackwood's* seized the occasion of the Queen's Jubilee celebrations for the retrospective 'Tis Sixty Years Since'. Despite her personal weariness and the opportunity the article afforded her to voice domestic prejudices against such innovations as antimacassars, the tyranny of William Morris patterns, and Liberty design concepts, she concluded the article with a panegyric to the reign's achievements in such matters as philanthropy and medical advances. She also announced herself unequivocally in favour of the revolution in the speed and convenience of transport that the period had seen.

Her earliest memories involved a canal journey to make the move from Edinburgh to Glasgow. Her father's job with the export department of the Excise Office in Liverpool had allowed her to witness the transition from the days of the great sailing-ships to the coming of those 'magic slaves', the paddle-steamers.[3] The subtitle of an early novel, *John Drayton: Being A History of the Early Life and Development of a Liverpool Engineer* (1851), suggests the world of romance and opportunity implicit in a career she was later eager to embrace for her own nephew, rather than the dry manual of self-improvement conjured up for twentieth-century readers. The novel itself charts a speed of social transformation bewildering to those deprived of community traditions. Boys from the rustic hinterlands of Liverpool have nothing of the moral and educational securities provided by the Scottish and Welsh exile communities. Nevertheless the outlook is optimistic: the lurking demons of Chartism, rationalism, and democracy can all be conquered by the love and devotion of a good woman of pious upbringing, and the hero manages to embody the continuity that can be achieved by obtaining a position as ship's engineer on a boat that, to the absolute disbelief of the old folk, can shuttle back and forth between England and the New World in ten-day crossings. All of which did not prevent Mrs Oliphant using, when occasion served, exceptionally lengthy, dangerous sea voyages to remove a husband or lover and wrench the heartstrings as character and reader alike wonder whether the deep will return their loved ones unharmed.[4] These tales, it is only fair to say, were usually located in fishing communities on the coast of Fife and attributed to tales her mother had told her.

The coming of the railway was for her, as for most Victorians, the greatest visible symbol of change. Despite the occasional, almost mandatory, conventional reference to the steam engine as 'raising feelings in bystanders like those experienced by Frankenstein after he had made his monster',[5] her attitude to it, in comparison with previously available modes of transport, was entirely positive. To someone who disliked sea travel as much as she did, the thought of the long, tedious, and frequently stormy removals that a previous generation had been forced to make from Scotland to the South down the east coast was dispiriting.[6] Channel crossings were a trial to her and she claimed that it was the thought of the voyage that prevented her from meeting her American reading public.[7] Melodramas such as *Salem Chapel* show her to have been fully alive to the nightmarish possibilities afforded by the railway, a form of transport which, since it was equally available to pursuer and pursued, could only introduce a note of hectic speed rather than favour the triumph of justice, but she never indulged in the suicides and accidental deaths attributed by many another Victorian novelist to the iron monster. Railway stations, junctions, or platforms did little more than provide an easy shorthand for the emotions connected with meetings, partings, and 'frail travelling coincidences'.[8] Travel, or the new speed of travel, did not fundamentally affect the moral quality of life: it merely provided a sharper focus for observing life. Only in very early novels does she pay lip-service to the notion that travel of itself broadens the mind.[9]

Her first journey abroad with Frank appears to have convinced her that the Grand Tour of Europe had become a much overrated distraction for disappointed lovers: those lacking the necessary intellectual preparation or interest were unlikely to find themselves suddenly 'inspired with real and elevating love for the great in art, and the beautiful in nature' and would do far better to throw themselves into hard work or try the rigours of India.[10] Her own experience taught her that a restless desire for travel was too often the result of a desire to achieve numbing distraction from pain. After her husband's death she had spent two years 'always moving about and changing from one place to another', so that everything might seem 'exceptional' before she could force herself to set out 'anew upon the dread reality' of returning to London.[11]

Henry James cruelly remarked of Mrs Stormer, his thinly veiled satirical portrait of Mrs Oliphant, that in her novels featuring passion and the English upper classes abroad, she never really saw Dresden or Florence, but merely took her old box of props and puppets abroad with her, fishing them out for whichever book she was currently writing.[12] There is an element of truth in this criticism. Unlike Henry James, who relished the chameleon-like opportunities foreign societies afforded to the permanent exile prepared to soak up the local colouring, Mrs Oliphant reputedly loathed sightseeing, preferring to soak up the atmosphere through observing the mores of the places she lived in or visited:[13] a country's eating habits or its attitudes to marriage provided the significant surface differences that were of interest to her. Her books on Italian history were similarly criticized. The *Saturday Review* claimed that while her anecdotal, biographical mode of history might be suitable for a city like Florence, it was wholly uncongenial to the spirit of Venice where an awareness of the contribution made by its political and commercial life was vital.[14] Where these critics went astray was in attributing this mode to mere laziness. Her method was the result of conviction. To give life to a story or a period, she claimed, it was no good relying upon transcribing 'originals' or using newspaper articles to achieve verisimilitude as was Charles Reade's practice. It was unsurprising that sociologists like Herbert Spencer and Henry Maine failed in their attempts to reconstruct a picture of Roman society for they lacked the one insight needful: 'The novelist working on the basis of humanity, which, though varying in its modes, is practically the same among all people and in all ages, has advantages over the scholars.'[15]

There was a further fundamental difference of attitude between Mrs Oliphant and James in their attitude to foreign parts. James was, not surprisingly, fascinated by those who had made the choice to be eternal expatriates. Mrs Oliphant found the claustrophobic, gossipy life lived by the English in cities like Rome rebarbative. To live as an alien outside this community was equally unthinkable for a mother of growing children. Parents, mainly widowed men, who subject their children to this rootless life, where they are bereft of other relations and yet never really accepted by the natives, are seen as indulging in a consummate act of selfishness. She never forgot Frank's act of treachery in leaving her to fend for herself in Italy, and novels of later years contain moving pictures of young wives and children leading lives of comparable isolation.[16]

Most of the members of her fictional expatriate communities are there as a consequence of their failure to address the 'dread reality', financial or emotional, of home. By parking 'poor brother Willie' with the Macphersons, who formed the hub of the 'noisy, Bohemian' expatriate artist society in Rome, Mrs Oliphant was in effect expressing her view of such social misfits. 'The Macphersons', she wrote years later, 'had a curious position in Rome, and it is difficult to describe them . . . he always had a curious position.' Her own choice of Windsor, and Eton as a school for the boys, represented the most definitive turning of the back upon the normal 'rut of the artist life'. Effectively this repudiation embraced the whole tenor of her married life. It is hard to imagine Frank's company of workmen or even Frank's artist friends with whom he 'smoked and talked' of the day's work in his studio, 'the drawingroom proper of the house',[17] finding a welcome in Mrs Oliphant's establishment in the upper-middle-class purlieu of Windsor.

In the thirtysomething years that remained to her she was to broaden her knowledge of Europe, and even make a two-month trip to Palestine and Egypt in her sixtieth year for her book entitled *Jerusalem: Its History and Hope* (1892), but it had been the earlier part of her life that offered her the greater variety and range of experience. Topographically speaking, at the age of 35 Mrs Oliphant undoubtedly had a wider knowledge than Charlotte Brontë, or, for that matter, Dickens or George Eliot. The social distance she had travelled is also remarkable. From the humble economic circumstances of a clerk's home, the passport of extensive reading and early writing had allowed her access to literary groups in Edinburgh and London. Perhaps marriage to a man bent upon raising himself from craftsman to artist status also served to ease the London stage of this transition in ways not available to Dickens, who as a man had to prove himself capable of making the transition unaided, before he could hope to gain a wife's support.

The exceptional mobility of her early life carried consequences for her writing, both in terms of attitude and content. Earlier chapters have pointed to the sharpness of observation honed by the experience of occupying so many border territories: the Scots–English divide, the woman in a man's world, the mother acting as male provider. The range of her opportunities for observing human nature in a wide variety of economic and national settings seems also to have fed into a cast of mind at once sceptical and open to a sense of the mysterious and unfathomable, convinced of the bedrock unalterability of the human character and experience and yet alive to every nuance of change in social mores. A short piece of journalistic ephemera, 'Heroes: Mortality and Immortality', provides a simple illustration of these apparently conflicting attitudes. The piece opens with a confident assertion, in keeping with the tone of voice of the 'dowager' figure under whose byline these articles have appeared: 'The hero of one age differs from the heroes of another as much as its clothes do and its ways of thought.' By way of a disquisition upon the nobly borne suffering of the short-lived German Emperor and the story of General Gordon's decision to offer himself up as a human sacrifice to prevent further bloodshed, the piece arrives three paragraphs later at a conclusion apparently wholly at odds with its beginning: 'the thing that hath been is, according to all experience, the thing that shall be'. The opening remark was founded upon a sense of the changes in fashion the centuries witness in attitudes to human suffering: whereas the eighteenth century would have found scope for moralizing an early death, late Victorians have elevated brave suffering to the heroic pantheon. These, however, are merely shifts of emphasis; of one thing only can we be certain, that both these heroic exemplars will soon be forgotten and further sacrificial victims be required, for 'humanity is sadly unteachable'. It was the pity inherent in this sceptical conviction of human waste that in turn fuelled the desire, openly admitted as emotional rather than rational, for an afterlife to provide a meaning that the experience of life so flagrantly denied.[18]

The capacity Mrs Oliphant had developed to adjust to different social milieux while also retaining a very firm sense of her own identity (she never, for instance, made any effort to lose her 'pretty racy Scotch accent',[19] and always despised those who sought to disguise their true social origins) seems to have had further implications for her craft. 'Anthony Trollope's talk about the characters in his books astonished me beyond measure', she wrote, and although she claimed that her writing 'often carried me away from myself and quenched, or at least calmed the troubles of life', she was forced to admit, 'I am no more interested in my own characters than I am in Jeanie Deans, and do not remember them half so well, nor do they come back to me with the same steady interest and friendship.' 'Perhaps people will say', she ruefully confessed, 'this is why they never laid any special hold upon the minds of others, though they might be agreeable reading enough.'[20] There is, certainly, a sense of distance between writer and character, even when the character is observably autobiographically generated, that offers the reader a wholly different experience from the almost total immersion in the heroine's fictional world afforded by a novel such as Charlotte Brontë's *Jane Eyre*. Nor are we as readers as abruptly discomforted as we sometimes are in George Eliot's novels by the interplay between the inner world of a particular character's thoughts and the contemplative philosophizings of a narrator whose outlook plays over 'that far greater range of relevancies called the universe'. Again an example may help to convey Mrs Oliphant's particular narrative stance. I have deliberately chosen a novel which enjoys high repute and makes no sustained use of the ironic gap between character and narrator that produces the overall mood of books like *Miss Marjoribanks*. The following passage is taken from *Kirsteen: The Story of a Scotch Family Seventy Years Ago* and describes Kirsteen's state of mind as she decides to emulate Jeanie Deans's journey south from Scotland to the unexplored territory of London. She is already sufficiently disorientated by her first journey away from the 'wilds of Argyllshire' to her long-estranged sister's house in Glasgow.

The Sunday which followed was strange yet delightful to Kirsteen. It was like the last day of a sailor on shore before setting forth upon the unknown, but rather of a sailor like Columbus trusting himself absolutely to the sea and the winds, not knowing what awaited him, than the well-guided mariners of modern days with charts for every coast and lighthouses at every turn. Kirsteen looked

> On land and sea and shore,
> As she might never see them more.

All was strange to her even here, but how much stranger, dark, undeciphered, unknown was that world upon the edge of which she stood, and where there was absolutely nothing to guide her as to what she should encounter! Kirsteen was not quite sure whether she could understand the language which was spoken in London; the ways of the people she was sure she would not understand. Somewhere in the darkness that great city lay as the western world lay before its discoverer. Kirsteen formed an image to herself of something blazing into the night full of incomprehensible voices and things; and she had all the shrinking yet eagerness of a first explorer not knowing what horrors there might be to encounter, but not his faith in everything good. The Sunday came like a strange dream into the midst of this eagerness yet alarm. She was almost impatient of the interruption, yet was happy in it with the strangest troubled happiness; though it was so real it was bewildering too, it was a glimpse of paradise on the edge of the dark, yet unreal in its pleasure as that vast unknown was unreal. She played with the children, and she heard them say their prayers, the two little voices chiming together, the two cherub faces lifted up, while father and mother sat adoring. It was like something she had seen in a dream—where she was herself present, and yet not present, noting what every one did. For up to this time everything had been familiar in her life—there had been no strangeness, no new views of the relationship of events with which she was too well acquainted to have any room for flights of fancy.[21]

The facility of the style, teetering dangerously on the brink of the facile when words like 'strange' and 'unknown' are so shamelessly overused, partly accounts for the ease with which readers devoured her three-deckers, but there are other devices at work here. The extraordinariness of the literal and metaphysical adventure that Kirsteen is embarking upon is at first conveyed by drawing upon common pools of imaginative reference. Repeatedly we are first offered the easily graspable experience—a sailor's last day on shore, or the fear of foreign languages and mores—before being given the more particular sensations of the heroine. The distance between narrator and character is not merely a matter of third-person narrative, but derives from the sense that the writer is closer to the readers' responses than to the character. That is not to suggest total complicity with readers: there is something, in her reminder of the difficulties that faced travellers of previous generations, of George Eliot's retrospective stance in relating the historic that manages to rebuke the unthinking process by which we equate past and present. A double layer of irony is also at work in her presentation of the idealized family scene Kirsteen witnesses: the novel encourages us to be critical about the self-centredness of her elder sister, who uses her loudly proclaimed devotion to her husband and children as a defence against her responsibilities to her parents and siblings. Kirsteen's sense of this as 'like something she had seen in a dream—where she was herself present and yet not present' is a telling comment upon the loving unity of family life for which she has so greatly yearned and of which she is always to be so conspicuously disappointed. This narrative pattern of encouraging the easy recognition of the familiar and following it up by the defamiliarizing observation that can stimulate 'flights of fancy' throws up in its wake the self-reflexive image of the traveller-writer 'herself present, and yet not present, noting what everyone did'.

The clearest register of the effect produced upon her fiction by her voyage from Scotland to England and through the social echelons was of course in the choice of fictional settings. The novels of her first decade frequently carried the subtitle 'A Story of Scottish Life' and employed both her own earliest memories and her mother's store of family legend. Alongside these tales she soon embarked upon novels where the vagaries of the hero or heroine's career were often attributable to the economic and social uncertainties of life in the industrial hinterlands of Liverpool, to which her father's work had brought her. After her marriage, life in 'Bohemian' London and the trips with Frank around the southern counties, where his stained glass was required, allowed her characters to explore fresh territory, but it was not until the early 1860s that she acquired the confidence to create her own English provincial community: Carlingford. Each of these successive settings, of course, also capitalized upon changing literary fashion and none more recognizably so than 'The Chronicles of Carlingford' which ruthlessly exploited the popularity of Trollope's Barsetshire format. The comparison is informative. The social range of Mrs Oliphant's fictional world is less surely handled, at this stage of her writing, than Trollope's. Lady Western, it has frequently been observed, is unlikely to have extended the hand of friendship to a Dissenting minister as she does in *Salem Chapel* (1863). Thirteen years later, after eleven years of gauging the niceties of life in the Anglican precincts of Windsor, Mrs Oliphant was a better judge of the degree of intimacy and patronage that might operate between the impoverished aristocracy and relatives unfortunate enough to have entangled themselves with wealthy Dissenters. The London-based chapters of *Phoebe Junior* (1876) are a tribute to this development of her social antennae.

There is a further aspect in which the Carlingford novels reflect the unsettled nature of Mrs Oliphant's early years: like Dickens, whose childhood homes had also experienced the arbitrary dislocations effected by his father's changing fortunes, she never seems to have developed much sense of the complex workings of small town or village life in England. We may hear of the wharf-men of St Roque's, or 'the bargemen at the top of Prickett's lane', but as readers we gain no insight into the fine threads of financial and social network that anchor these neighbourhoods to the households in Grange Lane. We may look in vain for the octopi tentacles of family relationship, that develop through intermarriage over the generations, of which we are made aware in George Eliot's novels of community life. Instead we meet discrete families drawn together by their need for society, or by such professional visitors as doctors, clergy, and lawyers. The family, which was always to be Mrs

Oliphant's essential fictional unit, dominated her outlook on all those vexed matters close to the heart of the Victorian value system: class, breeding, and philanthropy.

(b)   Class and breeding

Geographical mobility is a great aid to social mobility since it enables the individual or the immediate family to cast off the less desirable connections of previous incarnations. Such manœuvres could not always hope to be completely successful, and the fear of black sheep, such as her 'poor Willie', returning from exile haunts the novels in the shape of socially incompatible long-lost relations who appear without warning from the colonies.[22] A series of moves also helped a greater degree of selectivity in keeping up with more distant relations. Mrs Oliphant's mother seems to have been adept at this exercise. Despite her much vaunted general contempt for her husband's family, she was able to approach the intellectually successful family of Wilson cousins when the time came to launch her daughter on the Edinburgh literary scene. The case of these Wilson cousins is instructive in understanding Mrs Oliphant's social values. Her father's first cousin, Archibald, had been an Edinburgh wine merchant, but his two sons, Daniel and George, profited from the democratic traditions of the Scottish educational system and won themselves positions high up the professional ladder, the former becoming President of Toronto University and a knight, the latter Regius Professor of Technology at Edinburgh University and President of the Royal Scottish Society for the Arts. Their younger cousin was to use her intellectual abilities to effect a similar cultural leap. As one of her more acerbic obituarists expressed it, 'She had educated herself into the true aristocrat's view of life, and had a genuine contempt for the Philistine.'[23]

There is very little evidence that Mrs Oliphant ever recognized herself as 'coming from the wrong side of the tracks'. Indeed, in her *Autobiography* she took considerable pride in reflecting upon the distance her literary efforts had brought her from the simple cottage life of her childhood and the 'shabby' areas of London in which she had spent her early married life. Fictional characters who are forced to negotiate their way upwards in society, in ways that inevitably distance them from even their closest family, often find the strain almost unbearable. The gender divide is particularly remarkable here. Girls whom the random fortunes of love have displaced from very humble origins often find the early years of their marriage bedevilled by a combination of cultural vertigo and isolation from all the familial affection they have previously experienced, but love usually proves a sufficient inducement to the educational efforts necessary for becoming a true wifely companion.[24] Economic motives alone are unequal to detaching a girl from friends and family, and so Mrs Oliphant's fiction finds no place for the Becky Sharp manipulators of the marital market-place. The apparent exception to this rule occurs in her late, rather bitter social comedy, *The Cuckoo in the Nest* (1892), where a village girl wins her way through to the chance of a fortune and a title by persuading the simpleton son of the local landowner to marry her. Nevertheless, despite the girl's ambitions, energy, and competence, there is no basis of love to persuade her that it might be worthwhile to adopt her marital family's cultural assumptions. At the end of the novel, after her first husband's death, her social isolation becomes too great for her and 'the invincible vulgarity' that she has never shaken off finds more pleasure in the prospect of marrying a village man, who truly loves her and who is in the position to provide her with an ''Andsome 'Ouse', than in retaining the prospect of a title and a fortune.

For most men, however, the problem is more complex. On the one hand they appear to enjoy the advantage of greater flexibility: their identity is provided not solely by their family but by the status they enjoy in the wider world. On the other hand society had not trained them to adapt themselves to sudden changes of fate as it had women in those generations when the chances of marriage or a husband's bankruptcy were the determining factors in their lives. During the 1870s Mrs Oliphant became much preoccupied with the disorientation men sometimes suffered on account of the discrepancies between the expectations fostered by upbringing and the surprising fates meted out by life. It seems likely that the arrival on her doorstep in 1870 of her destitute brother Frank, whose happy household and settled life she had once had cause to envy, proved the catalyst. The puzzle and the pity of shared childhoods and wholly divergent capacities for meeting life's disasters were certainly firmly etched upon her mind by this turn of events: 'he and I, who had been so much to each other once, were nothing to each other now . . . we no longer thought alike on almost any subject: he had drifted one way and I another.'[25]

Squire Arden (1871) and its sequel *For Love and Life* (1874) take the case of a young man, Edgar, who discovers himself neither entitled to inherit the squirearchy to which he has believed himself heir, nor to be a part of the family by which he has been raised. The matter is further complicated by the fact that the old Squire's incomprehensible dislike of his 'son' has caused the young man to be brought up abroad so that he not only has to negotiate the labyrinthine complications of his paternity but divine for himself the rules that govern English society. (One reason that Frank 'settled down to a kind of quiet life, read his newspaper, took his walk, sat in his easy chair in the dining-room or in his own room for the rest of the day' might have been the difficulty he would have had integrating into his sister's Windsor society after a lifetime in Scotland and Liverpool.) If one is prepared to accept the incredible plot, the emotional complexities of the hero's position, cast adrift in a society where his gentlemanly upbringing seems to exclude as many careers as it opens to him and forced to recognize a relation of kinship rather than kindly patronage with a poor Scots family, are well handled. The following year saw the publication of *The Story of Valentine and His Brother*, of which Mrs Oliphant thought particularly highly, which postulates the case of twins, one of whom has been brought up as heir to a Scottish estate and the other by his gipsy mother. The novel ponders the extent to which nature and nurture are respectively responsible for an ability to handle life's sudden reversals. Two motifs constantly reappear in these novels: the Scots inheritance and the Etonian education, which Mrs Oliphant firmly believed taught boys the 'art of mastering themselves' and gave them the cachet of 'gentlemen'. There is a certain defensiveness in the way she distinguishes between the social-climbing that leads an Edinburgh lawyer to wish to send his son to Eton and the legitimate tradition that leads generations of Scots landowners to send their sons there.[26] Her proven ability to provide the trappings of English upper-middle-class life apparently formed her own justification for acquiring for her sons an education that she felt would firmly anchor them to the English establishment. To hope for boys of humble origins to advance themselves through scholarship alone was a fatal mistake, or this at least is the message behind a short story and a three-volume novel, published in quick succession, that share the same melodramatic plot of a young Scots peasant whose intellectual ability takes him beyond the reach of his family. The strain imposed by passing himself off as the social equal of Oxford men on a visit back to his birthplace results in insanity and violence. Several of these tales, *The Story of Valentine*, 'The Lily and the Thorn', and *Young Musgrave*, suffer from Mrs Oliphant's need to imagine a Scottish background so humble that educational opportunity can only be achieved at the expense of great family sacrifices while still upholding her view of Scottish society as essentially uncontaminated by English class divisions.

The Scots instead had a prejudice of liking people better for being 'well-born'.[27] This was a matter of name and 'old blood' rather than social rank. In the tale that gave her the name by which she was known to the Blackwoods, *Katie Stewart* (1853), the miller's wife is prepared to allow her youngest daughter to become a companion to the daughter of an English earl, but rebuffs any attempt at condescension with the claim that their own 'forebears and kin are as guid as most folk'. Mrs Oliphant's own mother had 'had a very high idea . . . of the importance of the Oliphant family, so that I was brought up with the sense of belonging (by her side) to an old, chivalrous, impoverished race'.[28] When she wrote this in 1885 she still regarded it as an amusing prejudice of her mother's which she herself had no desire to dispel. It was only when she started work on the biography of *Laurence Oliphant* (1891) that she discovered, to her surprise, that her mother had been right to claim descent from the Oliphants of Kellie, 'a race to which I also belong, both by birth on the mother's side and by marriage'.[29]

The rich compound of romantic nostalgia and a laughably pedantic attention to genealogy, involved in this Scottish reverence for 'old blood', provided Mrs Oliphant with the stuff of a fictional pathos that occasionally attained tragic dimension. Reverence for the name tended to go hand in hand with attachment to a particular locality or piece of land and depended upon all involved having a similar sense of history. A sense of consequence, derived from generations of respect from the local populace, is shown to be sadly provincial in *It Was a Lover and His Lass* (1883), where three Scottish sisters make their début on the London scene and realize that not only is the crush at the Court presentation a far dream from their visions of an intimate conversation with their sovereign, but that if they wish to be noticed at all in 'good society' they will have to avail themselves of the good services of the rich young man who is the adopted heir to their family's fortune, but who has, of course, 'no blood'. When the youngest sister marries the rich young man the novel tacitly acknowledges the folly of standing, upon the dignity of the family name if doing so must effectively put an end to it. In the late 1880s, as Mrs Oliphant contemplated the sacrifices she had made to hand on a name her relatives might be proud of, her treatment of the subject took a grimmer turn. Although *The Poor Gentleman* has a relatively happy ending, it contains pictures of lives spoilt or warped by the obsession with 'name'. The peevishly discontented 'poor gentleman' has waited too long to inherit a hereditary title and house which he lacks the income to support. The daughter of the current incumbent of both title and house has sacrificed her dreams of marital bliss to secure a 'nameless' husband prepared to take her own and bow to her autocratic understanding of what the family name demands. Worse still, in a sub-plot presumably fed by Mrs Oliphant's alarm about the unsuitable women with whom her son Cyril appeared to be involved, the 'poor gentleman's' son looks destined to squander the name and his chance of inheriting the family fortune, by dallying with a girl who has acquired 'London manners' but turns out to be without 'family' and irredeemably 'vulgar': niece to the local roadbreaker, and daughter of 'an actress'. *The Ladies Lindores* (1883) plays with a similar theme, but, despite the sad events of the novel, the plot fails to reach tragic dimensions because Mrs Oliphant clearly finds the new Scots lord's ambition to rise to the British peerage and the House of Lords insufficiently ingrained in the character to provide the weighty motive necessary for tragic conflict.

In *Kirsteen* (1890), partly by setting the tale back in the legendary mists of seventy years before, she manages to establish characters of the monolithically single-minded intensity necessary for tragedy. In the pursuit of reviving the name and home of the Douglases of Drumcarro, the present Laird has probably killed as a young man while involved in the slave-trade of the West Indies and kills again at the end of the novel when he finds his youngest daughter's honour threatened; the family banishes a daughter who dares defile the family name by marrying a mere nameless doctor; and Kirsteen submits to the family feeling that she has besmirched the name by engaging in the trade of 'mantua-making'. Nevertheless, it is this trade that finally restores the family estate. It is also her consciousness of the dignity of her name that sustains her throughout her endeavours to earn her own livelihood. Indeed, the success of the fashion house she joins is made as a result of her policy of taking no orders from commoners: she herself would have gone further than her partner:

'And there are many of the nobility. . . whom I would wish to be weeded out—for there are titles and titles, and some countesses are just nobodies however much they may think of themselves. You will never get to the first rank . . . unless ye just settle and never depart from it, who you are to dress, and who not.'[30]

Given Mrs Oliphant's penchant for using sewing as a metaphor for writing, it is perhaps not fanciful to see in this something of the reservations she had felt in the early days of her career when she contemplated accepting commissions from lesser periodicals than *Maga*.

Just as Mrs Oliphant gravitated towards the Established Church when it became clear that the English drew few distinctions among the Dissenting sects, so, we may infer from her fiction, she found the English class system insufficiently flexible in admitting her sense of the peculiarities of her own position. In the early novels, based either in Scotland or in the Celtic exile communities of Liverpool, there is little sense of class stratification, but by the time she created Carlingford an awareness of such matters has crept in. The pathos with which she treats the drawing-master's daughter and her naïve conviction that, in living the lives of artists, her family are exempt from society's rules has a ring of self-parody.

'We have a rank of our own', she said to herself, but with that tremor which always accompanies the transference of a purely fantastic rule of conduct into practical ground— 'We are everybody's equal, and we are nobody's equal.'

Seeing her fellow-creatures in the light of 'all good subjects, more or less . . . the consciousness that she could draw them and immortalise them' gave her the illusion of being a spectator outside the system.[31] In the days when she dwelt in London's Bohemian artist world, Mrs Oliphant had felt she enjoyed precisely this freedom. One of her earliest reviews is quite striking for its time in making so central a feature of the essentially 'middle-class' nature of Dickens's writing. Of David Copperfield she wrote, 'In the very heart and soul of him this young man is *respectable*.'[32] A couple of years later, despite her own upbringing in exactly similar circumstances, she subjected the terraced houses of 'clerkish suburbia' to scathing socio-aesthetic criticism. Each new terraced house in Islington, she claimed, built higher walls and closer railings than its predecessor in a desperate desire for distinctiveness and privacy, 'and it was edifying to observe everybody's virtuous resolution to see nothing where there was visibly nothing to see'.[33] By 1877, moving steadily up-market herself along the houses of an elegant Windsor crescent, she felt herself justified in caricaturing the interior of a rented 'suburban villakin' which was 'like a hundred, nay a million other semi-detached suburban villakins'.[34]

In as far as Mrs Oliphant understood English class issues she was better at observing the minutiae of everyday differentiation, much as a resident foreigner might have done, than in trying to articulate the code within the plot concerns of a novel. The loosely structured series of tales *The Neighbours on the Green*, whose setting was acknowledged as Englefield Green, the home of her friend R. H. Hutton, editor of the *Spectator*, on the whole proves acceptable because the middle-aged narrator, Mrs Mulgrave, a poor gentlewoman, is little more than an Angli-cized version of her first published narrator, Miss Margaret Maitland: she takes a similarly unprejudiced interest in the doings of her neighbours of whatever social class. Mrs Mulgrave's 'innocent' remarks upon the shame of unoccupied cottages in an area where homelessness was on the increase, or her observation that genteel gossips are uniformly hard in their judgements of the lower classes, sound less like the opinions of a dyed-in-the-wool inhabitant of the Green than of their immigrant author. There is one tale in this series, 'The Stockbroker at Dinglewood', which offends modern sensitivities in the way that the treatment of class prejudice does in the two novels *Mrs Arthur* (1877) and *Within the Precincts* (1879). All three stories flirt with the question which was a never-ending source of fascination to the English middle classes: how does one define a gentleman? Yet all three miss the moral dimension of the dilemma and become strident in their attempt to define the ideal by exposing a succession of lurid negatives such as stockbrokers, those lacking in cultural refinement, and those who presume gentility is defined by not needing to work. It is harsh, but perhaps not unjust, to suggest that, despite their Etonian education, her sons reflected her uncertainty in this respect by practising gentility more as a series of studied refusals than as a positive moral code.

Her tone was never more unpleasant than when she adopted that umbrella word of abuse, 'tradesman', favoured by the English upper-middle classes to describe those whom, despite their wealth, they wished to exclude from their circles. Nevertheless, her particular application of this pejorative term deserves comment. She was perfectly prepared, in the abstract, to admit that a man could be a gentleman and engage in commerce: *For Love and Life* (1874) includes the parable of an old Etonian who discovers to his chagrin that his family money came from a shop; he is taught by his aristocratic wife not to be ashamed of the name that he asks her to share, and proceeds to run his establishment with a display of feudal concern that would have warmed Thomas Carlyle's heart. Despite changes of circumstance, both he and the questing hero of this book will always have the education and cultural accessories of a gentleman upon which to fall back. What stuck in her craw was 'the invincible vulgarity' of those whom money alone placed in the position to patronize artists. From *The Three Brothers* (1870) onwards struggling artists of impeccable social credentials are forced to see their work hung as trophies upon the walls of undiscerning *nouveau-riche* cheesemongers and their like. As so often in her work, painting and writing were almost interchangeable. Publishing as a profession had had little more than a generation in most cases to separate itself from the humble booksellers' trade, and on many an occasion when Mrs Oliphant felt that her own publishers were behaving parsimoniously or without sufficient respect she would remind them of this fact. Although she moved to Ealing in October 1861 to be near her friends the Blacketts, by November Henry Blackett, in his role as publisher, had disappointed her and she wrote to John Blackwood, 'my excellent friend Blackett however is perhaps not exactly what you understand by a gentleman'.[35] On another occasion, angered by Macmillans' desire to offer less than she anticipated on her *Makers of Modern Rome*, she reported to Cecco the following conversation with their reader George Craik:

I said I thought there was an atmosphere of trade in all ways that was different from that among ordinary men and that people did things in the way of business which they would not do in other circumstances. He said with quiet innocence, spreading out his hands, that he was not conscious of any such thing but laughed and half assented when I said Fred Macmillan was a tradesman.[36]

Unlike many of his relatives who had been at Eton, Fred, it is true, had been at Uppingham and then learnt his 'trade' from the ground-floor and was inclined to take 'the business view' rather than relying upon his readers' decisions. Nevertheless, it must have been hard for wealthy and successful businessmen like William Valentine, the jute manufacturer from Dundee, that a clerk's daughter should use his 'bourgeois' mode of life as her chief objection to his marrying her niece and take every opportunity to demonstrate to him 'the kind of thing' his prospective wife's family would in future expect of him in terms of taste.[37]

It would be wrong to assume that Mrs Oliphant was alone among Victorian authors in her muddled thinking and double standards in this area. Admiration for self-help was easier than liking self-made men and money had a habit of seeming less vulgar if the bloom of its ostentatious mint condition had been rubbed smooth by several generations of the same family.[38] In Dickens's *Great Expectations*, where the issue of what constitutes a gentleman looms large, it is less than clear to a late twentieth-century mind why Pip should be ashamed to touch Magwitch's honestly earned money. One of Mrs Oliphant's late novellas, *Sons and Daughters* (1890), suggests something of the complicated elements that fuelled her prejudices in these matters. Gervase Burton, the dilettante hero, has enjoyed the type of education she afforded her own sons, and when he comes down from Oxford declines to join his merchant father, because in trade 'every transaction is not carried on as it would be between two men of the same social grade under the eyes of all the world'. Although these were almost exactly the words she had herself applied to Fred Macmillan, here Burton is felt to be both selfish and ungrateful, because he is by implication criticizing the honest labour of the previous generation which has won him his privileges. As the story continues Gervase is dispatched to the West Indies to sort out the family estate, thus proving himself to have the kind of business flair compatible with gentility. When his father is ruined Gervase displays an almost overrefined gentlemanly scrupulosity in repaying the firm's debts, and is then allowed to imagine that his father has responded in kind by sending him the large dowry his merchant father-in-law demands. The reader is aware, however, that this sum has been supplied courtesy of his fiancée, who has made wise investments of the private fortune her mother left her. Not only do private investments seem in no way tainted by their connections with either commerce or 'speculation', but women are able to put the care of their loved ones above abstract codes of behaviour. Madeline, Gervase's fiancée, we are told, thought as she contemplated his gloomy hatred of the work he has to undertake 'what she would do in his place. How little she would mind! How she would conquer any antipathy she had and put it under her feet, and scorn to confess it!' The problem here is partly that in order to make her the kind of girl in whom Gervase would be interested Madeline can have no opportunity to earn the money by her own endeavours. As a God-given talent, writing raised Mrs Oliphant's profession above mere money-making, but its pursuit as a breadwinning exercise had involved her in overcoming antipathies to the kind of people to whom she was sometimes forced to sell her wares, and, although she rejoiced in the gentleman's education she had bought her sons, it wounded her deeply that they took no account of the sacrifices she had made and assumed themselves entitled to continue their dilettante lives at her expense.

As she looked back at the end of her life she was inclined to feel that the perplexities that had surrounded her own struggles to balance an inherited fondness for good breeding with moral approbation of honest endeavour, a desire to bring her sons up as gentlemen with the harsh economic realities of the Victorian market-place, were symptomatic of a far larger socio-economic drift.

There was a time when the middle class was glorified above all other as the salt of the nation ... I do not quite know what was then understood by the term. It had something to do with the ten-pound householder, but rose up from him through all the rich shopkeepers and the poor professional classes, and the well-to-do who were nothing in particular, up to the edge of the county families and the 'old nobilitie' ... Still less do I know what the term means now. A middle-class school, for instance, means something quite inferior... The consequence of this is, that hundreds of people who cannot really be said to be anything but middle-class persons, send their sons to Eton and to the Universities, and thus are included somehow, vaguely, as belonging to the upper class in the shifting, shadowy nomenclature of position—they, or if not they, at least their sons after them. And accordingly the term uppermiddle class has been invented for them, which the young ones, I think, do not like, having had the same education as the greatest 'swells,' and feeling in no way inferior to them.[39]

If she was right in thinking that her experience had to some extent mirrored the 'rise and rise of the middle classes', this may help to account for the longevity of her popularity as an author. Unlike female authors whose very success seemed to secure them 'mental greenhouses' ever more remote from the characters they had originally excelled at describing,[40] Mrs Oliphant's experience, together with her constant monitoring of social change in her capacity as reviewer, actually allowed her to extend her range. Her last full-length novel, *Old Mr Tredgold* (1896), has travelled from the Fife settings of her early days to that fashionable late Victorian mecca, the Isle of Wight, discarded the fisherfolk, retained the gossiping genteel classes of Carlingford days, and added to this both the old aristocracy who feel themselves to be the natural lawgivers and the smart *demi-mondaine* set who hover nervously, in Jamesian mode, between the world of new riches and minor titles.

As a novelist Mrs Oliphant's vision was, in its very different way, just as middle class as Dickens's, partly because this was where she perceived the great bulk of her readers' interest to lie. Christian Socialism, she claimed, had been doomed to failure because, concentrating upon a feudal *rapprochement* between the élite and

the working classes, it had ignored the world of the shopkeeper and the tradesman.[41] These last were just within her grasp, though almost always in parodic
terms. The working poor, the fishermen, crofters, and occasional industrial workers
of the early novels are in essence judged by their capacity to approximate to a world
of middle-class values. Any attempt they make to better themselves by more radical
means, via Mechanics' Institutes or political agitation, is seen as a combination of
dangerously naïve idealism and the subversive discontent whipped up by dema-
gogues. The urban poor without either jobs or homes are virtually invisible in her
fictional world, except in the world of moral fable.[42] The working class who receive
the most detailed treatment within her novels are those with whom over the years
she enjoyed the most contact: servants. Her treatment of them is interesting because she had not always taken their presence for granted. Her own family is
unlikely to have employed anyone above the rank of a maid of all work, which
allowed her to make perceptive fun of rich women who imagine idyllic escapes to
small cottages, accompanied only by a lady's maid.[43] Such grand personages as
ladies' maids lacked the training for the back-breaking and versatile work this
would demand. When only one servant was employed, however, she became more
of a companion-help to the family, to whom the children became attached and who
in turn became devoted to her employer's family, as her own faithful Jane Hockey
had done. This position was compatible with a degree of independent-minded
criticism which particularly characterizes the servants of her Scottish novels. The
larger establishments necessitated by success in business demanded a more refined
servant structure dominated by awesome butlers, and littered with footmen. This
floating population are felt in her novels as a threat to family privacy, an omnipres-
ent force of eager gossips from whom the crises and scandals afflicting the family
must be kept hidden. In employment terms as well as in social structures the family
and family loyalty remained the only unit Mrs Oliphant fully understood. Writing
over thirty years after the event, she still did not understand the self-protective
motives that might have lain behind the inconsiderate behaviour of her husband's
workforce when ill-health and business uncertainty forced him to break up the
firm, and she continued to contrast their 'callousness and want of honour and
feeling' with the behaviour 'of my maids, who stood by me to the last moment
. . . loyal and true as the others were selfish and cruel'.[44]

(c) Philanthropy

It will come as no surprise that Mrs Oliphant's charitable theory and practice were
based upon the notion of private help, personally proffered; although the rigour
with which she clung to this view, over a lifetime which saw an explosion of
'professional' national charities, is remarkable. Outside the pages of Thomas
Carlyle's famous diatribes against the 'deep froth-oceans of "Benevolence", "Fraternity", "Emancipation-principle", "Christian Philanthropy" ',[45] it would be hard
to find a more systematic opponent of organized charities. Although Dickens railed

in *Bleak House* against all those who turned charity into a profession because they failed to perceive the cardinal truth that charity begins at home, Mrs Oliphant found his personal practice lamentably inconsistent with his fictional declarations. 'Hearth and home', she pronounced, were central to his middle-class Utopian vision; his desire to play a part upon a public stage and indulge in 'indifferent and doubtful pieces of philanthropy and social reform' unsuitable for a writer.[46] The coincidence of Mrs Oliphant's views with those of Thomas Carlyle is not accidental for both had come in contact with the teaching of Dr Chalmers, the Scottish proponent of 'a Godly commonwealth'.[47] Furthermore, in trying to describe her mother's own particular brand of 'inexhaustible' kindness and 'boundless' love, manifested in spontaneous charitable acts, such as 'tak[ing] off a warm garment of her own . . . to give it to a poor woman', Mrs Oliphant instinctively resorted to the Carlyles as a point of reference: 'I understand the Carlyles, both he and she, by means of my mother.' There was no objection to philanthropy as such. The entire Wilson family had become involved in charitable relief work in Liverpool in the troubled economic climate of the 1840s; her father was treasurer of the relief fund, and Willie, 'who was at home idle, took the charge of administering this charity, and used to go about the poor streets with a cart of coal behind him and his pockets stuffed with orders for bread and provisions of all kinds'. This 'organized' philanthropy seems to have been justified by two factors: its response to perceived local need and the practical individual involvement it generated. It had the additional benefit of bringing brother Frank 'up to this time everything that was good except in respect to the Church, to that last and crowning excellence'.[48]

In the days of Mrs Oliphant's more overtly pious novels the importance of a Christocentric charitable vision is emphasized. *John Drayton* (1851), whose message, 'know what thou canst work at and work at it', is articulated in Carlylean phraseology, repudiates the notion of a universal panacea such as Chartism because it ignores the intractability of the human material it must work upon, lessens the onus upon the individual conscience, and, worst of all, ignores God, who alone enjoys sufficient vision to be able to regulate the affairs of the macrocosm.[49] *Ailieford* (1853) offers a further gloss on this: human philanthropy tends all too often, the hero ruefully reflects, to the morally coercive. Confronted with his brother's irresponsible behaviour he would have backed a 'strong restrictive system . . . I would have improved upon it after my own vain fashion, and put the iron collar and fetters of uniform slavery where He only laid the silken ties and distinctions of individual love.'[50] Her experiences with 'poor brother Willie' lurk behind this perception as they do behind so many of her other pronouncements on the dilemmas involved in philanthropy. Early novels such as *Lilliesleaf* and *Merkland* are very strong on the general principle of spending inheritances upon redeeming the Prodigal rather than saving them for those who may be more conventionally deserving, but are capable of helping themselves. It remained only to give these propositions universality by providing a theological basis for her personal persuasion. It is from a young Scots minister in *The Laird of Norlaw* (1858) that we learn that we are to love the poor not for themselves but because God loved them. Instead of contradicting the notion of 'individual love' this principle is intended to carry the benefactor through those moments when recipients seem unworthy and ungrateful.[51] A book of practical piety produced the same year, *Sundays*, reiterated the rule of Christian charity only bringing benefit to giver and taker when practised at the personal level. In her own childhood, she tells her assumed audience of young readers, she was encouraged to deliver a portion of the family's Sabbath-day meal to the poor and invalid. Such a service performed 'by one's own hands, or by the hands of our children', rather than by dispatching a servant, teaches the importance of personal sacrifice and removes the element of obnoxious and demoralizing patronage.[52]

As her novels grew more secular in tone and she removed the specific references to a Christocentric charitable philosophy, her views took on an increasingly negative appearance. Those characters who show forth their author's good works in fictional form by devoting their money and time to their family as an immediate responsibility are increasingly forced to recognize that they have adopted a self-denying ordinance which can expect no recompense in public approbation or private gratitude. In 1858, when her unmarried heiress, Lucy Crofton, decides to throw open her home to poor kinsfolk whose 'far-off bonds of relationship . . . were just sufficient to add piquancy to dislike, and vehemence to emulation', her subsequent trials are great, but her God-given mission finds its eventual reward in a happy marriage.[53] In 1883, when Catherine Vernon, the disappointed spinster banker, does up the Heronry, or Vernonry as it is more popularly known, for her poor relations, gossip may be partially right in calling it her whimsical Folly. The absence of heavenly motivation and the toll of many years in which she experiences 'the half-resentment, half-exaction with which they received her benefits' does not make her misanthropic but 'cynical . . . She tolerated everything, and smiled at it; she became indulgent and contemptuous. What did it matter what they said or felt?'[54]

There is no doubt that Mrs Oliphant was herself in a position to understand the development of such a self-protective carapace. She knew only too well that it was easier to feel generous at a distance. 'Poor brother Willie's' long exile in Rome obviously prompted her picture of Lady William, who also supported a long-absent, wayward brother: 'Poor Ned! How often is there one in a family who is never spoken of but with that prefix, and how often he is the one who is best beloved.'[55]

As she looked back from the vantage-point of the 1890s she became acutely aware that her convictions about the private exercise of charity had, as in so many other matters of personal morality, caused her to grow increasingly out of step with society's preferred maxims. The very gesture of resorting to the non-realist domain of the 'Stories of the Seen and the Unseen' may indicate her sense of the disturbing power needed to overturn the norms of contemporary terrestrial society. In 'A Visitor and his Opinions' (1893) England is visited unawares by an angelic figure whose communings with various classes of society are designed to show how fallen man rarely intends evil but cannot consistently choose the good. Invited to a house-party of the governing classes, he draws attention to the futility of their discussion about the competing claims of the Service of Man and the Service of God schools of philanthropy: 'Because you have to do with a race which learns nothing, which makes no progress, which begins again afresh in every generation'. '*Dies Irae*' (1895) attempted to provide a respectable lineage to her own philosophy of good only being achieved by 'one loving woman' ministering to 'one struggling sister' by articulating it through the voices of spiritual authorities such as Dante and Coleridge. Money and institutionalized aid only serve to pauperize and demoralize the recipient.

From 1860, when she used the pages of *Maga* to denounce the interfering self-righteousness of committees of self-appointed do-gooders,[56] to her last stories and articles she clung to the notion that charitable work, especially as practised by women, was usually motivated by a desire for self-healing[57] or emancipation[58] and almost invariably encouraged self-display and insensitivity. She found this thesis helpful in explaining to her readers the attraction Alice Le Strange, Laurence Oliphant's first wife, had felt to the rigorous authoritarianism of Thomas Lake Harris's community.

The benevolences of country life had not seemed enough for her, as they do to some women, whom they enable to hold the balance more or less even between the dissipations of society and the requirements of serious existence.[59]

She denounced the handiwork on offer at the charitable Bazaars of high society, which threatened to deprive poor seamstresses of a living,[60] and, summoning Political Economy to her aid, supported a 'trickle-down theory' of social benefit because this would not be subject to the whimsical involvement and disengagement of the individual do-gooder.

Cousin Mary (1888) contains an interesting discussion between a rector and his wife as they watch the curate's wife relapse from the 'new broom' enthusiasm of her first parochial efforts as the needs of her own growing family begin to preoccupy her. With the capacity for self-criticism that sometimes marked her fictional explorations of personal prejudices, she attributed her own views to the childless and embittered rector's wife, who claims that the life of poor villagers is the worse for their brief glimpse of succour. The rector argues that good works are never wasted, but the novel as a whole endorses the values of former days 'when it was the fashion to believe that it was a woman's first duty to serve and care for those who were her own'.[61] Whether one sees Mrs Oliphant's own life as a practical application of these closely nursed theories or whether, less charitably, one sees the theories as a justi-fication of her almost exclusively family-centred benevolence, her theory and prac-tice never parted company. There is again an element of self-parody in the picture of Lucilla Marjoribanks rejecting the notion of running a House of Mercy or immersing herself in parish work when her father's death leaves her with a much reduced income.

The House of Mercy was not a thing to be taken into any serious consideration; but still there was something in the idea which Lucilla could not dismiss carelessly as her friends could. She had no vocation, such as the foundress of such an establishment ought to have, nor did she see her way to the abandonment of all projects for herself, and that utter devotion to the cause of humanity which would be involved in it; but yet, when a woman happens to be full of energy and spirit, and determined that whatever she may be she shall certainly not be a nonentity, her position is one that demands thought. She was very capable of serving her fellow-creatures, and very willing and well disposed to serve them; and yet she was not inclined to give herself up entirely to them, nor to relinquish her personal prospects—vague though these might be.

It is little Rose, the artist *manquée*, from whom the idea for the House of Mercy comes when she confides to Lucilla that she is less sure than she used to be of the moral influence of Art. Were she as clever as Lucilla, she argues, 'I would show all these poor creatures how to live and how to manage . . . and teach them and their children and look after them, and be a mother to them!'[62] When Mrs Oliphant had faced the world anew, alone and in debt, she had been luckier than Lucilla, for she had a vocation as a writer and was convinced that novels did in fact provide a pattern of life from which young girls might learn 'how to live and how to manage', while the obvious need of her young children protected her from the accusation of mere self-promotion. Looking back at a similar point of decision at the end of her life, she was convinced that hers had been the only choice for her. In the third chapter of *The Makers of Modern Rome* (1895) we are presented with one of those refracted autobiographies that make the generic divisions of literature seem so fragile. Melania was a wealthy Roman matron who, in a short space of time, lost her husband and the two eldest of her three children. The similarities are obvious. Abandoning her inheritance and her youngest child she made her way to Palestine and a monastic life where she endured 'a catalogue of privations, as privations are calculated in the history of the saints'. Horrified though she was by Melania's unmaternal behaviour, the story was one, Mrs Oliphant reflected, 'which the thoughtful spectator will scarcely dismiss with the common imputation of simple heartlessness and want of feeling'. Whatever had prompted it, Melania's dramatic action could not be accounted an act of self-sacrifice, for 'she had attained the full gratification of her own will and way, which is an advantage not easily or often computed'. Ironically, the picture of Melania's subsequent life, where, in her seclusion, 'she was in the way of the very best of company, receiving pilgrims of the highest eminence, bishops, scholars . . . bringing the great news of the world from every quarter', was not unlike that other retreat in Windsor which Mrs Oliphant's less dramatic vision of Christian self-sacrifice had secured. The story, as she tells it, reminds us how difficult it is ever to arrive at a true account of motivation: 'The disappearance of Melania made a great sensation in Rome, and no doubt discouraged Christian zeal and woke doubts in many minds even while proving to others the heights of sacrifice which could be made for the faith.' Such pictures show her fully alive to the different readings her own 'sacrifices' could be made to bear.

However, against Mrs Oliphant's refusal to give public countenance to charitable causes or openly to plead the cause of fellow women authors, one should place the numerous letters to publishers in which she sought to introduce friends' manuscripts or obtain employment for their children. Apart from the solid evidence her large household provides of her private acts of charity, perhaps the finest tribute to her generosity of spirit appears in the memoirs of her least complimentary close acquaintance, Janet Story. Although I have found no evidence to support her belief, she claimed that Mrs Oliphant had returned to 'rotting Rome' once more in 1878 to visit the dying Geraldine Macpherson and had promised her that she would take care of her children. It is certainly the case that she edited and saw through the press Geraldine's *Memoirs of the Life of Anna Jameson* (1878), just as ten years later she undertook another labour of love, *Memoir of the Life of John Tulloch*, both designed to raise incomes for the survivors. Whether she did in fact, as Janet Story believed, take in and bring up the little Macphersons, is hard to establish. What matters is that an unsympathetic observer believed that this was precisely the way in which her loyal friendship would manifest itself.[63]

Although Mrs Oliphant's upbringing and instincts colluded to make her prefer the exercise of private benevolence, her fiction makes it clear that she had given thought as to whether it was better to use her money and talent to provide a comfortable middle-class life for the few rather than to involve herself in projects to help the very poor. In two tales written in the 1870s, *Diana Trelawny: The History of a Great Mistake* and *The Greatest Heiress in England*, she explored two instances of this dilemma. Diana, having unexpectedly inherited wealth sufficient to free her from governessing, decides to give not to the obviously indigent but to those to whom greater comfort means much. The plot of this novella is strained to breaking-point by Mrs Oliphant's desire to provide Diana chances for the quiet suffering which must attach to her patronage of undeserving, slightly impoverished gentility. In *The Greatest Heiress* the germ of the plot once again lies in a lower-middle-class girl suddenly finding herself in the position to dispense great wealth. She is bound by the terms of her inheritance to dispense her money at an individual level, finding those to whom her gift will make most difference, rather than those whose cause is necessarily the most deserving. The fairy-tale format of this tale allows the story to concern itself more with a general lesson about life than with trying to provoke our interest in a particular character's emotional responses to a series of unlikely plot turns played out against a realistic domestic setting. The reader, if not the heiress, learns that her gifts do as much harm as they do good, and that the conscientious application to such a task is bound to be deemed mere folly by society at large. Eventually her innocence will best be preserved by marrying a man of no great moral reputation, but of boundless worldly wisdom.

(*d*) *Money*

> 'Unfortunately . . . we can do nothing without it. It means of course show and
> luxury, and gaiety, and all the things you despise; but at the same time . . . it
> means ease of mind, so that a man can rise every day without anxiety, knowing
> that he has enough for every claim upon him.'[64]

While it might be the mark of a Victorian gentleman that he neither talked of, nor
presumed upon, his money, to judge from the novels of many Victorian writers he
thought of little else. 'Those giant powers of Debt and Shame', Mrs Oliphant
declared in 1871, 'are to this generation what dragons and devouring monsters were
to the past.' She made this observation while contemplating the life and work of
Walter Scott, whose strengths and weaknesses of character she saw as directly
related to his nationality. The practicality in his daily approach to his relentless
work, his imprudent generosity, his 'proud inclination to be the bestower—to give
rather than receive', and his almost excessively honourable desire to discharge debt
are all depicted as essentially Scottish traits.[65] The identification is not accidental.
When, in the light of being 'assailed from a very unlikely quarter with furious
upbraidings as to my extravagance', she came to discuss her own approach to the
getting and spending of money, the same features appear.

> [I] made on the whole a large income—and spent it, taking no great thought of the morrow.
> Yes, on the whole taking a great deal of thought of the morrow in the way of constant work
> and constant undertaking of whatever kind of work came to my hand. . . . Indeed I do not
> defend myself. It would have been better if I could have added the grace of thrift, which is
> said to be the inheritance of the Scot, to the faculty of work.[66]

Her early novels alluded to the Scots dream of creating a merchant prince in each
family by dint of sending a son to India, but the 'steady monotony of self-denial'
involved in thrift was less appealing: 'When a man's first quality is to be honourable
and just above all other things, he has to assume a sternness of self-restraint which
sometimes makes him appear less amiable to superficial eyes.'[67] She could still
remember the 'small fierce measures' she had imposed upon brother Willie in an
effort to pay off his debts without troubling their mother: 'I ordained that for two
days in the week we should give up our mid-day meal.'[68] Nevertheless, those who
have not incurred debt, but merely fear it, such as those bachelors in her fiction who
cautiously count the cost of their proposal, always seem both romantically lack-
lustre and a little selfish.

Meanness was something she could not abide. Even her father, whose hatred of
strangers clashed so sharply with her mother's inclination to keep open house, is
defended from the charge of 'illiberality'. Her brothers did not, however, inherit
their mother and sister's capacity to 'manage'.

> Poor dear Frank! how well I remembered the use he made of one of my mother's Scotch
> proverbs to justify some new small expense following a bigger one which he would allow to

be imprudent. 'Well,' he would say, half-coaxing, half-apologetic, 'what's the use of eating the coo and worrying (choking) on her tail?'

His sister was more inclined to justify unnecessary expenditure on the grounds of convenience and good sense. She recalled the miseries of 'a cheap journey, second class, and monstrous in length' between London and Paris undertaken with other women and children.

We were all dead tired when we arrived, but when we reached our hotel and got round a table, and well warmed and refreshed with an innocent champagne, St. Peray, which I made them all drink, our spirits recovered. I was always great in the way of feeding my party,—would not hear of teas or coffee meals, but insisted upon meat and wine, to the horror but comfort of my companions.[69]

The truth was that she enjoyed spending money, and, as this story illustrates, derived considerable pleasure from demonstrating an ability to command lavish expenditure without the need for reference to a cautious or critical husband. Her friend, Lady Ritchie, who had endured the constant fretting over the minutiae of the household budget to which Leslie Stephen subjected his womenfolk, drew an admiring picture of Mrs Oliphant's ceaseless hospitality.

I knew her best sitting in her sunny room at Windsor, with her dogs at her feet, with flowers round about, with the happy inroads of her boys, their friends, with girls making the place merry and busy, and that curious bodyguard of older friends, somewhat jealous and intolerant of any affections of later date than their own.[70]

All the appurtenances of a prosperous upper-middle-class household are on display. Many accounts speak also of her love of fine clothes. She was not above female gossip on the subject. 'Tell Mrs Blackwood please', she wrote to John after a Lord Mayor's dinner she had attended, 'that Mrs Trollope was the greatest fright I ever saw, an object, as we would say in Scotland.'[71] She indulged in the contemporary mania for collecting costly lace.[72] The 1881 portrait, done by Frederick Sandys, makes full play of the contrast between her direct, no-nonsense demeanour and her flamboyantly patterned dress with its intricately ruched lace collar: her plainly dressed hair is surmounted by the most delicate of lace caps.[73] Yet all these were minor self-indulgences compared with Scott's purchase of Abbotsford or Dickens's acquiring Gadshill. Their grandiose purchases were made at a stage in their lives when it seemed important to prove that their popularity was in fact not a measure of vulgar success but compatible with the claim to gentility. Mrs Oliphant staked her claim, before she could be assured of her lasting success, in a way that displayed her usual mixture of good sense and daring. Having made her decision over the boys' education, she first rented her elegant Windsor houses and purchased only when this seemed to make good economic sense.

It seems that she grew to find 'alternations of anxiety and deliverance' congenial. Her habit of selling her work in advance, unlike the cautious Trollope, who usually had a spare manuscript in a desk drawer, accustomed her to trusting to future earning capacity to pay off accumulating debts. If her strength had failed or the market turned against her, 'I should have been left in the direst bankruptcy; and I had no right to reckon upon always being delivered at the critical moment.' In 1894 she wrote, 'I should think anyone who did so blamable now.' In retrospect her attitude came to seem like gambling.[74] Her commitment to the Victorian work ethic made her despise and distrust financial speculators. The bankrupt and dishonourable financier of *The Fugitives* (1879) continues to be careless with money, indulging himself from time to time in acts of thoughtless generosity, because 'he had never done much more than turn it over in his hands, gaining, yet sometimes losing, by chance, by luck, by hair breadth hazards, but never by the strain of daily toil'.[75]

However insouciant the actual bankrupt in her novels, there is always a price to be paid. Some bankrupts, like the demented old man hidden away in a locked wing in *Janet*, forfeit their health and sanity. Her brother Frank's ruin in 1868, which seemed to her to result from a combination of poor management and ill-health, left him 'like a man in a palsy' incapable of much feeling on any subject, even his inability to repay his debts.[76] His failure was, in fact just as likely to have occurred as a consequence of the collapses, in 1857 and again in 1866, of a number of great financial houses. Liverpool had been particularly hard hit because of the trade with America, where the financial crisis had originated. Mrs Oliphant, however, was more interested in the domestic repercussions of such events than in the world of high finance. It is the wives and children of bankrupts, in her tales, who bear the brunt of the blow. Kept in the dark until the crash comes, and often encouraged by their husbands to ever more hectic displays of lavish spending to convince creditors of continuing financial viability, the wives have to stay and face the music when the defaulting husband flees to the Continent. In the days immediately after Frank's flight to France, Mrs Oliphant went to join her distraught sister-in-law in Liverpool and together they 'did everything they could, but that was very little'. Reading between the lines it seems possible that Mrs Oliphant may not only have taken in his older children but paid off some of his debts. It is difficult otherwise to see how two years later, after his wife's death, Frank was able to return to England without a criminal prosecution ensuing. Two stories of bankruptcy, written in the aftermath of this event, would seem to corroborate this suspicion. In 'The Stockbroker at Dinglewood' and *At His Gates* (1872) artist figures suffer financially in the crash and play a part in saving the perpetrator of the crime. The children and other close relatives suffer doubly from the fall, first financially and then from the tarnish subsequently attaching to the family name. Yet for the children there is a glimpse of hope. As she wrote of her own nephews and nieces, 'They had their lives before them, and unbounded possibilities of making everything right.'[77] These tales do little more than use Frank's downfall as a plot source, but the ensuing years saw a more diffuse and subtle treatment of the fears of imminent insolvency. *Phoebe Junior* seems to have benefited from an unusually slow gestation period. Begun in October 1872,[78] it was not published until the year after her brother Frank's death. The years of Frank and three of his four children sharing the house in Windsor with her had perhaps made her ponder at greater length the character defects that had prompted his ruin. The portrait of Parson May, who is driven to forge his signature to a promissory note, dispenses with the absolute divide between callously selfish financiers and innocent dupes. May is a man who takes it

for granted, frankly and as a part of nature, that he himself was the first person to be considered in all matters. So he was of course—so the father, the breadwinner, the head of the family ought to be; and when he has a wife to keep him upon that pedestal, and to secure that his worship shall be respected, it becomes natural, and the first article of the family creed; but somehow when a man has to set forth and uphold this principle himself, it is less successful.[79]

Like Frank, May is a self-absorbed man, whose incompetence in financial matters scarcely justifies him in claiming a breadwinner's respect from his children. The vexed question of who would then constitute 'the head of the family' must have crossed Mrs Oliphant's mind when she decided to bring her elder brother's family under her own roof. Frank's habit of looking upon her 'as a kind of stepmother to his children'[80] must have been a further galling proof of the curious position she occupied, forced to take on 'a man's view of mortal affairs' and yet regarded by her brother as an appropriate person to be responsible for the day-to-day management of their large household.

Her novels frequently stress the different effect of financial worries upon wives and husbands. Men like Parson May, or the poor curate in *Cousin Mary*, may suffer from the gnawing worry of knowing their income to be inadequate to their needs, but the practical consequences and effective economizing are all undertaken by the wife.

It was she who had to bear the children, and nurse them, and have all the fatigue of them; it was she who had to scheme about the boys' shoes and their schooling, and how to get warm things for the winter, and to meet the butchers and bakers when they came to suggest that they had heavy payments to make and to bear all these burdens with a smile, lest *he* should break down.[81]

Men in debt in the world of her novels are often buoyed up by a feckless sense of optimism to throw good money after bad while even quite wealthy women care about 'sixpences given to railway porters';[82] a difference possibly attributable to women more usually living on a fixed income. Some of her travelling companions' horror at her bold ordering up of meat and wine in Paris may have stemmed from the prospect of having to go through these bills with their husbands at a later date. This ability to understand a variety of positions allowed her finally to transcend the limitations of the familiar Victorian bankruptcy plot in one of her finest novels, *Hester* (1883), where money becomes the mysterious force that rules lives in such a way as to contract a girl's expectations, rather than to expand them in the way the *Bildungsroman* overtones of the title imply, and prompts some men to see it as nothing less than 'blood, life and liberty'.[83] From the first page of the novel money attains the force of a touchstone, distinguishing men from one another.

John Vernon was one of those men in whose hands everything turns to gold. What the special gift is which determines this it is difficult to tell, but there can be little doubt that it is a special gift, just as it is a particular genius which produces a fine picture or a fine poem. There were wiser men than he, and there were men, as steady to their work and as constantly in their place, ready for all the claims of business, but not one other in whose hands eveything prospered in the same superlative way. His investments always answered, his ships always came home, and under his influence the very cellars of the banking house, according to the popular imagination, filled with gold. At one period of his career a panic seized the entire district, and there was a run upon the bank, by which it was evident anybody else must, nay, ought, to have been ruined; but John Vernon was not ruined. It was understood afterwards that he himself allowed that he did not understand how he had escaped, and nobody else could understand it: but he did escape, and as a natural consequence became stronger and richer, and more universally credited than ever.

Here the knack of making money is deliberately compared with artistic talent in that they are both a mystery even to successful practitioners. Moreover, once a name has been won, it is this unquantifiable commodity that keeps the thing afloat and guarantees further successes. The analogies are not hard to seek with a world where Mrs Oliphant was constantly involved in advance trading upon her name and yet where other writers, in her estimate less wise and certainly less industrious, seemed capable of commanding even more because of the credit others invested in their name. There are characters, like Edward Vernon, for whom the 'boiling of the daily pot' and the security of a solid provincial reputation grow stale, and for them the mere thought of speculation in dangerously new fields and gambling with 'direst bankruptcy' grows to have a compulsive attraction. It is also a world in which those who have no capital to invest can apparently make money by selling the romance of finance to others: stockbrokers become the publishers of the investment world. The role of being repeatedly forced to save the family name and bail out various members of her own family is entrusted to the shrewd businesswoman, Catherine Vernon. Yet it is she who suffers most in the tale. She is admitted to the position of an honorary male and accorded the respect due to a 'visible Providence', but these are double-edged tributes since they take from her any reputation for feeling and her patronage effectively distances her from those she had most wished to help. The only winners in this novel are those who learn to stand aloof, never risking their all, either emotionally or financially, learning always to watch the changing markets through the focus of absolute self-centredness.

Such people are history's heroes, because they embody the prevailing spirit of the nineteenth century: 'It is all for materialism, for profit, for personal advantage—the most self-interested, the least ideal of ages.'[84] Every rank of society was infested with the disease. Residence in Windsor had apparently taught her that the cathedral community was no less money-minded than the avowedly secular portions of society. *Within the Precincts* (1879) takes us to a dinner-party inside the Deanery where the Dean and his aristocratic wife, although not active instigators of gossip, liked to hear . . . who was going to marry who, and by what schemes and artifices the marriage had been brought about; and who had most frequently and boldly broken the marriage vow, and by whom it had been most politely eluded; and how everybody lived and cheated, and nothing was as it seemed; and all that is done for money, and that is done for pleasure, in that busy, small, narrow-minded village society—which is the world.[85]

Writing of John Millais's latest offering for the 1875 hanging at the Royal Academy, she complained that he had deserted the spiritual values implicit in his early paintings such as *The Huguenots* in favour of the subject-matter popular with wealthy British investors. Character portrayal had been abandoned in favour of meticulously detailed costumes from which viewers could tell at a glance what the sitters had paid for their dress.[86] 'Tis Sixty Years Since'[87] took a determinedly celebratory look at the period in keeping with the festive nature of the Queen's Jubilee, but her last novel, *Old Mr Tredgold* (1895), had offered, by way of an alternative assessment, the most embittered summation of her previous criticisms. It is her version of *The Way We Live Now* (1876), but where Trollope had diagnosed dishonesty and the worship of an essentially fraudulent reputation for wealth, Mrs Oliphant complained that money, however disgusting in its manifestation, really did now hold the reins of power. The vulgar, *nouveau-riche* city men of her earlier novels who, whatever their buying-power, were never really accepted by the society they naïvely coveted, have been succeeded by cynical old men who can command even those who heartily dislike and despise them. Old Mr Tredgold's conviction that money is the supreme value reaches its apotheosis in a scene where the values of the Victorian marriage market are put on crude display: he asks each of his younger daughter's suitors to match his dowry pound for pound. Although he is furious when she elopes to marry a man who cannot do this, he is so impressed by her forethought in obtaining 'portable property' from him in the shape of jewellery and dresses, acquired as a consolation prize for apparently complying with his wishes, that he secretly determines upon her as the suitable heir to his wealth. Even the brandishing of the will as a means to command a show of love or obedience that is so often the undoing of the elderly in former novels plays no part in this old man's cynical framework. Love does not prove triumphant: no overt reconciliation takes place before the old man dies, until which time the couple are kept in comparative luxury by secret gifts from the older, unmarried daughter's allowance. Her sisterly love receives no vindication when her younger sister unexpectedly inherits everything and claims that there is no point in sharing the spoils with a sister who has made do with so little for so long. If the rampant cynicism of the old man and the naked greed of his younger daughter might be thought monstrously exceptional, the smaller events of the novel illustrate how widespread throughout society is the supreme worship of material comfort. Two elderly, genteel spinsters, a couple who in former novels might have been expected to have embodied integrity, arrive to remonstrate with the young girl for her feckless disregard for propriety.

Tea singularly changed the face of affairs. Gossip may be exchanged over the teacups, but to come fully prepared for mortal combat, and in the midst of it to be served by your antagonist with a cup of tea, is terribly embarrassing . . . Mr Tredgold's tea was naturally the very best that could be got for money, and had a fragrance which was delightful; and there were muffins in a beautiful little covered dish, though October is early in the season for muffins. 'I'll give you some tea first,' cried the girl, 'and then you can come down upon me as much as you please.'

And it was so nice after that damp drive, after the jolting of the midge in the dull and dreary afternoon! It was more than female virtue was equal to, to refuse that deceiving cup.[88]

It seems possible that the wholesale sell-out of all society beneath the ranks of the old aristocracy, represented in this novel, may have owed something to the disgust Mrs Oliphant experienced at the marriage of Annie Coghill, who had been part of her household for eighteen years before accepting the proposal of an elderly widower of ten thousand a year. Subsequent visits to their opulent home did nothing to soften her. Staying over the New Year in 1893, she wrote to Cecco that she could not stand the way Coghill 'talked at dinner and looks at his wife in his jewels as a commercial proposition'.[89]

It may also have been the case that by the time she wrote this last novel she felt almost unbearably the bitter irony and hollowness of those years in which she herself had so often been accused of prostituting her art for the sake of an adequate income. In that very article where she had accused Millais of succumbing to the god of materialism she had mulled over the narrowness of the margin that separated the selfless sacrifice of the highest vision from mere bowing to the demands of the market.

And which is best? to do our duty to them [families], by doing easily just what we can in art, to the entire satisfaction of the picture-dealer, and delight of our sublime patrons, the wealthy British investors in pictures; or to keep ourselves always on the strain of a laborious effort, trying perhaps to do more than we can.

Only God, she concluded, could be the final judge of the higher duty and justly reward those emanations of 'a sublimer sentiment than ever could be put on canvas or paper'.[90] Through most of her adult life it had been the tension between her strong belief in spiritual values and the earthy realism that acknowledged that 'money is not a thing to be scorned'[91] that had prevented her pragmatic anti-idealist slant from turning into cynicism.

2. 'A Fuller Conception of Life'

(a) Anti-idealism[92]

When in 1864 Mrs Oliphant compared her work with Charlotte Brontë's she spoke of her own as looking 'perfectly pale and colourless beside hers—but yet', she added, 'I have had far more experience and, I think, a fuller conception of life'.[93] A remark she made at the end of her life, reviewing the work of all the Brontë sisters, made it clear that she was not merely thinking of the dramatic colouring lent by Charlotte's use of the Gothic. 'Their philosophy of life', she wrote, 'is that of a schoolgirl, their knowledge of the world almost *nil.*' Nor was it that she subscribed to the myth of three provincial girls, brought up in the seclusion of Haworth parsonage to be ignorant of everything that was mundane and sordid in life. What she despised, as the mark of the schoolgirl, was their tendency to absolutism: Branwell could not be seen as an 'ordinary ne'er-do-well' or Patrick as a high-spirited eccentric: they had to be transformed in their fiction to Byronic heroes or capricious tyrants.[94]

By contrast, the pervasive tone in Mrs Oliphant's work is supplied by an ironic perception of the discrepancy between the idealized vision of life, which occupies a portion of most people's thinking, and the compromises, accommodations, and failures that characterize awkward reality. It was her conviction that the tragic and the trifling met together everywhere and that 'this sudden breaking in of the ordinary and common-place' intensifies our sense of 'tragic misery'.[95] It was there-fore the duty of fiction to represent life's perplexing mixture. In this sense verisi-militude became her artistic ideal: when the Little Pilgrim encounters a poet in the heavenly city, telling his tale of earthly history, 'the poet and his audience were at one' and he receives the highest accolade of all when his audience declare, 'yes, it was that way'.[96] In her position as *Maga*'s literary reviewer Mrs Oliphant presumed to embody the heavenly reading community, and authors are judged in as far as their 'telling of life' accords with her own. This was not so much a question of subject-matter as the philosophical view embodied in its presentation. She was as opposed to the 'fine vein of feminine cynicism' in Jane Austen, which restricted her ability to 'touch the regions of higher feeling',[97] as to Charlotte Brontë's practice of regarding love as the only object in life,[98] or the 'sublimated schoolgirls of romance' idealized by George Eliot,[99] or to a view of life rendered entirely 'in shadow. No picture can be true in which all the figures are equally sordid, mean, and commonplace.'[100]

Realism, of itself, was not enough. Zola was bracketed with the Pre-Raphaelite artists in this condemnation.

The determination not to select, to paint what was real, led Millais into the mistake in which Holman Hunt persevered, of giving to the shavings of the carpenter's shop, and the tools on his bench, an importance as great as to the highest development of character and feelings.[101]

Although it might be supposed that she was making a particular objection to the Holy Family in Millais's *Christ in the House of His Parents* being occluded, in fact the rule she is applying to both representational art and fiction is the same: the insistence on character portrayal as its central interest. 'Works of fiction' might still be regarded by many as the lowest form of art, she wrote in 1871, but in her view they required 'imagination, feeling, wit, the power of seeing and representing human character, of entering into a hundred different conditions of mind and being, and doing justice to all'.[102] To achieve this variety it was not sufficient to employ 'the very common artifice which the majority of novelists give way to, of colouring all the secondary persons with an unpleasant tint in order to throw up the excellence of the favourite—an expedient which Miss Austen herself employs'.[103] The dictum delivered by a character in an early novel, *The Melvilles*, lays out Mrs Oliphant's artistic credo: 'In every heart there is a mixture . . . with the amiable, shadows of evil, and with the unamiable, suggestions of good.' The moral corollary is then spelt out: 'we would need to see all before we could absolutely judge'.[104] This observation is delivered by way of rebuke to a girl who too easily condemns her father's behaviour, but the application to novel-writers and readers is there to be gathered. Mrs Oliphant was to criticize Trollope's claims for the didactic function of the novel as too facile. The novel could not act as a direct guide to life because its examples must always be too specific.[105] This was to prove one of the many reasons for her growing preference for the biographical genre, which seemed to her to possess 'all the higher attractions of the art of fiction, with the inestimable advantage of fact and reality which add a charm to every picture. It requires not only labour and patient investigation but a power of insight at once poetic and philosophical, a faculty of generalisation, and of appreciating the minutest detail.'[106]

Nevertheless, since, in her view mistakenly, many young girls did seem to read all novels as an introduction to life, she felt it all the more imperative to use her own fiction to resist the 'schoolgirlish' tendency to idealize, lest disappointment should lead to the equally dangerous path of cynicism. The obligation she felt always to keep the young reader in mind offers in turn a further explanation of the enthusiasm she showed in later life in turning to biography or to the article of social commentary. As one elderly lady of a later novel, *The Ladies Lindores* (1883), explains it, when proffered the contents of the latest box of novels from the lending library, including both ' "Middlemarch" and one of Mr Trollope's':

'No "Middlemarch" for me,' said Miss Barbara, with a wave of her hand, 'I am too old for that. That means I've read it, my dear,—the way an experienced reader like me can read a thing—in the air, in the newspapers, in the way everybody talks. No, that's not like going into a new neighbourhood—that is getting to the secrets of the machinery, and seeing how everything, come the time, will run down, some to ill and harm, but all to downfall, commonplace, and prosiness. I have but little pleasure in that. And it's pleasure I want at my time of life. I'm too old to be instructed. If I have not learnt my lesson by this time, the more shame to me, my dear.'[107]

In her *Autobiography* Mrs Oliphant suggests that, as an adolescent, she had indulged in the visionary day-dreams involving 'those lofty poetical beings whom girls love', and mockingly outlined the novels to which these had given rise. Although in retrospect she found the episode of her romantic engagement at 17 to J.Y. 'on the eve of his going away' and her subsequent heartbreak at its failure 'amusing to look back upon', the incident may have taken her longer to get over than this suggests.[108] A biographer, who claimed to have enjoyed Denny's help, alleged that it was this incident that had been responsible for 'robbing her of all sentimentality' and rendering her indifferent to subsequent attempts on her heart.[109] Certainly her initial impressions of her cousin Frank are inextricably entwined with sensations of being 'angry, disappointed and cast down' because the art galleries and plays he showed her brought her 'tumbling down from all my ideal and my anticipations'. Her subsequent account of Frank's wooing, her 'alarmed negative' in response to his initial proposal and her bald statement, 'But in six months or so things changed', followed by the oblique, 'It is not a matter which I can enter here', do not suggest that her eventual marriage was embarked upon in 'lofty poetical' spirit.[110] *The Days of My Life: An Autobiography* (1857), in which pride, the fear of being pitied rather than loved, and a preference for novels over real life, almost deprive a girl of the genuine affection her cousin and 'arranged' husband feels for her, confirms that the subtitle held a more than fictional significance. Her preference for an entirely anonymous publication of a story 'of that playing with trouble, of which I myself have done a little in my day' was possibly prompted by a desire to conceal the autobiographical reference.[111] In the one full letter of this period to survive from Margaret to Frank she writes to him out of the misery of Willie's disgrace: 'I do not and cannot regret, dearest Frank, the engagement which has united us to each other, I gave you my promise when I was not secure of my heart—I give you my heart now without reserve, with joy and thankfulness, even in this affliction.'[112] A commonsensical accommodation to the actual, rather than a perpetual search for the ideal, often characterized the marriages quite happily undertaken from then on in her novels and made her particularly anxious to repudiate the myth that a girl's disappointment in love the first time precluded her from subsequent happiness. Nevertheless, as novels like *Kirsteen* demonstrate, she kept a lingering admiration for those who remained faithful to the memory of their first love: although it was also typical of her to add that fidelity to the memory of the untarnished dead is the easiest kind since, 'Now that fear was buried like the rest. There was no one to object any more than to praise.'[113] Perhaps yet more characteristic of the lesson her novels offered is the outcome of the history of Lottie Despard, a girl whose heart had been broken, not so much by the despicable behaviour of Rollo Ridsdale, whose very name proclaims him a cad to the experienced novel reader, but by her decision to find 'in him the ideal after which she had sighed all her life'. Deserted by Rollo she will eventually find solace in marriage to a middle-aged minor canon of unexciting aspect who has proved his loyalty and devotion in ways that may echo Frank's behaviour: he has given her money to help her brother emigrate and find a life remote from the temptations of this English town.[114] (The heroines of her novels often marry otherwise undistinguished young men who happen to have been able to be of service during some family crisis.) The narrator uses the concluding chapter to spell out the implications for a philosophy of life:

For one girl or boy whose life lies all fair before them after the first effort, how many are there who have to leave the chapter incomplete, and, turning their backs upon it, to try a second beginning, perhaps with less satisfaction, and certainly with a somewhat disturbed and broken hope.

If this implies that the chances of life fall equally for girls and boys, her *œuvre* as a whole would tend to suggest that women's comparative powerlessness to dictate their own fate is more likely to force them to learn the art of the possible. Men are afforded greater possibilities of hurting others beside themselves by clinging tenaciously to their vision in despite of the facts. The political radicalism that the hero of *He That Will Not When He May* (1880) embraces is at once so manifestly crack-brained and vague that it stands little chance of lasting, and it is never clear whether he abandons it because he is disgusted that the daughter of the artisan leader of the movement prefers social advancement to Utopian idealism, or whether he only finds renunciation of his title and estate palatable when it is voluntarily espoused. It seems likely that the idea came to her from watching Laurence Oliphant's curious flirtation with Thomas Lake Harris's American community, and in the concluding paragraph of her two-volume biography she described his eccentric career as a demonstration at its most extreme of her age's tendency to swing between the two poles of visionary idealism and deep cynicism: 'There has been no such bold satirist, no such cynic philosopher, no such devoted enthusiast, no adventurer so daring and gay, no religious teacher so absolute and visionary, in this Victorian age.'[115] The particular facts of this life allowed the exceptional case to be made, but the world of commonplace temperament to which she deliberately restricted her novels more usually depicted young men for whom perfectionism and strong convictions served as a mask for unbridled self-will, and women whose feeble consolation lies in doing their best, thinking as little as possible and hoping things will come right in the end.[116] Yet such ostrich-headed defeatism held little real attraction for Mrs Oliphant, whose interest had always been provoked by those who managed to hold worldliness in tension with other-worldliness, the scepticism born of experience with the pursuit of the ideal. As she grew older she found it hard to incarnate the pursuit of the ideal within the bounds of realistic domestic fiction. The way in which the spiritual challenge, extended in *The Wizard's Son*, not to accept 'second-best' in life has to be imagined in a magical Scottish loch setting, rather than in the staid English environs of provincial Sloebury, in which the novel starts, is symptomatic of her tendency to feel the need of 'another world' in which to locate the ideal. Those who prefer psychological to spiritual interpretations of mystical experiences may find it significant that Mrs Oliphant had already begun her 'Little Pilgrim' series, exploring the parameters of the afterlife, before that 'very black moment' in St Andrews when she received her first visitation of 'a kind of heavenly peace'.

Her several interesting studies of cynical women are written with sympathetic understanding. *At His Gates* (1872), written in the aftermath of the change of prospects which brother Frank and his family's arrival dictated, includes her first attempt at depicting this state of mind. Her own moral dilemma as to whether 'to give up what hopes I might have had of doing now my very best' or 'to set myself steadily to make as much money as I could'[117] is transferred to a wife who 'was too much of an idealist (without knowing it) to let proof invalidate theory' and her moderately talented painter husband. In the third volume of the novel, however, authorial interest is transferred to a woman whose character is overdeveloped for the part the plot demands of her. Mrs Burton has been introduced to us as a woman of cold stateliness, presiding over her fraudulent banker husband's dinner-table in full evening dress, even when dining *à deux*. She preserves her aloofness from his vulgar ostentation by a carefully nurtured private sense of mockery, wearing her finest jewellery at all times so as 'to make all her splendours common'. Her cold amusement at constantly having her low expectations of humanity fulfilled stands her in good stead when the crash comes. The only occasion when she finds her heart touched is by the prospect of her son's innocent suffering. Yet he 'could hardly be blamed for failing to guess at' the moment of emotion that might have saved her from her 'self-contained and self-sufficing character'. At the end of the novel she settles down in Mayfair to a life which is luxurious but curiously limited.

She did not care for luxuries; but she did care to watch the secret movements of life, to penetrate the secrets of human machinery, to note how men met the different emergencies of their existence. She gathered a little society round her who were as fond of this pursuit as herself; but unless they could have provided themelves with cases on which to operate, this association could not do them much good, and it was dry fare to be driven to scrutinising each other. She thought she was happier in her tiny house in Mayfair, where she kept three maids and a man, and was extremely comfortable; but I believe that in reality her time of highest enjoyment was also her time of greatest suffering, when she was ruling her own little world . . . and seeing her house tumble to pieces, and holding out against fate.[118]

Mrs Burton would appear to provide just as much a haunting mirror-image for Mrs Oliphant as the painter and his wife. Unlike Mrs Oliphant's later cynical women, such as Sophie Dorsett in *Phoebe Junior*, or Catherine Vernon in *Hester*, whose amused contempt for others is a form of self-protection, the original source of Mrs Burton's cynicism is never fully explained: it is just a given of her character. The sudden intrusion of a first-person narrator at this point in the novel would suggest that Mrs Oliphant is persuading herself as much as her reader that her recent anxieties are both a useful counterbalance against emotional aridity and will serve to provide grist to the mill of a novelist of domestic realism.

One other Victorian variant of female 'anti-idealism' caused Mrs Oliphant little but merriment. Lucilla Marjoribanks and Phoebe Beecham in their differing degrees incarnate the practical outlook of a generation brought up upon utilitarian principles. Lucilla makes proud boast of her schooling in Political Economy and does not hesitate to apply its lessons to the more intimate world of personal relations. 'I like to know exactly how far one can calculate upon everybody,' she claims, 'then one can tell, without fear of breaking down, just what one may venture to do.'[119] Much of the energy of *Miss Marjoribanks* derives from Lucilla's 'messianic fervour' which is so comically harnessed to calculating opportunism. In the hands of many another Victorian novelist the mechanical absolutism of Lucilla's 'programme' would have become monstrous in either its grotesqueness or its evil. John Blackwood clearly felt a certain unease about the consistent 'hardness of tone' he detected as he received the successive numbers. Mrs Oliphant's defence is interesting.

As for what you say of hardness of tone, I am afraid it was scarcely to be avoided. I hate myself the cold-blooded school of novel-writing, in which one works out a character without the slightest regard to whether it is good or bad, or whether it touches or revolts one's sympathies. But at the same time I have a weakness for Lucilla, and to bring a sudden change upon her character and break her down into tenderness would be like one of Dickens's maudlin repentances, when he makes Mr Dombey *trinquer* with Captain Cuttle.[120]

Lucilla's efforts are directed to the good of the community; nevertheless, it is only her energy that saves her from the absolute aridity of a 'self-sufficing' character like Mrs Burton. If 'sensible' Phoebe Beecham's pragmatism is more attractive it is because she catches a glimpse 'of a higher kind of existence' and cries over the self-enforced loss of 'reverential homage' and the 'romantic' when she prevents Reginald May from making his proposal.[121] After these full-scale studies of Political Economy as a philosophy by which to rule one's life, Mrs Oliphant continued to revert intermittently to drawing minor female characters such as Emma Ashton in *Hester*, Mary Douglas in *Kirsteen*, or Marion in *The Railwayman's Daughter*, who behave with a total disregard for any higher vision of life than their own practical needs. Their limited imagination prevents them from malice and, indeed, they would never harm others unless they felt them to stand in the way of their own success in life. So ignorant are they of an alternative guide to life that the very naïvety with which they proclaim their philosophy amuses those whom it does not scandalize. The texts in which they find themselves offer both visions of a higher path and examples of profound cynicism, compared with which these girls appear as misfits from a more primitive animal form of existence.

(b)   *Illness*

It might be said that there was one issue on which Mrs Oliphant had so hardened herself that even her closest friends found her insensitive. Adult illness, and particularly any form of nervous disorder or mental illness, was as likely to elicit her contempt as her pity. Lady Ritchie, who was closer to her than most, found this hard to understand until she read the posthumously published *Autobiography*.

I could then understand why she had been so scornful of mental difficulties which seemed real enough to some of us, and why she always spoke bitterly of problems of thought—she who had so many practical troubles to encounter.[122]

By her own account she had never made a sympathetic nurse. She had begun to write 'to secure some amusement and occupation for myself' while 'my mother had a bad illness, and I was her nurse, or at least attendant'. She felt that she was slow to notice when others were suffering: both her mother and her husband Frank managed to conceal their terminal illnesses from her for a considerable time after it had become obvious to others that there was little or no chance of recovery. In her mother's case she accused herself of having been reluctant to face 'something which would not lighten after a while as all my troubles had always done, and pass away'. Once her mother's condition could no longer be hidden Mrs Oliphant knew where a daughter's duty lay, but was honest enough to admit how hard she had found it.

Then there followed a struggle of a month or two, much suffering on her part and a long troubled watch nursing on mine. At the very end I remember the struggle against overwhelming sleep, after nights and days in incessant anxiety, which made me so bitterly ashamed of the limits of wretched nature. To want to sleep while she was dying seemed so unnatural and horrible . . . And, oh me! when all was over, mingled with my grief there was—how can I say it?—something like a dreadful relief.[123]

In Frank's case, after the first episode of coughing up blood, she was 'quite ready to believe . . . that it might turn out to be nothing . . . I was much intent upon going to Scotland that year . . . and I did go.' Once there, guilty panic ensued and she resorted to the new and expensive method of telegraphing to find out how he was. Even when Frank's health gave serious enough concern to persuade them to sell the business and go to Italy, she was still determined to make light of the hardships of the journey. In retrospect she saw how her bracing attitude and little extravagances must have added to his torture.

things were very cheap in Florence then, and I don't think I was at all afraid, nay, the reverse, always inclined to spend. Of course this must have added to Frank's depression, for which I was sometimes inclined to blame him, not knowing how ill he was. He got rheumatism in addition to other troubles; and I have the clearest vision of him sitting close by the little stove in the corner of the room, wrapped up, with a rug upon his knees, and saying nothing, while I sat near the window, trying with less success than ever before to write, and longing for a word, a cheerful look, to disperse a little the heavy atmosphere of trouble.

The woman's traditional image as caring nurse was antipathetic both to her personality and her chosen career. Her irritation at the drag upon the wheels of her natural energy and creativity that Frank's decrepitude represented is reflected in the ensuing picture of one of their visitors at this time, a Miss Macdonald, 'whose distinction was that she refused a duke! and who had dedicated herself to her old father and mother, then very old, and she no longer young,—a very attractive woman, whose sacrifice I grudged dreadfully, though she did not'.[124] The need for concentrated and self-disciplined work, demanded by her vocation as family breadwinner, did not, she persuaded herself, leave her the option of behaving like Geddie Macpherson, their new-found friend in Rome, who was 'incapable of the dull domestic life which seemed the right thing to me, ready to go off upon a merrymaking at a moment's notice, indifferent what duty she left behind, yet just as ready to give up night after night to nurse a sick friend'. In retrospect she realized that she had only been able to nurse her husband night and day at the end because she was buoyed up by pregnancy and laudanum in 'a kind of exaltation, as if I were walking upon air'.[125] When her brother Frank became 'feeble and less easy to take care of', she became 'anxious that he should live in a doctor's house and be watched and cared for as his state seemed to demand'. Although she was subsequently much 'vexed with thoughts that I might have been more tender to him', she knew that his death had been 'opportune', especially as his final attack, probably a stroke, made her feel that she could no longer abandon him to strangers during the two years during which the doctor said he might linger.[126] By the time that her adult sons fell seriously ill she was sufficiently wealthy not to hesitate in calling in professional nursing help. Such women, as she observed in *The Heir Presumptive and the Heir Apparent* (1891), were a long way removed from the Sairy Gamps of former days, usually 'almost ladies' in social status and capable of keeping as professional secrets the strange chapters of family history they frequently witnessed. It is also possible that by the time her sons were terminally ill she realized that her anxious fretting in their sick-rooms was an irritant rather than a balm to them. In a novel written shortly after her husband's death she had remarked that men were often abler at nursing one another than their womenfolk, who do it 'with their heart in their eyes . . . so marring the work we would give our lives to accomplish'.[127] *Innocent* (1873) contains a more developed, half-comic reworking of the theme, where an anxious mother, who has not heard from her son, who is in fact enjoying himself in Paris, expounds gender difference to her daughter.

'Now if it had been you or me, Nelly, we should have said, "I took cold, or I got a bad headache," or whatever it was, on such a day—and how it got worse or better; and when we were able to get up again, or to get out again. It is not Frederick alone, it is every man. They tell you just enough to make you unhappy—never any details. . . . We care so much that we can't think of anything else . . . And they have an advantage in it. Frederick is a very good son, but if I were to write to him, "I have been ill, and I am better," he would be quite satisfied, he would want nothing more.'[128]

When Cecco was abroad for his health, this increasingly taciturn man in his early thirties must occasionally have dreaded opening yet another letter pestering for details and offering endless advice as to the best posture for a weak chest or the ideal diet.[129]

Like most mothers, of course, Mrs Oliphant put in her fair share of agonizing over her children's cots through such crises as croup and febrile convulsions. She was also prepared to don 'Mrs Gamp's bonnet' to preside over the birth of the Tullochs' grandchild, Wladimir Tarver. Nevertheless, she was always painfully aware that these calls on her time had to compete with her duty to her publishers.

It is interesting to compare the tension she clearly felt between the two ways of demonstrating her ability to take 'care' of her responsibilities with the picture that Anthony Trollope left of his mother, whose time was split between sustaining the family with her writing and nursing her sick husband and dying adult son, Henry, yet was capable, according to an admiring male, of holding the two in perfect equilibrium.

The doctor's vials and the ink-bottle held equal place in my mother's rooms. I have written many novels under many circumstances, but I doubt much whether I could write one when my whole heart was by the bedside of a dying son. Her power of dividing herself into two parts . . . I never saw equalled.[130]

Mrs Trollope's adult children, however, succumbed to consumption, not alcoholism, and it seems likely that the effect on Mrs Oliphant of watching her mother's last days, 'wasted Love incarnate as she was', spent in an anguish of maternal solicitation over Willie, who behaved like an invalid 'tucked in the study that had been made for him, copying for me, reading old books, smoking and something worse than smoking', was to harden her heart against such an expense of spirit.[131] To represent alcoholism as an absolute evil and alcoholics as wicked was, she believed, neither 'just', 'wise', nor 'merciful',[132] but removing it from the category of moral disease allowed her to analyse its effects more dispassionately. *Harry Muir* (1853) devotes its three volumes to depicting the slow decline of 'poor Harry' from adored brother into the scourge of his womenfolk's lives as he sacrifices even an unanticipated inheritance to drink. Another novel of the same year that 'poor Willie' was set to copy and allowed to put his name to contains an episode that must have provided equally piquant family reading. The dreamily idealistic hero of *Ailieford: A Family History* (1853) becomes engaged to the daughter of a doctor whose alcoholism has advanced to the stage of recurrent outbreaks of *delirium tremens*. Mary performs her filial duty as nurse with a stoicism bordering on hardness, and the hero is shocked to see her seated again at the sewing, with which she earns her livelihood, on the very day after they have witnessed her father's shocking death, replete with visions of vengeful demons. Neither the girl's pragmatic attitude nor the boy's sensibilities gains absolute authorial approval, although both are sympathetically explored. This small domestic scene does, however, precipitate the eventual breakdown of their engagement because Mary sees in it evidence of their temperamental incompatibility. Twentieth-century readers may well be struck by the prescient irony of the hero finding the girl again, years later, married to, and again tending, a ne'er-do-well drunkard. Mary's refusal to do anything other than endure is responsible for driving her former suitor to take up a new life abroad. As so often in her novels, Mrs Oliphant has separated out the strands of her own reactions and allowed them incarnation in different characters. In real life a certain pragmatic hardness had been necessary to allow Willie and her withdrawn, apathetic father to go their separate ways after her mother's death, and yet she constantly questioned whether her ability to comport herself with dignity during her worst crises was, as others may have hinted, a mark of deep-seated insensitivity. *The Wizard's Son* (1884) effects a very deliberate contrast between two widows who believe their children to have been killed by falling ruins: one mother sits immobile and apparently passionless by the ruins all night, but the other, who is carried off weeping and hysterical, attracts all the bystanders' sympathy for her outspoken grief.[133] When Mrs Oliphant looked back at the way she had survived the darker moments in life she wrote slightly self-reprovingly: 'If I had not had unbroken health, and a spirit almost criminally elastic, I could not have done it.'[134]

From her letters it is clear that Mrs Oliphant did not enjoy unbroken good health, and was as subject to the occasional cold as the rest of us. What is equally clear, however, is that she was not one to make much of minor ailments. Doctor's orders to take a rest receive a brief mention, but do not seem to have affected the delivery of the next month's contribution to *Maga*.[135] Looking back on herself as a young married woman, from the vantage-point of 1885, she was pretty certain that she had been foolish ever to have put any credence in the old wives' tales told her by another prolific author, Mary Howitt, who was convinced that her loss of 'many babies . . . through some defective valve in the heart' was 'somehow connected with too much mental work on the part of the mother'.[136] The rheumatism of Mrs Oliphant's later years, for which she took the cure at Wiesbaden, caused her great pain, according to her niece, Denny, but is rarely mentioned in her correspondence.[137]

The habit of exaggerating her relentless good health began as a means of coping with single motherhood. Of the widowed Madonna Mary, in her novel of that name, she remarked, 'it had to be done . . . This was the view her mind took of most matters; and she had always been well, and never had any pretext to get out of things she did not like, as women do who have headaches and handy little illnesses.'[138] Such 'pretexts' she felt were part of the mid-Victorian woman's repertoire of learnt behaviour. When the young Hester Vernon is placed in an intolerable position at a ball, by the thoughtless young man she loves, she employs the stratagem for the first time: 'She had a headache, she said. It was her mother's way of getting free of every embarrassment, and Hester was acquainted with the expedient, though she had not hitherto been tempted to use it.'[139] The fits of the vapours to which eighteenth-century women were prone no longer formed a socially acceptable mode of expressing excitement or discontent. In *The Unjust Steward* (1896) another foolish widow takes to her bed, 'very hysterical, laughing and crying in a manner which was by no means unusual in those days, though we may be thankful it has practically disappeared from our experiences now—unfortunately not without leaving a deeper and more injurious deposit of the hysterical'.[140] The last observation may have been prompted by the presence of her semi-permanent house-guest, Fanny Tulloch, whose endless complaints about her ill-health took their toll on her hostess's good humour. Her mysterious bouts of illness did not, as Mrs Oliphant remarked, prevent her from 'eating like a hunter on the hill'. In more sympathetic moments she was prepared to admit that, whether Fanny's illnesses were real or imagined, she suffered from both.[141]

The sofa-bound, plaintive wives and mothers who reappear throughout her fiction do receive an element of pity from their creator. Those who do not survive their tyrannical or self-important husbands and tiresome children, to make a dramatic recovery in the liberation of widowhood, do slowly become the paralysed figures they have enacted. Kirsteen's mother may take the better part of three volumes to die, but from the start circumstances and her own temperament have been against her:

poor Mrs Douglas had no spirit, no health, little brains to begin with and none left now, after thirty years of domestic tyranny and a 'bairn-time' of fourteen children. What could such a poor soul do but fall into invalidism with so many excellent reasons constantly recurring for adopting the habits of that state and its pathos and helplessness—especially with Margaret to fall back upon, who, though she would sometimes speak her mind to her mistress, nursed and tended, watched over and guarded her with the most unfailing care?[142]

Physical illness is often the result or expression of an inner malady in her novels. Such afflictions vary from the permanent loss of voice suffered by a spoilt heiress in *The Last of the Mortimers*, when she fails to obtain her own way, to the more plausible breakdowns, presumably modelled on brother Frank's, suffered by a number of her bankrupts. Such afflictions, however, offer no moral lesson or opportunity for conversion; they merely test the love and devotion of the immediate families. Similarly, her cripples are rarely exemplars of unnatural piety.

Mrs Oliphant resolutely set her face against that favourite Victorian female novelist's practice of maiming men in order to humble them sufficiently for a strong heroine to achieve her victory. In her view men already carried a spiritual handicap by virtue of their gender. Secondly, the most cursory comparison of her own 'unbroken health' with the physical frailty of her two brothers, her husband, and her sons would not have encouraged her to see physical strength as a necessary male attribute.

The first handicapped person to appear in her fiction may well have been suggested by her encounters with Frank Smedley, author of such sporting novels as *Frank Farleigh* and *Vernon Lee*, 'an extraordinary being in a wheeled chair, with an imperfect face (as if it had been somehow left unfinished in the making)'. To her mind the efforts of this 'terrible cripple, supposed to be kept together by some framework of springs and supports', to maintain himself by authorship, despite allegedly being the son of a rich man, were 'pathetic'. His fictional counterpart is likewise an object of pity to the narrator, who describes a heartless girl deliberately arousing the desire of a man who can never hope to attract anything beyond sisterly compassion.[143]

It was only after those double strokes of misfortune, Frank and Maggie's deaths, that Mrs Oliphant recognized the metaphor of male crippling as peculiarly appropriate for bearing the burden of her own emotional disablement. *At His Gates* (1872) contains a figure entirely surplus to the plot's requirements, but important enough to carry the novel's concluding words. Haldane, the Dissenting minister, has lost his ministerial appointment as a consequence of a stroke and then, as his condition worsens, is relieved of his post as editor of a Dissenting journal. For much of the novel he stands surrogate for Willie's dispiriting experiences with the world of English Dissent, but, at the novel's close, the pathetic isolation to which his disabling strokes have brought him is suddenly made to do duty for Mrs Oliphant's sense of the pathos of her own position. He sits chair-bound next to a woman who, though she has long believed herself widowed, has had her husband restored to her and has only 'lost' her daughter in marriage. The husband offers comfort to his wife.

'Well, Helen', he said, with his cheery voice, 'she is gone as you went from your mother; and there are two of us still, whatever life may have in store.'

'If there had not been two of us,' the mother cried, with momentary passion, 'I think I should have died!'

Stephen Haldane took her hand in his, in sign of his sympathy. He held it tightly, swaying for a moment in his chair. And he said nothing, for there was no one whose ear was his, to whom his words were precious. But in his heart he murmured, God hearing him, 'There is but one of me; and I shall never die.'

The similarity of his silent plaint to the last words she had committed to her journal before leaving Rome, where Maggie had died, is unmistakable.

I have nobody to stand between me and the roughest edge of grief. All the terrible details have come to me. I have to bear the loss, the pang unshared. My boys are too little to feel it, and there is nobody else in the world to divide it with me. O Lord, Thou wouldest not have done it but for good reason! Stand by the forlorn creature who fainteth under Thy hand, but whom Thou sufferest not to die.[144]

The transfer of sympathy from her brother's plight to her own, and the occasion for it, enacted in the manipulation of Stephen Haldane as a figure of pathos is significant. It locates the moment at which Mrs Oliphant felt with such force the pitiableness of her own position that she simply had no compassion left to expend upon others. Her daughter Maggie's death occurred in the middle of an expedition undertaken, against her own better judgement, almost entirely out of compassion for others. Geddie Macpherson had been staying with Mrs Oliphant when she had an 'almost fatal' illness and now wanted her friend to accompany her back to Rome. Mrs Oliphant was further persuaded by the prospect it afforded to the Tullochs to break free from the effects of a long depressive spell from which he had been suffering. In her *Autobiography* she recorded at length the sympathetic attention she had given to what she subsequently saw as the risible source of his malady.

It originated, (or he thought it did) in (of all things in the world) a false quantity he had made in some Latin passage he had quoted in a speech at some Presbytery or Assembly meeting. He told it with such impassioned seriousness, with his countenance so full of sorrow and trouble, his big blue eyes full of moisture, that I was much impressed, and, I remember, gave him out of my sympathy and emotion the equally inconceivable advice to call the men together to whom that speech had been made, and make a clean breast of it to them. I remember he was staggered in the semi-insanity of his talk by this queer insane suggestion, and perhaps a touch more would have awakened the man's wholesome humour and driven the strange delusion away in a shout of laughter; but I was deadly serious, as was he.

She never entirely forgave either herself or him for the part his 'semi-insanity', and her over-sympathetic approach to it, played in precipitating the second bereavement in Rome. Thirty years later she was to recall that they all left Rome together after Maggie's death because 'I felt that if I left them then I could never bear to see them again'.[145] She certainly became 'so scornful' of the alleged cause of

Principal Tulloch's depression that she was prepared, while he was still alive, to use the precise 'mental difficulty' he had shared with her as the basis for a minor canon's nervous debility and lack of promotion in *Within The Precincts* (1879). Given that Tulloch suffered recurrent breakdowns, her behaviour seems particularly insensitive. Although their friendship survived to see a mutual dedication of books (his *Movements of Religious Thought in Britain during the Nineteenth Century*, her *Primrose Path*), she refused to encourage him in what seemed to her a self-indulgent preoccupation with his own misery. In September 1881 she wrote to him:

It wants patience, and I am sure you have had a very hard trial to go through in your banishment and loneliness; but God be thanked that it has had its effect, and I hope you will carry out your cure bravely, and not think of coming away till the doctors give you leave: as they have been justified in ordering you this very bitter medicine . . .

Yes, it is evident that I am much stronger than you are. I fancy that women are stronger than men, after they get over their special danger, though indeed the padrona is not a case in point. But think, please, if it had been me who had been ill, what would have become of me?—no income going on whether one could work or not—no wife to take care of me. You are far better off than I am in these respects, and, to tell the truth, I am often tired to death of work and care—always work, work, whether one likes or not. But I am wicked to complain.[146]

In fact, even before she had met Tulloch she had shown herself suspicious of the morbid introspection associated with such practices as keeping a diary to record one's spiritual frame of mind.

A sick man who watches his own symptoms falls most frequently into miserable hypochondriacism; and I confess it always grieves and distresses me to find good people commenting, in published books and diaries, upon the momentary vicissitudes of their own mind and spirit.[147]

It was perhaps not surprising therefore that she found the religious melancholy of William Cowper, the eighteenth-century poet, wholly unproductive of sympathy. He is dismissed as a self-centred bachelor who might have been saved from himself had he found true love.[148]

In the main her fictional depictions of madness demonstrate the saving power of love to redeem the temporarily insane. Even in that most melodramatic of novels, *Salem Chapel* (1863), which yields a daughter and a girl betrayed by love both driven distraught by the cruel deceptions of the villain, the girl is enabled to recover her senses, or emerge from total self-absorption, in the task of nursing the daughter, long considered half-witted, back to health. Mrs Oliphant declared herself opposed to hereditary insanity forming the central subject of a novel because it could yield no satisfactory result,[149] and only twice resorted to its use, in *Cousin Mary* (1888) and *A Cuckoo in the Nest* (1892). In both cases the role of half-witted, decadent scion of the aristocracy is to provide a suitable victim for the machinations of schemers intent upon wresting rightful inheritance away from the true line. Far more frequent are portraits of women who temporarily lose their senses as a result of some great shock, usually exacerbated by the premature birth of their child—a condition into which she presumably felt the untimely circumstances of Cecco's birth could have led her. The period, sometimes years, which it takes these women to recover from their brain-fever allows the author breathing-space to pick up the other threads of the plot and continue for a third volume. In the case of male characters the retreat into total madness, consequent upon some criminal act, provides the excuse for the subsequent complicated exertions of loving relatives to keep the madman from the hands of impartial justice.[150] Mrs Oliphant's determined grip upon reality, exercised both in the crises of her own life and in the matter of character portrayal, had the detrimental effect of allowing these plot crutches an unfortunate prominence. Though she was prepared to resort to melodramatic acts of violence for reasons of plot, she very rarely allowed her characters to relieve themselves in outbursts of hysterical passion or delirious confession. It is often the way in which a character's thoughts and emotions, particularly those of her female characters, are contrasted with the necessities of mundane social intercourse that lends passionate conviction to their inner state.

The naked intensity of some of the more private passages of reflection in her *Autobiography* underlines the very deliberateness with which she was wont to repress 'my own way of self-comment'. The text of this work as a whole shows a constant warring between the side of her that would dearly have loved to have been able to give open utterance to 'a grief that rends one asunder' or to succumb to the 'passion and agony' of her inner turmoil, and her determination to dismiss this as useless self-indulgence and force her thoughts back into 'a prosaic little narrative'. So deep had this habit of repression sunk after the terrible event of Maggie's death, that Cecco clearly felt it necessary for the family's good to force an open confrontation on the issue after Cyril's death. A week after the event found Cecco, his mother, and Denny in Switzerland.

In the middle of the day at our lunch my Cecco said, 'If all had been well we would have been drinking Tiddy's health. It might not be fit to do that now, but let us drink to our meeting with him' and we did so solemnly. This is how we are to take our sorrow, never to avoid his name. From the time of her death till now I have never named Maggie's name. I have avoided it and called her my child, my darling, never that familiar sound named. But Cecco will not have it so with his brother. He speaks of him constantly and I am training myself to do it too—nay, I think I can do it without difficulty—as yet.[151]

In the final portions of her *Autobiography*, written after Cecco's death, the collision between interiority and the attempt at public memoir threatened total fragmentation. Try though she might to laugh at the morbidly 'elaborate self-discussions' of John Addington Symonds's *Memoirs*, she was forced to admit that 'the movements of the mind are more interesting than those of the body, or rather of the external life. I might well given myself up to introspection at this sad postscript of my life.'[152] She had, after all, been one of the first to appreciate Anthony Trollope's capacity to unite the pleasures of the realist and sensational novel by the delicacy with which he conducted his psychological analyses of his more disturbed characters. Although she included *The Last Chronicle of Barset* under the rubric of the novel of sensation, she wrote of its central character, the Reverend Josiah Crawley: 'there is a grandeur about the half-crazed, wildered man—a mingled simplicity and subtlety in the conception—to which we cannot easily find a parallel in fiction'.[153] Her own fiction had also always been at its best when she had allowed it to act as the vehicle for examining 'movements of the mind'. The distance and focus lent by a narrative drive which allowed some resolution to the circling anxieties of real life enabled her to use and give covert expression to the personal mental susceptibilities she so greatly distrusted. When asked in 1888 to outline a course of study for tiros in the art of fiction she concluded by hypothesizing that the intending novelist 'would examine how men are affected by circumstances, and with what subtle strategies their minds work, making new paths wherever the old are blocked up. No doubt he would naturally think it out in the first place from what he himself would do, but the study would soon branch out into other lines . . .'.[154] Her own later fiction specialized in tracing the odd mental convolutions of those possessed by *idées fixes*. The doctor who figures in the margins of *A House in Bloomsbury*, deriving his income from treating his patients' dyspepsia, while pursuing his private hobby of playing 'medical detective', examining their mental disorders and obsessions, might well serve as a trope for Mrs Oliphant's habit of using her conventionally plotted novels to explore the eccentric positions to which 'elaborate self-discussions' might lead.[155]

(c) Anti-intellectualism

When they tried to characterize Mrs Oliphant, her close friends found it necessary both to attest to 'an intellect so alert that one wondered she ever fell asleep'; 'that chord of intelligent antagonism' that made her such a stimulating companion; and, at the same time, to emphasize her absolute detestation of 'mental speculation' or the highbrow discussion of abstract ideas.[156] It would be tempting to believe that her only interest in 'movements of the mind' was in following the dialogue of the heart and head in which so many of her characters partake, but the evidence suggests otherwise. Principal Tulloch claimed that the origins of the book he dedicated to her lay in 'our discussion many years ago, and in the treatment of which you were to bear what would have proved by far the most interesting part'.[157] Her determinedly anti-intellectual stance clearly became something of an affectation in later life. Tulloch's own son reported that 'After having had what she called a "course" of a very intellectual person, she would say she would like to have the cook up to talk to'.[158]

As with many prejudices, her anti-intellectualism seems to have been the by-product of other deeply cherished opinions, rather than based upon a logically coherent position. It stemmed partly from her mother's repudiation of anything that smacked of 'artificial aids'. She was by any standards a remarkably well-read woman, and a keen supporter of such projects as Blackwoods' Ancient Classics for English Readers, which brought the '*sine qua non*' of the cultivated mind within the reach of the formerly disenfranchised, such as Dissenters and women readers.[159] But she was outspoken in her criticism both of those who flaunted their auto-didact status and those who trailed the cloak of their more traditional scholarly attainments too openly. The clash between her instinctive preference for those who wore their learning lightly and the intellectual appetite that had spurred her on to become *Blackwood's* general utility woman of letters, rather than remain a popular novelist, is neatly captured in the dilemmas that face the heroine of *Joyce* (1888). Growing up in Scotland, the girl shares 'something of the Scotch indifference to recondite scholarship' and comes to dislike the intellectual pomposities of her betrothed, a hard-working Scottish schoolteacher. Nevertheless, when her long-lost father, an Indian colonel, transports her to genteel life in the Home Counties, she finds their total absence of shared literary interests an important factor in preventing a close relationship. Her heart is instead drawn to a Captain Bellendean who can make the passing apposite reference to Horace and Juvenal, though he has forgotten the actual vocabulary of the Latin he acquired at school.

The reference to Joyce's Thameside sojourn in the Home Counties was not accidental. The choice of Windsor as her home typified the complexity of the dilemmas Mrs Oliphant faced and the uneasy compromises she made. She disliked the arrogance of the Matthew Arnold coterie who dominated the male intellectual world in London and in any case knew herself debarred, as a woman, from its purlieus. Moreover, she felt there was something absurdly élitist and wasteful in a publication like Arnold's *Friendship's Garland*, which was intended to provide a useful critique of national behaviour while aiming itself well over the heads of the provincial Philistines whose mores it most deplored.[160] On the other hand, her tales, novels, and letters repeatedly indicate the mixture of prudish stuffiness, snobbery, and ignorant middle-class prejudice that characterized the social life of this Royal Borough. As she told John Blackwood, 'I am almost sorry to say I don't feel myself much sillier than the majority of men I meet, though perhaps that may be because the men in Windsor are not lofty specimens.'[161] An unkind critic might be prompted to suggest that Windsor allowed her a reputation for intellectual achievement without much effort on her part. The same was not true of Oxford. During a stay there she wrote to Blackwood,

Almost anybody who is anybody has called I think, but intellectualism like any other *ism* is monotonous, and the timidity and mutual alarm of the younger potentates strikes us a good deal. They are so much afraid of committing themselves or risking anything that may be found wanting in any minutiae of correctness. Scholarship is a sort of poison tree and kills everything.

Offering to do her Cervantes volume for the Foreign Classics series anonymously, she added, somewhat bitterly, 'My name seems to be sufficient warrant for all manner of accusations of incorrectness, from all the whipper-snappers of young scholars.'[162] It is true that she was a careless scholar and wrote at such speed that she rarely bothered to check her quotations, but she did resent the inference that she was an irresponsible reviewer. Defending herself to Blackwood about the furore her review of Augustus Hare's *Memorials of a Quiet Life* had produced, she wrote, 'Whatever the Universities may say, I read every word of both the books mentioned to my pain and sorrow.'[163] One of the reasons, indeed, that she liked and respected John Blackwood so well was that she saw him as a product of the same educational system as herself: his judgements were derived from long experience as a reader of books and human nature, unlike another printer who used to rush off to lectures in between setting up print to 'acquire doses of knowledge without the leisure to digest and apply them'.[164] She saw the intellectual pretensions of young Oxford dons like Walter Pater as part of the false dichotomy practised there between aestheticism and athleticism. She was herself more drawn to the Captain Bellendean school of casually allusive quotation: the brief French phrases and poetic quotations with which her novels are spattered make flattering reference to the cultural capital she and her readers might be supposed to share, without involving either author or reader in the further intellectual effort of consulting a dictionary or original text.

Eton, by contrast with Oxford, seemed to her to offer a good combination of scholarship and the sporting achievements befitting a gentleman,[165] and she herself undoubtedly enjoyed the intelligent, sociable company of those Eton masters who turned to schoolmastering in days when it was still impossible to combine scholarship and family life under the statutory provisions of the old universities. Yet, although she knew that her own education had not been acquired without much hard work, she was still inclined to posture as a supporter of 'the school of life' and pour contempt upon eminent names like Grote and Mill, whose ivory tower lives seemed to her both sterile and culpably remote from the world of the ordinary reader.[166] If it is possible to blame the sins of the children upon the mother, Cyril and Cecco were living proof of their mother's muddled thinking and prejudices on education and the life of the intellect. Like most parents she wanted them to acquire easily the cultural attainments and atmosphere for which she had had to strive, but failed to see that the relaxed, non-competitive style she coveted for them would prove wholly incompatible with success in the increasingly professional world of the late nineteenth century. This passage from the very end of her *Autobiography* bears reprinting if only because her analysis of her conflicting and ultimately destructive attitudes both reveals her prejudices and shows once again her characteristic capacity to be her own most perceptive critic.

My dearest, bright, delightful boy [Cyril] missed somehow his footing, how can I tell how? . . . He had done everything too easily in the beginning of his boyish career, by natural impulse and that kind of genius which is so often deceptive in youth, and when he came to that stage in which hard work was necessary against the competition of the hard working, he could not believe how much more effort was necessary. Notwithstanding all distractions he took a second-class at Oxford,—a great disappointment, yet not disgraceful after all . . .

perhaps he thought I took it lightly, and that it did not so much matter. Then it was one of my foolish ways to take my own work very lightly, and not to let them know how hard pressed I was sometimes, so that he never, I am sure, was convinced how serious it was in that way . . . Another theory I have thought of with many tears lately. I had another foolish way of laughing at the superior people, the people who took themselves too seriously,—the boys of pretension, and all the strong intellectualisms. This gave him, perhaps, or helped him to form, a prejudice against the good and reading men, who have so many affectations, poor boys, and led him towards those so often inferior, all inferior to himself, who had the naturalness along with the folly of youth . . . He went out of the world, leaving a love-song or two behind him and the little volume of 'De Musset', of which much was so well done, and yet some so badly done, and nothing more to show for his life . . .

My Cecco took the first steps in the same way, but, thanks be to God, righted himself and overcame—not in time enough to save his career at Oxford, but so as to be all that I had hoped.[167]

Part Three
The Professional Woman

7 *A Woman of Letters*

At the outset of her career as a *Maga* reviewer Mrs Oliphant drew a whimsical picture that seems to prefigure those brief portraits in which Virginia Woolf often sought to convey her sense of the difficulties against which women writers battled. In this passage Mrs Oliphant conjures up the complexity of the historical transformation she has observed. The Muse of History, a solemn matronly figure on a pedestal, who inspired the long line of male historians descending from Edward Gibbon, has metamorphosed into the woman as historian. The nineteenth-century Muse of History, substituted by Mrs Oliphant, has not just descended from her pedestal of classical privilege, but has quietly taken over and changed the nature of the historian's profession. The figure serves as a fitting introduction for a chapter discussing the problems and opportunities faced by a professional woman writer conscious of entering a market-place so long dominated by male traditions and practices.

There she is—behold her!—in the library of the British Museum, with her poke bonnet, her umbrella, her india-rubber overshoes; perhaps—most likely—some sandwiches in that pocket where weighty tablets and bits of antiquity alone were wont to be. There she sits all the dull November day, the London fog peering in at her through the big windows; nobody blowing a trumpet to clear the way as she goes home through the dingy streets of Bloomsbury,—instead of her triumphal car, putting up with an omnibus, and possibly carrying her notes in her little bag or basket, like any ordinary womankind who has been buying buttons or hooks-and-eyes.[1]

1. Making a Name

The famous cases of the Brontë sisters and Marian Evans have led to a popular myth that feminine modesty combined with the assumed superiority and marketability of male penmanship to force the majority of Victorian women novelists either into adopting male pseudonyms or remaining anonymous. The multifaceted nature of Mrs Oliphant's output makes her case unusually interesting in its revelation of the complicating factors that surrounded an individual woman's self-advertisement. Despite her mother's insistence that writing should not be given pride of place over more domestic skills, Mrs Oliphant was never made to feel that authorship was unbecoming in a woman, or might bring disgrace upon the family name. If anything, the reverse was true. Her mother acted as her first publicity agent, attempting to secure literary introductions for her talented daughter, and it was from her that she derived 'a very high idea, founded on I have never quite known what, of the importance of the Oliphant family'.[2] Contempt for the patronymic heritage had been early instilled in Mrs Oliphant, whose mother held the Wilson family, their name, breeding, and constitution, in great contempt. Mrs Oliphant's marriage to a maternal cousin, and her subsequent adoption of the initials M.O.W.O., effectively beleaguered the paternal name while also insisting upon a right, independent of her husband, to bear the name Oliphant. If this reading of her self-inscription seems unduly fanciful, it is worth remembering the narrator's farewell to Lucilla Marjoribanks on her marriage to her cousin Tom Marjoribanks: 'If there could be any name that would have suited her better, or is surrounded by more touching associations, we leave it to her other friends to find out; for at the moment of taking leave of her, there is something consoling to our mind in the thought that Lucilla can suffer no change of name.'

Her own pride in the possession of such a family name made her revert on at least three occasions in her fictional plots to the affront offered to men when a girl's family insist that he accept her name as a condition of marriage. In *Innocent* (1873), a tale written shortly after brother Frank's bankruptcy, she was prompted to reflect upon the importance men attached to their family name, despite their capacity for destroying its worth single-handed. In fact Mrs Oliphant never published anything under her maiden name of Wilson. Her first novel avoided this by claiming the status of fictional autobiography, and until her marriage those novels to which she laid direct claim were published as 'by the author of *Passages in the Life of Margaret Maitland, of Sunnyrise (Written by Herself)*'. The prestigious event of her first publication in book form by the reputable firm of Blackwoods occurred just after her marriage, and it was then that she expressed her preference for the initials M.O.W.O. on the title-page, although she claimed that she was also happy for Blackwoods to take 'the greater risk of nameless publication' since 'there seems to me something very disagreeably pompous and self-important in "the author"'.[3] By *Zaidee* (1856) she was insisting upon her right to appear at least under the name of Margaret Oliphant if her initials proved too cumbersome. She did not wish this novel to be attributed to the author of either *Katie Stewart* or *Margaret Maitland* since it bore no resemblance to them and in any case it was 'the most important book I have ever written and the one I should be best pleased to put my name to'.[4] The following year, 'not desiring to be stereotyped', she 'decided to kill off Margaret Maitland as a narrator' and designed *The Days of My Life: An Autobiography* as the first of a new anonymous series.[5] The desire to allow new departures in her fiction to make their own way without benefit or hindrance to her previous reputation stayed with her. Macmillans was offered her first 'Little Pilgrim' story on condition of total anonymity.[6] She first used the name by which she was to be best known, Mrs Oliphant, in the year of her widowhood,[7] and in the next decade had real reason to protect her trade mark zealously. She told Blackwood that she had no wish to see a piece of juvenilia, 'John Rintouil', republished with her name attached to it.[8] She apologized profusely when a family friend, Mrs S. C. Hall, pressured her into allowing her name to be used in the magazine she edited, since she was well aware that it was in a different league from *Maga*.[9] Mrs Oliphant shared George Eliot's conviction that 'a *name* is precisely the most highly-priced thing in literature', and where Eliot suspected sharp practice in the anonymous publication of Mrs Oliphant's 'Chronicles of Carlingford' series, which had led some people to attribute them to her, Mrs Oliphant herself was inclined to be resentful of Blackwood's 'fondness' for publishing her anonymously.[10]

Perhaps George Eliot's suspicions of opportunism on the publisher's part were well-founded. Certainly when Mrs Oliphant advised Blackwood against putting her name to *John: A Lover's Tale* in 1870, because it was unfortunately due to appear at the same time as Hurst and Blackett's named edition of *The Three Brothers*, he deliberately ignored her wishes and laid claim to her as a Blackwoods' author.[11] From the mid-1870s Mrs Oliphant was constantly worrying that the very frequency with which she had to publish was cheapening her name.

The alternation in the early years between named and anonymous publication makes the nature of the arrangement by which she allowed brother Willie to profit by four early novels easier to understand. Willie's precise stake in *John Drayton* (1851) is unclear, but Bentley, the publisher, clearly believed her to be the author and she agreed to accept a reduced fee for her next offering, *The Melvilles*, because she insisted on anonymous publication, without any reference to her previous work.[12] This publication produced a further alias under which her work could be published without direct falsehood. To advertise *The Melvilles* (1852) and *Ailieford* (1853) as 'by the author of *John Drayton*' was true to the letter if not the spirit of the law. The only exception to this rule was *Christian Melville* (1856), which was attributed to 'the author of *Mathew Paxton*' (1854), Willie's own work. In her *Autobiography* Mrs Oliphant refers to *Christian Melville* as the first novel she ever wrote and continues, 'It was published long after by Willie on his own account, and very silly I think it is, poor little thing.'[13] Given the concern she was already displaying about her own name as an artist, it is very unlikely that she would have wished to claim authorship of the piece, but it remains unclear whether the published attribution was straight literary theft by Willie or the device of an unscrupulous publisher.

Mrs Oliphant's generosity towards her brother was warranted to the extent that the 'literary priest' was encouraged to graduate from 'fair copyist' to authorship of four further novels. The episode also suggests how swiftly Mrs Oliphant became a thoroughly professional writer, able to turn her hand to editorial work and 'ghost' writing and yet determined to preserve the artistic standards that could select the corpus of work to which she would wish to attach her name. This discriminatory ability was to cost her dear in 1870 when Frank's bankruptcy faced her 'with a great decision, to give up what hopes I might have had of doing now my very best, and to set myself steadily to make as much money as I could, and do the best I could for the three boys'.[14] Yet, as her sons grew up, she thought much of the status her 'name' might win for them. In 1874 she told John Blackwood he could relax her usual principle of anonymity: 'one usually thinks much less of the praise when one is aware of the identity of the writer. However, as it is an object worth considering to commend the name which my boys, I hope, will make something of', she thought it would be sensible to tell Lord Lytton that she had been the author of a favourable review. A few years later, in asking John Blackwood for an introduction to Lord Salisbury, who, she hoped, would provide a Foreign Office post for one of the boys, she reminded him that 'his sons had been in the same Eton house with Salisbury's' and, she added, 'I suppose he will know my name.'[15] In the name, of which she was so fiercely proud, her work and her family, that so often seemed at odds, appeared to achieve identity of interest. Her decline in reputation in the years after her sons' death seemed to her to have an almost ironic fitness about it: 'I pay the penalty in that I shall not leave anything behind me that will live.'[16] It is also possible that her sense that she was preserving an old and honourable name rather than 'making a name for herself' played its part in her resistance to the notion of saving oneself to produce the great novel and in her sons' conviction that their mother's reputation was in such a high state of credit that no further investment could be required of them.

Perhaps the most significant gauge of the store she set by the name to which she was triply entitled by birth, marriage, and work, is provided by her youngest niece's decision in 1895 to try to give pleasure to her adoptive aunt by changing her own surname by deed poll from Wilson to Oliphant.

The self-consciousness of her attitude towards her name as something she could deploy at will emerges in the *Autobiography* as an amused sense of the contrast between the 'anonymity' of her social presence and the considerable audience her 'voice' could command. As a reviewer she set great store by the personal invisibility guaranteed by anonymity. In her case the assumption of the male voice helped to make the point of transition more precise, but she became firmly wedded to Blackwood's policy, notably old-fashioned by the closing years of the century, of anonymous reviewing. The 'anonymity principle', as she called it, was equally helpful to reviewer and reviewed, in her opinion, since it upheld the 'dignity of opinion' without recourse to the discounting process which came into play when personalities became involved.[17] Despite Henry James's assertion that 'no woman had ever, for half a century, had her personal "say" so publicly and irresponsibly', she certainly believed her exercise of the prerogative to be eminently responsible. It was, after all, the report of an *unfavourable* review of her own fiction that led her to declare to Blackwood that she did not want to discover the reviewer's identity and to conclude, 'Anonymity is a great institution—I think I shall go in for that henceforward in everything but novels.'[18]

2. The Hero as Woman of Letters

Carlyle's lecture 'The Hero as Man of Letters' defined the Victorian ideal of the writer as prophet, priest, or sage as exclusively male.[19] The rapid expansion of the periodical press in the opening years of the nineteenth century offered a profession to generalist writers who were able to interpret and expound rather than make original contributions to knowledge. It might have been supposed that this new job opportunity, which encouraged non-academic voices and could be practised at home, would have instantly attracted women writers; yet in the *Wellesley Index to Victorian Periodicals* only 11 women, out of 11,560 authors indexed, have more than fifty entries to their name. Margaret Oliphant easily tops this list with a total of 252 entries, two-and-a-half times as many as her nearest female competitor.[20] These entries include some of her serialized fiction and are not truly indicative of her non-fictional output in that they do not take account of the thirty or so articles contributed to the *St James's Gazette*, nor her contributions to the *Spectator* and others probably still unrecorded. The very marked gender exclusivity of the periodical press was associated with the view that women writers, who characteristically had less formal education than men, were better suited to fiction, the junior and inferior branch of prose-writing. Carlyle's lecture had literally marginalized women, who appear only 'as foolish girls . . . in remote villages', consumers seeking such direction as they were capable of comprehending from 'the wretchedest circulating library novels'. Carlyle's contempt for the novel was legendary. This letter from his wife, Jane Welsh Carlyle, to Mrs Oliphant, reporting her husband's backhanded compliment, may therefore seem surprising.

I do long to see you to tell you, not what *I* think of your book but what Mr. C. thinks, which is much more to the purpose! I never heard him praise *a woman's* book, hardly any man's as cordially as he praises this of yours! You are 'worth whole cartloads of Mulochs, and Brontës, and THINGS of that sort! . . . You are really [he says] 'a fine clear, loyal, sympathetic female being.'[21]

Despite the comparison with Mulocks and Brontës, the encomium from the great man was elicited not for one of Mrs Oliphant's novels, but for her first biography, the life of Carlyle's friend, Edward Irving. This foray into the world of real literature may have raised her above her female contemporaries in his opinion, but did not justify her admission into the stronghold of male heroes of literature.

Twentieth-century literary canonization has continued to exclude Mrs Oliphant from the pantheon of the great for a number of reasons, some of which can be traced back to Carlyle's influence. The posthumous publication of her *Autobiography*, with its wry, self-deprecating attempts to evaluate a life spent juggling the demands of her art with the needs of her family, appeared when it was no longer fashionable to question the supreme value of art. Yet Carlyle's legacy also played its part. Literary activity in the last decade of the nineteenth century was dominated by a male clubland taking its revenge for the long years of George Eliot's supremacy. Slowly a new literary myth evolved, the logic of which seems to have been something like this: George Eliot, now amongst the honoured dead, could be left upon her pedestal, with the sole proviso that she continued her act of cross-dressing into perpetuity. (If this seem far-fetched it is worth asking why the Brontë sisters' professional achievements are not discussed under their professional names: Acton,

Currer, and Ellis Bell.) As the *only* woman admitted to the great tradition, until recent years, George Eliot then became the paradigm for discussing the woman's experience as writer. This exception really did begin to prove the rule by which other women writers were judged. This has proved damaging because, as it so happened, George Eliot's life and work could very neatly be fitted into another male-centred, nineteenth-century myth: the myth of progress. Thus the fact that her literary career had its beginnings in the work of translation and reviewing—work which was laid aside when she began her career as novelist—established the notion that such work—the breadwinning activity of many a Victorian woman writer—was necessarily an apprentice stage to true creative talent: money-spinning rather than yarn-spinning. Mrs Oliphant's career presents an alternative lesson: she obtained her first commissions for review articles, which typically paid better than fiction, on the strength of her success as a novelist and short-story writer. George Eliot might have delayed her start as a novelist by filling the pages of the *Westminster Review* out of love for John Chapman, but Mrs Oliphant was firm in demanding £50 an essay from John Blackwood for her series of 'Historical Sketches of the Reign of George II' because they would 'involve much more labour than novel writing'.[22] She also felt that running the two careers of novelist and reviewer in tandem was advantageous for her work. In the midst of writing the episodes of *The Story of Valentine and His Brother*, she turned her attention to her review of the *Autobiography* of the popular preacher, Dr Guthrie. 'I don't mind doing it, even if you don't publish it at all,' she confided to John Blackwood, 'for it seems the purpose of one of those little walks an artist takes away from his picture which he is in the act of painting—letting me see my more important work from a little distance.'[23]

Mrs Oliphant's achievements were Herculean by any standard. Rumour even related that she had once written an entire issue of *Maga*, reviews, fiction, poetry, and all. Rumour, as always, exaggerated: nevertheless, she had sometimes written as much as one-third of a magazine which was always seen as predominantly masculine in its tone and intended readership. The pattern of her writing career also begins to make more sense if it is placed beside that of her next most prolific contemporary, Anthony Trollope. Like him it took her time to find her most characteristic *métier* as a novelist: both started with the genre of the regionally based novel, perhaps because, for different reasons, they felt themselves outsiders to the main English tradition; both briefly and unsuccessfully essayed the historical novel; and both their careers took off when they imaginatively appropriated a quintessentially English community and produced a series of works depicting it. Both attempted at various times to break their own mould by publishing a new departure in their fiction anonymously.[24] Both produced volumes of short stories; both wrote biographies; both recognized the profitability of books which recognized the middle-class Victorian's appetite for travel and allowed them also to experience its pleasure and rigours. Both were interested in literary history and helped feed the Victorian appetite for works by generalists on the subject. Both suffered from the conclusion that such unrelenting productivity must sacrifice quality to quantity and from the view that a consistency of tone, a characteristic approach to their subject-matter, however varied in itself, must be an indication of the second-rate order of their imaginative capacity. In one major respect, however, they differed. Where most of those who met Trollope, like those who met Robert Browning, were disconcerted by the contrast between the larger-than-life physical presence of this rumbunctious author and his subtle, psychologically probing novels, the Blackwoods immediately christened Margaret Wilson 'Katie' after her novel *Katie Stewart*,[25] and, at the very end of her life, J. M. Barrie saw her as 'less the novelist now than a pathetic figure in a novel', and from what he continued to say it is clear that he had in mind one of her own novels.[26] In this respect Mrs Oliphant needs to be compared with other women writers. Virginia Woolf, who saw her through the anti-Victorian eyes of her Bloomsbury contemporaries, may seem an unlikely figure to invoke at this point, apart from the fact that she recognized the *Autobiography*, however grudgingly, as 'a most genuine and moving piece of work'.[27] In the *Auto-biography* she would have recognized a woman writer, like herself, supremely conscious of entering a male-dominated world, but seeing it always through a woman's eyes, and constantly aware of the strain, amounting to a looming threat of fragmentation, that resulted from her desire to preserve a continuum between the life and the work. That the dangers of such self-awareness appeared only in Mrs Oliphant's more private writings was perhaps attributable to an upbringing in which she had always seen women as heroes, taking control, rather than an up-bringing like Virginia Woolf's where men, often pathetically, strove to perpetuate the myth of male heroism by exploiting and manipulating women.

Mrs Oliphant's remarkable success as 'woman of letters' would appear to be indirectly attributable to her mother's unlimited confidence in her daughter. Living 'much out of the world' in exile in Liverpool, and with her sons launched, her mother devoted herself to educating her daughter at home. She was an avid reader of periodicals, and despite her 'fervent Liberalism' she was prepared to allow the Tory *Blackwood's Edinburgh Magazine* to take its place alongside the Whiggish *Edinburgh Review*.[28] When the time came to launch her daughter, Mrs Wilson's idea of a 'coming out' party was to take her to Edinburgh and effect introductions to the literary set there. She was even prepared to put aside her contempt for her husband's family if it meant introductions to the Wilson boys, one of whom, Daniel, was then 'at the head (in a literary point of view) of the business of Messrs Nelson, reading for them and advising them about books'.[29] Best of all, she engineered an invitation for her daughter to stay on in Edinburgh under the care of their old family doctor, Dr David Macbeth Moir, *Blackwood*'s 'Delta', whom she had previously canvassed to secure his editor's attention for Margaret. Margaret herself was very anxious to make her passage through the 'Scylla and Charybdis of the novel craft',[30] formed by the publishers Bentley and Colburn, as swift as possible and join the more respectable ranks of Blackwoods' authors. Once having secured the publication of her seventh novel, *Katie Stewart*, under their auspices she lost no time in suggesting herself as an essayist or reviewer.[31] From John Blackwood's point of view she was a useful acquisition because she was not too disheartened when her ideas were turned down and always willing to include 'some of your likings among the crowd' when she was asked to review lesser writers.[32] Moreover, Thackeray and Bulwer Lytton, the 'big names' they entrusted to her in her third and fourth published articles, were both pleased with her comments. Thackeray especially must have reassured Blackwood, as to the risk he was taking, by attributing her article to Professor Aytoun, Blackwood's chief literary reviewer.[33] Delighted though she was to have signed up with Blackwoods, the contracts she continued to secure elsewhere (as her mother remarked, 'Mr Blackwood, honest man', did not suspect the true extent of young Katie's previous experience, being unaware of the novels she had made over to her brother[34]) lent her both a degree of assurance in nego- tiating her rates of pay and the courage to stand by her own literary judgements. When John Blackwood tried to influence her presentation of that staunch *Maga* man, Lockhart, he received this firm rebuff: 'I must judge for myself—I will pay, as I always do, the greatest attention to your personal objections; but it is I who will be responsible for the work.'[35]

In the long run, however, hitching her wagon to the Blackwoods' star may have done her as much harm as it did her good as a woman of letters. Although she became *Maga*'s 'general utility woman' she never enjoyed security of tenure and over the years this type of complaint became more frequent in her dealings with Blackwood: 'I don't think I am generally a difficult person to deal with—but perhaps you may find it difficult to realize the difference between working steadily on a settled plan and doing bits of work precariously, without knowing what one may calculate upon.'[36]

John Blackwood undoubtedly became her banker, reviewer, literary adviser, and friend, but the relationship remained essentially one of patronage. She had possibly reached the pinnacle of her dreams and the ceiling of her achievements as a professional writer too early in her career. By the late 1860s she always felt it right to offer her work first to Blackwood, partly out of a sense of obligation but also because, tempting though it was to consider an offer from a periodical like *Good Words*, it had to be seen as 'a kind of exceptional offer not standing in the same rank as a Magazine of *our* rank—if indeed there is any Magazine in the same category'.[37] Yet, because Blackwoods was so much a family firm with a clearly defined male succession, it offered no chance of promotion. Mrs Oliphant, indeed, wryly noted the publishing house's cleverness, on the book-selling side of their operations, in appointing two bachelors, devoid of ambition and without need for advancement, to manage their London and Edinburgh outlets.[38] *Maga*'s circulation, moreover, re- mained at around 7,000 and its style as well as its politics were conservative, so that it suffered in the burgeoning and highly competitive periodicals market of the 1870s. Perhaps again because of her close association with *Maga*, Mrs Oliphant managed to sell three novels and her series of stories, *Neighbours on the Green*, to the

Cornhill, but only once succeeded, with *Carità* (1877), in selling a novel in book form to that most generous of Victorian publishers, George Smith.

It was the failure to attain the security and prestige of an editorial chair that most rankled with Mrs Oliphant as the years passed by. In the heyday of her success with the 'Chronicles of Carlingford' she repeatedly tried to raise the matter by way of a joke, prophesying confusion if she were allowed to supplant John Blackwood during his vacations.[39] In the mid-1880s, when her sons' indifference to her wishes made her feel at her most powerless, she wrote the following letter to George Craik, a partner in Macmillans: 'Thank you very much for your good wishes. The only way such kind thoughts could come to practical benefit would be to find me something like an editorship where there would be steady income without perpetual strain, such as his friends have found more than once for Leslie Stephen, but then he is a man.'[40]

The problem, however, was not that Mrs Oliphant was a woman, but that she constantly compared herself to the best-paid literary men of her generation. Thackeray, Trollope, and Dickens had all secured themselves editorships of prestigious periodicals. Other women did in fact achieve the regular employment she coveted. In religious publishing there was a strong tradition of female editors, from 'Charlotte Elizabeth' Tonna to Emma Jane Worboise and Charlotte Yonge. On the secular front women also began to make headway: Mrs Henry Wood, who, in Mrs Oliphant's opinion, 'wrote like a respectable chambermaid',[41] was rich enough to buy a periodical as a vehicle for her own fiction, and Mary Elizabeth Braddon conducted a series of magazines. None of these periodicals conducted by women, however, was in the first rank to which Mrs Oliphant aspired, and, being so well known as a factotum of Blackwood's, she was unlikely to attract offers from competitors. On various occasions she approached the prestigious publishers to whom she was closest with ideas for periodicals which she felt she might be particularly equipped to edit. In the 1860s her connection with 'kirk men' like Tulloch and Story persuaded her that they needed organization, and eventually she took it upon herself to ask John Blackwood what he would say to the project of starting up 'an organ' in their interest.[42] As the years went by she became more blatantly commercial in her suggestions. Given Macmillans' history of educational literature, she thought they were the appropriate firm to approach to ask if they would consider starting a children's magazine on the lines of the 'pretty St Nicholas's', which she found paid generously in America.[43] There is evidence to suggest that the grievance she aired to George Craik arose from a belief she had cherished in the early 1880s, that she might be about to become editor of a periodical owned by Longmans. When her friend, Principal Tulloch, who, she opined, had neither 'the nerves or the temper' for such a post,[44] relinquished the editorship of *Fraser's Magazine* in 1880, her own hope rose to such an extent that she felt herself entitled to commission articles for Longmans' proposed new venture. Thomas Hardy, the recipient of the following letter, clearly interpreted her advances in this way, and replied direct to her, expressing interest in an idea that would finally see print as 'The Dorsetshire Labourer'.

Dear Sir

Messrs Longmans have the intention of changing the form of Fraser's Magazine or rather replacing it by one intended to bear their own name, and in talking with Mr Charles Longman on the subject I mentioned to him an idea of mine for a series of magazine articles which was to consist of sketches of the labouring poor, in the country, the English and Scotch peasant in fact—which had occurred to me some time since when planning a magazine that never came to anything . . . I mentioned to Mr Longman your name as eminently qualified for such a piece of work. I write to you now at his request to ask whether you would be disposed to do it for him? . . . Will you . . . write either to Mr Charles Longman or myself to say whether you would be disposed to aid in the series he contemplates?[45]

Of course, it is possible, as Trollope suggested, that Mrs Oliphant was simply temperamentally unfitted for such a post. He claimed that, even in the minor role of series editor for the Blackwood's Foreign Classics series she was, by turn, indifferent, imperious, and overbearing in her dealings with his son Henry Merivale; though this may have been the effect of a parental pride every bit as sensitive as Mrs Oliphant's own to justifiable attacks upon a son's indolence.[46] On one occasion even William Blackwood accused her of exceeding her authority as editor, and her complaints about the collaborative volume on Molière she undertook with the Eton schoolmaster Frank Tarver suggest that she was not cut out to work in harness with others who invariably seemed to lack her speed and stamina.[47] As Denny remarked ten days after her aunt's death, 'lately she let me do more and told me more than before. Still you know how entirely she did everything herself.'[48]

Even the minor post of series editor had had to be fought for tenaciously. Despite the fact that she had suggested the publishing concept to Blackwood and then earmarked the money to provide Cyril's allowance, she feared that it might slip from her grasp and be given to the Reverend W. Lucas Collins, whom she generously admitted to have done a fine job as editor and contributor to the Ancient Classics for English Readers.[49] Security of tenure and a guaranteed income continued to elude her, but she was endlessly inventive in her endeavours to find 'solid underground work' which would not necessitate 'the constant reproduction of one's name to the weariness of the world'. This argument was put forward to John Blackwood in support of the suggestion that she should compile 'an encyclopaedia of literature', listing 'every current book published in any amount of languages'. Blackwood's notable lack of enthusiasm for the project did not defeat her, she merely reshaped the notion into an 'encyclopaedia of classic literature'.[50]

Hampered and boxed in as Mrs Oliphant increasingly felt herself to be, she nevertheless ran as full a gamut of the non-fiction areas as any of her male contemporaries. Politics alone remained beyond her *Maga* remit until the end of her career. She had openly declared her radical affiliation to the Tory John Blackwood at the beginning of their relations and their correspondence kept up the joking allusions to his entrenched position. Over the years her own position seems to have changed:

in 1876 the tone was still humorous but she was prepared to tell Blackwood, apropos of an article on Macaulay she was sending him for the May number, 'I do not mind if you throw in a bit of Toryism on your own account, though I think I am gloriously Tory now and then.'[51] By the time of her 'Old Saloon' articles in the mid-1880s the personalities involved had changed: Mrs Oliphant now seemed to share *Maga*'s detestation of Gladstone and all he stood for. Perhaps William Blackwood also realized that the firm had been underestimating the range of her accomplishments when he received a letter telling him how she had been endeavouring to explain to Queen Victoria how Gladstone still managed to retain favour with the Scots. Queen Victoria apparently found her new political adviser's explanation of Gladstone's deep-seated vanity very convincing; they agreed that someone must be guarding him from reading the newspaper criticism of his policies.[52] The climate of editorial opinion as to a woman's sphere seems also to have undergone a change. The *St James's Gazette* found it perfectly acceptable to have Mrs Oliphant speaking out as 'A Dowager' upon matters of contemporary concern, and even *Maga* was prepared to accept the extension of subject-matter as long as it was voiced through a male mouthpiece.[53]

Science and philosophy were the other major areas of nineteenth-century prose, identified by her and Cecco in *The Victorian Age of English Literature*, that she avoided. She felt that spiritually and educationally she belonged to a pre-scientific age and could never see why the craze for keeping aquaria or attending lectures on the origins of the universe were regarded as intrinsically superior pastimes to embroidery.[54] These subjects attracted her only through the human interest of watching eminent scientists and philosophers, as they were revealed in biographies and autobiographies, attempting to grapple with problems that seemed for the most part so remote from everyday life.[55] Amongst the other categories of prose non-fiction she identified she was prepared to review books concerned with biography, history, theology, and art, and to some of these categories she made notable contributions herself.

Her husband Frank had introduced her both to the world of galleries, museums, and pictures and to contemporary talk about art. Her account in the *Autobiography* of Frank squiring her round the National Gallery and registering 'astonished disappointment' at her total 'want of appreciation' of the visual arts suggests her own embarrassment at the gap in her education this represented. It is improbable that the humble circumstances of her upbringing would have afforded even the basic instruction in water-colours that formed part of many middle-class girls' range of accomplishments. (She was never to acquire any pleasure from that other staple middle-class female accomplishment—music.)[56] Towards the end of her life she claimed that although she could make landscape pencil sketches she had never achieved any proficiency with colours.[57] Marriage to Frank had provided an education for which she was to be both emotionally and professionally grateful and she was careful to include exhibition attendance as part of her sons' extracurricular cultural activities.[58] In her novels an ignorance as profound as her own had been is one of the features that marks the class gap and suggests the divide that will have to be scaled if marriages between upper-class husbands and girls from working-class backgrounds are ever to succeed.[59] Escorting Frank on his work for his stained-glass-window commissions gave her access to the vocabulary and views of the Camden school of ecclesiastical architecture and Pugin's Gothic revival, while the painterly talk he indulged in with friends like William Frost, Alexander Johnstone, and George Lance gave her an insight into the problems of the art business.[60] She never fully comprehended the seriousness of Frank's devotion to his art—a commitment that would lead him to donate his windows where no fee was forthcoming, and become profoundly depressed by his first exposure to the Italian masters, whom he could never hope to emulate.[61] She continued to be fascinated by an art which demanded formal training and hard work, even though these counted for so little in the face of genius.[62] Perhaps the growing technical competence of her nieces reinforced the deliberately amateur stance of her exhibition reviews: in the same letter in which she approached Macmillans for an introduction for Madge to a wood-engraver she declined their invitation to review an exhibition of sketches of Venice on the grounds of insufficient technical expertise: 'I know what I like, but not why I like it.'[63] Like Virginia Woolf with her sister Vanessa, she was to find that living at close quarters with artist husband and nieces provided her with a fruitfully different medium through which to explore at one remove the problems of her own. Beautiful views were always more likely to retain a place in her memory than pictures or statues, yet her capacity to respond to representational skill or narrative meaning made her an attractive proposition to publishers who wanted art made accessible to the general public. Character, situation, and emotional significance were what she took from pictures: she had herself been drawn to commune with Albertinelli's picture, *The Visitation*, showing 'the tender old Elizabeth' visiting a pregnant Mary, when she found herself pregnant, motherless, and without another woman's support in Florence.[64] The sections of her Macmillans series of historical guides that dealt with the lives and times of the painters of Florence and Venice often offered word-paintings of the stories their pictures told that would hold some appeal even to those who had little hope of travelling to see the original.

Biography became her preferred genre because it possessed 'all the higher attractions of the art of fiction, with that inestimable advantage of fact and reality which add a charm to every picture'.[65] Like fiction it was still a comparatively young art form and therefore practised by rank amateurs who paid scant regard to its possibilities.[66] Biography, she swiftly recognized, conformed very closely, in the demands it made and the possibilities it offered, to the kind of fiction to which she aspired: 'For a human life is generally a very illogical performance, take it from beginning to end; it is seldom an epic, and it is never an antithesis, and before it can be made to back out any foregone conclusion, or prove any formal argument, must suffer such violence as in most instances denudes it of all its individual grace.'[67] Biography favoured character at the expense of plot, fidelity to the significant minutiae of life rather than formulaic shape and definitive closure. Indeed, biography made high demands upon the artist since it necessitated discovering the shape that would best suit the individual subject.

By the mid-1870s John Blackwood told her that he considered biography to be 'about the greatest of your many fortes'.[68] Yet when she had first attempted the genre she had felt some temerity as a woman in displaying 'the presumption of undertaking so serious a work'. Her preface to her signed biography of Edward Irving takes the form of a lengthy apology that she, 'a person without authority', should undertake 'to pronounce judgement' on a man of such heroic stature. She had plucked up courage to essay the genre because she had been approached by Irving's relations, who had shown her friendship when she first came to London to housekeep for brother Willie.[69] Being the authorized biographer probably predisposed her to cast Irving in the mould of a romantic hero, and contemporary reviews accused her of being over-sympathetic;[70] nevertheless, the novelist's appraising eye was at work during her researches, and she wrote to John Blackwood that she found Henry Drummond, the English financier behind the Holy Catholic Apostolic Church, 'a very good type of your English country gentleman and almost too tempting a study for a novel writer'.[71] Twentieth-century historians have claimed that Mrs Oliphant resolved her ambivalent reactions as biographer to Irving's religious position by casting him as the sacrificial victim of the Holy Catholic Apostolic Church. The more complex mixture of sympathy and scepticism that Irving's activities aroused in her was to surface more fully in the sub-plot of *The Minister's Wife* (1869), which contains a perceptive assessment of the emotional weaknesses that Irvingite religion exploited both in the preacher and his followers.

Her next major commission as biographer arose partly as a consequence of her subject's good opinion of her work on Irving, and partly from the humble work of translation that 'women of letters' often found themselves undertaking if they wished to earn a living. The young George Eliot had begun her literary life as translator of Strauss and Feuerbach, and, as Mrs Oliphant herself remarked, 'It is easier than letting lodgings or going out governessing.'[72] After her husband's death Mrs Oliphant was reduced to accepting translation work. The articles and fiction written during her miserable sojourn in Italy are among her weakest and it must have looked as if her talent had been extinguished by the weight of her troubles. She was only too aware that Blackwoods' proposal that she should translate Montalembert's *Les Moins d'Occident* was an act of charity and she had no hesitation in asking for a dictionary to help her in a translation that she feared might even then be too poor to use.[73] In happier days, after her success with the early Carlingford volumes, she was able to joke to Blackwood, 'Perhaps I may be able to fall back upon translating in my old days, instead of writing wretched novels like other poor old women who profess the trade of fiction—but my own opinion is that we ought to be killed off by act of parliament at fifty and so avoid that lamentable conclusion.'[74] The role of Blackwood's publishing house in providing her first with adolescent education through the pages of *Maga* and subsequently with 'on the job' training should not be underestimated.[75] Montalembert was sufficiently pleased with her work to invite her to complete further volumes of his massive work, and the fluency in French that this project and her subsequent stay in France, after Maggie's death, secured her, meant that she was unintimidated by the research necessary to produce Montalembert's biography.

The ten years that had elapsed between her work on Irving and the life of Montalembert had boosted her confidence so that she no longer approached the genre apologetically. She wrote to Blackwood demanding to know how much she might expect from the completed work, so that she could devote 'three months or so' to ensuring that her life came out before any French competitors as she had no intention of being reduced to the position of translator again. A few months later she told him that she was writing 'much of Montalembert twice over. I get more difficult to please with my work as I get older.' The seriousness with which she took this project can be judged by her being prepared to spend two days in the British Museum searching for a particular letter in *The Times* for 1851.[76] She was never to display the same conscientiousness in her fiction and journalism, where she evidently rarely stopped to check a reference or a quotation.[77] The peculiar burden incumbent upon a 'woman of letters' was shown when Madame Montalembert descended on Mrs Oliphant on the day she was moving house, insisting on reading the complete book, much of which was at the printers, and fussing abour four more letters while her hostess was trying to get the curtains up in the guest bedroom and sending off two desperate letters to Blackwood asking for the instant return of her manuscript so as to evade the threatened return of her guest later that year. After publication Mrs Oliphant, for once, showed herself interested in seeing the reviews.[78]

The way in which Mrs Oliphant had turned the apparent shame of her banishment to translating work, traditionally regarded as less creative and therefore suited to women, into a triumphant assertion of her right to be considered not merely as a biographer but as the biographer of a European intellectual is a measure of her determination and her ambition. Her suggestion in 1877, when the last volumes of *Les Moins d'Occident* were ready for translation, that Annie Walker 'I feel sure . . . would gladly undertake the work at half the sum you paid me', for 'it would be an advantage for her to have it to do . . . and in French she is more correct than I am to whom the gift of correctness has not been given', marks her transition from patronized to patron. Although this letter may at first suggest a lack of sisterly solidarity in matters of pay, it is worth remembering that Mrs Oliphant was providing Cousin Annie with the basic necessities of life and pleasing to note that when the later volumes proved to be longer than the earlier ones Mrs Oliphant insisted that Blackwood renegotiate the rate of pay.[79] Her own command of French was sufficient in later life, she felt, to enable her to disapprove strongly of an unauthorized translation of *The Little Pilgrim*, by the Swiss Madame de Witt, as more of a paraphrase than a translation.[80] Her acquaintance with French life and mores had also given her, in effect, a cosmopolitan stance from which to view English affairs. Although she did not essay the large-scale socio-political comparisons of such Victorian sages as Carlyle or Arnold, she was able to employ this new-found knowledge to open up new areas in her domestic fiction. Sometimes the comparisons were made explicit, as in 'The Count's Daughters'[81] or *Whiteladies* (1875). More often she was able to sustain the *longueurs* of the three-decker by transporting her characters to France or Italy where she could discourse knowledgeably upon the insular, gossipy nature of English colonies abroad.

The Montalembert venture paid off handsomely in other directions too. It won for her an increasing portion of *Maga*'s reviewing of French literature and the editorship of the Blackwood's Foreign Classics series. Within a year of its appearance another of her regular publishers, Macmillans, put a new proposition to her, suggesting a volume on Italian poets. She feared that Dante would overshadow such an enterprise, but welcomed the notion of a book that would tap the growing market for books in English about Europe. Topographical studies held no allure for her, but she swiftly saw how Macmillan's proposal might be tailored to suit her talents and be dovetailed with other projects in such a way as to maximize her income. She offered Macmillan what was to prove an infinitely extendable format. *The Makers of Florence: Dante, Giotto, Savonarola, and their City* (1876) purveyed cultural history in a series of biographical sketches. She told Macmillan that it could run to one or two volumes as he pleased: 'Either way would be the same to me as Biography is always so pleasant to me and I have such thorough enjoyment in it.'[82] This was to be the first of a series of handsomely bound, copiously illustrated 'coffee-table' publications: *The Makers of Venice: Doges, Conquerors, Painters and Men of Letters* (1887), *Royal Edinburgh: Her Saints, Kings, Prophets and Poets* (1890), and *The Makers of Modern Rome* (1895). The way in which she had been able to evolve a genre peculiarly fitted to her strengths and weaknesses is perhaps best seen in the first section of *The Makers of Modern Rome* where she draws a picture of the early Church by depicting the lives of the Roman matrons who had wealth, education, and position enough to influence the forms of Christian piety in the fourth-century Roman Empire. These six chapters of confident, witty commentary and speculation upon the excesses, the unconscious self-deception, and the nobility of these early female devotees provide a succinct demonstration of Mrs Oliphant's power to recognize the demands of the market and transform these into a vehicle for her own talents. A letter written in the last year of her life, before she set off on a research trip for the book J. M. Dent had commissioned on Siena, divulged the recipe that had formed the basis of these books: 'My great desire is that the book should be readable and amusing as well as accurate and valuable.'[83]

It was also in these books of European cultural history that she found a way of venturing to comment upon the prevailing Victorian ideologies in her own voice, rather than resorting to the male mouthpiece of her periodical articles. The ability she developed in these books to concentrate long periods of history in the telling anecdote, married with her experience and range as a reviewer, resulted in other commissions where her own voice provided the continuity necessary to link disparate material. *The Victorian Age of English Literature* (1890) and *Annals of a*

Publishing House (1897) still repay reading, in a way that the drier *Literary History of England in the Eighteenth and Beginning of the Nineteenth Century* (1882) does not, because they do not pretend to encyclopaedic coverage but confront us with the personal view of a 'woman of letters' confident of her right to assess her peers.

As reviewer and practitioner she came to hold firm views on the biographer's art: in the Preface to her *Memoir of Count de Montalembert* she asserted that 'while receiving with gratitude the kind communication made to me, I reserved my own opinion on all points—the only possible means by which an artist of whatever description, can hope to produce a genuine and recognisable portrait'. So seriously did Mrs Oliphant take biography that she was prepared to make a rare *ex cathedra* pronouncement upon the responsibilities attaching to the genre. Consequent upon one of her many attacks upon Froude for traducing his subject, Thomas Carlyle, she spoke out in a signed article on 'The Ethics of Biography': the biographer had a moral responsibility to readers and subject alike to judge how successful and how honest the subject had been in putting into practice the beliefs that governed his life. Finally, the imagination should also be brought into play as 'an adjunct of the biographer's sympathies'.[84] Sadly, Mrs Oliphant did not survive to compose the fully fledged official biography that it was rumoured Queen Victoria wished her to write.[85] Yet the incomplete, posthumously published 'sketch' suggests how far she had come in developing her own brand of biography since the days of her work on Irving. She no longer allowed piety to dictate the selection and arrangement of material, but chose a stance that allowed readers to appreciate both the exceptionalities of the individual case and the extent to which all mortals are subject to the frailties of the human condition. Queen Victoria is presented and judged through the eyes of a middle-class nineteenth-century professional woman. The sketch is 'personal' not because it trades upon the intimate glimpses of her sovereign that Mrs Oliphant had enjoyed at Windsor, but because it frankly displays the biographer's own criteria for evaluating the life of a professional woman. Portraying the Queen as a woman of similar standing, forced, like herself, to work until 'two o'clock in the morning before her task was done', also allowed Mrs Oliphant to arrive at the more trenchant judgements to which she would have subjected any other successful rival: where their spheres overlapped she declared Queen Victoria's tastes to be 'those of the multitude. She reads without very much critical discernment.'[86]

3. 'Writing Ran Through Everything'

Writing had begun for Mrs Oliphant as a pastime 'to secure some amusement and occupation' while nursing a sick mother. Just as Trollope's posthumously published autobiography managed to reduce his artistic status to that of honest craftsman, so Mrs Oliphant's accounts of 'the boiling of the daily pot' served to align her work with that of contemporary female drudges.[87] Yet even when writing became a financial necessity for her she was able to express herself 'grateful to God that it was work I liked and that interested me in the doing of it, and it has often carried me away from myself and quenched, or at least calmed, the troubles of life'.[88] Mrs Oliphant may have been the exception in her generation of female artists in not needing to seek male approbation for her writing activities, but this seems only to have internalized the need to reconcile pleasure in writing, the Scottish Puritan work ethic, and the notion of a woman's proper sphere. Preaching against 'idleset' or time-wasting is a constant refrain in the early novels. Girls, we are told, should be taught from the earliest age to have a piece of sewing in hand.[89] She came to feel that she had been lucky not to have been born into a family like Jane Austen's who 'were half-ashamed to have it known that she was not just a young lady like the others, doing her embroidery'. Since, as a young girl, she had an aversion to needlework she was permitted a seat 'at the corner of the family table with my writing-book, with everything going on as if I had been making a shirt instead of writing a book . . . My mother sat always at needle-work of some kind, and talked to whoever might be present, and I took my share in the conversation, going on all the same with my story, the little groups of imaginary persons, these other talks evolving themselves quite undisturbed.'[90]

The 'plain sewing' at which her mother excelled was easily identifiable as woman's work because it made a visible contribution to the family's needs and could be construed as a practical expression of loving sacrifice of time for the benefit of others.[91] Writing could less easily be interpreted as a selfless activity, even when reading it aloud provided family entertainment. Writing novels, like reading them, seemed a potential threat to the altruistic ideal because it provided a retreat from actual responsibilities in a world of imaginary pleasure, but, worse still, rather than favouring self-obliteration, writing offered a space for self-definition. Her mother dealt with the matter by a literal restriction of space. Any suggestion that 'special facilities or retirement was necessary . . . would at once have made the work unnatural to her eyes, and also to mine'. Mrs Oliphant was to wrestle with the contradictory images her upbringing had given her for the rest of her life. Her family had been 'quite pleased to magnify me, and to be proud of my work, but always with a hidden sense that it was an admirable joke'. On the one hand her mother and her brother Willie had taken her seriously enough to seek out publishers, but had also taught her that writing must be 'subordinate to everything'. This left her stranded between feeling that it should have been sufficient 'to have kept the daily pot boiling and maintained the cheerful household fire so long' and resenting the way in which others mistook her deliberate sacrifices for lack of talent. The care with which the dangers of self-importance had been etched into her adolescent conciousness emerged in the adult's acerbic comments about contemporaries who were able to cosset their genius, yet she belonged to a generation attached to the Romantic notion of an artistic daemon that demanded acknowledgement. It is a telling moment in her *Autobiography* when, having outlined the career decision necessitated by the new responsibility for two families, she wrote, 'One can't be two things or serve two masters. Which was God and which was mammon in that individual case it would be hard to say.'[92]

Looking back from the vantage-point of 1894 she also admitted that 'there is no doubt that it was much more congenial to me to drive on and keep everything going, with a certain scorn of the increased work, and metaphorical toss of my head, as if it mattered! than it ever would have been to labour with an artist's fervour and concentration to produce a masterpiece'. The previous year she had been riled by the visit of a Mrs Templeton who had advised her ('keeping her cab waiting all the while') to struggle to be silent for as long as ten years in the endeavour to produce a book worth waiting for. 'All this would be simple enough if I had a great and burning conviction that such a thing was required of me but to set out in cold blood to work oneself up to such a point seems the strangest idea.'[93] Such a deliberate act would have smacked of the 'unnaturalness' her mother so deplored. This resistance to 'working oneself up' seeped into the very texture of the writing. She had advised Cecco only a few days before this unwelcome visit to 'let himself go' in his writing as she had never been able to do on account of being 'shy'.[94] Mrs Oliphant's style as a reviewer and novelist characteristically depended upon establishing an intimate conversational relationship with the reader: to refine and polish would disturb the balance by drawing attention to the artistic pretensions of the writer. Nevertheless, the fashionable aestheticism of the 1890s caused even Mrs Oliphant to question whether she had too greatly neglected her reputation as an artist. 'Do you know', she wrote to Emily Lawless, a fellow novelist, 'I am sometimes inclined to think that a little pomposity is coming on! I begin to have a faint consciousness of stilts, and of an inclination to think that a person of my standing should be treated with respect, which amuses me as a new feature in what Colonel Lockhart used to call "the other fellow" who is one's self.'[95] It was only in the three years that remained to her after her sons' death that she was able to place the problems of that ' "other fellow" who is one's self' at the centre of her fiction. It is possible that the reaction which had set in against the high Victorian doctrine of resistance to any implied split between the artist's morality and talent, and manifested itself in James and Stevenson's tales of dual personality written in the late 1880s, also played its part in allowing these issues to surface in her work. Yet the problems of the artist, and in particular the anxieties of the woman writer, had hovered on the margins of her tales from a very early period.

4. Figuring her Art

Unsurprisingly, her earliest attempts at figuring the anxieties besetting the woman who decides to turn a domestic occupation into a money-spinner appeared in portraits of women taking to sewing for a living. The training she had received from her mother had offered an implicit analogy and, in the class from which she came, sewing, like writing, offered the possibility of paid employment within the home

without the forfeit of gentility consequent upon entering a commercial establishment. The purity of feminine status assured by sewing in comparison with writing
emerges in the way that women not only work silently but in such a way that their
menfolk do not even notice the difference between commissioned garments and
ordinary domestic tasks. Determined attention to the piece in hand could provide
a retreat every bit as secure as 'the corner of the table' which Margaret Wilson was
given for writing. In houses so humble that there was no space for a woman to seek
solitude, resolute sewing in silence provided an effective barrier, and male loafers
could be 'needled' into repentance by 'a quick needle making itself heard in the
silence' as effectively as they could be by the written word.[96] To the very end of her
life, when the 'plain sewing' that had bored her as an adolescent had been replaced
by 'dainty sewing or knitting'[97] the analogue appealed to her because of its conno-
tations of self-sacrificial labour. The comparison is both literally and metaphor-
ically present in the proud complaint she voiced to Blackwood in her sixty-sixth
year: 'I have worked a hole in my right forefinger—with the pen, I suppose!—and
can't get it to heal,—also from excessive use of that little implement.'[98] Even sewing
could, like writing, be misinterpreted or misappropriated. When an orphaned girl
takes up her needle the day after her father's death it is registered as a sign of her
phlegmatic nature:[99] Mrs Oliphant found it difficult to forgive herself the ease and
the speed with which she resumed writing after each bereavement. The liberty to
'take a share in the conversation', afforded to travelling dressmakers, could so easily
become a licence to gossip.

As a writer Mrs Oliphant had been forced to draw a distinction between legitimate and illegitimate uses of the sociable atmosphere in which her writing was
conducted. Her firm disapproval of sketches from life being transliterated into
fiction seems to have stemmed from distrust of her own pronounced abilities as a
mimic. The *Cornhill*'s critic found himself amazed by 'some of the kit-cat sketches'
of acquaintances appearing in her *Autobiography* which appeared to have been
'drawn in vitriol'.[100] When she did include a mimic within her fictional world, the
way in which the socially unproductive nature of her talent is imaged reminds us
how deeply the 'craftwork' implications of her mother's regimen had been ingrained. Mrs Woodburn's capacity to 'take off' her neighbours 'did not make the
offender unpopular—for there were very few people in Carlingford who could be
amusing, even at the expense of their neighbours—but made it quite impossible
that she should ever do anything in the way of knitting people together, and making
a harmonious whole out of the scraps and fragments of society'.[101] The move into
metaphor reminds us too how the simple substitution of needlewoman for writer
became less possible as Mrs Oliphant's fiction became more fully entrenched in
middle-class domesticity, where doing one's own 'plain sewing' had become a badge
of poverty. A *Blackwood's* review of 1883 was surely right to find her decision to
hide the wronged society wife under the guise of a seamstress one of the more
irritating and implausible aspects of her melodrama, *Salem Chapel* (1863); yet the
extent to which Mrs Oliphant had conflated earning a living by the pen and the

needle is suggested when we see this character, Mrs Hilyard, working to support her daughter, 'happy to continue amid others' conversation', with her 'constantly moving fingers', 'stained with the coarse blue stuff' of her trade.[102]

The force which this analogy still held for Mrs Oliphant emerged in its most striking form in *Kirsteen: A Story of a Scotch Family Seventy Years Ago* (1890), a tale in which the heroine is able to support her ungrateful family by the proceeds of the dressmaking business she enters in London. Lest late nineteenth-century readers should miss the nuances of the sacrifices required, an early chapter is devoted to making explicit the fact that a dressmaker 'is an artist in her way' and that, rightly understood, dressmaking is 'just like a' the airts I ever heard tell of, a kind of epitome of life'.[103]

One or two of her early novels directly portray characters with authorial ambitions. *The Quiet Heart* features two contrasting writers, one an arrogant man who despises steady labour and rests upon the laurels of his one book, the other a humble printer (unashamed of his dressmaking sister) who, by dint of constant application to his writing, becomes an influential editor. The moral application to Mrs Oliphant's burgeoning career is not hard to fathom, nor is the heroine's role: circumstances force her to become a professional portrait painter and in her pictures she is able to deliver the unflattering commentaries upon her loved ones that she is unable to articulate directly. *The Athelings* (1857) carries Mrs Oliphant's only fictional portrait of a woman novelist. The girl, whose humble suburban family circumstances bear some resemblance to those of the Wilsons, is at first destined to be a dressmaker, but to everyone's surprise her fiction begins to pay. Her gift, however, is used by Mrs Oliphant as little more than a vehicle for introducing the reader to the minor literary circles of publishers, lion-hunters, and journalists that Frank Oliphant had introduced her to in London. Serious issues look as if they are about to be broached when her clergyman lover voices his objections to her chosen career:

'I admire, above all things, understanding and quick intelligence. I can suppose no appreciation so quick and entire as a woman's; but she fails of her natural standing to me, when I come to hear of her productions, and am constituted a critic—that is a false relationship between a woman and a man.'[104]

Further discussion of this matter is sidestepped, however, and the demands of a romantic plot triumph over any deeper exploration of the woman writer's life.

It was only after Frank's death that the question of a woman with family responsibilities earning her living by her art became pressing. In *Miss Marjoribanks* (1866) both the heroine's and the would-be design artist, Miss Lake's, careers have to yield to the force of economic circumstance.

Ten years after Frank's death, in *The Three Brothers*, Mrs Oliphant was able to draw a thinly fictionalized self-portrait of a widowed artist 'happy in her work, and her freedom and her independence and children'. In Mrs Severn, Mrs Oliphant drew a somewhat self-indulgent picture of her life as it was in that period between the success of the Carlingford series and the change in prospects heralded by her brother Frank's total dependency. 'Mrs Severn was not a partisan of work for women, carrying out her theory, but a widow, with little children, working with the tools that came handiest to her for daily bread.'[105] Like her author, Mrs Severn specializes in domestic scenes, popular on account of their artful mixture of realism and sentiment. Although her work is legitimated by financial need she still retains sufficient artistic ambition to feel angered by taunts about overproductivity made by male practitioners of her art who have the time to perfect their work. Although the artistic *métier* chosen plunders the world of pictorial art, to which her husband had introduced her, Frank Oliphant's professional life is virtually expunged in the brief allusion to Mrs Severn's dead husband, who had not been a great painter and who had dragged his family around Europe after him in his search for 'inspiration'.

Only when Mrs Oliphant felt herself truly constricted by the weight of a second family did she begin to show signs of re-evaluating her husband's artistic life with a sympathy that refrained from merely appropriating it to translate her own situation. *At His Gates* (1872), written in the aftermath of her brother's bankruptcy, tells the story of a painter, Robert Drummond, who works 'contentedly, conscientiously, doing everything well and satisfied with the perfection of his work as work, though he was not unaware of the absence from it of any spark of divinity'. His wife, however, is discontented, 'hungry for excellence' in the pictures of the man she loves. Gradually Drummond grows to feel himself 'sapped at the foundations' by his wife's lack of confidence and sympathy and invests their income foolishly in a joint-stock venture so as to console his wife with material comforts. When the venture fails Drummond believes his best plan is to stage his own suicide and leave the family he could not satisfy. Six years later a new picture of genius, which yet bears strong resemblances to Drummond's work, turns up, to acclaim, at the Royal Academy Exhibition. It is the work of Drummond's miserable exile. The novel closes sombrely with his wife recognizing that the price to be paid for such work is too great.

Accordingly, fortified and consoled by the one gleam of glory which had crowned his brows, Helen smiled upon her painter, and took pleasure in his work, even when it ceased to be glorious. That was over; but the dear common life—the quiet, blessed routine of everyday— that ordinary existence, with love to lighten it, and work to burden it, and care and pleasure intermingled, which apart from the great bursts of passion and sorrow and delight that come in from time to time, is the best blessing God gives to men—that had come back, and was here in all its fulness, in perfect fellowship and content.[106]

The redistribution of roles, possible in fictionalizing the past, allowed Mrs Oliphant to reassure herself that in subjugating her art to her family she was serving God not mammon, to give vent to her hurt at Frank's concealment of his approaching death, but also to recognize the part her own naïvely intransigent standards might have played in Frank's decision. Yet, for all the fine talk about the blessings to be found in the unexceptional, the end of the novel betrays this with a fantasy of 'the one great work' which has appeared to due acclaim.

Some twenty years later Mrs Oliphant redeployed the essentials of this plot in two short stories, 'Mr Sandford' and 'The Wonderful History of Robert Dalyell', eventually published together under the title of *The Ways of Life*. Into the second of these tales she siphoned off the suicide *revenant* theme, leaving the first tale less hampered by melodramatic trappings. 'Mr Sandford' again presents us with a painter, whose subject-matter is reminiscent of Frank's penchant for the historical genre, popular in mid-century. Over the years he has received a steady tribute of 'praise and pudding' from his public, but at the age of 60 he suddenly becomes aware that his work is played out as far as inspiration goes and his pictures are hanging fire on the market, where a change of fashion has made his output seem old-fashioned. Nevertheless, he still has a family to support, containing idle adult children who have grown more accustomed to 'cake and wine' than to being thankful for his capacity to provide their daily bread. This story, however, was written after Mrs Oliphant's sons had died, and, like the autobiographical passages written at this time, shows a desire to separate out the roles of artist and family provider that she had so strenuously sought to unite throughout the majority of her career. It is the departure of his wife and children for a seaside holiday that suddenly provides Sandford with the unwelcome solitude to focus upon his artistic predicament. He forces himself to acknowledge that he does not have the facility to produce the impressionist paintings now in vogue; nevertheless, the occasional touch in his daily work both consoles and depresses him. Reviewing his morning's painting, 'he recognised in a moment the jogtrot, the ordinary course of life, and against it the flush of the sudden inspiration, the stronger handling, the glory and glow of the colour'. A rare prefatory note leaves us in no doubt that this tale is autobiographical, written when Mrs Oliphant too believed herself to be 'on the ebb-tide', and its integrity lies in its awareness that for prolific artists like Sandford or Mrs Oliphant the evidence of their genius is inextricably embedded in 'the jogtrot' of their customary work and cannot be summoned up to produce the one great masterpiece. The extent of her identification with this artist figure can best be judged by a self-exculpatory letter she wrote to the editor of a transatlantic periodical to which she was a contributor:

I feel inclined to explain that I don't really work at the breakneck pace my kind reviewer supposes, but am, in fact, very constant, though very leisurely, in my work . . . and my faults must be set down to deficiencies less accidental than want of time. The occasions, now and then, when I am hurried, are those on which I usually do my best.[107]

'Mr Sandford' also pays tribute to the gift of an artistic temperament that has a value quite separate from its power to achieve masterpieces or to command money and respect: Sandford derives profound, if melancholy, satisfaction from the sensibility that allows him to appreciate the landscapes of his long solitary walks. Nevertheless, mulling over her tale, she felt that she had not fully expressed the harshness of her own self-judgement. She felt the tale displayed the lack of that courage that would have characterized the greater artist: instead of pursuing

Sandford's predicament to the full depths of its misery she permits him the death she so strongly craved for herself at this time. Characteristically, however, she did permit herself a wry paragraph in which Mrs Sandford finds widowhood not so desolate a state as she feared and the family is saved from destitution by the upturn in the market for 'Sandfords' created by the artist's death.

'The Library Window', published in the year before her death,[108] is perhaps at once the most accomplished and least self-indulgent account of the woman writer's predicament that Mrs Oliphant ever produced. The title openly heralds the tale's bookish concerns, and a brief résumé of some of the central images serves to reveal the significant correlation between the heroine's narrative and the metaphors and spaces with which Mrs Oliphant associated her own writing practices. The story opens with the narrator recalling her stay at St Rule's (a thinly disguised St Andrew's), where her tolerant, elderly aunt allows her to occupy the recessed window-seat of the large drawing-room in a house across the street from the university Library. The title points to the Library as the main source of interest, but the first-person narration of a young girl suggests that the true focus may lie elsewhere, in her developing consciousness. She starts the story from the vantage-point of her aunt's drawing-room window, 'that deep recess where I can take refuge from all that is going on inside, and make myself a spectator of all the varied story out of doors'. This window, which she interprets as a refuge from the boredom of the boring female rituals within, also provides tantalizing glimpses of a life outside, and we are reminded of Mrs Oliphant's Windsor 'study', which consisted of 'the little second-drawing room of my house, with a wide opening into the other drawing-room where all the (feminine) life of the house goes on'.[109] The girl narrator's opening paragraph may persuade us into seeing her as a marginal, spectator figure, looking back into the confines of 'drawing-room' life, but her account also leaves her silhouetted against the window as the main source of interest. Like the young Margaret Wilson, her spare time is divided between books and the sewing, which receives only 'a few stitches when the spirit moved me'. The account the narrator gives of her reading habits is sharply reminiscent of her creator's remark, 'I wrote as I read, with much the same sort of feeling':[110]

and if the book was interesting, I used to get through volume after volume sitting there, paying no attention to anybody. And yet I did pay attention. Aunt Mary's old ladies came in to call, and I heard them talk, though I very seldom listened; but for all that, if they had anything to say that was interesting, it is curious how I found it in my mind afterwards, as if the air had blown it to me.

If the girl's status as spectator-narrator, or the story's subject, is deliberately left uncertain, so is her temperament. It is never entirely clear whether she has been sent to St Rule's as a place of seaside recuperation, or whether her extreme sensitivity is merely a mark of adolescence to be expunged by exposure to 'the rules' of this conservative community. She has been repeatedly described as 'fantastic and fanciful and dreamy, and all the other words with which a girl who may happen to like poetry, and to be fond of thinking, is often made uncomfortable'. She interprets her capacity for being able to do two things at once or enjoying 'second-sight' as a talent; others see it as a strange eccentricity, which they condemn with their use of words like 'fantastic', which sounds, as the girl complains, akin to the madness of 'Madge Wildfire or something of that sort'.

Behind the narrative we are also made strongly aware of the lurking presence of fairy-tale devices and rituals, often the mark in twentieth-century feminist writings of the desire to address collective rather than individual patterns of female experience. Mrs Oliphant's own previous experience in using her stories of the Seen and the Unseen (to which this tale belongs) as a genre for the oblique exploration of gender issues certainly prevents this tale from drifting into the detailed circumstantiality of personal reference to which her other attempts at rendering the artist's predicament had too often succumbed.

The heroine becomes enchanted by a window in the Library opposite, not visible to all, where in the twilight she gradually makes out, on subsequent evenings, a room, a bookcase, and then a writing-desk. Finally she sees a young man writing continuously, much in the manner attributed to Sir Walter Scott. His total absorption stirs the girl into a reciprocal attentiveness to her vision, but she is humiliated and furious when older women believe her to be dreaming of 'some man that is not worth it'. Her vision increasingly alienates her from the values of the older generation by whom she is surrounded. As the story progresses the only person to whom she draws closer, at least in her imagination, is her father, who has provided her with a model of devotion to writing by returning every night after his day's labours at the Treasury. Her father is described as a man who believes in the romantic daemon: 'He says things blow through his mind as if the doors were open, and he has no responsibility.' Her mother, by contrast, is portrayed as a woman who considers it her duty to keep nonsense out of her daughter's head by constantly occupying her in useless errands. She has little understanding of the writing process, often looking up as if to rebuke her husband when he wanders from the desk to the window to seek inspiration or a more precise wording. Her aunt, and her aunt's fearsome friend Lady Carnabee (Cannot Be?), who bears a marked resemblance to the wicked fairy in Sleeping Beauty, may, the story implies, have enjoyed similar visions in their youth. It is the prick the heroine receives from Lady Carnabee's diamond ring that appears to trigger the first vision, and it is she who provides the first clue in the mystery story when she ironically enquires, 'whoever has heard of a window that was no to see through?' Having delivered the prick from a ring that we learn first belonged to a scholar-writer, she claims not, like her fairy-tale predecessor, to have put the girl to sleep, but to have 'waked you to life' from the habit of idle dreaming. It is Lady Carnabee too who delivers the deathblow, willing the vision to disappear because its glittering illumination is dangerous. These women, of the same blood, gifted with the power to see far into things, have renounced the enticing dream as dangerous: that they are both spinsters, who have known the seduction of the vision and therefore rejected human suitors, is perhaps an indication of the fate they fear for this young girl. Her aunt's sympathy is tempered by sadness: even she feels the time has come to deflect the girl's attention to specifically feminine pursuits by inviting her 'to learn my old lace stitches'. An elderly male friend of her aunt's, a man of scientific disposition, and a university professor also play their part in denying the possibility of her vision. Eventually her aunt tells her of a family legend concerning a previous daughter of the house who had enjoyed a similar silent companionship with a Scholar seen at the same window. When that girl had attempted to realize their friendship by summoning him to come to her, motives had been misconstrued and her brothers had killed the Scholar.

Hard though she tries, the heroine cannot initially make out the features of the man across the street, whose recognition she craves: even when she sees him face on, we are only told that he is young and beardless, and indeed the last phase of the story, written many years later, suggests that he is a companionable familiar rather than possessing an individual identity. The story suggests, though never crudely states, that the girl, who finds that when she can delineate him clearly 'my look went with his look, following it as if I were his shadow', has all the time been seeing, though not recognizing, her mirror-image, thrown upon the recessed window of the drawing-room by the lamps brought in at twilight. It is always at *undermeles*, the liminal time of medieval romance when the boundaries between the world of faery and the moral world are particularly fragile, that the vision appears. The girl herself describes it as a time when the quality of the light was such that it made it appear 'as if every object was a reflection of itself'. To an imaginative girl, nurtured in an environment that sees writing as a male prerogative, the prospect of attaining the fellowship of the pen is alluring, but fraught with the danger of disappointment and the alternative taunts of eccentricity bordering upon madness, or impropriety. And yet, traumatic though the vision has been, its effects are not wholly effaced. At first the case looks hopeless, especially if the vision is, as she assumes, local. Her mother comes to remove her, and 'At first I thought I would not go. But how can a girl say I will not, when her mother has come for her, and there is no reason, no reason in the world, to resist, and no right!' Nevertheless, the combined action of the adult female community and the external accidents of a woman's life, marriage, childbirth, and widowhood, cannot obliterate the experience. Not only do we have the evidence of the tale itself that the girl has become a narrator, but she tells us that, best of all, the face she had seen at the window appeared again when she had most need, waving to her from the crowd of unknown faces that met the ship when she returned, newly widowed, from abroad. The diamond ring, willed to her by Lady Carnabee, becomes, in the final paragraph, token for the double-edged gift of a woman writer's imagination. It stays locked away 'in the lumber-room in the little old country house which belongs to me, but where I never live'. It would be hard not to see the author herself planning her last move away from Windsor and its graveyard in this and the ensuing remark: 'If any one would steal it, it would be a relief to my mind', but the distinguishing excellence of this tale lies in its last writerly trick. The last paragraph refers us back to those other characters, Aunt Mary and Lady Carnabee. Like the naïve narrator the naïve reader comes to realize that the story's focus was not confined to the library window, nor to the girl's own maturing consciousness, but was invested in a multiplicity of roles and characters. Put more simply, Mrs Oliphant is present not merely as the female story-teller, but also as the elderly aunt with an eventful past, now very old and quiet and feeling a protective pity for the next generation of female writers and their struggles. She is also there in Lady Carnabee, the acerbic patron, bringing others' talents to light, but more often feared for her capacity to pour critical cold water on the younger generation's enthusiasms, and more than half-inclined to link arms with the rational gentlemen whom she took so much pleasure in contradicting.

5. Working Conditions

Read as an expression of the female writer's desires, the tale of 'The Library Window' provides a haunting image of a girl who has glimpsed 'the real place'.

There was another small window above, which twinkled very much when the sun shone, and looked a very kindly bright little window, above that dullness of the other which hid so much. I made up my mind this was the window of his other room, and that these two chambers at the end of the beautiful hall were really beautiful for him to live in, so near all the books and so retired and quiet nobody knew of them. What a fine thing for him!

That any writer in his or her late sixties should be moved to yearn for the convenience of an arrangement which prevented the necessity for laborious research trips to the British Museum is unremarkable. Over the years Mrs Oliphant had also experienced every inconvenience possible to a reviewer, travelling all over Europe and daily awaiting her source material to arrive by post. The more immediate piquancy of the image, however, derives from the girl's sense of her male counterpart's good fortune. The yearning implicit in this image carries the experiential thrust of keenly felt deprivation we recognize when Dickens describes a child's face pressed up against the pastry-cook's window. One compelling impression left by the fifty-year span of Mrs Oliphant's letters is the arduous task faced by a woman in carving out time and space for her breadwinning activities. In one respect the mere act of writing constitutes a woman's assertion of a right to a space for self-definition, but creating the conditions necessary for such fulfilment proved a harder challenge. The sense of literal space being in question comes out very clearly in the way Mrs Oliphant expressed her slightly bitter amusement at the privileges enjoyed by some contemporary writers. In 1868 she wrote to Blackwood that she had seen a letter from Ruskin which she imagined would 'throw you into fits of laughter. He is "about to enter on some work which cannot well be done except without interruption" he says, and therefore begs his friends "to think of me as if actually absent from England, and not to be displeased though I must decline all correspondence"! Shouldn't you like to follow such a splendid example? It is positively sublime.'[111] Almost twenty years later, after reading Cross's *Life of George Eliot*, she was driven to ask herself, 'Should I have done better if I had been kept, like her, in a mental greenhouse, and taken care of?'[112] While she often displayed, as in the case of Dinah Mulock's later years as Mrs Craik, a not unnatural propensity to envy those women writers cosseted by devoted attendants, men were the more usual target, for they always seemed to have some study, or library, or club to which to retire. To an extent women had themselves to blame because 'it was the fashion of our generation' that 'our pride [should] consist, not in literary reputation, which was a thing apart, but in the household duties and domestic occupations which are the rule of life for most women'.[113] Her later writing demonstrated a certain self-consciousness about the way in which 'a fashion' had been metamorphosed into 'a rule'. It is not surprising that her *Autobiography*, which overtly addresses her joint roles as author and mother, should privilege the domestic scene. It is more noteworthy that when she came to describe her professional relations with her publishers, in the *Annals of a Publishing House*, she should feature a disastrous dinner she had prepared for her editor and illustrate her arrival at the position of being Blackwoods' 'general utility woman' by choosing the day in 1856, when, having been asked to produce a review of Laud's sermons at short notice, she wrote 'in the midst of removal, with a flying pen, in a room unoccupied as yet by anything but dust and rolled-up carpets, where a table and an inkpot had been hurriedly set out for me'.[114] Just as Trollope's open proclamation of the mechanics of his craft has created an image of absolutely regular productivity, not entirely in line with the evidence of his work diaries, so Mrs Oliphant fashioned a consistent self-image for herself that held its own self-perpetuating mystique. Indeed, one of her own letters demonstrates the potency such myths attained, even with other authors. Just six years after Trollope's *Autobiography* had been published she wrote to Cecco,

I have had today one of those languid days when one does no work which occur without any particular cause now and then . . . I have been working very hard and should have got on particularly fast this morning as I expect J.M. this afternoon, but instead of that I have done nothing, a page only in place of a chapter. I suppose these accidents must occur, though they did not do so with Anthony Trollope—and it is a great nuisance.[115]

All the memoirs written by intimates testify to their boundless amazement at the way in which she contrived to be the gracious hostess and caring mother in the face of her awesome productivity. Blackwood's daughter-in-law claimed that as a guest at Strathytyrum Mrs Oliphant always put in an appearance at the golfers' early breakfast, joined in sociable chat with the ladies, and made no fuss about the requirements of her work. 'She worked early and she worked late, and yet there was no time in the day when she could not be seen. She may be said to have been always working, yet her work was never obtruded.'[116] Howard Overing Sturgis (Henry James's dilettante friend) spoke of her 'passion of ministering' to others and marvelled at the schoolboy egotism with which he had presumed upon her time and interest.[117] Henry James himself, who knew that she was 'a night-working spinner', declared that her work demonstrated 'a sort of sedentary dash—an acceptance of the day's task and an abstention from the plaintive note from which I confess I could never withhold my admiration'.[118] Lady Ritchie, her closest surviving friend, painted what she regarded as a typical picture of Mrs Oliphant in the 'sunny room at Windsor, with her dogs at her feet, with flowers round about, with the happy inroads of her boys and their friends, with girls making the place merry and busy, and that curious bodyguard of older friends, somewhat jealous and intolerant of any affection of later date than their own'.[119] The slightly discordant note struck by the final phrase finds its echo elsewhere. Sturgis too commented upon 'the constant circle of intimates some unworthy' and concluded, 'It seemed as if the call for the highest and most absorbing power of loving of which her nature was capable, some element of weakness was necessary in the beloved object, to serve, to cherish, to protect—these were her functions; the mother instinct was so strong in her.' Unfair though this may seem in the face of the dependants who fell, through no fault of her own, upon her doorstep, there is perhaps a germ of truth in the hidden implication that Mrs Oliphant had assembled the type of household her career required.

This bodyguard of rival supplicants for her affectionate support may not have been 'the reverential circle' that gathered around George Eliot, 'agape for every precious word that might fall from her mouth', but they paid for themselves by being the visible guarantee of her successful mingling of the roles of writer and caring woman. Their perpetual recital of needs and grievances kept her in touch with the source material of her domestic fiction: she was to marvel at the way in which George Lewes had protected Eliot from 'unnecessary contact with life' in a way that she believed to be inimical to most forms of literary genius.[120] Yet her own circle of dependants could also be deployed to fend off unwelcome encroachments upon her time. It was perfectly possible to run up to town from Windsor by train, see her publishers, and perhaps take luncheon, but she was able to attribute her inability to attend literary dinners, which ate into her best working hours, to pressing demands at home.[121] This excuse could then be parlayed into a further handicap. Delighted by a rare puff from *Maga*, she wrote to Blackwood that 'she supposed Mr Trollope and Mr Reade . . . are deeply learned in all these byways: which a poor woman out of the way never knows of'.[122] This remark, which happened to be grossly unfair to Trollope, who disliked 'puffing', was made when her boys were of undergraduate age and her nieces still abroad at school. Young children at first necessitated working into the early hours, but she also admitted to finding this routine congenial and continued it long after the initial justification had disappeared. In her sixties she was still making New Year resolutions to change her habits. The eleventh of January 1893 found her, still in bed after lunch, writing to Cecco, 'I suffered greatly from it (late rising) in all my earlier life. In short I think I only vanquish it now by working in bed as I have always done more or less under one pretence or another.' Dating a letter of 16 January 1893, '1.00 p.m. and still in bed', she concluded the battle was lost for that year.[123] In widowhood of course, the bedroom provided another variant of 'a room of one's own'.

Her circle of dependants could be deployed in other positive ways. Brother Willie had been useful as a fair copyist for a writer whose handwriting was notoriously illegible. When Willie moved away, after their mother's death, Mrs Oliphant found herself artistically incommoded: 'I always write with greater comfort when I have the freedom of writing illegibly which is secured by copying my manuscript before dismissing it from my hands—and the chief part of this article was written under the effort of writing a readable hand.'[124] The succession of young ladies, coming for the long visits to which Mrs Oliphant was partial in early widowhood, no doubt provided company, additional childcare, and possibly a little secretarial assistance. The story she gleefully recorded, about the mother of one such girl, elsewhere identified as Janie Moir, whispering to her on parting that her daughter 'had been *praying for strength* to pay me this visit' is perhaps more revealing than Mrs Oliphant intended.[125] The departure of her trusted maid-of-all-work, Jane Hockey, in 1866, was attended by the arrival of Annie Walker, who seems to have combined the roles of housekeeper and literary amanuensis. Dependent relatives formed for Mrs Oliphant, as for many Victorians, a surplus labour pool to relieve her of many of the daily tasks of running the household. Annie stayed for nearly twenty years before her sudden marriage, and even after she had been married for nine years, Mrs Oliphant found it hard to get used to the fact that Annie now had other calls upon her time. In 1893 she wrote to Cecco from the Coghills' house complaining that Annie had retired 'calmly to the library' to join her husband even though she knew that, given Mrs Oliphant's schedule, it was the only time they could have together![126] By the time that Annie had left her house her nieces were old enough to start shouldering some of the burden of dealing with their often churlish cousins and attending to household affairs. When she was hard-pressed even her sons were occasionally invited to perform secretarial tasks such as sending off proofs or writing letters. Cyril's fair copies were usually accompanied by the whiff of smoke, which must have been a further reminder to her of his Uncle Willie.[127] Once Madge married, in 1894, Denny became doubly precious, and although her aunt constantly complained about Denny's reluctance to pursue a career she lived in fear of her decamping to reside permanently with Madge in Dundee.[128] A grumbling insecurity emerges in the letters of the last years as if Mrs Oliphant realized that it was too late to mould any of her other dependants or visitors into precisely the role she had in mind. Her oldest niece, Nellie, was tried out, but her obsessional fiddling with the 'white ropes of her fancy work' forced her aunt to cut short her summer visit to St Andrews.[129] Fanny Tulloch, though 'dear' to her and a fully paid-up participant in the troubled Oliphant family saga, would never read to Mrs Oliphant in the evening as Denny did.[130]

It is easy to deplore the fractious note about the disruptions to her life as a writer that sometimes crept into Mrs Oliphant's letters, but this becomes more comprehensible in the light of the prodigious tasks she set herself. In May 1867 she was travelling in Germany, troubled by how inadequate her German was for her researches, worrying about the proofs of the Montalembert translation, and in the throes of writing her novel, *The Brownlows*, when she complained to John

Blackwood, 'I can work fifteen hours a day at home—but I can't do that when abroad upon the world in this way cultivating the German clergy and other strange species.' At home in Windsor in August that year she was far more complacent. 'I am working doubletides on Montalembert, or rather would have been doing so— as today I stop and go into Brownlows—I admire my own methodical way of getting through my work and I hope you will also applaud its regularity and precision.'[131]

After she had struck the rich vein of the 'Chronicles of Carlingford', Blackwood had attempted to persuade her to concentrate her energies upon the *Perpetual Curate* and abandon her reviewing until it was finished, but she had replied, 'you must let me do a little now and then for the disease has got to be chronic with me and I must work or die, not to speak of the daily nay hourly necessity of bread and butter.'[132] Writing, and particularly the habit of keeping different tasks on the boil at the same time, was both a stimulus and an anodyne: turning from one type of work to another seems to have refreshed her. *The Curate in Charge* was begun in the middle of *The Makers of Florence* 'by way of unfurling myself'.[133] *Phoebe Junior* was begun 'partly to amuse myself, and on a sudden impulse' during a period when she had established a rhythm of monthly articles for *Maga*.[134] The average *Maga* review of new books covered four or five works which all had to be read, and the pieces of her later years, under the title 'The Looker-On', also involved her in reviewing plays and exhibitions. Back in the 1860s, Mrs Oliphant recalled, she had once found herself 'Having done nothing on the 20th of the month, to the next number of a story then running in the Magazine, the said Magazine being due in London by the first of the next month', but this was memorable as an exception.[135] Like other hard-pressed, prolific contemporaries, Mrs Oliphant learnt to count words 'much and very carefully', which 'I did not do in the happier days of my youth'.[136] She had adopted the practice of word-counting by the 1880s when she was almost always busy producing material to pay off sums of money already spent, and therefore anxious to proceed fast to the next task. Before that it had been her practice, like Dickens, to estimate by the average page of her handwriting. This rough guide usually worked well for the comparatively short length of an article for *Maga*, or over the length of an entire three-decker, or serialization, where there was leeway to vary the length between individual episodes, but it served less well in the tighter form of the short story. When William Isbister complained to her that the short story he had commissioned for *Good Words* ran over-length, she replied, 'my calculation is that two pages of my writing makes about a page of Good Words— and there is I think as near as I can remember 100 pages of my MS including small half pages—so that I had no idea I was too long.' She was forced to offer to cut her story because she had nothing else put by that would answer.[137] In her early days she had been able to afford the luxury of a conscious decision not to imitate Trollope's habit of attempting to keep a complete novel ahead of her publishers. In the course of *Salem Chapel*'s serialization she wrote to John Blackwood, 'I am tempted to write the next number immediately, but refrain, since the result seems more satisfying when it swims in my mind for the full interval.'[138]

When her family responsibilities demanded a steadier flow of income her practice changed. The *Autobiography* tells us how in the early 1870s she had 'a novel written, but did not know where I should find a place for it. Literary business arrangements were not organised then as now—there was no such thing as a literary agent.' Acting on her own behalf, she went to London to try to place the novel with George Smith, who refused it. Fortunately, the *Graphic* approached her for a tale, but she felt that the novel she had just completed was inappropriate for their pages and so she 'began another instantly, and went on with it in instalments'.[139] Sometimes she had so many things on the go that she could not keep track of all her manuscripts. *Diana Trelawney: The History of a Great Mistake* was first published in 1892, but had been written in June 1877 and sent straight off to Blackwoods. Later that month she had attempted to withdraw it and replace it with a three-decker.[140] When John Blackwood died in 1879 nothing had been decided, and although she was absolutely certain the firm still had her manuscript,[141] the tale simply lay dormant until rediscovered by his successor.

Only the act of composition itself could be protected from the welter of surrounding complications. Lady Ritchie 'was always struck, when I saw her writing, by her concentration and the perfect neatness of her arrangements—the tiny inkstand of prepared ink, into which she poured a few drops of water, enough for each day's work, the orderly manuscript, her delicate, fine pen . . .'.[142] Travelling played havoc with her filing system, however, and when she later wanted to dispute a contract she was sometimes driven to admit that she simply could not track down the original correspondence.[143] Such incidents serve to remind us of the variety of demands upon the time of a successful freelance writer unequipped with agents, accountants, telephones, or word-processor. A letter to John Blackwood of 1875, addressed from 'London, Paddington Station' and starting, 'I write to you from the Railway Station Waiting room that I may not lose a post', suggests that in a later age she might have relished such aids as the cellphone and the dictating machine.[144] Just occasionally the juggling act failed. On 23 May 1883 she wrote to Craik at Macmillan, 'I begin for the first time to get quite muddled about my work and to be overwhelmed by the various requirements—but I am under the grip of a miserable cold for the moment and I hope this is only temporary.'

Most ordinary mortals would not have needed the excuse of a heavy cold to excuse a certain confusion over current commitments such as these: Morley, Macmillans' reader, was suddenly asking for cuts and corrections, at the second proof stage, to her book on Sheridan in the English Men of Letters series—a book from which she now felt so remote that she could no longer remember her authorities.[145] Her novel *Hester*, also appearing under the Macmillans imprint, had had to be 'put off' and 'put off' because there was a newspaper story (probably *Oliver's Bride*) which needed to be 'put up'. Meanwhile she was almost half-way through writing *The Wizard's Son*, already appearing in monthly instalments in *Macmillan's Magazine*, and found Morley's attitude unhelpful since she had been ready to spread herself but inferred that Morley wanted to cut her short. In the same letter she also offered *Macmillan's Magazine* the first refusal of an anonymous review of a privately printed book recounting Sir Arthur Gordon's colonization of the mountain tribes of Fiji. Since her eldest son was about to become Gordon's private secretary she attached some importance to the piece, which eventually saw print in the October number of *Maga*.[146] By October, however, the contours of her working life had changed: *Sir Tom*, already published in serial form, had arrived in book proof; Morley was once again trying to cut short *The Wizard's Son*, which she promised to revise heavily for its publication in book form; no articles had been promised to *Maga*, and, having no engagements other than a mere thirteen-part novel (*Madam*) due to start in *Longman's Magazine* in January, she felt able to plan a holiday.[147]

Her complaints about Macmillans' new reader presuming to offer fresh criticisms at the stage of the second proof were, in part, the expression of indignation by 'an older person with more literary reputation to stand upon than Mr Morley himself', but were also a reaction against interference with her long-established working procedures. After Willie's departure as fair copyist even John Blackwood was soon complaining of her illegibility, and it seems to have become accepted practice for time to be built into the publishing schedule for her to make extensive and definitive alterations at the first proof stage.[148] The hapless Macmillans' editor who, in 1877, not only failed to forward the proofs of *Young Musgrave* to her but added a paragraph by another hand to the September number was made to feel her wrath.[149] Given the extensive corrections sometimes demanded, it was not surprising that she should claim 'proofs drive me frantic—they are the one thing intolerable in literature'.[150] Impatient though she was of the time they consumed, she was well aware of the extent to which her own practice was to blame. 'It is curious,' she reflected in later life, 'the anger with which some writers rage at the mistakes (or perhaps impertinences) of the printer, which to others are a fruitful source of amusement.'[151] Her experience with the index of *Royal Edinburgh* (1892) was a case in point.

This has been done in great part on the attractive assumption that all persons with similar names must be the same. This is very much the plan on which the early historians and genealogists worked, and it certainly made their task easier, but the results were not perhaps always so satisfactory as might have been wished. When Mahomet for instance tells us that Mary, the mother of Jesus, was the same person with Miriam, the sister of Moses, one feels a little abroad in one's chronology. The identifications in the index are less startling, but still it is not usual to represent old Bell-the-Cat as the Earl of Angus who married the widow of James IV. I myself had distinguished these personages,—who were in fact grandfather and grandson—but the printer knew better and put them under one head. Was not the name of both Archibald? More amusing is the case of an unhappy Earl of Douglas of whom it was stated in the proof as I received it that he was 'treacherously executed: p. 99'; 'marries the maid of Galloway: p. 100' and after various other strange feats was assassinated on p. 114. Now a great deal of trouble was caused by this assassination, and to think that it might all have been saved, if it had only been generally known that the poor man had been beheaded some years before, so that it was really quite unnecessary to murder him. Unfortunately the generally prevailing opinion was that the person executed was the latter earl's cousin and predecessor, who happened to bear the same Christian name, and such, indeed had been my own theory till I came upon this new and surprising version of the facts.[152]

Mrs Oliphant welcomed Macmillans' acquisition in 1886 of a 'type printer', but clearly regarded the typed version of her manuscript as an alternative version of the first proof rather than as a means of achieving a fair copy for editors too hard-pressed to make out her handwriting. When the editor of *Macmillan's Illustrated Magazine* had the temerity to reject a commissioned story that had already been typed up, she expostulated that although he was entitled to express editorial preferences he was not free to reject the work at this stage and she requested the summary return of the typewritten version: 'I do not choose that an original story of mine should be lying about on anybody's table.'[153]

Despite the asperity with which she resisted editorial attempts to change her working habits, there were some alterations effected by time that she was powerless to prevent. In her parents' home 'it came to be the custom that I should every night "read what I had written" to them before I went to bed. They were very critical sometimes, and I felt while I was reading whether my little audience was with me or not, which put a good deal of excitement into the performance.' This serves as an important reminder of the extent to which early Victorian novels at least were involved with the oral tradition of story-telling. In Mrs Oliphant's case the practice lends a further dimension to her pleasure at having 'found unawares an image' that expressed her writerly pleasure: 'i.e. that I wrote as I read, with much the same sort of feeling.' If one can judge by her evaluation of her own style, the imminent prospect of reading one's work aloud may have had effects every bit as profound upon prose rhythms and dialogue as they have long been acknowledged to have had in poetry: 'I have always had my sing-song, guided by no sort of law, but by my ear, which was in its way fastidious to the cadence and measure that pleased me.'[154]

The following letter to her publisher John Blackwood, written whilst composing *The Story of Valentine and His Brother*, starts by reiterating the stylistic benefits of the practice but goes on to suggest other consequences. 'I wish I could have the advantage of reading the rest to you—even the mere fact of hearing it read is such an advantage to a writer and it is one of the drawbacks of getting old that domestic criticisms become impossible—at least to a person in my position.'[155]

Whether family life was too busy or whether she felt that it would detract from her dignity as head of the household to invite criticism from Annie and her sons is unclear. At the close of the 1870s reading aloud from *Maga* certainly continued to be part of the family's entertainment, but in the next decade it is difficult to imagine her reading aloud the manuscripts of novels such as *The Wizard's Son* in the bosom of a family whose own problems and disappointments it so clearly mirrored.[156] In fact, the practice of reading her manuscripts aloud came and went as the immediate circumstances of her life changed. In 1863, when her Maggie, the oldest child, was only 9, she wrote apropos of *The Perpetual Curate* to John Blackwood,

I am very much comforted and exhilarated by your favourable opinion of his Reverence . . . I think, if it suits you, I should rather like the first part to appear next month. Though I am not sure that I approve of it in theory, it seems to suit me in practice, and the publication and the talk stimulates and keeps me up. Very likely this is because I have nobody at home nowadays to talk it over with; but I think it is for the advantage of the work to be written just as it is published . . .[157]

These remarks demonstrate how even a Victorian novelist as resistant to any invasion of her privacy as Mrs Oliphant craved the audience response which could be fed back into the novels and served to keep authors in touch with their readers' tastes. She was never greatly interested in the criticisms levelled at her novels by her fellow band of professional critics. She turned to the reactions of John Blackwood or the letters and conversation of other close friends as substitutes for a more immediate circle of listeners, much as Dickens, in the aftermath of the disruption to his domestic circle effected by the collapse of his marriage, was to give as a reason for his reading tours his need of that 'particular relationship (personally affectionate and like no other man's) which subsists between me and the public'.[158]

The long time-span covered by her novel-writing also saw significant changes in the publishing format available to authors and favoured by publishers. Out of her first twenty-three novels only three were serialized. In the case of the first, *Katie Stewart*, she quite simply left the work of dividing the story into parts to John Blackwood, on the grounds that she could no longer carry the story in her mind 'even if I had any knowledge of this mode of publication, which I have not'.[159] By 1856, when her third, *The Athelings*, appeared in *Maga*, she had begun to realize the complications involved. She accused John Blackwood of making 'petty calculations' when he complained that the last episode she had sent, containing thirty-seven manuscript pages, fell well short of the agreed portion. Her answer was to send him chapter 15 as well as the portion ending at chapter 14, her preferred break-point in the story.[160] 'The Chronicles of Carlingford' had first been conceived in short-story form. After adding two long novels, *Salem Chapel* and *The Perpetual Curate*, Mrs Oliphant intended to add just one more short tale in four numbers, 'Miss Marjoribanks'. The difficulties of continuing with the serial parts of *The Perpetual Curate* over the traumatic period of Maggie's death had probably sapped her enthusiasm for a longer run. When she sent John Blackwood the second episode in February 1865 she still intended it to appear in four or five numbers, although she felt that 'not enough progress had been made and I am afraid that I am getting into a habit of over-minuteness'. Nevertheless, she continued, with sublime disregard for *Maga*'s editorial planning, 'it seems to suit my demon best to let it have its way'. By April, having decided to let the story blossom into a novel, she reassured Blackwood that she would not rely on melodramatic 'complications of plot' to extend the tale, but concentrate on 'bringing out' the central character. Nevertheless, the exigencies of plot were worrying her in May because she had begun 'to get into the middle, that fatal period which is always my most dangerous moment'. 'The two ends', she later told him, 'can usually take care of themselves.' By August she reported, 'I feel a little too *fluent* as if I had all run to words.' When she sent off the ninth number in September she warned him that a twist in the plot was about to occur: 'The present complication of affairs will end with the next number—but naturally her own story is all to come yet and I hope you will not find it a dangerous experiment with the public.' The next month's letter suggests that Blackwood clearly did feel that the novel's shapelessness was indeed beginning to be 'a dangerous experiment'. She replied, 'The story is a story without a plot from its very nature, as must have been apparent from the first', although in November she did seek his permission 'to kill off the doctor'.[161] Despite the fact that his forward planning had been seriously affected by the prolongation of *Miss Marjoribanks*, she accused him of 'shabby' behaviour when he excluded her number from the Christmas issue of *Maga*: 'I have kept up to time so often when I might have had a very good excuse for indolence.' Six months after the novel had run its course she was still defending her plot development with Blackwood, 'the only publisher in the world in whom the rebellious subject has such perfect confidence'. He had not liked her marrying Lucilla off to Tom, to which she responded that he had started by disliking Lucilla's coldness and now he was attributing too much feeling to her, and besides, she added, with an irony John Blackwood would surely have enjoyed, 'It is the sad fate of gifted women in general never to be appreciated.'[162]

Having accustomed herself to monthly serialization, she was taken aback by a 'curious proposal' made to her by the proprietor of the Glasgow paper *The Star*, for a story to publish in daily instalments. At this stage of her life she still often had a novel put by in reserve, so it was not the fear of 'bursting the boiler', as Dickens had phrased it, but the question of reputation that made her consult John Blackwood. Glasgow seemed sufficiently remote for the experiment not to worry her unduly: 'Had it been in London I should probably never have given it a thought.' In the event her fears were justified: she became involved in expensive legal action, which she won, but without recouping the money she had hoped to make.[163] On the next occasion when she was approached by a newspaper she took the trouble to enquire who else had been signed up.[164] She had been accustomed to associate weekly publication with the hectic pace of 'sensation novels', but since Trollope had agreed to follow her in this new venture of adding fiction to the *Graphic*, which claimed 'a circulation far exceeding that of any magazine', she agreed.[165] This time the pressure was considerable, for she did not consider the novel she had in reserve suitable and the *Graphic* wanted something to begin 'within a week or two'. When she recalled the book she remembered that 'the trial scene in it was very badly managed—not unnatural, for I never was present at a trial, though that, of course, was no excuse'. Writing for weekly publication at the same time as sending off her monthly *Maga* articles did not leave a great deal of time for visiting courts for background material.

Looking back some twenty years later on the *Graphic* episode, Mrs Oliphant felt that, although there had been fewer outlets for her work then, there had been time to enjoy 'a number of mild amusements' with her young family. 'Serials in magazines were published in much less number, magazines themselves being not half so many (and a good thing too!).'[166] By the end of the century reading habits had changed, and so perforce had authorial practices. 'We know one admirable reader,' wrote Mrs Oliphant in 1889, 'a man too, and a busy one—fair be his lot!—who confesses to having eighteen stories in progress, which makes the course of the month a real happiness.'[167] Such a wealth of publications did seem to permit greater diversity of subject-matter, allowing authors to escape from the endless treadmill of romance, but the shorter span of reading attention encouraged by serialization had also had consequences for form. It encouraged writers to what Mrs Oliphant deplored as the lazy habit of republishing essays in collected form and readers to practise the art of dipping rather than 'reading the night through'.[168] It also favoured the rapid expansion of the short-story form, about which Mrs Oliphant had mixed feelings.

They are what the thrifty novelist might well call a great waste of material on the part of the writer, for a successful short story could in almost every case be spun out into three volumes. But as they encourage fine workmanship, and cultivate that power of taking infinite deal of trouble which Carlyle defined as the greater part of genius, they are very much in the interest of the public.[169]

Like Trollope, Mrs Oliphant had always rather disliked the publishing concept, encouraged by Dickens, of the short story got up for the Christmas market.[170] Nor did she like the habit that grew as the century progressed of magazine editors specifying both the length and the nature of the story. *Good Words*, she complained, had dissipated the effect of a story, whose length she had calculated for its overall effect, by breaking it up into two numbers and placing it side by side 'with a busy companion'.[171] The truth was that although she was prepared to try her hand at the new vogue for carefully crafted short stories, and had indeed found the format perfect for her tales of the supernatural, she still preferred the old three-volume format that allowed a novelist room for movement and did not necessitate the 'dry concentration' on plot, which the single-volume six-shilling novella now demanded.[172] Her own short-story writing had begun in the days when there was no clear agreement as to what the genre constituted, and she had variously used it as a trial run for the plots of three-volume novels, an opportunity for anecdote or character sketch, for collections of stories 'with a slight thread of connection—though independent of each other', or for her tales of the supernatural.

As the competition between publishers grew, so did their endeavours to find additional charms beyond the printed word to woo their readers. Later in her career it was customary for cheap editions of novels to carry illustrations, but her suggestion to John Blackwood that *Katie Stewart* (1852) should make an appearance with six figures and six landscapes as 'a pretty book' for the Christmas market seems to have been a matter of much negotiation. (His refusal to contemplate illustrations in his periodical, *Maga*, may have been one reason for its declining share of the market after 1860.) Mrs Oliphant's one reservation as to the *Katie Stewart* project had been that she knew 'how slow people are to think of picturebooks as intended for reading'. Her husband does not seem to have thought book illustration worth his while. His ostensible excuse was that there was no lack of good artists in Edinburgh capable of producing pictures of the Fife landscape, and he may have been fully committed to his expanding firm and his large-scale historical paintings.[173] In the event he provided only a frontispiece and title-page illustration, both of which he asked to have removed from the second edition.[174] Thirty years later, however, the *English Illustrated Magazine* had set high standards on the home market and American periodicals were making headway with their excellent pictures,[175] and so it now seemed a sensible proposition to train her niece Madge in the respectable craft of engraver: moreover, she had the contacts to whom to introduce her. As Mrs Oliphant branched out into her European history books, Denny was encouraged to attempt sketches from which her sister could take the engravings.[176] She already had some experience in trying to place this kind of work, for she had busied herself trying to secure commissions for her friend Geddie Macpherson and had succeeded in getting her employed by *Good Words* to illustrate *Madonna Mary*. A further advantage of having an 'in-house' artist was that she could discuss the illustration with the artist. As she told John Blackwood, her friend's illustration might have 'suffered a little in the cutting, but I think though it be a little deficient in technical qualities, it is very much superior in meaning and expression to the general run of such illustrations'.[177] More typical of her remarks about the illustrations commissioned for her tales by the publisher himself was the sarcastic comment she made to Isbister, 'If the artist would take the trouble to read it before he makes the illustrations it would be an advantage I think.'[178] In the concluding chapter of *The Curate in Charge* (1876) she had allowed herself the luxury of a fictionalized lecture on the engraver's role. Mab, the orphaned daughter of a poor clergyman, has embarked upon such a career.

Do not let the reader think less well of Mab because this was not the highest branch of art which she was contemplating. It was not that she hoped at eighteen and a half to send some great pictures to the Academy, which should be hung on the line, and at once take the world by storm. What she thought of was the homelier path of illustrations. 'If, perhaps one was to take a little trouble, and try to find out what the book means, and how the author saw a scene', Mab said; 'they don't do that in the illustrations one sees; the author says one thing, the artist quite another—that, I suppose, is because the artist is a great person and does not mind. But I am nobody. I should try to make out what the reading meant, and follow that.'[179]

The story first appeared in *Macmillan's Magazine* and its proprietors had clearly not heeded her warning. In 1883 she reminded them that the reign of fiction was not yet over despite the endeavours George Craik was making with their two periodicals, *The Century* and the *Illustrated*, to reduce the novelist's role to providing 'letterpress' only.[180] The problem became worse if anything when Macmillans undertook to provide the illustrations for her history books. Although she had approved Craik's choice of artist, George Reid, for *Royal Edinburgh*, he had not deemed it necessary, during her absence abroad, to consult her about the individual illustrations as his predecessor, Mr Duckworth, had over *The Makers of Florence*. She would have been happy, she said, to have provided letterpress to accompany an illustrated guide to the city in a light article for the magazine, 'but this is too much!'.[181] Actually Mrs Oliphant does seem to have had a good eye; her complaints that Reid's picture of the statue of Allan Ramsay was 'more worthy of a shilling guide book than a volume like ours', and her question as to why 'in the name of all that is ridiculous . . . Sir Walter Scott [should] have had a bit of thistle stuck behind him?', seem entirely justifiable. Macmillans told her that they could not cut off 'the ludicrous adjunct', as she called it, for fear of offending the artist, whom they regarded as an equal collaborator. She replied that their view of illustrated books as a collaboration between two equals was 'quite new to me' and that, save for the bonus of the artist's signature, she would have preferred photographs.[182] A year later she was again complaining that she had not been shown the engravings for *Jerusalem: Its History and Hope*.[183] She was well aware that, as paymasters, her publishers had the upper hand, but throughout her career she was always prepared to strike a symbolic blow for the dignity of the writer against the mercenary considerations of 'the book trade'.

6. The Business of Books

When Henry James wrote of Mrs Oliphant as 'a person whose eggs are not all in one basket, nor all her imagination in service at once', his juxtaposition of commercial and artistic language says as much about the values and practices of the Victorian literary market-place, in which he had also worked, as it does about his ostensible subject.[184] From the vantage-point of the late 1890s, James could see the rift opening up between highbrow writers, whose very assurance of their own artistic worth and integrity would lie in being published in small circulation, avant-garde periodicals, and the purveyors of popular culture, who were keen to exploit the railway-station bookstall and mass-circulation newspapers. The 1881 Elementary Education Act, which had finally made literacy freely available to all of school age, was to change the practices and values of the literary market within a generation. When late nineteenth-century aesthetes castigated the likes of Anthony Trollope and Mrs Oliphant for their businesslike attitude to the literary trade they showed themselves ignorant of the speed at which change had occurred. Victorian novelists were accustomed to judge their relative success by using a financial yardstick. Yet 'success in fiction' remained a curiously ambiguous phrase. Asked in 1888 by an American periodical to write an article on this subject, Mrs Oliphant spent the first half of her piece addressing the incalculable nature of 'the power to touch the public mind' which resulted in 'a triumph which was good for everybody all round', author, publisher, and reader; and the second half discussing the aesthetic rules which might be said to constitute the art of fiction.[185] A novelist's capacity to attract advance bids from Mudie's Select Library or to increase the circulation figures of a periodical was what told most with publishers in the payment they offered their authors for successive novels.

Novelists were accustomed to use a sense of their comparative selling power in negotiating their own advances. Mrs Oliphant's *Autobiography* repeatedly expressed her puzzlement over the way in which Dinah Mulock had used her introduction to her publisher friend, Henry Blackett, to 'spring . . . quite over my head':

Success as measured by money never came to my share. Miss Mulock in this way attained more with a few books, and that of very thin quality, than I with my many. I don't know why. I don't pretend to think that it was because of their superior quality. [186].

Expressing her disappointment to John Blackwood for offering her only two-thirds of the £1,500 he had paid for *The Perpetual Curate*, for the serialization rights to its Carlingford successor, *Miss Marjoribanks*, she again invoked Dinah Mulock, and added Wilkie Collins for good measure, as authors whom she knew to be better paid.[187] Mrs Oliphant was herself used as a yardstick by competing novelists. Eliza Lynn Linton, the longevity of whose writing career matched Mrs Oliphant's own, wrote to George Bentley, her publisher in 1885, complaining that she did not understand 'why I do not make so much as others. Chambers gives Mrs Oliphant £700 for the magazine rights of her story (*A House Divided Against Itself*), which is not up to my work.—I think you could afford me half of that for [my new novel].'[188]

The implicit threat of 'taking one's trade elsewhere' is everywhere present in correspondence between novelists and their publishers. Very early in her career the young Margaret Wilson found herself telling Richard Bentley, publisher of *John Drayton* and *The Melvilles*, that dealing with him was not as satisfactory as it had been with Mr Colburn, with whom her first three novels had been published. Despite an earlier protestation that she knew 'little of business' and found it difficult to work out the 'half-profits' deal he was offering her, she speedily discovered that such coyness cut no ice and became more peremptory in her demands. She was astute enough to dismiss his offer of a 'note of hand', which she would be forced to discount, and insist on payment in banknotes. An 'on account payment' was eventually sent in mid-March, by way of the two halves of a £50 note in separate envelopes. In her letter of receipt she declared herself sorry that the second edition of *John Drayton* was not selling as well as the first; nevertheless, this did not prevent her trying to strike a hard bargain at the beginning of April for *The Melvilles*. She declared herself willing to accept a £50 reduction on her initial asking price of £250, on the grounds of this being an anonymous work, but only if she kept the copyright. That, she remarked, was her final offer: 'any lower offers I do not feel I should be justified, since one may do injustice to one's self as well as to one's neighbours, in entertaining!' [189]

It had taken only three years and six published novels for her to acquire this professional mantle in her negotiations. When Colburn had offered her £150 for her first publication, *Margaret Maitland*, she had 'thanked him *avec effusion*' and remembered 'walking along the street with delightful elation, thinking that, after all, I was worth something—and not to be hustled aside'.[190]

It is well-nigh impossible to work out what Mrs Oliphant earned *in toto* during her working life, partly because she dealt with so many publishers, some of whose records do not survive, partly because she herself frequently became muddled about what any one initial contract had originally promised, but mainly because she increasingly used her various major publishers, such as Blackwoods and Macmillans, as bankers, drawing credit in advance for novels as yet unwritten and occasionally paying off parts of her accumulating debts by way of the odd article. By the mid-1870s she would even ask Blackwood for advances against books, as yet unwritten, commissioned by less accommodating publishers like Hurst and Blackett.[191] What is perhaps more interesting is to gain some impression of the trajectory of her earnings during her long writing career and some sense of her comparative earning capacity. When her will was brought to probate in 1897 it is true that the £4,932. 14s. 11d. she left behind her seemed in some sort to justify her sense of grievance that although she had published more than her most prolific popular rival, Anthony Trollope, she had done nothing like so well.[192] The gross value of his personal estate, as published on 23 January 1883, came to £25,892.19s. 3d.[193] Yet at the outset of their respective careers she had seemed at least as successful as he was. Even in the aftermath of the success of *The Warden* and *Barchester Towers*, Trollope found himself selling his sixth novel, *The Three Clerks* (1857), for £250 outright, to the same Richard Bentley with whom Mrs Oliphant had dealt so firmly—and that after having first offered it to Longmans, who stalled, unwilling to risk so large a lump sum, and Hurst and Blackett, who failed to keep their appointment with the author.[194] By her twelfth novel, *Zaidee* (1856), she was prepared to acknowledge Blackwood's offer of £800 'very liberal',[195] from a man whom Trollope claimed 'never let anything worth doing slip through his fingers, rated a manuscript's novel too high or too low, or ever misjudged the humour of the hour and the taste of the public'.[196] Mrs Oliphant's misfortune was that Blackwood, apparently put off by the harshness of tone of *Miss Marjoribanks*, which many subsequent readers have found her most accomplished work, refused to recognize her Carlingford series as the financial equal of Trollope's Barsetshire series. When he paid her £1,500 in 1864 for the three volumes of *The Perpetual Curate* she would have been justified in thinking herself as very much on a par with Trollope, who had sold *Orley Farm* as a five-volume package to Chapman and Hall in 1860 for £2,500 and half-profits after the first 10,000, by which system he contrived to garner a further £600. Yet even at this stage, before Trollope forged ahead in 1864 to earn £3,525 in all for *Can You Forgive Her*, his highest-earning fiction, significant differences began to emerge. The £1,500 payment she had received for *The Perpetual Curate* covered both the magazine serial rights and the subsequent copyright for its publication in book form. When Trollope sold *The Small House at Allington* to George Smith in 1862, for publication in twenty instalments in his *Cornhill* magazine, he refused the offer of £3,500 for the entire copyright, thinking he could do better by separating magazine rights from book copyright. In the event he was to lose £500 by this calculation. In 1877 he told Thomas Hardy, 'I sell everything out and out to my publishers, so that I may have no further bargainings . . . There can be no doubt that the royalty system is the best if you can get a publisher to give you a royalty, & if you are not in want of immediate money.' There precisely lay the rub for Mrs Oliphant, who invariably kept at least the copyright reversion for Tauchnitz editions as a source for a quick cash sale. Trollope had waited until in 1867, two-thirds of his way through his publishing career, he was assured that the editorship of *St Paul's Magazine* would net him about the same £750 per annum as his Post Office salary before he resigned his Civil Service career.[197]

Mrs Oliphant was almost certainly right to place the second turning-point in her literary fortunes in that period after her brother Frank's return to England, in 1870, when she gradually realized that she would have to assume responsibility for his family as well as her own. From then on the need for a regular annual income was the driving force behind every contract she made, and she never knew 'quite at the beginning of the year how the ends would come together at Christmas, always with troublesome debts and forestalling of money earned, so that I had generally eaten up the price of a book before it was printed'. By contrast in 1865 a sense of relative ease had been apparent when she had contemplated a contract for *Madonna Mary*. She told Blackwood that *Good Words* had offered her £1,000 together with the reversion of the copyright to her—a prospect, in fact, of something like the money she had earned for *The Perpetual Curate*. She admitted herself tempted, but told him that if he disliked the thought of his contributor appearing in the pages of another publisher's magazine she would turn this lucrative offer down. Having accepted the contract with *Good Words*, she was feeling sufficiently secure financially in the October of the same year to feel she could devote an American fee, probably a payment from Fletcher Harper for the first American edition of *Miss Marjoribanks*, to the purchase of a pony for Tiddy. The margin between her income and expenditure was sufficiently small, even during her most successful period, for her to need continuous work, but the statement she made about her affairs to John Blackwood in 1871 suggests that she had matters under control. Shocked by hearing that Henry Blackett had failed to make provision for his family, and doubtless remembering how her own husband's death had left her '£1,000 of debt' and 'a small insurance of, I think, £200 on Frank's life', she appointed John Blackwood and Principal Tulloch, together with Cecco's tutor, as guardians to the boys and reckoned that, were she to die, they would have the Civil List pension, which she had been awarded in 1868, of £100 per annum until they came of age, £1,000 apiece, and £500 to pay off debts. The following year she told Blackwood she had taken out £1,000 life insurance.[198]

A recent study in the sociology of publishing takes the case of two 'second-rate novelists', published by Macmillans: Mrs Oliphant and the prolific American male novelist, F. Marion Crawford, and compares their earnings between 1870 and 1891.[199] Her earnings during this period are estimated to have amounted to £10,125, or £500 per annum, while the American was paid some £600 per annum: from which it is concluded that critical double standards were echoed by contractual double standards. While this conclusion, which may well be correct, supports every suspicion under which Mrs Oliphant ever laboured, the figures used are misleading as a guide to her real financial position. The analysis omits to mention that only twenty-three of the sixty-four books she published over this period came out under the Macmillans imprint. While this does not invalidate the view that she was receiving lower pay than her male counterpart, it does overlook other factors. In these years she was gainfully employed elsewhere, producing regular articles for *Maga*, and other periodicals, editing the Blackwood's Foreign Classics series, and publishing novels under the imprints of Blackwoods; Hurst and Blackett; Longmans; Maclehose and Son; Partridge; Sampson Low; Scribners; Smith, Elder & Co.; and Ward and Downey. This affects the picture in two ways. First, she was sometimes simply too busy to pursue her threats of taking her merchandise elsewhere. Negotiations with Macmillans over a one-volume book she had offered them in March 1879 on Margaret of Scotland seemed to her to be dragging on interminably, and in June she eventually accepted their terms of £150 plus 'half-profits' on the grounds that 'One can write a good slice of another in the time it would take to haggle'.[200] Secondly, her very literary fecundity, she worried, had adverse effects on the sums she could command. Prolific authors like Mrs Oliphant and Trollope were always haunted by the spectre of flooding their own market. At the very outset of her career she had eight novels published between 1851 and 1853, and felt it necessary to mention to John Blackwood, under whose prestigious imprint she was appearing for the first time, 'It seems to me that there is a disagreeable impression produced by two books by the same author appearing about the same time.'[201] Reviewers were quick to conclude that such 'industry' was a sign of 'mass-production' techniques taking over from hand-crafted art, and publishers were reluctant to pay top prices for a commodity that, however agreeable and popular, did not distinguish the pages of their own magazine from its numerous competitors. Mrs Oliphant's products may sometimes have had to give way in Blackwood's *Maga* to a star turn like George Eliot,[202] but her letters to publishers show far more anxiety over the irritation her 'self-competition' may be causing them. For instance, she wrote to Blackwood apologizing for the fact that his publication in book form of *John: A Love Story*, currently appearing in serial form in *Maga*, should have coincided with Hurst and Blackett's three-volume version of *The Three Brothers*, currently being serialized in *St Paul's*. 'I have never had anything republished before until it had ended its periodical course and was quite unprepared for it!—though it seems the fashion now.' Not wanting Blackwoods to suffer by this, she asked 'whether it would be better to publish it [*John*] without my name as you are fond of doing'.[203]

Finally, by presenting only aggregate figures and a hypothesized annual income, the Tuchman and Fortin analysis neglects the decline over the years of Mrs Oliphant's power to command the prices she had fomerly expected for individual pieces of work. In 1874 she agreed with Blackwood that £1,000 was about right for the serialization of *The Story of Valentine and His Brother*, subsequently to be published by him in book form. The following year she accepted £500 from Macmillans for a similar deal for a two-volume work, *The Curate in Charge*. This was not a real fall in price because the material occupied six months rather than twelve in serial form. In 1877 she seems to have agreed to accept £700 from Macmillans for a three-volume work, *Young Musgrave*, which occupied twelve months of their periodical.[204] She was particularly hard pressed this year financially and the results showed both in the contracts she made and in the quality of her work. The last two years had seen heavy expenditure in equipping Cyril for Oxford and Frank junior for India.[205]

Cyril began to run up unforeseen debts at Oxford and then, in the spring of 1877, her house in Windsor came up for sale. It seemed a bargain: 'It is supposed it will go for something about £1,600 and I pay £105 of rent, which is a large percentage.' 'It would be so easy to buy it in a book!' she told Blackwood, explaining to him that she hoped to persuade him, and another unnamed publisher, to advance her £1,000. Perhaps feeling herself on a less sound footing with Macmillans, she delayed approaching them for a whole year; she wrote to them on 27 April 1878 with great urgency saying that the house was to be sold 'Thursday next', Blackwood was on holiday, and could they please advance her £500 in addition to her 'normal bread-and-butter' even though she knew they were not in a position to use more of her work at this juncture. When she had approached Blackwood the previous year she had made a similar point as to the timing of publications: 'If I were to die the said novel would be a little more than less valuable (Mr Trollope tells me he has more than one thus prepared for posthumous issue).'[206] That observation is interesting both for what it tells us of the hard-headed calculations of popular novelists and as providing an additionally ironic gloss on a short story, 'Mr Sandford', written *twenty* years later, where we are told that, despite the anxieties of the artist's family when he died, 'he did better still, as he had foreseen, by dying. Daniells sold the three pictures at prices higher than he had dreamed of, for a Sandford was now a thing with a settled value, it being sure that no new flood of them would ever come into the market.'[207]

Meanwhile, in 1877, she had approached William Isbister, now the managing proprietor of *Good Words*, whom Trollope, also committed to him at this period, described as being 'a fairly honest fellow but dilatory and vague'. Reminding him of a casual conversation they had once had on the subject, she offered him a story for the magazine's Christmas number *Good Cheer*, again giving as her reason her desire to buy her rented house. Her refusal a couple of years later to waste time by haggling with Macmillans may well have been a reaction to her correspondence with Isbister. Her side of the correspondence makes dispiriting reading. She claimed that he repeatedly failed to reply to her letters, underpaid her according to her calculations of £3 a printed page, asked for cuts, which she refused, telling him, 'you must operate on the other people and let me alone', and, in later years, sailed dangerously close to the wind in the matter of ignoring copyright reversion conventions.[208] He too might justifiably claim to have been short-changed. *Young*

Musgrave, which had been running from January to December 1877, in *Macmillan's Magazine*, took as its germ the sacrifices paid by two generations to cover up and make amends for the murder committed by an over-educated, mentally unbalanced peasant lad. 'The Lily and the Thorn', which Mrs Oliphant sold Isbister for his 1877 Christmas number, was not only highly unseasonal in subject-matter and tone, ending with the observation that nothing mattered since death comes to all eventually, but simply told the story of *Young Musgrave*'s germinal incident in greater detail. Although her account of the practice she elsewhere adopted of using different stages of the same story is true, the proximity of their appearance, in reverse order, without any hint to the reading public, beyond the similarity in names, of the tales' relatedness, lends an air of sophistry to her argument and more than a suggestion that she was now using his vagueness to her own advantage.

Dear Mr Isbister,

Your critic is very unpleasant and very unjust and more than that quite wrong. Young Musgrave is the sequel to the Lily and the Thorn. When I had written the longer story I felt it would be a pity not to make use of the dramatic advantage of the incident, which is supposed to have happened nearly twenty years before the story of Young Musgrave begins and which is simply referred to in that book—I told you I think (did I not?) at the time I sent you the story, that the two were thus connected—believing that it would be rather an advantage to both—of course there are different opinions as to the advantages of continuing the same characters from one story to another, but it is a thing which all the best writers have done and some of them largely. I don't know who the person is who has written to you but his criticism is evidently malignant—I will write to the Athenaeum on the subject—but no, I do not see why I should, unless this is positively repeated—though I feel deeply the malice of the suggestion that a story which I feel to be one of the most telling I have written is a sign of exhaustion on my part.[209]

If the late 1870s had been increasingly hectic, the 1880s saw her trapped in a situation where she had almost always mortgaged her work in advance and was therefore not in a position to make terms according to the individual merits of a piece. In 1878 she had still been able to command £750 for the three-volume *He That Will Not When He May*.[210] On 28 July 1882, claiming that successive negotiations delayed and annoyed her, she proposed a bulk deal to Macmillan: in return for a regular income over two years of £1,000 per annum, paid quarterly, she would supply him with three full-length novels. For a predictable income she was prepared to sacrifice £250.

Elsewhere, meanwhile, she was taking risks. Possibly as a gambit to persuade Longmans to entrust their proposed periodical to her as editor, she allowed them to use her three-volume novel, *In Trust* (1881), to attempt to break the stranglehold over the fiction industry achieved by Mudie's Select Library. For his advance purchases of the three-decker novels, which he favoured because it enabled him to lend separate volumes to three customers simultaneously, Charles Mudie expected a very substantial discount which, in turn, kept the price of this publishing format artificially high. Longmans brought out *In Trust* for 12*s*. 6*d*., less than half the price of the £1. 11*s*. 6*d*. which had become the standard. As the *Athenaeum* pointed out, *In Trust* was not a weighty enough missile to launch in this trade war: 'it is not a work of genius, such as the public would buy at any price; it is an excellent representative of the better class of current fiction, such as most intelligent people ask for at the circulating library, but have not hitherto been in the habit of buying and placing on their shelves.' It was, perhaps, just as well that it was not a novel of Mrs Oliphant's that was destined to spearhead the publishers' attack on Mudie's lending library; for she continued to appear on their lists and the year after her death eighty-nine of her titles remained in their annual catalogue.[211]

The *Athenaeum*'s judgement that her fiction was better borrowed than purchased did not improve her position with the publishing fraternity. During the mid-1870s she had been confident enough of her own reputation to try persuading Blackwood to bring out a collected edition of her work. She had floated the notion of 'an author's edition' which would involve buying up the copyright of her early Scottish books, 'because they are exhausted apparently, even in the railway issues which it has always moved my soul to see them in'. She never succeeded in this ambition, but continued to publish her novels separately, resorting increasingly frequently in later days to offering Macmillan even those novels which had appeared in competitors' magazines: Macmillans paid £400 a piece for the book rights to *A Country Gentleman and His Family* (1886), *Joyce* (1888), and *A Poor Gentleman* (1886).[212]

The drain on her income caused by Cyril's life-style and intermittent ill-health in the late 1880s involved her in increasingly complex financial negotiations with her publishers, which, in turn, reduced her freedom for manœuvre. Cyril's fainting attack in Paris in early January 1888, and the consequent expense of having him treated and attended, had involved Mrs Oliphant, who was already considerably in debt to Macmillan, in 'terrible expense'. A year and a half later she was still in dire straits. Looking about her for something on which to raise some ready money, she lit upon the notion of selling Macmillans the copyright of *The Heir Presumptive and the Heir Apparent*. There was only one flaw in this plan: Macmillans had already advanced her £200 against Tillotson's payments for the serialization of the book. Her suggestion was that Macmillans should advance her, at three-monthly intervals, the complete fee due from Tillotsons, and, in return, they could purchase the copyright for the knock-down price of £250. A further complication entered when Tillotsons proved reluctant to send their payment direct to Macmillan: declaring herself unwilling to offend her 'most liberal customers, so to speak', she promised to remit the money in instalments as she received it. By November she discovered that Tillotsons had delayed publication by three months, but she implored Macmillans to keep up payments to her bank: this they did, paying her a further £400 on 9 November against the serialization instalments. In the event the novel did not start its serial publication until 18 October 1890 and she was still promising Macmillans their money when she set off in March for Jerusalem, having received a further advance of £550 out of a total payment of £1,200 towards

Jerusalem: Its History and Hope. Not surprisingly, she expressed herself 'a little uneasy in the thoughts of the ever present possibility of my death before I am able to accomplish the work'. She therefore sought to reassure Macmillans by claiming that she had directed her sons to repay outstanding debts out of her literary remains: 'sundry stories left behind which have not been republished and various fragments of autobiography'.[213] Worse was to follow. Despite the fact that Macmillans had come through, on 18 July 1890, with their £250 for the book copyright of *The Heir Presumptive*, thirteen months later Mrs Oliphant tried to urge them to accept *The Railwayman and His Children* in lieu of the revised manuscript of *The Heir Presumptive*, offering as her reason that she was only half-way through the revision and she wanted to get *The Railwayman and His Children* out fast because its Continental publishers, Heineman and Balestier, were pushing for an early date. The respective publication dates suggest that Macmillans accommodated her once again, but not without reminding her of the terms of their initial agreement. Given the continuous demands she had made of them as bankers, the tone of her response is remarkably grand. As to the extract of a letter of some two years ago, which they had forwarded and she had completely forgotten,

I can of course have nothing to say. I am curious however to know whether all my private letters treating of my most intimate affairs go into the hands of your clerks to be copied out by any one who may happen to be in your employment—because in this case I must learn to be more careful how I write—such a detail had not occurred to me. It is a little alarming in the case of letters that are written to a friend.

Finding an opportunity for speaking *de haute en bas* may have relieved her feelings, but she was doomed to lose the larger war. Having conceded a price cut for the book copyright of *The Heir Presumptive*, she could not regain her former bargaining position and her next two novels to appear with them, *The Railwayman and His Children* and *Lady William*, were also sold at the lower price of £250.[214]

Time and again in her dealings with publishers Mrs Oliphant was, or at least claimed to be, astonished at the way in which they failed to respect their separate roles as friend and businessman, while herself trading remorselessly upon the special relations built up over long years of mutual hospitality. Such letters may of course reflect an instinctive swing of the mercurial personality that J. M. Barrie described as 'most sympathetic when she unbent and a ramrod if she chose' (or, as one of the Tulloch boys less kindly characterized it, wholly unable 'to understand or sympathise with those who took differing views from her own').[215] On the other hand there is something a little trumped up in a righteous indignation that so deliberately aims to sidetrack the nature of Macmillans' specific complaint. In less embattled circumstances she was quite clear as to the distinction she wished to keep between business transactions and the claims of friendship. In 1875, for instance, she wrote to ask John Blackwood if she might extend a loan, made that quarter, for a further nine months, saying that two women friends of hers, one of them his sister Isabella Blackwood, had offered to lend her the money, but she preferred to avoid private transactions and stick to legitimate business arrangements. Only at the very end of her life, when even her most long-standing publisher, Blackwoods, seemed alarmed 'lest I should leave you in the lurch' and proved reluctant to advance her money, did she resort to borrowing the travel money to Siena to do research for her forthcoming book from Cousin Annie. Cousin Annie could now afford to return some of the bounty she had received for so long, and Mrs Oliphant's code permitted drawing upon relatives.[216]

It has been suggested that women novelists of the mid-Victorian period tended to form longer-lasting relations with their publishers than their male contemporaries. This may well be because they found the transition between the middle-class female world of social relationship and the male world of commerce between gentleman and tradesman a hard one to negotiate, and were therefore reluctant to have to repeat the process too often.[217] Mrs Oliphant certainly made frequent display of this unease, but the very frequency with which she voiced it gives rise to the suspicion that she also knew how to 'make play' with it. Consider, for instance, this letter written to Macmillans when she thought they were trying to short-change her in their payments for her twenty-sixth novel, *A Son of the Soil*.

I have always been accustomed to go on the perhaps erroneous idea that publishers knew best what they could afford to offer—but when I have gotten other people in my trade who do otherwise, I begin to think that I ought to act more energetically, for my little boys' sakes.[218]

The subtext implies that she has been forced by her publishers' meanness and the rapacity of others, not even worthy of a name, to abandon a natural womanly passivity and trust, and furthermore that even these considerations would have told for nothing had she not had her little boys to consider. Langford, Blackwood's London business manager, was accustomed to claim that George Eliot and Lewes ran a 'Spenlow and Jorkins' routine in their business negotiations with the firm. Mrs Oliphant's business manner more often resembled the behaviour of another Dickensian lawyer, Vholes, who justifies 'the distrustful eye of business' dominating all his business relations by constant reference to three daughters and an ageing father in the Vale of Taunton.[219] Mrs Oliphant's genuine need to make a paying business of her work is not in doubt, and she was right to feel that many literary women had husbands behind whose business expertise they could shelter in making their negotiations. Yet it is also noteworthy that, with the sole exception of brother Willie's initial negotiations on her behalf with a London firm, she had always dealt direct with her various publishers and, conscious of her husband's ineptitude as a businessman, had never made any pretence of sheltering behind an appeal to his views or wishes. While she learnt to take 'a man's view of mortal affairs', however, she was careful not to lose any advantage femininity might confer. When she came to write of her most desperate appeal to a publisher in the cruel Scottish winter of her early widowhood, she recalled the picture as if it had been carefully composed. John Blackwood and his wife were already fairly frequent visitors, but she sought this interview at their place of business.

I think I see their figures now against the light, standing up, John with his shoulders hunched up, the Major with his soldierly air, and myself all blackness and whiteness in my widow's dress, taking leave of them as if it didn't matter, and oh! so much afraid that they would see the tears in my eyes.[220]

She was no less resourceful, six years later, in dressing the part of the successful author. Pencilled in against her account to John Blackwood of a visit she had paid to the George St., Edinburgh end of the firm, where she claimed that 'neither Mr Simpson nor anybody else knew me', is the observation, 'No wonder! the style of ladies' dress now defies recognition—that of Mrs Oliphant on the occasion referred to impressed me so that I expected I was about to address a Duchess.'[221] This scene of her majestic descent upon those to whom she had formerly to sue for her widow's mite bears comparison with better-known pictures such as Trollope's arrival at Chapman and Hall's, clad in his pink coat and brandishing a hunting crop. It is also worth setting it alongside the alternative self-presentation she offers in the *Autobiography* of the time, after the publication of *Salem Chapel*, which '*almost* made me one of the popularities of literature', not because the one discountenances the other, but because taken together they suggest something of the complexity of her experience and personality.

The story was successful, and my fortune, comparatively speaking, was made. It has never been very much, never anything like what many of my contemporaries attained, and yet I have done very well for a woman, and a friendless woman with no one to make the best of me, and quite unable to do that for myself. I never could fight for a higher price or do anything but trust to the honour of those I had to deal with. Whether this was the reason why, though I did very well on the whole, I never did anything like so well as others, I can't tell, or whether it was really inferiority on my part.[222]

George Reid's 'Sir Walter Scott'

I have so far discussed the particularities of Mrs Oliphant's life and work, rather in the manner she herself suggested when sketching the outlines of one of her own female characters:

Mrs Everard also was a widow. This fact acts upon the character like other great facts in life. It makes many and important modifications in the aspect of affairs. Life à deux (I don't know any English phrase which quite expresses this) is scarcely more different from the primitive and original single life than is the life which, after having been à deux, becomes single, without the possibility of going back to the original standing ground. That curious mingling of a man's position and responsibilities, cannot possibly fail to mould a type of character in many respects individual. A man who is widowed is not similarly affected, partly because in most cases he throws the responsibility from him, and either marries again or places some woman in the deputy position of governess or housekeeper to represent the feminine side of life, which he does not choose to take upon himself. Women, however, abandon their post much less frequently, and sometimes, I suspect get quite reconciled to the double burden . . . Sometimes they attempt too much, and often enough they fail; but so does everybody in everything, and widows' sons have not shown badly in general life.[1]

The novel in which this remark occurs was written in 1872, before her sons were old enough to be judged to have made a lamentable failure 'in general life', but Mrs Oliphant was in no doubt that it was in this wider arena that they must make their mark. She was similarly aware that her other creations, her fiction and non-fiction, would achieve a valuation in the general market-place, irrespective of the special circumstances of her own life. Feminist studies have often been accused of evading critical responsibility, either in the interests of the prior task of reclaiming neglected voices, or from a desire to resist the contamination of the male values so firmly imprinted on the traditional tests of literary greatness. Unfortunately, neither of these positions do much credit to their women subjects or to literary studies: rather they imply a view that reduces literature, of whatever calibre, to the status of a useful historical source; and the refusal to engage in critical dialogue only re-inforces the suspicions indulged in by those outside the ghetto thus created.

Mrs Oliphant herself would have been irritated by any reluctance to apply the contemporary critical standards used to judge male writing to her work. As she grew older and more certain of her professional status, she became increasingly irritated by various positions which seemed to undermine or threaten a woman's right to enter the literary market-place and aim for its top prizes. The hordes of new authors who apparently regarded writing as 'the easiest trade, requiring no training at all'[2] offered an implicit attack upon her hard-won professional status and seemed to reinforce the previously fashionable thesis that, since genius was unlikely to occur in a woman, different standards of judgement were appropriate.

In this respect, she felt, women artists had been their own worst enemies. They had been so anxious to avoid the stigma of abnormality or deviance from conventional notions of female propriety that they had vied with each other 'in denying all eccentricity and claiming the reputation of good housekeepers, good economists, seamstresses, and all that goes with these famous domestic qualities'. Reviewing *The Life of Harriet Beecher Stowe*, she registered her annoyance with a passage that evaluated the art in terms of the author's ability to earn mattresses for her family.

This admirable confession of poverty and virtuous striving and the prosaic uses of the literary gift, was considered engaging and delightful to the highest degree in those days. But it has been repeated a great many times since: and we are not sure that it would not please us more now to hear that our poet authoress was a little out of the common way, that there was a touch of frenzy in her poetic eye, and that she did not think of feather-beds, but let her money drop through her fingers, and knew nothing of business.[3]

It might at first sight seem as if Mrs Oliphant's *Autobiography* was itself responsible for encouraging the application of exactly those different standards for female achievements that her criticism so strenuously repudiated. In one respect that work follows a well-documented tendency for the autobiographies of nineteenth-century women to display a degree of self-denigration wholly at odds with the evidence and spirit of either their letters or their less personal public writings.[4] Though she was inclined to minimize the quality of her achievements, she did not fall into the other well-established trait of making gestures to woman's essentially passive role as a channel through which external inspiration and energies might flow. She was not in the habit of attributing her success to good luck or the generosity of others, but stressed her own unremitting labours and the conscious choices she had made in what to us might seem fairly constricted circumstances. Nor is the passage where she asserts that her status as mother and friend was always more important than her reputation at the circulating library a plea for critical leniency on grounds of gender. Bereavement had made her sharply aware how little human consolation literary reputation could offer and, *sub specie aeternitatis*, any artistic achievement seemed both trivial and evanescent:

And now that there are no children to whom to leave any memory; and the friends drop day by day, what is the reputation of a circulating library to me? Nothing, and less than nothing—a thing the thought of which now makes me angry, that any one should for a moment imagine I cared for that, or that it made up for any loss. I am perhaps angry, less reasonably, when well-intentioned people tell me I have done good, or pious ones console me for being left behind by thoughts of the good I must yet be intended to do. God help us all! what is the good done by any such work as mine, or even better than mine.[5]

By the time that she wrote this final part of her autobiographical account she was an old woman and had been deprived of the goal and purpose which had served to legitimate her work as a female writer. She therefore felt entitled to speak out about the hollowness she had discovered behind that ideal of women as patient sufferers and inspirers of virtue. Silent suffering, or the ironic displacement of grievance, has here been replaced by the energy of openly expressed anger. It was this anger that fuelled the powerful work which was still to come in such pieces as 'The Anti-Marriage League', *The Makers of Modern Rome*, or *Old Mr Tredgold*. The passage which had begun in apparent nihilism went on to arrive at an expression of the transcendent value of art.

'if any man build upon this foundation . . . wood, hay, stubble . . . if the work shall be burned, he shall suffer loss; but he himself shall be saved; yet so as by fire'. An infinitude of pains and labour, and all to disappear like the stubble and hay. Yet who knows? The little faculty may grow a bigger one in the more genial land to come, where one will have no need to think of the boiling of the daily pot.

In the depression she experienced in the early months after Cecco's death she felt that she had lost on all fronts: her children were dead and all she had to show for a life of toil was a collection of pot-boilers. 'I pay the penalty in that I shall not leave anything behind me that will live.'[6] The obituaries that immediately followed her death were by and large respectful in tone, but a series of longer, more magisterial assessments of Mrs Oliphant's achievements were to follow consequent upon the publication of her *Autobiography* in 1899. These were inclined to take her own dispiriting self-evaluation of 1894 as the definitive account, and she was laid to rest as a dreary survival of antiquated Victorian values by those anxious to embrace the artistic preoccupations of the new century. The coincidence of her death with that of the century metamorphosed her career into a symbolic watershed: the point can be conveniently illustrated by comparing Leslie Stephen's evaluation of her with that of his daughter, Virginia Woolf.[7] He presented her as a test case in considering the problem of morality versus art. At one end of the spectrum he placed Southey, who had been prepared to sacrifice all else for the chance of a seat beside Milton or Spenser; at the other he placed Mrs Oliphant, who, on the evidence of 'that most pathetic autobiography', resigned her chance of writing a novel 'to stand on the same shelf as *Adam Bede* . . . because she wished to send her boys to Eton'. Dismissing the thought that she could perhaps have sent them to 'some humbler school and have kept her family without sacrificing her talents to over-production', as not germane to his argument, he concluded that he honoured and respected her decision. His daughter, on the other hand, produced the autobiography as 'a most genuine and indeed moving piece of work' in which she found all the evidence she wanted to convince herself that in her fiction, her 'innumerable faded articles, reviews [and] sketches of one kind and another', she had 'sold her brain, her very admirable brain, prostituted her culture and enslaved her intellectual liberty in order that she might earn her living and educate her children'. Neither of them saw good reason to challenge Mrs Oliphant's own evaluation of her writings, but each confidently claimed her as a trophy for diametrically opposed prejudices, Leslie Stephen being perhaps the more open in his admission, 'I have a low opinion of the intrinsic value of artistic masterpieces.'

And there matters stood until very recently. Robert and Vineta Colby's very thorough study, *The Equivocal Virtue: Mrs Oliphant and the Victorian Literary Market Place* (1966), presented an advance in scholarship, but, as the title's reference to her unflagging industry and eye to the market indicates, did little to change her reputation. The slow change that occurred as women critics, in particular, began to recognize that her anti-feminist conclusions were predicated upon a thoroughly feminist analysis, can be gauged by the way in which the Colbys' assessment of her *Autobiography* changed from their 1966 opinion that 'Her life records are a dreary chronicle', to their description of it in 1979 as 'the most beautiful and moving of all her works'.[8] The title of Merryn Williams's very serviceable study, to which all recent researchers are indebted, *Margaret Oliphant: A Critical Biography* (1986), asserts that its subject merits critical attention, but the effect is slightly undermined by taking so many chapter-headings from Mrs Oliphant's own self-marginalizing remarks: 'General Utility Woman', 'Never Penetrating Beyond the Threshold', and 'On the Ebb Tide'. Once again, too, a slight hesitancy manifests itself as to the nature of Mrs Oliphant's true significance for twentieth-century readers: a book that 'began as a study of her major novels' reached the book-buying public as 'the first full biography'.[9]

The old tug-of-war between the life and the art as evaluative guidelines, lent heavyweight leadership by Leslie Stephen and his daughter at the turn of the century, has become yet more intense in the late twentieth century when biographies have gained in best-seller appeal in almost direct correlation to literary criticism's increasing scepticism as to the validity and ideological respectability of using such extra-textual material.

Even were it possible or desirable to jettison the biographical dimension from the discussion, it is still not easy to assess the history of the reputation of Mrs Oliphant's writings. There has never been an informed consensus as to which works best show off her characteristic virtues. Many of her early works were out of print long before she died and, since the obituaries were often written by a later generation, one cannot but suspect that the praise meted out to her early Scottish novels was often the effect of reading *Kirsteen* (1890) rather than *Passages in the Life of Margaret Maitland*, which had last been republished in the Parlour Library in 1876, or its immediate successors, or of their gaining a reflected glory from the sudden vogue for kailyard novels at the time of her death.[10] 'The Chronicles of Carlingford', which had secured her claim to be considered in the major league of Victorian novelists, offered an easy peg upon which those with a slim acquaintance with her work could hang her reputation. Given the vagaries of republication this proved a mixed blessing: *Salem Chapel* happened to be the representative volume from this series to enter Everyman's Classics, and this encouraged many twentieth-century readers to regard her genius as irretrievably flawed by a penchant for succumbing to the 1860s fashion for the melodramatic appeal of the 'sensation novel'. In her own lifetime it would seem that the 'Little Pilgrim' series, for which she had not initially 'thought of pay at all', was to prove the best seller. She was herself amazed to discover that Macmillans had printed their twenty-first thousand of this within five years of its initial publication. She enquired whether this was 'to be received as genuine? or does the trade add on a little'. A pencilled note in the margin of this letter mentioned that the twenty-second thousand was already in print.[11] The popularity of this work was again to prove counterproductive to her reputation, since these religious allegories and fables belonged to a genre which was to fall wholly outside the boundaries of serious twentieth-century literature. The only other work to survive the almost total oblivion into which her work fell for some sixty years was *A Beleaguered City*: this was kept alive by the continuing market for tales of the supernatural. Even this may have skewed her reputation, allowing her to appear as a writer who had accidentally produced one or two worthwhile stories of the supernatural in the midst of piles of eminently forgettable three-deckers. Among her non-fiction, *The Life of Edward Irving* and her *Annals of a Publishing House* were to remain the standard works for many years; but the romantic bias of the former and the anecdotal style of the latter, both aimed at pleasing a general readership, were to attract the criticism of an unscholarly disregard for accurate detail from the very different type of reader who had reason to consult them in the following century. Yet the fact that the major reputable publishing houses went on publishing her work for over half a century bespeaks an achievement greater than the production of formula best-sellers, which might have found their niche with second-rank publishers like the Tinsley Brothers. Nor was her appeal solely to the middle-brow English tastes of the readers whose daily lives her work might be thought to have reflected. She had a considerable following in America, was swiftly made available to English-speakers on the Continent by the Tauchnitz editions, and some of her fiction was certainly translated into French and Russian.[12]

On the face of it, her popularity abroad, with a readership remote from the domestic concerns her novels depicted, seems surprising. *The Second Son* (1888), for instance, was written specifically for the American market, and Mrs Oliphant empowered T. B. Aldrich, editor of Boston's *Atlantic Monthly*, to make any changes he deemed necessary; but the plot, with its complicated use of English laws of primogeniture and entailment of estates, made no concessions to a transatlantic readership.[13] Mrs Oliphant, it seems, was right to identify her strength as her ability for character depiction and to assume that a 'novelist working on the basis of humanity, which though varying in its modes, is practically the same among all people and in all ages', has advantages over every other writer attempting to interest readers in the reconstruction of the circumstances of a particular society.[14] From her very first short story, 'John Rintoul', it is easy to see that she compensated for her self-acknowledged limitations at plot invention and structure by relying on closely delineated character.[15] This sometimes led to problems in her longer fiction. Occasionally, as in *Squire Arden*, it seems that, starting with only the most basic outlines of the plot in her mind, she only discovered the incumbent complications as she wrote. Sometimes Mrs Oliphant's interest in the plot from which the novel's action arises is simply superseded, as in *Madam*, by the interest she develops in a new generation of characters, who take centre-stage to the detriment of the novel's advertised centre of interest. On the other hand, habits encouraged by three-volume novels, such as following the fortune of *two* sets of characters, or moving the characters from one place to another, could sometimes be made to work to her benefit, as in *Phoebe Junior* or *The Wizard's Son*, where a clash of cultures, or the provision of an alternative world of opportunities, proves vital to the novels' thematic interests.

It was also her very strength as a character painter that threw the remaining weakness in her plots into high relief. Morally reprobate male characters occasionally disappear from her novels in a flurry of melodramatic villainy, killing any man they fear will expose them or, at the very least, indulging in hoarse curses or bitter laughter. These sudden denouements clashed crudely with her bent for meticulously tracing the after-effects of these characters' actions upon those remaining, and, however long she managed to delay such crises, they always produce a disappointing sense of being returned to the stereotypical world of sensationalism after the promise afforded by glimpses into these characters' inner self-justifications. For the ability to show both men and women in highly wrought states from which there is no obvious or immediate release was one of her most striking talents. Since the effect of her style so often relies upon a cumulative sense of image, rhythm, and cadence it is difficult to illustrate this briefly, but the capacity to allow her style to respond to the changing exigencies of plot and character is rarely shown to better effect than in *The Second Son* (1888), which contains two chapters focusing on different levels of emotional desperation. In the first, chapter 28, 'A Night in the Streets', we see a country girl taking panicky flight from her would-be seducer in London. Gradually her anger, self-pity, and shame subside into a desperate weariness as she finds herself alone and not knowing which way to turn in her predicament. The landscape of the suburbs in the small hours provides the perfect complement to her situation: the endless labyrinth of Roads, Gardens, and Places through which she walks coalesces into 'an awful desert of houses'. Each new turning offers simultaneously the hope of a new direction and the conviction of being utterly lost. Row upon row of doors, remaining firmly closed, mock her desire for comfort and solace. Worse still, despite her inner turmoil, she is forced to maintain an even pace throughout the small hours so as not to attract attention to herself and feels obliged to shun even those figures who might have been able to set her right upon her path.

The second chapter, 44, 'The Squire Goes Home', depicts an irascible, unpleasant old man, who has been used to imposing his own will on others through a combination of bullying and intimidation. Thwarted by a mere bunch of women, and shaking with impotent rage and shame at the revelation that his youngest son's failed seduction is well known in the neighbourhood, he decides to make his way home in the heat of the midday sun. His anger and perturbation make themselves felt in the raised beat of his pulse, which is in turn reflected in the insistence of the short clauses and phrases that describe his long and arduous walk home. The domestic turmoil that has already struck the traditional life of this very conservative squirearchy, and will result in the Squire dying of a stroke before he rescinds the will unjustly debarring his second son from the inheritance, is neatly encapsulated in the Squire's sudden eruption into the house during the afternoon period when the butler is 'dozing pleasantly'. Wanting to block out the penetrating sun and the 'derisive laughter of the county' that echoes in his ears, the Squire demands that the shutters be closed. The narrative focus then slides to the butler, who makes his ponderous preparations with a marked deliberation, where the various hiatuses and the syntactical inversion give pride of place to the butler's sense of grievance, and the reader's anxiety as to how long the Squire will be able to contain the temper that has nowhere to put itself is heightened by the premonitory release in the opening of the bottles: 'He sent for the various bottles, there was a popping of corks which occupied some time: and finally he took in himself to the library a tray, which the footman carried to the door.'

It was Mrs Oliphant's choice of narrative stance that allowed her to move in and out of her various characters at will, offering them up to the reader at their own evaluation, as other characters saw them, and brooded over by the narrator's voice. Her first published novel had employed a first-person narrator, an elderly single woman whose relative freedom from ties, financial and emotional, allowed her to move between and comment upon the rest of the cast. This voice blended easily with Mrs Oliphant's own authorial persona and came into its own again in the short-story cycle 'Neighbours on the Green'. She was to find the narrative voice of female characters whose opinions diverged from her own less useful, or perhaps less appealing.[16] It was one thing to comment ironically, at times even fondly, upon the foibles of her own sex, and another to serve up their weaknesses naked, without the benefit of authorial protection, to the general reader's eye. A long career in learning to use the male voice against itself as *Maga*'s literary critic had freed her from any such reservations in disclosing male vanities. The distinction is illuminatingly and fruitfully deployed in *A Beleaguered City*, where the main narrative thrust is carried by the pompously authoritative tones of the Mayor and the female point of view separated between two versions of Mrs Oliphant, the wifely advocate of female self-sacrifice, and the slightly querulous mother whose pride in her son's achievement is almost matched by her resentment of his adult autonomy.

In the majority of her fictions an impersonal voice carries the overview, lending a characteristically ironic tone by exploiting the gaps between the characters' perception of their own and each other's lives. This does not necessarily reduce all the characters within a particular tale to peep-show dimensions, but offers the reader the kind of pleasure that one might derive from being unexpectedly offered a new and privileged view of a well-known building. The point can be briefly illustrated. In an unremarkable short story, 'A Party of Travellers', we are speedily introduced to one of their number as 'one of those quiet women who, without any unkindness in them, nay, with the most devoted and true affection, yet cannot help seeing the foibles of their belongings, and get a gentle fun from out of them in spite of themselves'. Such characteristics might well have qualified this woman as a narrator for a tale by Mrs Oliphant, so it comes as a surprise, which is germane to the tale's outcome, when the narrator draws us back apace to see the character from a different angle. She is observed walking on the beach, unconscious of the incongruous picture her silken dress creates there. The narrator pauses to remark what a good thing it is that few of us recognize our own distinguishing idiosyncrasies, 'for what would become of all our little individualities, our angles, the rough places which distinguish us one from another, if we could see how droll we appear—just as droll, or more so, than the other people are?'[17] As Mrs Oliphant recognized, she had to nourish this skill for sustaining an illusion of an ever-receding series of perspectives, to fight off the opposing temptation of reductionism, of which the *Saturday Review* held her guilty.

Mrs Oliphant, in her long observation of mankind and her abundant practice in giving it to the world, seems to have come to the conclusion that—vulgarly speaking—men are much of a muchness, and that if you represent one and all as influenced by other motives than those they acknowledge, you can never be far wrong . . . She finds an easy amusement in bringing together by the ears men of different religious creeds and professions, and subduing them to uniformity by their weaknesses. A sort of unity indeed is established by this means; if people do not think all alike, at the end of the book they are all alike, which comes to much the same thing.[18]

This reviewer seems to have mistaken a strongly held philosophical conviction for artistic laziness. The circumstances of her own life, from which she drew her creative sustenance, had done much to convince her of an obstinately repetitive disposition in human affairs. Try though she might to provide different conditions for her sons' upbringing, their adult lives replicated almost exactly the depressing decline into indolent dependence that her own brothers' lives had each, very separately, taken. Place as well as character conspired to give this dreary impression of circularity: it was to be 'rotting Rome' that twice bereaved her.

Deployed at its best, this conviction that human nature is 'practically the same in all times and in all ages', but has an almost infinite capacity for discovering individually quirky variations, gave rise to a delicate capacity to hover on the borders of tragicomic irony. There are a series of family confrontations between the thrice-married Squire Wentworth and his very disparate progeny in *The Perpetual Curate* that measure up to the finest of Trollope's comic scenes. In this scene the irascible Squire, a well-intentioned father, holding the traditional views of the English squirearchy, is discussing with the son of his middle wife, the perpetual curate of the novel's title, the plight of the second son of his first wife, Gerald, whose excessively refined conscience has led him to believe he must abandon the family living and his wife and family, to become a Roman Catholic priest,

'There never was any evil in him, that I could see, from a child; but crotchety, always crotchety, Frank. I can see it now. It must have been their mother,' said the Squire, meditatively; 'she died young, poor girl! her character was not formed. As for *your* dear mother, my boy, she was always equal to an emergency; she would have given us the best of advice, had she been spared to us this day. Mrs Wentworth is absorbed in her nursery, as is natural, and I should not care to consult her much on such a subject . . . I consider you very like your mother, Frank. If anybody can help Gerald, it will be you . . . You have only to talk to him, and clear up the whole affair', said the Squire, recovering himself a little. He believed in 'talking to', like Louisa [Gerald's pathetic wife], and like most people who are utterly incapable of talking to any purpose . . . 'There is the bell for luncheon, and I am very glad of it', he said; 'a glass of sherry will set me all right . . . If the worst should come to the worst, as you seem to think', he said, with a kind of sigh, 'I should at least be able to provide for you, Frank. Of course, the Rectory would go to you . . .'

So saying, the Squire led the way into the house; he had been much appalled by the first hint of this threatened calamity, and was seriously distressed and anxious still; but he was the father of many sons, and the misfortunes or blunders of one could not occupy all his heart. And even the Curate, as he followed his father into the house, felt that Louisa's words, so calmly repeated, 'Of course the Rectory will go to you', went tingling to his heart like an arrow, painfully recalling him in the midst of his anxiety, to a sense of his own interests and cares. Gerald was coming up the avenue at the moment slowly, with all the feelings of a man going to the stake . . . He thought nothing less than that his father and brother were discussing him with hearts as heavy and clouded as his own; for even he, in all his tolerance and impartiality, did not make due account of the fact, that every man has his own concerns next to him, close enough to ameliorate and lighten the weight of his anxieties for others.[19]

While the last remark from the narrator draws attention to the common denominator in human behaviour, it in no way diminishes the oddity of such a blunt, and naïvely transparent, man as the Squire having fathered two men of such refined conscience as Frank and Gerald. While counting entirely upon the principle that 'breeding will out', the proud patriarch fails to perceive the part his own obstinate, if simple-minded, convictions have played in giving his sons a similarly blinkered view of their own rightness. Conscious of his duties and responsibilities as head of this long-established family, he has deployed money, land, livings, and wives to secure the succession, without any real glimmer of the individual susceptibilities standing in his way. The benevolent but incompetent authoritarianism that shines through his ramblings inclines us to sympathize with the sons whose life of intellectual and spiritual agonizings have so repeatedly had to encounter this brick wall. Frank and Gerald, however, are then disclosed to us as being not only motivated by equally rigid, though different, agenda, but also as more or less locked into the egocentricity of the human condition. Readers familiar with Mrs Oliphant's point of view will appreciate the unwitting accuracy with which the Squire has pinpointed Frank's good sense and willingness to make an effort on the family's behalf as proof of his strong maternal inheritance. It is a mark of Frank's 'female' sensitivity of conscience that the arrow of his selfish concerns goes 'painfully' to its mark, whereas his brother Gerald approaches the house, to which he has been invited for lunch, unshaken in his ability to transform the scene into a martyrdom which will secure him the unchallenged central role. The passage is rich both in humour and pathos, for the occasion of this gathering, the crisis of conscience that threatens to wrench the family asunder, would have tapped deeper wells of suffering in many Victorian families, where differing religious conviction had caused separation. One phrase in this passage may have caused surprise. We are told not that Gerald, '*despite* all his tolerance and impartiality', did not take account of the absolute egocentricity of every man's view of life, but that '*in* all his tolerance and impartiality' he failed to recognize this fact. As so often, Mrs Oliphant hides within her narrative a figure who serves as a reminder to her of the temptation she had most to guard against. It is because Gerald's estimation of life is conducted from a grandly Olympian viewpoint that he can recognize neither the deep-seated selfishness of his own position nor that others, however feeble or muddle-headed they may seem, are demonstrating their humanity by the tenacity with which they cling to other viewpoints. Of his wife's, to us entirely understandable, objections to the step he is proposing, all he can say is, 'It is a strange view of life, to look at it from Louisa's point.'[20] Mrs Oliphant recognized that if she confined herself to the impartial tolerance of others' 'peccadilloes' adopted by a Gerald Wentworth or a Catherine Vernon, this would reduce her writing to a uniformly cold cynicism and forfeit the ability to offer pleasure through her sense of her characters' widely differing 'views of life'. It was her greatest reservation about Jane Austen that her 'involuntary training' in silent observation and a tolerance devoid of moral anger or 'human charity' had made her slow to see 'that even the most stupid and arrogant of mortals has his rights'.[21]

Her ability to give individuality to her characters, while at the same time making us conscious of a consistent line of authorial point of view, was related to her style. She had both the mimic's ability to capture individual turns of phrase and nuance and a very sure sense of her own cadences. Her first novel, *Christian Melville*, is flawed by the over-use of rhetorical questions, pretentious phraseology, arch descriptions, and the resort to the graphic present to provide dramatic intensity; but this was the novel of a 17-year-old, and George Eliot was almost 40 when she wrote *Scenes of Clerical Life*, which manifested each of these stylistic flaws. A couple of early historical novels she wrote early in her career, *Caleb Field* and *Magdalen Hepburn: The Story of the Reformation*, though more competent pieces of work, bear the sign of the labour they cost, because both of them resort to stylistic devices alien to her normal mode: the former in 'taking a great deal of trouble about a Nonconformist minister who spoke in antitheses very carefully constructed',[22] and the latter in her endeavours to reproduce an authentic dialect regardless of its comprehensibility. Honing and polishing were wholly alien to her talent; her poetry was utterly unmemorable because the constraints of conventional metrical discipline never allowed her to do more than imitate other poets' rhythms or pad out her verses with line-fillers.

As with other very prolific artists who have been quick to discover their own voices, yet have been capable throughout their careers of curious lapses of tone and control, it has seemed most profitable to attempt to identify the constituent parts of her writing which from time to time coalesced in such a way that she hit her truest vein. We have her own authority for this approach in the story of Mr Sandford, the elderly and much respected painter, who learns to see that his finest work has always arisen 'out of the jogtrot' of his ordinary work, not from conscious attempts to change artistic direction.[23]

One of the most impressive aspects of Mrs Oliphant's achievements as a writer was the speed with which she used her prolific output to cast her juvenilia behind her, find her own voice, and achieve a resistance to the infection of other styles. Her early reviews give some indication that this was at least a semi-conscious process for they were particularly strong in noting such weaknesses in others' writing. Mrs Gore's artificiality was in part a product of 'her regular sentences . . . the dialogue which chimes in exactly the same measure, whether the speakers speak in a club, or in the dowager duchess's sombre and pious boudoir';[24] those prominent non-fiction writers Macaulay and Ruskin were judged to have developed style at the expense of content.[25] Similarly towards the end of her career she noted an attentiveness to style, bordering upon obsessiveness, as characterizing the work of Henry James or George Meredith, both of whom she felt were writing with an eye to the critics rather than the general reader.[26] Mrs Oliphant's *Autobiography* is notably free from the desire to respond to professional criticisms of her work. Fifty years of literary journalism had taught her how ephemeral such judgements were and reaffirmed her conviction that the general reader, at whom she aimed, valued the reassurance of a distinctively individual style.

She had not long been launched in her career by the time that she found the self-confidence to dismiss the comments of a certain Ann Mozley (a fellow essayist), reported to her by John Blackwood.

As to your courteous critic's remarks, I am quite conscious of the 'to be sure's' and the 'naturally', but then a faultless style is like a faultless person, highly exasperating, and if one did not leave those little things to be taken hold of perhaps one might fare worse.[27]

She recognized these phrases, which have been interestingly linked both to the conditions under which her mother had allowed her to legitimate her writing and to the appeal to experience that constitutes the realist writer's claim to authority, as absolutely characteristic of her style.[28] Taken together, these desires to imply inspiration rather than careful craftsmanship, and a simplicity which bespoke its origins in the truth of experience, were the hallmarks of a female tradition that had long found its natural medium in realist fiction, within whose elastic form it might also enjoy the freedom to employ, more or less covertly, the authorities and professional rhetoric marked out by education and cultural prejudice as male territory. In Mrs Oliphant's case it was the very flexibility of the realist domestic fiction, acknowledged as an appropriate sphere for women writers, that permitted the characteristic intrusions of her very personal observations into the narrator's otherwise distanced tones. She was astute enough to recognize that, given the fluctuations in narratorial distance, her 'readability' relied heavily upon a fluent style. Her chosen medium imitated and exploited all the parenthetical tricks of the colloquial register, but this, in turn, encouraged mannerisms that she dared not iron out for fear of losing 'my sing-song, guided by no sort of law, but by my ear, which was in its way fastidious to the cadence and measure that pleased me'.[29]

Despite the rebuff she offered, via John Blackwood, to Ann Mozley, she had occasionally been prepared to accept criticisms of her own style from people whose opinion she respected. In 1862 she had told Blackwood that she agreed with the strictures of the Reverend Lucas Collins, a respected clerical scholar who marched under the Blackwoods' banner, about 'her tricks of style': they were 'not conscious but natural', she claimed, and, now that they had been brought to her attention, she would try and iron them out.[30] Blackwood did not think she had tried hard enough. After receiving an instalment of *The Perpetual Curate*, he wrote, 'Observe the repetition of your favourite words, "perplexed", "troubled", "little", "poor" . . . and *strike* them out as often as you can.'[31] It seems possible that the title of the 1883 *Maga* article about her work, 'A Little Chat about Mrs Oliphant' concealed an affectionate joke, rather than being offensively patronizing. The writer referred to the 'air of almost garrulous ease about her best work', noting that she did not trouble like Matthew Arnold or Thackeray to polish her periods, but went on to remark that, 'like Scott', the novelist so long acknowledged as without peer in the nineteenth century, she had 'something better than style'.[32] It was this 'something' that fascinated many of her obituarists writing in the more literary journals. As Stephen Gwyn of the *Edinburgh Review* expressed it,

As for her style, it certainly does not conform to the prevailing standards. It does not keep one on the stretch with continual expectation of the unexpected word: it is never contorted or tormented, never emphatic, never affected. The words flow simply and smoothly, like the utterance of a perfectly well-bred woman.

Then, perhaps aware of the note of condescension that had crept in, he tried to capture the flavour of her syntax, which had 'always . . . a certain looseness of texture', and yet never lost control of its long sentences. Speaking of *Miss Marjoribanks*, he also commended 'the neatly turned sentences which round off each chapter clearly, as if with the crack of a whip'.[33]

This chapter contains two quite lengthy quotations, chosen for other reasons than the stylistic, which, nevertheless, serve quite well to show something of her manner. The first on p. 289, takes the occasion of introducing a minor character, Mrs Everard, for launching into a disquisition on widowhood. Its tone is conversational: the narrator appears parenthetically, ostensibly admitting a degree of ignorance, while actually introducing a hint of worldly experience. The passage builds upon repetition and qualification, in a way that contrives to suggest an intimate, spoken aside to 'the gentle reader', but the sentences themselves display a far more certain sense of balance than they would normally enjoy in spoken discourse. The long, convoluted sentence beginning 'Life *à deux*' is carefully hedged about with three short emphatic sentences, all of which make much the same point, though the third ('That curious mingling . . .') serves to advance the argument by introducing the notion of role and gender. The long, intervening sentence, that manages to take us from the single life, through marriage, to a recognition of a new quality of singleness, offers us perches from which to recover our balance, before taking flight again, but avoids the monotony of mere repetition. The second use of 'original', earlier defined as a synonym for 'primitive', reminds us that we are being returned to a contemplation of 'single life', but one that has been dislocated from its previous semantic partner. By the end of the sentence we are brought to 'standing ground', while simultaneously having that security denied. The next two sentences clearly signal their related positions in the argument as a whole by locating their subjects firmly at the beginning of the sentence, before embarking upon more complicated syntactical games. Men's moral inferiority is underlined by means of twice repeating the allegation that remarriage is tantamount to a denial of duty, which then becomes women's 'burden'. The final sentence begins well, with a nicely graduated decline and fall achieved by depriving the key word 'fail' of the qualifier the previous parallel phrase enjoyed; the afterthought ('but so does . . .') perhaps shows something of the naïve charm, verging on clumsiness, of a conversational style attempting to wrench the tone back from elegiac reverie to the exigencies of the particular occasion for this digression.

So little manuscript material remains that it is difficult to get a clear picture of Mrs Oliphant's proof revision procedures: the speed of their turnaround would suggest, however, that she had no time for polishing the individual sentence. Although one might allow for the lassitude of her final year, this response to William Blackwood's request for the tidying of a manuscript was not atypical: 'As for the mingling of *I* and *me* in the narrative: I see no objection to retaining it as it is natural to me to use the pronouns indifferently and would be troublesome and unnecessary to change.'[34]

The second lengthy passage quoted (pp. 296–7) demonstrates her ability to use dialogue imaginatively. It was no less true in her fiction than in her everyday life that she had the gift 'of making people talk': 'like the art of driving a hoop . . . I give a little touch now and then, and my victim rolls on and on.'[35] Squire Wentworth is neither an important figure in the plot, nor an intrinsically interesting character, yet his almost uninterrupted monologue manages to convey the calibre of the man, ponderous, well-meaning, and insensitive. Like Jane Austen, Mrs Oliphant had learned that bores are best left to convey their weakness directly to the reader. Though the mode of his speech to Frank is described as meditative, his thought processes, nudged slowly forward by repetition and digression, are not. And yet these characteristics are swiftly and economically established. Although the Squire talks to no purpose in terms of the particular problem he is addressing, the reader is not left to flounder amongst a heap of irrelevancies and meaningless platitudes. As in her use of dialect, Mrs Oliphant soon discovered that the secret of verisimilitude lay not in reproducing obscure vocabulary, but in using the occasional appropriate idiom and catching the particular rhythm of sentence construction. The

Squire provides an exemplary illustration of the rule that Mrs Oliphant herself expounded in her article 'Success in Fiction', where she said that dialogue should be 'an ideal representation of what people in certain circumstances would be likely to say, leaving out the repetition, the pointless remarks, the meaningless digressions with which most of us actually dilute our conversation'.[36] Moreover, the flexibility of her impersonal narrator's medium, varying, as Gwyn put it, from 'the utterance of a perfectly well-bred woman' to the whiplash crack of a well-turned epigram, was particularly adept at gliding smoothly from a character's questions or self-communings, to the observations of a sharper, overarching intelligence. The habit of using an ironically distanced narrator could be put to good effect in passages such as this where the individual characters are so self-absorbed that we might become uncomfortably conscious of their conversational partners as frozen into a series of Browningesque 'listeners'. Sometimes her characters are inarticulate, or reluctant to commit themselves for fear of being misunderstood, and on these occasions her power to weave back and forth between the inconsequential surface of their conversation and the thread of their inner thoughts bears comparison with such famous scenes as Virginia Woolf's Mr and Mrs Ramsay discussing whether the stocking she is knitting will be finished in time to take to the lighthouse.

It is perhaps in her use of imagery that Mrs Oliphant is most markedly in the female tradition. Although the mock-heroic metaphors that pervade *Miss Marjoribanks* show her to have been capable of the consistent application and development of a particular trope, this is not her most characteristic mode. More frequently everyday objects and pastimes become briefly invested with a significance that transcends their literal status. This happens in much the same way that Mrs Ramsay's knitting vouches for the insistent practicality of the bounty she bestows upon all with whom she is connected, measures time passing, and can be used to convey her emotional response to the conversation flowing around her, yet obstinately refuses symbolic status. *The Perpetual Curate* supplies several examples of this process at work. Mrs Morgan, the rector of Carlingford's wife, finds that her dissatisfaction with the marriage that she and her husband have so long and so prudently deferred becomes, albeit unconsciously, almost entirely expressed in a series of trivial domestic preoccupations. The large floral pattern of the drawing-room carpet, left by a predecessor, serves as a constant reminder of the continued need for irksome frugality; her husband's tolerance of the curate's intrusions when he realizes a particular pudding is in the offing, speaks of that male collegiate world that takes servants and women for granted, and from which it is her business to wean her husband; her endless replanning of the garden and her obsessive tending of her favourite 'maidenhair fern' suggest a woman desperate to enjoy the fruits of an establishment of her own, together with her habit of resorting to memories of her single life to comfort herself for the disappointments of the married state. Mrs Morgan's expression of her anxieties and ambitions through the daily routine of managing her household is replicated time and again in Mrs Oliphant's fiction, where the pleasures and responsibilities of furnishing a house enjoy both actual and metaphorical significance for women. By such means as buying a new carpet, or repapering a room, women demonstrate their power to impose their will, and show the extent to which all but the most independent were hedged about, even in this confined sphere of operations, by the capacity or desire of their menfolk to provide the wherewithal to realize their dreams.

The psychological habit of investing objects with emotional significance is not limited to women. Gerald Wentworth, the apostate clergyman of the same novel, finds that inner struggles have become 'twined in the most inextricable way' into the form of the majestic cedar tree outside his library window. The cedar's solid shadow, untroubled by any passing breeze, recalls his ever-present trouble and reminds him that he stands to lose all that is most familiar to him. Its very passive immobility serves to reveal the intensity of inarticulate need that leads even men and women surrounded by loving families to the desperate, and to an extent risible, device of using objects as recipients and expressions of their innermost emotions.[37]

Besides the homes and feminine activities, such as sewing, discussed elsewhere in this book, two other facets of daily life seem, in Mrs Oliphant's fiction, to be capable of carrying a significance beyond the merely practical: food and dress. The capacity to provide good food for one's family or guests demonstrated, in measurable form, a woman's quality as a carer, and her wider abilities as a woman capable of organizing a household. The grandeur of Lucilla Marjoribanks' first victory is demonstrated by the manner in which she outflanks her father's housekeeper, not by imposing her own recipes, but by occupying the higher moral ground. Cutlets, gravy-beef, and the accuracy of the household accounts are as nothing in comparison to the underlying purpose they serve:

'Now we are two women to manage everything, we ought to do still better. I have two or three things in my head that I will tell you after; but in the meantime I want you to know that the object of my life is to be a comfort to my poor papa; and now let us think what we had better have for dinner', said the new sovereign.[38]

A late tale, 'Who Was Lost and Is Found', presents, as its title suggests, a muted retelling of the tale of the Prodigal Son, seen from the mother's point of view. The killing of the fatted calf, which celebrated the repentant homecoming, is here rewritten as a series of daily meals by which this anxious mother can judge her son's mood. She learns to take pleasure from the occasions when, despite his continual drinking and smoking, her son is capable of consuming the enormous meals she lays before him: 'It is a kind of certificate of morality which many a poor woman has hailed with delight.'[39] The pathos of this remark lies not only in the recognition that the mother is forced to use such trivial methods of assessing her own 'morality' as well as that of her son but in its patent reference to Mrs Oliphant's anxious supervision of her grown sons' meals. Her earliest memory of maternal love featured just such a scene of her own mother, 'who never seemed to sit down in the strange, little, warm bright picture, but to hover about the table pouring out tea, supplying everything he wanted to her boy (how proud, how fond of him!—her eyes liquid and bright with love as she hovered about)'.[40] The arbitrary particularity with which, in her *Autobiography*, Mrs Oliphant recalls the menus of meals she had provided did not spring from their being grand set-pieces, but because they were recollected in loving detail as examples of her ability to provide in maternal fashion for her party when travelling, or to create happy, informal supper parties for the young. By contrast, to the end of her life Mrs Oliphant remembered 'with a shudder a certain dish of chicken cutlets intended to be particularly delicate and dainty' that she had prepared for a dinner party with her own hands, the cook being indisposed, at the start of her association with the Blackwood family.[41] Even when her income enabled her to employ adequate domestic help, she still imaged her role as provider and carer in terms of the practical expression of domestic love. The phrase she chose, 'the boiling of the daily pot', has most often been read as a straightforward admission that she wrote 'pot-boilers', but far more illuminating is the way in which she recaptured the phrase from the language of cliché to reinvest her writing with the trappings of maternal solicitude: 'it was good to have kept the pot boiling and maintained the cheerful household fire, though it is smouldering out in darkness now.'[42]

Food might be the most basic commodity through which to express female values, but clothing ran it a close second. Again, childhood memories of her mother played their part:

My clothes were all made by her tender hands, finer and more beautifully worked than ever child's clothes were; my under garments fine linen and trimmed with little delicate laces, to the end that there might be nothing coarse, nothing less than exquisite, about me; that I might grow up with all the delicacies of a woman's ideal child.[43]

One of the Tulloch boys claimed in his obituary that 'She wished every girl about her to be dressed as nicely as possible', and 'never thought money was thrown away on dress'.[44] She was sufficiently interested in 'dress' to contribute a book on the subject to Macmillans' Art in the Home series and to welcome the proliferation of women's fashion magazines at the end of the century.[45] The book remains of more than period interest because she sees dress as more than either merely functional or wholly superficial adornment. Carlyle's *Sartor Resartus* had alerted her to the subject's metaphorical application, but whereas Carlyle had used clothes as a means of investigating his philosophy of life, Mrs Oliphant used them as a mode of discussing art. The following passage, discussing the rules of good dress sense, could have served equally well as a guide to her position as literary critic:

Reformation without revolution, reasonable conservatism without obstinacy, a certain reserve in respect to the new, a certain reverence for the old, combined with candour and generous appreciation of what is best in both, form the ideal temper . . .[46]

She develops the subject's moral aspect and its gender implications, dismissing those who would see it as vanity and rebutting those who see it as trivial and therefore an exclusively feminine preoccupation. Critical attention to the changing conventions of fashion is recommended, rather than slavish pursuit or arrogant dismissal. In her fiction this area of a woman's life receives attention because it shows up so clearly the strait-jacket of convention from which women sometimes yearn to escape, tempered by the realization that, like most conventions, the rituals of dress have their use, not merely to provide a social grammar but to give disciplined expression to intense emotions. Many of her fictional families find themselves simultaneously irritated and soothed by the incongruous juxtaposition of the grave and the trivial brought about by the effort to assemble mourning clothes. As a writer she was fascinated by the contrast between the intransigent materialism of clothes themselves and the subtle gradations of inner feelings they could disguise or reveal. Those novels, such as *At His Gates*, *Hester*, and *Kirsteen*, where money and integrity of character are drawn into a complex web of relationship, also make notable use of dress as a mirror for this curious matrix. Other values often lurked behind the simple figures of a cash transaction, as they might in the decision of what to wear. A woman could manage to subvert her husband's vulgar intention of displaying her as a clothes-horse tribute to his own earning power, by privately regarding the very frequency with which she sports these trophies as a sign of her contempt for them. 'Dressing down', on the other hand, could express sulky aggression, or an act of kindly condescension.[47]

Mrs Oliphant's use of metaphor is less dramatically signposted than it is in the writings of a Charlotte Brontë or a George Eliot, but it is none the less certainly part of that female tradition of quasi-metaphorical writing which, drawing upon women's intimacy with the deepest emotions and the daily drudge of household responsibilities, was able to establish in domestic fiction a path back and forth between the two by using familiar objects as both material setting and emotional reference points. In Mrs Oliphant's case the use of material objects provides one other dimension to her writing: their very solidity serves as an ironic contrast with the sense of life's arbitrariness, and its potential at any given moment for tragic or comic development. Her account of the time when she heard of the first ominous signs of her husband's fatal disease offers a fine illustration.

In the early summer one evening after dinner (we dined, I think, at half-past six in those days) I went out to buy some dessert-knives on which I had set my heart—they were only plated, but I had long wanted them, and by some chance was able to give myself that gratification. I had marked them in a shop not far off, and was pleased to get them, and specially happy. Some one had dined with us, either Sebastian Evans or my brother-in-law Tom,—some one familiar and intimate who was with Frank. When I came back again there was a little agitation, a slight commotion which I could not understand; and then I was told that it was nothing—the merest slight matter, nothing to be frightened at. Frank had, in coughing, brought up a little blood.

The dessert-knives and the dinner hour provide that sense of the commonplace necessary to domestic realism's verisimilitude; their very ordinariness is then used as a reliable marker in the shifting fragments of experience and sensation that make up human life. The dessert-knives remain sharply etched while the people involved in the episode have sunk into shadowy oblivion. This episode, constituting another of those 'turning-points' by which she marked her life, provides a convenient halting place in the process of making the case for Mrs Oliphant as 'worth reading'. It offers evidence of an artistry, so 'natural' as to be overlooked, in the ease with which she brings us from the loose, conversational structure of that long opening sentence to the carefully controlled *frisson* in which the passage finds its temporary resting-place. The shaping and selective powers that separate art from reportage are there in the initial decision to feature the dessert-knives, the careful isolation of the reader's naïve expectation of happiness from the narrator's tragic hindsight, and finally in the writer's ability to preside over and maintain a distance from the figures within her tale, so that the drama of the particular moment is uncontaminated by sympathetic identification. This small vignette constitutes a compelling example of the experimental egos with which the autobiographer and novelist plays, and of Mrs Oliphant's professionally astute recognition that her *métier* lay in exploiting a woman's sense of the artificiality of all attempts to draw boundaries between the life and the writing, between experience and its various representational forms. Perhaps the chief reason that she was to remain such a baffling enigma to Henry James was his conviction that he had always, unlike her, striven to ensure that his fiction should 'be in some direct relation to life'.[48]

It is, however, with the immediately preceding passage from her *Autobiography* that I should like to end my study; for in it I think we catch a glimpse of that process by which the life became transmuted into the characteristic modes of her fiction. From the 'common and homely origins', apparently containing nothing of note, and in the interstices of her roles as mother and writer, came those moments of 'fantasticating' where she saw the silhouetted figures that were her various selves— now 'eight-and-twenty, going down stairs as light as a feather', now an elderly, rheumaticky widow—so separated by 'the salt and bitter waves' of experience that only the imagination could give them the transient illusion of unity. In such a passage we see how she became 'a fiction to herself'.

When I look back on my life, among the happy moments which I can recollect is one which is so curiously common and homely, with nothing in it, that it is strange even to record such a recollection, and yet it embodied more happiness to me than almost any real occasion as might be supposed for happiness. It was the moment after dinner when I used to run upstairs to see that all was well in the nursery, and then to turn into my room on my way down again to wash my hands, as I had a way of doing before I took up my evening work, which was generally needlework, something to make for the children. My bedroom had three windows in it, one looking out upon the gardens I have mentioned, the other two into the road. It was light enough with the lamplight outside for all I wanted. I can see it now, the glimmer of the outside lights, the room dark, the faint reflection in the glasses, and my heart full of joy and peace—for what?—for nothing—that there was no harm anywhere, the children well above stairs and their father below. I had few of the pleasures of society, no gaiety at all. I was eight-and-twenty, going down-stairs as light as a feather, to the little frock I was making. My husband also gone back for an hour or two after dinner to his work, and well—and the bairns well. I can feel now the sensation of that sweet calm and ease and peace.[49]

Notes

Place of publication is London, unless otherwise stated. Since there is no collected or authoritative edition of Mrs Oliphant's works, and her works survive in motley form, I have supplied chapter rather than page references for the novels. Dates for Mrs Oliphant's published works have not been given in the notes but can be found by referring to the list in the Select Bibliography.

LIST OF ABBREVIATIONS USED IN THE NOTES

A&L   *Autobiography and Letters of Mrs Margaret Oliphant*, ed. Mrs Harry Coghill (Edinburgh and London, 1899; reprinted with an introduction by Q. D. Leavis, Leicester, 1974)

Annals   M. O. W. Oliphant, *Annals of a Publishing House: William Blackwood and His Sons: Their Magazine and Friends* (2 vols., 1897; the first volume was proofread by the author before her death, the second by William Blackwood). Volume iii, *The Life of John Blackwood* (1898), is by Mrs Gerald Porter, John Blackwood's daughter

BL   British Library
Blackwood's   *Blackwood's Edinburgh Magazine*
Blackwood MS   Mrs Oliphant's letters to the Blackwoods, lodged in the National Library of Scotland. Unless otherwise stated, all letters indicated under this heading are to John Blackwood, until his death on 29 Oct. 1879. Thereafter they are to his nephew, William Blackwood

JAL   *The Autobiography of Margaret Oliphant: The Complete Text*, ed. Elisabeth Jay (Oxford and New York, 1990)

Macmillan MS   Mrs Oliphant's letters to Macmillan, lodged in the BL Macmillan Archive 54919

MOWO   Margaret Oliphant Wilson Oliphant
NLS   National Library of Scotland
Williams   Merryn Williams, *Margaret Oliphant: A Critical Biography* (1986)

PREFACE

1. *A&L* 186–7. Also 'Edward Irving', *Reminiscences*, ed. J. A. Froude (2 vols., 1881), i. 334–5.
2. *A&L* 389.
3. Mrs Oliphant spoke of Darwin as 'a reader of whom one was so much inclined to boast'. 'A Preface: On the Ebb-Tide', *The Ways of Life*, 15. Darwin's son's claim would seem to offer support: 'He did not often read out-of-the-way books, but generally kept to the books of the day obtained from a circulating library.' *Charles Darwin: His Life*

Told in an Autobiographical Chapter, and in a series of his published letters, ed. F. Darwin (1892), 77.

4. Ibid. 50. Mrs Oliphant was sufficiently struck by his attitude to mention it twice in *Blackwood's*: Apr. 1895, p. 630; Oct. 1896, p. 562.

5. H. Tennyson, *Alfred Lord Tennyson: A Memoir* (2 vols., 1897), ii. 372.

6. Letter quoted in Williams, 119.

7. J. M. Barrie gave the address when on 16 July 1908 a plaque was unveiled in St Giles' Cathedral, Edinburgh.

8. Introduction to *A&L* 9.

9. *Virginia Woolf and the Madness of Language*, trans. G. Bennington and R. Bowlby (1990), 150.

10. *The Athelings, or, The Three Gifts*, ch. 103.

11. *Blackwood's* (June 1888), 841–3; (Sept. 1884), 296; (Sept. 1888), 423.

12. Toril Moi, for instance, has found fault with the form of feminist criticism practised by Elaine Showalter on the assumption that women's writing in the realist tradition attracts her because of its strong projection of a unitary self, offering autobiographical authority to the text it constructs and banishing 'from itself all conflict, contradiction and ambiguity'. *Sexual/Textual Politics: Feminist Literary Theory* (1985), 4–8.

13. *JAL* 14, 17.

14. *May*, ch. 43.

15. *JAL* 118.

16. *JAL* 39.

CHAPTER 1: RELATING THE LIFE

1. A. Cross, *A Trap for Fools* (1989), ch. 10.

2. Unless otherwise signalled, the information in the following section, and the autobiographical quotations in this chapter, are taken from *JAL*.

3. C. Dickens to Miss Coutts, 4 Feb. 1850 (*The Letters of Charles Dickens*, ed. G. Storey, K. Tillotson, and N. Burgis (6 vols., 1965–88), vi. 28); C. Brontë to Ellen Nussey, Dec. 1851 (*The Brontës: Their Lives, Friendship, and Correspondence*, ed. T. J. Wise and J. A. Symington (4 vols., 1932), iii. 299.

4. Willie's troubled sojourn at Etal is anecdotally recounted in G. McGuffie, *The Priests of Etal; or, Annals of Tillside* (4th edn. Edinburgh, 1904), ch. 11.

5. Quoted in Williams, 16.

6. The evidence for the authorship of these novels is presented in J. S. Clarke, 'Mrs Oliphant's Unacknowledged Social Novels', *Notes and Queries* (Oct. 1981), 408–13.

7. Blackwood MS 4111, 8 Mar. 1855.

8. Blackwood MS 4106, 28 Mar. 1854.

9. *Annals*, ii. 475.

10. *Autobiographical Notes of the Life of William Bell Scott: And Notices of his Artistic and Poetic Circle of Friends 1830–1882*, ed. W. Minto (2 vols., 1892), i, ch. 15.

11. Quoted by Peter Cunningham, 'William Dyce, RA and the High Church Movement', MA thesis (East Anglia, 1972), 43.

12. F. W. Oliphant, *A Plea for Painted Glass: Being an Inquiry into its Nature, Character, and Objects and its Claims as an Art* (Oxford, 1855).

13. E. and C. S. Story, *Memoir of Robert Herbert Story, by his Daughters* (Glasgow, 1909), 288.

14. For Mrs Story's account of their acquaintance see *Later Reminiscences* (Glasgow, 1913), 47–53. In 1921 Denny wrote to Mr Grant, then minister of Rosneath, protesting against his plans to move Maggie's memorial window so as to make way for a war memorial window, financed by Princess Louise, regretting 'the complete overthrow of former standards and the merging of all personal feeling in that of the whole'. NLS 23204, 18 Jan. 1921.

15. Blackwood MS 4621, 7 Dec. 1894.

16. *A&L* 197–8.

17. 'It is our own strong conviction, matured by much study and experience, that there are no really *nice* people in the world who do not love dogs.' *Blackwood's* (Nov. 1889), 708.

18. Blackwood MS 4364, 28 Mar. 1877.

19. See her Preface to *Memoir of the Life of Laurence Oliphant*, i, p. vi: 'I have one other acknowledgement to make, which in happier circumstances would have been said only to the private ear of him to whom it is due. A great part of the letters quoted here were selected, arranged, and connected for me by my dear son, Cyril Francis Oliphant.'

20. *Blackwood's* (July 1890), 1–18. *Memoir of Laurence Oliphant*, ii. 249–51.

21. NLS 23195, 12 Jan. 1893.

22. NLS 23196, 16 Aug. 1894.

23. Blackwood MS 4664, 26 June 1897.

24. *Blackwood's* (Jan. 1896), 1–30.

25. Blackwood MS 4664, 19, 25 Mar., 7 May 1897.

26. Blackwood MS 4664, 16 June 1897.

27. *A&L* 438–40.

28. Henry James wrote her obituary for *London Notes*, Aug. 1897. This is reprinted in *Notes on Novelists* (1914), 357–60.

29. *Queen Victoria: A Personal Sketch*, 114.

30. *The Autobiography of Isaac Williams*, ed. G. Prevost (1892), p. vii.

31. [John Skelton], *Blackwood's* (Jan. 1883), 73–91.

32. *Blackwood's* (Jan.), 1–30; (Mar.), 385–410; (May), 617–39; (Aug.), 229–47; (Dec. 1881), 516–41; (July 1882), 79–101; (Apr. 1883), 485–511.

33. *JAL*, pp. vii–xvii.

34. *A&L*, p. x.

35. Probably the friend to whom H. O. Sturgis referred as 'a clever agreeable woman, who took her full share in all the innocent enjoyments Mrs Oliphant loved to plan, but who was always big with sighs over her own departed happiness, and the cruelty with which the world had used her'. 'A Sketch from Memory', *Temple Bar* (Oct. 1899), 233–48. The identification cannot be certain because Christina Rogerson and Fanny Tulloch are almost equally plausible candidates.

36. *A&L*, p. viii.

37. Macmillan MS.

38. *Blackwood's* (Dec. 1881), 517.

39. *Blackwood's* (Jan. 1881), 2.

40. *Edinburgh Review* (Apr. 1885), 552.

41. *Blackwood's* (Sept. 1880), 32.

42. See G. Bachelard, *The Poetics of Space*, trans. M. Jolas (Boston, 1969): a work of 'topoanalysis', or 'the systematic psychological study of the sites of our intimate loves'.
43. *Haps and Mishaps of a Tour in Europe* (1854), 57–8.
44. *Effie Ogilvie: The Story of a Young Life*, ch. 6.
45. Blackwood MS 4323, 24 July 1874.
46. NLS MS 23195, MOWO to Cecco, 10 Jan. 1893.
47. NLS MS 23194, 6 Aug. n.d.
48. *Notes on Novelists*, 358.
49. The matter is discussed at length in J. S. Clarke, 'The "Rival Novelist"—Hardy and Mrs Oliphant', *The Thomas Hardy Journal* (Oct. 1989), 51–61.
50. Blackwood MS 4323, 24 July 1874.
51. *Blackwood's* (Feb. 1868), 195–221.
52. As suggested by S. M. Gilbert and S. Gubar, 'Tradition and the Female Talent', in N. K. Miller (ed.), *The Poetics of Gender* (New York, 1986), 183–207.
53. Both 'The Private Life' (1892) and 'Greville Fane' (1892) are reprinted in *The Complete Tales of Henry James* (1963), 189–228, 433–52.
54. See L. Edel, *Henry James: The Treacherous Years, 1895–1901* (1969), 233.
55. The remark was made by Sir George Douglas, as quoted in J. S. Clarke, *The Thomas Hardy Journal* (Oct. 1989), 51–61.
56. A. I. Ritchie, *From the Porch* (1913), 25.
57. Introductory Note to *A Widow's Tale*, p. v.
58. *Later Reminiscences*, 48.
59. NLS MS, 1 Jan. 1893.
60. *Notes on Novelists*, 360.
61. Ritchie, *From the Porch*, 25.
62. W. W. Tulloch, *The Bookman* (Aug. 1897), 114.
63. A. C. Benson, *Memories and Friends* (1924), 79.
64. e.g. in 1877, recognizing that Principal Tulloch 'is not (entre nous) the active kind of father who pushes on his family', Mrs Oliphant was agitating on behalf of one of the Tulloch brothers who had confided his discontent with his lowly office job to his sister, Sarah Tarver. Macmillan MS, 2 Feb. 1877. She was even prepared to see what she could do trying to gain a Nautical Surveyorship for one of his younger brothers. BL Add. MS 42576, MOWO to J. Bryce, 20 June 1894.
65. NLS MS 23194, 26 Nov. 1878.
66. Letters to Blackwood, dated 8, 13, 15, 24 Mar. 1886, all refer to her careful handling of negotiations with the Queen, who was in residence at Windsor and agreed a Privy Purse and Civil List pension for the space of Mrs Tulloch's lifetime. 'In short my maids are getting quite used to the sight of the orderly.' NLS MS 23194.
67. NLS MS 23198, MOWO to Madge, 19 Nov. 1895.
68. Benson, *Memories and Friends*, 79.
69. Ibid. 81.
70. *Church Quarterly Review* (Oct. 1899), 143.
71. NLS MS 23196, 29 Sept. 1893.
72. NLS MS 23195, Saturday, Jan. 1893, from Coghurst, n.d.
73. NLS MS23196, MOWO to Denny, 8 Oct. 1893.
74. NLS MS 23195, 4 Jan. 1893.

75. NLS MS 23196, 27 Mar. 1892, 24 Feb. 1896.
76. NLS MS 23196, 8 Oct. 1893.
77. NLS MS 23196, MOWO to Denny, 8 Oct. 1893; MOWO to Madge, 30 Mar. 1894.
78. NLS MS 23196, MOWO to Madge, 31 Oct. 1895.
79. NLS MS 23196, 7 Apr. 1895.
80. See 'An Anxious Moment', *The New Amphion: Being the Book of the Edinburgh University Union Fancy Fair* (1886), 39–99.
81. For the following account of the Ward family I am indebted to J. A. Sutherland, *Mrs Humphry Ward: Eminent Victorian, Pre-Eminent Edwardian* (1990).

CHAPTER 2: WOMEN'S SPHERE

1. M. O. W. Oliphant, *Young Musgrave*, ch. 6.
2. Reprinted in R. Strachey, *The Cause: A Short History of the Women's Movement in Great Britain* (1928; repr. 1974), 395–418.
3. See above, ch. 1 n. 48.
4. *Blackwood's* (Apr. 1856), 379–87; and Blackwood MS 4111, 1855 n.d, and *Annals*, iii. 164.
5. MOWO with F. R. Oliphant, *The Victorian Age of Literature*, i, ch. 6; ii, ch. 5.
6. Z. Austen, 'Why Feminist Critics are Angry with George Eliot', *College English*, 37 (1976), 549–61.
7. *JAL* 19–20, 25–6; and *St James's Gazette* (11 Jan. 1888), 5–6.
8. *Blackwood's* (Apr. 1856), 379–87.
9. *A&L* 211; *Blackwood's* (Aug. 1866), 367–79.
10. *Edinburgh Review* (Oct. 1869), 572–602.
11. *Fraser's Magazine* (May 1880), 698–710.
12. *Edinburgh Review* (Oct. 1869), 572–602.
13. *Blackwood's* (Aug. 1889), 258.
14. *Edinburgh Review* (Oct. 1869), 95, 586.
15. Their comparative lack of formal training worries all the women artists who work for a living in her novels: see *The Quiet Heart, Zaidee*, and *The Three Brothers*.
16. Quoted in Williams, 172.
17. *Miss Marjoribanks*, chs. 11, 17, 26, 35.
18. *JAL* 132.
19. Williams, 172.
20. First published in *Cornhill Magazine*, Nov. and Dec. 1880; collected in *Neighbours on the Green*.
21. *Blackwood's* (Feb. 1879), 206–24.
22. *The Athelings*, ch. 86.
23. *Within the Precincts*, ch. 32.
24. Ibid., ch. 34.
25. *Daniel Deronda* (1876), ch. 51.
26. *Blackwood's* (Dec. 1889), 869.
27. e.g. *St James's Gazette* (23 Apr. 1888), 5–6.
28. *Edinburgh Review* (Oct. 1869), 572–602; *Fraser's Magazine* (May 1880), 698–710.
29. *Sir Tom*, ch. 25.

30. *The Railwayman and His Children*, chs. 38, 47.
31. *The Marriage of Elinor*, ch. 33.
32. Ibid., ch. 35.
33. *Merkland*, ch. 15.
34. *St James's Gazette* (23 Apr. 1888), 5–6.
35. Ibid.
36. NLS MS 23196.
37. *Orphans: A Chapter in a Life*, chs. 6, 19.
38. *JAL* 25.
39. *Christian Melville*, ch. 7.
40. *JAL* 8.
41. *Blackwood's* (May 1855), 554–68.
42. *Janet*, ch. 11.
43. The following novels and short stories contain comments on the role of the governess: *Adam Graeme of Mossgray, Zaidee, Orphans, Lucy Crofton, Miss Marjoribanks, Cousin Mary, The Prodigals and their Inheritance, The Two Marys*, 'Mademoiselle', 'The Story of a Wedding Tour' (in *A Widow's Tale and Other Stories*).
44. *Janet*, ch. 21.
45. *The Victorian Age of Literature*, i, ch. 6.
46. *Janet*, ch. 45.
47. Ibid., ch. 47, and *Blackwood's* (Sept. 1888), 441–3.
48. C. Brontë, *Jane Eyre* (1847), ch. 15.
49. NLS MS 23196, MOWO to Denny, 23 Oct. 1895.
50. *Blackwood's* (Sept. 1888), 443.
51. See above, ch. 1, n. 6.
52. *The Last of the Mortimers*, ch. 19.
53. *JAL* 132.
54. *Innocent*, ch. 28.
55. *Blackwood's* (Mar. 1870), 294.
56. *Hester*, ch. 45.
57. *Orphans*, ch. 6.
58. *Joyce*, ch. 14.
59. Ibid., chs. 41 and 42.
60. Cf. MOWO's state of mind on Christmas night 1887, the year in which she wrote this novel: 'I don't know how to stop, to change, to make another way of living, everything is so perplexed and hard . . . there are all the helpless young people, boys who ought to be earning their own living, girls who can't, but would somehow if I was out of the way, servants, dependants—all accustomed to have anything that is wanted and only me to supply all, and I will be sixty in a few months . . . What a situation to contemplate if one did face it fairly.' *JAL* 155.
61. *JAL* 145–6.
62. *Kirsteen*, ch. 5.
63. Ibid., ch. 18.
64. Ibid., ch. 40.
65. Ibid., ch. 23.
66. Ibid., ch. 46.
67. William Wordsworth, 'Lines composed a few miles above Tintern Abbey', lines 33–5.

68. *Kirsteen*, ch. 46.
69. *Old Mr Tredgold*, ch. 9.
70. *JAL* 150.
71. *The Melvilles*, ch. 5.
72. *Sir Robert's Fortune*, ch. 7.
73. *Hester*, ch. 36.
74. *The Prodigals and their Inheritance*, chs. 2, 6, 9, and 15.
75. Strachey, *The Cause*, 395–18.
76. *Fraser's Magazine* (May 1880), 698–710.
77. MOWO frequently drew upon this biblical narrative, which has continued to provide a serviceable source for feminist commentary: e.g. A. Loades, *Searching for Lost Coins: Explorations in Christianity and Feminism* (1987), 61–77.
78. *Innocent*, ch. 16.
79. *Passages in the Life of Margaret Maitland*, ch. 3; *Blackwood's* (Feb. 1858), 139–54.
80. *Phoebe Junior, A Last Chronicle of Carlingford*, for instance, makes unabashed use of the incident of a clergyman being in possession of a stolen or forged cheque central to A. Trollope's *The Last Chronicle of Barset* (1867), and Parson May and his family owe their names and some of their circumstances to C. M. Yonge's central family in *The Daisy Chain* (1856). The names, Lucilla and Phoebe, also appear in conjunction in another of C. M. Yonge's novels, significantly named *Hopes and Fears: Or Scenes from The Life of a Spinster* (1860).
81. *Miss Marjoribanks*, chs. 1, 40.
82. Ibid., chs. 7, 26, 37.
83. Ibid., ch. 42.
84. *A&L* 204–5.
85. *Blackwood's* (May 1870), 629; (Apr. 1871), 458–60.
86. *Phoebe Junior*, ch. 13.
87. *Miss Marjoribanks*, ch. 1, and *Phoebe Junior*, ch. 3.
88. *Phoebe Junior*, ch. 5.
89. Ibid., ch. 4.
90. Ibid., chs. 4, 45.
91. Ibid., ch. 37.
92. Ibid., chs. 37, 45.

CHAPTER 3: A WOMAN IN A MAN'S WORLD

1. *The Son of His Father*, ch. 7.
2. *JAL* 93.
3. NLS MS 23194, Robert Macpherson to MOWO, 26 Apr. 1868.
4. *Daily Chronicle* (28 June 1897).
5. *Blackwood's* (Jan. 1855), 94–6.
6. *The Marriage of Elinor*, ch. 1.
7. *Westminster Review* (Oct. 1856), 442–61; (Oct. 1854), 448–73.
8. M. Jacobus, *Reading Women: Essays in Feminist Criticism* (1986), 254.
9. *Westminster Review* (Oct. 1854), 448–9.
10. *A&L* 167.

11. *A&L* 160.
12. *JAL* 36.
13. *Annals*, iii. 73.
14. *JAL* 41–2.
15. *St James's Gazette* (25 July 1888), 6; (28 July 1888), 5–6.
16. Blackwood MS 4119, 1856 n.d.
17. *Annals*, i. 128.
18. Blackwood MS 4349, 1876 n.d.
19. Blackwood MS 4111, 1855 n.d.
20. *A&L* 171.
21. *Blackwood's* (May 1875), 633.
22. *Blackwood's* (June 1887), 745.
23. *Blackwood's* (May 1855), 558.
24. P. Nestor, *Female Friendship and Communities* (Oxford, 1985), 25, 30.
25. *Blackwood's* (Sept. 1874), 378.
26. *Blackwood's* (May 1855).
27. Blackwood MS 4364, 9 July 1877.
28. *Blackwood's* (Dec. 1886), 798.
29. *A&L* 221.
30. *Blackwood's* (Mar. 1869), 252–76.
31. *Whiteladies*, ch. 25.
32. *Blackwood's* (Apr. 1856), 379–87.
33. *Annals*, iii. 183–4
34. *Blackwood's* (Dec. 1872), 746–65; *A&L* 241.
35. *St James's Gazette* (9 May 1988), 5–6.
36. 'A Preface: On the Ebb Tide', *The Ways of Life* (1897), 1–20.
37. *Blackwood's* (Jan. 1887), 126–53.
38. *Blackwood's* (Nov. 1889), 696.
39. *JAL* 10.
40. Mrs Oliphant thoroughly endorsed this 'delicious' view of the advantage of polygamy to women expressed by Lady Ashburton. *Blackwood's* (Sept. 1873), 389.
41. *Daily News* (28 June 1897), 8.
42. NLS MS 23193, MOWO to Blackwood, n.d., encloses a letter from G. Eliot to Blackwood, dated 1 Apr. 1858, which MOWO had presumably found while combing through the firm's correspondence for the *Annals*. This letter, containing the 'more elegant rendering' of the reply John Blackwood himself used to choke off unwanted contributors, is recorded as lost in *The George Eliot Letters*, ed. G. S. Haight (9 vols., New Haven, Conn., 1954–6, 1978), ii. 447.
43. *Blackwood's* (May 1855), 554–68; (Sept. 1867), 257–80.
44. *The Literary History of England in the End of the Eighteenth and the Beginning of the Nineteenth Century* (3 vols., 1882), ii. 252.
45. *Blackwood's* (Sept. 1867), 257–80.
46. *A&L* 178.
47. 'The Two Mrs Scudamores', *Blackwood's* (Jan. 1872), 46–67.
48. 'The Sisters Brontë', *Women Novelists of Queen Victoria's Reign*, 3–61.
49. *Blackwood's* (Oct. 1896), 481–507.
50. *Blackwood's* (Jan. 1896), 135–49.

51. *Blackwood's* (Jan. 1894), 203.
52. *Annals*, ii. 177–8.
53. *He That Will Not When He May*, ch. 15.
54. Ibid., ch. 10.
55. A. Tennyson, 'The Two Voices', lines 127–32, 145–50.
56. *The Perpetual Curate*, ch. 3.
57. Ibid., ch. 40.
58. *JAL* 9.
59. *A Son of the Soil*, ch. 21.
60. Ibid., ch. 37.
61. *The Perpetual Curate*, ch. 37.
62. *Margaret Maitland*, ch. 24.
63. *Blackwood's* (Sept. 1867), 275–6.
64. 'The Lily and the Thorn', *Good Cheer* (Dec. 1877), 19–65. *Good Cheer* was the Christmas number of the magazine *Good Words*.
65. *John*, chs. 24, 25.
66. *Madam*, ch. 32.
67. Cf. the nabob who appears in *The Melvilles*, ch. 19; and the Indian railwayman of *The Railwayman and His Children*.
68. *Ailieford*, ch. 41.
69. *The Doctor's Family*, ch. 14.
70. *Whiteladies*, ch. 12.
71. *Salem Chapel*, ch. 30.
72. *Miss Marjoribanks*, chs. 51, 52.
73. 'The Little Pilgrim Goes Up Higher', *Macmillan's Magazine* (Sept. 1882), 337–55.
74. Blackwood MS 4364, 16 Nov. 1877.
75. 'A Girl of the Period', *The English Illustrated Magazine* (Feb. 1892), 418–32.
76. *May*, ch. 39.
77. NLS MS 23195, MOWO to Cecco, Friday (n.d.) Jan. 1893.
78. *Ombra*, ch. 61.
79. *Agnes Hopetoun's Schools and Holidays*, ch. 7.
80. *The Story of Valentine and His Brother*, ch. 13.
81. Blackwood MS 4364, n.d. Mar. 1877.
82. *Blackwood's* (Mar. 1876), 314–31; (July 1880), 62–80; (June 1896), 904.
83. *Blackwood's* (Mar. 1876), 330.
84. *Blackwood's* (July 1880), 68.
85. *JAL* 153.
86. 'The Whirl of Youth', *A Widow's Tale and Other Stories*, ch. 1.
87. *Blackwood's* (July 1880), 77–8; *He That Will Not When He May*, ch. 8.
88. *Blackwood's* (Nov. 1873), 604–8.
89. The tone and vocabulary employed in the last-mentioned article bear interesting comparison with that of her article 'Lace and Bric-a -Brac', *Blackwood's* (Jan. 1876), 59–78.
90. *Blackwood's*, (Nov. 1873), 609.
91. In *The Portrait of a Lady* (1881).
92. *The Curate in Charge*, ch. 9.

93. Ibid., ch. 20.
94. 'Isabell Carr', *St James's Magazine* (Oct. and Nov. 1861), 271–82, 399–412.

CHAPTER 4: WOMEN IN RELATIONSHIP

1. *The New Review* (Mar. 1896), 241–7.
2. 'The Sisters Brontë', *Women Novelists of Queen Victoria's Reign*, 3–61.
3. *Blackwood's* (Sept. 1867), 257–80.
4. 'Christabel' (1816).
5. *Ombra*, ch. 10.
6. e.g. *Merkland, Agnes*.
7. *The Wizard's Son*, ch. 25.
8. NLS MS 23195, MOWO to Cecco, 1 July 1893.
9. *Miss Marjoribanks*, ch. 38, and 'A Chance Encounter', *Black and White* (12 Dec. 1891), 786–90.
10. 'Thomas Carlyle', *Macmillan's Magazine* (Apr. 1881), 482–96.
11. *JAL* 75.
12. *Sir Tom*, ch. 10.
13. 'The Little Pilgrim Goes Up Higher', *Macmillan's Magazine* (Sept. 1882), 337–55.
14. *JAL* 113.
15. e.g. *Innocent* and *For Love and Life*.
16. *A Son of the Soil*, ch. 38.
17. *JAL* 73.
18. *JAL* 139; *Edinburgh Review* (Apr. 1885), 514–53.
19. *A&L* 177–8.
20. *The Three Brothers*, ch. 38.
21. 'Lady Isabella', ch. 5; *Neighbours on the Green*.
22. 'A Party of Travellers', *Good Words* (June 1879), 423.
23. *Blackwood's* (June 1871), 763–93.
24. *Blackwood's* (Apr. 1874), 457.
25. *Old Mr Tredgold*, ch. 8.
26. *The Marriage of Elinor*, ch. 7.
27. Cf. *Merkland*, ch. 25.
28. *Hester*, ch. 45.
29. *The Railwayman and His Children*, ch. 2.
30. *The Wizard's Son*, ch. 19, and letter quoted in Williams, 124.
31. *The Heir Presumptive and the Heir Apparent*, ch. 14.
32. *Miss Marjoribanks*, ch. 44.
33. Ibid., ch. 49.
34. 'Prelude' to *Middlemarch*.
35. *JAL* 10.
36. *Phoebe Junior*, ch. 3.
37. Ibid., ch. 43.
38. Examples can be found in *Ombra*, *The Wizard's Son*, and *A Poor Gentleman*.
39 J. Austen, *Northanger Abbey* (1818), ch. 10.

40. *The Perpetual Curate*, ch. 12.
41. *The Three Brothers*, ch. 35.
42. Julia Herbert in *The Wizard's Son*, ch. 50; cf. Beatrice in *Agnes* and the subject of *The Sorceress*.
43. *Daily News* (28 June 1897), 8.
44. *Blackwood's* (July 1874), 89; *May*, ch. 45.
45. *The Perpetual Curate*, ch. 37.
46. Central to the plot of *Ombra*.
47. 'The Story of Anne Maturin', *Scribner's Monthly* (New York), Nov. 1875, p. 53.
48. e.g. *The Primrose Path, Effie Ogilvie*, and *Joyce*.
49. *The Story of Valentine and His Brother*, ch. 38.
50. NLS MS 23196, MOWO to Denny, 6 Aug. 1884.
51. NLS MS 23196, MOWO to Denny, n.d. Apr. 1892, and 1 May 1892.
52. See 'Norah, the Story of a Wild Irish Girl', *Scribner's Monthly* (May 1871), 49–61; (June 1871), 149–62; and *The Second Son*.
53. *The Mystery of Mrs Blencarrow*, chs. 9, 10.
54. *A&L*, p. viii.
55. *Salem Chapel, Within the Precincts, The Second Son*.
56. Cf. the allegorical '*Dies Irae*' (1895), ch. 5, where one makes her appearance 'in satin and pearls, with rouged cheek and glittering white teeth, that laughed us to scorn. She was a NANA.'
57. *Blackwood's* (May 1855), 560; *Victorian Age of English Literature*, i, ch. 6.
58. *JAL* 115.
59. 'Thomas Carlyle', *Macmillan's Magazine* (Apr. 1881), 488.
60. *Blackwood's* (May 1862), 564–84.
61. *Blackwood's* (Oct. 1862), 440–1.
62. *A Country Gentleman and His Family*, ch. 25.
63. *Within the Precincts*, ch. 36.
64. e.g. *May* and *A Country Gentleman*. For the shame such women feel at a male relative's attempted trickery in such affairs see *For Love and Life* and *Lady Car*.
65. *Edinburgh Review* (Apr. 1885), 514–53.
66. *The Wizard's Son*, ch. 34.
67. Ibid., ch. 41.
68. Ibid., ch. 44.
69. *JAL* 81.
70. *The Cuckoo in the Nest*, ch. 13.
71. For publishing details see above, n. 52.
72. *Blackwood's* (Jan. 1896), 142–3; (July 1874), 72–91.
73. *The Ladies Lindores*, ch. 8.
74. Blackwood's MS 4280, 2 Dec. 1871.
75. *Blackwood's* (Jan. 1896), 135–49.
76. 1912 Preface to *Jude the Obscure* (1895).
77. 'Janet's Repentance', *Scenes of Clerical Life* (1858) and *Middlemarch* (1872).
78. *Blackwood's* (Jan. 1896), 144.
79. *A Country Gentleman*, ch. 28.
80. Ibid., ch. 51.
81. *A House Divided Against Itself*, ch. 22.

82. *The Duke's Daughter*, ch. 9. This tale was first published as 'Lady Jane', *Good Words* (Jan.–June 1882).
83. *The Marriage of Elinor*, ch. 3.
84. Collected in *A Widow's Tale and Other Stories*, ch. 1.
85. *The Ladies Lindores*, ch. 26; and see above, p. ••.
86. *JAL* 38, 79.
87. *Annals*, i. 4.
88. NLS MS 23196, 15 Oct. 1893.
89. NLS MS 23196, 8 Oct. 1893.
90. 'The Story of a Wedding Tour', 'John', and 'The Whirl of Youth' were all reprinted in *A Widow's Tale and Other Stories*, 301–20, 321–38, 339–68. 'A Mysterious Bridegroom', *Pall Mall Magazine* (Mar. 1895), 354–68.
91. *JAL* 90.
92. *JAL* 13.
93. *In Trust*, ch. 10.
94. *A Poor Gentleman*, chs. 26, 46.
95. *Miss Marjoribanks*, ch. 1.
96. *A Son of the Soil*, ch. 46.
97. *In Trust*, ch. 35.
98. *Blackwood's* (Nov. 1863), 628–9.
99. *Orphans*, ch. 18.
100. *Blackwood's* (Mar. and Apr. 1863), 284–300, 414–36.
101. *JAL* 4.
102. *A Country Gentleman and His Family*, ch. 26.
103. *JAL* 6–7, 13.
104. *The Greatest Heiress in England*, ch. 8. Cf. *The Curate in Charge* and *The Primrose Path*.
105. *The Greatest Heiress*, ch. 8.
106. See *Carità*, *Within the Precincts*, and *The Greatest Heiress*.
107. Blackwood MS 4380, 18 Jan. 1878.
108. A. Taylor, *Laurence Oliphant, 1829–1888* (Oxford, 1982), 247.
109. *Agnes*, ch. 53.
110. *Madonna Mary*, ch. 10.
111. *The Three Brothers*, ch. 41.
112. *JAL* 12.
113. V. Cunningham, *Everywhere Spoken Against: Dissent and the Victorian Novel* (Oxford, 1975), 232.
114. E. Showalter, *A Literature of Their Own: British Women Novelists from Brontë to Lessing* (1978; 1982), 179.
115. Blackwood MS 4111, n.d. 1855.
116. *A&L* 177.
117. *JAL* 36–7.
118. *Lilliesleaf*, ch. 2.
119. *The Quiet Heart* and *The House on the Moor*.
120. 'Grove Road, Hampstead', *The Two Marys*.
121. *Kirsteen*, ch. 33.
122. *JAL* 47, 81.
123. *The Wizard's Son*, ch. 3.

124. Showalter, *A Literature of Their Own*, 178–9.
125. *JAL* 151.
126. *Harry Joscelyn*, chs. 1, 15, 46.
127. *John*, ch. 14.
128. 'The Member's Wife', *The National Observer* (4, 11 Mar. 1893), 391–3, 415–7.
129. e.g. 'An Anxious Moment', *The New Amphion: Being the Book of the Edinburgh University Union Fancy Fair* (1886), 39–99; *The Melvilles*, ch. 43.
130. Cf. the excuses made to himself by the soul of the young man in limbo in 'The Land of Suspense', *Blackwood's* (Jan. 1897), 131–57.
131. *Blackwood's* (July 1872), 54–5.
132. 'The Portrait', *Blackwood's* (Jan. 1885), 1–28.
133. *JAL* 20.
134. e.g. *Sundays* and *Agnes Hopetoun's Schools and Holidays*.
135. Letter from MOWO to Mary Mapes Dodge dated 8 Oct. 1884, lodged in the Donald and Robert M. Dodge Collection, Box 2, folder 50, in the Library of Princeton University.
136. 'Mary's Brother', *Atalanta* (Oct. 1892), 44–9.
137. e.g. in *The Cuckoo in the Nest* and *Two Strangers*. Twenty years earlier she had been amused by the portrait of the 8-year-old Montalembert drawn by his grandfather: 'There is a fashion in character as well as costume; and good Mr Forbes was of the Sandford and Merton period, and unconsciously makes his darling talk in those pleasantly precise little sentences which belong as much to the last century as its lace ruffles and gold lace.' *Memoirs of the Count de Montalembert*, i, ch. 2.
138. *Blackwood's* (Apr. 1855), 451–66.
139. *JAL* 46 and 78.
140. *The Story of Valentine*, ch. 13.
141. Showalter, *A Literature of Their Own*, 178–80.
142. *The Ladies Lindores*, chs. 8 and 11.
143. Ibid., ch. 26, and *Spectator* (23 June 1883), 805–6.
144. *Blackwood's* (Feb. 1868), 203.

CHAPTER 5: A SCOTTISH WIDOW'S RELIGIOUS SPECULATIONS

1. *British Weekly* (1 July 1897), 177.
2. *Blackwood's* (July 1855), 72–86.
3. *JAL* 11.
4. NLS, Mrs Craik to MOWO, 2 Nov. 1865, also enclosing a letter from a Jane Hooper to Mrs Craik, on the same subject.
5. 'The Little Pilgrim in the Seen and the Unseen', *The Land of Darkness, along with some Further Chapters in the Experiences of the Little Pilgrim*, 143.
6. *Christian Melville*, written 1845; chs. 4 and 12.
7. e.g. in *Heart and Cross, Primrose Path, Lady Car.*
8. *Blackwood's* (Nov. 1856), 614; *JAL* 62.
9. The clearest example forms the subject of *The Unjust Steward; or, The Minister's Debt.*
10. 'The Golden Rule', *Stories from Black and White*, 273–312.
11. 'A Mysterious Bridegroom', *Pall Mall Magazine* (Mar. 1895), 354–68.

12. 'The Rector', ch. 3.
13. *Blackwood's* (Jan. 1871), 22–47.
14. Blackwood MS 4111, n.d. 1855.
15. *Memoir of the Life of John Tulloch*, 357.
16. In her very last letter to her old friend Story, Mrs Oliphant was still asking, 'Have you any light to give?' NLS MS, 4 Jan. 1896.
17. *JAL* 6.
18. *Blackwood's* (Mar. 1872), 278.
19. *Memoir*, 184.
20. *The Bookman* (Aug. 1897), 115.
21. *JAL* 159.
22. *The British Weekly* (1 July 1897), 177.
23. *Blackwood's* (Nov. 1858), 567–86.
24. *JAL* 94.
25. *Reminiscences*, i. 334–5.
26. *A&L* 197–9; *JAL* 111–12.
27. NLS MS 23194, Emily Lawless to MOWO, 25 May 1891.
28. *JAL* 93 n. and 111.
29. *Blackwood's* (July 1855), 72–86.
30. Blackwood MS 4141, 13 Jan. 1859.
31. *JAL* 26, 31.
32. *Passages in the Life of Margaret Maitland*, ch. 24; *Thomas Chalmers: Preacher, Philosopher and Statesman*, 230.
33. *JAL* 26, 23.
34. McGuffie, *The Priests of Etal*, 64.
35. *JAL* 23–5.
36. *Blackwood's* (Dec. 1858), 728–42.
37. Blackwood MS 4111, n.d. 1855.
38. McGuffie, *The Priests of Etal*, 68.
39. *The George Eliot Letters*, iv. 25–6.
40. *The Literary History of England* (3 vols., 1882), ii, ch. 6.
41. Quoted in Cunningham, *Everywhere Spoken Against*, 239.
42. *JAL* 39, 88, 166.
43. Ibid. 40–1.
44. *Macmillan's Magazine* (Dec. 1887), 81–5.
45. *JAL* 128.
46. *Memoir of the Life of Laurence Oliphant, and of Alice Oliphant, his Wife*.
47. *JAL* 58–60.
48. e.g. in *The Last of the Mortimers, A Son of the Soil, Innocent*, and 'Madame Saint-Ange', *Good Cheer* (Dec. 1867), 33–44.
49. Blackwood MS 4152, n.d. 1861.
50. *Macmillan's Magazine* (July 1863), 208–19.
51. Blackwood MS 4172, n.d. 1862.
52. Blackwood MS 4184, n.d. 1863.
53. Blackwood MS 4251, n.d. 1869.
54. *A Son of the Soil*, ch. 46.
55. *Church Quarterly Review* (Oct. 1899), 150; *A&L* 415.

56. *The Bookman* (Aug. 1897), 115.

57. NLS MS 23196, MOWO to Denny, 15 Oct. 1893.

58. *A&L* 191–2.

59. *The Perpetual Curate*, ch. 15.

60. *Blackwood's* (July 1871), 75.

61. *The Bookman* (Aug. 1897), 115; *Blackwood's* (Feb. 1894), 190–209.

62. *Blackwood's* (Nov. 1889), 719.

63. NLS MS 23196, MOWO to Denny, 15 Oct. 1893; *A&L* 415.

64. *JAL* 84–5.

65. *JAL* 125.

66. *A&L* 415.

67. *JAL* 56.

68. See E. K. Helsinger, R. L. Sheets, and W. Veeder (eds.), *The Woman Question 1837–1883* (3 vols., 1983), pp. xiv–xv, i. 3–20, and ii. 165–211.

69. *JAL* 32, 37.

70. F. D. Maurice, *The Kingdom of Christ* (2nd edn., 1842).

71. *Blackwood's* (July 1855), 72–86.

72. *Blackwood's* (Oct. 1896), 555–71.

73. This section is indebted to an unpublished Ph.D. thesis by C. Dormandy, 'George Eliot's Religious Consciousness and its Role in her Life and Work', (CNAA, 1992).

74. *JAL* 7.

75. *Agnes*, ch. 63.

76. Ibid., ch. 60.

77. Ibid., ch. 47.

78. Cf. *JAL* 8, 10.

79. *JAL* 134–5.

80. *A&L* 439.

81. *JAL* 44.

82. *JAL* 48.

83. *Blackwood's* (Feb. 1895), 237–55.

84. A useful discussion of the genre may be found in R. Jackson, *Fantasy: The Literature of Subversion* (1981).

85. *Blackwood's* (Apr. 1893), 481–511.

86. *Blackwood's* (Jan. 1884), 1–45. The publishing history of the tales of the supernatural and the tales of the afterlife is extremely complex and no complete edition of either category seems to exist. To distinguish between tales with deceptively similar names I have therefore supplied the first place of publication for each tale.

87. *A&L* 321–2.

88. *Blackwood's* (Jan. 1857), 74–86; *Tales from Blackwood* (1879).

89. See the chapter on 'The Occult' in J. R. Reed, *Victorian Conventions* (Athens, Ohio, 1975).

90. *Blackwood's* (Oct. 1871), 446–9.

91. *Blackwood's* (Nov. 1871), 552–76.

92. *JAL* 18.

93. Luke 2: 19.

94. *Blackwood's* (Mar. 1867), 338–40.

95. 'Old Lady Mary', ch. 1.

96. *Blackwood's* (Dec. 1876), 706–29.
97. Williams, 114.
98. *A&L* 275, 286.
99. R. A. and V. Colby, '*A Beleaguered City*: A Fable for the Victorian Age', *Nineteenth Century Fiction* (Mar. 1962), 283–301; *JAL* 137.
100. *Blackwood's* (Oct. 1864), 417–31.
101. Blackwood MS 4360, 12 Dec. 1877; 4380, 21 Jan. 1878. *Dante: Foreign Classics for English Readers.*
102. NLS MS 23194, Blanche Airlee to MOWO, 7 Jan. 1880.
103. *Fraser's Magazine* (May 1880), 698–710.
104. *Fraser's Magazine* (Jan. 1880), 118–44.
105. See above, p. 68 and ch. 2, n. 77.
106. *Purgatorio*, Canto XXI. 64.
107. *Blackwood's* (Jan. 1882), 1–30.
108. *Blackwood's* (Jan. 1885), 1–28.
109. *Longman's Magazine* (Dec. 1882), 229–52; (Jan. 1883), 341–64.
110. Cf. *The Bride of Lammermoor* (1819).
111. *The Wizard's Son,* ch. 41.
112. Ibid., chs. 1 and 19.
113. *A&L* 438.
114. *JAL* 124.
115. 'The Little Pilgrim Goes Up Higher', *Macmillan's Magazine* (Sept. 1882), 337–55.
116. See above, p. 99 and ch. 4, n. 13.
117. 'A Little Pilgrim in the Unseen', *Macmillan's Magazine* (May 1882), 1–19.
118. *A&L* 430.
119. *Blackwood's* (Jan. 1897), 131–57.
120. For a useful discussion of this point see P. Fiddes, *Past Event and Present Salvation* (1989), 199–200.
121. *Blackwood's* (Feb. 1895), 237–55.
122. *A&L* 439.
123. *JAL* 53.
124. *JAL* 157; 'The Little Pilgrim in the Seen and the Unseen', *The Scottish Church* (July 1885), 93–109, 102; 'Mr Sandford', *The Ways of Life*, ch. 5.
125. Cf. 'The Fugitives', *Good Cheer* (Dec. 1879 number of *Good Words*), 72; and 'The Little Pilgrim in the Seen and the Unseen', 125.
126. e.g. Williams, 133; and V. and R. A. Colby, *The Equivocal Virtue: Mrs Oliphant and the Victorian Market Place* (New York, 1966), 103.
127. For further discussion of Victorian writers' treatment of post-terrestrial states see G. Rowell, *Hell and the Victorians: A Study of the Nineteenth-Century Controversies Concerning Eternal Punishment and the Future Life* (Oxford, 1974), and M. Wheeler, *Death and the Future Life in Victorian Literature and Theology* (Cambridge, 1990).
128. F. Wendel, *Calvin: The Origin and Development of his Religious Thought*, trans. P. Mairet (1965), 287.
129. *A&L* 292.
130. *JAL* 150.
131. *Blackwood's* (Oct. 1896), 568.
132. *Dante*, chs. 4 and 5.

133. 'Old Lady Mary', ch. 3.
134. 'A Little Pilgrim in the Unseen', *Macmillan's Magazine* (May 1882), 16–18.
135. '*Dies Irae*: The Story of a Spirit in Prison' (1895).
136. Cf. *Blackwood's* (Oct. 1896), 564–71, and 'The Land of Suspense', *Blackwood's* (Jan. 1897), 131–57.
137. These thoughts on Judgement are to be found in 'The Little Pilgrim in the Seen and the Unseen'.
138. 'A Little Pilgrim in the Unseen.'
139. *JAL* 6.
140. As she does in 'The Little Pilgrim in the Seen and the Unseen'.
141. 'On the Dark Mountains', *Blackwood's* (Nov. 1888), 646–63.
142. 'A Little Pilgrim in the Unseen' (May 1882).
143. R. H. Story, *Memoir of the Life of the Rev. R. Story* (1862), 145 ff.
144. *Macmillan's Magazine* (July 1863), 208–19.
145. Rowell, *Hell and the Victorians*, 70–5.
146. *Blackwood's* (Oct. 1896), 568.
147. '*Dies Irae*', ch. 2.
148. 'On the Dark Mountains.'
149. 'The Land of Darkness', *Blackwood's* (Jan. 1887), 1–36.
150. *Letters of Anne Thackeray Ritchie*, ed. H. Ritchie (1924), 242.
151. J. M. Barrie, Introductory Note, *A Widow's Tale*, p. vii.
152. *Blackwood's* (June 1858), 703–18. For further discussion of this religious biography and of the genre's influence upon fictional deathbed scenes of the period see E. Jay, *The Religion of the Heart* (Oxford, 1979), 153–68.
153. *The Son of His Father*, ch. 12.
154. *Blackwood's* (June 1858), 706.
155. *Squire Arden*, ch. 67.
156. *The Life of Edward Irving*, ch. 19.
157. *Memoir of the Life of John Tulloch*, 476.
158. *Memoir of the Life of Laurence Oliphant and of Alice Oliphant, his Wife*, chs. 10, 12.
159. Blackwood MS 4295, 13 Apr. 1872.
160. *JAL* 130.
161. *JAL* 44–9.
162. *JAL* 80.
163. *JAL* 5, 84.
164. *Blackwood's* (June 1889), 828.
165. *JAL* 12, 16.
166. Blackwood MS 4202, 10 May 1864.
167. *Blackwood's* (Feb. 1876), 236.
168. *Forum* (New York, 1887–91), Aug. 1889, pp. 314–22.
169. *A Widow's Tale and Other Stories*, 57–113.
170. *Carità*, chs. 7, 31.
171. *The Sorceress*, chs. 17–20.
172. *May*, chs. 6 and 11.
173. *JAL* 47, 49.
174. *The Laird of Norlaw*, chs. 3, 47, 61.
175. *The Melvilles*, ch. 39.

176. *Blackwood's* (June 1871), 690.
177. *Agnes*, ch. 60.
178. The endings respectively of *Phoebe Junior* and *Effie Ogilvie*.
179. 'The Little Pilgrim in the Seen and the Unseen.'
180. *Blackwood's* (Feb. 1895), 252.
181. *JAL* 78.
182. *Agnes*, ch. 42.
183. *The Primrose Path*, chs. 13, 15, 18, 21.
184. *Innocent*, ch. 34.
185. *Harry Muir: A Story of Scottish Life*, ch. 46.
186. *A Rose in June*, ch. 7.

CHAPTER 6: A WOMAN AND THE WIDER WORLD

1. *JAL* 10.
2. *Blackwood's* (June 1862), 663-72.
3. *Blackwood's* (May 1897), 599-624.
4. e.g. 'John Rintoul; or, the Fragments of a Wreck, *Blackwood's* (Mar. 1853), 329-47; *Katie Stewart: A True Story*; 'Eben, A True Story', *The National Magazine* (1858), 67-71, 82-5; 'The Ship's Doctor', *Good Words* (Apr. 1868), 236-43.
5. *Blackwood's* (May 1897), 606-9.
6. *The Quiet Heart*, ch. 5.
7. Letter from MOWO to Mr Seymour dated 22 Sept. n.d. Archives of Charles Scribner's Sons, Author Files, Box 108, folder 'O', lodged in the Library of Princeton University.
8. e.g. 'A Railway Junction; or, the Romance of Ladybank', *Blackwood's* (Oct. 1873), 419-41; and 'The Story of a Wedding Tour', *A Widow's Tale and Other Stories*, 301-19.
9. *Caleb Field*, ch. 2.
10. *Lucy Crofton*, ch. 24.
11. *A&L* 176.
12. 'Greville Fane', *The Complete Tales of Henry James*, 433-52.
13. *Daily News* (28 June 1897), 8.
14. *Saturday Review* (28 Jan. 1888), 106-7. Nevertheless, another publisher, J. M. Dent, was sufficiently impressed by her books on Florence and Venice to commission a similar volume on Siena from her. *Memoirs of J. M. Dent, 1849-1926* (1928).
15. *Blackwood's* (June 1888), 850.
16. e.g. *Agnes, Innocent, Mrs Arthur, Harry Joscelyn, A House Divided Against Itself.*
17. *JAL* 44.
18. *St James's Gazette* (20 June 1888), 6.
19. Ritchie, *From the Porch*, 22.
20. *JAL* 14, 118.
21. *Kirsteen*, ch. 20.
22. See *The Doctor's Family, He That Will Not When He May, The Son of His Father*, and *Two Strangers*.
23. *The British Weekly* (1 July 1897), 177.
24. See *Agnes* and *Mrs Arthur*.

25. *JAL* 132.
26. *The Story of Valentine and His Brother.*
27. *Margaret Maitland*, ch. 5.
28. *JAL* 21.
29. *Memoir of Laurence Oliphant*, ch. 1.
30. *Kirsteen*, ch. 29.
31. *Miss Marjoribanks*, ch. 17.
32. *Blackwood's* (Apr. 1855), 451–66.
33. *The Athelings*, ch. 1.
34. *Mrs Arthur*, ch. 31.
35. Blackwood MS 4163, 6 Nov. 1861.
36. NLS MS 23195, 10 Jan. 1893.
37. NLS MS 23195, MOWO to Cecco, 9 Jan. 1893.
38. *Blackwood's* (Aug. 1883), 244–63, uses the astronomer James Ferguson as the occasion for a disquisition upon Victorian attitudes to self-help.
39. *Blackwood's* (Oct. 1896), 487.
40. See *JAL* 15, and above, ch. 1 n. 40.
41. *Blackwood's* (Feb. 1877), 188.
42. 'Dies Irae', and 'A Visitor and His Opinions', *Blackwood's* (Apr. 1893), 481–511.
43. In *The Days of My Life*, and *Old Mr Tredgold*.
44. *JAL* 65.
45. *Fraser's Magazine* (Dec. 1849), 671.
46. *Blackwood's* (Apr. 1855), 451–3.
47. For an account of Chalmers, see S. Brown, *Thomas Chalmers and the Godly Commonwealth* (Oxford, 1982).
48. *JAL* 22–3.
49. *John Drayton*, ch. 6.
50. *Ailieford*, ch. 41.
51. *The Laird of Norlaw*, ch. 31.
52. *Sundays*, 9–11.
53. *Lucy Crofton*, ch. 6.
54. *Hester*, ch. 7.
55. *Lady William*, ch. 1.
56. *Blackwood's* (Dec. 1860), 698–715.
57. As in *The Days of My Life*, ch. 16, and *Ombra*, ch. 60.
58. As in *The Marriage of Elinor*, ch. 29.
59. *Memoir of Laurence Oliphant*, ch. 10.
60. See *The Last of the Mortimers*, ch. 7, and *Joyce*, ch. 25.
61. *Cousin Mary*, chs. 9 and 12.
62. *Miss Marjoribanks*, ch. 46.
63. Story, *Later Reminiscences*, 50–1.
64. *Hester*, ch. 36.
65. *Blackwood's* (Aug. 1871), 229–56.
66. *JAL* 136.
67. 'The Fugitives', *Good Cheer* (Dec. 1879 number of *Good Words*), 49.
68. *JAL* 27.
69. *JAL* 22, 107, 129.

70. Ritchie, *From the Porch*, 22.
71. Blackwood MS 4323, 24 July 1874.
72. *A&L* 275.
73. See Plate.
74. *JAL* 135, 136.
75. 'The Fugitives', *Good Cheer* (Dec. 1879), 49.
76. *JAL* 131.
77. *JAL* 129.
78. Blackwood MS 4295, 22 Oct. 1872.
79. *Phoebe Junior*, ch. 10.
80. *JAL* 132.
81. *Cousin Mary*, ch. 12.
82. *Marriage of Elinor*, ch. 5.
83. *Hester*, ch. 25.
84. *Blackwood's* (Feb. 1889), 296.
85. *Within the Precincts*, ch. 36.
86. *Blackwood's* (June 1875), 751–3.
87. *Blackwood's* (May 1897), 599–624.
88. *Old Mr Tredgold*, ch. 8.
89. NLS MS 23195, 31 Dec. 1892.
90. *Blackwood's* (June 1875), 750.
91. *Mrs Arthur*, ch. 3.
92. In her use of the term 'ideal' Mrs Oliphant seems to have followed the distinction, drawn by Ruskin and favoured by many who wrote in the Victorian realist tradition, between the True and the False ideal. See J. Ruskin, *Works*, ed. E. T. Cook and A. Wedderburn (39 vols., 1908), v. 140–7; also Jay, *Religion of the Heart*, 210 ff.
93. *JAL* 10.
94. *Women Novelists of Queen Victoria's Reign*, 3–61.
95. *The Minister's Wife*, ch. 48.
96. 'The Little Pilgrim Goes Up Higher.'
97. *Blackwood's* (Mar. 1870), 294.
98. *Blackwood's* (Sept. 1880), 382.
99. *Blackwood's* (Jan. 1896), 142.
100. *Blackwood's* (Mar. 1890), 415.
101. *Blackwood's* (Feb. 1886), 253.
102. *Blackwood's* (Oct. 1871), 477.
103. *Blackwood's* (Sept. 1880), 398.
104. *The Melvilles*, ch. 25.
105. *Blackwood's* (Sept. 1880), 380.
106. *Blackwood's* (Jan. 1875), 114.
107. *The Ladies Lindores*, ch. 8.
108. *JAL* 24–5.
109. I. C. Clarke, *Six Portraits* (1935), 196.
110. *JAL* 28, 33.
111. Blackwood MS 4119, 1856 n.d.
112. Quoted in Williams, 16.
113. *Kirsteen*, ch. 33.

114. *Within the Precincts.*
115. *Memoir of Laurence Oliphant*, ch. 12.
116. *A Country Gentleman and His Family*, ch. 34.
117. *JAL* 132.
118. *At His Gates*, chs. 4, 14, and 45.
119. *Miss Marjoribanks*, ch. 5.
120. *A&L* 204–5.
121. *Phoebe Junior*, ch. 35.
122. *From the Porch*, 23.
123. *JAL* 24, 37–8.
124. *JAL* 64, 70.
125. *JAL* 75, 78.
126. *JAL* 145–6.
127. *Heart and Cross*, ch. 23.
128. *Innocent*, ch. 9.
129. See above, p. 43.
130. A. Trollope, *An Autobiography*, ed. F. Page (Oxford, 1950), 29.
131. *JAL* 37.
132. *Blackwood's*, (Jan. 1883), 160.
133. *The Wizard's Son*, ch. 48.
134. *JAL* 135.
135. Blackwood MS 4266, Mar. 1870, n.d.
136. *JAL* 40.
137. Clarke, *Six Portraits*, 221.
138. *Madonna Mary*, ch. 11.
139. *Hester*, ch. 36.
140. *The Unjust Steward; or, The Minister's Debt*, ch. 20.
141. NLS MS 23196, MOWO to Denny, 2 Mar. 1896, 21 Nov. 1895.
142. *Kirsteen*, ch. 50.
143. *JAL* 43; *Heart and Cross.*
144. *JAL* 9.
145. *JAL* 106, 109.
146. *A&L*, 299–300.
147. *Sundays*, ch. 1.
148. *Blackwood's* (June 1871), 763–93.
149. *Blackwood's* (May 1855), 561.
150. e.g. *Merkland*, 'The Lily and the Thorn', and *Young Musgrave.*
151. *JAL* 46.
152. *JAL* 99.
153. *Blackwood's* (Sept. 1867), 277–8.
154. 'Success in Fiction', *Forum* (Aug. 1889), 321–2.
155. *A House in Bloomsbury*, ch. 5.
156. J. M. Barrie, Introductory Note, *A Widow's Tale*, p. vi; and Ritchie, *From the Porch.*
157. *Movements of Religious Thought in Britain during the Nineteenth Century*, p. iii.
158. *The Bookman* (Aug. 1897), 114.
159. Blackwood's (Sept. 1874), 365–86; (Nov. 1874), 599–620; and, for her private estimate, see Blackwood MS 4323, 12 Oct. 1874: 'I agree with you that Mr Collins' volumes are

very good, but I dont agree with you about Mr Trollope, whose Caesar I cannot read without laughing. It is so like Johnny Eames.'

160. *Blackwood's* (Apr. 1871), 458–60.
161. Blackwood MS 4349, n.d. 1876.
162. Blackwood MS 4396, 16 Mar. 1879.
163. Blackwood MS 4309, 6 Feb. 1873.
164. *Annals*, i. 10.
165. *Blackwood's* (July 1880), 62–80.
166. *Blackwood's* (Sept. 1873), 376; (Apr. 1874), 443.
167. *JAL* 152–3.

CHAPTER 7: A WOMAN OF LETTERS

1. *Blackwood's* (Oct. 1855), 437.
2. See above, p. 201.
3. Blackwood MS 4103, 1 Nov. 1853.
4. Blackwood MS 4111, 8 Nov. 1855 and n.d. 1855.
5. Blackwood MS 4111, 1855 n.d.
6. Macmillan MS, 19 Apr. 1882.
7. *Agnes Hopetoun's Schools and Holidays.*
8. Blackwood MS 4152, n.d. 1860.
9. Blackwood MS 4163, n.d. 1861.
10. *The George Eliot Letters*, iv. 25; Blackwood MS 4172, 1862 n.d.; 4266, 1870 n.d.
11. Blackwood MS 4266, 1870 n.d.
12. BL Add. MS 46616, 6 Aug. 1851, 2 Apr. 1852.
13. *JAL* 25.
14. *JAL* 132.
15. Blackwood MS 4323, 9 Feb. 1874; 4396, 28 Feb. 1879.
16. *JAL* 136.
17. Macmillan MS, 23 May 1883; *Blackwood's* (Jan. 1883), 88; Blackwood MS 4323, 9 Feb. 1874.
18. Blackwood MS 4266, 1870 n.d.
19. *The Works of Thomas Carlyle*, Centenary Edn., ed. H. D. Traill (30 vols., 1886–99), v. 154–95.
20. I am here indebted to C. Christ, '"The Hero as Man of Letters", Masculinity and Victorian Nonfiction Prose', in T. E. Morgan (ed.), *Victorian Sages and Cultural Discourse: Renegotiating Gender and Power* (1990), 19–31.
21. *A&L* 186.
22. Blackwood MS 4225, 27 Oct. 1867.
23. Blackwood MS 4323, 12 Mar. 1874.
24. [MOWO], *The Days of My Life*; [A. Trollope], *Nina Balatka* (1867).
25. *JAL* 36.
26. Introductory Note, *A Widow's Tale*, p. vi.
27. V. Woolf, *The Three Guineas* (1938; Oxford, 1992), 287.
28. *Annals*, i. 128.
29. *JAL* 34.

30. The description was Mrs C. F. Gore's and was quoted by MOWO in *Annals*, ii. 349.
31. Blackwood MS 4106, 28 Mar. 1854.
32. Blackwood MS 4111, 5 Feb. 1855.
33. Blackwood MS 4111, n.d., Feb. 1855.
34. NLS MS, Margaret Wilson, née Oliphant, to her brother, Thomas, n.d. 1852.
35. Blackwood MS 4238, n.d. 1868.
36. Blackwood MS 4225, n.d. Nov. 1867.
37. Blackwood MS 4202, 11 June 1865.
38. *Annals*, i. 417.
39. Blackwood MS 4172, n.d. 1862; 4184, n.d. 1863.
40. Macmillan MS, 10 Oct. 1885.
41. *Blackwood's* (June 1888), 841.
42. Blackwood MS 4184, n.d. 1863; 4213, 13 Jan. 1866.
43. Macmillan MS, 2 Dec. 1880.
44. Blackwood MS 4396, 2 May 1879.
45. Quoted in Clarke, 'The "Rival Novelist"', 51–61.
46. *The Letters of Anthony Trollope*, ed. N. J. Hall (2 vols., Stanford, Calif., 1983), ii. 840, 856–7, 868.
47. Blackwood MS 4364, MOWO to William Blackwood, 5 Nov. 1877; 4396, 25 Jan. 1879.
48. Blackwood MS 4664, 4 July 1897.
49. Blackwood MS 4364, n.d. 1877; 4323, 25 Aug. 1874, 2 Oct. 1874.
50. Blackwood MS 4337, n.d.1875; 4349, 4 Jan. 1876.
51. Blackwood MS 4349, 15 Apr. 1876.
52. NLS MS 23194, 13 Mar. 1886.
53. Articles signed 'A Dowager', or 'M', in *St James's Gazette*, Jan.–Aug. 1888; *Blackwood's* (Jan. 1895), 148–70.
54. *Blackwood's* (Aug. 1855), 215–30; (Apr. 1895), 624.
55. 'The Scientific Gentleman', *Neighbours on the Green*, is her only fictional attempt at giving the subject pride of place. At least one obituarist, however, felt that pride of place should be given to 'her masterly analysis of Bishop Berkeley's philosophy', *Daily News* (28 June 1897), 8.
56. *JAL* 27–8, 123–4.
57. NLS MS 23196, MOWO to Denny, 11 June 1892.
58 *Blackwood's* (Feb. 1873), 224–7.
59. *Agnes* and *Mrs Arthur*.
60. Blackwood MS 4119, 1856 n.d.; 4163, 1861 n.d.; *Autobiographical Notes of the Life of William Bell Scott*, ed. W. Minto (2 vols., 1892), i. 188; *JAL* 43–4, 61–2.
61. Something of his dedication can be felt in F. W. Oliphant, *A Plea for Painted Glass; Annals*, ii. 472; *JAL* 70.
62. *Blackwood's* (Aug. 1894), 303–4.
63. Macmillan MS, 4 Oct. 1882.
64. *JAL* 73.
65. *Blackwood's* (Jan. 1875), 114.
66. *Blackwood's* (Apr. 1895), 620–50.
67. *Blackwood's* (Apr. 1858), 708.
68. *Annals*, iii. 347.
69. *JAL* 27; Blackwood MS 4133, n.d. 1858.

70. [W. Lucas Collins], *Blackwood's* (June 1862), 737–57.
71. Blackwood MS 4133, n.d. 1858.
72. *Blackwood's* (Aug. 1876), 172.
73. Blackwood MS 4152, July and n.d. 1860.
74. Blackwood MS 4202 (4 Sept. 1865).
75. 'How largely you, by means of the Magazine, have contributed to my education!', Blackwood MS 4295, n.d. 1872.
76. Blackwood MS 4280, 9 Oct. 1871, 4295, 20 Mar. 1872, 26 Apr. 1872.
77. In this respect she clearly became a legend in her own lifetime. Edith Simcox reported that the conversation at the home of G. H. Lewes and George Eliot on 26 May 1878 focused upon 'translations, ignorance in print and the unprincipledness of even good people like Mrs Oliphant who write of that whereof they know nothing'. Quoted in *The George Eliot Letters*, ix. 228.
78. Blackwood MS 4295, 10, 18 June and 28 Sept. 1872.
79. Blackwood MS 4364, 2 Feb. 1877 and n.d. 1877.
80. Macmillan MS, 26 Jan. 1886.
81. *Good Cheer* (Dec. 1874), 1–31.
82. Macmillan MS, 30 June and 14 Aug. 1873, 8 June 1875.
83. Blackwood MS 4664, 11 Jan. 1897.
84. *Contemporary Review* (July 1883), 76–93.
85. *Daily Chronicle* (27 June 1897).
86. *Queen Victoria: A Personal Sketch*, 142, 154.
87. For a dispiriting account of this breed see N. Cross, *The Common Writer: Life in Nineteenth-Century Grub Street* (Cambridge, 1985), ch. 5.
88. *JAL* 117–18.
89. *John Drayton*, ch. 25.
90. *JAL* 30.
91. *Blackwood's* (Jan. 1876), 59–60.
92. *JAL* 30, 132, 136.
93. *JAL* 132; NLS MS 23195, MOWO to Cecco, 5 July 1893.
94. NLS MS 23195, 1 July 1893.
95. *A&L* 387.
96. *John Drayton*, chs. 10, 13.
97. *A&L*, p. viii.
98. *A&L* 426.
99. *Ailieford*, ch. 23.
100. Meredith Townsend, *The Cornhill* (June 1899), 773–9.
101. *Miss Marjoribanks*, ch. 4.
102. *Blackwood's* (Jan. 1883), 79; *Salem Chapel*, ch. 11.
103. *Kirsteen*, ch. 8.
104. *The Athelings*, ch. 77.
105. *The Three Brothers*, ch. 16.
106. *At His Gates*, ch. 45.
107. Letter to Thomas Aldrich, quoted by Harriet Waters Preston in *Atlantic Monthly* (Sept. 1897), 425.
108. 'The Library Window', *Blackwood's* (Jan. 1896), 1–30.
109. *JAL* 30.

110. *JAL* 118.
111. *A&L* 219.
112. *JAL* 15.
113. 'Mrs Craik', *Macmillan's Magazine* (Dec. 1887), 81–5.
114. *Annals*, ii. 475–7.
115. Blackwood MS 23195, 30 Jan. 1890.
116. *Annals*, iii. 350.
117. 'A Sketch from Memory', *Temple Bar* (Oct. 1899), 233–48.
118. *Notes on Novelists*, 359.
119. *From the Porch*, 22.
120. *Edinburgh Review* (Apr. 1885), 552.
121. *JAL* 137.
122. Blackwood MS 4396, 28 Feb. 1879.
123. NLS MS 23195.
124. Blackwood MS 4111, 19 Dec. 1855.
125. *JAL* 106; NLS MS 23196, MOWO to Madge, 27 Nov. 1895.
126. NLS MS 23195, 4 Jan. 1893.
127. Blackwood MS 4396, Cyril Francis Oliphant to John Blackwood, 1879; 4360, 28 Mar. 1877.
128. NLS MS 23196, MOWO to Madge, 30 Mar. 1894.
129. NLS MS 23196, MOWO to Madge, 27 Nov. 1895.
130. NLS MS 23196, MOWO to Denny, 27 Feb. 1896.
131. Blackwood MS 4225, 15 May, 1 Aug. 1867.
132. Blackwood MS 4184, 19 May 1863.
133. Macmillan MS, 10 Feb. 1875.
134. Blackwood MS 4295, 22 Oct. 1872.
135. *Annals*, i. 293.
136. Macmillan MS, 26 Mar. 1883.
137. William Isbister Collection, Box 3: Folder 'O'. Letter from MOWO to Isbister, n.d. (sent from 2 Pockington Terrace, Barmouth). Lodged in Princeton University Library.
138. Blackwood MS 4172, n.d. 1862.
139. *JAL* 133–4.
140. Blackwood MS 4364, 22 June 1877.
141. Blackwood MS 4396, Christmas Eve 1879.
142. *From the Porch*, 23.
143. Macmillan MS, 3, 5 Dec. 1887, 20 Mar. 1889.
144. Blackwood MS 4337, n.d. 1875.
145. Macmillan MS, 29 May 1883.
146. Macmillan MS, 23 May 1883; *Blackwood's* (Oct. 1883), 486–507.
147. Macmillan MS, 3 Oct. 1883.
148. Blackwood MS 4133, n.d. Feb. 1858; 4295, 5 Apr. 1872.
149. Macmillan MS, 27 Aug. [1877]. (Wrongly catalogued as for Aug. 1892.)
150. Macmillan MS, 22 July [1864].
151. *Annals*, ii. 440–1.
152. Macmillan MS, 5 June 1891.
153. Macmillan MS, 7 Apr. 1892.
154. *JAL* 30, 104, 118.

155. Blackwood MS 4323, 9 Feb. 1874.

156. Blackwood MS 4396, 2 Apr. 1879.

157. *A&L* 191.

158. *Charles Dickens: The Public Readings*, ed. P. Collins (Oxford, 1975), p. xxii.

159. Blackwood MS 4099, 25 Mar. 1852.

160. Blackwood MS 4119, n.d. 1856.

161. Blackwood MS 4191, 5 Dec. 1864; 4202, 7 Feb., 19 Apr., 10 May, 20 Sept., 2 Aug., n.d. [Sept.], 11 Oct., 13 Nov. 1865.

162. Blackwood MS 4213, 2 Jan., 20 Mar., 29 Nov. 1866.

163. *JAL* 133. Blackwood MS 4266, n.d. 1870; 4280, 1 Aug. 1871.

164. Blackwood MS 4295, 4 Oct.1872.

165. *Blackwood's* (May 1862), 584. The boast of Arthur Locker, editor of the *Graphic*, quoted in *Letters of Anthony Trollope*, ii. 565.

166. *JAL* 133–5.

167. *Blackwood's* (Nov. 1889), 705.

168. *Blackwood's* (Mar. 1889), 423–4; (Jan. 1890), 146.

169. *Blackwood's* (June 1889), 833.

170. Blackwood MS 4099, 13 Aug. 1852; also *The Victorian Age of English Literature*, i, ch. 6.

171. William Isbister Collection, Box 3: Folder 'O'. Letter from MOWO to Isbister dated 27 Aug. n.d.

172. *Blackwood's* (Apr. 1897), 484.

173. Blackwood MS 4099, 13 Aug., 21 Oct. 1852.

174. Blackwood MS 4099, Frank Oliphant to John Blackwood, 8 Oct. 1852; 4103, 5 Jan. 1853.

175. *The Victorian Age of English Literature*, ii, ch. 8; *Blackwood's* (Jan. 1883), 138.

176. William Isbister Collection, Box 3: Folder 'O'. Letter from MOWO to Isbister dated 23 Sept. n.d., refers to engravings Madge has done for *Good Words*. Also Macmillan MS, 3 Dec. 1883, expresses the hope that Denny's sketches from photographs of Heidelberg will be good enough to merit engravings being made from them.

177. William Isbister Collection, Box 3: Folder 'O'. Letters from MOWO to Isbister dated 16, 27 Nov [1877] suggest that Mrs Oliphant redoubled her efforts on her friend's behalf when she became a widow. The illustration for *Madonna Mary* is reproduced in Williams, pl. 5. Blackwood MS 4202, 22 Dec. 1865.

178. William Isbister Collection, Box 3: Folder 'O'. Letter from MOWO to Isbister dated 23 Aug. [1880s].

179. *The Curate in Charge*, ch. 20.

180. Macmillan MS, 4 Dec. 1883.

181. Macmillan MS, n.d. 1889.

182. Macmillan MS, 21, 26 Aug. 1890.

183. Macmillan MS, 5 Sept. 1891.

184. *Notes on Novelists*, 360.

185. *Forum* (New York, 1887–91), Aug. 1889, pp. 314–22.

186. *JAL* 91, 102.

187. Blackwood MS 4213, 3 Apr. 1866.

188. N. F. Anderson, *Women against Women in Victorian England: A Life of Eliza Lynn Linton* (Bloomington, Ind., 1987), 181.

189. BL Add. MS 46616, MOWO to Richard Bentley, 20 Nov., 5 Nov., 12 Nov. 1851; ?Mar., 2 Apr. 1852.
190. *JAL* 28.
191. Blackwood MS 4337, 8 Sept. 1875.
192. NLS MS 23204.
193. Hall, *Trollope*, 494 n.
194. Ibid. 154–5.
195. Blackwood MS 4106, 29 Nov. 1854.
196. Quoted in Hall, *Trollope*, 199.
197. *JAL* 102. Hall, *Trollope*, 207, 248, 259, 312.
198. *JAL* 132–3. Blackwood MS 4202, 11 June, 11 Oct. 1865; 4280, n.d. 1871; *JAL* 79; Blackwood MS 4295, 30 Mar. 1872.
199. G. Tuchman and N. E. Fortin, *Edging Women Out: Victorian Novelists, Publishers and Social Change* (New Haven, Conn., 1989), 194 ff. Their choice of comparison would have irritated Mrs Oliphant, who classified Crawford as a 'hybrid American' of the Jamesian school, déraciné without having achieved an understanding of English mores. She also questioned whether he was writing too much too fast! *Blackwood's* (Sept. 1884), 298–308.
200. Macmillan MS, 27 Mar., 1 Apr., 5 June 1879. Possibly she had lost interest in the idea herself by then. I cannot trace this publication, but, canny as ever, she used whatever material she had already gathered as the first part of *Royal Edinburgh: Her Saints, Kings, Prophets and Poets*, 1–37.
201. Blackwood MS 4099, 12 Feb. 1852.
202. As claimed in Showalter, *A Literature of Their Own*, 105.
203. Blackwood MS 4266, 24 May 1870.
204. Blackwood MS 4323, 3 Oct. 1874; Macmillan MS, 1 Apr. 1875, 1 Jan., n.d. June 1877.
205. Blackwood MS 4337, 20, 26 Sept., 27 July 1875.
206. Blackwood MS 4364, 28 Mar. 1877.
207. 'Mr Sandford', *Ways of Life*, ch. 7.
208. Quoted in Hall, *Trollope*, 419. William Isbister Collection, Box 3: Folder 'O'. Letters from MOWO to Isbister dated 6 Mar., 26 Jan., 17 Sept., 28 Oct., 26 Nov. [1877]; 8 Sept. [1880/1], and undated letter from 14 Victoria Square.
209. William Isbister Collection, Box 3: Folder 'O'. Letter from MOWO to Isbister dated only Thursday from Windsor, [1878].
210. Macmillan MS, 24 Oct. 1878.
211. Quoted in G. Griest, *Mudie's Circulating Library and the Victorian Novel* (Bloomington, Ind. and London, 1970), 73–4 and 186; *Athenaeum* (11 Feb. 1882), 186; *Catalogue of the Principal English Books in Circulation at Mudie's Select Library* (Jan. 1898). It is perhaps one measure of the growing split between the literary avant-garde and the book-borrowing public that, despite Edwardian sneering, Mudies still stocked 73 of these 89 fiction titles in 1918, together with 13 works of non-fiction.
212. Blackwood MS, n.d. 1877. Macmillan MS, 28 Aug. 1885, n.d., 2 Mar., 9 July 1887.
213. Macmillan MS, 23 Jan. 1888, 31 July, 11 Aug., 6, 8, 9 Nov. 1889, 11 Mar. 1890.
214. Macmillan MS, 28 Aug., 5 Sept., 8 Oct. 1891; 21 June 1892.
215. 'Introductory Note', *A Widow's Tale*, p. v; and *The Bookman* (Aug. 1897), 115.
216. Blackwood MS 4337, 26 Oct. 1875; 4664 , 25 Mar., 3 May 1897. Once her nephew Frank was earning a living in India it did not seem unreasonable to ask him to

contribute to the upkeep of his sister Nellie, who had failed to find a permanent home with her mother's side of the family. NLS MS 23194, MOWO to Frank, nephew, 27 June 1879. This relief was to be short-lived, however, for Frank died on 30 Oct. 1879.

217. J. A. Sutherland, *Victorian Novelists and Publishers* (1976), 84.
218. Macmillan MS, 8 Feb. [1866].
219. Sutherland, *Victorian Novelists*, 201; C. Dickens, *Bleak House*, ch. 39.
220. *JAL* 91.
221. Blackwood MS 4213, n.d. 1866.
222. *JAL* 91.

CHAPTER 8: THE WOMAN AND HER ART: AN ASSESSMENT

1. *Innocent*, ch. 9.
2. *Blackwood's* (Feb. 1886), 258.
3. *Blackwood's* (Mar. 1890), 409–10.
4. e.g. in M. G. Mason, 'The Other Voice: Autobiographies of Women Writers', in J. Olney (ed.), *Autobiography: Essays Theoretical and Critical* (Princeton, NJ, 1980), 207–35; and P. Spacks, 'Selves in Hiding', in E. C. Jelinek (ed.), *Women's Autobiography*, (Bloomington, Ind., 1980),112–32.
5. *JAL* 136.
6. Ibid.
7. L. Stephen, *National Review* (July 1899), 740–57; V. Woolf, *The Three Guineas* (1938; Oxford, 1992), 287.
8. V. and R. A. Colby, *The Equivocal Virtue* (New York, 1966), 208; R. A. and V. Colby, 'Mrs Oliphant's Scotland: The Romance of Reality', in I. Campbell (ed.), *Nineteenth Century Scottish Fiction*, ed. I. Campbell (Manchester, 1979), 89–104.
9. Williams, p. xi.
10. A vogue that Mrs Oliphant herself deplored; see *Blackwood's* (Aug. 1889), 265–6.
11. Macmillan MS, 19 Apr. 1882, 5 Dec. 1887.
12. See above, ch. 7, n. 80. *A Rose in June* appeared in Russian in 1875, *He That Will Not When He May* in 1881, and *Lady Car* in 1893. For this information I am indebted to Mr Paul Foote of Queen's College, Oxford.
13. Macmillan MS, 26 July 1887.
14. *Blackwood's* (June 1888), 850–2.
15. 'John Rintoul; or, the Fragment of a Wreck', *Blackwood's* (Mar. 1853), 329–47; (Apr. 1853), 410–30.
16 As in *The Days of My Life* or one of the narrators in *The Last of the Mortimers: A Story in Two Voices*.
17. 'A Party of Travellers', *Good Words* (Mar.), 211–6; (June), 423–9; (Oct. 1879), 698–705.
18. *Saturday Review* (22 July 1876), 112–13.
19. *The Perpetual Curate*, ch. 17.
20. Ibid., ch. 16.
21. *Blackwood's* (Mar. 1870), 294–6.
22. *JAL* 30.
23. 'Mr. Sandford', *The Ways of Life*, ch. 4.
24. *Blackwood's* (May 1855), 555.

25. *Blackwood's* (Aug. 1856), 128–9.
26. *Blackwood's* (Sept. 1880), 401; (Oct. 1896), 503.
27. Quoted in a letter from J. Blackwood to A. Mozley, 31 Mar. 1865; *Annals*, iii. 338.
28. P. M. Davis, *Memory and Writing: From Wordsworth to Lawrence* (Liverpool, 1983), 316–17.
29. *JAL* 104.
30. Blackwood MS, n.d. 1862.
31. NLS, Blackwood Letter Books. Acc. 5643, D5, 3 May 1864. In the margin of the copy of her 1858 novel, *Orphans*, held by the London Library, a reader has noted a page where 'little' occurs nine times.
32. [John Skelton], *Blackwood's* (Jan.1883), 73–91.
33. *Edinburgh Review* (July 1899), 26–47.
34. Blackwood MS, 15 Feb. 1897.
35. *JAL* 98.
36. *Forum* (New York, 1887–91), Aug. 1889, p. 321.
37. *Perpetual Curate*, ch. 16.
38. *Miss Marjoribanks*, ch. 4.
39. *Who Was Lost and Is Found*, ch. 7.
40. *JAL* 18–19.
41. *Annals*, ii. 477.
42. *JAL* 136–7.
43. *JAL* 20.
44. *The Bookman* (Aug. 1897), 114.
45. *Blackwood's* (June 1895), 907.
46. *Dress*, ch. 1.
47. *At His Gates*, ch. 14; 'A Maiden's Mind', *Atalanta* (Dec. 1895), ch. 5; *Miss Marjoribanks*, ch. 10; *Hester*, ch. 4.
48. *Notes on Novelists*, 358; 'Greville Fane', *The Complete Tales*, 438–9.
49. *JAL* 63–4.

The Family Tree of MARGARET OLIPHANT WILSON OLIPHANT

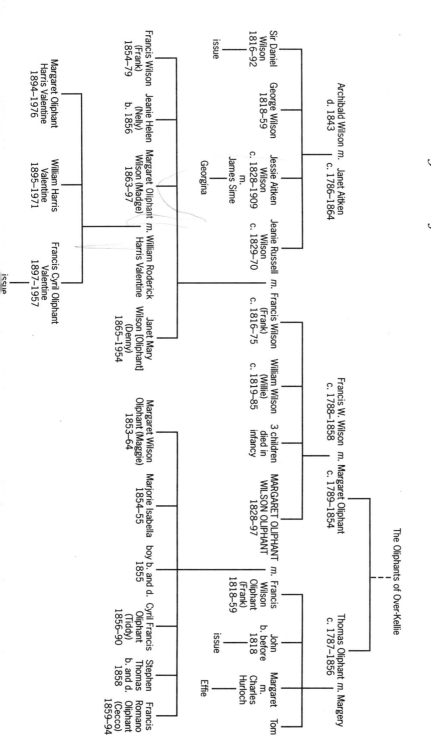

A Chronology of Margaret Oliphant

1828   4 April: Margaret Oliphant Wilson born at Wallyford, Midlothian, youngest child of
        Francis W. Wilson (c.1788–1858), clerk, and Margaret Oliphant (c.1789–1854). Her
        two elder brothers are Francis (Frank) and William (Willie). During her first ten
        years the family move first to Lasswade, near Edinburgh, and then to Glasgow.

1838   Family move to Liverpool.

1845   Margaret suffers broken engagement.

1849   Publication of Margaret's first novel. She spends three months in London as house-
        keeper for Willie and there meets her cousin, Francis Wilson Oliphant (Frank).

1851   Margaret and her mother visit Edinburgh.

1852   Willie leaves his first ministerial post in Etal, Northumberland, and returns home,
        disgraced.
        4 May: Margaret marries her cousin Frank (1818–59), artist and stained-glass-
        window designer, and moves to London. In August her parents and Willie move to
        London to be near her.

1853   21 May: Birth of daughter, Margaret Wilson Oliphant (Maggie).

1854   22 May: Birth of second daughter, Marjorie Isabella.
        17 September: Death of Margaret's mother.

1855   8 February: Death of Marjorie Isabella.
        November: Death of third child, a son, after only one day.

1856   16 November: Birth of fourth child, Cyril Francis (Tiddy or Tids).

1857   First signs of Frank Oliphant's tubercular condition.

1858   28 May: Death of fifth child, Stephen Thomas, aged nine weeks.

1859   Margaret, Frank, and the children leave for Italy hoping to improve Frank's health.
        Margaret's regular contributions to *Blackwood's Magazine* provide the family
        income.
        20 October: Frank dies in Rome.
        12 December: Birth of last child, Francis Romano (Cecco).

1860   February: Margaret and her children return to England to stay with her brother
        Frank and his family in Birkenhead. Summer spent in Fife. In October Margaret and
        her children move to Edinburgh.

1861   Begins *Chronicles of Carlingford* series. Moves to Ealing in October to be close to
        friends.

1863   Margaret and her children accompany friends to Italy.

1864   27 January: Eldest child, Maggie, dies in Rome; remainder of the year spent in Italy,
        Switzerland, and France.

1865   September: Returns from France to London. In December moves to Windsor for
        boys' schooling at Eton.

1866   Annie Louisa Walker (future Mrs H. Coghill, editor of *Autobiography*), becomes Margaret's housekeeper and secretary.

1868   Brother Frank suffers financial ruin. Margaret takes in his two eldest children and sends Frank junior to Eton when his parents go abroad.

1870   Margaret's recently widowed brother Frank returns to England, apparently having suffered a nervous breakdown. He and his two youngest children, Margaret Oliphant (Madge) and Janet Mary (Denny), become wholly dependent upon Oliphant.

1875   July: Margaret's brother Frank dies.
        August: Madge and Denny sent to school in Germany.
        October: Tiddy goes up to Balliol College, Oxford, and Margaret's nephew Frank, a qualified engineer, sails for India.

1879   Madge and Denny return from Germany in the spring, Madge to train as a wood-engraver and Denny to attend boarding-school in Windsor. In October their brother Frank dies in India.

1884   Tiddy leaves for Ceylon to be private secretary to the Governor, but soon returns in poor health. In the summer Margaret enjoys her first mystical experience, in St Andrews.

1885   Margaret's brother Willie dies in Rome where he had been supported by her for quarter of a century.

1890   Margaret, accompanied by her sons and Madge, travels to Jerusalem in the spring for research purposes. In November her eldest son, Tiddy, dies.

1893   July: Madge marries William Valentine, jute manufacturer.

1894   In October Margaret's last surviving child, Cecco, dies. Denny changes her name by Deed Poll to Oliphant.

1896   April: Final move to Wimbledon.

1897   25 June: Margaret Oliphant Wilson Oliphant dies.

Select Bibliography

Place of publication is London, unless otherwise stated.

PRIMARY SOURCES

Manuscript material

The largest collection of Mrs Oliphant's papers is held by the National Library of Scotland. The Blackwood MS contains letters to her publisher (1851–97) and a handful of letters from other relatives to Messrs Blackwoods. MSS 23193–23204 comprise general correspondence, letters to her sons and nieces, their correspondence, and miscellaneous papers.

The British Library holds her correspondence with two other publishers, Bentley and Macmillan, and a letter to J. Bryce.

Mrs Oliphant's letters to William Isbister, editor of *Good Words*, are lodged in the Library of Princeton University, as is her correspondence with Mrs Mapes Dodge, editor of the *St Nicholas*, her letters to the firm of Scribner's in whose magazine she published, and a letter of 1895 to James Payn, then editor of the *Cornhill Magazine*.

Margaret Oliphant Wilson Oliphant's published works

For a comprehensive listing of all editions of Mrs Oliphant's fiction see J. S. Clarke, *Margaret Oliphant (1828–1897): A Bibliography*, Victorian Fiction Research Guides XI, Dept. of English, University of Queensland, 1986. This supersedes the previous fullest listing to be found in *Autobiography and Letters of Mrs Margaret Oliphant*, ed. Mrs Harry Coghill (Edinburgh and London, 1899; reprinted with an introduction by Q. D. Leavis, Leicester, 1974). This edition of the *Autobiography* currently contains the fullest listing of her contributions to *Blackwood's Edinburgh Magazine*. J. S. Clarke and D. Trela are working upon a bibliographical guide to the full range of her non-fiction. References to some of the articles she contributed to the *Spectator* (to be found under the heading 'A Commentary from an Easy Chair' between 7 Dec. 1889 and 8 Nov. 1990) and the *St James's Gazette* (to be found under the heading 'A Fireside Commentary' between 11 Jan. 1888 and 24 Aug. 1888) will be found in the Endnotes and in the Index.

The following list of Margaret Oliphant's major works is based upon the information provided in J. S. Clarke's bibliographical guide to the fiction. I have cited the first date of publication in book form (whether here or in America) together, where relevant, with periodical publication dates. The books are listed so as to suggest Mrs Oliphant's probable order of writing.

1849 *Passages in the Life of Margaret Maitland, of Sunnyside, written by Herself*
1850 *Merkland: A Story of Scottish Life*
1851 *Caleb Field: A Tale of the Puritans*

1851   (Aug.) *John Drayton: Being a History of the Early Life and Development of a Liverpool Engineer*
1852   *Memoirs and Resolutions of Adam Graeme of Mossgray*
1852   (Apr.) *The Melvilles*
1852   *Katie Stewart: A True Story* (*Blackwood's*, July–Nov. 1852)
1853   *Harry Muir: A Story of Scottish Life*
1853   *Ailieford: A Family History*
1854   *The Quiet Heart* (*Blackwood's*, Dec. 1853–May 1854)
1854   *Magdalen Hepburn: A Story of the Scottish Reformation*
1856   *Zaidee: A Romance* (*Blackwood's*, Dec. 1854–Dec. 1855)
1855   *Lilliesleaf: Being a Concluding Series of Passages In the Life of Mrs Margaret Maitland, of Sunnyside, Written by Herself*
1856   *Christian Melville*
1857   *The Athelings, or The Three Gifts* (*Blackwood's*, June 1856–June 1857)
1857   *The Days of My Life: An Autobiography*
1858   *Sundays*
1858   *Orphans: A Chapter in a Life*
1858   *The Laird of Norlaw: A Scottish Story*
1859   *Agnes Hopetoun's Schools and Holidays: The Experiences of a Little Girl*
1859   *Lucy Crofton*
1861   *The House on the Moor*
1862   *The Last of the Mortimers: A Story in Two Voices*
1862   *The Life of Edward Irving, Minister of the National Scotch Church, London*
1862   *The Rector and The Doctor's Family* (*Blackwood's*, Sept. 1861–Jan. 1862)
1863   *Heart and Cross*
1863   *Salem Chapel* (*Blackwood's*, Feb. 1862–Jan. 1863)
1864   *The Perpetual Curate* (*Blackwood's*, June 1863–Mar. 1864, May 1864–Sept. 1864)
1865   *A Son of the Soil* (*Macmillan's Magazine*, Nov. 1863–Apr. 1865)
1865   *Agnes*
1866   *Miss Marjoribanks* (*Blackwood's*, Feb.–Dec. 1865, Feb.–May 1866)
1866   (Dec.) *Madonna Mary* (*Good Words*, Jan.–Dec. 1866)
1868   *Brownlows* (*Blackwood's*, Jan. 1867–Feb. 1868)
1868   *Francis of Assisi*
1869   *Historical Sketches of the Reign of George II* (*Blackwood's*, Feb.–Aug. 1868)
1869   *The Minister's Wife*
1870   *The Three Brothers* (*St Paul's* and *Appleton's Journal*, June 1869–Sept. 1870)
1870   *John: A Love Story* (*Blackwood's*, Nov. 1869–July 1870)
1871   *Squire Arden* (*The Star, Glasgow Evening Post*, June–Sept. 1870)
1872   *At His Gates* (*Good Words* and *Scribner's Monthly*, Jan.–Dec. 1872)
1896   *The Two Marys* (*Macmillan's Magazine*, Sept., Nov., Dec. 1872; Jan. 1873). Published in book form together with 'Grove Road, Hampstead' (*Good Words*, Dec. 1880)
1872   *Memoirs of the Count de Montalembert, A Chapter of Recent French History*
1872   *Ombra*
1873   *May*
1873   *Innocent* (*The Graphic*, Jan.–June 1873)
1875   *The Story of Valentine and His Brother* (*Blackwood's*, Jan. 1874–Feb. 1875)

1874   *A Rose in June* (*Cornhill Magazine*, Mar.–Aug. 1874)

1874   *For Love and Life*

1875   *Whiteladies* (*Good Words*, Jan.–Dec. 1875)

1876   *The Curate in Charge* (*Macmillan's Magazine*, Aug. 1875–Jan. 1876)

1876   *An Odd Couple* (*The Graphic*, Dec. 1875)

1876   *Phoebe Junior: A Last Chronicle of Carlingford*

1876   *Dress*

1876   *The Makers of Florence: Dante, Giotto, Savonarola and Their City*

1877   *Carità* (*Cornhill Magazine*, June 1876–Aug. 1877)

1892   *Diana Trelawny: The History of a Great Mistake* (*Blackwood's*, Feb.–July 1892), written in 1877

1877   *Dante: Foreign Classics for English Readers*

1877   *Cervantes: Foreign Classics for English Readers*

1877   *Young Musgrave* (*Macmillan's Magazine*, Jan.–Dec. 1877)

1877   *Mrs Arthur*

1879   *A Beleaguered City* (*New Quarterly Magazine*, Jan. 1879)

1879   *Molière: Foreign Classics for English Readers* (with F. B. C. Tarver)

1879   *Within the Precincts* (*Cornhill Magazine*, Feb. 1878–Apr. 1879)

1878   *The Primrose Path*

1879   *The Greatest Heiress in England*

1879   *The Fugitives* (*Good Words*, Dec. 1879)

1880   *He That Will Not When He May* (*Macmillan's Magazine*, Nov. 1879–Nov. 1880)

1881   *In Trust* (*Fraser's Magazine*, Feb. 1881–Jan. 1882)

1881   *Harry Joscelyn*

1882   *Lady Jane* (*Good Words*, Jan.–June 1882). Retitled *The Duke's Daughter* and published together with *The Fugitives* (1890)

1882   *Literary History of England in the End of the Eighteenth and Beginning of the Nineteenth Century*

1882   *A Little Pilgrim in the Unseen.* Includes the short story of this name (*Macmillan's Magazine*, May and Sept. 1882), and 'The Little Pilgrim Goes up Higher' (*Macmillan's Magazine*, Sept. 1882)

1883   *The Ladies Lindores* (*Blackwood's*, Apr. 1882–May 1883)

1883   *The Lady's Walk* (*Longman's Magazine*, Dec. 1882, Jan. 1883)

1883   *Sheridan*

1884   *The Wizard's Son* (*Macmillan's Magazine*, Nov. 1882–Mar. 1884)

1883   *Sir Tom* (*Bolton Weekly Journal*, and other papers, Jan.–July 1883)

1883   *Hester*

1883   *It Was a Lover and His Lass*

1884   *Madam* (*Longman's Magazine*, Jan. 1884–Jan. 1885)

1885   *The Prodigals and Their Inheritance* (*Good Words*, Dec. 1884)

1886   *A Country Gentleman and His Family* (*Atlantic Monthly*, Jan. 1885–Feb. 1886)

1886   *A House Divided Against Itself* (*Chambers's Journal*, Jan.–Dec. 1885)

1885   *Oliver's Bride: A True Story* (*Bolton Weekly Journal*, and other papers, Apr.–May 1885)

1886   *Effie Ogilvie: The Story of a Young Life* (*The Scottish Church*, June 1885–May 1886)

1886   *A Poor Gentleman* (*The Leisure Hour*, Jan.–Dec. 1886)

1886   *The Son of His Father* (*Bolton Weekly Journal*, and other papers, Apr.–Oct. 1886)

1887   *The Makers of Venice: Doges, Conquerors, Painters, and Men of Letters*

1888   *The Second Son* (*Atlantic Monthly*, Jan. 1887–Feb. 1888)

1888   *Joyce* (*Blackwood's*, May 1887–Apr. 1888)

1888   *Cousin Mary*

1888   *Memoir of the Life of John Tulloch*

1888   *The Land of Darkness*. Includes the short story of this name (*Blackwood's*, Jan. 1887), 'The Little Pilgrim in the Seen and the Unseen' (*The Scottish Church*, July 1885), and 'On the Dark Mountains' (*Blackwood's*, Nov. 1888)

1889   *Neighbours on the Green*

1897   *The Ways of Life*. Includes 'Mr Sandford' (*Cornhill Magazine*, Apr., May 1888) and 'The Strange Story of Mr Robert Dalyell' (*Cornhill Magazine*, Jan.–Mar. 1892)

1889   *Lady Car: The Sequel of a Life* (*Longman's*, Mar.–July 1889)

1890   *Kirsteen: The Story of a Scotch Family Seventy Years Ago* (Macmillan's Magazine, Aug. 1889–Aug. 1890)

1890   *Royal Edinburgh: Her Saints, Kings, Prophets and Poets*

1890   *The Mystery of Mrs Blencarrow* (*Manchester Weekly Times*, and other papers, Nov.– Dec. 1889)

1890   *Sons and Daughters* (*Blackwood's*, Mar., Apr. 1890)

1891   *The Railway Man and His Children* (*The Sun*, Oct. 1890–Sept. 1891)

1891   *The Heir Presumptive and the Heir Apparent* (*Birmingham Weekly Post*, and other papers, Oct. 1890–Apr. 1891)

1891   *Jerusalem: Its History and Hope*

1891   *A Memoir of the Life of Laurence Oliphant, and of Alice Oliphant, His Wife*

1893   *Lady William* (*Lady's Pictorial*, Jan.–June 1891)

1891   *The Marriage of Elinor* (*Good Words*, Jan.–Dec. 1891)

1891   *Janet*

1892   *The Cuckoo in the Nest* (*The Victorian Magazine*, Dec. 1891–Nov. 1892)

1892   *The Victorian Age of English Literature* (with F. R. Oliphant)

1893   *The Sorceress* (*The Gentlewoman*, and other papers, July 1892–Jan. 1893)

1893   *Thomas Chalmers, Preacher, Philosopher, and Statesman*

1894   *A House in Bloomsbury* (*The Young Woman*, Oct. 1893–Sept. 1894)

1894   *Sir Robert's Fortune: The Story of a Scotch Moor* (*Atalanta*, Oct. 1893–Sept. 1894)

1894   *Who Was Lost and Is Found* (*Blackwood's*, June–Nov. 1894)

1894   *Historical Sketches of the Reign of Queen Anne*

1894   *Two Strangers*

1895   *'Dies Irae': The Story of a Spirit in Prison*

1895   *A Child's History of Scotland*

1895   *The Makers of Modern Rome*

1895   *Old Mr Tredgold* (*Longman's Magazine*, June 1895–May 1896)

1896   *The Unjust Steward, or The Minister's Debt*

1896   *Jeanne d'Arc: Her Life and Death*

1897   *Annals of a Publishing House: William Blackwood and His Sons, Their Magazine and Friends*

1897   'The Sisters Brontë', *Women Novelists of Queen Victoria's Reign*

1898   *A Widow's Tale, and Other Stories* (with an Introductory Note by J. M. Barrie)

1898   *That Little Cutty.* Includes the short story of this name (*Home*, Dec. 1880), 'Dr Barrère' (*The English Illustrated Magazine*, Dec. 1884), and 'Isabel Dysart' (*Chambers's Journal*, Jan. 1893)

1899   *The Autobiography and Letters of Mrs M. O. W. Oliphant*, arranged and edited by Mrs Harry Coghill

1990   *Queen Victoria, A Personal Sketch*

SECONDARY SOURCES

Books and Articles

ANDERSON, N. F., *Women against Women in Victorian England: A Life of Eliza Lynn Linton* (Bloomington, Ind., 1987).

ANDERSON, R. D., *Education and Opportunity in Victorian Scotland* (Oxford, 1983).

Athenaeum, review of M. O. W. Oliphant's *In Trust* (11 Feb. 1882), 186.

AUERBACH, N., *Woman and the Demon: The Life of a Victorian Myth* Cambridge, Mass., 1982).

AUSTEN, Z., 'Why Feminist Critics are Angry with George Eliot', *College English*, 37 (1976), 549–61.

BACHELARD, G., *The Poetics of Space* (1958), trans. M. Jolas (Boston, 1969).

BARRIE, J. M., Introductory Note to M. O. W. Oliphant's *A Widow's Tale* (1898).

BEER, G., *Darwin's Plots: Evolutionary Narrative in Darwin, George Eliot, and Nineteenth-Century Fiction* (1983).

BENSON, A. C., *Memories and Friends* (1924).

The Brontës: Their Lives, Friendship, and Correspondence, ed. T. J. Wise and J. A. Symington, 4 vols. (1932).

BROWN, S., *Thomas Chalmers and the Godly Commonwealth* (Oxford, 1982).

CARLYLE, T., 'Edward Irving', in *Reminiscences*, ed. J. A. Froude, 2 vols. (1881).

—— *The Works of Thomas Carlyle*, Centenary Edition, ed. H. D. Traill, 30 vols. (1886–99).

Catalogue of the Principal English Books in Circulation at Mudie's Select Library (Jan. 1898).

CHRIST, C., ' "The Hero as Man of Letters": Masculinity and Victorian Nonfiction Prose', in T. E. Morgan (ed.), *Victorian Sages and Cultural Discourse: Renegotiating Gender and Power* (1990), 19–31.

CLARKE, I. C., *Six Portraits* (1935).

CLARKE, J. S., 'Mrs Oliphant's Unacknowledged Social Novels', *Notes and Queries*, (Oct. 1981), 408–13.

—— 'The "Rival Novelist"—Hardy and Mrs Oliphant', *The Thomas Hardy Journal* (Oct. 1989), 51–61.

COLBY, R. A. and V., '*A Beleaguered City*: A Fable for the Victorian Age', *Nineteenth Century Fiction*, (Mar. 1962), 283–301 and *JAL* 137.

———— 'Mrs Oliphant's Scotland: The Romance of Reality', in I. Campbell (ed.), *Nineteenth Century Scottish Fiction* (Manchester, 1979), 89–104.

COLBY, V. and R. A., *The Equivocal Virtue: Mrs Oliphant and the Victorian Market Place* (New York, 1966).

[COLLINS, W. LUCAS], Review of M. O. W. Oliphant's *Life of Edward Irving, Blackwood's* (June 1862), 737–57.

COSSLETT, T., *Woman to Woman: Female Friendship and Community in Victorian Fiction* (Brighton, 1988).

CROSS, A. [C. Heilbrun], *A Trap for Fools* (1989).

CROSS, N., *The Common Writer: Life in Nineteenth-Century Grub Street* (Cambridge, 1985).

CUNNINGHAM, V., *Everywhere Spoken Against: Dissent and the Victorian Novel* (Oxford,1975).

DARWIN, F. (ed.), *Charles Darwin: His Life Told in an Autobiographical Chapter, and in a series of his published letters* (1892).

DAVIS, P. M., *Memory and Writing: From Wordsworth to Lawrence* (Liverpool, 1983).

DENT, J. M., *Memoirs of J. M. Dent, 1849–1926* (1928).

DICKENS, C., *The Letters of Charles Dickens*, eds. G. Storey, K. Tillotson, and N. Burgis, 6 vols. (1965–88).

—— *Charles Dickens: The Public Readings*, ed. P. Collins (Oxford, 1975).

EDEL, L., *Henry James: The Treacherous Years, 1895–1901* (1969).

ELIOT, G., 'Woman in France: Madame de Sablé', *Westminster Review* (Oct. 1854), 448–73.

—— 'Silly Novels by Lady Novelists', *Westminster Review* (Oct. 1856), 442–61.

—— *The George Eliot Letters*, ed. G. S. Haight, 9 vols. (New Haven, Conn., 1954–6, 1978).

FAWCETT, T., *The Rise of English Provincial Art: Artists, Patrons and Institutions outside London, 1800–30* (Oxford, 1974).

FERRER, D., *Virginia Woolf and the Madness of Language*, trans. G. Bennington and R. Bowlby (1990).

FIDDES, P., *Past Event and Present Salvation* (1989).

FLINT, K., 'The Woman Reader and the Opiate of Fiction: 1855–1870', in J. Hawthorn (ed.), *The Nineteenth-Century British Novel* (1986), 47–62.

GILBERT, S. M., and GUBAR, S., 'Tradition and the Female Talent', in N. K. Miller, *The Poetics of Gender* (New York, 1986), 183–207.

GREENWOOD, G., *Haps and Mishaps of a Tour in Europe* (1854).

GRIEST, G., *Mudie's Circulating Library and the Victorian Novel* (Bloomington, Ind. and London, 1970).

HALL, N. J., *Trollope: A Biography* (Oxford, 1991).

HARDY, T., 1912 Preface to *Jude the Obscure* (1895).

HARVEY, J. R., *Victorian Novelists and Their Illustrators* (1970).

HELSINGER, E. K., SHEETS R. L., and VEEDER, W. (eds.), *The Woman Question 1837–1883*, 3 vols. (1983), pp. xiv–xv, i. 3–20, and ii. 165–211.

HOMANS, M., *Bearing the Word: Language and Female Experience in Nineteenth-Century Women's Writing* (Chicago and London, 1986).

JACKSON, R., *Fantasy: The Literature of Subversion* (1981).

JACOBUS, M., *Reading Women: Essays in Feminist Criticism* (1986).

JAMES, H., 'The Private Life' (1892) and 'Greville Fane' (1892), in *The Complete Tales of Henry James* (1963), 189–228; 433–52.

JAY, E., *The Religion of the Heart* (Oxford, 1979).

JOHNSON, B., *A World of Difference* (Baltimore and London, 1987).

LOADES, A., *Searching for Lost Coins: Explorations in Christianity and Feminism* (1987), 61–77.

LOVELL, T., *Consuming Fiction* (1987).

McGUFFIE, G., *The Priests of Etal, or Annals of Tillside* (4th edn., Edinburgh, 1904).

MASON, M. G., 'The Other Voice: Autobiographies of Women Writers', in J. Olney (ed.), *Autobiography: Essays Theoretical and Critical* (Princeton, NJ, 1980), 207–35.

MOI, T., *Sexual/Textual Politics: Feminist Literary Theory* (1985).

MOTT, F. L., *A History of American Magazines, 1741–1850; 1850–65*, 2 vols. (New York, 1930).

NESTOR, P., *Female Friendship and Communities* (Oxford, 1985).

NIGHTINGALE, F., *Cassandra*, in R. Strachey, *The Cause: A Short History of the Women's Movement in Great Britain* (1928; repr. 1974), 395–418.

OLIPHANT, F. W., *A Plea for Painted Glass: Being an Inquiry into its Nature, Character, and Objects and its Claims as an Art* (Oxford, 1855).

OREL, H., *The Victorian Short Story: Development and Triumph of a Literary Genre* (Cambridge, 1986).

PARKER, R., *The Subversive Stitch: Embroidery and the Making of the Feminine* (1984).

PETERSON, L., 'Audience and the Autobiographer's Art: An Approach to the Autobiography of Mrs M. O. W. Oliphant', in G. P. Landow (ed.), *Approaches to Victorian Autobiography* (Athens, Ohio, 1979).

PORTER, MRS GERALD, *The Life of John Blackwood* (1898).

REED, J. R., *Victorian Conventions* (Athens, Ohio, 1975).

RITCHIE, A. I., *From the Porch* (1913).

—— *Letters of Anne Thackeray Ritchie*, ed, H. Ritchie (1924).

ROWELL, G., *Hell and the Victorians: A Study of the Nineteenth-Century Controversies Concerning Eternal Punishment and the Future Life* (Oxford, 1974).

Saturday Review, review of *Phoebe Junior*, 22 July 1876; review of M. O. W. Oliphant's *The Makers of Venice*, 28 Jan. 1888.

SCOTT, W. B., *Autobiographical Notes of the Life of William Bell Scott: And Notices of His Artistic and Poetic Circle of Friends 1830–1882*, ed. W. Minto, 2 vols. (1892).

SHOWALTER, E., *A Literature of Their Own: British Women Novelists from Brontë to Lessing* (1978; 1982), 179.

—— (ed.), *The New Feminist Criticism: Essays on Women, Literature and Theory* (1986).

[JOHN SKELTON], 'A Little Chat about Mrs Oliphant', *Blackwood's* (Jan. 1883), 73– 91.

SPACKS, P., 'Selves in Hiding', in E. C. Jelinek (ed.), *Women's Autobiography* (Bloomington, Ind., 1980), 112–32.

STANTON, D. C., *The Female Autograph* (Chicago and London, 1987).

STEPHEN, L., *National Review* (July 1899), 740–57.

STORY, E. and C. S., *Memoir of Robert Herbert Story, by His Daughters* (Glasgow, 1909).

STORY, J. L., *Later Reminiscences* (Glasgow, 1913).

STORY, R. H., *Memoir of the Life of the Rev. R. Story* (Cambridge, 1862).

—— *The Life and Remains of Robert Lee DD*, with introductory chapter by Mrs Oliphant, 2 vols. (1870).

—— *The Risen Christ: A Sermon Preached at Rosneath Church on the Lord's Day after the Death of John McLeod Campbell* (Glasgow, 1872).

STRACHEY, R., *The Cause: A Short History of the Women's Movement in Great Britain* (1928; repr. 1974).

SUTHERLAND, J. A., *Victorian Novelists and Publishers* (1976).

—— *Mrs Humphry Ward: Eminent Victorian, Pre-Eminent Edwardian* (1990).

TAYLOR, A., *Laurence Oliphant, 1829–1888* (Oxford, 1982).

TENNYSON, H., *Alfred Lord Tennyson: A Memoir*, 2 vols. (1897).

TERRY, R. C., *Victorian Popular Fiction 1860–80* (1983).

TRELA, D. (ed.), *Margaret Oliphant: Essays on a Gentle Subversive* (Susquehanna, Penn., 1994).

TROLLOPE, A., *An Autobiography*, ed. F. Page (Oxford, 1950).
—— *The Letters of Anthony Trollope*, ed. N. J. Hall, 2 vols. (Stanford, Calif., 1983).
TUCHMAN, G., and FORTIN, N. E., *Edging Women Out: Victorian Novelists, Publishers and Social Change* (New Haven, Conn., 1989).
TULLOCH, J., *Movements of Religious Thought in Britain during the Nineteenth Century* (1885).
WHEELER, M., *Death and the Future Life in Victorian Literature and Theology* (Cambridge, 1990).
WILLIAMS, M., *Margaret Oliphant: A Critical Biography* (1986).
WILSON, W., *Andrew Ramsay of Errol*, 3 vols. (1865).
WOOLF, V., *The Three Guineas* (1938; Oxford, 1992), 287.

Posthumous appreciations

These appeared in two waves, as obituaries, and as reviews of her *Autobiography* (1899).
British Weekly (1 July 1897), 177.
Church Quarterly Review (Oct. 1899), 143.
Daily Chronicle (28 June 1897).
Daily News (28 June 1897), 8.
JAMES, HENRY, *London Notes* (Aug. 1897), reprinted in *Notes on Novelists* (1914), 357–60.
PRESTON, HARRIET WATERS, *Atlantic Monthly* (Sept. 1897), 425.
STEPHEN, LESLIE, *National Review* (July 1899), 740–57.
STURGIS, HOWARD OVERING, 'A Sketch from Memory', *Temple Bar* (Oct. 1899), 233–48.
TOWNSEND, MEREDITH, 'Mrs Oliphant', *The Cornhill* (June 1899), 773–9.
TULLOCH, W. W., *The Bookman* (Aug. 1897), 113–15.

Unpublished dissertations

CUNNINGHAM, P., 'William Dyce, R.A. and the High Church Movement', MA thesis (East Anglia, 1972).
DORMANDY, C., 'George Eliot's Religious Consciousness and its Role in her Life and Work', Ph.D. thesis (Westminster College, CNAA, 1992).
JASPER, D., 'The Reconstruction of Christian Belief in the Late Victorian Novel with Particular Reference to the Works of Mrs Margaret Oliphant, Mrs Humphry Ward, Mark Rutherford and Samuel Butler', BD thesis (Oxford, 1979).
MOSIER, W. E., 'Mrs Oliphant's Literary Criticism', Ph.D. thesis (Northwestern University, 1967).
WATSON, K., 'The Use of Religious Diction in the Nineteenth-Century Novel with Special Reference to George Eliot', D. Phil. thesis (Oxford, 1970).

Index